# THE ANNALS
# OF
# AMERICA

# THE ANNALS OF AMERICA

## Volume 16

## 1940 - 1949

### The Second World War and After

William Benton, *Publisher*

## ENCYCLOPÆDIA BRITANNICA, INC.

*Chicago London Toronto Geneva Sydney Tokyo Manila*

The editors wish to express their gratitude for permission to reprint
material from the following sources:

Art News for Selection 43 (Stuart Davis, "The Dynamic American Scene"), from *Art News*, Copyright 1943 The Art Foundation, Inc.

Arts and Architecture for Selection 43 (Jackson Pollock, "Universal Art"), from *Arts and Architecture*, February 1944.

Atlantic-Little, Brown and Company for Selection 41, from *U.S. Foreign Policy: Shield of the Republic*, by Walter Lippmann, Copyright 1943 by Walter Lippmann.

The Atlantic Monthly and James B. Conant for Selection 7, from *The Atlantic Monthly*, Copyright © 1940 by The Atlantic Monthly Company, Boston, Mass.

Basic Books, Inc. for Selections 64, 105, from *The Atomic Age*, ed. by Morton Grodzins and Eugene Rabinowitch, © 1963 by Basic Books, Inc., Publishers, New York.

William Benton for Selection 47, from *The Economics of a Free Society*, Committee for Economic Development Supplementary Paper No. 1.

Brandeis Lawyers Society for Selection 113, from *The Emerging Common Law of Free Enterprise*, by Adolf A. Berle, Jr., Philadelphia: Brandeis Lawyers Society, Copyright 1951 by Brandeis Lawyers Society.

Brandt & Brandt for Selection 4, from *The Selected Works of Stephen Benét*, Holt, Rinehart and Winston, Inc., Copyright 1940 by Stephen Vincent Benét.

Columbia University Press for Selection 32 ("I Got My Questionnairy"), from *Negro Folk Music, U.S.A.*, ed. by Harold Courlander.

Henry Steele Commager for Selection 92, from *Harper's Monthly Magazine*, September 1947, Copyright © 1947 by Harper's Magazine, Inc.

Avis M. De Voto for Selection 119, from *Harper's Magazine*, October 1949, Copyright by Mrs. Bernard De Voto.

Dodd, Mead & Company, Inc. for Selection 8, from *This Is Wendell Willkie*, by Wendell Willkie.

Doubleday & Company, Inc. for Selection 109, from

# CODED SOURCES IN THIS VOLUME

*Bulletin*

*Department of State Bulletin.* Published weekly by the Office of Public Services, Bureau of Public Affairs. Supersedes two previous publications: *Press Releases* and *Treaty Information Bulletin.* Washington, July 1, 1939 *et seq.*

FDR

*The Public Papers and Addresses of Franklin D. Roosevelt.* Compiled by Samuel P. Rosenman. In 13 vols. New York, 1938-1950.

PRFA

[United States Department of State] *Papers Relating to Foreign Affairs.* Compiled annually since 1861 except for 1869 with supplements issued periodically. Title changed to *Papers Relating to Foreign Relations of the United States* in 1870 and to *Foreign Relations of the United States* in 1947. Washington, 1862 *et seq.*

*Record*

*Congressional Record.* A record of the proceedings of Congress from March 3, 1873, to date, arranged by number of Congress and by session. Washington, 1874 *et seq.*

*Record, App.*

*Congressional Record Appendix.* A supplement to the *Congressional Record* (see above), paged separately and also arranged by Congress and session.

*United States Reports* [Supreme Court]

| | |
|---|---|
| 319 U.S. 624 | Vol. 319, pp. 624ff.; |
| 323 U.S. 214 | Vol. 323, pp. 214ff.; |
| 328 U.S. 303 | Vol. 328, pp. 303ff. |

VSD

*Vital Speeches of the Day.* Published twice a month. New York, 1934 *et seq.*

# Contents

Introduction, xvii
Chronology, 1940-1949, xxiv
Maps, xlviii

## 1948

# THE SECOND WORLD WAR AND AFTER
## In Pictures

When war broke out in Europe again in 1939, America was
little better prepared than it had been in 1914. Isolationism
was still strong, and the Neutrality Acts embodied the desire
of many to avoid the "mistake" of 1917. But sympathy for
Britain and France was also strong and widespread, both
officially and among the people. As the Axis powers continued
successful, the wall of neutrality was breached to render all
possible aid to the Allies "short of war."

Isolationism and the clinging to the remnants of neutrality
ended abruptly at Pearl Harbor. Fully committed, America
could as yet only play a defensive role until the mobilization
of men and material matched the massive requirements of global
war. The tide had definitely turned by 1943; Japan's navy had
been mastered, the U-boat no longer fatally menaced Atlantic
shipping, the first invasions had successfully pushed back Axis
forces in Africa, Italy, and the Pacific.

The activities of the several New Deal programs had prepared
both Washington and the nation's business for the economic
controls required for total mobilization. Control by government far
exceeded that of World War I and was much more successful in
averting severe economic dislocations. The unemployment that had
not yet been eliminated by one New Deal agency or another now
disappeared entirely as the economy attained new productive peaks.

## An Uncertain Victory . . . . 375-390

It had taken nearly five years of war to prepare for D-Day in June
1944; from then on it took just eleven months to defeat Germany
utterly. This success was repeated, on the whole less spectacularly,
in the Pacific, where the capture of nearby islands permitted the
daily bombardment of Japan itself. The Japanese war came to
an abrupt end with the dropping of the atomic bomb; the end of
war did not, however, signal the beginning of peace.


## The Cold War . . . . 475-486

The traditional arrangements of world power were permanently
disrupted by the war. Already in 1945 it was clear that the
United States and Russia were now dominant; it was further clear
that from their deep and growing hostility would come a
realignment of the world into two opposing camps. The structure
of postwar Europe reflected this, as did the new alliances that
came from it — NATO and the Cominform.


## Adjusting to Peace . . . . 547-560

Reconversion to peace was also more successful than it had been
in 1919. The postwar depression that many thought inevitable failed
to occur; the problem was, in fact, just the opposite: the inflation
that had been held off for so long. It seemed a simple step to
sustained prosperity. The political scene was marred by a
recurrence of Red-chasing, this time bolstered by the discovery of a
few actual Communists in relatively minor government positions.

# Introduction

Anger, greed, and distrust all played major parts in bringing about World War II. Germany had not gotten over its anger about the Treaty of Versailles; Adolf Hitler fanned the smoldering passions into flame. Germany and Italy in Europe, and Japan in the Far East, were greedy for their neighbors' territory; but their greed was shared by the Western democracies. The latter's distrust of the Soviet Union and its enigmatic leader, Joseph Stalin, and Stalin's distrust of England and France, made collective defense against Fascist aggression impossible until it was almost too late. The failure of any combined Anglo-French-Russian policy to contain Germany cost the Soviet Union unbelievable destruction and death, brought France utter defeat, and led England and the whole civilized world to the brink of ruin.

None of this was as apparent in 1939 as it is now. The opposition to America's becoming involved in the war that broke out in Europe on September 1, 1939, was even more vocal, and a great deal better organized, than had been the opposition against entry into World War I. "America First!" was the motto of those who disapproved of President Roosevelt's efforts in behalf of beleaguered Britain and who believed that it would be possible for the United States to stay out, this time, of a war that, as Charles Lindbergh said, was just one more in those age-old conflicts that from time immemorial had ravaged a corrupt and decadent Europe.

The arguments against American involvement were not always as simple as that, and the spectrum of opposition was very wide, ranging as it did all the way from the American Nazi Party to men like Chancellor Robert M. Hutchins of the University of Chicago, who feared that America's great promise to the world could not be fulfilled if the country entered the conflict. All told, their numbers and influence were great enough to keep America out of the war until Japan forced the country's hand in December 1941. [For various statements of the America First position, see Selections 10, 13, 16-17, and 24. See also Selection 19 for another antiwar view.]

There were many, of course, who differed with them, holding that the United States was in peril if England was, and that Hitler's aim was not merely hegemony in Europe, but also world domination. To Archibald Mac-Leish, the America Firsters were "The Irresponsibles," and it seemed of dire moment to him and to others that Hitler be stopped immediately, before his power was extended too far. The President and many of his advisors agreed; and they did what they could to help Britain and to place the country in a position where it could move quickly if attacked — as they were sure it would be eventually. These efforts were largely ineffectual — the United States has never entered a major war prepared — but they may have saved England, and perhaps they were better than nothing would have been. (For Selections dealing with this problem up until the end of 1941, see numbers 1-4, 9-12, 14-15, and 22-23.)

The staggering blow suffered by the United States in the Japanese attack on Pearl Harbor of December 7, 1941, was close to being the worst in the country's history and was almost decisive in the Pacific, if not in the whole war. The Pacific Fleet was crippled in the attack, leaving the Japanese — who were negotiating with Secretary of State Cordell Hull in Washington at the moment when the bombs began to fall — free to create their Greater East Asia Co-Prosperity Sphere. One of the largest empires ever ruled over by one man, it was comprised of Japan itself, much of eastern China (including the great British base at Hong Kong), French Indochina (including Vietnam), Burma, Thailand, and Malaya (including Singapore), almost all of the Netherlands East Indies, the Philippines, the Solomon, Caroline, and Marianas Islands, and a portion of the Aleutian Island chain stretching eastward to Alaska. It would cost many thousand American lives and billions of dollars to repair the damage done in a day. (For Roosevelt's message to Congress requesting a declaration of war and his Fireside Chat to the American people describing the events at Pearl Harbor, as well as a later discussion of the controversy about that terrible Sunday in December, see Selections 25 and 73.)

The United States struck back quickly, not only at Japan but also at Germany and Italy, but the going was slow and for at least a year resulted in little ground gained and many casualties. The reconquest of the Solomons was initiated in August 1942 with the famous attack on Guadalcanal, but a bloody six months battle had to ensue before the Japanese left. Island-hopping was the term used by the Marines and Seabees to describe the long drawn out campaign to retake, one by one, the outposts that had cost the Japanese almost nothing to acquire in the first place. Typically, an island would be "softened up" with bombardment by carrier-based planes, then the battleships and cruisers would steam close enough to bring their big guns into play. But there was always fierce opposition from the deeply entrenched defending troops, and the sparkling sands of the lovely sun-drenched beaches ran with blood, while over them the remaining fronds of the shattered palm trees waved in the gentle Pacific breeze.

By the end of 1942, it was clear that the high tide of Japanese conquest had been reached, but it was 1944 before it began noticeably to ebb. The same could be said of events in the European theater. North Africa was retaken in late 1942 and early 1943. The invasion of Sicily — to remind the Italians that the Mediterranean was not, after all, as Mussolini had boasted, an "Italian lake" — occurred in July 1943, and General Mark Clark's Fifth Army landed at Salerno Beach, just south of the glittering Bay of Naples, in September. By that time Mussolini had been deposed and Italy had surrendered — "ONE DOWN, TWO TO GO" was the headline in hundreds of U.S. newspapers — but it was not to be that easy. Salerno was sobering; German panzer units, a far cry from the bumbling Italians, nearly wiped out the landing force, and the fighting continued throughout the winter. Not until June 4, 1944, did Rome fall, and the campaign dragged on for months after that, with terrible losses to both sides.

Hitler had attacked Russia on the first day of summer, 1941. The action, taken against the advice of many of his generals, gave him what he had been warned against — a second front in the east — and flew in the face of the shocking Russo-German Pact, signed in late August 1939. For a time it looked as if Hitler had been right and the generals wrong; the Germans seized most of western, or European, Russia by the end of the summer, and ruled a domain stretching from Moscow in the east to the Atlantic, and from Narvik in northern Norway to the North African littoral. But here too the bloody reconquest proceeded steadily, though slowly, as the months wore on. The Russians held at Leningrad (where half the population starved to death during a two-year siege), at Moscow, at Stalingrad; the Russian winter took its toll of Hitler's armored and mechanized battalions as it had of Napoleon's invaders a century and a half before. (No one failed to see the analogy, least of all the Russians, whom it encouraged, and the Germans, whom it disheartened.) By the end of 1944, Soviet troops had burst out of Russia itself, had passed through Hungary on the south and Poland on the north, and were standing at the very borders of the German *Festung*, or fortress, readying themselves for the last great offensive of the war.

They had come so far and moved so fast in the preceding months mainly because of "Operation Overlord," the code name of the Allied invasion of western Europe that began before dawn on June 6, 1944. American GIs, British Tommies, Canadians and Anzacs, and troops of other allied nations poured ashore at beaches in Britanny whose new American names — Omaha, Utah — became household words overnight. (Omaha Beach was the worst; there the Allies were almost thrown back into the sea.) After weeks of hard fighting General Patton's American Third Army burst out of its beachhead and on August 25, Paris fell. It was a near thing; the city was saved from complete destruction only by the refusal of the German commandant to obey Hitler's order to burn it to the ground. By the middle of December the Allies were poised on Germany's western borders, ready for their last surge to meet the Russians at Berlin — or so everyone hoped. (For an eloquent recital of some of the major victories of this crucial year of 1944, see Selection 54.)

The year 1945 saw the end of the war and the beginning of a new world order. But the war ended more easily than the new world was born. After the last German counterattack, centering on Bastogne from December 16, 1944, to January 16, 1945, the Allies moved quickly inward. The Canadians struck north, the Americans straight east, the French south; and the Russian armies raced westward across the plains of eastern Germany. They reached Berlin first, at the end of April, and swept onward to meet the Americans and British at the Elbe. Hitler killed himself on April 30, and the shooting stopped a week later. The Third Reich that he had boasted would endure for a thousand years had in fact lasted for twelve years and four months.

That was two down; the third had still to fall. The Japanese fought with ever greater ferocity as the iron ring tightened on their homeland; thousands killed themselves rather than surrender, and off Okinawa kamikaze suicide pilots sank 15 U.S. ships and damaged scores of others. But the American bases were close enough now so that raids with incendiary bombs could be launched almost nightly, and the Japanese cities, with their flimsily built buildings, flared up one by one. The first atomic bomb fell on Hiroshima on August 6, the second on Nagasaki three days later, and Japan surrendered on August 15. The third was down, and the end of the end had come. (For Selections in this volume dealing with various events of the war, see numbers 27, 32-33, 36, 38-40, 44-46, 49 and 72, 61-62, and 69.)

The success of the new world that was born at San Francisco in April 1945 was more hoped-for than real, at least at first. Fifty nations took part in the meeting and all signed the Charter of the United Nations, as they called it (see Selection 65); the Charter was to take effect the following October. The first meeting of the General Assembly was held at London on January 10, 1946, and the Security Council met for the first time in the same month.

There were serious problems from the beginning, mainly involving the ideas of national sovereignty and national security. The one implied the other, but there were those who said that the sovereignty that few if any nations were willing to give up meant nothing because national security was now an empty term. The reason, of course, was the atomic bomb, which had made mincemeat of Hiroshima and Nagasaki and seemed capable of erasing any and all national boundaries, to say nothing of obliterating national defenses. If a nation's life could no longer be safe in the jungle that the world of nations obviously was, did it not make sense to try at last to live under the law? Had not the American colonies done much the same thing in 1776? Since they had managed to give up sovereignty in order to gain collective security, could not the whole world do it now?

So some said, but the logic of the argument, persuasive as it seemed, was not persuasive enough. No one gave up much sovereignty to the United Nations; it was a place to talk, to air problems, perhaps to patch up differences, but it had no real power. The power was in Washington and Moscow, not in UN headquarters, which was first at London, then at Paris, finally — from 1952 on — at New York, which thereby, according to E. B. White, was by way of becoming the capital of the world. (For discussion of some of these problems, especially that of the fearsome power of the new weapon, see Selections 41-42, 64, 66-68, 70-71, 74-75, 77-78, 103-105, and 120-121.)

Sovereignty was not the only problem; ideological differences and the distrust generated by them created another. Winston Churchill, who had distrusted the Soviets in the 1930s, did not feel much more sanguine in the '40s about the possibilities of peaceful coexistence between East and West, and at Fulton, Missouri, on March 5, 1946, he used a phrase that helped to crystallize the division (see Selection 76). An iron curtain, he said, had fallen in eastern Europe, and henceforth international affairs would take on the character of a great siege or armed truce. The phrase caught the public imagination and was used by everyone to describe a situation that came into existence at least in part because Churchill had predicted it would.

Doubtless there were good reasons for Churchill's distrust. The cold war (this was another phrase that had vast influence — Herbert Bayard Swope always claimed he had invented it, inserting it in a speech by Bernard Baruch in April 1947) was not, could not have been, the doing of one side alone. In that respect the cold war was like any other war, but in almost every other respect it was different. Troops were trained, arms were produced, and immense sums of money were spent, but American and Russian soldiers did not actually fight each other. There was fighting, but it was confined to what came to be called brushfire wars, the participants in which were the more or less irregular forces of the smaller nations. The great powers guided and watched, but they did not engage.

Hope — of some future resolution of differences, and fear — of the bomb, were about equally important causes of the long détente (it did not begin to be called that until after Korea, the most dangerous and frightening of the cold war outbreaks). In the meantime the lines were drawn ever tighter, alliances were formed, and the U.S. and the U.S.S.R. both spent money to shore up the sagging economies of their friends and cohorts. Despite the anxieties of the time, almost everyone agreed that a cold war was better than a hot one. (For some events of the cold war, and statements about it, see Selections 61, 71, 87-89, 98, 105, and 115-116.)

Perhaps the most serious effect of the cold war in the United States was on public opinion. It was a time of revolution in the world, but most Americans turned their backs on revolution more sharply and emphatically than they had ever done. Men like Senator Joseph R. McCarthy of Wisconsin saw their chance and took it, and widespread fear, distrust, and frustration were converted into what seemed to some to be a new kind of witch hunt, the victims of which were not religious dissenters but political ones. A similar phenomenon had been apparent after World War I, but this time it was much worse, partly because it lasted longer — going well beyond the terminal date of this volume — and partly because communism was now a much more powerful force in the world.

Harry S. Truman, who had succeeded to the presidency after the sudden death of President Roosevelt in April 1945 (only three months after his inauguration for an unprecedented fourth term), played a curiously paradoxical part in the affair. On the one hand, he may be said to have given McCarthyism its first impetus with his Loyalty Order of 1947; but on the other hand, he often seemed, in those dark years, to be a lonely figure of sanity in the general madness of the time. The question of his role is tied up with the larger question of his stature as an American President; some hold him to have been one of the best, others to have been one of the worst. At any rate, he won one of the most astonishing victories in our history in the 1948 election, when all the experts were sure that he would lose to Republican Thomas E. Dewey.

"The people," the sardonic humorist Ed Howe once said, "are always worsted in an election." But this was one time that he was wrong. Truman was a scrapper, and the people liked that and voted for him. He won despite the fact that a States' Rights candidate captured four Southern states, and that ex-Vice President Henry Wallace, running on a Progressive Party platform that was thought dangerously leftist, took many Northern liberal votes. (For Selections dealing with the questions of loyalty and internal security against the threat of communism, see numbers 81, 90-93, 100, 106-107, and 117-119. See also Selections 111 and 112.)

We are reminded of other occurrences of the 1940s by Selections in this volume. The American Negro, for example, suffered important defeats and experienced important victories during the decade; an example of the first was Truman's failure to get his Civil Rights bill passed (it had to wait for Lyndon Johnson), of the second, the desegration of the armed forces, which Truman brought about by executive order rather than trusting its implementation to Congress. (See Selections 20, 31, 51, 82, 94, and 101-102.) Labor also experienced vicissitudes during the decade, and although here too defeats probably outweighed victories, the increasing prosperity of the country helped make everyone more comfortable. (See Selections 5-6, 34, 44, 47, 55-56, 83-86, and 113.) The controversy about American education also continued in these years. The tendency was for more and more young people to stay longer and longer in school. Here the GI Bill, with its provision for federal aid to returning veterans who wanted to complete their educations, was a vastly important factor. But at the same time the indictments of the quality of the education provided by the schools became ever louder. Quantity versus quality had been the basic terms of the argument for more than a century, and old habits were not to be discarded in a day. (See Selections 7, 30, 37, 45, 50, 58, 80, 97, and 114.)

Two other Selections deserve special mention here. One (Selection 26) is a poem by Robert Frost, who became in this decade the grand old man of American letters. He read it at a Phi Beta Kappa exercise in December 1941, published it early the next year, and read it again at John F. Kennedy's inauguration nearly twenty years later. It was an attempt to sum up the American's relation to his country, an extraordinarily difficult task but, in this case, consummately performed.

The land was ours before we were the land's.
She was our land more than a hundred years
Before we were her people. She was ours
In Massachusetts, in Virginia,
But we were England's, still colonials,
Possessing what we still were unpossessed by,
Possessed by what we now no more possessed.
Something we were withholding made us weak
Until we found out that it was ourselves
We were withholding from our land of living,
And forthwith found salvation in surrender.
Such as we were we gave ourselves outright
(The deed of gift was many deeds of war)
To the land vaguely realizing westward,
But still unstoried, artless, unenhanced,
Such as she was, such as she would become.

Selection 109 is an extract from John Kouwenhoven's book *Made in America*, a study of American arts. In it, Kouwenhoven attempted to identify the characteristic strain in those arts, and concluded that much of the best American work is largely unconscious and is not thought of by many of us as art at all: bridges, for example, and jazz, and the skylines of cities, and Hollywood movies — the arts of the vernacular, as he called them. The traditional question that has disturbed so many Americans for so long is whether we have produced a great art, comparable to that of other cultures. Kouwenhoven's answer was simple and arresting. We have, he said, without noticing it; we have been at our best — and then very good indeed — when we haven't tried too hard. The point was not a new one — it had been made, for example, during the 1920s. But Kouwenhoven made it with eloquence and force.

# Chronology: 1940 - 1949

## 1940

**Jan. 26.** Japan's commercial treaty with the U.S. expires, and Secretary of State Cordell Hull tells Japan that the U.S. is not going to renew it. By end of March, Japan has established a puppet government in China.

**April 7.** Socialist Party convention nominates Norman Thomas of New York for President. **April 28.** Socialist Labor Party nominates John W. Aiken of Massachusetts. **May 10.** Prohibition Party nominates Roger W. Babson of Massachusetts. **June 2.** Communist Party nominates Earl Browder of Kansas. **June 28.** Republicans at Philadelphia nominate dark-horse candidate Wendell L. Willkie of New York for President and Senator Charles L. McNary of Oregon for his running mate. **July 18.** Democrats renominate President Roosevelt, although he has told the convention that he does not want a third term; Secretary of Agriculture Henry A. Wallace of Iowa is chosen for his running mate. Republican and Democratic platforms both support current foreign and defense policies and oppose involvement in foreign wars. Republicans approve most New Deal reforms but attack methods.

**April 9.** German troops invade Norway and Denmark; French and British forces sent to help resistance in Norway are unsuccessful and withdraw in June, but British troops occupy Iceland to prevent Germany from using it as a base.

**April 20.** Radio Corporation of America laboratories demonstrate first electron microscope; instrument is 10 feet high, weighs 700 pounds, and has magnification power of 20,000 to 25,000 diameters.

**May 10.** Germany invades Belgium, the Netherlands, and Luxembourg. Prime Minister Neville Chamberlain of England resigns and is replaced by Winston Churchill, heading a coalition government.

**May 28.** Belgian Army surrenders on orders from King Leopold; this strands English and French troops in Belgium, and more than 340,000 men are forced to withdraw across English Channel from Dunkirk, France. Operation takes a week; more than 850 vessels, from warships to private power boats, carry troops to England. **June 3.** During evacuation, the U.S. agrees, in answer to Prime Minister Churchill's appeal, to send Britain outdated and surplus war supplies, including aircraft.

**May 31.** By this date, President Roosevelt has requested defense appropriations amounting to $4,260,000,000 and has proposed production of 50,000 airplanes per year.

**June 5.** Battle of France begins when German Army crosses the Somme River, reaching Paris by June 14. Italy has declared war on Britain and France and attacked France from the south on June 10. **June 13.** Premier Paul Reynaud of France asks the U.S. for aid, but Marshal Henri Philippe Pétain succeeds Reynaud as head of government; Pétain negotiates peace with Germany on June 22 and with Italy two days later. Free French government moves to London, and Marshal Pétain sets up government of occupation at Vichy on July 2.

**June 15.** U.S. National Defense Research Committee is established; it is headed by Dr. Vannevar Bush.

**June 15-17.** Soviet Army occupies Lithuania, Latvia, and Estonia, which become part of the Soviet Union in August.

**June 16.** Pittman Resolution provides for sale of armaments to Latin-American countries; Germany and Italy are informed that the U.S. will not recognize transfer from one non-American country to another of any geographic region of the Western Hemisphere.

**June 22.** Congress passes tax measures that will raise $3-4 billion per year. National debt limit is increased from $45 billion to $49 billion.

**June 26.** Reconstruction Finance Corporation, established in 1932, is authorized to make loans to plants producing war materials.

**June 29.** Alien Registration (Smith) Act requires registration and fingerprinting of about 5 million aliens; Act also makes unlawful influences designed to overthrow any government in the U.S. by force.

**July 20.** President Roosevelt signs act providing for a $4 billion two-ocean Navy of 200 ships.

**July 30.** In order to forestall take-over by Germany of European possessions in the Western Hemisphere, 21 American nations sign Act of Havana. Agreement provides that as a measure of defense, any or all of American republics may assume protection of any European possession that seems to threaten aggression against it.

**Aug. 8.** Battle of Britain begins when Germany launches huge air offensive against coasts, cities, and installations of British Isles in effort to soften them up for planned invasion; British lack planes but secretly have developed radar. By October 12, after sustaining very heavy losses in aircraft, Germany is forced to give up idea of invasion, although extensive bombing continues.

**Aug. 18.** President Roosevelt and Canada's Prime Minister MacKenzie King establish Permanent Joint Board of Defense.

**Aug. 27.** President Roosevelt signs bill authorizing him to call out the National Guard and the organized reserves for a year's service.

**Sept. 3.** The U.S. announces transfer of 50 overage destroyers to Britain in exchange for 99-year leases of air and naval bases on Newfoundland, British Guiana, Bermuda, and islands of the West Indies.

**Sept. 4.** Secretary Hull notifies Japan that the U.S. will oppose Japanese aggression in French Indochina, but three weeks later Japan signs treaty with governor general of Indochina, who is loyal to French Vichy government, and gains air and troop bases there.

**Sept. 14.** Congress passes Selective Training and Service Act, first U.S. compulsory military training in peacetime; Act calls for registration of men between 21 and 35 years and training of a limit of 900,000 in first year. First draft numbers are chosen on October 29.

**Sept. 26.** President Roosevelt proclaims an embargo on export of scrap iron and steel to all countries except Britain and those in the Western Hemisphere. **Oct. 8.** Japanese ambassador terms measure an "unfriendly act."

**Sept. 27.** Japan signs military and economic pact with Germany and Italy, pledging mutual assistance.

**Oct. 25.** Strongly anti-Roosevelt labor leader John L. Lewis urges all members of Congress of Industrial Organizations (CIO) to vote for Willkie, saying he will resign the presidency of the CIO if Roosevelt wins election.

**October.** Germans occupy Rumania, and Italy invades Greece. British land forces on Greek islands, including Crete.

**Nov. 5.** President Roosevelt wins election by popular vote of 27,308,000 to Willkie's 22,321,000. Electoral vote is Roosevelt, 449; Willkie, 82. Democrats retain control of Congress.

**Nov. 21.** Lewis resigns as head of CIO; Philip Murray becomes president on following day.

**Dec. 9.** British forces attack Italians in

North Africa and within two months have destroyed Rodolfo Graziani's army, taking about 130,000 prisoners.

**Dec. 20.** U.S. Office of Production Management for Defense (later OPM) is set up, headed by William S. Knudsen; Office is coordinating agency for defense plants and is to send all possible aid to nations fighting the Axis. On the next day, Germany calls U.S. help to Britain "moral aggression."

1940 census shows U.S. population of 131,669,000, including 528,000 immigrants arrived since 1930; this is lowest immigration in more than a century, the result of 1927 quota law and world conditions. More than 56 percent of people live in places of 2,500 or more population. Average life expectancy has increased to about 63 years. Illiteracy is 2.9 percent, 1.4 percent less than in 1930.

Research on radar is intensified by National Defense Research Committee.

Richard Wright publishes *Native Son*, novel of a young Negro in an antagonistic society. *You Can't Go Home Again* by Thomas Wolfe is published, two years after his death.

# 1940 - 1941

Edwin M. McMillan and Philip H. Abelson discover first transuranium element, atomic number 93, which they call neptunium; early in 1941, McMillan, Glenn T. Seaborg, and others discover plutonium; both elements are radioactive.

# 1941

**Jan. 6.** In annual message that asks for further aid to anti-Axis nations, President Roosevelt enumerates "four freedoms" that he feels are necessary to postwar world:

freedom of speech and expression, freedom of worship, freedom from want, and freedom from fear.

**January-March.** U.S. and British military leaders hold secret talks in Washington; plan arrived at is for both countries to concentrate on conquering Germany first in the event that the U.S. should become involved in war against Japan.

**March 3.** Panama agrees for the duration of the war to allow the U.S. to maintain air defense installations beyond the limit of the Canal Zone.

**March 11.** Lend-Lease Act is signed by President Roosevelt. Congress authorizes the President to lend an initial $7 billion worth of war matériel to any nations whose defense he considers vital to that of the U.S. Measure is primarily intended to aid Great Britain, whose credit is rapidly becoming exhausted.

**March 24.** Axis forces begin counteroffensive against British troops in North Africa, forcing their withdrawal to Egypt.

**April 6.** Germany invades Yugoslavia and Greece; by April 23, both have surrendered, and British troops have withdrawn to Crete, which Germany, using airborne troops, subdues by June 1 after 11 days of fighting.

**April 9.** Feeling that defense of Greenland is necessary to that of the Western Hemisphere, U.S. Secretary of State Cordell Hull and Danish Minister Henrik de Kauffmann sign agreement that U.S. will defend Greenland against aggressors in return for right to build and maintain military installations there.

**April 11.** President Roosevelt tells Prime Minister Churchill that henceforth U.S.

ocean security zone to be patrolled will be extended to longitude 26° west, a line about halfway between England and U.S. East Coast. German submarines, working in packs, have done enormous damage to Allied and neutral shipping, especially in the North Atlantic.

**April 11.** Office of Price Administration and Civilian Supply (later OPA) is established to recommend price controls for prevention of wartime inflation. First act is to freeze steel prices. In September, secretary of the treasury says that price controls must be more stringent to ward off inflation. **Dec. 26.** OPA announces tire rationing, which eventually cuts down civilian consumption by 80 percent.

**April 13.** The Soviet Union and Japan sign nonaggression pact at Moscow.

**May 27.** President Roosevelt declares an unlimited national emergency; three weeks later the U.S. suspends diplomatic relations with Germany and Italy and freezes all their assets in the U.S. Germany and Italy immediately order closing of U.S. consulates in all countries controlled by the Axis.

**June 22.** Germany (and later Rumanian and Finnish troops) invades the Soviet Union along an 1,800-mile front from Finland to the Black Sea. **June 24.** President Roosevelt pledges U.S. assistance to the Soviet Union. **July 13.** Britain and the Soviet Union sign pact at Moscow agreeing that neither will make a separate peace with Germany.

**June 25.** Fair Employment Practices Committee is established to promote Negro equality in defense industries and government employment. The measure is a forerunner of later laws designed to establish economic opportunity and effective equality for Negroes.

**July 7.** The U.S., by agreement with the Icelandic government, occupies Iceland for the duration of the war to prevent its use by Germany for military bases; this move frees the large majority of British troops already there.

**July 23-26.** Japan occupies French Indochina. **July 25.** The U.S. and Britain halt all trade with Japan by freezing Japan's credits. On the following day, President Roosevelt calls Philippine armed forces into the service of the U.S under Lieutenant General Douglas MacArthur and names MacArthur commander of all U.S. and Philippine forces. Japanese ambassador to the U.S. is warned that further aggression by Japan in the Far East will lead to U.S. move to protect American rights.

**Aug. 14.** President Roosevelt and Prime Minister Churchill, having met off Newfoundland in two warships a few days earlier, issue joint statement of eight war and peace aims their governments wish to pursue; they pledge themselves to a common goal of destroying Nazi tyranny. By September 24, 11 anti-Axis countries have endorsed the Atlantic Charter.

**Aug. 18.** Term of service of U.S. Army draftees is extended for 18 months.

**Sept. 4.** U.S. destroyer *Greer*, in defensive waters off Iceland, is attacked by German submarine. A week later, President Roosevelt warns that German and Italian ships will cross American defense zones at their own risk and issues orders to U.S. Navy vessels to shoot on sight any Axis ships encountered in these zones.

**Sept. 29.** Missions from Britain and the U.S. consult in Moscow on war needs of the Soviet Union. By this time Germany has conquered most of the Ukraine and reached Leningrad. **Oct. 1.** The U.S. and Britain agree to give Soviet Union war matériel, and U.S. about a month later extends $1 billion of lend-lease credit. Russians suffer food shortage during ensuing winter.

**Oct. 11.** President Roosevelt secretly suggests to Britain that the two countries make joint effort to develop an atomic bomb.

**Oct. 17.** German submarine torpedoes U.S. destroyer *Kearny* near Iceland, with loss of 11 lives. At the end of October, U.S. destroyer *Reuben James*, convoying merchant ships between U.S. and Iceland, is sunk by German submarine; only 44 of the 120-man crew are rescued.

**Nov. 13.** Following President Roosevelt's request of October 9, Congress amends Neutrality Act of 1939 to permit arming of U.S. merchant ships and authorizes them to go to belligerent ports.

**Nov. 17.** Joseph C. Grew, U.S. ambassador to Japan, warns President Roosevelt that Japan may attack the U.S.

**Nov. 20.** Secretary Hull talks with Japanese representatives in Washington, who demand that the U.S. reestablish normal trade relations with Japan, give up interests in China, and stop naval expansion in the Pacific. **Nov. 26.** Secretary Hull proposes Japanese withdrawal from China and Indochina and a nonaggression pact in return for reestablishment of commercial relations. **Nov. 27.** Commanders of U.S. Pacific forces are warned that a Japanese carrier force has left Japan and that an attack may be imminent.

**Nov. 22.** Germans take Rostov-on-Don. **Nov. 29.** Soviet troops retake Rostov and in next two weeks start counteroffensive.

**Dec. 6.** President Roosevelt appeals to Japanese emperor to keep peace.

Dec. 7. Japanese carrier-based planes attack U.S. naval base at Pearl Harbor (at same time in Washington that Japanese representatives are delivering to Secretary Hull Japan's rejection of November 26 proposals); also attacked are Guam, the Philippines, Midway Island, Hong Kong, and the Malay Peninsula. Surprise attack on Pearl Harbor at 7:55 A.M. Sunday finds most U.S. warships docked or at anchor and planes on the ground; 19 ships are sunk or disabled, including 8 battleships and 3 destroyers; about 140 U.S. planes are destroyed; about 2,300 people, mostly sailors and soldiers, are killed, and 1,200 are wounded. Japanese lose 29 planes and 5 midget submarines.

Dec. 8. Congress declares war on Japan with only one dissenting vote. Dec. 11. Germany and Italy declare war on the U.S., and Congress adopts resolution recognizing a state of war with them.

Dec. 8-25. Japan, having crippled U.S. Pacific fleet and begun invasion of Malaya and Thailand, invades the Philippines and captures Guam, Wake Island, and Hong Kong.

Dec. 17-23. Conference attended by representatives of industry and labor votes no-strike and no-lockout policy for war industries and recommends a board to settle differences. National War Labor Board (WLB) is established in the following month, supplanting the National Defense Mediation Board.

Dec. 19. Congress extends Selective Service ages to 20 to 44 years.

In *United States* v. *Classic,* the Supreme Court upholds federal power to regulate state primary elections involving candidates for federal office; decision tends to increase Negro vote in Southern states.

The Supreme Court upholds Fair Labor Standards Act of 1938 on the ground that commerce is a national function and cannot be regulated in part by the states and in part by the federal government. Decision follows opinion in dissent of Justice Oliver Wendell Holmes, Jr., in 1918.

Sir Howard Florey, who has been working on large-scale manufacture of penicillin in England, comes to the U.S. to persuade drug manufacturers of its great value in saving lives; penicillin is soon turned out in large quantities, though not for unlimited civilian use until after the war.

# 1941 - 1946

The Supreme Court calls unconstitutional a California law that excludes "Okies," calling it a barrier to interstate commerce. In 1946 the Court makes a similar ruling in the case of a Jim Crow law involving interstate travel of Negroes.

# 1942

Jan. 1. Declaration of the United Nations is signed in Washington, D.C., by 26 countries, including the U.S., Great Britain, the Soviet Union, and China; each country pledges maximum war effort against the Axis and agrees not to sign a separate armistice or peace treaty.

Jan. 2. The Japanese occupy Manila, the Philippines; General MacArthur's troops retreat to Bataan Peninsula, with headquarters on Corregidor.

Jan. 11. Japan invades the Dutch East Indies, completing, except for a portion of New Guinea, occupation by the following summer.

Jan. 12. The U.S. and Mexico form mutual defense commission. In the following two weeks at Rio de Janeiro conference of American nations, all 21 delegates approve discontinuing diplomatic relations with the Axis; 19 governments follow delegates' recommendations at once, Chile one year later, and Argentina two years later.

**Jan. 16.** President Roosevelt establishes War Production Board (WPB), which is to be in charge of all war production and supply; this board supplants OPM.

**Jan. 24.** Three-day naval battle begins in Makasar Strait between Celebes and Borneo; Japanese invasion ships sustain major damage inflicted by Allied air and sea forces.

**Jan. 30.** President Roosevelt signs Emergency Price Control Act to curb rising prices and to put ceilings on rents in war industry areas. During World War II, retail price increases are considerably less than in World War I.

**Jan. 31.** U.S. carrier-based planes bombard Gilbert and Marshall islands. On the same day, British forces retreat from Malaya to Singapore but are forced to surrender that island to Japan on February 15.

**January.** Battle for North Africa between Germany and Britain continues, with Axis forces halted 60 miles west of Alexandria, Egypt, by the end of June.

Soviet forces continue counter-offensive begun at end of previous year toward the Ukraine; Red Army advances cease by March 15, but not before German forces are turned back from Moscow, Leningrad, and the Caucasus.

**January-June.** U.S. and Great Britain form special joint agencies to deal with raw materials, armaments, and foods. Most conferences are held in Washington.

**Feb. 7-Nov. 21.** Special wartime agencies are established to direct and control almost all aspects of national life; among others are strategic intelligence, housing, alien property, shipping, public information, and foreign relief. Among agencies formed in previous year are those that direct Western Hemisphere affairs, civilian defense, scientific research, lend-lease to Allies, censorship, and transportation.

**Feb. 25.** British are forced to withdraw from Rangoon, Burma, which makes it possible for Japan to cut off the Burma Road, main supply route between Allies and China. Japanese have attacked through forests from Thailand instead of by sea as expected.

**Feb. 27.** U.S. fleet starts three-day battle of the Java Sea in effort to delay Japanese invasion of Java; Allied losses are enormous at little cost to Japan.

**March 5-9.** Japan takes Batavia (present-day Jakarta), capital of Dutch East Indies, lands on island of New Guinea, and takes all of Java.

**March 17.** General Douglas MacArthur, on presidential orders, arrives in Australia from the Philippines to take command of Southwest Pacific Allied forces. In April, when Bataan falls, American forces on Bataan withdraw to Corregidor.

**March.** Federal government moves more than 110,000 Japanese from the West Coast to inland relocation camps; about 75,000 of these are American-born citizens of Japanese ancestry. Exclusion lasts until January 1945, is later called "our worst wartime mistake."

**April 18.** In surprise raid, U.S. carrier-based bombers reach and damage Tokyo and other Japanese cities; some crews are downed for lack of fuel to reach bases in China; others land in Japanese-occupied

China but are helped to escape by Chinese underground.

**April 18.** President Roosevelt establishes War Manpower Commission to supervise war training and recruiting, the draft, and industrial and agricultural war efforts.

**May 4-7.** U.S. forces frustrate Japan's plan to capture Port Moresby, New Guinea, in Battle of the Coral Sea, first naval engagement in which there is no contact of ships, all fighting being done by planes.

**May 6.** At end of month-long siege, 11,500 American and Filipino forces and refugees on Corregidor surrender to Japanese when lack of food and supplies makes further resistance impossible.

**May 14.** Congress passes measure providing for formation of the Women's Army Auxiliary Corps (WAAC, later WAC), which is soon followed by Women Accepted for Volunteer Emergency Service (WAVES, Navy); Women's Auxiliary Ferrying Squadron (WAFS, Air Force); Women's Reserve of the Coast Guard Reserve (SPARS, derived from Coast Guard motto, *Semper Paratus* [Always Ready]); and the Women's Reserve of the U.S. Marine Corps (WM).

**May 30.** British Royal Air Force, which advocates night saturation bombing, attacks Cologne, Germany, in 1,000-bomber raid and in June makes equally large raids on Essen and Bremen.

**June 3-6.** In most decisive naval battle of the war, Japanese lose 4 carriers and about 275 planes when they attempt to seize the Midway Islands, as a base for attack on Hawaii and the U.S. West Coast. This is first major defeat of modern Japanese Navy, and losses equalize Allied and Japanese naval power.

**June 3-21.** Japanese planes twice bomb Alaskan coastal town, two western islands of the Aleutians are occupied, and the coast of Oregon is shelled by a Japanese ship.

**June 10.** To avenge killing of Gestapo official, Germans destroy entire town of Lidice, Czechoslovakia, killing all men and removing all women and children to camps.

**June 27.** Federal Bureau of Investigation (FBI) announces capture of eight German saboteurs brought by submarines to Florida coast and Long Island, New York. Six are executed and two imprisoned.

**June.** By this month, shipyards of Henry J. Kaiser on the West Coast have been assigned one-third of U.S. wartime shipbuilding. Assembly-line methods, in which ships are made in parts that are welded together instead of built from the keel up, make it possible for a ship to be completed in less than a week; Kaiser's record is four days from start to finish.

**July 21.** Japanese land troops near Gona, New Guinea, with intent to launch an overland attack on Port Moresby, crossing mountains toward the south coast, but by mid-November Allied forces have forced them back across the mountains to Buna and Gona and taken several other New Guinea positions.

**July 22.** German Army crosses Don in two-pronged drive toward the Caucasus and Stalingrad (present-day Volgograd), which they enter in mid-September.

**July.** Joint Chiefs of Staff, meeting in London, plan invasion of Axis-held North Africa and increased activity against Japan in the Pacific, postponing second front in Europe (attack from French coast). **Aug. 12.** Soviet Premier Joseph Stalin, Prime Minister Winston Churchill, and W. Averill

Harriman (representing President Roosevelt) meet in Moscow. Stalin is told that the Allies cannot relieve hard-pressed Soviet forces by opening a second front in 1942.

**Aug. 7.** In first major offensive against Japan, U.S. Marines land on Guadalcanal in Solomon Islands and take airport. Sea, air, and land battles for the island seesaw back and forth for six months; losses are heavy on both sides. By February 9, 1943, all Japanese are cleared from the island.

**Aug. 17.** U.S. 8th Air Force makes first independent U.S. bombing attack in Europe when B-17s raid railroad yards near Rouen, France. U.S. advocates pinpoint bombing by daylight.

**Aug. 19.** British and Canadian troops, with a few U.S. Rangers, raid Dieppe on coast of France; about half of force is killed, wounded, or taken prisoner. In previous months, commando raids have been made on other parts of French coast.

**September.** Brigadier General Leslie R. Groves is appointed military head of Manhattan District for development of atomic bomb. Major construction on three plants — at Oak Ridge, Tennessee; Los Alamos, New Mexico; and Richland, Washington — does not begin until following year.

**Oct. 1.** Test pilot for Bell Aircraft Corporation flies first American jet airplane in California.

**Oct. 9.** Britain and the U.S. declare that they will give up extraterritorial rights in China and in January of the following year sign treaties with China to this effect; treaties give China equal status among world powers.

**Nov. 3.** In fall elections Democrats keep majorities in House and Senate, although Republicans gain 9 Senate seats and 46 in the House.

**Nov. 8.** U.S. and British amphibious operation begins in North Africa under Lieutenant General Dwight D. Eisenhower and Admiral Sir Andrew Cunningham. Landings are made at Casablanca, Oran, and Algiers; Oran is taken on November 10. **Nov. 11.** In effort to minimize casualties, Allies make treaty with Admiral Jean Darlan, representative of French Vichy government, that involves his becoming high commissioner of French North Africa. Immediately German forces are sent into unoccupied France. **Nov. 27.** French fleet at Toulon is sunk by its crews to prevent take-over by Germans.

**Nov. 13.** Draft age is lowered to 18 years, and all men between 18 and 38 become eligible; at the same time, voluntary enlistments are ended. Some industrial and agricultural workers, as well as clergymen, are deferred.

**Dec. 2.** First controlled self-sustaining nuclear chain reaction, set off by Enrico Fermi and associates at the University of Chicago, demonstrates feasibility of atomic bomb and potentiality of nuclear power for peacetime uses.

**December.** By end of 1942, Japan has taken control of an area that reaches from Burma on the west to the Marshall and Gilbert islands on the east, from the western Aleutian Islands on the north to the Dutch East Indies on the south, and includes Korea, Manchuria, Thailand, French Indochina, and much of mainland China.

# 1942 - 1945

Rationing of foods and materials essential to the war effort begins generally in 1942 (although auto tire rationing has begun almost immediately after Pearl Harbor); sugar, coffee, fuel oil, gasoline, fats, oils, butter, meats, cheese, canned and processed foods, and, finally, shoes are rationed. Except for sugar, all products are off rationing lists by end of 1945; sugar rationing is discontinued 18 months later.

# 1943

**January.** President Roosevelt and Prime Minister Churchill meet at Casablanca, Morocco; decisions made are that unconditional surrender of Axis powers will be the only acceptable basis for ending the war; a second front must be launched (although no date or place is fixed); Sicily and Italy will be invaded as a separate operation from second front; General Dwight D. Eisenhower is to command all of North African campaign.

**March-September.** Battle of the Bismarck Sea results in the sinking of 12 Japanese transports and 10 warships; by September 16, Allied forces have retaken Lae in New Guinea.

**April 7.** British and U.S. forces under command of General Eisenhower join lines in Tunisia in campaign to drive Axis forces out of Africa. With U.S. forces attacking from the west and British from the east, Axis are encircled and a month later retreat to Cap Bon Peninsula, where on May 12, more than 200,000 surrender in end of North African phase of war.

**April 8.** Because of threatened inflation, President Roosevelt freezes wages, salaries, and prices. **April 17.** War Manpower Commission freezes 27 million workers in essential industries in their jobs.

**April 26.** Soviet Union breaks off diplomatic relations with Polish government-in-exile.

**May 27.** President Roosevelt directs that all war contracts must include clauses prohibiting racial discrimination in war industries. Upgrading of Negroes results in riots; rioters controlled by federal troops.

**May.** President Roosevelt, Prime Minister Churchill, and many British and U.S. officials, meeting in Washington, D.C., settle May 1, 1944, as date for invasion of northwestern Europe.

**May.** After three weeks of fighting, U.S. forces retake Attu Island in the western Aleutians; three months later U.S. and Canadian forces attack Kiska but find that Japanese have abandoned it.

**June 3.** Generals Henri Giraud and Charles de Gaulle, after meeting in French Algiers, announce establishment of French Committee of National Liberation (later French Provisional Government-in-Exile); the two generals are to be co-presidents. Committee pledges maximum support of the Allies against the Axis.

**June 14.** Supreme Court reverses 1940 decision and holds that children cannot be required to salute the flag in school if their religion prohibits it; case has been brought by Jehovah's Witnesses.

**June 25.** War Labor Disputes (Smith-Connally) Act is passed over President Roosevelt's veto. Act authorizes the President to prevent labor disputes from interfering with war production by having government operate industry. This authority is later used in mine and railroad disputes.

**June 30-December.** U.S. naval and amphibious forces begin "island hopping" campaign in Solomon Islands; strategy is to take key islands as bases for attacking next target and bypassing others, since seizure of every Japanese-occupied island will be too costly. By end of the year, the U.S. has gained control of the Solomons (except Bougainville) and landed at two points on New Britain.

July 10. U.S., British, and Canadian forces begin sea and air invasion of Sicily from bases in Tunisia. By August 17, Sicily has been captured, to be used as takeoff point for invasion of the Italian mainland.

July 19. "Big Inch," world's longest oil pipeline, is dedicated. It has been laid over about 1,300 miles from Texas to Pennsylvania, crossing about 230 rivers and streams.

July 25. Italy's Premier Mussolini and his Cabinet resign; new government is headed by Marshal Pietro Badoglio. July 28. Italian Fascist Party is dissolved.

August. Russians battle fiercely against German offensive begun on July 5 and by November 6 have retaken Orel, Belgorod, Smolensk, Dnepropetrovsk, and Kiev. By beginning of 1944 they have pushed Germans back west of Kiev and entered Poland.

Quebec Conference meets, attended by President Roosevelt, Prime Minister Churchill, chiefs of staff, and other advisers. May 1, 1944, date for invasion of Europe is discussed, as well as supplementary invasion of southern France. Plans are made for increased military operations in the Far East, especially Burma.

Sept. 3. British and Canadians invade Italy from Sicily. Sept. 8. Italy surrenders unconditionally. Sept. 9. U.S. forces land south of Naples and meet determined German resistance, which ends by September

15. By this time, Germany has taken Rome, and the Italian fleet has surrendered to the Allies. Sept. 12. Mussolini, who has been arrested by new Italian government, escapes and sets up Fascist government in German-occupied parts of Italy, where German armies continue to fight until end of war.

Sept. 21. House of Representatives adopts Fulbright Resolution, which advocates formation of "international machinery" to achieve and keep a "just and lasting peace." Nov. 5. Senate adopts resolution introduced by Senator Tom Connally of Texas that is similar but requires Senate ratification of any international agreement made to this end.

Oct. 13. Italy declares war on Germany.

October. Representatives of Britain, the U.S., and the Soviet Union meet in Moscow; the U.S. and Britain tell Russians of second front preparations; Soviets pledge declaration of war on Japan once Germany is beaten and refuse to recognize Polish government-in-exile. Allies set up European Advisory Commission to work out basic principles for postwar treatment of Germany and Italy. All three powers declare that they recognize the necessity of an international organization to maintain world peace.

Nov. 9. Assistance for victims of war is planned when 44 nations meeting in Washington establish United Nations Relief and Rehabilitation Administration (UNRRA). In next two years, member nations agree to contribute $4 billion for relief.

Nov. 22. Generalissimo and Madame Chiang Kai-shek of China meet in Cairo, Egypt, with President Roosevelt and Prime Minister Churchill; in Declaration of Cairo they agree to demand unconditional surrender of Japan, declare that their countries do not aim for territorial expansion, state that

Japan must be deprived of all Pacific islands gained since 1914 and must return Chinese territories to China, and agree that Korea must become independent as soon as possible. Soviet Union does not attend, not being at war with Japan.

**Nov. 23.** After three days of bloody fighting, U.S. Marines take Tarawa and Makin islands in the Gilberts in second step toward Japan via Solomon, Gilbert, Marshall, Mariana, and Bonin islands.

**Nov. 28.** President Roosevelt, Prime Minister Churchill, and Premier Stalin meet at Teheran, Iran, and plan second front in Western Europe; Stalin again promises to enter war against Japan. General Eisenhower is named commander of the invasion of Western Europe on Dec. 24.

**Dec. 17.** President Roosevelt signs bill repealing Chinese Exclusion Acts and setting annual Chinese immigration quota at 105.

**Dec. 31.** By this date, Allied forces have control of southern Italy to a line across the peninsula about halfway between Naples and Rome.

By end of 1943, Allies have taken the initiative in all theaters of war: Pacific, Mediterranean, Eastern Europe, and Southeast Asia; air attacks on Germany are constant from Allied bases in England.

Wendell Willkie publishes his *One World,* following his 31,000-mile, 49-day journey around the world; a strong plea for international cooperation, it sells 1 million copies within two months and eventually more than 2 million. Other best sellers of this year are *A Tree Grows in Brooklyn* by Betty Smith and *Here Is Your War* by Ernie Pyle; the latter is one of many war books, mostly by correspondents. Pyle is killed on island near Okinawa in April 1945.

Regional painting thrives in this period, especially Middle Western subjects, such as those by Grant Wood, Thomas Hart Benton, and John Steuart Curry. At the same time, many refugee artists work in the U.S., among them Piet Mondrian, Marc Chagall, and Fernand Léger. Most original painting is by Jackson Pollock, who gives his first one-man show in this year.

## 1943 - 1944

**1943.** The Supreme Court declines to consider case involving exclusion of Japanese from the West Coast but upholds military curfew in that area. **1944.** Court upholds Japanese exclusion (*Korematsu* v. *U.S.*), although dissent calls relocation unconstitutional; however, in another case, the Court finds that no person whose loyalty to the U.S. has been established may be relocated.

## 1943 - 1945

**May 15, 1943.** The Soviet Union dissolves the Third International (Comintern). A year later, U.S. Communist Party is dissolved but reformed as the Communist Political Association. This group is discontinued in 1945 and again becomes the Communist Party.

## 1943 - 1948

U.S. scientists begin research on antihistamines for use in treatment of allergies. Several have been discovered by 1948, including Dramamine, which is found to be effective in controlling motion sickness.

## 1944

**Jan. 11.** Allies begin air attacks against Germany from Britain in preparation for invasion of France. **March 4.** Berlin is bombed for first time by U.S. planes;

bombing reaches height in April and in May just before invasion begins. General Eisenhower establishes Supreme Headquarters, Allied Expeditionary Force (SHAEF), in Britain immediately after start of air attacks.

**Jan. 18-March 3.** Having begun counter-offensive on three fronts late in previous year, Russians relieve Leningrad defenders, who have been besieged for 17 months, and retake Stalingrad, Rostov-on-Don, Kharkov, and Rzhev.

**January.** General Joseph ("Vinegar Joe") Stilwell, U.S. commander in Southeast Asia, launches campaign in northern Burma aimed at capturing airfield at Myitkyina to gain Allied access to China. By May 17, 1944, airfield is taken.

**March 19.** U.S. forces conquer essential parts of Admiralty Islands and one month later capture Japanese airfields at Hollandia, on north coast of Netherlands (present-day West) New Guinea.

**March 20.** German forces occupy Hungary. **April 10.** Soviet forces retake Odessa and, a month later, Sevastopol; at beginning of year, German invaders have been cleared from the area between Moscow and Leningrad.

**June 4.** U.S. 5th Army liberates Rome, having landed to the south with other Allied units in January.

**June 6.** D-Day invasion of Europe begins; date in early May has been changed because of necessity of shipping landing craft from Mediterranean theater, and because tides, the moon, daylight, and weather conditions must be favorable to amphibious landings, as well as paratroop landings inland. Invasion, along 50-mile Normandy coastline, is spearheaded by about 175,000 troops carried in 4,000 landing craft and supported by 600 warships and about 11,000 planes. **June 13.** Germans counterattack by bombarding England, especially London, with V-1 rockets, pilotless and jet propelled.

**June 15.** B-29 long-range Superfortresses bomb Kyushu from bases in China and India in first raid of campaign against Japanese home islands. In November, raids are carried out from rebuilt airfields on captured Saipan Island, in the Marianas.

**June 21.** Three-day air and naval battle of Philippine Sea costs Japan 450 planes and 3 carriers, as well as crippling 4 carriers, a battleship, and a cruiser. The U.S. losses include 20 aircraft and negligible ship damage.

**June 22.** President Roosevelt signs Servicemen's Readjustment Act ("G.I. Bill of Rights"); it establishes educational and other benefits for veterans after demobilization. By end of 1946, two million veterans are beneficiaries of this law, mostly in colleges and universities.

**June 23.** Soviet forces launch offensive south of Leningrad along 300-mile line.

**June 26.** Republicans meet at Chicago and nominate Governor Thomas E. Dewey of New York for President and Governor John W. Bricker of Ohio for Vice-President. **July 20.** Democrats at Chicago renominate President Roosevelt but choose Senator Harry S. Truman of Missouri for Vice-President instead of Vice-President Wallace. Minor party candidates are: Norman Thomas of New York, Socialist; Claude A. Watson of California, Prohibition; and Edward A. Teichert of Pennsylvania, Socialist Labor. Platforms of both Democrats and Republicans advocate membership in an international organization to maintain world peace. CIO Political Action Committee supports Democrats.

**July 1-22.** United Nations Monetary and Financial Conference is held at Bretton Woods, New Hampshire, with 44 nations attending. Policies and plans are developed for mutual assistance in economic recovery and restoration of trade; International Monetary Fund is established for currency stabilization, along with International Bank for Reconstruction and Development. The Soviet Union takes part in Conference but does not join new financial institutions.

**July 2.** By this date Allies have taken Cherbourg, France, and landed about 1 million troops in Normandy, with vehicles and supplies to support them. **July 18.** British have taken Caen, and U.S. forces take Saint-Lô. Advancing from Saint-Lô a week later, armored forces penetrate Brittany and by August 9, Americans have laid siege to ports of Brest, Lorient, and Saint-Nazaire.

**July 18.** Premier Hideki Tojo, disgraced by loss of Saipan, resigns as head of Japanese government; his Cabinet follows suit.

**July 19.** U.S. forces capture Leghorn, on west coast of Italy. **Aug. 12.** Allies take Florence, forcing Germans to line north of the Arno River.

**July 20.** German Army factions attempt bomb assassination of Adolf Hitler; following its failure, many high-ranking officers, including Field Marshall Rommel, are executed or commit suicide.

**July 27.** The Soviet Union, opposed strongly by the U.S. and Britain, recognizes as government of Russian-occupied Poland the Polish Committee of National Liberation, which is later seated in Lublin.

**Aug. 9.** By this date, Pacific island-hopping campaign has resulted in establishment of U.S. footholds in the Marshalls and the Marianas.

**Aug. 14.** War Production Board authorizes partial conversion of war industries to civilian output. Office of War Mobilization and Reconversion is established in October in anticipation of economic and social problems in transition from war to peace.

**Aug. 15.** Southern France is invaded by Allied forces, which land between Marseilles and Nice and fight up the Rhône River Valley toward armies in northern France. **Aug. 25.** French 2nd Armored Division enters Paris, and three days later U.S. 3rd Army reaches the Marne River. **Sept. 4.** British and Canadian troops capture Brussels and badly needed port of Antwerp, which is also German V-2 rocket launching site. By this time the Allies have landed more than 2 million men and their supplies on the Continent.

**Aug. 21-Oct. 7.** Representatives of the U.S., Britain, China, and the Soviet Union meet at Dumbarton Oaks, Washington, D.C., to discuss postwar world organization. Proposals agreed on later serve as basis for United Nations Charter. Security Council is planned as executive branch, but the Soviet Union does not agree on voting plan, refusing to consent to the rule that a Security Council nation may not vote in an issue involving itself.

**Aug. 22.** Allied forces, having circled Germans and attacking from north and south, close German escape gap between Falaise and Argentan, killing or capturing about 500,000 German troops.

**Sept. 11.** U.S. forces enter Germany through Luxembourg. In next two weeks, in largest airborne operation ever attempted, Allies land more than 20,000 paratroops and their equipment in the Netherlands to secure bridgeheads for advancing ground troops. **Oct. 21.** U.S. forces take Aachen, Germany, after three-week battle, and one month later Metz and Strasbourg are captured.

**Sept. 11-16.** President Roosevelt and Prime Minister Churchill meet in Quebec to discuss European and Pacific battle plans, occupation zones after defeat of Germany, and treatment of Germany after the war.

**Sept. 15.** Invasion of Palau Islands begins; about two weeks later, marines take Peleliu, about 500 miles from the Philippines.

**Sept. 29.** President Roosevelt, concerned over increase of Nazi and Fascist influence in Argentina and lack of cooperation against Axis, accuses Argentina of reneging on inter-American obligations.

**Oct. 20.** U.S. forces headed by General MacArthur return to Philippines, landing on Leyte. Six-day naval battle in Leyte Gulf (actually four separate operations), with loss of 24 Japanese carriers, battleships, cruisers, and destroyers, marks end of Japanese fleet as an effective force.

**October.** Prime Minister Churchill and Premier Stalin, meeting in Moscow, plan division of postwar influence in southeastern Europe; the Soviet Union is to control Hungary, Bulgaria, and Rumania; Britain is to predominate in Greece; and Yugoslavia is to be divided between Great Britain and Soviet Union. President Roosevelt, not present at the conference, announces that he will not be obligated by British-Soviet decisions.

**Nov. 7.** President Roosevelt is elected for a fourth term with popular vote of 25,607,000 to Dewey's 22,015,000; vote includes several million absentee ballots sent by members of the armed forces. Minor candidates receive less than 1 percent of vote. Electoral vote is Roosevelt, 36 states with 432 votes; Dewey, 12 states with 99 votes. About 70 percent of U.S. press has supported Dewey. CIO Political Action Committee claims that its support has helped elect 120 Democratic representatives and 17 senators.

**Dec. 15.** Congress creates new rank, General of the Army ("five-star general"), for Generals Eisenhower, Henry Arnold, MacArthur, and George C. Marshall.

**Dec. 16-27.** In Battle of the Bulge, last major Axis counteroffensive of the war, German armored forces drive toward Antwerp, attacking thinly defended Allied line, in hope of splitting British-U.S. armies. Delayed by defenders of Bastogne, which is almost surrounded, Germans are finally defeated with heavy losses on both sides. By January 31, 1945, Allied forces have regained former line in the Ardennes.

**Dec. 26.** Russians, driving westward on all fronts, have by this date taken Estonian port of Tallinn, entered East Prussia, with Yugoslav forces taken Belgrade, and laid siege to Budapest. In addition, British and Greek forces have driven Germans out of Greece.

U.S. Supreme Court, in Texas case involving exclusion of Negroes from Democratic Party, and consequently from participating in primaries, holds that exclusion from a political party on ground of race is tantamount to a denial of suffrage and hence a violation of the Fifteenth Amendment.

# 1944 - 1945

By 1944, military goods are about 65 percent of total U.S. production as opposed to 2 percent in 1939. Aluminum production, mainly for aircraft, has increased 500 percent; synthetic rubber production has risen from 2,000 tons in 1939 to more than 900,000 tons in 1945.

## 1944 - 1950

Glenn Seaborg and associates produce four man-made elements, americium, curium, berkelium, and californium, element numbers 95 through 98.

## 1945

**Jan. 23.** Soviet troops reach Oder River on border of Germany after offensive that has begun in Poland on January 12.

**Feb. 4-11.** President Roosevelt, Prime Minister Churchill, and Premier Stalin meet in the Crimea at Yalta. Their agreements (many of which are not made public until after the war) give the Soviet Union extensive territorial and other rights in the Far East in return for promise to enter war against Japan; they also work out plans for treatment of Germany and liberated nations, and reparations are discussed. Voting in United Nations Security Council is agreed on, and date is set for San Francisco Conference on Charter.

**Feb. 8.** Allied drive across Germany begins with attacks in northern, central, and southern Germany. **March 2.** U.S. troops have crossed the Saar River, entered the Ruhr Valley, and are approaching Düsseldorf. **March 23.** Allies cross Rhine near Wesel. **March 26.** U.S. forces cross Rhine at Worms and push northward into the Ruhr. **March 29.** Mannheim and Frankfurt am Main captured. **April 11.** U.S. forces reach Elbe River. **April 17.** Düsseldorf surrenders, and on following day Ruhr pocket is liquidated; German prisoners total 325,000, including 30 generals.

**Feb. 10.** B-29s raid Tokyo nine days before U.S. marines land 750 miles from Japan on Iwo Jima; island is taken only after major struggle lasting for almost a month; casualties are heavy. **March 24-27.** Carrier-based planes pound Japanese in Okinawa, 350 miles from Japan, in preparation for invasion that begins on April 1. Japanese air attacks on invasion forces, continuing into June, result in heaviest losses of war, about 45,000 killed or wounded. Okinawa is taken by June 21.

**Feb. 24.** After battle of almost three weeks, U.S. forces take Manila, capital of the Philippines; this marks end of campaign in these islands.

**March 3.** Finland, out of the war since end of 1941, declares war on Germany.

**March 3.** In Act of Chapultepec, all American nations except Argentina sign mutual security pact that permits "use of armed force to prevent or repel aggression" by one state against another. **March 12.** Argentina is admitted to Pan American Union and 15 days later declares war on the Axis.

**April 5.** Soviet Union abrogates nonaggression pact with Japan but does not declare war. On same day, Japanese premier and his Cabinet resign.

**April 12.** President Roosevelt dies of a cerebral hemorrhage at Warm Springs, Georgia, after less than three months of his fourth term. Vice-President Harry S. Truman becomes thirty-third President.

**April 20.** U.S. forces take Nürnberg, and three days later Russians enter Berlin. **April 25.** Soviet troops from the east and U.S. forces from the west meet on the Elbe River at Torgau. On the next day, British take Bremen.

**April 25-June 26.** United Nations Charter is drafted at San Francisco. Fifty nations take part in meeting; Charter is signed by all and becomes effective October 24.

**April 28.** As Allied armies invade Po Valley in Italy, Italian partisans capture and kill Benito Mussolini and his mistress as they are trying to escape to Switzerland.

**May 2.** Berlin is taken a day after announcement by provisional German government that Hitler has committed suicide. Germans in Italy surrender on the same day, and two days later German forces in Denmark, the Netherlands, and northwest Germany follow suit. **May 7.** Unconditional German surrender is signed at Allied Reims headquarters; it becomes effective at midnight May 8-9. A month later, Germany is divided into four sectors by European Advisory Commission; northwestern area is to be controlled by Britain, the Rhineland and the Saar by France, southwestern area by the U.S., and eastern area by the Soviet Union; Berlin, within Soviet area, is divided into four similar sectors.

**May 3.** Rangoon captured by Allies. This virtually closes Burma campaign.

**May-December.** Immediately after end of war in Europe, the U.S. begins to convert to peacetime economy. Rationing on all items but sugar is ended; War Production Board lifts ban on manufacture of consumer goods, removing 210 controls on August 20 and, except for shortage materials, ending Controlled Materials Plan on September 30; production of military aircraft by December is one-half that of previous year, manpower controls are ended in August; and by end of the year, National War Labor Board is replaced by National Wage Stabilization Board.

**July 16.** First atomic bomb is exploded in the desert at Alamogordo, New Mexico. President Truman informs Churchill and Stalin at Potsdam Conference of successful test, but public announcement is not made until August 6.

**July 17-Aug. 2.** U.S., Great Britain, and Soviet Union hold Potsdam Conference. Unconditional surrender of Japan is reaffirmed as war aim, and ultimatum is sent to Japanese government; treaties with Germany and her allies are discussed; war crimes trials are planned.

**July 28.** U.S. Senate ratifies United Nations Charter, with two dissenting votes.

**July 29.** Japan rejects unconditional surrender demand sent from Potsdam Conference, although mainland of Japan has been heavily bombed by U.S. forces since beginning of May.

**Aug. 6.** Atomic bomb is dropped on Hiroshima, Japan; about four square miles of the city are devastated by explosion equal to 20,000 tons of TNT; more than 135,000 people are killed or injured.

**Aug. 8.** The Soviet Union declares war on Japan and invades Manchuria; declaration comes three months after Germany's surrender as promised.

**Aug. 9.** The U.S. drops second atomic bomb, this time on Nagasaki, a provincial capital and naval base in southern Japan.

**Aug. 15.** V-J Day ending war in Pacific is proclaimed after Potsdam ultimatum has been accepted by Japanese on August 10 and unconditional surrender has been agreed to on August 14; Emperor Hirohito is allowed to retain his throne. Occupation of Japan begins two weeks later, and formal surrender is signed aboard battleship *Missouri* in Tokyo Bay on September 2. **Sept. 9.** At Nanking, Japanese sign formal surrender of forces in China.

Aug. 21. Lend-lease program ends. Total U.S. receipts during the war have been about $8 billion; outlay has been almost $50 billion. U.S. aid for recovery of war-torn nations is continued by UNRRA and, later, the Marshall Plan (European Recovery Program).

Sept. 11-Oct. 2. Council of Foreign Ministers of principal Allies meets at London to draft treaties with former Axis powers. Failure to agree on proposed treaty with Germany is first serious breach between the Soviet Union and the other major Allies. A second conference, held at Moscow from December 16 to 26, considers Far East questions also, as well as eventual international atomic energy control.

Dec. 22. President Truman orders special arrangement for admission of displaced persons to U.S. Forty thousand are admitted under this order before legislation in 1948 authorizes increases in immigration quotas for war victims. At end of World War II, fought by 57 Allied and Axis countries, military personnel killed and missing are: Allies, 10,650,000; Axis, 4,650,000. This does not include estimated equal number of civilian deaths resulting from starvation, bombing of cities, and mass murders by Axis powers. The U.S., Britain, the Soviet Union, China, France, Germany, Italy, and Japan have borne major cost in dollars and lives. In proportion to population, the U.S. killed and missing figures are lightest: 292,000, or 1 per 450 of population; U.S.S.R. figures are heaviest: 7,500,000, or 1 per 22 of population. Proportion of deaths to total casualties in World War II (less than 1 to 4) is less than half that of World War I because of more efficient and rapid methods of evacuation of wounded, use of blood plasma, and control of disease and infection with penicillin and sulfa drugs. Cost to the U.S. in loans and matériel supplied is about $350 billion. About 16 million U.S. citizens have served in military units. At end of the war, about 10 million European civilians are out of their own countries as refugees, prisoners, or slave laborers.

Although U.S. citizens and corporations have been taxed more than ever before, revenue from all taxes has amounted to less than half of wartime expenditures. Government borrowing to raise the remainder increases the national debt from 1940 level of per capita $325 to $1,849.

During the war, the U.S. government has, through the Defense Plant Corporation, financed about 85 percent of new war plants; by 1945 it owns about nine-tenths of aircraft, shipbuilding, magnesium, and synthetic rubber plants; about three-quarters of aluminum producers; and about half of machine-tool manufacturers.

Arthur M. Schlesinger, Jr., publishes his Pulitzer Prize history *The Age of Jackson*.

# 1946

Jan. 10. First meeting of the General Assembly of the United Nations is held in London; 51 nations take part. Security Council meets in the same month.

Jan. 19. Iran protests to the United Nations Security Council against presence of Soviet troops in Iran after agreed-on date for Allied withdrawal. U.S. supports Iran. In April the Soviet Union states that troops will withdraw on May 6.

Feb. 21. Office of Economic Stabilization is reestablished within Office for Emergency Management. June 30. Price control expires, but some controls are reestablished on July 25 and continue until following June; however, most wage and price controls are terminated in this year.

**March 5.** Winston Churchill, in speech at Fulton, Missouri, asserts that an "iron curtain" has come down across Europe "from Stettin in the Baltic to Trieste in the Adriatic," ending an era of hopeful wartime collaboration between Western Allies and the Soviet Union. President Truman is in the audience.

**April 1.** Strike of 400,000 United Mine Workers begins; workers, whose wages have been fixed for several years, demand more money and fringe benefits. President Truman seizes mines and threatens to continue operating them under government authority when employers refuse government-negotiated contract. Second strike in November, defying an injunction, leads to contempt citation against John L. Lewis, who is fined $10,000, and union, which is fined $3,500,000. Almost all the largest labor unions call strikes this year after lifting of wartime restrictions.

**April 18.** League of Nations dissolves itself, transferring its properties to the United Nations.

**April 25.** Council of Foreign Ministers meets at Paris to discuss peace treaties for satellites of the Axis and arrives at terms by July 4. Council calls a meeting of 21 nations to consider treaty drafts, but there are persistent disagreements between Western countries and the Soviet Union, which finally objects to participation of smaller nations. Conference breaks up in October with agreement on only minor issues.

**May 20.** General George C. Marshall, special envoy to China with rank of ambassador, accuses both sides in Chinese civil war of generating hate campaigns. **June 24.** Head of Communist Chinese, Mao Tse-tung, insists that the U.S. cease supplying arms to Nationalist Chinese and evacuate its forces from China. Seven months later, Communists and Nationalists are informed that the U.S. has given up efforts at mediation of the conflict. In 1949, Nationalists, under Chiang Kai-shek, withdraw to island of Formosa, leaving mainland to Communists.

**June 14.** Bernard Baruch, U.S. delegate to UN Atomic Energy Commission, proposes plan to outlaw manufacture of atomic bombs, dismantle those already existing, and share atomic energy secrets with other nations. Plan includes right of international inspection of manufacturing facilities, but the Soviet Union, which has a similar plan, does not accept international inspection.

**July 4.** The U.S. grants full independence to the Philippines as provided in the Philippine Commonwealth and Independence (Tydings-McDuffie) Act of 1934. Republic of the Philippines remains allied to the U.S. and leases military bases to U.S. forces.

**July 7.** Mother Frances Xavier Cabrini is canonized; she is first U.S. citizen to become a saint.

**July.** U.S. explodes two atomic bombs off Bikini Atoll in Pacific in first test of effect on military equipment, especially warships.

**Aug. 1.** U.S. Atomic Energy Commission is established. Five-man civilian board headed by David E. Lilienthal is authorized to develop and control all military and peaceful aspects of atomic energy.

**Aug. 1.** President Truman signs bill implementing proposal of Senator J. William Fulbright of Arkansas to use funds from postwar sale of wartime surplus goods to Allies to pay for international exchange of students and teachers, on model of educational use of Boxer Rebellion indemnity funds in 1901. Action creates world's largest international fund for such purposes; program continues to the present day.

**Aug. 2.** U.S. Senate resolution accepts compulsory jurisdiction of new International Court of Justice under United Nations Charter.

**Sept. 20.** President Truman dismisses Henry Wallace, secretary of commerce, following Wallace's advocacy of continued cooperation with the Soviet Union. Dismissal ends debate in U.S. government on "hard" or "soft" policy toward Soviets.

**Oct. 1.** After ten-month trial at Nürnberg, Germany, of 24 major Nazis for crimes against peace, humanity, and the laws of war, 12 are sentenced to death. In U.S. zone of occupation, 12 other trials of major war criminals are subsequently held at Nürnberg under international authority.

**Oct. 1.** Acting Secretary of State Dean Acheson states that the U.S. will keep occupation forces in South Korea until North Korea is evacuated by Soviet troops and a free government is formed for the unified country.

**Nov. 5.** In fall elections, Republicans win enough seats to control both House and Senate for first time in 16 years.

**Dec. 2.** Britain and the U.S. sign agreement for economic merger of their occupation sectors of Germany. Previously in this year, the U.S. has slowed down dismantling of West German industrial equipment for reparations payments.

**Dec. 14.** The UN accepts John D. Rockefeller's $8,500,000 gift site in New York City for its headquarters.

Robert Penn Warren publishes *All the King's Men*, his novel of Southern politics;

it wins the Pulitzer Prize in the following year.

# 1946 - 1949

**June 4, 1946-Oct. 19, 1949.** Trial of high-ranking Japanese leaders results in sentences of hanging for 7 (after U.S. Supreme Court has denied its right to hear appeal), life imprisonment for 16, and shorter terms for 2 by November 12, 1948. Local trials held at sites of Japanese wartime military activity result in 4,200 convictions and 720 executions by the time they are officially announced closed on October 19, 1949.

# 1947

**Feb. 10.** The U.S. Supreme Court upholds a state law permitting parochial school children to ride on public school buses. This is the first of many cases in this period on separation of church and state in relation to schools.

**March 10-April 24.** Secretary of State George C. Marshall and British Foreign Minister Ernest Bevin meet in Moscow with Soviet officials; they are unable to agree on type of government for Germany, Britain and the U.S. advocating a federal form and the Soviet Union a centralized form. Britain and the U.S. refuse the Soviet demand for $10 billion in reparations from Germany.

**March 12.** President Truman asks economic and military aid for Greece and Turkey to strengthen them against "attempted subjugation by armed minorities or by outside pressures" and announces the principle of containment of Soviet expansion (the Truman Doctrine). Congress later approves and allocates an initial $400 million to immediate aid of Greece and Turkey. **Sept. 18.** The Soviet Union attacks the U.S. as "warmongers" in UN General Assembly.

**March 31.** Wartime draft ends. Because of political pressures to return everyone to civilian life, demobilization proceeds faster than at first planned, but enough men are available to maintain armies of occupation.

**April 11.** Jack Roosevelt ("Jackie") Robinson becomes first Negro major-league baseball player in this century when he signs contract with the Brooklyn Dodgers.

**June 5.** The U.S. ratifies peace treaties with minor Axis nations — Italy, Hungary, Bulgaria, and Rumania. All agree to pay reparations and to return land occupied; some cede to the Soviet Union and its satellites land within their prewar boundaries; Italy also cedes land to France and Greece.

**June 5.** Secretary of State Marshall proposes that the U.S. contribute to economic recovery of those European countries that will determine their needs and cooperate economically. Although Great Britain and France invite 22 nations to meet in Paris to draft plans, only 16 participate, since the Soviet Union and its satellites denounce plan as one to enslave Europe and withdraw to form their own mutual assistance system. **July 12.** Marshall Plan Conference creates Committee of European Economic Cooperation, which two months later reports that Europe's needs over the next four years will require aid of between $19 billion and $22 billion. In April 1948 Congress votes funds for four-year plan; aid eventually amounts to $12 billion.

**June 23.** Labor Management Relations (Taft-Hartley) Act is passed over President Truman's veto. Act, which seeks to swing balance of power in management-union relationships away from "excess" privileges unions have gained during New Deal, is bitterly opposed by unions, especially because of strike and closed shop restrictions; Act also provides for supervision of finances and limitation of political activities.

**July 7.** Hoover Commission is created to investigate inefficiency and to recommend reorganization of the executive branch of the government. Former President Hoover is chairman.

**July 11.** General Albert C. Wedemeyer is appointed to analyze and report on situation in China and Korea. In August he attacks use of force by Communists, as well as economic policies and corruption of Nationalists.

**July 18.** President Truman signs Presidential Succession Act, which changes line of succession after the Vice-President to speaker of the House, president pro tempore of the Senate, and Cabinet members according to rank.

**July 26.** President Truman signs National Security Act, which unifies all branches of the armed services as the National Military Establishment under a secretary of defense. Department is reorganized and renamed Department of Defense in 1949.

**Oct. 30.** At Geneva Trade Conference, 23 nations (comprising three-fourths of world's commerce) agree on tariff reductions for about two-thirds of their international trade items.

**October.** U.S. Air Force pilot tests first airplane that exceeds the speed of sound, X-1 research model made by Bell Aircraft Corporation.

The U.S. accepts UN trusteeship over the Carolines, the Marshalls, and the Marianas; all are in the Pacific and are former Japanese possessions or League of Nations mandates.

Transistor, which, substantially smaller, replaces the vacuum tube in electronic communications equipment, is invented at Bell Telephone Laboratories by three scientists, who in 1956 receive Nobel Prize for their work.

# 1947 - 1951

**March 22, 1947.** President Truman orders investigation into loyalty of all employees of the Executive branch of the government; check begins in August and continues until April 1951. The vast majority of those investigated (more than 3 million) are cleared; at least 3,000 others resign, while only 212 are dismissed.

# 1948

**Jan. 23.** Split between Soviet-held North Korea and U.S.-occupied South Korea broadens when the Soviet Union announces that UN Temporary Commission on Korea will not be allowed to enter North Korea. **May 10.** Korean elections are held, but they are boycotted by the North. **Aug. 15.** Republic of Korea is formed at Seoul, South Korea. **Sept. 9.** North Korea proclaims Democratic People's Republic of Korea, which claims to be government of entire country.

**March 8.** The Supreme Court holds that released-time religious education given on public school property, even though by private teachers, is a violation of the First Amendment of the Constitution.

**April 30.** Organization of American States (OAS) is formed at Bogotá, Colombia, by the U.S. and 20 Latin-American nations; OAS is a regional group for mutual defense and general cooperation. Organization becomes legally effective in 1951, when two-thirds of nations have ratified charter.

**May 14.** The U.S. recognizes the new state of Israel, but surrounding Arab countries do not, vigorously protesting existence of new nation. **Sept. 17.** Ralph J. Bunche of the U.S. succeeds Swedish Count Folke Bernadotte as UN mediator of Israel-Arab conflicts after Bernadotte's assassination in Jerusalem. Bunche is successful in working out armistice agreements.

**May 25.** General Motors Corporation signs first sliding wage scale union contract with United Automobile Workers; it includes clause that adjusts wages to cost of living index.

**May 30.** U.S. Supreme Court holds that enforcing a private contract restricting sale or rental of property because of race is a violation of the Fourteenth Amendment.

**June 11.** U.S. Senate approves Vandenberg Resolution, which favors U.S. participation in regional security agreements within the UN framework; principle is widely applied in succeeding years.

**June 21.** Republican Party meets at Philadelphia and nominates Governor Thomas E. Dewey of New York for President and Governor Earl Warren of California for Vice-President. **July 15.** Democrats at Philadelphia renominate President Truman, with Senator Alben W. Barkley of Kentucky as his running mate. Southern Democrats walk out of convention, refusing to support strong civil rights platform; they meet in the same month in Alabama, where they nominate Governor J. Strom Thurmond of South Carolina to run on a States' Rights ticket. **July 24.** Newly formed Progressive Party, partly made up of Democrats who oppose Truman's foreign policy and others who feel he cannot win election, nominates former Vice-President Henry A. Wallace for President. Minor party candidates are: Socialist, Norman Thomas of New York; Prohibition, Claude A. Watson of California; and Socialist Labor, Edward A. Teichert of Pennsylvania. Republican platform is dedicated to maintenance of peace and the principles of Taft-Hartley

Act. Democrats demand repeal of the Taft-Hartley Act, as well as civil rights legislation.

**June 24.** New Selective Service Act is signed to provide manpower for occupation of Germany and Italy and expanding military aid programs. Men of 19 to 25 are inducted for 21 months' service; 18-year-olds are permitted to volunteer for one year in any of the regular services.

**June 25.** Displaced Persons Act is signed, providing for admission to the U.S. of displaced persons from Europe; about 400,000 persons enter the U.S. under Act and later amendments.

**Nov. 2.** President Truman unexpectedly wins election in spite of States Rights' Party split-off. *Chicago Tribune* has been so sure of his defeat that it has gone to press with headline announcing it. Popular vote is Truman, 24,106,000; Dewey, 21,970,000; Thurmond, 1,169,000. Electoral vote is Truman, 303; Dewey, 189; Thurmond, 39. Democrats regain control of Congress, with majorities in both houses.

Atomic particle (pi-meson) is created synthetically (a possibility implicit in Einstein formula $E = mc^2$) by University of California scientists in synchrocyclotron.

Zoologist Alfred C. Kinsey and associates publish *Sexual Behavior in the Human Male*, a study based on thousands of personal interviews; report shows, among other things, wide differences between actual sex practices and conventional beliefs about them. *Sexual Behavior in the Human Female* is published in 1953.

Norman Mailer publishes *The Naked and the Dead*, his best-selling war novel.

# 1948 - 1949

**Jan. 17, 1948.** As a result of UN mediation (participated in by U.S.), truce is signed between the Republic of Indonesia, which has proclaimed its independence in 1945, and the Netherlands, which still considers Indonesia a group of Dutch colonies; in December, however, the UN condemns the Netherlands for violating truce by military action. **Dec. 27, 1949.** The Netherlands formally transfers its sovereignty to the United States of Indonesia.

**May 1948.** The U.S. announces testing of three new atomic weapons at Eniwetok Atoll in the Pacific. **Nov. 4.** U.S. proposal for international control of atomic energy is approved by UN General Assembly. **Sept. 1949.** The U.S. announces that the Soviet Union has exploded an atomic bomb.

**June 1948.** The Soviet Union begins blockade of ground and water transportation routes into Berlin from the West in effort to force Western Allies to give up control of western part of the city, which is in the center of the Soviet occupation zone. U.S. and British air forces ship food and other vital supplies into West Berlin for almost 16 months by air transport. By the time the Soviet Union has canceled the blockade in May 1949, about 1,600,000 tons of supplies have been airlifted to 2,500,000 Berliners. Airlift continues until September 30, increasing total tonnage to more than 2,300,000.

# 1949

**Jan. 20.** President Truman's Inaugural Address stresses international cooperation through the UN, the Marshall Plan, and regional security pacts and adds "Point Four" proposal for U.S. technical assistance to economically underdeveloped countries. By 1952, 37 nations outside the Communist bloc have benefited by this program.

**Feb. 24.** Highest altitude ever reached by a man-made projectile is achieved by guided missile Wac-Corporal when it travels to a height of 250 miles.

**April 4.** North Atlantic Treaty Organization (NATO) is formed by the U.S., Canada, Great Britain, Denmark, Norway, Iceland, France, Belgium, the Netherlands, Luxembourg, Italy, and Portugal when they sign mutual security pact; U.S. Senate ratifies agreement in July. Greece and Turkey join NATO in 1952.

**May 8.** West Germany adopts federal system of government at Bonn. **June 20.** Paris Conference of Council of Foreign Ministers again fails to agree on question of German unity. **Sept. 21.** U.S. replaces West German military occupation forces by

civilian commission. **Oct. 7.** East Germany becomes German Democratic Republic.

**June 20.** President Truman signs Reorganization Act of 1949, which permits the President to reorganize the executive branch of the government; Act follows recommendations by the Hoover Commission.

**June 29.** U.S. troops are withdrawn from Korea, leaving only military advisers. **Sept. 8.** UN Korean commission announces that it has not been able to settle conflict between North and South Korea, and that it fears country is close to civil war.

**Oct. 14.** Under the Smith Act of 1940, 11 leaders of U.S. Communist Party are sentenced to fines and prison terms for conspiracy to overthrow the government of the U.S. by force.

*Death of a Salesman,* tragedy by Arthur Miller, opens on Broadway and wins Pulitzer Prize.

# World War II

World War II was the first global conflict. Europe, Asia, Africa, and Australia, and the nations of the Western Hemisphere all participated. For the United States it was the first two-ocean war; in fact it seemed to be two different wars fought at the same time. By December 1941, when Pearl Harbor was attacked, Japan was already dominant in the Far East and Germany controlled most of Europe.

In the Pacific, the war with Japan was an arduous three and a half year struggle of island-hopping and naval battles with the goal of getting near enough to Japan to launch an invasion. The development of atomic bombs in 1945 made an invasion unnecessary.

The war with Germany first focused on the Mediterranean: in Africa, where a desert campaign was waged in 1942-1943; and in Italy, where a bitter campaign lasted from 1943-1945. Strategic bombing of Germany was kept up all during the war, with the heaviest destruction of industrial sites coming in 1944. The main, and direct, assault on the Third Reich began on June 6, 1944, with the invasion of the heavily fortified French coast by an Allied armada of 5,000 ships. With the establishment of this "second front," Germany was hard pressed both on the east and on the west. The end of the European war came in May 1945, the end of the Pacific war in August of the same year.

Following World War II there was no "return to normalcy" for the United States, but instead unrelieved involvement in foreign affairs in an era of world revolution. The globe was almost immediately divided into spheres of influence between Communist and non-Communist nations. Russia dominated eastern Europe, and Red China, after 1949, became the prevailing influence in the Far East. Old forms of colonialism were discarded, and dozens of new nations attained independence. The United States made military and financial commitments in all parts of the world, to reconstruct postwar Europe and Asia and to stave off growing Communist influence.

Maps prepared by Uni-Map Inc., Palatine, Ill.
for Encyclopaedia Britannica, Inc.

WORLD WAR II IN EUROPE
TO MAY 1943

Allies and Allied
Controlled Areas

Axis Powers

Vichy France and Vichy
Controlled Areas

Axis Allied States

Axis Occupied Areas

Neutral States

Thrusts | Allied ➡ | Victor of Battle | Allied ✳ ANZIO
        | Axis ➡   |                  | Axis ✳ DUNKIRK

ARCTIC OCEAN

ATLANTIC OCEAN

Murmansk

Archangel

British Landings April-May 1940

Narvik

Namsos

Trondheim

FINLAND

Russo-Finnish War
Nov. 1939-March 1940

Bergen

NORWAY
May 1940

Oslo

SWEDEN

Helsinki

Leningrad

UNION OF SOVIET

Gorki

NORTH SEA

DEN.
April 1940

Copenhagen

Stockholm

BALTIC SEA

EST.
Invaded by Russia June 1940

Riga

LAT.

LITH.

Smolensk
July 1941

Moscow

SOCIALIST

REPUBLICS

Glasgow

IRELAND

GREAT
BRITAIN

NETH.
May 1940

Berlin

Danzig

Minsk

STALINGRAD,
NOV. 1942-
FEB. 1943

London

DUNKIRK
MAY-JUNE 1940

BELG.

GERMANY

POLAND

Warsaw
Sept. 1939

Russia Attacks
Poland Sept. 1939

Kursk

Kharkov

Voronezh

Paris

LUX.
May 1940

Prague

CZECH.
March 1939

Germany Invades Poland
and Initiates W.W. II
Sept. 1, 1939

Kiev

Germany Invades
Russia June 1941

Rostov
Nov. 1941

FRANCE
June 1940

Munich

Vienna

AUSTRIA
March 1938

HUNGARY
Nov. 1940

RUMANIA
Nov. 1940

Odessa

Sevastopol

Bordeaux

SWITZ.

VICHY
German Occupied
Nov. 1942

Milan

Belgrade

Bucharest

BLACK SEA

PORT.

SPAIN

Marseilles

CORSICA

ITALY

YUGO.
April 1941

Sofia

BULGARIA
March 1941

Istanbul

Ankara

Lisbon

Madrid

Barcelona

Rome

SARDINIA

ADRIATIC SEA

ALB.
April 1939

TURKEY

CYPRUS
(Br.)

SYRIA
(Fr.)

Gibraltar
(Br.)

SP.
MOROCCO

Oran

Algiers

Allied Landings Nov. 1942

MEDITERRANEAN

SICILY

GREECE
April 1941

Athens

SEA

CRETE
British Evacuate
Crete May 1941

EL ALAMEIN,
OCT.-NOV.
1942

PAL.
(Br.)

MOROCCO
Joined Allies
Nov. 1942

Tunis
Axis Forces in
North Africa
Surrender
May 1943

Mareth Line
March 1941

Arrival of German
Afrika Korps
Feb. 1941

Tripoli

Bengasi

Cairo

TUNISIA
Joined Allies
Nov. 1942

ALGERIA
Joined Allies Nov. 1942

Line Feb. 1941

Italians invade Egypt
Sept. 1940
Repulsed by British
Dec. 1940-Feb. 1941

LIBYA

EGYPT

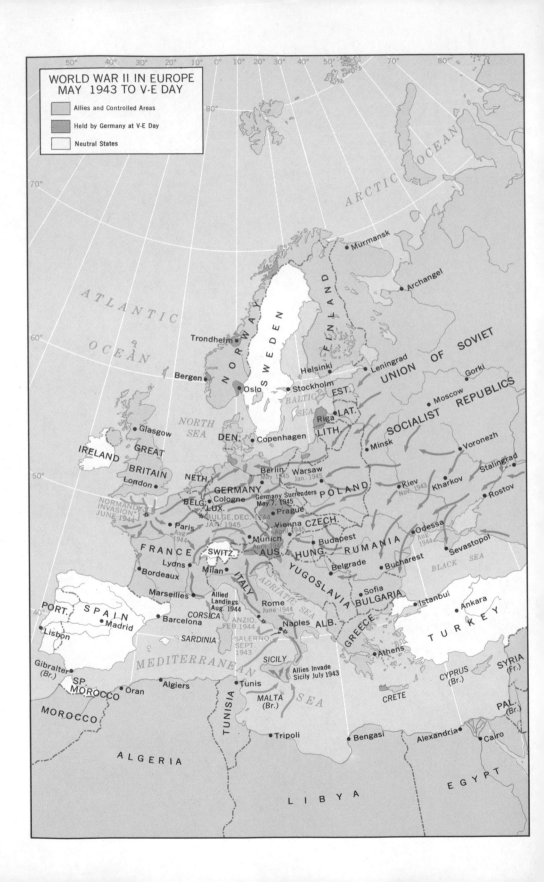

WORLD WAR II IN EUROPE
MAY 1943 TO V-E DAY

Allies and Controlled Areas

Held by Germany at V-E Day

Neutral States

ARCTIC OCEAN

ATLANTIC OCEAN

NORWAY

SWEDEN

FINLAND

UNION OF SOVIET

Murmansk

Archangel

Trondheim

Bergen

Oslo

Helsinki

Leningrad

Gorki

Stockholm

BALTIC SEA

EST.

Moscow

SOCIALIST REPUBLICS

Glasgow

NORTH SEA

DEN.

Copenhagen

Riga

LAT.

LITH.

Minsk

Voronezh

IRELAND

GREAT BRITAIN

London

NETH.

Berlin
May 1945

Warsaw
Jan. 1945

POLAND

Kiev
Nov. 1943

Kharkov

Stalingrad

NORMANDY INVASION
JUNE 1944

BELG.

LUX.

Cologne

GERMANY

Germany Surrenders
May 7, 1945

Prague

CZECH.

Rostov

BULGE, DEC. 1944
JAN. 1945

Paris
Aug.
1944

Vienna
April 1945

Odessa
Aug.
1944

Sevastopol

FRANCE

SWITZ.

Munich

AUS.

HUNG.

Budapest

RUMANIA

Lyons

Milan

Belgrade

Bucharest

BLACK SEA

Bordeaux

ITALY

YUGOSLAVIA

Sofia

Marseilles

ADRIATIC SEA

BULGARIA

Istanbul

Ankara

PORT.

SPAIN

Madrid

CORSICA

Allied
Landings
Aug. 1944

Rome
June 1944

Naples

ALB.

GREECE

TURKEY

Lisbon

Barcelona

ANZIO,
FEB. 1944

SARDINIA

SALERNO,
SEPT.
1943

Athens

Gibralter
(Br.)

SP.
MOROCCO

Oran

Algiers

MEDITERRANEAN SEA

SICILY

Tunis

MALTA
(Br.)

Allies Invade
Sicily July 1943

CRETE

CYPRUS
(Br.)

SYRIA
(Fr.)

PAL.
(Br.)

MOROCCO

ALGERIA

TUNISIA

Tripoli

Bengasi

LIBYA

Alexandria

Cairo

EGYPT

STRATEGIC BOMBING OF GERMANY

Petroleum Field and/or Refinery ∴
Aircraft Plant ✚
Submarine Base ☐
Concentration and/or Extermination Camp ✧
Chemical Plant ✱
Major Industrial Area ■
Rocket Site ▲
Progressive Range of Fighter Escort
Axis Controlled Areas
Neutral States ☐

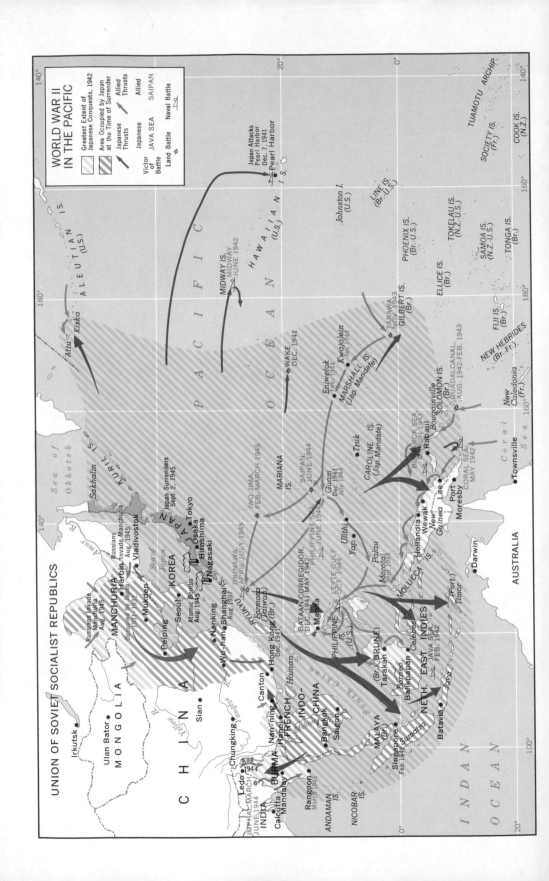

## WORLD WAR II IN THE PACIFIC

Greatest Extent of Japanese Conquests, 1942

Area Occupied by Japan at the Time of Surrender

Japanese Thrusts

Allied Thrusts

Victor of Battle    JAVA SEA    SAIPAN

Japanese Thrusts    Land Battle    Naval Battle

POST-WAR EUROPE
→ Air Corridors to Berlin
Occupation Zones of Germany
and Austria 1945-1950

U.S.    French
British    Russian

ATLANTIC OCEAN

FAEROE IS.
(Den.)

SHETLAND IS.
(Br.)

N O R W A Y

Murmansk

Archangel

S W E D E N

F I N L A N D

L. Onega

Trondheim

Bergen

Oslo

Helsinki

L. Ladoga

Leningrad

Göteborg

Stockholm

UNION    OF

Baltic Sea

Riga

Moscow

SOVIET

Dvina R.

Minsk

IRELAND

Dublin

GREAT

Glasgow

NORTH
SEA

DEN.

Copenhagen

Kaliningrad

SOCIALIST

Leeds

Liverpool

Birmingham

Amsterdam

NETH.

Hamburg

Hannover

Berlin

POLAND

Warsaw

REPUBLICS

Dnieper R.

Kiev

London

BRITAIN

Brussels

BEL.

GERMANY

Bonn

Russians blockade Berlin
June 1948
Airlift till May 1949

Le Havre

Paris

LUX.

Frankfurt

CZECHOSLOVAKIA

Prague

Cracow

Merger of Communist and
nationalist parties win elections
1948

Dniester R.

Odessa

Nantes

Loire R.

Rhine R.

SWITZ.

Munich

AUSTRIA

Vienna

Budapest

HUNGARY

RUMANIA

Black

F R A N C E

Bay of
Biscay

Lyons

Rhône R.

Austria ind. neutral
state; occupation
ended July 1955

Trieste

Po R.

YUGOSLAVIA

Belgrade

Bucharest

R.

Sea

Bordeaux

Garonne R.

Milan

Genoa

Tito becomes premier March 1945;
breaks from Kremlin summer 1948

Danube

Marseilles

I T A L Y

Adriatic Sea

Sofia

BULGARIA

Istanbul

Douro R.

AND.

Corsica

Rome

Tirane

Salonika

TURKEY

Madrid

Tagus R.

Ebro R.

Barcelona

Sardinia

Naples

ALB.

GREECE

Izmir

PORTUGAL

S P A I N

Valencia

BALEARIC IS.

M E D I T E R R A N E A N

Civil War
Dec. 1944
to Oct. 1949

Athens

Lisbon

Seville

Palermo

Crete

Gibraltar
(Br.)

SP. MOROCCO

Algiers

Tunis

Sicily

Malta
(Br.)

S E A

Casablanca

Oran

MOROCCO
(Fr.)

A L G E R I A
(Fr.)

T U N I S I A
(Fr.)

Tripoli

Bengasi

L I B Y A

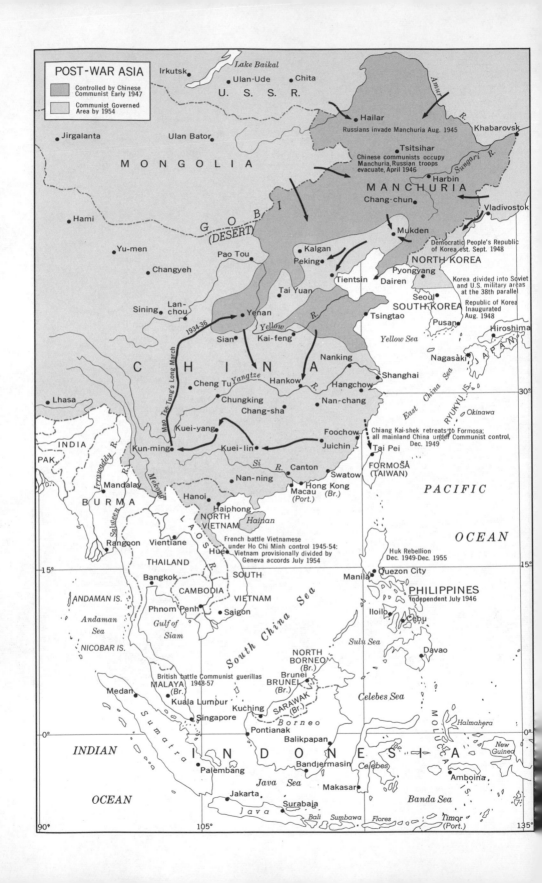

POST-WAR ASIA

Controlled by Chinese Communist Early 1947
Communist Governed Area by 1954

*Lake Baikal*
Irkutsk
Ulan-Ude
Chita
Jirgalanta

U. S. S. R.

*Amur R.*

Hailar
Russians invade Manchuria Aug. 1945
Khabarovsk

Ulan Bator
MONGOLIA

Tsitsihar
Chinese communists occupy Manchuria, Russian troops evacuate, April 1946

*Sungari R.*

Hami

Harbin
MANCHURIA
Chang-chun

Vladivostok

Yu-men
Changyeh
Pao Tou

GOBI
(DESERT)

Kalgan
Peking
Tientsin
Mukden
Democratic People's Republic of Korea est. Sept. 1948
NORTH KOREA
Pyongyang
Dairen

Korea divided into Soviet and U.S. military areas at the 38th parallel

Sining
Lan-chou
Tai Yuan

Republic of Korea Inaugurated Aug. 1948

1934-36

Yenan
Sian
Kai-feng
*Yellow R.*

SOUTH KOREA
Seoul
Tsingtao
Pusan
*Yellow Sea*

Hiroshima

Lhasa

CHINA

Nanking

Nagasaki

INDIA
PAK.

Cheng Tu
*Yangtze R.*
Hankow
Chungking
Chang-sha
Nan-chang
Hangchow
Shanghai

*East China Sea*

RYUKYU IS.
Okinawa

30°

Kuei-yang
Kun-ming
Kuei-lin
Juichin
Foochow
Chiang Kai-shek retreats to Formosa; all mainland China under Communist control, Dec. 1949
Tai Pei
FORMOSA (TAIWAN)

PACIFIC

Nan-ning
*Si R.*
Canton
Swatow
Hong Kong (Br.)
Macau (Port.)

Mandalay
BURMA
Hanoi
Haiphong
NORTH VIETNAM
*Hainan*

OCEAN

Rangoon
Vientiane
Hue
French battle Vietnamese under Ho Chi Minh control 1945-54: Vietnam provisionally divided by Geneva accords July 1954

Huk Rebellion Dec. 1949-Dec. 1955

15°

THAILAND
Bangkok
CAMBODIA
Phnom Penh
SOUTH VIETNAM
Saigon

Manila
Quezon City
PHILIPPINES
Independent July 1946

15°

ANDAMAN IS.
*Andaman Sea*
NICOBAR IS.

*Gulf of Siam*

*South China Sea*

Iloilo
Cebu

*Sulu Sea*

Davao

NORTH BORNEO (Br.)
Brunei
BRUNEI (Br.)

*Celebes Sea*

Medan
British battle Communist guerillas 1948-57
MALAYA (Br.)
Kuala Lumpur
Singapore
Kuching
SARAWAK (Br.)

*Borneo*

MOLUCCA

Halmahera

New Guinea

0°

INDIAN

*Sumatra*
Pontianak
Balikpapan

INDONESIA

0°

OCEAN

Palembang
Jakarta
Surabaja
*Java*

Bandjermasin
*Java Sea*
Makasar
*Celebes*

*Banda Sea*

Amboina

*Bali* *Sumbawa* *Flores*

Timor (Port.)

90°
105°
135°

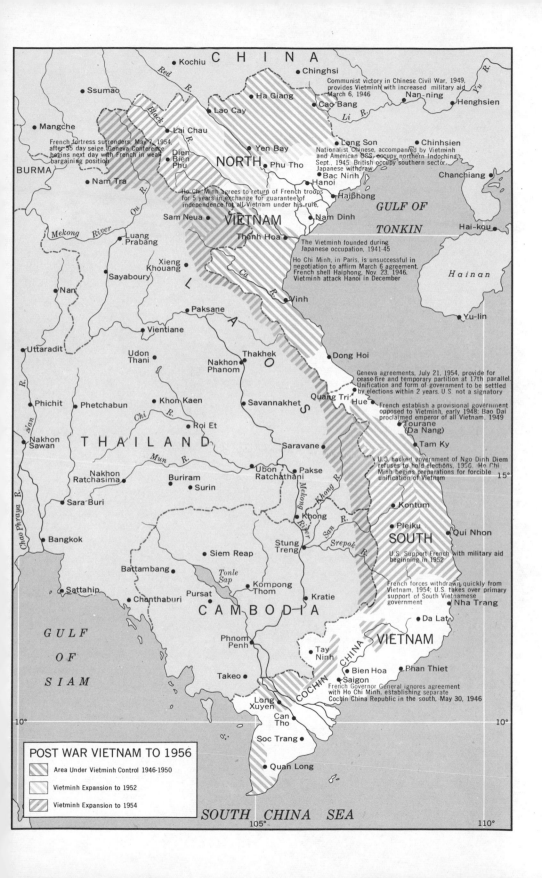

POST WAR VIETNAM TO 1956 map

**CHINA**

- Kochiu
- Ssumao
- Chinghsi
- Ha Giang
- Nan-ning
- Cao Bang
- Henghsien
- Lao Cay
- Mangche
- Lai Chau
- Leng Son
- Chinhsien
- Yen Bay
- Dien Bien Phu
- NORTH VIETNAM
- Phu Tho
- Chanchiang
- Nam Tra
- Bac Ninh
- Hanoi

**BURMA**

Communist victory in Chinese Civil War, 1949, provides Vietminh with increased military aid March 6, 1946

French fortress surrenders, May 7, 1954, after 55 day seige. Geneva Conference begins next day with French in weak bargaining position

Nationalist Chinese, accompanied by Vietminh and American OSS, occupy northern Indochina, Sept., 1945. British occupy southern sector. Japanese withdraw.

Ho Chi Minh agrees to return of French troops for 5 years in exchange for guarantee of independence for all Vietnam under his rule.

- Sam Neua
- Haiphong
- Nam Dinh
- Thanh Hoa

**GULF OF TONKIN**

- Hai-kou

*Hainan*

The Vietminh founded during Japanese occupation, 1941-45

Ho Chi Minh, in Paris, is unsuccessful in negotiation to affirm March 6 agreement. French shell Haiphong, Nov. 23, 1946. Vietminh attack Hanoi in December

- Luang Prabang
- Xieng Khouang
- Sayaboury
- Nan
- Paksane
- Vinh
- Vientiane
- Yu-lin
- Uttaradit

*Mekong River*

**L A O S**

- Udon Thani
- Thakhek
- Dong Hoi
- Nakhon Phanom
- Phichit
- Phetchabun
- Khon Kaen
- Savannakhet
- Quang Tri
- Hue
- Roi Et

**THAILAND**

Geneva agreements, July 21, 1954, provide for cease-fire and temporary partition at 17th parallel. Unification and form of government to be settled by elections within 2 years. U.S. not a signatory

French establish a provisional government opposed to Vietminh, early 1948; Bao Dai proclaimed emperor of all Vietnam, 1949

- Tourane (Da Nang)
- Tam Ky
- Nakhon Sawan
- Saravane
- Ubon Ratchathani
- Pakse
- Nakhon Ratchasima
- Buriram
- Surin
- Sara Buri
- Khong
- Kontum

U.S. backed government of Ngo Dinh Diem refuses to hold elections, 1956. Ho Chi Minh begins preparations for forcible unification of Vietnam

- Pleiku
- Qui Nhon
- Bangkok
- Siem Reap
- Stung Treng
- **SOUTH**

U.S. Support French with military aid beginning in 1952

- Battambang
- *Tonle Sap*
- Kompong Thom
- Kratie

French forces withdrawn quickly from Vietnam, 1954; U.S. takes over primary support of South Vietnamese government

- Nha Trang
- Sattahip
- Chanthaburi
- Pursat
- **CAMBODIA**
- Da Lat

**GULF OF SIAM**

- Phnom Penh
- Tay Ninh
- **VIETNAM**
- Bien Hoa
- Phan Thiet
- Takeo
- Saigon

French Governor General ignores agreement with Ho Chi Minh, establishing separate Cochin China Republic in the south, May 30, 1946

- Long Xuyen
- **COCHIN CHINA**
- Can Tho
- Soc Trang
- Quan Long

**SOUTH CHINA SEA**

POST WAR VIETNAM TO 1956

- Area Under Vietminh Control 1946-1950
- Vietminh Expansion to 1952
- Vietminh Expansion to 1954

# 1940

1.

## Archibald MacLeish: The Irresponsibles

*Archibald MacLeish was one of the few men of letters during the 1930s to dramatize the threat of totalitarianism to American society. In his writings of that period, The Fall of the City (1937) and Air Raid (1938), he repeatedly urged action to save the democracies. The Irresponsibles (1940), written during his service (1939-1944) as librarian of Congress and reprinted here in part, attacked the moral lassitude of writers who failed to take an active stand in defense of freedom and democracy. The very detachment and objectivity that heightened the intellectual's social awareness and made it so valuable to society under normal circumstances served, MacLeish felt, to undermine the sense of responsibility and commitment that were urgently needed during periods of crisis.*

Source: *The Irresponsibles*, New York, 1940.

HISTORY — if honest history continues to be written — will have one question to ask of our generation, people like ourselves. It will be asked of the books we have written, the carbon copies of our correspondence, the photographs of our faces, the minutes of our meetings in the famous rooms before the portraits of our spiritual begetters. The question will be this: Why did the scholars and the writers of our generation in this country, witnesses as they were to the destruction of writing and of scholarship in great areas of Europe and to the exile and the imprisonment and murder of men whose crime was scholarship and writing — witnesses also to the rise in their own country of the same destructive forces with the same impulses, the same motives, the same

means — why did the scholars and the writers of our generation in America fail to oppose those forces while they could — while there was still time and still place to oppose them with the arms of scholarship and writing?

It is a question the historians will ask with interest — the gentle, detached, not altogether loving interest with which historians have always questioned the impotent spirits of the dead. Young men working in the paper rubbish of our lives, the old journals, the marginal notations, the printed works, will discover (or so they will think) that the scholars and the writers of our generation in this country had been warned of danger as men were rarely warned before. They will discover (or so they will think) that the common inherited culture of the West, by which alone our scholars and our writers lived, had been attacked in other countries with a stated and explicit purpose to destroy. They will discover that that purpose had been realized. They will discover that a similar purpose backed by similar forces, created by similar conditions, was forming here. And it will seem to them strange — ironical and strange — that the great mass of American scholars and American writers made no effort to defend either themselves or the world by which they lived.

They will make of course the necessary reservations. They will note that societies of scholars and associations of writers adopted resolutions declaring their devotion to civilization. They will note that certain young novelists and poets, the most generous and gallant of their time, unable to endure the outrage and injustice, gave up their lives as writers and enlisted in the hopeless armies to fight brutality with force. But of those who truly faced this danger not with their bodies but their minds, of those who fought the enemies of the intellect with the weapons of the intellect, devoting to that warfare all the strength, all the imagination, all the resources of courage and inventiveness, all the watchfulness by day and night, all the last reserves of hope and skill and pain which men must use whose lives and more than lives are put in danger — of those who fought this danger with the weapons by which this danger could be overcome, they will record the names of very few. And they will ask their question. Why did we, scholars and writers in America in this time, we who had been warned of our danger not only by explicit threats but by explicit action, why did we not fight this danger while the weapons we used best — the weapons of ideas and words — could still be used against it? . . .

The study of beauty, the study of history, the study of science, has occupied our whole hearts and the misfortunes of our generation are none of our concern. They are the practical and political concern of practical and political men but the concern of the scholar, the concern of the artist, is with other, purer, more enduring things.

This is the answer we have written down for history to find. . . . We say this with all the authority of the political scientists of the past to whom the misfortunes of the people were always political and economic and of no concern to the poet, the pure scholar, the artist intent upon his art. We say it also with the authority of the political scientists of the present to whom all phenomena of whatever kind are, by hypothesis, economic and political. But though we say it we do not believe it. For we have observed these misfortunes. They have been acted out for us to see. And what we have seen is this: that the misfortunes of our time are not the misfortunes the philosophers, the theorists, the political scientists have described to us. They are not the practical concern of the practical man and therefore matters of indifference to the scholar. On the contrary, it is the practical man and the practical man alone — the man whose only care is for his belly and his roof — who can safely be indifferent to these troubles. The things he lives by are not menaced. And it is precisely the scholar, the poet — the man whose care is for the structures of the intellect, the houses of the mind — whose heart is caught. For it is the scholar's goods which are in danger.

It is perhaps because we have seen this and yet refuse to see it — because we know one thing and yet continue to declare another — that our minds are so confused and our counsels so bewildering. Nothing is more characteristic of the intellectuals of our generation than their failure to understand what it is that is happening to their world. And nothing explains that failure as precisely as their unwillingness to see what they have seen and to know what they do truly know. They have seen the crisis of their time — they have seen it spelled out, played out, fought out as few observers ever before in history saw the tragedy exposed. They know its ending. And yet they continue to pretend that they do not know. They continue to speak of the crisis of their time as though the war in Europe were that crisis — and the war, they say, is no concern of theirs. They continue to speak of the crisis as though the imperialistic maneuvers, the struggles for markets, the propaganda in the newspapers and the radio, were the crisis — and the maneuvers of imperialism, the propaganda of the press and the struggles for trade they say are no concern of theirs. And yet they know — they know very well because they have seen — that these things are not the crisis but merely its reflections in the mirrors of action. They know that behind the war, behind the diplomatic gestures, behind the black print on the page and the hysterical voices on the air there is something deeper and more dangerous — more dangerous to *them*. They know that it is a condition of men's minds which has produced these things — a condition which existed and exists not only in Europe but in other parts of the world as well and not least in our own country. And they know that this condition of men's minds is not a practical, a political, phenomenon of no concern to the scholar and the man of thought but something very different. . . .

What is new and unexampled in the times we live in is *the repudiation of the forms*. What is new is a cynical brutality which considers moral self-justification unnecessary and therefore — and this is perhaps its worst indecency — dispenses even with the filthy garment of the hypocrite. To use brutality and force, not in the name of Right nor in the name of God, but in the name of force alone, is to destroy the self-respect and therefore the dignity of the individual life without which the existence of

art or learning is inconceivable. To lie, not in the name of truth, but in the name of lies, is to destroy the common basis of communication without which a common culture cannot exist and a work of learning or of art becomes unintelligible.

The truth is — the plain and simple truth of which we have so many painful evidences — that the disorder of our time, whatever else it may now be or may become, is in its essentials a revolt against the common culture of the West. For against what but the common culture did this disorder continue to struggle in Germany long after it had overthrown the former state? There was no domestic danger for it to fear. Against what but the Western respect for the dignity of the individual was aimed the long series of outrages against the Jews? The Jews were impotent when they were subjected to the worst abuses. Against what but the Western respect for the common, the nationless, creation of the artist was aimed the destruction of the work of men like Thomas Mann? Thomas Mann had already been repudiated by his people when they accepted the government of his enemies. Against what but the Western belief in the wholeness of Western civilization was aimed the assault upon a church which was no longer a danger to any ruler and the fabrication of a paganism which needed only the blond sopranos on the ends of wires to be Wagner at his worst?

Intellectuals in America and elsewhere — writers, scientists, the men of learning — have attempted to ignore these questions. They have pretended to themselves that the burning of books, the exiling of artists, the invention of mythologies were merely incidents — afterthoughts — decorations: that the true crisis was the crisis of food, the crisis of arms, the crisis created by political forces, by economic collapse — that they had, and needed have, no truck with it. They have been wrong. These things are not incidents. They are not afterthoughts.

They are the essential nature of the revolution of our age. For without this attack upon the habits of the mind, the reliances of the spirit, that revolution could not, by any possibility, have succeeded.

The revolution of our age — the revolution which has finally emerged and declared itself in action — is not the great revolution of the masses of which generous men once dreamed: and which other and less generous men have now so meanly and so bloodily betrayed. The revolution of the masses was a revolution which proposed to set up one faith against another faith, one culture against another culture: a faith in man, a faith in the power of the patterns of men's lives, against a faith in institutions and in money; a culture of the people against a culture of the exploiters of the people. The revolution which has finally and successfully emerged in action has no such faith and no such culture.

It is a revolution of negatives, a revolution of the defeated, a revolution of the dispossessed, a revolution of despair. It is a revolution created out of misery by dread of yet more misery, a revolution created out of disorder by terror of disorder. It is a revolution of gangs, a revolution *against*. And the enemy it is against, the enemy it must destroy, is the enemy which, in all times and in all civilizations, has stood against the revolutions of the gangs — the rule of moral law, the rule of spiritual authority, the rule of intellectual truth. To establish the negative revolutions, the revolutions of which the only aim is power, the revolutions which have no means but force, it is necessary first to destroy the authority of the unseen sayings of the mind. It is necessary to destroy the things the mind has made. Caliban in the miserable and besotted swamp is the symbol of this revolution. As long as the unseen beauty in the air retains its voices and its seductive music and its stinging whips the revolutions of the gangs are clumsy, blundering, grotesque and foolish. They can bellow and threaten and boast and gesture with their arms but in the end the invisible voices of the air, the invisible power of the ideal will master them. They have one hope of success and only one — the destruction of the whole system of ideas, the whole respect for truth, the whole authority of excellence which places law above force, beauty above cruelty, singleness above numbers.

It is the distinction of our time — perhaps unhappily its most memorable distinction — that it and it alone has provided the formula by which this overthrow could be achieved. Only in our time has the revolution of the gangs discovered a strategy and a leadership brutal enough, cynical enough, cunning enough to destroy the entire authority of the inherited culture and thereafter to seal the doors against the searching and the asking of the scholar's mind, the artist's mind, so that the revolution of force, the revolution of despair could flower and fulfill its possibilities. Only in our time has the revolution of the gangs shown itself openly and admittedly as the thing it is — a revolution of cruelty, cunning and despair against the authority and the discipline of the mind.

It is to this disorder and not to some political and partisan dissension, not to some accidental economic breakdown — practical and political matters for the men of politics and practice — it is to this direct, explicit and intentional attack upon the scholar's world and the scholar's life and the scholar's work that American scholarship has been indifferent. Or if not indifferent, then inactive, merely watchful — fearful, watchful and inactive. And it is there that history will place its questions.

How could we sit back as spectators of a war against ourselves?

Did we suppose the newly discovered techniques of deception, of falsehood as a military force, of strategic fraud, were incapable of reaching us — incapable of crossing sea water? We had seen their methods drive their conquests through the countries of the world more rapidly than Alexander or Napoleon or Tamerlane or any other conqueror or killer.

Or was it something else we thought? Did we believe others would defend us? Did we think the issue was an issue of strategy, an issue of battles? Did we think the British and the French would win their war and so defend us? But we knew very well, because we had seen, that this war was not a war fought in the open on the military front, but a war fought in the back street and the dark stair — a war fought within the city, within the house, within the mind — a war of treason: a war of corruption: a war of lies. And against treason and corruption and lies, battle fleets and grand armies are impotent. . . .

Had the intellectuals of our time been whole and loyal — it would, I think, have been impossible for the revolution of the gangs to have succeeded where success has been most dangerous — in the perversion of the judgments of the mind. Murder is not absolved of immorality by committing murder. Murder is absolved of immorality by bringing men to think that murder is not evil. This only the perversion of the mind can bring about. And the perversion of the mind is only possible when those who should be heard in its defense are silent. . . .

There are examples in history of civilizations made impotent by excesses of culture. No one, I think, will say of us that we lost our intellectual liberties on this account. But it may well be said, and said with equally ironic emphasis, that the men of thought, the men of learning in this country, were deceived and rendered impotent by the best they knew. To the scholar impartiality, objectivity, detachment were ideal qualities he taught himself laboriously and painfully to acquire. To the writer objectivity and detachment were his writer's pride. Both subjected themselves to inconceivable restraints, endless disciplines to reach these ends. And both succeeded. Both writers and scholars freed themselves of the subjective passions, the emotional preconceptions which color conviction and judgment. Both writers and scholars freed themselves of the personal responsibility associated with personal choice. They emerged free, pure and single into the antiseptic air of objectivity. And by the sublimation of the mind they prepared the mind's disaster.

If it is a consolation to the philosophers of earlier civilizations to know that they lost the things they loved because of the purity of their devotion, then perhaps this consolation will be ours as well. I doubt if we will profit by it or receive much praise.

---

*Frankly, my dear, I don't give a damn.*
    MARGARET MITCHELL [Rhett Butler (Clark Gable) to Scarlett O'Hara (Vivien Leigh)], *Gone With the Wind*

2.

## Stop Hitler Now!

*Events in Europe during the first six months of 1940 worked a great change in the popular mood of isolationism that had been predominant in America since 1937. The possibility of a worldwide Axis victory now loomed as a distinct threat to America's future. Wendell Willkie expressed the general sentiment when he said: "An overwhelming number of people in this country believe that we should give all possible aid, short of war, of course, to the Allies." An effort to bring this sentiment to fruition was made by the Committee to Defend America by Aiding the Allies, organized in the spring of 1940 under the chairmanship of William Allen White. One of the committee's most effective promotional pieces was an advertisement written for the committee by Robert E. Sherwood and published on June 10, 1940, the day Italy declared war on France.*

Source: *New York Times,* June 10, 1940.

## STOP HITLER NOW!

WE AMERICANS have naturally wished to keep out of this war — to take no steps which might lead us in. But —

We now know that every step the French and British fall back brings war and world revolutions closer to US — our country, our institutions, our homes, our hopes for peace.

Hitler is striking with all the terrible force at his command. His is a desperate gamble, and the stakes are nothing less than domination of the whole human race.

If Hitler wins in Europe — if the strength of the British and French armies and navies is forever broken — the United States will find itself alone in a barbaric world — a world ruled by Nazis, with "spheres of influence" assigned to their totalitarian allies. However different the dictatorships may be, racially, they all agree on one primary objective: *"Democracy must be wiped from the face of the earth."*

The world will be placed on a permanent war footing. Our country will have to pile armaments upon armaments to maintain even the illusion of security. We shall have no other business, no other aim in life, but primitive self-defense. We shall exist only under martial law — or the law of the jungle. Our economic structure will have to be adjusted to that of our gangster competitors. We shall have to change ourselves from easy-going individuals into a "dynamic race."

"Government of the people, by the people, for the people" — if Hitler wins, this will be the discarded ideal of a decayed civilization.

*Is this "Alarmism"?* Then so is the challenging scream of an air-raid siren, warning civilians that death is coming from the skies. We have ample cause for deepest alarm. It should impel us, not to hysteria, but to resolute action.

It is obvious that there is no immediate danger of direct invasion of the United States. Hitler doesn't strike directly when he doesn't have to. He edges up on his major victims, approaching through the territory of small and defenseless neighbors.

We have twenty-one neighbors in this hemisphere, in addition to the colonial possessions of Britain, France, Holland and Denmark. We must not forget that however wide the Atlantic and Pacific oceans may be, the Canadian and Mexican borders are no barriers to invasion.

The Monroe Doctrine is not an automatic safety catch, securing the entrance to our hemisphere from all intruders. We have to enforce it — all the way from Greenland and Alaska to Cape Horn. Furthermore, we have to guard night and day against the manifold enemies from within. We can not ignore the fact that Trojan horses are grazing in all the fertile fields of North and South America.

The Western Hemisphere contains the richest territory for exploitation on earth today. And the international gangsters want it. They have already started the process of taking it. For many years the agents of the Nazis have been effectively at work in Latin America, gaining ground by persuasion, bribery, intimidation. They have been fighting a trade war and a political war; and what we have lately seen in Norway and Holland and Belgium proves to us that these agents are ready to fight a military war when the orders come through from home.

"Divide — and conquer!" has been the Nazi watchword in the insidious invasion of all countries. The preliminary work of division has been carried on here with devastating success.

We can and should and will devote ourselves to a vast program of defense. But we must not try to fool ourselves into thinking that security can be bought. It will be achieved only by unity of purpose among ourselves, by the spirit of sacrifice that we can summon from our own hearts and minds. Overwhelming destiny will not be stopped "with the help of God and a few Marines."

This is a job for *all* of us! It will take years for us to build the necessary machines and to train the men who will run them. Will the Nazis considerately wait until we are ready to fight them?

Anyone who argues that they will wait is either an imbecile or a traitor.

How long shall *we* wait before making it known to Hitler and the masters of all the slave states that we are vitally concerned in the outcome of this war — that we would consider a victory for them an unmitigated calamity for civilization?

Whatever our feelings about the tragic mistakes of statesmanship in England and France we know now that the free people of those nations are willing to fight with inspiring heroism to defend their freedom. We know now that such men will die rather than surrender. But the stoutest hearts can not survive forever in the face of superior numbers and infinitely superior weapons.

There is nothing shameful in our desire to stay out of war, to save our youth from the dive bombers and the flame throwing tanks in the unutterable hell of modern warfare.

But is there not an evidence of suicidal insanity in our failure to help those who now stand between us and the creators of this hell?

WE CAN HELP — IF WE WILL ACT NOW
— before it is forever too late.

We can help by sending planes, guns, munitions, food. We can help to end the fear that American boys will fight and die in another Flanders, closer to home.

The members of our government are your servants. In an emergency as serious as this, they require the expression of your will. They must know that the American people are not afraid to cast off the hypocritical mask of neutrality, which deceives no one, including ourselves.

*Send a postcard, a letter, or a telegram, at once* — to the President of the United States, to your Senators and your Congressmen — urging that the *real* defense of our country must begin NOW — with aid to the Allies!

The United States of America is still the most powerful nation on earth — and the United States of America is YOU!

---

3.

# FRANKLIN D. ROOSEVELT: The Hand That Held the Dagger

*By June 1940 the debate within the Roosevelt administration and in Congress over whether the United States should extend material aid to the Allies was in full cry. British and French leaders, supported by American liberals, had sent numerous warnings of what would happen if aid were withheld, but American military leaders were loath to weaken further what they considered to be already overextended defenses, and many congressmen, fearing an adverse public reaction, opposed any aid at all. On June 5 Germany invaded France, and five days later Italy declared war on France and England. On the same day — June 10 — President Roosevelt was scheduled to address the graduating class at the University of Virginia. Despite his awareness that the majority of the students in the country were against any involvement in the European war, he concluded his speech with an unqualified commitment to give aid to all nations under attack by Germany and Italy. A portion of the address is reprinted here.*

Source: *Record, App.*, 76 Cong., 3 Sess., pp. 3740-3741.

---

PERCEPTION OF DANGER, danger to our institutions, may come slowly or it may come with a rush and a shock as it has to the people of the United States in the past few months. This perception of danger, danger in a worldwide area — it has come to us clearly and overwhelmingly — we perceive the peril in a worldwide arena — an arena that may become so narrowed that only the Americas will retain the ancient faiths.

Some, indeed, still hold to the now somewhat obvious delusion that we of the United States can safely permit the United States to become a lone island, a lone island in a world dominated by the philosophy of force.

Such an island may be the dream of those who still talk and vote as isolationists. Such an island represents to me and to the overwhelming majority of Americans today a helpless nightmare, the helpless nightmare of a people without freedom; yes, the nightmare of a people lodged in prison, handcuffed, hungry, and fed through the bars from day to day by the contemptuous, unpitying masters of other continents.

It is natural also that we should ask ourselves how now we can prevent the building of that prison and the placing of ourselves in the midst of it.

Let us not hesitate — all of us — to proclaim certain truths. Overwhelmingly we, as a nation — and this applies to all the other American nations — are convinced that military and naval victory for the gods of force and hate would endanger the institutions of democracy in the Western world, and that equally, therefore, the whole of our sympathies lies with those nations that are giving their lifeblood in combat against these forces.

The people and the government of the United States have seen with the utmost regret and with grave disquiet the decision of the Italian government to engage in the hostilities now raging in Europe. More than three months ago the chief of the Italian government sent me word that because of the determination of Italy to limit, so far as might be possible, the spread of the European conflict, more than 200 million people in the region of the Mediterranean had been enabled to escape the suffering and the devastation of war.

I informed the chief of the Italian government that this desire on the part of Italy to prevent the war from spreading met with full sympathy and response on the part of the government and the people of the United States, and I expressed the earnest hope of this government and of this people that this policy on the part of Italy might be continued. I made it clear that in the opinion of the government of the United States any extension of hostilities in the region of the Mediterranean might result in a still greater enlargement of the scene of the conflict, the conflict in the Near East and in Africa, and that if this came to pass no one could foretell how much greater the theater of the war eventually might become.

Again, on a subsequent occasion, not so long ago, recognizing that certain aspirations of Italy might form the basis of discussions between the powers most specifically concerned, I offered, in a message addressed to the chief of the Italian government, to send to the governments of France and of Great Britain such specific indications of the desires of Italy to obtain readjustments with regard to her position as the chief of the Italian government might desire to transmit through me. While making it clear that the government of the United States in such an event could not and would not assume responsibility for the nature of the proposals submitted nor for agreements which might thereafter be reached, I proposed that if Italy would refrain from entering the war, I would be willing to ask assurances from the other powers concerned that they would faithfully execute any agreement so reached and that Italy's voice in any future peace conference would have the same authority as if Italy had actually taken part in the war as a belligerent.

Unfortunately, to the regret of all of us and to the regret of humanity, the chief of the Italian government was unwilling to accept the procedure suggested and he has made no counterproposal.

This government directed its efforts to doing what it could to work for the preservation of peace in the Mediterranean area, and it likewise exercised its willingness to endeavor to cooperate with the government of Italy when the appropriate occasion arose for the creation of a more stable world order through the reduction of armaments and through the construction of a more liberal international economic system, which would assure to all powers equality of opportunity in the world's markets and in the securing of raw materials on equal terms.

I have likewise, of course, felt it necessary in my communications to Signor Mussolini to express the concern of the government of the United States because of the fact that any extension of the war in the region of the Mediterranean would inevitably result in great prejudice to the ways of life and government and to the trade and commerce of all of the American republics.

The government of Italy has now chosen to preserve what it terms its "freedom of action" and to fulfill what it states are its promises to Germany. In so doing it has manifested disregard for the rights and security of other nations, disregard for the lives of the peoples of those nations which are directly threatened by this spread of the war, and has evidenced its unwillingness to find the means through pacific negotiations for the satisfaction of what it believes are its legitimate aspirations.

On this 10th day of June, 1940, the hand that held the dagger has struck it into the back of its neighbor.

On this 10th day of June, 1940, in this university, founded by the first great American teacher of democracy, we send forth our prayers and our hopes to those beyond the seas who are maintaining with magnificent valor their battle for freedom.

In our unity — in our American unity — we will pursue two obvious and simultaneous courses; we will extend to the opponents of force the material resources of this nation, and at the same time we will harness and speed up the use of these resources in order that we ourselves in the Americas may have equipment and training equal to the task of any emergency and every defense.

All roads leading to the accomplishment of these objectives must be kept clear of obstructions. We will not slow down or detour. Signs and signals call for speed — full speed ahead.

Yes; it is right that each new generation should ask questions. But in recent months the principal question has been somewhat simplified. Once more the future of the nation, the future of the American people is at stake.

We need not and we will not in any way abandon our continuing effort to make democracy work within our borders. Yes; we still insist on the need for vast improvements in our own social and economic life. But that, that is a component part of national defense itself.

The program unfolds swiftly, and into that program will fit the responsibility and the opportunity of every man and woman in the land to preserve his and her heritage in days of peril.

I call for effort, courage, sacrifice, devotion. Granting the love of freedom, all of these are possible. And — and the love of freedom is still fierce, still steady in the nation today.

———◆———

*I say this in dead earnest — if, because of some fine speeches about humanity, you return this administration to office, you will be serving under an American totalitarian government before the long third term is finished.*
    WENDELL L. WILLKIE, speech during campaign, 1940

4.

## STEPHEN VINCENT BENÉT: "Nightmare at Noon"

*By the middle of 1940 Germany had conquered France, Holland, Belgium, Denmark, and Norway, and the "Battle of Britain" was about to begin. Against this background of European crisis, poet Stephen Vincent Benét looked at an America where no bombs had yet fallen and where blackouts were as yet unnecessary and wondered what it would be like when — as seemed inevitable — the war clouds drifted across the Atlantic. "Nightmare at Noon" was the result.*

Source: *Selected Poetry and Prose*, Basil Davenport, ed., New York, 1960.

### NIGHTMARE AT NOON

There are no trenches dug in the park, not yet.
There are no soldiers falling out of the sky.
It's a fine, clear day, in the park. It is bright and hot.
The trees are in full, green, summer-heavy leaf.
An airplane drones overhead but no one's afraid.
There's no reason to be afraid, in a fine, big city
That was not built for a war. There is time and time.

There was time in Norway and time, and the thing fell.
When they woke, they saw the planes with the black crosses.
When they woke, they heard the guns rolling in the street.
They could not believe, at first. It was hard to believe.
They had been friendly and thriving and inventive.
They had had good arts, decent living, peace for years.
Those were not enough, it seems.
There were people there who wrote books and painted pictures,
Worked, came home tired, liked to be let alone.
They made fun of the strut and the stamp and the stained salute,
They made fun of the would-be Caesars who howl and foam.
That was not enough, it seems. It was not enough.
When they woke, they saw the planes with the black crosses.

There is grass in the park. There are children on the long meadow
Watched by some hot, peaceful nuns. Where the ducks are fed
There are black children and white and the anxious teachers
Who keep counting them like chickens. It's quite a job
To take so many school-kids out to the park,

But when they've eaten their picnic, they'll go home.
(And they could have better homes, in a rich city.)
But they won't be sent to Kansas or Michigan
At twenty-four hours' notice,
Dazed, bewildered, clutching their broken toys,
Hundreds on hundreds filling the blacked-out trains.
Just to keep them safe, just so they may live not die.
Just so there's one chance that they may not die but live.
That does not enter our thoughts. There is plenty of time.

In Holland, one hears, some children were less lucky.
It was hard to send them anywhere in Holland.
It is a small country, you see. The thing happened quickly.
The bombs from the sky are quite indifferent to children.
The machine-gunners do not distinguish. In Rotterdam
One quarter of the city was blown to bits.
That included, naturally, ordinary buildings
With the usual furnishings, such as cats and children.
It was an old, peaceful city, Rotterdam,
Clean, tidy, full of flowers.
But that was not enough, it seems.
It was not enough to keep all the children safe.
It was ended in a week, and the freedom ended.

There is no air-raid siren yet, in the park.
All the glass still stands, in the windows around the park.
The man on the bench is reading a Yiddish paper.
He will not be shot because of that, oddly enough.
He will not even be beaten or imprisoned.
Not yet, not yet.
You can be a Finn or a Dane and an American.
You can be German or French and an American,
Jew, Bohunk, Nigger, Mick — all the dirty names
We call each other — and yet American.
We've stuck to that quite a while.
Go into Joe's Diner and try to tell the truckers
You belong to a Master Race and you'll get a laugh.

*What's that, brother? Double-talk?*
*I'm a stranger here myself but it's a free country.*
*It's a free country . . .*
Oh yes, I know the faults and the other side,
The lyncher's rope, the bought justice, the wasted land,
The scale on the leaf, the borers in the corn,
The finks with their clubs, the grey sky of relief,
All the long shame of our hearts and the long disunion.
I am merely remarking — as a country, we try.
As a country, I think we try.

They tried in Spain but the tanks and the planes won out.
They fought very well and long.
They fought to be free but it seems that was not enough.
They did not have the equipment. So they lost.
They tried in Finland. The resistance was shrewd,
Skilful, intelligent, waged by a free folk.
They tried in Greece, and they threw them back for a while
By the soul and spirit and passion of common men.
Call the roll of fourteen nations. Call the roll
Of the blacked-out lands, the lands that used to be free.

But do not call it loud. There is plenty of time.
There is plenty of time, while the bombs on London fall
And turn the world to wind and water and fire.
There is time to sleep while the fire-bombs fall on London.
They are stubborn people in London.

We are slow to wake, good-natured as a country.
(It is our fault and our virtue.) We like to raise
A man to the highest power and then throw bricks at him.
We don't like war and we like to speak our minds.
We're used to speaking our minds. There are certain words,
Our own and others', we're used to — words we've used,
Heard, had to recite, forgotten,
Rubbed shiny in the pocket, left home for keepsakes,
Inherited, stuck away in the back-drawer,
In the locked trunk, at the back of the quiet mind.
Liberty, equality, fraternity.
To none will we sell, refuse or deny, right or justice.
We hold these truths to be self-evident.

I am merely saying — what if these words pass?
What if they pass and are gone and are no more,
Eviscerated, blotted out of the world?
We're used to them, so used that we half-forget,
The way you forget the looks of your own house
And yet you can walk around it, in the darkness.
You can't put a price on sunlight or the air,
You can't put a price on these, so they must be easy.
They were bought with belief and passion, at great cost.
They were bought with the bitter and anonymous blood
Of farmers, teachers, shoemakers and fools
Who broke the old rule and the pride of kings.
And some never saw the end and many were weary,
Some doubtful, many confused.
They were bought by the ragged boys at Valmy mill,
The yokels at Lexington with the long light guns
And the dry, New England faces,

The iron barons, writing a charter out
For their own iron advantage, not the people,
And yet the people got it into their hands
And marked it with their own sweat.
It took long to buy these words.
It took a long time to buy them and much pain.

Thenceforward and forever free.
Thenceforward and forever free.
No man may be bound or fined or slain till he has been judged
    by his peers.
To form a more perfect Union.

The others have their words too, and strong words,
Strong as the tanks, explosive as the bombs.

The State is all, worship the State!
The Leader is all, worship the Leader!

Strength is all, worship strength!
Worship, bow down or die!

I shall go back through the park to my safe house,
This is not London or Paris.
This is the high, bright city, the lucky place,
The place that always had time.
The boys in their shirtsleeves here, the big, flowering girls,
The bicycle-riders, the kids with the model planes,
The lovers who lie on the grass, uncaring of eyes,
As if they lay on an island out of time,
The tough kids, squirting the water at the fountain,
Whistled at by the cop.
The dopes who write "Jimmy's a dope" on the tunnel walls.
These are all quite safe and nothing will happen to them.
Nothing will happen, of course.
Go tell Frank the Yanks aren't coming, in Union Square.
Go tell the new brokers' story about the President.
Whatever it is. That's going to help a lot.
There's time to drink your highball — plenty of time.
Go tell fire it only burns in another country,
Go tell the bombers this is the wrong address,
The hurricane to pass on the other side.
Go tell the earthquake it must not shake the ground.

The bell has rung in the night and the air quakes with it.

I shall not sleep tonight when I hear the plane.

5.

# Philip Murray: Collective Bargaining and Industrial Democracy

*The New Deal inaugurated a new era in industrial-labor relations. The National Labor Relations Act of 1935 had immensely strengthened labor's ability to organize unions and to engage in collective bargaining. In Senate committee hearings during February 1940, Philip Murray, leader of the Steel Workers Organizing Committee, testified concerning labor's progress as a result of the 1935 Act and denounced proposed amendments that would weaken the law. A portion of his testimony is reprinted below.*

Source: *National Labor Relations Act and Proposed Amendments, Hearings Before the Committee on Education and Labor, U.S. Senate*, 76 Congress, 3 Session, Washington, 1940, Pt. 24, pp. 4635-4665.

I WELCOME THE OPPORTUNITY to appear before the honorable committee on behalf of the Steel Workers Organizing Committee, as its chairman, to present the point of view of my organization on the proposed amendments to the National Labor Relations Act, which are now pending before the Congress.

In presenting this point of view I do not propose to deal with the conflicting legal and technical points involved in this controversy. Instead I wish to take the honorable members of this committee, in the course of my discussion, behind the stage of collective bargaining in the great iron and steel industry. I want to show you the inside workings of collective bargaining in the industry. As a participant in the development of employee-employer relations on a democratic basis during the past few crucial years, I have a human story to relate about the steel industry. It is the story of management and workers adjusting themselves to new kinds of relationships, orienting themselves in their everyday economic activities to the democratic ways of our political life, and resolving their differences around the conference table.

My story is a personal one, a human drama. It has been the good fortune of living generations to witness the start of a new cycle in worker-management relations in the basic steel-producing industry. From the historic, and bloody, Homestead, Pa., strike of 1892 until the equally historic, but peaceful, signing of the March 1937 collective-bargaining contract between the Steel Workers Organizing Committee (SWOC) and the United States Steel Corporation and subsidiaries, a period of forty-five years, one single policy governed the relations between steelworkers and their employers. That policy was, as steel employers put it: "We will deal with our employees as individuals only, and refuse to recognize or deal with them as an organized group or trade union."

That policy was undemocratic, inhuman, and contravened the fundamental tenets of the federal Constitution. It was undemocratic because it denied the steelworkers their rights of free association for their mutual protection. It was inhuman because it pitted the overpowering corporate wealth of giant industrialists against the puny strength of a single, individual workingman. It violated the federal Constitution because it forbade the individual worker to join hands with his fellow workers so that together, as an organized trade union, their power might begin to equal that of the huge corporation which gave them employment. That policy was enforced by coal and iron police, labor spies, tear and sickening gas, and other reprehensible means that mark the history of the 1901 and 1909 strikes against United States Steel, the 1910 strike against Bethlehem Steel, the 1917 strike against Youngstown Steel, the 1919 strike against the entire industry, and the 1933 strike against the Weirton Steel Co.

The cycle of industrial relations, which ran from 1892 to 1937, was marked by recurrent warfare between steel employers and their workers, who periodically strove to end the cycle. They strove, at great sacrifice and the loss of many lives, to start a new cycle of industrial relations. Not until 1937 were the steelworkers successful in their trying efforts. In the spring of that year the basic steel-producing industry embarked upon a new cycle of industrial relations which was based on the fundamental democratic principles, as stated by Mr. Myron C. Taylor, then chairman of the board of the United States Steel Corporation, to wit:

The company recognizes the right of its employees to bargain collectively through representatives freely chosen by them. . . . It will negotiate and contract with the representatives of any group of its employees so chosen and with any organization as the representatives of its members. . . .

Three-fourths of the steel industry followed the lead of United States Steel. My story is concerned primarily with the peaceful development of collective bargaining during the past two years, which represent the first two years of a new cycle of industrial relations for the steel industry, except for a minority segment of the industry which has tried, in vain, to prolong the cycle of industrial relations which started in 1892 and ended in 1937.

This new cycle of industrial relations, based on the fundamental principles of a political democracy, has been encouraged and guided by the industrial-relations policy of the federal government. This policy has been to encourage industry to operate its plants on the same democratic basis that our federal, state, and local governments operate, namely, that:

(a) Workers may associate themselves together into a group or trade union for their mutual protection;

(b) Workers may select representatives of their own choosing to advance their mutual interests; and

(c) Workers may enjoy these rights without interference from their employers, and the federal government, as it protects the other rights of its citizens, will protect these rights of the workers with its power.

This policy of the federal government has been administered by the National Labor Relations Board since July 5, 1935, although the administration of this policy was delayed and impeded by the gratuitous opinions of self-appointed kangaroo courts, until the Supreme Court of the United States validated the National Labor Relations Act on April 12, 1937, twenty-one months later.

The major experience of the SWOC with the National Labor Relations Board has been either as an alternative to the stoppage of work or as a means to facilitate the settlement of an industrial dispute already in progress. One of the chief functions of the board is to administer in industry the democratic principle of majority rule. Prior to the creation of the board, workers were forced to engage in a strike through their trade union to prove to their employer that a majority of his workers belonged to the union. There was no other way of establishing their majority claims. There were no elections, since no impartial board existed to conduct them. The union's majority could not be established by comparing its membership cards with the company's payroll because the union justly feared its members would be fired and blacklisted if their names were divulged to the company. Under these conditions, in pre-board days, the only way left open to establish its majority for a group of workers, who had managed to organize into a trade union despite the belligerent opposition of their employer, was to go on strike. When the employer challenged the majority claims of a union, its leaders could only say: "If you doubt our majority, then we will have to show you it on the picket line." The consequence, as a rule, was costly warfare, bloodshed, the loss of lives, and other irreparable losses. . . .

To illustrate how the National Labor Relations Board has actually rendered invaluable public service when the question of majority rule has been the chief point of controversy, I shall recite our experiences with the Jones & Laughlin Steel Corporation. I want to take the honorable members of this committee in my discussion to a point twenty miles below Pittsburgh on the Ohio River to the steel town of Aliquippa, Pa. Approximately 13,000 steelworkers are employed in the huge works of Jones & Laughlin, which stretch for more than four miles along the Ohio River in Aliquippa. When the Aliquippa steelworkers attempted to organize a trade union in 1933, ten of their leaders were discharged. It was their case which was settled by the United States Supreme Court in April of 1937. A long history of antiunionism is the story of Aliquippa prior to 1937. I shall not take the

time of this committee to tell this story, although it has a vital bearing on the problems this committee is considering, but I am appending a brief history of Aliquippa to my statement, and I commend it to the honorable members of this committee for their careful study. My present purpose is to tell the story of Aliquippa since 1937.

By May 1937 a distinct majority of Aliquippa's steelworkers had become members of the SWOC. In addition, a majority of the Jones & Laughlin Steel Corporation's 12,000-odd employees in its Pittsburgh Works had also become members of the SWOC. On behalf of these members the SWOC requested a conference with the corporation's officials early in May. The United States Steel Corporation had already recognized SWOC and signed a collective-bargaining contract with it. The same form of recognition was requested from Jones & Laughlin, which hesitated to grant it. Instead, Jones & Laughlin rushed plans to convert its company union, or employee representative plan, into a so-called independent union to compete with the SWOC. This brought negotiations to a head, and in self-defense the Jones & Laughlin workers went on strike.

The strike, at once, was successful; in fact, it was 100 percent. When the Jones & Laughlin officials saw their works completely closed down for the first time in their history, they reentered negotiations with the SWOC. The corporation officials told me and my associates that they would sign a contract similar to the one between the SWOC and U.S. Steel, provided we could show that a majority of Jones & Laughlin's workers were SWOC members. Unlike the case of Judge Elbert Gary in 1919, these Jones & Laughlin officials were sincere. The real question in dispute was not the right of the union to exist, as was the case in 1919, but merely whether the union actually represented a majority of the workers.

Happily for the workers and the corporation, the National Labor Relations Board was in existence. Because of the existence of the board, the Jones & Laughlin strike was one of the shortest on record, involving approximately 25,000 workers. It lasted just thirty-six hours.

In the past there would have been no other way out than a long-drawn-out battle, but here under the Wagner Act there was a definite, sane, constitutional, and democratic way of settling our differences. The company said we did not really represent its men. SWOC insisted that it did. The obvious way to settle it, therefore, was to hold an election.

The National Labor Relations Board provided the machinery for this, and the strike was settled with an agreement that the terms of the U.S. Steel contract would be in effect until an election was held by the National Labor Relations Board within ten days to determine whether or not the Steel Workers Organizing Committee represented a majority of the Jones & Laughlin employees. The result was a smashing victory — 17,208 for the union and 7,207 against the union.

The Jones & Laughlin Steel Corporation thereupon signed a collective-bargaining contract with the SWOC, recognizing it as the sole bargaining agency for all of its production and maintenance workers. This contract was the beginning of the extension of democratic principles and procedures into the operation of the Jones & Laughlin works. Twenty-five thousand workers who had been governed for years by the dictatorial rules that management arbitrarily promulgated elected their own representatives. These representatives sat around the conference table with management and negotiated fair, democratic rules to govern the operations of the Jones & Laughlin mills. Here was an overt experiment in democratic ways. I am happy to report to this committee, as a firm believer in democratic principles, that this experiment in industrial democracy has been altogether successful. . . .

Today, employers no longer publicly state that they will only deal with their workers as individuals. All employers, from enlightened ones down to Tom Girdler, publicly proclaim their belief in collective bargaining and the free right of their workers to organize into unions of their own choosing. The actual practices of some employers, however, have been much at variance with these public statements. While, on the one hand, they publicly recognize the right of their workers to organize freely, on the other hand, they secretly strove to control the organization of their workers by creating company unions. Beginning with the NIRA in 1933 and continuing through 1936, American industry saw the mushroom growth of company unions. They seemed to grow up from almost nowhere, although with just enough exceptions to prove the rule they were hatched in the offices of corporation attorneys. . . .

Meanwhile, the Steel Workers Organizing Committee had grown in industry-wide proportions. It was obvious that a majority of the steel workers in the United States had joined the union and that they wished to be represented by it. On March 2, 1937, Carnegie-Illinois Steel Corporation, largest subsidiary of the United States Steel Corporation, signed a preliminary recognition contract with the Steel Workers Organizing Committee. Two weeks later this contract was expanded into a formal contract embodying definite terms and conditions of employment for a specific period of time.

This Carnegie-Illinois-U.S. Steel contract served as a standard for the entire industry. It provided for recognition of the Steel Workers Organizing Committee as bargaining agent for its members; it raised wages 10 cents an hour over and above a 10 percent wage raise of five months previous and established an eight-hour day, forty-hour week with time and one-half for overtime; it granted vacations with pay; it introduced seniority rights in layoffs and recall; it set up a democratic machinery for the adjustment of grievances, with arbitration as the final step; it outlawed strikes and lockouts during the term of the contract; it reaffirmed the basic rights of ownership to management; it made safety and health a matter of joint company-union concern; it enumerated holidays; it set a date at which joint conferences for renewal were to take place; and, lastly, defined the terms of the contract.

Shortly thereafter the other U.S. Steel units signed identical contracts with the Steel Workers Organizing Committee. This is the first time United States Steel Corporation was under contract for all its producing subsidiaries at the same time and with the same union. Various steel plants of the company had had labor contracts before but those had been inherited and were discarded as soon as possible.

On April 26, 1937, the Carnegie-Illinois Steel Corporation, through its counsel, appeared before the National Labor Relations Board and made a statement for the record with reference to the proceedings based on charges of company violation of the Wagner Act. The corporation stated that it would not interfere with the employees' rights under the act; that it would not dominate or interfere with the formation or administration of any labor organization, or contribute financial or other support to it; that it would not contribute any support to or participate in and would withdraw all recognition from and would completely disestablish its relations with the existing plans of employee representation; and that a copy of the statement would be posted on all bulletin boards of its plants. On the same day President B. F. Fairless of the Carnegie-Illinois Steel Corporation announced

the corporation's new policy to its employees. It should be noted that this company-dominated employee representative plan was inaugurated in 1933, two years before the passage of the Wagner Act. Thus ended U.S. Steel's venture into organizing unions. It washed its hands of company unions and adopted a policy of bargaining collectively with a bona fide trade union democratically controlled by U.S. Steel workers. . . .

This collective-bargaining development is unparalleled in American industrial and labor history. A great change has taken place in management's attitude toward its workers. In view of the fact that the character of industrial relations, by and large, is determined by the attitude of management, this new and changed attitude is a healthy sign. It is a bulwark to our democratic form of government. I am happy to report that not a single company that embarked upon contractual relations with the SWOC beginning in 1937 has severed relations with SWOC. Every single firm has renewed its collective-bargaining contract with SWOC, and others have since signed SWOC contracts. The part the industrial-relations policy of the federal government, as administered by the National Labor Relations Board, played in this development, and continues to play in it, is indeterminable. But to the credit and glory of our political democracy, it has been substantial, and rightly so.

Up to the present date, three-fourths of the steel industry has followed the lead of U.S. Steel and embarked upon a new cycle of industrial relations. Unfortunately, a minority of the basic steel industry took a different course in 1937. The so-called Little Steel firms attempted, in vain, to prolong the cycle of industrial relations which began with the bloody Homestead strike of 1892. In their futile attempt to stop the development of collective bargaining in the steel industry which has since taken place, the Little Steel firms designed and provoked a bloody strike more murderous than the Homestead strike in 1892.

The strike took place in the summer of 1937. Its leader was Tom Girdler. In contrast to the Jones & Laughlin Steel Corporation situation, the National Labor Relations Board was powerless to render any service. The question in dispute was not whether SWOC represented a majority of the workers involved, as in the Jones & Laughlin case. Instead the issue was the same as in the 1919 steel strike, namely, does the union, in this instance the SWOC, have a right to exist. Tom Girdler provoked the Little Steel strike for the sole purpose of maintaining his unfair advantage over his workers. Backed by huge financial and industrial interests, Tom Girdler was able to beat down any single individual worker his management employed. Tom Girdler opposed the organization of his workers because he knew that as an organized trade union his workers could meet him on equal grounds. . . .

The number of companies under contract with us has now reached 638. . . . These contracts are for the most part patterned after the standard U.S. Steel agreement. Variations and allowances are made for peculiar industrial and special local conditions. Quite frequently, certification by the NLRB is embodied in the recognition clause which has accordingly been expanded from limitation for members only to sole bargaining rights. Generally, one contract covers all the production and maintenance workers at all the plants of a particular company. However, there are some instances where separate agreements are entered into for each plant.

The members of the Steel Workers Organizing Committee are organized into 1,100 lodges, or local unions, on the basis of 1 for each plant. Thus there may be a number of local unions for a single company. These lodges have elected over 10,000 officers and grievance committeemen, each of whom is an employee of the respective company or plant, and therefore a fellow worker of the persons who elected him. Here is industrial democracy patterned after our old New England town meetings, for the general body of workers convene regularly, usually once a month, to discuss and decide upon the policies their officers are to pursue.

Steelworkers are now more than employees. They are citizens of the steel industry. They have just as strong an interest in its welfare as management. And through the Steel Workers Organizing Committee they are taking part in its development and improvement. They are making a real contribution. In 1938 the SWOC issued a handbook, a copy of which I should like inserted in the record, entitled *Production Problems.* This handbook sets forth a joint program for management and men to improve productive efficiency and thereby enlarge their participation in the national income.

I want to bring the first part of my discussion to a close by observing that a new cycle of industrial relations is now in its fourth year for a majority of the basic steel-producing industry. Despite the ill-advised and futile efforts of Tom Girdler and the misguided steel employers that followed his lead, a majority of the steelworkers and steel employers of this country now determine their relationships by democratic means. Whether this economic and industrial development of democracy shall continue in the steel industry, or whether the industry shall revert to the chaotic and barbarous ways Tom Girdler is trying to perpetuate will be determined, in large measure, by the action of the federal Congress. The SWOC is doing its part to bolster democracy in America, and most certainly the Congress should not do anything to frustrate this development or encourage the decaying seed of the old autocracy now represented by Tom Girdler.

6.

## Woody Guthrie: "Union Maid"

*Women in the labor movement are often forgotten or ignored, but as early as 1834
women textile workers in Massachusetts had struck against wage cuts. Again in
New York City in 1909, 20 thousand shirtwaist-makers — mostly women — struck
against the deplorable conditions of the sweatshops. Women continued to be active
in the labor movement, achieving their most notable success in organizing the
Communications Workers Association of America. Woody Guthrie, who composed
songs about most of the important social movements of the 1930s and 1940s, wrote
"Union Maid" in 1940. It became the most popular song about women in the labor
movement. The heroine of Guthrie's song was, however, a "union widow" — the wife
of a union man, who spent many lonely hours tending the home while her husband was
away organizing.*

Source: *Songs of Work and Freedom*, Edith Fowke and Joe Glazer, eds., New York, 1960.

### ❧ UNION MAID

There once was a union maid;
She never was afraid
Of goons and ginks and company finks
And the deputy sheriffs that made the raid.
She went to the union hall
When a meeting it was called,
And when the company boys came 'round
She always stood her ground.

*Chorus:*
Oh, you can't scare me, I'm sticking to the
  union.
I'm sticking to the union, I'm sticking to
  the union.
Oh, you can't scare me, I'm sticking to the
  union,
I'm sticking to the union till the day I die.

This union maid was wise
To the tricks of company spies;
She couldn't be fooled by company stools —

She'd always organize the guys.
She'd always get her way
When she struck for higher pay;
She'd show her card to the
  National Guard
And this is what she'd say:

You girls who want to be free
Just take a tip from me!
Get you a man who's a union man
And join the Ladies' Auxiliary.
Married life ain't hard
When you've got a union card;
A union man has a happy life
When he's got a union wife.

7.

## JAMES BRYANT CONANT: Education for a Classless Society

*On March 28, 1940, James B. Conant delivered the Charter Day Address at the*
*University of California. Conant, president of Harvard, reviewed what he called*
*the Jeffersonian tradition of education — "freedom of the mind, social mobility*
*through education, [and] universal schooling" — and stressed that the establishment*
*of a classless society where "equality of opportunity" was a reality depended*
*upon major readjustments in the American educational system. A portion of his*
*speech is reprinted below.*

Source: *Atlantic Monthly*, May 1940.

UNTIL FAIRLY RECENTLY it was taken for granted that the American republic could be described as classless. For a century and a half Americans have been saying with pride, "This is a free country. There are no classes in the United States." Note these words carefully, for the denial of classes in America is the denial of hereditary classes, not the denial of temporary groupings based on economic differences. "Caste" and "class" are equated by the average American, and I shall follow this usage. "This is a free country. There are no classes in the United States." The number of times these two sentences have been sincerely spoken could be recorded only by a figure of astronomical magnitude. Were they ever an approximately accurate description of typical American society? My answer would be yes. Have they today sufficient vitality and validity to be the basis for a continuation of Jefferson's educational program? A crystal gazer alone could tell. But I think the chance is good enough to demand our careful consideration of the possibility. For my own part, I risk with enthusiasm an affirmative answer and stand on the hope of our reconstituting a free and classless nation.

Phrases descriptive of a free, casteless, or classless society have not only represented an American belief of great potency in the past but have described actual conditions in many sections of this republic. As compared with the situation in even such free countries as England and France, this country was unique in being without hereditary classes. The importance of this fact, I believe, has not been fully emphasized. But, I hasten to add, the social changes which have altered the situation during the last fifty years have all too often been ignored.

American society in some localities has always been organized on definite class lines; money and power have been passed on from father to son. The different strata have been relatively rigid and impenetrable. But until recently such situations were the exception rather than the rule. Now we see in progress the rapid extension of such stratification over the whole land. We see throughout the country the development of a hereditary aristocracy of wealth. The coming of modern industrialism and the passing of the frontier with cheap lands mark the change. Ruthless and greedy exploitation of both natural and human resources by a small privileged class founded on recently acquired ownership of property has hardened the social strata and threatens to provide explosive material beneath.

Let us not shut our eyes to the realities. The vanishing of free lands, the spread of large-scale manufacturing units, the growth of cities and their slums, the multiplication of tenant farmers and despairing migratory laborers are signs of the passage from one type of social order to another. The existence of vast unemployment only emphasizes the evil significance of an unwelcome change. Have we reached a point where the ideal of a peculiar American society, classless and free, must be regarded as of only historical significance?

Our friends on the Left will, I imagine, say yes. A class struggle is inevitable, they declare. Forget the dreams of a pioneer civilization, the early American town or farm, and face the modern capitalistic world, they urge. From their viewpoint no discussion of present problems which refuses to fit every fact into the framework of a class struggle can be realistic. The extremists will add, at least to themselves, that the outcome of the struggle is also inevitable — a classless society, not of the early American type but on the Russian model.

On the extreme Right we may find an equally clear renunciation of the ideal — equally clear, but not, as a rule, equally outspoken, for the underlying assumptions here are often entirely unconscious. Throughout the history of this republic there has been among a small group undue admiration for the educational system of England, a system built largely on class lines. Among such people Jefferson's idea of careers open to all the talented has evoked little enthusiasm. There has been little concern with recruiting the professions from every economic level. The ideal has been education of a ruling caste rather than a selective system of training leaders.

Yet the unique character of the American way of life has been repeatedly emphasized since Jefferson's time. Lincoln in his first message to Congress declared that "the leading object of the Government for whose existence we contend" is "to elevate the condition of men; to lift artificial weights from all shoulders; to clear the paths of laudable pursuit for all; to afford all an unfettered start and a fair chance in the race of life." The historian F. J. Turner, writing at the beginning of the present century, summed up the case as follows: "Western democracy through the whole of its earlier period tended to the production of a society of which the most distinctive fact was freedom of the individual to rise under conditions of social mobility. . . ."

It is not within my province to consider what political measures should be taken if we reject the idea of an inevitable stratification of society. It is not for me to say what legislation is in order if we desire to implement the ideal of a free classless society. My unwillingness to discuss this important aspect of the problem is not to be taken as a measure of my dissatisfaction with the rapidly growing social and economic differentiation of the United States. On the contrary, if the American ideal is not to be an illusion, the citizens of this republic must not shrink from drastic action. The requirement, however, is not a radical equalization of wealth at any given moment; it is rather a continuous process by which power and privilege may be automatically redistributed at the end of each generation. The aim is a more equitable distribution of opportunity for all the children of the land. The reality of our national life must be made a sufficiently close approximation to our ideal to vitalize a belief in the possibility of the envisaged goal.

I am wary of definitions — even in expounding the exact sciences to an elementary class. It is often more profitable to explain the nature of a concept by illustration than to attempt a definition. Both the words "free" and "classless," as I am employing them, have a relative, not an absolute, meaning. They are useful, I believe, even in a rough quantitative sense, in contrasting different types of social organizations which have existed in the last few centuries in the Western World. It is easy to imagine a small segment of any country where one would be hard put to it to say whether the society in question was free and classless, or the contrary. To pass a judgment on larger social units is even more difficult, but I should not hesitate to say that Russia today is classless but not free; England, free but not classless; Germany, neither free nor classless. . . .

It seems to me that in this century, as in a much earlier period of our history, an imported social philosophy has strongly influenced radical thought. I am not referring to orthodox Marxism, but rather to the general slant of mind inevitable among English and Continental reformers whose basis of reference is a society organized on hard-and-fast class lines. The original American radical tradition has been given a twist by the impact of these alien ideas. As far as the role of government is concerned, the political reformer has swung completely round the circle. On this issue, Jefferson with his almost anarchistic views would find difficulty, indeed, in comprehending his modern political heirs.

Native American radicalism has all but disappeared. Our young people now seem forced to choose between potential Bourbons and latent Bolsheviks. But without a restoration of the earlier type of radical the Jeffersonian tradition in education will soon die. Obviously it cannot long survive a victory of the socialistic Left — there is no place for such ideas in a classless society on the Russian model. And it will likewise disappear automatically unless a high degree of social mobility is once again restored. To keep society fluid, the honest and sincere radical is an all-important element. Those in positions of power and privilege (including college presidents) need to be under constant vigilant scrutiny and from time to time must be the objects of attack. Tyrannies of ownership and management spring up all too readily.

In order to ensure that the malignant growths of the body politic will be destroyed by radiations from the Left, much abuse of healthy and sound tissue must be endured. Reformers and even fanatical radicals we must have. But if the unique type of American society is to continue, those who would better conditions must look in the direction of the progressive or liberal movements of an earlier period. The Left must consider returning to the aim of checking tyranny and restoring social mobility. Reformers must examine every action lest they end by placing in power the greatest tyrant of all — organized society.

THERE ARE PROBABLY SOME who feel that I am indulging in nostalgic fancy when I hope for the evolution of a less stratified and more fluid society. You may say that the modern world of large cities, vast industries, and scientific methods of communication has made the America of a hundred years ago as irrelevant as the Middle Ages. You may argue that a way of life which was possible in the 1840s is impossible in the 1940s; that in the near future we shall all of us have to move in a quite contrary direction. You may contend that soon we shall have to take sides in a bitter class struggle and choose between an American brand of Fascism and an American brand of Socialism.

I know that many believe this to be inevitable. I venture to disagree. And here is the reason for my rash dissent. In my opinion, our newly erected system of public education has potentialities of which we little dream. In this century we have erected a new type of social instrument. Our secondary-school system is a vast engine which we are only beginning to understand. We are learning only slowly how to operate it for the public good. But I have hope that it will aid us in recapturing social flexibility in regaining that great gift to each succeeding generation — opportunity, a gift that once was the promise of the frontier.

Let me explain. Today some 6 million

boys and girls attend our secondary schools, ten times the number enrolled a half century ago. Today nearly three-quarters of those of high school age are enrolled as pupils; fifty years ago schooling at this level was a privilege of less than 10 percent of those who might attend. Opportunity can be evaluated only in terms of personal capacity. What is opportunity for one young man is a blind alley for another. In rapidly expanding pioneer communities, openings for capabilities of all sorts automatically appeared. Only doctors, lawyers, and ministers needed an extensive education. Opportunities were ready at hand for all other types of talent.

In our highly industrialized, relatively static society, the situation is otherwise. The personal problem of each boy or girl is much more difficult. Abilities must be assessed, talents must be developed, ambitions guided. This is the task for our public schools. All the future citizens pass through these institutions. They must be educated as members of a political democracy, but, more important still, they must be equipped to step on to the first rung of whatever ladder of opportunity seems most appropriate. And an appropriate ladder must be found for each one of a diverse group of students. This may seem an overwhelming burden to put upon our educational system. But is it not possible that our public schools, particularly our high schools, can be reconstructed for this specific purpose?

Jefferson thought of universal schooling of younger children chiefly in terms of educating potential voters. His selective process for higher studies was conceived in terms of intellectual pursuits — of preparation for the learned professions such as law and medicine. To continue the tradition he started, we must expand both of his ideas today. The roads which lead to those careers which depend on aptitude for "book learning" still run through the universities. We must fight to keep them open. State-supported universities have blazed the way. But the task is far from done. In many lo-

calities the opportunities for the children of the really poor are lamentable indeed. Outside of metropolitan areas and college towns, the privileges of a professional training are hard to win. An expanded scholarship policy in our privately endowed universities is imperative. Wisely administered student aid will go far to right the balance. Perhaps this device merits more attention even by institutions supported by the state.

The changes required to provide adequately for the intellectually gifted are relatively slight. The real problems of reconstruction of our schools and colleges do not lie in this area. The real difficulties are with the careers of a different sort. Our schools must be concerned with educating for a useful life a great variety of boys and girls. They must be concerned not only with the able scholar but with the artist and the craftsman. They must nourish those whose eye or ear or manual dexterity is their greatest asset. They must educate others whose gifts lie in an ability to understand and lead their fellowmen. The school curricula must include programs for developing the capacities of many who possess intuitive judgment on practical affairs but have little or no aptitude for learning through the printed page.

It has been a natural consequence of our history that many false values now permeate the entire educational system. "Book learning" is placed too high in the scale of social ratings by some; too low by others who profess to scoff at "brains." That type of ability which can handle easily the old-fashioned subjects of the curriculum is often glorified by being equated with "intelligence" by educational snobs. On the other hand, the same ability often suffers from lack of stimulation when there is failure to maintain high standards. As a result, we have a great deal of make-believe in our schools and colleges — too many feeble attempts at tasks which are proper only for a restricted type of individual; too many failures to explore talents which fall outside orthodox academic bounds. Jefferson in the simpler society of his day naturally thought of only a few avenues of opportunity open through education. Today we must recognize the existence of many and strive for the social equality of all.

Parents who expect miracles worked upon their children must be reminded of the limitations imposed by nature. In athletics, at least, the coaches are expected to develop only promising material. No one complains if his undersized son with awkward legs does not become a football hero. Some fathers, however, seem to demand the intellectual equivalent of such a miracle. We expect our college health departments to direct each student into that form of sport which is suited to his physique and power. We need a parallel form of educational guidance in both schools and colleges to assist the development of the skills of brain and hands.

But again I venture to be optimistic. I see signs everywhere of enormous strides forward in such matters. Our educational pattern is becoming daily more diversified; a recognition of the need for a radically different type of education is growing. We look forward to the opening of many channels which lead to a variety of attractive goals; we can envisage the building up of more than one "élite."

Of course, in any realistic discussion of these problems we cannot neglect the social and economic factors. As long as the shadow of unemployment is upon the land, some method of providing food and clothing for the children of many families must be found. For even free schools offer little real opportunity to famished youngsters; public education is only theoretically available to those in rags. Providing food and clothing for those to whom assistance is essential is clearly necessary for a satisfactory functioning of the entire educational system. Many a talented youth is lost by dropping out of the competition, for financial reasons, during the high school years. In short, we must explore every method of developing the individual capacity of each future citizen for useful labor based on individual initiative.

Political and economic changes must go hand in hand with educational innovations — the revision of methods of perpetuating control of many large industries, the overthrow of nepotism and patronage wherever possible, the stimulation of small enterprises, the spreading of private ownership. All this and more is needed if a free classless society is to become once again an ideal which affects our lives.

FREEDOM OF THE MIND, social mobility through education, universal schooling — these, let me repeat, are the three fundamentals of the Jeffersonian tradition. They have represented the aspirations and desires of a free people embarked on a new experiment, the perpetuation of a casteless nation. Popular enthusiasm for enlightenment, for overturning dogmas, for intellectual exploration, has temporarily waned. I have given my reasons for hoping that the black reaction of these years is only a passing phase. The ideal of a free republic without classes has likewise suffered an eclipse. To many of the present college generation the phrase "equality of opportunity" seems a mockery, a trite collection of idle words. In this I see the major challenge to our educational system, a challenge which can be met only by a radical reconstruction. If the nation wants to bend its efforts to have as free and classless a society *as possible,* then for those of us concerned with schools and colleges our course is clearly plotted.

So it seems to me. If we as educators accept the American ideal, then this acceptance must be the major premise for all our thinking. Without neglecting the older roads designed for those of academic brilliance, we must construct many new approaches to adult life, and we must do so very soon. Extreme differentiation of school programs seems essential — differentiation of instruction, but not necessarily a division into separate schools. From this it follows that rapid improvement in our testing methods must be forthcoming; a much more conscientious and discriminating form of educational guidance must be developed soon if we are not to fail. In short, a horde of heterogeneous students has descended on our secondary schools; on our ability to handle all types intelligently depends in large measure the future of this country.

Is it too late — too late for our schools to revitalize the idea of a classless nation? Can we complete the necessary major readjustments in our educational system in time to prevent the extinction of the Jeffersonian tradition? I believe we can, if we make haste. I predict at least another century of vigor for the American ideal. I envisage a further trial on this continent for many generations of our unique type of social order. I look forward to a future American society in which social mobility is sufficient to keep the nation in essence casteless — a society in which the ideals of both personal liberty and social justice can be maintained — a society which through a system of public education resists the distorting pressures of urbanized, industrial life. I have faith in the continuation of a republic composed of citizens each prepared to shoulder the responsibility for his own destiny. And if at each step in the educational journey opportunity truly beckons, will not each student rejoice in the struggle to develop his own capacities? Will he not be proud of the continuing American tradition and find in contemplation of our national history ample courage to face those risks and hazards that come to all who would be free?

8.

# WENDELL L. WILLKIE: Acceptance Speech

*The three leading Republican contenders for the presidency in 1940 were Senator Robert A. Taft of Ohio, Senator Arthur H. Vandenberg of Michigan, and Thomas Dewey, later governor of New York. Wendell Willkie, without a political organization and with little party support, was a dark horse. However, by the time the Republican Convention opened in June there was a rising tide for Willkie, and he was nominated on the sixth ballot. On August 17 Willkie delivered his acceptance speech, a portion of which is reprinted here, in his hometown of Elwood, Indiana. In the election Willkie carried only ten states, but he polled over 22 million votes, more than any previous Republican candidate.*

Source: *This is Wendell Willkie: A Collection of Speeches and Writings on Present-Day Issues,* New York, 1940, pp. 259-280.

No MAN IS SO WISE as to foresee what the future holds or to lay out a plan for it. No man can guarantee to maintain peace. Peace is not something that a nation can achieve by itself. It also depends on what some other country does. It is neither practical nor desirable to adopt a foreign program committing the United States to future action under unknown circumstances.

The best that we can do is to decide what principle shall guide us.

For me, that principle can be simply defined: In the foreign policy of the United States, as in its domestic policy, I would do everything to defend American democracy and I would refrain from doing anything that would injure it.

We must not permit our emotions — our sympathies or hatreds — to move us from that fixed principle.

For instance, we must not shirk the necessity of preparing our sons to take care of themselves in case the defense of America leads to war. I shall not undertake to analyze the legislation on this subject that is now before Congress, or to examine the intentions of the Administration with regard to it. I concur with many members of my party, that these intentions must be closely watched. Nevertheless, in spite of these considerations, I cannot ask the American people to put their faith in me without recording my conviction that some form of selective service is the only democratic way in which to secure the trained and competent manpower we need for national defense.

Also, in the light of my principle, we must honestly face our relationship with Great Britain. We must admit that the loss of the British Fleet would greatly weaken our defense. This is because the British Fleet has for years controlled the Atlantic, leaving us free to concentrate in the Pacific. If the British Fleet were lost or captured, the Atlantic might be dominated by Germany, a power hostile to our way of life, controlling in that event most of the ships and shipbuilding facilities of Europe.

This would be calamity for us. We might be exposed to attack on the Atlantic. Our defense would be weakened until we could build a navy and air force strong enough to defend both coasts. Also, our foreign trade would be profoundly affected. That trade is vital to our prosperity. But if we had to trade with a Europe dominated by the present German trade policies, we might have to change our methods to some totalitarian form. This is a prospect that any lover of democracy must view with consternation.

The objective of America is in the opposite direction. We must, in the long run, rebuild a world in which we can live and move and do business in the democratic way.

The President of the United States recently said: "We will extend to the opponents of force the material resources of this nation, and at the same time we will harness the use of those resources in order that we ourselves, in the Americas, may have equipment and training equal to the task of any emergency and every defense."

I should like to state that I am in agreement with these two principles, as I understand them — and I don't understand them as implying military involvement in the present hostilities. As an American citizen I am glad to pledge my wholehearted support to the President in whatever action he may take in accordance with these principles.

But I cannot follow the President in his conduct of foreign affairs in this critical time. There have been occasions when many of us have wondered if he is deliberately inciting us to war. I trust that I have made it plain that in the defense of America, and of our liberties, I should not hesitate to stand for war. But like a great many other Americans I saw what war was like at first hand in 1917. I know what war can do to demoralize civil liberties at home. And I believe it to be the first duty of a President to try to maintain peace.

But Mr. Roosevelt has not done this. He has dabbled in inflammatory statements and manufactured panics. Of course, we in America like to speak our minds freely, but this does not mean that at a critical period in history our President should cause bitterness and confusion for the sake of a little political oratory. The President's attacks on foreign powers have been useless and dangerous. He has courted a war for which the country is hopelessly unprepared — and which it emphatically does not want. He has secretly meddled in the affairs of Europe, and he has even unscrupulously encouraged other countries to hope for more help than we are able to give.

"Walk softly and carry a big stick" was the motto of Theodore Roosevelt. It is still good American doctrine for 1940. Under the present administration the country has been placed in the false position of shouting insults and not even beginning to prepare to take the consequences.

But while he has thus been quick to tell other nations what they ought to do, Mr. Roosevelt has been slow to take the American people into his confidence. He has hesitated to report facts, to explain situations, or to define realistic objectives. The confusion in the nation's mind has been largely due to this lack of information from the White House.

If I am elected President, I plan to reverse both of these policies. I should threaten foreign governments only when our country was threatened by them and when I was ready to act; and I should consider our diplomacy as part of the people's business concerning which they were entitled to prompt and frank reports to the limit of practicability.

Candor in these times is the hope of democracy. We must not kid ourselves any longer. We must begin to tell ourselves the truth — right here — and right now.

We have been sitting as spectators of a great tragedy. The action on the stage of history has been relentless. For instance, the French people were just as brave and intelligent as the Germans. Their armies were considered the best in the world. France and her allies won the last war. They possessed all the material resources they needed. They had wealth and reserves of credit all over the earth. Yet the Germans crushed France like an eggshell.

The reason is now clear: The fault lay with France herself. France believed in the forms of democracy and in the idea of freedom. But she failed to put them to use. She forgot that freedom must be dynamic, that it is forever in the process of creating a new world. This was the lesson that we of America had taught to all countries. . . .

We must face a brutal, perhaps, a terrible fact. Our way of life is in competition with Hitler's way of life. This competition is not merely one of armaments. It is a competition of energy against energy, production against production, brains against brains, salesmanship against salesmanship.

In facing it we should have no fear. History shows that our way of life is the stronger way. From it has come more wealth, more industry, more happiness, more human enlightenment than from any other way. Free men are the strongest men.

But we cannot just take this historical fact for granted. We must make it live. If we are to outdistance the totalitarian powers, we must arise to a new life of adventure and discovery. We must make a wider horizon for the human race. It is to that new life that I pledge myself.

I promise, by returning to those same American principles that overcame German autocracy once before, both in business and in war, to outdistance Hitler in any contest he chooses in 1940 or after. And I promise that when we beat him, we shall beat him on our own terms, in our own American way.

The promises of the present administration cannot lead you to victory against Hitler, or against anyone else. This administration stands for principles exactly opposite to mine. It does not preach the doctrine of growth. It preaches the doctrine of division. We are not asked to make more for ourselves. We are asked to divide among ourselves that which we already have. The New Deal doctrine does not seek risk, it seeks safety. Let us call it the "I pass" doctrine. The New Deal dealt it, and refused to make any more bets on the American future.

Why, that is exactly the course France followed to her destruction! Like the Blum government in France, so has our government become entangled in unfruitful adventures. As in France, so here, we have heard talk of class distinctions and of economic groups preying upon other groups. We are told that capital hates labor and labor, capital. We are told that the different kinds of men, whose task it is to build America, are enemies of one another. And I am ashamed to say that some Americans have made political capital of that supposed enmity.

As for me, I want to say here and now that there is no hate in my heart, and that there will be none in my campaign. It is my belief that there is no hate in the hearts of any group of Americans for any other American group — except as the New Dealers seek to put it there for political purposes. I stand for a new companionship in an industrial society.

Of course, if you start, like the New Deal, with the idea that we shall never have many more automobiles or radios, that we cannot develop many new inventions of importance, that our standard of living must remain what it is, the rest of the argument is easy. Since a few people have more than they need and millions have less than they need, it is necessary to redivide the wealth and turn it back from the few to the many.

But this can only make the poor poorer and the rich less rich. It does not really distribute wealth. It distributes poverty.

Because I am a businessman, formerly connected with a large company, the doctrinaires of the opposition have attacked me as an opponent of liberalism. But I was a liberal before many of these men had heard the word, and I fought for many of the reforms of the elder La Follette, Theodore Roosevelt, and Woodrow Wilson before another Roosevelt adopted — and distorted — liberalism.

I learned my liberalism right here at home. From the factories that came into this town many years ago, large fortunes were made by a few individuals, who thereby acquired too much power over our community. Those same forces were at work throughout the rest of the nation. By 1929 the concentration of private power had gone further than it should ever go in a democracy.

We all know that such concentration of power must be checked. Thomas Jefferson disliked regulation, yet he said that the prime purpose of government in a democracy is to keep men from injuring each other. We know from our own experience that the less fortunate or less skillful among us must be protected from encroachment. That is why we support what is known as the liberal point of view. That is why we believe in reform.

I believe that the forces of free enterprise must be regulated. I am opposed to business monopolies. I believe in collective bargaining, by representatives of labor's own free choice, without any interference and in full protection of those obvious rights. I believe in the maintenance of minimum standards for wages and of maximum standards for hours. I believe that such standards should constantly improve. I believe in the federal regulation of interstate utilities, of securities markets, and of banking. I believe in federal pensions, in adequate old-age benefits, and in unemployment allowances.

I believe that the federal government has a responsibility to equalize the lot of the farmer with that of the manufacturer. If this cannot be done by parity of prices, other means must be found — with the least possible regimentation of the farmer's affairs. I believe in the encouragement of cooperative buying and selling, and in the full extension of rural electrification.

The purpose of all such measures is indeed to obtain a better distribution of the wealth and earning power of this country. But I do not base my claim to liberalism solely on my faith in such reforms. American liberalism does not consist merely in reforming things. It consists also in making things. The ability to grow, the ability to make things, is the measure of man's welfare on this earth. To be free, man must be creative.

I am a liberal because I believe that in our industrial age there is no limit to the productive capacity of any man. And so I believe that there is no limit to the horizon of the United States.

I say that we must substitute for the philosophy of distributed scarcity the philosophy of unlimited productivity. I stand for the restoration of full production and reemployment by private enterprise in America.

And I say that we must henceforth ask certain questions of every reform, and of every law to regulate business or industry. We must ask: Has it encouraged our industries to produce? Has it created new opportunities for our youth? Will it increase our standard of living? Will it encourage us to open up a new and bigger world?

A reform that cannot meet these tests is not a truly liberal reform. It is an "I pass" reform. It does not tend to strengthen our system, but to weaken it. It exposes us to aggressors, whether economic or military. It encourages class distinctions and hatreds. And it will lead us inevitably, as I believe we are now headed, toward a form of government alien to ours, and a way of life contrary to the way that our parents taught us here in Elwood.

It is from weakness that people reach for dictators and concentrated government power. Only the strong can be free.

---

9.

## Franklin D. Roosevelt: The Destroyer Deal

*With the surrender of France in June 1940 England was left open to attack by the Axis powers and in dire need of ships to protect her coasts. President Roosevelt was alarmed by the possibility of an English defeat that would give Germany control of the Atlantic, but because of the Neutrality Act (1939) he was prohibited from trading naval units to Britain. Pessimistic about the chances of getting the Senate to ratify a military aid treaty, Roosevelt called upon Attorney General Robert Jackson to find some legal justification for independent presidential action. On September 2 Roosevelt, armed with Jackson's legal defense, signed an executive agreement with Great Britain that provided her with fifty "mothball" U.S. destroyers in return for 99-year leases on naval and air bases in British possessions. On September 3 the President announced his destroyer-bases deal at a press conference on board a train en route to Washington. Portions of the press conference are reprinted below.*

Source: FDR, IX, pp. 375-390.

*The President:* Hello, good people, how are you? This was an easy trip for you, an awfully easy trip with no news. Why, there is old Fred [Mr. Essary]. Fred, who let you come?

*Q.* [Mr. Essary] I did not ask anybody's permission. I just came.

*The President:* You just came. Gosh, I am glad that somebody got up to give the lady [Miss Fleeson] a seat. Fred, you have become a trouper again; it is all right.

*Q.* [Mr. Essary] So I have.

*The President:* Sit on the floor, Felix [Mr. Belair]; you are too big to stand up.

*Q.* This is the first train press conference since Germany moved into Denmark.

*The President:* I guess that's right.

*Q.* We had a big talk with you at that time about Iceland and Greenland.

*The President:* You are learning geography. There was another press conference where we talked about the Celebes Islands. [*Laughter.*]

*Q.* We were clear to the Cocos before we knew. [*Laughter.*]

*The President:* I have today nothing for you as news from here, although I have something for you for your own information. It is a Washington story that will be out there in twenty-two minutes, so the story will come from Washington. I cannot add to it, but you ought to know about it because you will probably get all kinds of flashes, "For God's sake, get some news." Well, there isn't any news.

In twenty minutes there is going to the Congress the following message, which I am going to read from the only copy I have, which is a rough copy, so there is no use taking it down.

*Mr. Early:* The text will be released there [in Washington].

*The President:* It is probably the most important thing that has come for American defense since the Louisiana Purchase. [*Turning to Mr. Essary.*] That goes back before you and me.

*Q.* [Mr. Essary] That is quite far.

*The President:* How far? About 1803?

*Q.* [Mr. Essary] About.

*The President:* [*Reading.*]

"To the Congress of the United States:

I transmit herewith for the information of the Congress notes exchanged between the British ambassador at Washington and the secretary of state on September 2, 1940"

— in other words, that is yesterday — [*Reading.*]

"under which this government has acquired the right to lease naval and air bases in Newfoundland, and in the islands of Bermuda, the Bahamas, Jamaica, St. Lucia —"

*Q.* [*Interposing*] What is that last one?

*The President:* St. Lucia.

*Q.* How do you spell it?

*The President:* S-t. L-u-c-i-a, period. Now, I am not fooling on those. These are real places. [*Laughter.*] [*The President continued reading.*]

"— Trinidad, and Antigua, and in British Guiana —"

Get out the map. We haven't even got an atlas on board. That is terrible. [*Reading.*]

"— also a copy of an opinion of the attorney general dated August 27, 1940, regarding my authority to consummate this arrangement."

*Q.* [*Interposing.*] What was the date?

*The President:* August 27. And also [*Reading.*]

"The right to bases in Newfoundland and Bermuda are gifts — generously given and gladly received."

Mind you, all these places being mentioned are what they call Crown colonies.

*Q.* Are these ninety-nine-year leases, Mr President?

*The President:* Yes. [*Reading.*]

"The other bases mentioned have been acquired in exchange for fifty of our over-age destroyers."

*Q.* This is breaking out of Washington? [*Laughter.*]

*The President:* This is breaking out of Washington. This is not a press conference, just a little information conference.

*Q.* No connection between those bases and the destroyers?

*Q.* Which of the bases are being leased?

*The President:* They are all ninety-nine years, but Newfoundland and Bermuda are gifts. In other words, there is no exchange in relation to them.

*Q.* No *quid pro quo?*

*The President:* No *quid pro quo* on those at all. You see the point? . . .

*Q.* The release clause applies also to the two gifts?

*The President:* Yes. [*Reading.*]

"This is not inconsistent in any sense with our status of peace. Still less is it a threat against any nation. It is an epochal and far-reaching act of preparation for continental defense in the face of grave danger.

"Preparation for defense is an inalienable prerogative of a sovereign state. Under present circumstances this exercise of sovereign right is essential to the maintenance of our peace and safety. This is the most important action in the reinforcement of our national defense that has been taken since the Louisiana Purchase. Then, as now, considerations of safety from overseas attack were fundamental.

"The value to the Western Hemisphere of these outposts of security is beyond calculation. Their need has long been recognized by our country, and especially by those primarily charged with the duty of charting and organizing our own naval and military defense. They are essential to the —" a lot more geography for you — [*Reading.*]

"protection of the Panama Canal, Central America, the northern portion of South America, the Antilles, Canada, Mexico, and our own Eastern and Gulf seaboards. Their consequent importance in hemispheric defense is obvious. For these reasons I have taken advantage of the present opportunity to acquire them."

That is all.

*Q.* Mr. President, when will the destroyers be sent to Great Britain?

*The President:* Oh, some of them are — I don't know; reasonably soon.

*Q.* Would it be a fair assumption to say that some are on the way?

*The President:* No, I would not say that.

*Q.* Will the British send crews over to take the destroyers?

*The President:* I don't know; I don't know.

*Q.* Where are the destroyers now?

*The President:* I don't know.

*Q.* Mr. President, does this require Senate ratification?

*The President:* Listen: [*Reading.*]

"I transmit herewith for the information of the Congress —"

these notes and the opinion. And, at the end, I say [*Reading.*]

"For these reasons I have taken advantage of the present opportunity to acquire them."

*Q.* Mr. Jackson's opinion?

*The President:* It is all over; it is all done.

*Q.* Mr. President, when might work start on these bases?

*The President:* Don't, please, go any further than this. As soon as we can. In other words, I cannot tell anything about it — they are all "if" questions. If you go beyond this, they are all "if" questions. . . .

*Q.* Can you say which will be naval bases and which air bases?

*The President:* That is an "if" question. You will see by the notes that accompanied this that there is to be created, on both sides, a board which will take up the question of the location; and that board either has been announced in Washington, or will be very soon. It either has proceeded, or is about to proceed, with its duty.

*Q.* Might that be comprised of officers from the services?

*The President:* That board is proceeding or will proceed almost immediately on its duties.

*Q.* How close is the formula that you have used to make this public to the procedure President Monroe used in announcing the Monroe Doctrine? Wasn't there an exchange of correspondence?

*The President:* I think that was employed too.

*Q.* An exchange of correspondence?

*The President:* Of course there was no mutuality in the Monroe Doctrine. There is mutuality here.

This has to be for background — it is for your own information, historical, without attribution. In about — I cannot give you the exact dates — about 1803, Napoleon was at war with Great Britain. France was a belligerent, and we were scared pink because France had bought from Spain the whole of the Louisiana Territory, and especially the mouth of the Mississippi. That was the important thing to our defense. France had a very weak army down there in Louisiana. I think they had one regiment, something like that, for the whole of the territory. We were scared to death that there might be, as an outcome of the Napoleonic Wars, some threat or some danger of some power going in there and going up the valley to connect up with Canada, the back part of Canada, thereby confining the states practically to this side of the Mississippi.

There was an awful lot of discussion about it and everybody was yelling, "For God's sake, protect us," all over the country, "by acquiring, if you can, this mouth of the Mississippi." Of course in those days they, none of them, realized what they were getting with the Louisiana Purchase, that they were getting that tremendous back country that went clear up to Montana, but they saw it primarily from the standpoint of the mouth of the Mississippi and the control of the main stem of the Mississippi.

So Jefferson sent Monroe and Chancellor Robert R. Livingston over to Paris —

*Q.* [*Interposing.*] One of your relatives, wasn't he?

*The President:* Relative, yes. He was my wife's great-grandfather. [*Laughter.*]

And they went to Paris and negotiated with Napoleon, who was a belligerent fighting Great Britain at the time. In fact, he was fighting over most of Europe. They made this deal for the purchase of the whole thing from Napoleon for a price of — as I remember it — what was it, $15 million?

*Q.* Yes, sir.

*The President:* And Napoleon, at the same time, verbally agreed that a portion of that money would be spent over here in buying certain naval supplies and certain food supplies that he needed over there for the continuation of his wars. The contract was signed over there in Paris. Monroe and, I think, Livingston hopped the first sailboat they could and came back to Washington and announced that the thing had been done. Thereupon there ensued a long session in the Cabinet and every other place as to whether such a thing could be done. You see, there was nothing said about it in the Constitution.

*Q.* I thought Jefferson did it — made the Louisiana Purchase?

*The President:* But it was Monroe and Livingston who made the actual purchase. They brought back a signed contract to him. He said, "Fine; I accept it," and then there ensued this discussion in the early days when the Constitution had never been tried out very much. There wasn't anything in the Constitution about it, and to put the thing up to Congress would have involved a delay. Now, the main thing was to put our hands on it, to take it, to get it; and Jefferson, thereupon, as soon as word came from the two commissioners, proceeded to take over Louisiana. It was a *fait accompli.* He got the opinion of the attorney general that he could do it without a treaty, do it for the national defense as commander in chief, and do it as President, as well, in an obvious emergency.

And, later on, he asked, not the Senate but he asked the Appropriations Committee of the House to please appropriate $15 million to him as an item in an appropriation bill, which was done. There was never any treaty, there was never any two-thirds vote in the Senate, and today Louisiana is about one-third of the whole of the United States.

And we are going back 100 — about 137 years — for our historical precedent and authority. It is a very interesting thing.

Q. Did Mr. Jackson, in setting up his opinion saying that you had authority to do that, set forth the Louisiana Purchase as a historical precedent?

*The President:* I think that is mentioned in it. . . .

Q. Any value placed upon the destroyers?

*The President:* You are thinking in terms of dollars and cents and pounds and shillings and pence and you should, in a great emergency, remove pure figures from your mind. Some people will say, undoubtedly — this is still off the record — that, from the point of view of dollars and cents, it is not a good deal. And others will say, "My God, the old Dutchman and Scotchman in the White House has made a good trade." Personally, you can take your money and take your choice. Personally, I think it is a good trade.

Q. Are we back on the record again?

*The President:* No, you are not on the record.

Q. For the record, Mr. President, is it proper to say that these destroyers are released to the British in fee?

*The President:* Yes, in fee.

I have not finished the story. There is also to be given out in Washington, simultaneously — you will have to leave this off the record as coming from me; make it just pure information — a restatement by Prime Minister Winston Churchill on what he said on the 4th of June to Parliament, and this is a restatement to the effect that the British Fleet, in case it is made too hot for them in home waters, is not going to be given to Germany or sunk.

Q. What is the status of that statement? Are they using it?

*The President:* They are using it, I do not know how. In other words, the declaration of June 4, which was perfectly clear and obvious, is reiterated and restated now.

Q. In this correspondence that will accompany this [release]?

*The President:* Yes.

Q. Is that part of the *quid pro quo?*

*The President:* What?

Q. Is that part of the deal?

*The President:* No, it happens to come along at the same time.

Q. Fortuitously?

*The President:* Fortuitously, that is the word. . . .

Q. Will there be any joint control of the base or will there be sovereignty?

*The President:* Nobody knows what sovereignty is. There will be complete American control. That word "sovereignty," you know, went out some years ago.

Q. Did the British lay down any conditions, sir, that the fifty destroyers, including the twenty mosquito boats, must be in condition?

*The President:* No.

Q. They practically all are?

*The President:* They practically all are.

Q. Mosquito boats are not mentioned.

*The President:* No, mosquito boats are not mentioned in there.

Q. Will this apply to airplanes as well as ships?

*The President:* All it says is "air and naval bases." I think it is the other way around, "naval and air bases."

10.

# Franklin D. Roosevelt: Martin, Barton, and Fish

*Both Roosevelt and the Republican candidate, Wendell L. Willkie, wanted to keep foreign policy out of the 1940 presidential campaign. As the campaign wore on, however, Willkie, goaded by his advisers, began first to suggest and then to assert that Roosevelt's reelection would mean war within a year. On October 28 at Madison Square Garden, Roosevelt, in one of his most famous and effective campaign speeches, answered the Republican charges. The reiterated phrase that is used here as the title of the piece was one of Mr. Roosevelt's most effective political inventions. The speech is reprinted here in part.*

Source: *Record, App.,* 76 Cong., 3 Sess., pp. 6533-6534.

TONIGHT I TAKE up again the public duty — the far from disagreeable duty — of answering major campaign falsifications with facts.

Last week in Philadelphia I nailed the falsehood about some fanciful secret treaties to dry on the barn door. I nailed that falsehood and other falsehoods the way when I was a boy up in Dutchess County we used to nail up the skins of foxes and weasels. Tonight I am going to nail up the falsifications that have to do with our relations with the rest of the world, and with the building up of our Army, Navy, and air defense. It is a very dangerous thing to distort facts about such things. If repeated over and over again, it is also apt to create a sense of fear and doubt in the minds of some of the American people.

I now brand as false the statement being made by Republican campaign orators, day after day and night after night, that the rearming of America was slow, that it is hamstrung and impeded, that it will never be able to meet threats from abroad. That par-

ticular misstatement was invented about the time of the Republican National Convention. Before that the responsible Republican leaders had been singing an entirely different song.

For almost seven years the Republican leaders in the Congress kept on saying that I was placing too much emphasis on national defense. And now, today, these men of great vision have suddenly discovered that there is a war on in Europe and another one in Asia. And so, now, always with their eyes on the good old ballot box, they are charging that we have placed too little emphasis on national defense.

But, unlike them, the printed pages of the *Congressional Record* cannot be changed or suppressed at election time. And based on that permanent record of their speeches and their votes, I make this assertion — that if the Republican leaders had been in control of the Congress of the United States during the past seven years, the important measures for our defense would not now be law, and that the Army and Navy of the

United States would still be in almost the same condition in which I found them in 1933.

I make these charges against the responsible political leadership of the Republican Party. There are millions of patriotic Republicans who have at all times been in sympathy with the efforts of this administration to arm itself adequately for defense.

To Washington in the past few months have come not two or three or a dozen, but several hundred of the best business executives in the United States — Republicans and Democrats alike. Not holding company lawyers or executives, but men experienced in actual production — production of all the types of machines and tools and steel that have made this nation the industrial leader of the world.

I asked Mr. Knudsen and Mr. Stettinius and Mr. Harriman and Mr. Budd and the many others to serve because I believe they are certainly among the ablest men in the country in their own fields. I do not know their politics. I do not care about their politics. All I know is that they are cooperating 100 percent with this administration in our efforts for national defense. And this government is cooperating with them 100 percent.

All of these men — all of American industry and American labor — are doing magnificent and unselfish work. The progress today proves it. . . .

When the First World War ended we were one of the strongest naval and military powers in the world. When this administration first came into office fifteen years later, we were one of the weakest.

As early as 1933 the storm was gathering in Europe and in Asia. Year by year I reported the warnings of danger from our listening posts in foreign lands. But I was only called "an alarmist" by the Republican leadership and by the great majority of the Republican papers. Year by year I asked for

more and more defense appropriations. In addition, I allocated hundreds of millions of dollars for defense work from relief funds, from Civilian Conservation Corps funds, and from Public Works funds, as was understood by the Congress when the funds were voted.

Today, our Navy is at a peak of efficiency and fighting strength. Ship for ship and man for man it is as powerful and efficient as any that ever sailed the seas in the history of the world. Our Army and our air forces are now at the highest level they have ever been in peacetime. But in the light of existing dangers they are not great enough for the absolute safety of America.

While this great, constructive work was going forward, the Republican leaders were trying to block our efforts toward national defense. They not only voted against these efforts but they stated time and again through the years that they were unnecessary and extravagant, that our armed strength was sufficient for any emergency.

I propose now to indict these Republican leaders out of their own mouths — these leaders who now disparage our defenses — indict them with what they themselves said in the days before this election year, about how adequate our defenses already were. Listen to this statement, for instance. I quote: "The facts are that we have the largest and most powerful Navy we ever had, except for two years after the World War, and the greatest air forces we ever had, and a match for any nation."

Now, who do you think made this statement in June 1938? It was not I. It was not even a member of this administration. It was the ranking Republican member of the House Committee on Foreign Affairs, Republican leader Hamilton Fish.

And now listen to ex-President Hoover, speaking in that same year of 1938. I quote: "We shall be expending $900 million more than any nation on earth," he complained. "We are leading in the arms race."

And now listen to Republican leader Senator Vandenberg, also speaking in 1938. He said that our defense expenditures had already brought us — and I quote — "an incomparably efficient Navy"; and he said further, "I rise in opposition to this super-super Navy bill. I do not believe it is justified by any conclusive demonstration of national necessity."

And now listen to Republican leader Senator Taft — the runner-up this year for the Republican presidential nomination — speaking in February 1940. I quote: "The increase of the Army and Navy over the tremendous appropriations of the current year seems to be unnecessary if we are concerned solely with defense."

There is the record; there is the permanent, crystal-clear record. Until the present political campaign opened, Republican leaders, in Congress and out, shouted from the housetops that our defenses were fully adequate. Today they complain that this administration has starved our armed forces, that our Navy is anemic, our Army puny, our air forces piteously weak. This is a remarkable somersault. . . .

The Republican campaign orators and leaders are all now yelling "Me, too," on help to Britain. But last fall they had their chance to vote to give aid to Britain and other democracies — and they turned it down. This chance came when I recommended that the Congress repeal the embargo on the shipment of armaments and munitions to nations at war and permit such shipment on a cash-and-carry basis. It is only because of the repeal of the Embargo Law that we have been able to sell planes and ships and guns and munitions to victims of aggression.

How did the Republicans vote on the repeal of this embargo? In the Senate the Republicans voted 14 to 6 against it. In the House the Republicans voted 140 to 19 against it.

The act was passed by Democratic votes but it was over the opposition of the Republican leaders. And just to name a few, the following Republican leaders voted against the act: Senators McNary, Vandenberg, Nye, and Johnson; Congressmen Martin, Barton, and Fish.

Now, at the eleventh hour, they have discovered what we knew all along — that overseas success in warding off invasion by dictatorship forces means safety to the United States as well as to those smaller nations which still retain their independence and the restoration of sovereignty to those smaller nations which have temporarily lost it. One of the keystones of American policy is the recognition of the right of small nations to survive and prosper.

Great Britain would never have received an ounce of help from us if the decision had been left to Martin, Barton, and Fish.

Let us come down to one more example, which took place just two months ago.

In the Senate there was an amendment to permit the United States government to prevent profiteering or unpatriotic obstruction by any corporation in defense work. It permitted the government to take over, with reasonable compensation, any manufacturing plant which refused to cooperate in national defense. The Republican senators voted against this Russell-Overton amendment on August 28, 1940, eight to six.

The bill was adopted all right — by Democratic votes. But the opposing vote of those eight Republican leaders showed what would happen if the national government were turned over to their control. Their vote said, in effect, that they put money rights ahead of human lives — to say nothing of national security.

You and I, and the overwhelming majority of Americans, will never stand for that.

Outside the halls of Congress eminent Republican candidates began to turn new somersaults. At first they denounced the bill. Then, when public opinion rose up to demand it they seized their trapeze with the greatest of ease and reversed themselves in midair. This record of Republican leadership — a record of timidity, weakness, and shortsightedness — is as bad in international as in military affairs. It is the same record of timidity, weakness, and shortsightedness which they showed in domestic affairs when they were in control before 1933. . . .

In July 1937, Japan invaded China. On January 3, 1938, I called the attention of the nation to the danger of the whole world situation. It was clear that rearmament was now a necessary implement of peace. I asked for large additions to American defenses. I was called an alarmist — and worse names than that.

In March 1938, German troops marched into Vienna. In September 1938, came the Munich crisis. German, French, and Czech armies were mobilized. The result was only an abortive armistice.

I said then, "It is becoming increasingly clear that peace by fear has no higher nor more enduring quality than peace by the sword."

Three months later, at Lima, the twenty-one American republics solemnly agreed to stand together to defend the independence of each one of us. The declaration at Lima was a great step toward peace. For unless the hemisphere is safe, we are not safe.

Matters grew steadily worse in Europe. Czechoslovakia was overrun by the Nazis. General war seemed inevitable. Yet, even then, Republican leaders kept chanting, "There will be no war."

A few months later — on the 1st of September, 1939 — war came. The steps which we had carefully planned were put into effect. American ships were kept from danger zones. American citizens were helped to come home. Unlike 1914, there was no financial upheaval.

The American republics set up at Panama a system of patrolling the waters off the whole Western Hemisphere. I ask you to support a continuance of this type of affirmative, realistic fight for peace. The alternative is to risk the future of the country in the hands of those with this record of timidity, weakness, and shortsightedness or in the inexperienced hands of those who, in these perilous days, are willing recklessly to imply that our boys are already on their way to the transports.

This affirmative search for peace calls for clear vision. It is necessary to mobilize resources, minds, and skills, and every active force for peace in the world.

We have steadily sought to keep mobilized the greatest force of all — religious faith, devotion to God. Your government is working at all times with representatives of the Catholic, Protestant, and Jewish faiths. Without these spiritual forces we cannot make or maintain peace, and all three of them work with us toward that great end.

Shadows, however, are still heavy over the faith and hope of humankind. We who walk in the ways of peace and freedom and light have seen the tragedies enacted in one free land after another. We have not been blind to the causes or to the consequences of these tragedies.

We guard ourselves against all evils — spiritual as well as material — which may beset us. We guard against the forces of anti-Christian aggression, which may attack us from without and the forces of ignorance and fear which may corrupt us from within.

We shall continue to go forward in firm faith. We shall continue to go forward in peace.

11.

# Franklin D. Roosevelt: Proposal for Lend-Lease

*As Britain's situation in the war grew more desperate, her ability to pay for needed arms and material rapidly diminished. Following his election to a third term in November 1940, President Roosevelt determined to find some means of underwriting an Allied victory over Germany without huge intergovernment loans. In mid-December he hit upon the idea of Lend-Lease; the materials of war would be turned over to Allied nations now, and would be paid for at the end of the war in goods and services. In a press conference on December 17, Roosevelt outlined in simple terms the underlying premises of the Lend-Lease program. Two weeks later, in an effort to rally public opinion behind his program, Roosevelt delivered one of his most famous "Fireside Chats" — the "arsenal of democracy" speech — on December 29, in which he called upon the American people to assume new responsibilities as guardians of the freedom of the world. A portion of the December 17 press conference is reprinted here.*

Source: FDR, IX, pp. 604-615.

IN THE PRESENT WORLD SITUATION of course there is absolutely no doubt in the mind of a very overwhelming number of Americans that the best immediate defense of the United States is the success of Great Britain in defending itself; and that, therefore, quite aside from our historic and current interest in the survival of democracy in the world as a whole, it is equally important, from a selfish point of view of American defense, that we should do everything to help the British Empire to defend itself. . . .

It isn't merely a question of doing things the traditional way; there are lots of other ways of doing them. I am just talking background, informally; I haven't prepared any of this — I go back to the idea that the one thing necessary for American national defense is additional productive facilities; and the more we increase those facilities — factories, shipbuilding ways, munition plants, et cetera, and so on — the stronger American national defense is.

Orders from Great Britain are therefore a tremendous asset to American national defense because they automatically create additional facilities. I am talking selfishly, from the American point of view — nothing else. Therefore, from the selfish point of view, that production must be encouraged by us. There are several ways of encouraging it — not just one, as the narrow-minded fellow I have been talking about might assume, and has assumed. He has assumed that the only way was to repeal certain existing statutes, like the Neutrality Act and the old Johnson Act and a few other things like that, and then to lend the money to Great Britain to be spent over here — either lend it through private banking circles, as was done in the earlier days of the previous war, or make it a loan from this government to the British government.

Well, that is one type of mind that can think only of that method somewhat banal.

There is another one which is also somewhat banal — we may come to it, I don't know — and that is a gift; in other words, for us to pay for all these munitions, ships, plants, guns, et cetera, and make a gift of them to Great Britain. I am not at all sure that that is a necessity, and I am not at all sure that Great Britain would care to have a gift from the taxpayers of the United States. I doubt it very much.

Well, there are other possible ways, and those ways are being explored. All I can do is to speak in very general terms, because we are in the middle of it. I have been at it now three or four weeks, exploring other methods of continuing the building up of our productive facilities and continuing automatically the flow of munitions to Great Britain. I will just put it this way, not as an exclusive alternative method but as one of several other possible methods that might be devised toward that end.

It is possible — I will put it that way — for the United States to take over British orders and, because they are essentially the same kind of munitions that we use ourselves, turn them into American orders. We have enough money to do it. And thereupon, as to such portion of them as the military events of the future determine to be right and proper for us to allow to go to the other side, either lease or sell the materials, subject to mortgage, to the people on the other side. That would be on the general theory that it may still prove true that the best defense of Great Britain is the best defense of the United States, and therefore that these materials would be more useful to the defense of the United States if they were used in Great Britain than if they were kept in storage here.

Now, what I am trying to do is to eliminate the dollar sign. That is something brand new in the thoughts of practically everybody in this room, I think — get rid of the silly, foolish old dollar sign.

Well, let me give you an illustration: Suppose my neighbor's home catches fire, and I have a length of garden hose 400 or 500 feet away. If he can take my garden hose and connect it up with his hydrant, I may help him to put out his fire. Now, what do I do? I don't say to him before that operation, "Neighbor, my garden hose cost me $15; you have to pay me $15 for it." What is the transaction that goes on? I don't want $15 — I want my garden hose back after the fire is over. All right. If it goes through the fire all right, intact, without any damage to it, he gives it back to me and thanks me very much for the use of it. But suppose it gets smashed up — holes in it — during the fire; we don't have to have too much formality about it, but I say to him, "I was glad to lend you that hose; I see I can't use it any more, it's all smashed up." He says, "How many feet of it were there?" I tell him, "There were 150 feet of it." He says, "All right, I will replace it." Now, if I get a nice garden hose back, I am in pretty good shape.

In other words, if you lend certain munitions and get the munitions back at the end of the war, if they are intact — haven't been hurt — you are all right; if they have been damaged or have deteriorated or have been lost completely, it seems to me you come out pretty well if you have them replaced by the fellow to whom you have lent them.

I can't go into details; and there is no use asking legal questions about how you would do it, because that is the thing that is now under study; but the thought is that we would take over not all, but a very large number of, future British orders; and when they came off the line, whether they were planes or guns or something else, we would enter into some kind of arrangement for their use by the British on the ground that it was the best thing for American defense, with the understanding that when the show was over, we would get repaid sometime in kind, thereby leaving out the dollar mark in the form of a dollar debt and substituting for it a gentleman's obligation to repay in kind. I think you all get it.

# 1941

12.

## FRANKLIN D. ROOSEVELT: The Four Freedoms

*In his annual message to Congress on January 6, 1941, President Roosevelt called upon Congress to enact the Lend-Lease program that he had first proposed at a press conference the previous December. Though the first part of the message concerned itself with the war in Europe and sought to define America's war aims, the latter part was more significant as an expression of Roosevelt's vision of the future. Known as the Four Freedoms Speech, it was a formulation of the social and political goals that the President hoped to attain for the American people, as well as the people of the world, following the war.*

Source: *Record*, 77 Cong., 1 Sess., pp. 44-47.

JUST AS OUR NATIONAL POLICY in internal affairs has been based upon a decent respect for the rights and dignity of all our fellowmen within our gates, so our national policy in foreign affairs has been based on a decent respect for the rights and dignity of all nations, large and small. And the justice of morality must and will win in the end.

Our national policy is this:

First, by an impressive expression of the public will and without regard to partisanship, we are committed to all-inclusive national defense.

Second, by an impressive expression of the public will and without regard to partisanship, we are committed to full support of all those resolute peoples, everywhere, who are resisting aggression and are thereby keeping war away from our Hemisphere. By this support, we express our determination that the democratic cause shall prevail, and we strengthen the defense and security of our own nation.

Third, by an impressive expression of the public will and without regard to partisanship, we are committed to the proposition that principles of morality and considerations for our own security will never permit us to acquiesce in a peace dictated by aggressors and sponsored by appeasers. We know that enduring peace cannot be bought at the cost of other people's freedom.

In the recent national election there was no substantial difference between the two great parties in respect to that national policy. No issue was fought out on this line before the American electorate. Today it is abundantly evident that American citizens everywhere are demanding and supporting speedy and complete action in recognition of obvious danger. Therefore, the immediate need is a swift and driving increase in our armament production.

Leaders of industry and labor have responded to our summons. Goals of speed have been set. In some cases these goals are being reached ahead of time; in some cases we are on schedule; in other cases there are slight but not serious delays; and in some cases — and I am sorry to say very important cases — we are all concerned by the slowness of the accomplishment of our plans. The Army and Navy, however, have made substantial progress during the past year. Actual experience is improving and speeding up our methods of production with every passing day. And today's best is not good enough for tomorrow.

I am not satisfied with the progress thus far made. The men in charge of the program represent the best in training, ability, and patriotism. They are not satisfied with the progress thus far made. None of us will be satisfied until the job is done.

No matter whether the original goal was set too high or too low, our objective is quicker and better results.

To give two illustrations:

We are behind schedule in turning out finished airplanes; we are working day and night to solve the innumerable problems and to catch up.

We are ahead of schedule in building warships; but we are working to get even further ahead of schedule.

To change a whole nation from a basis of peacetime production of implements of peace to a basis of wartime production of implements of war is no small task. And the greatest difficulty comes at the beginning of the program, when new tools and plant facilities and new assembly lines and shipways must first be constructed before the actual

materiel begins to flow steadily and speedily from them.

The Congress, of course, must rightly keep itself informed at all times of the progress of the program. However, there is certain information, as the Congress itself will readily recognize, which, in the interests of our own security and those of the nations we are supporting, must of needs be kept in confidence.

New circumstances are constantly begetting new needs for our safety. I shall ask this Congress for greatly increased new appropriations and authorizations to carry on what we have begun. I also ask this Congress for authority and for funds sufficient to manufacture additional munitions and war supplies of many kinds to be turned over to those nations which are now in actual war with aggressor nations.

Our most useful and immediate role is to act as an arsenal for them as well as for ourselves. They do not need manpower. They do need billions of dollars' worth of the weapons of defense.

The time is near when they will not be able to pay for them in ready cash. We cannot, and will not, tell them they must surrender merely because of present inability to pay for the weapons which we know they must have. I do not recommend that we make them a loan of dollars with which to pay for these weapons — a loan to be repaid in dollars. I recommend that we make it possible for those nations to continue to obtain war materials in the United States, fitting their orders into our own program. Nearly all of their matériel would, if the time ever came, be useful for our own defense.

Taking counsel of expert military and naval authorities, considering what is best for our own security, we are free to decide how much should be kept here and how much should be sent abroad to our friends who, by their determined and heroic resistance, are giving us time in which to make ready our own defense. For what we send abroad we shall be repaid, within a reasonable time following the close of hostilities, in similar materials or, at our option, in other goods of many kinds which they can produce and which we need.

Let us say to the democracies, "We Americans are vitally concerned in your defense of freedom. We are putting forth our energies, our resources, and our organizing powers to give you the strength to regain and maintain a free world. We shall send you, in ever increasing numbers, ships, planes, tanks, guns. This is our purpose and our pledge."

In fulfillment of this purpose we will not be intimidated by the threats of dictators that they will regard as a breach of international law and as an act of war our aid to the democracies which dare to resist their aggression. Such aid is not an act of war, even if a dictator should unilaterally proclaim it so to be. When the dictators are ready to make war upon us, they will not wait for an act of war on our part. They did not wait for Norway or Belgium or the Netherlands to commit an act of war. Their only interest is in a new one-way international law, which lacks mutuality in its observance and, therefore, becomes an instrument of oppression.

The happiness of future generations of Americans may well depend upon how effective and how immediate we can make our aid felt. No one can tell the exact character of the emergency situations that we may be called upon to meet. The nation's hands must not be tied when the nation's life is in danger. We must all prepare to make the sacrifices that the emergency — as serious as war itself — demands. Whatever stands in the way of speed and efficiency in defense preparations must give way to the national need.

A free nation has the right to expect full cooperation from all groups. A free nation has the right to look to the leaders of business, of labor, and of agriculture to take the lead in stimulating effort, not among other groups but within their own groups.

The best way of dealing with the few slackers or troublemakers in our midst is, first, to shame them by patriotic example; and if that fails, to use the sovereignty of government to save government.

As men do not live by bread alone, they do not fight by armaments alone. Those who man our defenses and those behind them who build our defenses must have the stamina and courage which come from an unshakable belief in the manner of life which they are defending. The mighty action which we are calling for cannot be based on a disregard of all things worth fighting for.

The nation takes great satisfaction and much strength from the things which have been done to make its people conscious of their individual stake in the preservation of democratic life in America. Those things have toughened the fiber of our people, have renewed their faith and strengthened their devotion to the institutions we make ready to protect.

Certainly this is no time to stop thinking about the social and economic problems which are the root cause of the social revolution which is today a supreme factor in the world. There is nothing mysterious about the foundations of a healthy and strong democracy. The basic things expected by our people of their political and economic systems are simple. They are: Equality of opportunity for youth and for others; jobs for those who can work; security for those who need it; the ending of special privilege for the few; the preservation of civil liberties for all; the enjoyment of the fruits of scientific progress in a wider and constantly rising standard of living. These are the simple and basic things that must never be lost sight of in the turmoil and unbelievable complexity of our modern world. The inner and abiding strength of our economic and political systems is dependent upon the degree to which they fulfill these expectations.

Many subjects connected with our social economy call for immediate improvement. As examples:

We should bring more citizens under the coverage of old-age pensions and unemployment insurance.

We should widen the opportunities for adequate medical care.

We should plan a better system by which persons deserving or needing gainful employment may obtain it.

I have called for personal sacrifice. I am assured of the willingness of almost all Americans to respond to that call. A part of the sacrifice means the payment of more money in taxes. In my budget message I recommend that a greater portion of this great defense program be paid for from taxation than we are paying today. No person should try, or be allowed, to get rich out of this program; and the principle of tax payments in accordance with ability to pay should be constantly before our eyes to guide our legislation. If the Congress maintains these principles, the voters, putting patriotism ahead of pocketbooks, will give you their applause.

In the future days, which we seek to make secure, we look forward to a world founded upon four essential human freedoms.

The first is freedom of speech and expression everywhere in the world.

The second is freedom of every person to worship God in his own way everywhere in the world.

The third is freedom from want, which, translated into world terms, means economic understandings which will secure to every nation a healthy peacetime life for its inhabitants everywhere in the world.

The fourth is freedom from fear — which, translated into world terms, means a worldwide reduction of armaments to such a point and in such a thorough fashion that no nation will be in a position to commit an act of physical aggression against any neighbor — anywhere in the world.

That is no vision of a distant millennium. It is a definite basis for a kind of world attainable in our own time and generation. That kind of world is the very antithesis of the so-called new order of tyranny which the dictators seek to create with the crash of a bomb.

To that new order we oppose the greater conception — the moral order. A good society is able to face schemes of world domination and foreign revolutions alike without fear.

Since the beginning of our American history, we have been engaged in change — in a perpetual peaceful revolution — a revolution which goes on steadily, quietly adjusting itself to changing conditions — without the concentration camp or the quicklime in the ditch. The world order which we seek is the cooperation of free countries, working together in a friendly, civilized society.

This nation has placed its destiny in the hands and hearts of its millions of free men and women, and its faith in freedom under the guidance of God. Freedom means the supremacy of human rights everywhere. Our support goes to those who struggle to gain those rights or keep them. Our strength is in our unity of purpose. To that high concept there can be no end save victory.

---

*America to me is not a territory and not a code, but a way of life. It is, in words that David Starr Jordan taught me, the land where hate dies away.*

ALBERT GUÉRARD

13.

# Burton K. Wheeler: The Menace of Lend-Lease

*President Roosevelt formally presented his Lend-Lease proposal to Congress on January 6, 1941. Congressional debate on the bill was fierce. Senator Burton K. Wheeler of Montana, a leading Republican isolationist, bitterly attacked the President's proposal in a symposium on the Lend-Lease question held on January 12, 1941. Wheeler's remark that Lend-Lease would "plow under every fourth American boy" provoked Roosevelt to respond that it was "the rottenest thing that has been said in public life in my generation." Despite isolationist opposition, Congress passed the Lend-Lease Act on March 11, 1941. The terms of the agreement with Britain, which marked a turning point in the war against Hitler, were later extended to Soviet Russia and other Allied countries.*

Source: *Record, App.,* 77 Cong., 1 Sess., pp. A178–A179.

THE LEND-LEASE POLICY, translated into legislative form, stunned a Congress and a nation wholly sympathetic to the cause of Great Britain. The Kaiser's blank check to Austria-Hungary in the First World War was a piker compared to the Roosevelt blank check of World War II. It warranted my worst fears for the future of America, and it definitely stamps the President as war-minded.

The lend-lease-give program is the New Deal's triple-A foreign policy; it will plow under every fourth American boy.

Never before have the American people been asked or compelled to give so bounteously and so completely of their tax dollars to any foreign nation. Never before has the Congress of the United States been asked by any President to violate international law. Never before has this nation resorted to duplicity in the conduct of its foreign affairs. Never before has the United States given to one man the power to strip this nation of its defenses. Never before has a Congress coldly and flatly been asked to abdicate.

If the American people want a dictatorship — if they want a totalitarian form of government and if they want war — this bill should be steam-rollered through Congress, as is the wont of President Roosevelt.

Approval of this legislation means war, open and complete warfare. I, therefore, ask the American people before they supinely accept it — Was the last World War worthwhile?

If it were, then we should lend and lease war materials. If it were, then we should lend and lease American boys. President Roosevelt has said we would be repaid by England. We will be. We will be repaid, just as England repaid her war debts of the First World War — repaid those dollars wrung from the sweat of labor and the toil of farmers with cries of "Uncle Shylock." Our boys will be returned — returned in caskets, maybe; returned with bodies maimed; returned with minds warped and twisted by sights of horrors and the scream and shriek of high-powered shells.

Considered on its merits and stripped of its emotional appeal to our sympathies, the

Isolationists Burton Wheeler and Robert Taft, who led prewar opposition to Roosevelt

lend-lease-give bill is both ruinous and ridiculous. Why should we Americans pay for war materials for Great Britain who still has $7 billion in credit or collateral in the United States? Thus far England has fully maintained rather than depleted her credits in the United States. The cost of the lend-lease-give program is high in terms of American tax dollars, but it is even higher in terms of our national defense. Now it gives to the President the unlimited power to completely strip our air force of its every bomber, of its every fighting plane.

It gives to one man — responsible to no one — the power to denude our shores of every warship. It gives to one individual the dictatorial power to strip the American Army of our every tank, cannon, rifle, or antiaircraft gun. No one would deny that the lend-lease-give bill contains provisions that would enable one man to render the United States defenseless, but they will tell you, "The President would never do it." To this I say, "Why does he ask the power if he does not intend to use it?" Why not, I say, place some check on American donations to a foreign nation?

Is it possible that the farmers of America are willing to sell their birthright for a mess of pottage? Is it possible that American labor is to be sold down the river in return for a place upon the Defense Commission, or because your labor leaders are entertained at pink teas? Is it possible that the American people are so gullible that they will permit their representatives in Congress to sit supinely by while an American President demands totalitarian powers — in the name of saving democracy?

I say in the kind of language used by the President — shame on those who ask the powers — and shame on those who would grant them.

You people who oppose war and dictatorship, do not be dismayed because the warmongers and interventionists control most of the avenues of propaganda, including the motion-picture industry. Do not be dismayed because Mr. Willkie, of the Commonwealth & Southern, agrees with Mr. Roosevelt. This merely puts all the economic and foreign "royalists" on the side of war.

Remember, the interventionists control the moneybags, but you control the votes.

14.

## Frank Knox: Lend-Lease and National Defense

*Congressional debate continued for over two months on the Lend-Lease Bill urged by President Roosevelt early in January 1941. The House Foreign Affairs Committee and the Senate Foreign Relations Committee heard testimony for and against the bill, which, by coincidence, had received the number 1776. Secretary of the Navy Frank Knox, publisher of the* Chicago Daily News *and the 1936 vice-presidential candidate of the Republican Party, voiced his support for Lend-Lease in the following statement before the Senate Foreign Relations Committee, which met from January 27 to February 3, 1941.*

Source: *To Promote the Defense of the United States, Hearings Before the Committee on Foreign Relations, U.S. Senate,* 77 Congress, 1 Session, Washington, 1941, Pt. 1, pp. 180-183.

BEFORE COMING HERE, your chairman advised me that he would permit me to develop further some of the points which I made in my statement before the House Foreign Affairs Committee on Bill 1776, Lend-Lease Bill. . . .

In Europe the military situation is far from stable, and I believe that there are few British who would care to accept German peace commitments at their face value.

I should like to quote three short paragraphs from my statement given before the House committee:

To keep our land secure we must prevent the establishment of strong aggressive military power in any part of the New World. We can keep non-American military power out of our hemisphere only through being able to control the seas that surround its shores. Once we lose the power to control even a part of those seas, inevitably the wars of Europe and Asia will be transferred to the Americas.

We need time to build ships and to train their crews. We need time to build up our outlying bases so that we can operate our fleets as a screen for our continent. We need time to train our armies, to accumulate war stores, to gear our industry for defense.

Only Great Britain and its fleet can give us that time. And they need our help to survive.

I reiterate here my belief that the chief question that confronts us is whether we shall now take steps to keep Europe's wars in Europe, or shall drift along and permit those wars to be transferred to the Americas. We need time to get ready to meet out at sea a strong, aggressive Germany if we are to keep the fighting away from the lands of this hemisphere. You may remember that in my statement before the House committee I gave a comparative table of naval tonnage which might oppose us, both in the immediate future and over the next several years, if Britain does not survive Germany's attack. I would not have you draw the implication from my statement and from those figures that I fear that the

United States will not fully realize in time the danger that confronts them. But they have no time to waste and must act at once.

In public speeches I have warned the American people that if Britain is defeated, we ought then to be fully prepared to repel attempts by Germany to seize bases on this side of the Atlantic. Germany would use these bases either to attack us directly or else first to establish herself solidly in South America. Many of our people and many of the speakers who have opposed giving ample aid to Great Britain apparently believe it fantastic to think that there is any real danger of invasion. I disagree with such people and believe that a victorious Germany would move over to this hemisphere just as soon as she could accumulate the strength to do so, and certainly very soon unless we now take the steps to check her career of reckless aggression.

Admiral General Raeder, chief of the German Navy, recently made a speech to the shipyard workers in Bremen. The significant portion of his speech to the United States was a promise that after the war Germany would have — I quote —

A fleet developed and enlarged to a size befitting a world power, and overseas naval bases where there would be plenty of work of all kinds.

There can be little doubt as to German ambitions for world sea power in the event of victory.

The existence of the British Navy and a balance of power in Europe have operated to give us military security against aggressions from that region. For many years we actually have had the benefits of a two-ocean Navy instead of only the one-ocean Navy that flies the American flag. The defeat of Great Britain would definitely carry with it the destruction of the British Fleet, or would transfer it to German hands to be used against us when Germany has trained German naval personnel to operate it.

Even were there no danger of invasion, and I may say that I believe building up our Navy and our Army in the way we are now doing will give us the means to defeat invasion, provided we have the time to complete our plans I repeat, even if there [were] no danger of invasion, I ask the committee whether they can face calmly the prospect of all of Europe completely dominated by the Hitler regime? The question to decide is — Would we rather see Europe dominated by a democratic system, or would we rather see Europe dominated by a Hitler system?

What would be our relative positions under those very different sets of circumstances? If the Hitler system is victorious, can any of us imagine that we can return freely to the ways of peace which we have known in the past? For my part, I believe that so long as the Hitler system endures we will be forced to maintain a tremendous Navy and a very large Army in order to continue any sort of national existence. I well realize the sacrifices that our people will have to make to maintain their liberties in such a world, and I believe that we should now do everything that we can do to keep the British Commonwealth of Nations from being overcome by this terrible new system of government that has arisen in Germany. For myself, I prefer to live in a world governed by a victorious democracy rather than by a victorious Hitler.

Suppose, contrary to my own view, we concentrate our full effort on building up our own ships, and troops, and aircraft, and stand aside and accept the chance of a complete German victory over Britain. As I understand their arguments, that is the course that the opponents of the lend-lease plan would have this government pursue. I am ready to admit that we might be able to arm ourselves so heavily that it would become impossible for the Axis Powers to bring their military power directly against us across the seas and to defeat us here in our own territory. The costs of such armaments would be great, and they would bear very heavily upon our people. But let us admit, for the sake of the argument, that we could bear these burdens, and that we could build up the fleets and armies we would need to fend off a direct invasion: Would we, then, be safe from Axis attack?

I say that no, decidedly, we would not be safe. The Nazi method is plain to all, and it is to win by any means, direct or indirect.

Latin America has great potential wealth, principally in raw materials. Its natural customer is Europe, because the United States can only consume a part of the Latin-American exports. Heretofore Great Britain, Germany, Italy, and other European nations have competed for the greater part of these exports, and the competition has been to the advantage of our neighbors. But with the Nazis in supreme control there would be but one European customer.

We can be very sure that the devious diplomatic, economic, and political methods which Germany has employed toward all the countries near her would also in the future be employed in the regions to the south of us. First would come economic penetration, next economic dependence, then political immigration and political interference. After that we would see the establishment of puppet regimes under Nazi or native control, and finally the arming of those countries and their military domination by Nazis. The cycle would be complete. European militarism would be established in a world that has had the atmosphere of peace and freedom.

Whether the methods are direct or indirect, this hemisphere is now in grave danger of invasion.

Aside from reasons of national safety, we have many other selfish reasons for desiring to see the British nation continue in existence. The type of civilization that has been developed in the United Kingdom has conditioned the development of American civilization. Our social, our economic, and our political systems were brought to this New World many years ago as transplantations from the British systems. Close personal contacts and a constant exchange of ideas between the American and the British peoples have nourished the sturdy growth of the American national life, whose roots lie embedded in British soil. From a cultural standpoint it would be a calamity for us if British life were uprooted and replaced by a Nazi growth. Even those of our citizens whose lineage leads back to parts of the world other than Britain must feel that their greatest benefits from life in this country are connected with the stability of the institutions which Britain originated and which we have adapted to our own form of civilization.

I have a high appreciation of the keen sense of national strategy inherent in the American character, and I believe that our people now are determined to put forth their full efforts for saving Britain and thus saving themselves from the burdens of future militarism and war and from an overturn of American life.

I believe they want this bill to pass.

---

*We must be the great arsenal of democracy*
FRANKLIN D. ROOSEVELT, "Fireside Talk," Dec. 29, 1940

Wide World

Hitler rejoicing at the terms he dictated in the armistice for conquered France, 1940

# WAR IN EUROPE

Roosevelt made no effort to follow Wilson's impossible ideal of neutrality in thought, word, and deed. His foreign policy began with an understood spiritual alliance with the "embattled democracies," chiefly Britain and France, and developed with the course of events into an explicit determination to render all possible aid short of entering the war. Despite the arguments for isolation and neutrality grounded in tradition, distrust of foreign nations generally, and the disillusionment of World War I, there was a tacit belief within the administration and among its supporters that America could not hope for security if the Axis powers were allowed to dominate the rest of the world. In this feeling even many neutralists shared, to the extent of supporting the programs of hemisphere defense set up at conferences in Panama and Havana in 1939 and 1940. Convinced, however, that more direct action was necessary, that, indeed, the defense of Britain was imperative, the President pressed Congress for modifications of the Neutrality Acts. The "cash-and-carry" plan of 1939 was supplemented by the destroyer deal of 1940, an executive act that traded fifty overage destroyers to Britain for military bases in British possessions in the Caribbean area. In March 1941 the Lend-Lease Act empowered the President to supply threatened nations with defense articles when he deemed it in the national interest. This broad authority, coupled with the huge preparedness funds and the peacetime conscription voted by Congress in 1940, directly involved America in nearly every aspect of the war but actual combat.

**Mussolini welcomes Hitler to Florence in 1940 to discuss their plans for Europe**

Germany and Italy entered into a series of diplomatic and cultural alliances from 1936 onward, and Japan joined the "Axis" in 1937. German Fascism dominated the policies and propaganda of the Axis powers; the anti-Communist line typical of Fascism was quickly dropped after the Russo-German pact was signed, and the anti-Semitic campaign was substituted, even in Japan where there were no Jews.

(Below) Sign in a German town stating that Jews were not welcome; (right) Jews wearing yellow stars

Wide World

Wide World

(Above) Speaker at a Bastille Day ceremony in Paris in 1937; (below) signing the Russo-German contract in Moscow, August 1939. Russian representative Molotov is signing the agreement

(Above) German soldiers break barriers at the Polish border, 1939; (left) German troops storm a Polish city in September 1939; (bottom) Jewish refugees fleeing the Nazi advance in Poland

Wide World

(Top) German Stukas over Poland in 1939; (center) homeless citizens after the bombing of Rotterdam by the German Air Force in 1940; (bottom) British soldiers on the beach at Dunkirk queue up during rescue operations in June 1940

Kramer Hofmeester

"The Times," London — Pictorial Parade

Heinrich Hoffman

Keystone Press

**Rouen burning after a German attack, June 1940**

Though Britain and France had declared war in September 1939 following Hitler's attack on Poland, there was no military activity for eight months. In April, Allied forces tried vainly to defeat the German invasion of Norway. On May 10 Hitler launched the major Western offensive; the armored divisions roared through the Low Countries and in little more than a month Paris was occupied. Britain was left alone and isolated.

**(Left) Bulletin board listing transportation available for evacuating Paris; (below) French prisoners in a Nazi camp after the fall of France, 1940**

Dever from Black Star

Keystone Press

London Civil Defense team removing victim from building destroyed in a German bombing raid, an almost nightly occurrence during Hitler's two-year air siege of Britain

(Right) Winston Churchill, who succeeded Chamberlain as prime minister and led England through the war years; (below) British fighter pilots running for their planes during training exercises, 1939

Keystone Press

Pictorial Parade

(Above) "New Kind of 'Pump Priming'" accuses Roosevelt of using war production and the risk of involvement as a means of stimulating the economy; (above right) Secretary of State Cordell Hull signing the Neutrality Proclamation, 1939; (right) Ambassador to Britain Joseph P. Kennedy arriving in New York for consultations, 1939. Kennedy continued to advise accommodation with the Axis long after this approach had been abandoned by the President. Feeling the real threat to be the Soviet Union, he advised staying out of the war. (Below) Old submarines taken over by British sailors under Lend Lease

Every step taken or proposed by Roosevelt to deal with the worsening situations in Europe and Asia was stoutly opposed by a powerful isolationist group in Congress. Ranging from La Follette Progressives to flatly anti-administration members, the isolationists were committed to absolute neutrality and avoiding the "mistake" of 1917. This group was supported by a number of popular organizations devoted to non-intervention. The fascist German-American Bund, Father Coughlin's anti-Semitic Christian Front, the more respectable America First Committee with many prominent isolationists on its rolls: all campaigned vigorously to offset the growing Allied support both in the administration and at large.

(Top) Four prominent Americans at an America First rally in Madison Square Garden, New York, 1941. From left are Burton K. Wheeler, Charles Lindbergh, Kathleen Norris, and Norman Thomas; (center) volunteers of the War Resister League conduct a poster walk down a city street; (right) "Wake Up, You're On Next!"; cartoon by Herb Kruckman

**(Top) German troops and equipment in pursuit of the Russian Army; (right) Hitler and aides study Russian war map**

After taking over the Balkan area, Hitler felt that he must secure his Eastern frontier before moving on to the invasion of Britain. The attack on Russia in June 1941 broke the almost intolerable tension in Britain; London was clearly safe with Hitler fully committed in the East. The Russian campaign, intended to be a swift summer victory, dragged on into a major defeat the following year.

**Russians burn railway station to prevent German seizure of equipment**

15.

# Joseph C. O'Mahoney: The Defense of Economic Freedom

*In 1938 President Roosevelt had established the Temporary National Economic Committee (TNEC) to investigate what was considered to be the growing concentration of economic power in the United States. The TNEC conducted research for almost three years and, on March 31, 1941, issued its final report and recommendations. The report's main conclusion was that "the system of free enterprise for profit" had not so much failed "in this generation" as that, owing to more and more stringent controls exerted by big business, it had never been given a chance. Senator Joseph C. O'Mahoney of Wyoming, chairman of the TNEC, summarized his committee's findings and recommended government policies to deal with industrial concentrations in a report submitted on March 11, part of which is reprinted here.*

Source: 77 Congress, 1 Session, Senate Document No. 35, pp. 671-687.

IF WE ARE AGREED, and we all seem to be agreed, at least here in the United States, that we want to preserve free enterprise, it becomes apparent that we had better get about the task; and a good way to begin, it seems to me, would be to make up our minds exactly what we want to do about our problem instead of trying to blame one another for its existence. The representatives of business, as well as the representatives of government, those who are engaged in agriculture, those who are engaged in industry, all are vitally concerned, and it must be perfectly clear that any remedy which does not stop the steady progress of concentration will be utterly futile and will end only in an all-powerful government. If we want to remedy these obvious ills, we'd better stop scolding one another and begin to cooperate.

Business leaders who object to any government action overlook the plain fact that there is no possible way of bringing about the coordination which we need except through government action. To refuse to cooperate means only to accentuate the present drift toward centralism which has produced the authoritarian government in Europe and brought the democratic nations of the Old World to the very brink of disaster. It is more important to business than to any other group to cooperate in the reestablishment of free individual, local, private enterprise and full employment if it desires to remain free from complete government control.

The first and most necessary step is to recognize that we must have a national rule for national business. We must be able to differentiate between that business which is naturally and properly national in scope and that business which is naturally and properly local in scope. If we desire to have business carried on by collective units, and it must be carried on thus in the modern world, then we must find the way to make these units thoroughly democratic. Economic freedom and political freedom go hand in hand. Neither can survive without the other, and since it must be acknowledged that in a republic the government of all the people must be able to speak for all the people then we have no recourse except to have that government define the rights, duties, and responsibilities of the organized agencies which conduct and control the commerce on which its citizens depend for employment and income.

It is idle to think that the huge collective institutions which carry on our modern business can continue to operate without more definite responsibility toward all the people of the nation than they now have. To do this it will be necessary, in my judgment, to have a national charter system for all national corporations. Whether this system should operate through licenses or through direct charters seems to me to be of little importance. One thing is certain — we cannot hope to stop the processes of concentration if we are willing to continue to allow the states to create agencies through and by which the concentration has been brought about.

I am aware that many businessmen, fortunately not so many now as formerly, look upon this plan for federal charters as merely another step in the growth of all-powerful government. That is an error. It is only through a charter system that the growth of government can be prevented. For fifty years, federal regulation, and, in some instances, even federal control of business, has been steadily increasing. It is unnecessary to recite here the laws by which, during the past generation, new bureaus and commissions have been established in Washington. Without regard to which political party happened to be in power, one bureau after another has been created and, necessarily so, because without them the public interest would have been completely neglected.

Businessmen have resisted every such law, but once a new agency has been created it has never been abandoned. From the establishment of the Interstate Commerce Commission down to the establishment of the Securities and Exchange Commission, the same story has been told; and although each in its turn has been roundly denounced by the organized agencies which were to be regulated, the necessity of the regulation has always been recognized by most of those affected and no political leader has ever dared to propose the abolition of such a commission after its establishment and the restoration of the conditions that existed before its creation.

But these bureaus and boards have been unable to solve the problem. Concentration has proceeded without interruption because those who wish to avoid the objectives of regulation in the public interest were always able through the corporate charter of some state to find a way around the law. The Insulls and the Hopsons, the Coster-Musicas have been able to prey upon the economic system of all the people solely because they were able to secure the separate states' charters which enabled them to engage in national commerce although their creators had neither the desire nor the governmental power to regulate the commerce in which they were engaged.

I see no other way to avoid the continued expansion of government debt and the continued expansion of government control over private business except through a national charter system. Such a system would make unnecessary the creation of new boards and commissions because it could be used to define so clearly the responsibilities and the duties of all national corporations that discretionary regulation would be unnecessary.

Over and over again it ought to be asserted that a corporate charter is a contract between individuals who want the privilege of doing business in corporate form and a government which speaks, or ought to speak, for all the people. Here in the United States the separate states do not have the constitutional power to speak in the public interest. Only the federal government has that power so far as interstate and foreign commerce is concerned. If we believe that the framers of the Constitution acted wisely when they gave to the federal Congress the power to regulate interstate and foreign commerce, then we cannot fail to acknowledge that the federal Congress should exercise that power by insisting upon writing the contracts which call into existence the corporations which carry on that commerce. Until that is done there can be no effective regulation except by piecemeal through the continued multiplication of government boards and commissions. That system will inevitably be accompanied by continued evasions, continued abuse, continued concentration, and continued expansion of government.

The maintenance of free private enterprise demands, first of all, that small enterprise should be effectively protected against attack by what we call monopoly. The big company which crushes its small competitor by underselling, that is to say, by selling at a loss, commits the unforgivable economic sin. That is not competition. That is economic war. The national oil company, for example, which enters a little community and builds a filling station across the street from an independent dealer and, by selling at a loss, forces him to sell out or suspend, destroys the very basis of a free economy. The monopolistic practices which kill free enterprise and which are without justification are so well known that they need not be restated here, but certainly the great crisis which the world now faces in the conflict of democracy and dictatorship should be enough to convince every business executive, as well as every government spokesman, that the time has come to outlaw all such practices in a way that will be effective.

That such practices exist in the United States in violation of well known law is demonstrated by the antitrust record of the Department of Justice under the direction of one of the members of this committee. The defendants who have been charged with violations of the antitrust law in the past three years have, for the most part, walked into court and pleaded guilty. The cases were so clear that there was no resistance. That the practices of which they were accused should not be tolerated in any society which even pretends to believe in free private enterprise no one can possibly deny, yet it is perfectly evident that the Sherman Antitrust Law can be effectively enforced only so long as we have an attorney general who is disposed to enforce it and a Congress that is willing to make the appropriations necessary to maintain a sufficient staff. That such a staff has not been maintained during the past fifty years except under Thurman Arnold is one of the reasons why the concentration of economic power and wealth so clearly demonstrated by the hearings and publications of this committee has not been prevented.

It would not be difficult so to draft a national charter law as to reduce materially not only the possibilities of evasion of the antitrust law but the difficulties of its enforcement. A charter law which, for example, would make corporate directors trustees in fact as well as in law and, at the same time, make them personally liable for violations of the antitrust law which they themselves conceived and directed, a law which would clearly define the fields into which a corporation might enter through subsidiaries and one which would standardize intercorporate financing, would not only tend to prevent some of the worst infractions of both ethics and law, which have contributed to the creation of our dilemma, but would also tend to open new fields for small enterprise.

This, however, is not the place to discuss the details of a federal charter system. I am concerned now only with urging the acceptance of the principle. For the details I think it would be wise to have Congress formally authorize a national conference on corporation law to suggest the form a statute should take. There is a rapidly increasing number of persons affiliated with modern business management who realize in much greater degree than ever before that national business does have social responsibilities which extend beyond the primary financial interests of stockholders. Once it is made clear that the purpose of such a law is to stop the trend toward concentration both in business and in government and to protect the interests of employees and the consuming public as well as stockholders, a broader opportunity would probably be presented for the drafting of a national law to meet acknowledged national needs. Business leaders who resist national charters for national business are standing in their own light.

It may be proper at this time to remark that in the first Federal Charter Bill which I introduced several years ago there was provision for the summoning of a national industrial conference "to develop a general program for the coordination, stabilization, and orderly development of the basic industries of the United States and for a more equitable distribution of the earnings of commerce, trade, and industry to these employed therein and to the investors of capital therein." Since that time, national organizations, both in agriculture and in industry, have suggested the desirability of some such conference. Within the week the National Farm Bureau, through its Executive Board, made such a recommendation.

I believe it to be an important step in the reestablishment of our national economy. The reception which has been accorded to the publications of this committee throughout the country, the interest which has been evoked in its studies among all classes of the population indicate that the time is ripe for such a conference and that it would be productive of constructive results. The present conditions from which we suffer have been brought about largely by restrictive practices, the chief object of which has been to restrain production and maintain price. Combinations and agreements in restraint of trade have always revolved around these objectives and were to be found in commerce long before the corporation attained its modern power. They are more disastrous in their effect now because of the high degree of concentration of economic power.

Agriculture seems to realize that it, too, is suffering from restrictions of production to maintain price, and in the field of labor the same evil may be found. It is altogether possible that such a conference as this would show the way by which our whole economy could reverse its unfortunate trend and show the way to increased production and lowered price, the only means through which we may hope to make use of the unlimited resources which nature supplies by devising a practical and equitable system of distribution.

Pending such a conference, however, we should undertake without delay an immediate program for the encouragement of small business. The first step, of course, is the continued vigorous enforcement of the antitrust laws; the second, a sound and feasible plan for providing venture capital to those who need it to establish new business and new industry. I see no hope of successfully stimulating small business merely by providing government loans.

The government should not be the source of such capital. The capital which is needed and which ought to be utilized is the private capital which now lies idle in the banks. Expanding government loans only tends to encourage the invasion of the field of private business by government. We must attack this task by making it more attractive than it now is for the owners of private capital to invest their funds. Surely, if we seek the reestablishment of active private enterprise, we must direct our efforts toward the independent employment of private funds rather than an attempt to loan nonexistent government funds. . . .

The discussion I have undertaken today was not intended to be all-inclusive. I have ventured merely to point to the alternative which is now squarely presented to the people of the United States — free private enterprise or government planning.

For two generations, the concentration of economic power and wealth has proceeded at such a pace that the welfare of the masses in agriculture and industry has been seriously jeopardized. Small business has been swallowed up by big business and big business is now confronted with the danger of being swallowed up by government. The way to reverse this trend is not to be found in further expanding the powers of government, nor releasing big business from so-called government interference. The only remedy to save a democratic economy is to be found in making the economy democratic. If we are to avoid an all-powerful central government, we have no recourse but to reestablish and encourage free private enterprise; that is to say, private enterprise which will be free from the arbitrary control of private organizations as well as of public organization.

Therefore, I recommend:

1. National charters for national corporations, in order that these agencies may have a definite and a free place in our economy and local business may be differentiated and protected from national business.

2. The effective and thorough enforcement of the antitrust laws to maintain competition and to prevent all combinations and agreements that destroy business.

3. The encouragement of new business and small enterprise by revision of the tax laws for the purpose of encouraging new employment and new industry.

4. A national conference called by Congress of the various organizations representative of business, labor, agriculture, and consumers, which have for years been working on diverse phases of this central problem, might concentrate public thought and action on the objectives on which there is general agreement instead of, as now, on the objectives concerning which there is only misunderstanding, suspicion, and disagreement.

In an hour of political uncertainty 153 years ago, the Continental Congress called a national convention to draft a national political constitution. That conference of American leaders was successful beyond the dreams of any of those who authorized it. Our need today is a national economic constitution which shall abolish the economic uncertainties which seem to threaten even our political system. I have an abiding faith that the patriotism and ability of the people of America is equal to the task.

In defense of democracy we must find the way to maintain and defend economic freedom for all.

---

*When you speak of better times, Hubert, do you mean when the war is over or when the Democrats are over?*

GARDNER REA, cartoon caption, *New Yorker*, 1940s

16.

## ROBERT M. HUTCHINS: America and the War

*President Roosevelt's Lend-Lease proposal of January 6, 1941, sparked vigorous discussion, not only in Congress but also across the nation. Most Americans were aware that the proposal represented a significant step toward American involvement in the war, and a large segment of public opinion, for many reasons, opposed it. Robert M. Hutchins, a leading American educator and president of the University of Chicago, contributed the following speech to the debate. Broadcast on January 23 over a nationwide radio hookup, the speech contained Hutchins' reasoned argument against any further extension of aid to the Allies. Hutchins supported the war effort fully after Pearl Harbor, but his view — that America must devote its resources to the task of making good on its age-old promises of freedom and abundance for all — was stated with eloquence and was widely discussed at the time.*

I SPEAK TONIGHT because I believe that the American people are about to commit suicide. We are not planning to. We have no plan. We are drifting into suicide. Deafened by martial music, fine language, and large appropriations, we are drifting into war.

I address you simply as an American citizen. I do not represent any organization or committee. I do not represent the University of Chicago. I am not a military expert. It is true that from the age of eighteen to the age of twenty I was a private in the American Army. I must have somewhere the very fine medal given me by the Italian government of that day in token of my cooperation on the Italian front. But this experience would not justify me in discussing tactics, strategy, or the strength to which our armed forces should now attain.

I wish to dissociate myself from all Nazis, Fascists, Communists, and appeasers. I regard the doctrine of all totalitarian regimes as wrong in theory, evil in execution, and incompatible with the rights of man. I wish to dissociate myself from those who want us to stay out of war to save our own skins or our own property. I believe that the people of this country are and should be prepared to make sacrifices for humanity. National selfishness should not determine national policy.

It is impossible to listen to Mr. Roosevelt's recent speeches, to study the Lease-Lend Bill, and to read the testimony of Cabinet officers upon it without coming to the conclusion that the President now requires us to underwrite a British victory, and apparently a Chinese and a Greek victory, too. We are going to try to produce the victory by supplying our friends with the materials of war. But what if this is not enough? We have abandoned all pretense of neutrality. We are to turn our ports into British naval bases. But what if this is not enough? Then we must send the navy, the air force, and, if Mr. Churchill wants it, the army. We must guarantee the victory.

We used to hear of "all aid short of war." The words "short of war" are ominously missing from the President's recent speeches. The Lease-Lend Bill contains provisions that we should have regarded as acts of war up to last week. The conclusion is inescapable that the President is reconciled to active military intervention if such intervention is needed to defeat the Axis in this war.

I have supported Mr. Roosevelt since he first went to the White House, I have never questioned his integrity or his goodwill. But under the pressure of great responsibilities, in the heat of controversy, in the international game of bluff, the President's speeches and recommendations are committing us to obligations abroad which we cannot perform. The effort to perform them will prevent the achievement of the aims for which the President stands at home.

If we go to war, what are we going to war for? This is to be a crusade, a holy war. Its object is moral. We are seeking, the President tells us, "a world founded on freedom of speech, freedom of worship, freedom from want, and freedom from fear." We are to intervene to support the moral order. We are to fight for "the supremacy of human rights everywhere."

With the President's desire to see freedom of speech, freedom of worship, freedom from want, and freedom from fear flourish everywhere we must all agree. Millions of Americans have supported the President because they felt that he wanted to achieve these four freedoms for America. Others, who now long to carry these blessings to the rest of the world, were not conspicuous on the firing line when Mr. Roosevelt called them, eight years ago, to do battle for the four freedoms at home. But let us agree now that we want the four freedoms; we want justice, the moral order, democracy, and the supremacy of human rights, not here alone but everywhere. The question is whether entrance into this war is likely to bring us closer to this goal.

How can the United States better serve suffering humanity everywhere: by going into this war, or by staying out? I hold that the United States can better serve suffering humanity everywhere by staying out.

But can we stay out? We are told it is too late. The house is on fire. When the house is on fire, you do not straighten the furniture, and clean out the cellar, or ask yourself whether the house is as good a house as you would like. You put out the fire if you can.

The answer is that the house is not on fire. The house next door is on fire. When the house next door is on fire you do not set fire to your own house, throw the baby on the floor, and rush off to join the fun. And when you do go to quench the fire next door, you make sure that your bucket is full of water and not oil.

But, we are told, we are going to have to fight the Axis sometime. Why not fight it now, when we have Britain to help us? Why wait until we have to face the whole world alone?

Think of the mass of assumptions upon which this program rests. First, we must assume that in spite of its heroic resistance and in spite of the enormous supplies of munitions which it is yet to receive from America the British Empire must fall.

Second, we must assume that the present rulers of totalitarian states will survive the conflict.

Third, we must assume that if these regimes survive they will want to attack us.

Fourth, we must assume that they will be in a position to attack us. This involves the assumptions that they will have the resources to do so, that their people will consent to new and hazardous ventures, that their task of holding down conquered nations will be easily completed, and that the ambiguous attitude of Russia will cause them little concern.

Next, if Britain falls, if the totalitarian regimes survive, if they want to attack us, if they are in a position to do so, we must further assume that they will find it possible to do so. The flying time between Africa and Brazil, or Europe and America, does not decide this question. The issue is what will be at the western end of the line? This will depend on our moral and military preparedness. A lone squadron of bombers might conquer a continent peopled with inhabitants careless of safety or bent on slavery. We cannot assume that any combination of powers can successfully invade this hemisphere if we are prepared to defend ourselves and determined to be free.

On a pyramid of assumptions, hypotheses, and guesses, therefore, rests a decision to go to war now because it is too late to stay out. There is no such inevitability about war with the Axis as to prevent us from asking ourselves whether we shall serve suffering humanity better everywhere by going into this war or by staying out.

The chances of accomplishing the high moral purposes which the President has stated for America, even if we stay out of war, are not bright. The world is in chaos. We must give our thought and energy to building our defenses. What we have of high moral purpose is likely to suffer dilution at home and a cold reception abroad. But we have a chance to help humanity if we do not go into this war. If we do go into it, we have no chance at all.

The reason why we have no chance to help humanity if we go into this war is that we are not prepared. I do not mean, primarily, that we are unprepared in a military sense. I mean that we are morally and intellectually unprepared to execute the moral mission to which the President calls us.

A missionary, even a missionary to the cannibals, must have clear and defensible convictions. And if his plan is to eat some of the cannibals in order to persuade the others to espouse the true faith, his convictions must be very clear and very defensible indeed. It is surely not too much to ask of such a missionary that his own life and

works reflect the virtues which he seeks to compel others to adopt. If we stay out of war, we may perhaps some day understand and practise freedom of speech, freedom of worship, freedom from want, and freedom from fear. We may even be able to comprehend and support justice, democracy, the moral order, and the supremacy of human rights. Today we have barely begun to grasp the meaning of the words.

Those beginnings are important. They place us ahead of where we were at the end of the last century. They raise us, in accomplishment as well as in ideals, far above the accomplishment and ideals of totalitarian powers. They leave us, however, a good deal short of that level of excellence which entitles us to convert the world by force of arms.

Have we freedom of speech and freedom of worship in this country? We do have freedom to say what everybody else is saying and freedom of worship if we do not take our religion too seriously. But teachers who do not conform to the established canons of social thought lose their jobs. People who are called "radicals" have mysterious difficulties in renting halls. Labor organizers sometimes get beaten up and ridden out of town on a rail. Norman Thomas had some troubles in Jersey City. And the Daughters of the American Revolution refused to let Marian Anderson sing in the national capital in a building called Constitution Hall.

If we regard these exceptions as minor, reflecting the attitude of the more backward and illiterate parts of the country, what are we to say of freedom from want and freedom from fear? What of the moral order and justice and the supremacy of human rights? What of democracy in the United States?

Words like these have no meaning unless we believe in human dignity. Human dignity means that every man is an end in himself. No man can be exploited by another.

Think of these things and then think of the sharecroppers, the Okies, the Negroes, the slumdwellers, downtrodden and oppressed for gain. They have neither freedom from want nor freedom from fear. They hardly know they are living in a moral order or in a democracy where justice and human rights are supreme.

We have it on the highest authority that one-third of the nation is ill-fed, ill-clothed, and ill-housed. The latest figures of the National Resources Board show that almost precisely 55 percent of our people are living on family incomes of less than $1,250 a year. This sum, says *Fortune* magazine, will not support a family of four. On this basis more than half our people are living below the minimum level of subsistence. More than half the army which will defend democracy will be drawn from those who have had this experience of the economic benefits of "the American way of life."

We know that we have had till lately 9 million unemployed and that we should have them still if it were not for our military preparations. When our military preparations cease, we shall, for all we know, have 9 million unemployed again. In his speech on December 29, Mr. Roosevelt said, "After the present needs of our defense are past, a proper handling of the country's peacetime needs will require all of the new productive capacity — if not still more." For ten years we have not known how to use the productive capacity we had. Now suddenly we are to believe that by some miracle, after the war is over, we shall know what to do with our old productive capacity and what to do in addition with the tremendous increases which are now being made. We have want and fear today. We shall have want and fear "when the present needs of our defense are past."

As for democracy, we know that millions of men and women are disfranchised in this country because of their race, color, or con-

dition of economic servitude. We know that many municipal governments are models of corruption. Some state governments are merely the shadows of big city machines. Our national government is a government by pressure groups. Almost the last question an American is expected to ask about a proposal is whether it is just. The question is how much pressure is there behind it or how strong are the interests against it. On this basis are settled such great issues as monopoly, the organization of agriculture, the relation of labor and capital, whether bonuses should be paid to veterans, and whether a tariff policy based on greed should be modified by reciprocal trade agreements.

To have a community men must work together. They must have common principles and purposes. If some men are tearing down a house while others are building it, we do not say they are working together. If some men are robbing, cheating, and oppressing others, we should not say they are a community. The aims of a democratic community are moral. United by devotion to law, equality, and justice, the democratic community works together for the happiness of all the citizens. I leave to you the decision whether we have yet achieved a democratic community in the United States.

In the speech in which Mr. Roosevelt told us, in effect, that we are headed for war, he said, "Certainly this is no time to stop thinking about the social and economic problems which are the root cause of the social revolution which is today a supreme factor in the world." But in the same speech he said, "The need of the moment is that our actions and our policy should be devoted primarily — almost exclusively — to meeting this foreign peril. For all our domestic problems are now a part of the great emergency." This means — and it is perfectly obvious — that if any social objective interferes with the conduct of the war, it will be, it must be instantly abandoned. War can mean only the loss of "social gains" and the destruction of the livelihood of millions in modest circumstances, while pirates and profiteers, in spite of Mr. Roosevelt's efforts to stop them, emerge stronger than ever.

The four freedoms must be abandoned if they interfere with winning a war. In the ordinary course of war most of them do interfere. All of them may. In calmer days, in 1929, the *New York Times* said, "War brings many collateral disasters. Freedom of speech, freedom of the press suffer. We think we shall be wiser and cooler the next time, if there is one; but we shan't." The urge to victory annihilates tolerance. In April 1939, Alfred Duff-Cooper said that "hatred of any race was a sign of mental deficiency and of lack of a broad conception of the facts of the world." In April 1940, Mr. Duff-Cooper said that the crimes of the German militarists were the crimes of the whole people and that this should be kept in mind when the peace treaty was written.

We cannot suppose, because civil liberties were restricted in the last war and expanded after it, that we can rely on their revival after the next one. We Americans have only the faintest glimmering of what war is like. This war, if we enter it, will make the last one look like a stroll in the park. If we go into this one, we go in against powers dominating Europe and most of Asia to aid an ally who, we are told, is already in mortal danger. When we remember what a short war did to the four freedoms, we must recognize that they face extermination in the total war to come.

We Americans have hardly begun to understand and practise the ideals that we are urged to force on others. What we have, in this country, is hope. We and we alone have the hope that we can actually achieve these ideals. The framework of our government was designed to help us achieve them.

We have a tremendous continent, with vast resources, in a relatively impregnable position. We have energy, imagination, and brains. We have made some notable advances in the long march toward justice, freedom, and democracy.

If we go to war, we cast away our opportunity and cancel our gains. For a generation, perhaps for a hundred years, we shall not be able to struggle back to where we were. In fact the changes that total war will bring may mean that we shall never be able to struggle back. Education will cease. Its place will be taken by vocational and military training. The effort to establish a democratic community will stop. We shall think no more of justice, the moral order, and the supremacy of human rights. We shall have hope no longer.

What, then, should our policy be? Instead of doing everything we can to get into the war, we should do everything we can to stay at peace. Our policy should be peace. Aid to Britain, China, and Greece should be extended on the basis most likely to keep us at peace and least likely to involve us in war.

At the same time we should prepare to defend ourselves. We should prepare to defend ourselves against military or political penetration. We should bend every energy to the construction of an adequate navy and air force and the training of an adequate army. By adequate I mean adequate for defense against any power or combination of powers.

In the meantime, we should begin to make this country a refuge for those who will not live without liberty. For less than the cost of two battleships we could accommodate half a million refugees from totalitarian countries for a year. The net cost would not approach the cost of two battleships, for these victims, unlike battleships, would contribute to our industry and our cultural life, and help us make democracy work.

But most important of all, we should take up with new vigor the long struggle for moral, intellectual, and spiritual preparedness. If we would change the face of the earth, we must first change our own hearts. The principal end that we have hitherto set before ourselves is the unlimited acquisition of material goods. The business of America, said Calvin Coolidge, is business. We must now learn that material goods are a means and not an end. We want them to sustain life, but they are not the aim of life. The aim of life is the fullest development of the highest powers of men. This means art, religion, education, moral and intellectual growth. These things we have regarded as mere decorations or relaxations in the serious business of life, which was making money. The American people, in their own interest, require a moral regeneration. If they are to be missionaries to the world, this regeneration must be profound and complete.

We must try to build a new moral order for America. We need moral conviction, intellectual clarity, and moral action: moral conviction about the dignity of man, intellectual clarity about ends and means, moral action to construct institutions to bring to pass the ends we have chosen.

A new moral order for America means a new conception of security. Today we do not permit men to die of starvation, but neither do we give them an incentive to live. Every citizen must have a respected place in the achievement of the national purpose.

A new moral order for America means a new conception of sacrifice, sacrifice for the moral purposes of the community. In the interest of human dignity we need a rising standard of health, character, and intelligence. These positive goals demand the devotion and sacrifice of every American. We should rebuild one-third of the nation's homes. We must provide adequate medical care in every corner of the land. We must

develop an education aimed at moral and intellectual growth instead of at making money.

A new moral order for America means a new conception of mastery. We must learn how to reconcile the machine with human dignity. We have allowed it to run wild in prosperity and war and to rust idly in periodic collapse. We have hitherto avoided the issue by seeking new markets. In an unstable world this has meant bigger and bigger collapses, more and more catastrophic war. In Europe and Russia the efforts to master the machine are carried out by methods we despise. America can master the machine within the framework of a balanced democracy, outdistance the totalitarian despotisms, and bring light and hope to the world. It is our highest function and greatest opportunity to learn to make democracy work. We must bring justice and the moral order to life, here and now.

If we have strong defenses and understand and believe in what we are defending, we need fear nobody in the world. If we do not understand and believe in what we are defending, we may still win, but the victory will be as fruitless as the last. What did we do with the last one? What shall we do with this one? The government of Great Britain has repeatedly refused to state its war aims. The President in his foreign policy is pledged to back up Great Britain, and beyond that, to the pursuit of the unattainable. If we go to war, we shall not know what we are fighting for. If we stay out of war until we do, we may have the stamina to win and the knowledge to use the victory for the welfare of mankind.

The path to war is a false path to freedom. A new moral order for America is the true path to freedom. A new moral order for America means new strength for America and new hope for the moral reconstruction of mankind. We are turning aside from the true path to freedom because it is easier to blame Hitler for our troubles than to fight for democracy at home. As Hitler made the Jews his scapegoat, so we are making Hitler ours. But Hitler did not spring full-armed from the brow of Satan. He sprang from the materialism and paganism of our times. In the long run we can beat what Hitler stands for only by beating the materialism and paganism that produced him. We must show the world a nation clear in purpose, united in action, and sacrificial in spirit. The influence of that example upon suffering humanity everywhere will be more powerful than the combined armies of the Axis.

---

17.

## Charles A. Lindbergh: America First

*In March 1932 Charles A. Lindbergh's two-year-old son was kidnapped from his home near Hopewell, New Jersey, and murdered. Partly because of Lindbergh's worldwide fame, this became the most celebrated crime of the 1930s. The incessant publicity finally became so distasteful to Lindbergh and his wife, the former Anne Morrow, that they took refuge in Europe. There Lindbergh visited various German centers of aviation, and, though he warned the United States of Germany's growing air power, he nevertheless accepted a decoration from the German government in 1938. He returned to find himself the subject of much criticism, a situation that did not improve when, in 1940 and 1941, he made a series of impassioned isolationist speeches opposing the President's pro-Allied foreign policy. Lindbergh became an important spokesman for the America First Committee, a group established in September 1940 to obstruct America's participation in the war, and it was in that capacity that he delivered the following speech in New York on April 23, 1941. As a result of the critical attacks on him Lindbergh resigned his colonelcy in the Air Force in the same month, but when war came he worked hard though unobtrusively for the American cause and was named a brigadier general in the Air Force Reserve by President Eisenhower in 1954.*

Source: *Record, App.,* 77 Cong., 1 Sess., pp. A2152-A2154.

THERE ARE MANY VIEWPOINTS from which the issues of this war can be argued. Some are primarily idealistic. Some are primarily practical. One should, I believe, strive for a balance of both. But, since the subjects that can be covered in a single address are limited, tonight I shall discuss the war from a viewpoint which is primarily practical. It is not that I believe ideals are unimportant, even among the realities of war; but if a nation is to survive in a hostile world, its ideals must be backed by the hard logic of military practicability. If the outcome of war depended upon ideals alone, this would be a different world than it is today.

I know I will be severely criticized by the interventionists in America when I say we should not enter a war unless we have a reasonable chance of winning. That, they will claim, is far too materialistic a viewpoint. They will advance again the same arguments that were used to persuade France to declare war against Germany in 1939. But I do not believe that our American ideals and our way of life will gain through an unsuccessful war. And I know that the United States is not prepared to wage war in Europe successfully at this time. We are no better prepared today than France was when the interventionists in Europe persuaded her to attack the Siegfried Line.

I have said before and I will say again that I believe it will be a tragedy to the entire world if the British Empire collapses. That is one of the main reasons why I opposed this war before it was declared and why I have constantly advocated a negotiated peace. I did not feel that England and France had a reasonable chance of winning. France has now been defeated; and despite the propaganda and confusion of recent months, it is now obvious that England is losing the war. I believe this is realized even by the British government. But they have one last desperate plan remaining. They hope that they may be able to persuade us to send another American Expeditionary Force to Europe and to share with England militarily as well as financially the fiasco of this war.

I do not blame England for this hope, or for asking for our assistance. But we now know that she declared a war under circumstances which led to the defeat of every nation that sided with her, from Poland to Greece. We know that in the desperation of war England promised to all those nations armed assistance that she could not send. We know that she misinformed them, as she has misinformed us, concerning her state of preparation, her military strength, and the progress of the war.

In time of war, truth is always replaced by propaganda. I do not believe we should be too quick to criticize the actions of a belligerent nation. There is always the question whether we, ourselves, would do better under similar circumstances. But we in this country have a right to think of the welfare of America first, just as the people in England thought first of their own country when they encouraged the smaller nations of Europe to fight against hopeless odds. When England asks us to enter this war, she is considering her own future and that of her Empire. In making our reply, I believe we should consider the future of the United States and that of the Western Hemisphere.

It is not only our right but it is our obligation as American citizens to look at this war objectively and to weigh our chances for success if we should enter it. I have attempted to do this, especially from the standpoint of aviation; and I have been forced to the conclusion that we cannot win this war for England, regardless of how much assistance we extend.

I ask you to look at the map of Europe today and see if you can suggest any way in which we could win this war if we entered it. Suppose we had a large army in America, trained and equipped. Where would we send it to fight? The campaigns of the war show only too clearly how difficult it is to force a landing, or to maintain an army, on a hostile coast.

Suppose we took our Navy from the Pacific and used it to convoy British shipping. That would not win the war for England. It would, at best, permit her to exist under the constant bombing of the German air fleet. Suppose we had an air force that we could send to Europe. Where could it operate? Some of our squadrons might be based in the British Isles, but it is physically impossible to base enough aircraft in the British Isles alone to equal in strength the aircraft that can be based on the continent of Europe.

I have asked these questions on the supposition that we had in existence an army and an air force large enough and well enough equipped to send to Europe; and that we would dare to remove our Navy from the Pacific. Even on this basis, I do

Wide World

Charles Lindbergh speaking to a Manhattan meeting of the America First movement in 1941

not see how we could invade the continent of Europe successfully as long as all of that continent and most of Asia is under Axis domination. But the fact is that none of these suppositions are correct. We have only a one-ocean Navy. Our Army is still untrained and inadequately equipped for foreign war. Our air force is deplorably lacking in modern fighting planes.

When these facts are cited, the interventionists shout that we are defeatists, that we are undermining the principles of democracy, and that we are giving comfort to Germany by talking about our military weakness. But everything I mention here has been published in our newspapers and in the reports of congressional hearings in Washington. Our military position is well known to the governments of Europe and Asia. Why, then, should it not be brought to the attention of our own people?

I say it is the interventionists in America, as it was in England and in France, who give comfort to the enemy. I say it is they who are undermining the principles of de-

mocracy when they demand that we take a course to which more than 80 percent of our citizens are opposed. I charge them with being the real defeatists, for their policy has led to the defeat of every country that followed their advice since this war began. There is no better way to give comfort to an enemy than to divide the people of a nation over the issue of foreign war. There is no shorter road to defeat than by entering a war with inadequate preparation. Every nation that has adopted the interventionist policy of depending on someone else for its own defense has met with nothing but defeat and failure.

When history is written, the responsibility for the downfall of the democracies of Europe will rest squarely upon the shoulders of the interventionists who led their nations into war, uninformed and unprepared. With their shouts of defeatism and their disdain of reality, they have already sent countless thousands of young men to death in Europe. From the campaign of Poland to that of Greece, their prophecies have been false and their policies have failed. Yet these are the people who are calling us defeatists in America today. And they have led this country, too, to the verge of war.

There are many such interventionists in America, but there are more people among us of a different type. That is why you and I are assembled here tonight. There is a policy open to this nation that will lead to success — a policy that leaves us free to follow our own way of life and to develop our own civilization. It is not a new and untried idea. It was advocated by Washington. It was incorporated in the Monroe Doctrine. Under its guidance the United States became the greatest nation in the world.

It is based upon the belief that the security of a nation lies in the strength and character of its own people. It recommends the maintenance of armed forces sufficient to defend this hemisphere from attack by any combination of foreign powers. It demands faith in an independent American destiny. This is the policy of the America First Committee today. It is a policy not of isolation but of independence; not of defeat but of courage. It is a policy that led this nation to success during the most trying years of our history, and it is a policy that will lead us to success again.

We have weakened ourselves for many months, and, still worse, we have divided our own people by this dabbling in Europe's wars. While we should have been concentrating on American defense we have been forced to argue over foreign quarrels. We must turn our eyes and our faith back to our own country before it is too late. And when we do this a different vista opens before us. Practically every difficulty we would face in invading Europe becomes an asset to us in defending America. Our enemy, and not we, would then have the problem of transporting millions of troops across the ocean and landing them on a hostile shore. They, and not we, would have to furnish the convoys to transport guns and trucks and munitions and fuel across 3,000 miles of water. Our battleships and submarines would then be fighting close to their home bases. We would then do the bombing from the air and the torpedoing at sea. And if any part of an enemy convoy should ever pass our Navy and our air force, they would still be faced with the guns of our coast artillery and behind them the divisions of our Army.

The United States is better situated from a military standpoint than any other nation in the world. Even in our present condition of unpreparedness no foreign power is in a position to invade us today. If we concentrate on our own defenses and build the strength that this nation should maintain, no foreign army will ever attempt to land on American shores.

War is not inevitable for this country.

Such a claim is defeatism in the true sense. No one can make us fight abroad unless we ourselves are willing to do so. No one will attempt to fight us here if we arm ourselves as a great nation should be armed. Over 100 million people in this nation are opposed to entering the war. If the principles of democracy mean anything at all, that is reason enough for us to stay out. If we are forced into a war against the wishes of an overwhelming majority of our people, we will have proved democracy such a failure at home that there will be little use fighting for it abroad.

The time has come when those of us who believe in an independent American destiny must band together and organize for strength. We have been led toward war by a minority of our people. This minority has power. It has influence. It has a loud voice. But it does not represent the American people.

During the last several years I have traveled over this country from one end to the other. I have talked to many hundreds of men and women, and I have letters from tens of thousands more who feel the same way as you and I. Most of these people have no influence or power. Most of them have no means of expressing their convictions except by their vote, which has always been against this war. They are the citizens who have had to work too hard at their daily jobs to organize political meetings. Hitherto, they have relied upon their vote to express their feelings; but now they find that it is hardly remembered except in the oratory of a political campaign.

These people, the majority of hardworking American citizens, are with us. They are the true strength of our country. And they are beginning to realize, as you and I, that there are times when we must sacrifice our normal interests in life in order to insure the safety and the welfare of our nation.

Such a time has come. Such a crisis is

here. That is why the America First Committee has been formed — to give voice to the people who have no newspaper or newsreel or radio station at their command; to the people who must do the paying and the fighting and the dying if this country enters the war.

Whether or not we do enter the war rests upon the shoulders of you in this audience; upon us here on this platform; upon meetings of this kind that are being held by Americans in every section of the United States today. It depends upon the action we take and the courage we show at this time. If you believe in an independent destiny for America, if you believe that this country should not enter the war in Europe, we ask you to join the America First Committee in its stand. We ask you to share our faith in the ability of this nation to defend itself, to develop its own civilization, and to contribute to the progress of mankind in a more constructive and intelligent way than has yet been found by the warring nations of Europe. We need your support, and we need it now. The time to act is here.

## 18.

# ZECHARIAH CHAFEE: Free Speech in America

*Periods of national emergency in America have often been marked by widespread disregard of the guarantees of the Bill of Rights. Dissent becomes intolerable, and patriotism demands, or seems to demand, one uniform and uncritical public opinion on the issues confronting the nation. So it had been during the Civil War and so it had been during and after World War I. In 1941 Professor Zechariah Chafee of Harvard expressed concern lest dissent and the right to freedom of discussion be threatened once again. A portion of his* Free Speech in the United States *is reprinted here.*

Source: *Free Speech in the United States,* Cambridge, 1941, pp. 559-566.

SPEECH SHOULD BE FRUITFUL as well as free. Our experience introduces this qualification into the classical argument of Milton and John Stuart Mill, that only through open discussion is truth discovered and spread. In their simpler times, they thought it enough to remove legal obstacles like the censorship and sedition prosecutions. Mill assumed that if men were only left alone, their reasoning powers would eventually impel them to choose the best ideas and the wisest course of action.

To us this policy is too exclusively negative. For example, what is the use of telling an unpopular speaker that he will incur no criminal penalties by his proposed address, so long as every hall owner in the city declines to rent him space for his meeting and there are no vacant lots available? There should be municipal auditoriums, schoolhouses out of school hours, church forums, parks in summer, all open to thresh out every question of public importance, with just as few restrictions as possible; for otherwise the subjects that most need to be discussed will be the very subjects that will be ruled out as unsuitable for discussion.

We must do more than remove the discouragements to open discussion. We must exert ourselves to supply active encouragements.

Physical space and lack of interference alone will not make discussion fruitful. We must take affirmative steps to improve the methods by which discussion is carried on. Of late years the argument of Milton and Mill has been questioned, because truth does not seem to emerge from a controversy in the automatic way their logic would lead us to expect. For one thing, reason is less praised nowadays than a century ago; instead, emotions conscious and unconscious are commonly said to dominate the conduct of men. Is it any longer possible to discover truth amid the clashing blares of advertisements, loud speakers, gigantic billboards, party programs, propaganda of a hundred kinds? To sift the truth from all these half-truths seems to demand a statistical investigation beyond the limits of anybody's time and money.

So some modern thinkers despairingly conclude that the great mass of voters cannot be trusted to detect the fallacies in emotional arguments by Communists and so on, and hence must be prevented from hearing them. Even the intellectuals do not seem to do much better in reaching Truth by conflicting arguments. For example, take controversies between professors. They talk and talk, and at the end each sticks to his initial position. On which side does Truth stand? We still do not know. Then, too, the emergencies seem greater and more pressing than of yore. We are less willing to await the outcome of prolonged verbal contests. Perhaps Truth will win in the long run; but in the long run, as Walter Lippmann says, we shall all be dead — and perhaps not peacefully in our beds either. Debating is only fiddling while Rome burns.

Away with all this talk; let's have action — now.

Nevertheless, the main argument of Milton and Mill still holds good. All that this disappointment means is that friction is a much bigger drag on the progress of Truth than they supposed. Efforts to lessen that friction are essential to the success of freedom of speech. It is a problem, not for law but for education in the wide sense that includes more than schools and youngsters. The conflict of oral evidence and arguments can be made increasingly profitable by wise improvements in technique. Anybody who has attended a forum knows how much depends on an able chairman and on sensible rules enforced by him. Journalists and other writers value accuracy of facts far more than formerly — we can expect even more from them in the future. None of us can get rid of our emotions, but we can learn to drive them in harness. As for blazing propaganda on both sides, young Americans can be trained to keep alive the gumption which comes down to us from Colonial farmers; this will make them distrust all men who conceal greed or a lust for power behind any flag, whether red or red-white-and-blue.

Reason is more imperfect than we used to believe. Yet it still remains the best guide we have, better than our emotions, better even than patriotism, better than any single human guide, however exalted his position.

A second point deserves renewed emphasis. The effect of suppression extends far beyond the agitators actually put in jail, far beyond the pamphlets physically destroyed. A favorite argument against free speech is that the men who are thus conspicuously silenced had little to say that was worth hearing. Concede for the moment that the public would suffer no serious loss if every communist leaflet were burned or if some prominent pacifist were imprisoned, as perhaps he might be under the loose language of the unprecedented federal sedition law passed last year, for discouraging drafted men by talk about plowing every fourth boy under. Even so, my contention is that the pertinacious orators and writers who get hauled up are merely extremist spokesmen for a mass of more thoughtful and more retiring men and women, who share in varying degrees the same critical attitude toward prevailing policies and institutions. When you put the hotheads in jail, these cooler people do not get arrested — they just keep quiet. And so we lose things they could tell us, which would be very advantageous for the future course of the nation. Once the prosecutions begin, then the hush-hush begins too. Discussion becomes one-sided and artificial. Questions that need to be threshed out do not get threshed out.

The evils of such a policy of suppression are especially acute during a national emergency like the World War or the present rapid development of national defense. Because of the 1916 prosecutions brought under the Espionage Act, tens of thousands among those "forward-looking men and women" to whom President Wilson had appealed in earlier years were bewildered and depressed and silenced by the negation of freedom in the twenty-year sentences requested by his legal subordinates from complacent judges. So we had plenty of patriotism and very little criticism, except of the slowness of munition production. Wrong courses were followed like the dispatch of troops to Archangel in 1918, which fatally alienated Russia from Wilson's aims for a peaceful Europe. Harmful facts like the secret treaties were concealed while they could have been cured, only to bob up later and wreck everything. What was equally disastrous, right positions, like our support of the League of Nations before the armistice, were taken unthinkingly merely because the President favored them; then they collapsed as soon as the excitement was over, because they had no depth and had never been hardened by the hammerblows of open discus-

sion. And so when we attained military victory, we did not know what to do with it. No well-informed public opinion existed to carry through Wilson's war aims for a new world order to render impossible the recurrence of disaster.

In 1941 the same problem confronts us, only it is infinitely more difficult. The task of today is to produce airplanes, guns, and battleships. The task of tomorrow is to throw out the half-crazed ruler who threatens to destroy the civilization painfully built up since Marathon. The task of the day after tomorrow is to rebuild that civilization far more solidly than in 1919. . . .

In this tremendous task of the day after tomorrow, the United States will be forced to take a major share. We cannot afford to turn away from it in disgust as in 1920 and let Europe plunge eventually into a third and still more frightful disaster in 1960. The Atlantic will then be more easily crossed by bombers than the English Channel is now. The American arsenal of munitions will be the first enemy objective. In short, so long as we permit Europe to be divided into competing armed groups, we shall be inevitably obliged to save the British Empire every other decade at increasing cost to ourselves in money and blood. Adequate national defense under such conditions will absorb most of the national life. . . .

The Supreme Court, though much more anxious to support liberty of speech than it was twenty years ago, can do nothing to keep discussion open during an emergency. Cases of suppression will get to Washington long after the emergency is over. What counts is what the local United States judges do. Still more important is the attitude of the prosecutors and police, because they can stifle free speech by breaking up meetings by arrests and confiscating pamphlets, and then not bothering to bring many persons to trial.

Above all, the maintenance of open discussion depends on all the great body of unofficial citizens. If a community does not respect liberty for unpopular ideas, it can easily drive such ideas underground by persistent discouragement and sneers, by social ostracism, by boycotts of newspapers and magazines, by refusal to rent halls, by objections to the use of municipal auditoriums and schoolhouses, by discharging teachers and professors and journalists, by mobs and threats of lynching. On the other hand, an atmosphere of open and unimpeded controversy may be made as fully a part of the life of a community as any other American tradition. The law plays only a small part in either suppression or freedom. In the long run the public gets just as much freedom of speech as it really wants. . . .

Behind the dozens of sedition bills in Congress last session, behind teachers' oaths and compulsory flag salutes, is a desire to make our citizens loyal to their government. Loyalty is a beautiful idea, but you cannot create it by compulsion and force. A government is at bottom the officials who carry it on: legislators and prosecutors, school superintendents and police. If it is composed of legislators who pass shortsighted sedition laws by overwhelming majorities, of narrow-minded school superintendents who oust thoughtful teachers of American history and eight-year-old children whose rooted religious convictions prevent them from sharing in a brief ceremony — a government of snoopers and spies and secret police — how can you expect love and loyalty? You make men love their government and their country by giving them the kind of government and the kind of country that inspire respect and love: a country that is free and unafraid, that lets the discontented talk in order to learn the causes for their discontent and end those causes, that refuses to impel men to spy on their neighbors, that protects its citizens vigorously from harmful acts while it leaves the remedies for objectionable ideas to counterargument and time.

Plutarch's Lives were the favorite reading of the men who framed and ratified our Constitution. There they found the story of Timoleon who saved his native city of Syracuse from the Carthaginian tyrants. In later years young hotheads used to get up in the public assembly and abuse Timoleon as an old fossil. His friends urged him just to say the word, and they would soon silence his detractors. But Timoleon insisted on letting the vituperative youngsters have their say. "He had taken all the extreme pains and labor he had done, and had passed so many dangers, in order that every citizen and inhabitant of Syracuse might frankly use the liberty of their laws. He thanked the gods that they had granted him the thing he had so oft requested of them in his prayers, which was, that he might some day see the Syracusans have full power and liberty to say what they pleased."

It is such a spirit that makes us love the United States of America. With all the shortcomings of economic organization, with all the narrowness and ignorance of politicians, we know that we are still immeasurably freer than we should be in Italy, Germany, or Russia to say what we think and write what we believe and do what we want. "There's a looseness about this here freedom that I likes."

Let us not in our anxiety to protect ourselves from foreign tyrants imitate some of their worst acts, and sacrifice in the process of national defense the very liberties which we are defending.

---

*America — a place where the people have the right to complain about the lack of freedom.*

Louis Hirsch

19.

# Donald Benedict *et al.*: Why We Refused to Register for the Draft

*The Selective Service and Training Act of 1940, the first peacetime conscription in the nation's history, established Civilian Public Service camps as an alternative to military service. Persons who opposed participation in war as conscientious objectors were assigned work on various public projects, such as land reclamation, forest-fire fighting, and hospital work. It has been estimated that over 12,000 conscientious objectors performed noncombatant service in these camps during World War II. In October 1940, eight students in New York City refused even to register for the draft, claiming that civilian public service was but another aspect of a government policy of which they disapproved. The group, which had been living in voluntary poverty in Harlem as a symbol of protest while attending the Union Theological Seminary, issued the following statement to a court in 1941.*

Source: *Nonviolence in America: A Documentary History*, Staughton Lynd, ed., Indianapolis, 1966, pp. 296-299.

IT IS IMPOSSIBLE FOR US to think of the Conscription Law without at the same time thinking of the whole war system, because it is clear to us that conscription is definitely a part of the institution of war. . . .

To us, the war system is an evil part of our social order, and we declare that we cannot cooperate with it in any way. War is an evil because it is in violation of the Way of Love as seen in God through Christ. It is a concentration and accentuation of all the evils of our society. War consists of mass murder, deliberate starvation, vandalism, and similar evils. Physical destruction and moral disintegration are the inevitable result. The war method perpetuates and compounds the evils it purports to overcome. It is impossible, as history reveals, to overcome evil with evil. The last World War is a notorious case of the failure of the war system, and there is no evidence to believe

that this war will be any different. It is our positive proclamation as followers of Jesus Christ that we must overcome evil with good. We seek in our daily living to reconcile that separation of man from man and man from God which produces war.

We have also been led to our conclusion on the Conscription Law in the light of its totalitarian nature. It is a totalitarian move when our government insists that the manpower of the nation take a year of military training. It is a totalitarian move for the President of the nation to be able to conscript industry to produce certain materials which are deemed necessary for national defense without considering the actual physical needs of the people. We believe, therefore, that by opposing the Selective Service Law, we will be striking at the heart of totalitarianism as well as war. . . .

We feel a deep bond of unity with those

who decide to register as conscientious objectors, but our own decision must be different for the following reasons:

If we register under the act, even as conscientious objectors, we are becoming part of the act. The fact that we as conscientious objectors may gain personal exemption from the most crassly un-Christian requirements of the act does not compensate for the fact that we are complying with it and accepting its protection. If a policeman (or a group of vigilantes) stops us on the street, our possession of the government's card shows that we are "all right" — we have complied with the act for the militarization of America. If that does not hurt our Christian consciences, what will? If we try to rationalize on the theory that we must go along with the act in order to fight the fascism and militarism of which it is a part, it seems to us that we are doing that very thing which all pacifist Christians abhor: we are consciously employing bad means on the theory that to do so will contribute to a good end. . . .

In similar vein, it is urged that great concessions have been won for religious pacifists and that we endanger these by our refusal to accept them. Fascism, as it gradually supplanted democracy in Germany, was aided by the decision of Christians and leftists to accept a partial fascism rather than to endanger those democratic concessions which still remained. It is not alone for our own exemption from fighting that we work — it is for freedom of the American people from fascism and militarism.

Partial exemption of conscientious objectors has come about partly through the work of influential pacifists and partly through the open-mindedness of certain nonpacifists. But it has also been granted because of the fear of the government that, without such a provision, public opposition to war would be too great to handle. In particular, it seems to us that one of the reasons the government has granted exemption to ministers and theological students is to gain a religious sanction for its diabolical war. Where actual support could not be gained, it hoped to soothe their consciences so that they could provide no real opposition.

We do not contend that the American people maliciously choose the vicious instrument of war. In a very perplexing situation, they lack the imagination, the religious faith, and the precedents to respond in a different manner. This makes it all the more urgent to build in this country and throughout the world a group trained in the techniques of nonviolent opposition to the encroachments of militarism and fascism. Until we build such a movement, it will be impossible to stall the war machine at home. When we do build such a movement, we will have forged the only weapon which can ever give effective answer to foreign invasion. Thus, in learning to fight American Hitlerism, we will show an increasing group of war-disillusioned Americans how to resist foreign Hitlers as well.

For these reasons we hereby register our refusal to comply in any way with the Selective Training and Service Act. We do not expect to stem the war forces today; but we are helping to build the movement that will conquer in the future.

---

*I believe that we are lost here in America, but I believe we shall be found. . . . I think that the true discovery of America is before us. I think the true fulfillment of our spirit, of our people, of our mighty and immortal land, is yet to come.*
THOMAS WOLFE, *You Can't Go Home Again*

20.

# Franklin D. Roosevelt: Discrimination in Wartime Employment

*During the spring of 1941, leaders of the Negro community laid plans for a march on Washington on the 1st of July. A. Philip Randolph, president of the Brotherhood of Sleeping Car Porters and one of the most influential Negro leaders of this century, explained the reasons for the march, which in fact did not occur. "When the defense program began and billions of the taxpayers' money were appropriated for guns, ships, tanks, and bombs," Randolph later said, "Negroes presented themselves for work only to be given the cold shoulder. . . . Not until their wrath and indignation took the form of a proposed protest march on Washington . . . did things begin to move in the form of defense jobs for Negroes." The march was averted by President Roosevelt's Executive Order No. 8802, issued June 25, which established the President's Committee on Fair Employment Practices.*

Source: U.S. Congressional Service, 77 Congress, 1 Session, No. 8802.

*Reaffirming policy of full participation in the defense program by all persons, regardless of race, creed, color, or national origin, and directing certain action in furtherance of said policy*

*Whereas* it is the policy of the United States to encourage full participation in the national defense program by all citizens of the United States, regardless of race, creed, color, or national origin, in the firm belief that the democratic way of life within the nation can be defended successfully only with the help and support of all groups within its borders; and

*Whereas* there is evidence that available and needed workers have been barred from employment in industries engaged in defense production solely because of considerations of race, creed, color, or national origin to the detriment of workers' morale and of national unity:

*Now, Therefore,* by virtue of the authority vested in me by the Constitution and the statutes, and as a prerequisite to the successful conduct of our national defense production effort, I do hereby reaffirm the policy of the United States that there shall be no discrimination in the employment of workers in defense industries or government because of race, creed, color, or national origin; and I do hereby declare that it is the duty of employers and of labor organizations, in furtherance of said policy and of this order, to provide for the full and equitable participation of all workers in defense industries, without discrimination because of race, creed, color, or national origin;

*And it is hereby ordered as follows:*

1. All departments and agencies of the government of the United States concerned with vocational and training programs for defense production shall take special measures appropriate to assure that such programs are administered without discrimination because of race, creed, color, or national origin.

2. All contracting agencies of the government of the United States shall include in all defense contracts hereafter negotiated by them a provision obligating the contractor not to discriminate against any worker because of race, creed, color, or national origin.

3. There is established in the Office of Production Management a Committee on Fair Employment Practice, which shall consist of a chairman and four other members to be appointed by the President. The chairman and members of the committee shall serve as such without compensation but shall be entitled to actual and necessary transportation, subsistence, and other expenses incidental to performance of their duties. The committee shall receive and investigate complaints of discrimination in violation of the provisions of this order and shall take appropriate steps to redress grievances which it finds to be valid. The committee shall also recommend to the several departments and agencies of the government of the United States and to the President all measures which may be deemed by it necessary or proper to effectuate the provisions of this order.

---

## 21.

# W. C. HANDY: How the Blues Came To Be

*The son of a minister, W. C. Handy was born in Alabama in 1873. He was first a schoolteacher but his love of music led him to become a bandmaster. Although blind at the age of thirty, Handy nevertheless conducted his own orchestra for the next eighteen years. In 1911 he wrote and orchestrated "Memphis Blues" for the mayor of Memphis, Edward H. "Boss" Crump, which, in combination with his "St. Louis Blues" of 1914, made him the most famous jazz musician in the land and earned him the title "Father of the Blues." Ragtime was the prevalent jazz style at the time, but Handy introduced a nostalgic element, chiefly by means of the "blue" lowered seventh, that became the characteristic feature of all Blues written thereafter. "Most white people," Handy once said, "think that the Negro is always cheerful and lively, but he isn't, though he may seem that way when he is most troubled. The Negro knows the Blues as a state of mind, and that's why his music has that name." The following selection is taken from Handy's autobiography, published in 1941.*

Source: *Father of the Blues*, Arna Bontemps, ed., New York, 1941, pp. 71-88.

SOUTHERN NEGROES sang about everything. Trains, steamboats, steam whistles, sledge hammers, fast women, mean bosses, stubborn mules — all become subjects for their songs. They accompany themselves on anything from which they can extract a musical sound or rhythmical effect, anything from a harmonica to a washboard.

In this way, and from these materials, they set the mood for what we now call blues. My own fondness for this sort of thing really began in Florence, back in the days when we were not above serenading beneath the windows of our sweethearts and singing till we won a kiss in the shadows or perhaps a tumbler of good home-made wine. In the Delta, however, I suddenly saw the songs with the eye of a budding composer. The songs themselves, I now observed, consisted of simple declarations expressed usually in three lines and set to a kind of earthborn music that was familiar throughout the Southland half a century ago. Mississippi with its large plantations and small cities probably had more colored field hands than any other state. Consequently we heard many such song fragments as *Hurry Sundown, Let Tomorrow Come,* or

> Boll Weevil, where you been so long?
> Boll Weevil, where you been so long?
> You stole my cotton, now you want my
>  corn.

Clarksdale was eighteen miles from the river, but that was no distance for roustabouts. They came in the evenings and on days when they were not loading boats. With them they brought the legendary songs of the river.

> Oh, the Kate's up the river,
>  Stack O' Lee's in the ben',
> Oh, the Kate's up the river,
>  Stack O' Lee's in the ben',
> And I ain't seen ma baby since
>  I can't tell when. . . .

At first folk melodies like these were kept in the back rooms of my mind while the parlor was reserved for dressed-up music. Musical books continued to get much of my attention. There was still an old copy of Steiner's *First Lessons in Harmony,* purchased back in Henderson for fifty cents. While traveling with the minstrels I had bought from Lyon and Healy a copy of Moore's *Encyclopedia of Music.* For a time books became a passion. I'm afraid I came to think that everything worthwhile was to be found in books. But the blues did not come from books. Suffering and hard luck were the midwives that birthed these songs. The blues were conceived in aching hearts.

I hasten to confess that I took up with low folk forms hesitantly. I approached them with a certain fear and trembling. Like many of the other musicians who received them with cold shoulders at first, I began by raising my eyebrows and wondering if they were quite the thing. I had picked up a fair training in the music of the modern world and had assumed that the correct manner to compose was to develop simples into grandissimos and not to repeat them monotonously. As a director of many respectable, conventional bands, it was not easy for me to concede that a simple slow-drag and repeat could be rhythm itself. Neither was I ready to believe that this was just what the public wanted. But we live to learn.

My own enlightenment came in Cleveland, Mississippi. I was leading the orchestra in a dance program when someone sent up an odd request. Would we play some of "our native music," the note asked. This baffled me. The men in this group could not "fake" and "sell it" like minstrel men. They were all musicians who bowed strictly to the authority of printed notes. So we played for our anonymous fan an old-time Southern melody, a melody more sophisticated than native. A few moments later a second request came up. Would we object if a local colored band played a few dances?

Object! That was funny. What hornblower would object to a time-out and a smoke — on pay? We eased out gracefully as the newcomers entered. They were led by a long-legged chocolate boy and their band consisted of just three pieces, a battered guitar, a mandolin, and a worn-out bass.

The music they made was pretty well in keeping with their looks. They struck up one of those over-and-over strains that seem to have no very clear beginning and certainly no ending at all. The strumming attained a disturbing monotony, but on and on it went, a kind of stuff that has long been associated with cane rows and levee camps.

United Press International

W. C. Handy (right) at the Cotton Makers' Jubilee Coronation festivities, 1946

Thump-thump-thump went their feet on the floor. Their eyes rolled. Their shoulders swayed. And through it all that little agonizing strain persisted. It was not really annoying or unpleasant Perhaps "haunting" is a better word, but I commenced to wonder if anybody besides small town rounders and their running mates would go for it.

The answer was not long in coming. A rain of silver dollars began to fall around the outlandish, stomping feet. The dancers went wild. Dollars, quarters, halves — the shower grew heavier and continued so long I strained my neck to get a better look. There before the boys lay more money than my nine musicians were being paid for the entire engagement. Then I saw the beauty of primitive music. They had the stuff the people wanted. It touched the spot. Their music wanted polishing, but it contained the essence. Folks would pay money for it. The old conventional music was well and good and had its place, no denying that, but there was no virtue in being blind when you had good eyes.

That night a composer was born, an *American* composer. Those country black boys at Cleveland had taught me something that could not possibly have been gained from books, something that would, however, cause books to be written. Art, in the highbrow sense, was not in my mind. My idea of what constitutes music was changed by the sight of that silver money cascading around the splay feet of a Mississippi string band. Seven years prior to this, while playing a cornet solo, Hartman's *Mia,* on the stage in Oakland, California, I had come to the conclusion, because of what happened in this eleven minute solo, that the American people wanted movement and rhythm for their money. Then too, the Broadway hits *Yankee Grit* and *Uncle Sammy* — two-steps in six-eight time that we featured in Mississippi — did not have this earthy flavor.

Once the purpose was fixed I let no grass grow under my feet. I returned to Clarksdale and began immediately to work on this type of music. Within a day or two I had orchestrated a number of local tunes, among them *The Last Shot Got Him, Your*

*Clock Ain't Right,* and the distinctly Negroid *Make Me a Pallet on Your Floor.* My hunch was promptly justified, for the popularity of our orchestra increased by leaps and bounds. But there was also another consequence. Bids came to us to play in less respectable places. We took these in our stride on the grounds that music, like joy, should be unconfined. Moreover there was money to be made, and who were we to turn up our noses?

Across the tracks of the Y. & M. V. railroad in Clarksdale there was a section called the "New World." It was the local red-light district. To the New World came lush octoroons and quadroons from Louisiana, soft cream-colored fancy gals from Mississippi towns. Just beyond this section lived some of the oldest and most respectable Negro families. On their way to the Baptist or Methodist churches they were required to pass before the latticed houses of prostitution. Occasionally they caught glimpses of white men lounging with the pretty near-white "imports." By using their imaginations they could assume what went on in the dim rooms beyond.

As musicians we didn't have to guess. As musicians, too, hired to play music rather than to discuss morals, we kept our mouths shut. We knew that big shot officials winked at the New World, but that was neither here nor there to the men with the horns and the fiddles. What was important was that these rouge-tinted girls, wearing silk stockings and short skirts, bobbing their soft hair and smoking cigarets in that prim era, long before these styles had gained respectability, were among the best patrons the orchestra had. They employed us for big nights, occasions when social or political figures of importance were expected to dine and dance with their favorite creole belles. Contacts made in these shady precincts often led to jobs in chaste great houses of the rich and well-to-do.

The shuttered houses of the New World called for appropriate music. This led us to arrange and play tunes that had never been written down and seldom sung outside the environment of the oldest profession. Boogie-house music, it was called. Much of it has since been fumigated and played in the best of society, but then Dopy McKnight thumped out the tunes on a rickety piano. We took them up, arranged orchestrations and played them to the wild approval of the richly scented yellow gals and their company. I have intimated that silver money had always been plentiful in the Delta; now at last we began to come in for our share of it.

The Delta had also its share of melodrama. Engagements in the New World plunged us into the tide. One evening a vivid octoroon, who had been winking at our violinist, shared a drink with him. Her ofay (white) company turned and put a pistol to the musician's temple. He promised to pull the trigger if he opened his mouth. He'd just as soon do it immediately, he said, if the boy felt like giving any back talk. When it was over, I recalled a saying that is almost an axiom among Negroes of the South. The thought of it is that more black men are killed by whites for merely conversing with colored girls of this type than for violating, as the orators like to put it, the sanctity of white womanhood. Ho-hum. The world is powerfully big, and a queer place.

As a sideline in Clarksdale I did a kind of bootleg business in Northern Negro newspapers and magazines. Not only did I supply the colored folks of the town but also got the trade of the farmers, the croppers, and the hands from the outlying country. They would come to my house on their weekly visits to the city, give me the high sign, and I would slip them their copies of the *Chicago Defender,* the *Indianapolis Freeman* or the *Voice of the Negro.* This may sound like a tame enough enterprise to those whose memories are short, but oldsters of those parts will not have to be told that I was venturing into risky business.

Negro newspapers were not plentiful in those days, and their circulation in cities like Clarksdale was looked upon with strong disfavor by certain of the local powers. But because I was favorably known to most of the white folks as the leader of the band that gave the weekly concerts on the main street, they never suspected me of such dark business as distributing Northern literature to Negroes of the community. In fact, Clarksdale and I remained on such good terms that when there came a time to call upon the well-to-do townsfolk to help us foot the bill for new uniforms, instruments, and other equipment for the men, the needed amount was oversubscribed before the bank closed on the day when the campaign was begun.

When we blossomed forth in the glad rags, the town stuck out its chest proudly. We were theirs, they had helped dress us up and everybody was pleased with the results, including ourselves. Senator John Sharp Williams, a great favorite of the people, came to town, giving us our first opportunity to show our appreciation by welcoming him with good music and gay uniforms. The occasion, as much as it pleased us all, was of no long-range consequence, so far as I recall, but it represents another line of the work that fell to our band during those days and in the years that followed. We were frequently hired, as on this occasion, to furnish music for political rallies.

This meant that we had to absorb a "passel" of oratory of the brand served by some Southern politicians just this side of the turn of the century. We appeared with one gubernatorial candidate who regularly treated his audiences to the following titbit:

Ladies and Gentlemen:

I come before you as a candidate for the governorship of the grand old state of Mississippi. And I pledge you my sacred word of honor that if you elect me your governor, I shall not spend one dollar for nigger education.

Now I want to tell you why I will not spend one dollar of the state's money for nigger education; education unfits the nigger. Let me prove it to you conclusively. I am right.

When this great country of ours was torn by strife, and we followed the fortunes of the Confederacy, we left behind our mothers, our daughters, our sweethearts, and our wives; and we left them behind with our niggers, and they guarded them like so many faithful watchdogs. Now what kind of nigger did we leave them with? It was the uneducated nigger.

Suppose we again had to go to war, would you trust them with the nigger of today? (A chorus of no's came in answer.) That's why I wouldn't spend one dollar for nigger education.

His voice quavered and a mist came to his eyes as he extended one arm while resting the other dramatically over his heart. Then as the concluding words trailed off, we struck up *Dixie*. Outside we exchanged amazed glances among ourselves and laughed. He was not elected.

Each time we played for him, I was reminded of the first time I had listened to oratory of this sort. As a schoolboy in Florence I had gone home, buried my head in a pillow and wept after listening to sentiments like these uttered from the courthouse steps by a politician of the same stripe. Later I had wandered off alone in the woods across the road from the cabin in which I was born. There, point by point, I had undertaken to answer the man of ill will. Slowly, deliberately, I had torn his arguments to bits. At the top of my voice I had hurled the lie into his teeth. The woodland took up my shouts. The words of my defiance echoed and reechoed. That pleased me. I went home and slept well, a great burden removed. In Clarksdale the members of my band nudged one another with their elbows when we were safely out of the crowd. Then we all laughed — laughed. But playing for the political campaigns was not always the bitter pill this particular candidate made it. We were engaged for ex-Governor Earl Brewer when he made a delayed entrance into a red-hot, seven-cornered race for the governorship. Here the story was not the same. The ex-governor did not hesitate to touch on the Negro, but no tirade came from him. Instead he gave the finest tribute to Negro music that I had ever been permitted to hear. A tribute deeply felt and moving when he referred to our loyalty. He was not elected that year, but later when the time came for another campaign, he was not even opposed — elected unanimously.

Either way, however, we were undismayed. We could laugh and we could make rhythm. What better armor could you ask?

Negroes react rhythmically to everything. That's how the blues came to be. Sometimes I think that rhythm is our middle name. When the sweet good man packs his trunk and goes, that is occasion for some low moaning. When darktown puts on its new shoes and takes off the brakes, jazz steps in. If it's the New Jerusalem and the River Jordan we're studying, we make the spirituals. The rounders among us, those whose aim in life is just to become bigger rounders — well, they're the ones we can thank for the Frankie and Johnnie songs. In every case the songs come from down deep. . . .

More than once during my travels in the North and South I had passed through towns with signs saying, "Nigger don't let the sun go down on you here." And once, at least, we played in a town where the boot was on the other foot. Though Mound Bayou had no such words addressed to "peckerwoods" or "rednecks," the sentiment among its all Negro population was perhaps in some ways similar. Yet salesmen and other white visitors who found it necessary to spend the night there received all possible hospitality.

This town, thirty miles south of Clarks-dale on the Y. & M. V. railroad, was founded by Isaiah T. Montgomery, former bodyguard and slave of Jeff Davis, President of the Confederacy. The occasion for our band's visit was the dedication of the Bank of Mound Bayou, and we came largely through the instigation of Charles Banks the cashier. A Clarksdale boy himself, Banks had gained his training in the same Planters Bank that now employed our Stack. We carried the band to Mound Bayou to pay our respects to this home town boy, but we stayed on to admire the new Carnegie Library and blink in amazement at colored railroad ticket agents, colored telegraph operators, and pretty brownskins at telephone switchboards.

My personal admiration for the enterprise of the Negroes of Mound Bayou was so great that later, when they held the grand opening of their oil mill, I brought a band from Memphis at my own expense just to help them do the thing up brown. Booker T. Washington was the speaker for this occasion. After the address I dined with him in the home of Mr. and Mrs. Charles Banks and began to feel that the privilege of knowing the educator was ample recompense for my small contribution to the event. Later, however, Banks and his associates insisted on sending us a check in token of their gratitude for our contribution.

A picture of Clarksdale during the years I spent there would be incomplete without the blind singers and footloose bards that were forever coming and going. Usually the fellows were destitute. Some came sauntering down the railroad tracks, others dropped from freight cars, while still other caught rides on the big road and entered town on the top of cotton bales. A favorite hangout with them was the railroad station. There, surrounded by crowds of country folks, they would pour out their hearts in song while the audience ate fish and bread chewed sugarcane, dipped snuff while waiting for trains to carry them down the line.

They earned their living by selling their own songs — "ballets," as they called them — and I'm ready to say in their behalf that seldom did their creations lack imagination. Many a less gifted songsmith has plied his trade with passing success in Tin Pan Alley. Some of these country boys hustled on trains. Others visited churches. I remember buying such a ballet (ballad) entitled *I've Heard of a City Called Heaven*. It was printed on a slip of paper about the size of a postcard. Fifty years later, after I had published a choral arrangement of that piece, I heard the number sung with great success by the Hall Johnson Singers in *The Green Pastures*.

Mature years and a busy life have not enabled me to shake off a certain susceptibility to these dusky bards. Every time I put by enough money for a trip to Europe, I end up by purchasing a ticket to one of the more remote sections of the deep South, knowing fully in my mind that Europe and all its environs carry no such rich traditions and inspirational fertility as are embodied in this section of our America.

---

## 22.

# The Atlantic Charter

*From August 9 to 12, 1941, President Roosevelt and Prime Minister Churchill held a secret meeting on a ship off the coast of Newfoundland, the first of the conferences between the heads of the anti-Axis powers. At the conclusion of the conference they issued the Atlantic Charter, a declaration of Anglo-American goals for a better world, written largely by Churchill. Although the document was neither a treaty nor a signed official paper, but merely a press release, it nonetheless marked the beginning of the close cooperation between America and Britain that characterized the war years. The aims of the Atlantic Charter were later embodied in the Declaration of the United Nations in January 1942.*

Source: 77 Congress, 1 Session, House Document No. 358.

JOINT DECLARATION of the President of the United States of America and the Prime Minister, Mr. Churchill, representing His Majesty's government in the United Kingdom, being met together, deem it right to make known certain common principles in the national policies of their respective countries on which they base their hopes for a better future for the world.

First, their countries seek no aggrandizement, territorial or other.

Second, they desire to see no territorial changes that do not accord with the freely expressed wishes of the peoples concerned.

Third, they respect the right of all peoples to choose the form of government under which they will live; and they wish to see sovereign rights and self-government restored to those who have been forcibly deprived of them.

Fourth, they will endeavor, with due respect for their existing obligations, to further the enjoyment by all states, great or small, victor or vanquished, of access, on equal terms, to the trade and to the raw materials of the world which are needed for their economic prosperity.

Fifth, they desire to bring about the fullest collaboration between all nations in the economic field with the object of securing, for all, improved labor standards, economic advancement, and social security.

Sixth, after the final destruction of the Nazi tyranny, they hope to see established a peace which will afford to all nations the means of dwelling in safety within their own boundaries, and which will afford assurance that all the men in all the lands may live out their lives in freedom from fear and want.

Seventh, such a peace should enable all men to traverse the high seas and oceans without hindrance.

Eighth, they believe that all of the nations of the world, for realistic as well as spiritual reasons, must come to the abandonment of the use of force. Since no future peace can be maintained if land, sea, or air armaments continue to be employed by nations which threaten, or may threaten, aggression outside of their frontiers, they believe, pending the establishment of a wider and permanent system of general security, that the disarmament of such nations is essential. They will likewise aid and encourage all other practicable measures which will lighten for peace-loving peoples the crushing burden of armaments.

---

## 23.

## Franklin D. Roosevelt: Total National Defense

*With the Lend-Lease program in operation, President Roosevelt found it necessary to order the U.S. Navy to patrol the waters of the North Atlantic in order to protect the British convoys that were carrying "defense articles" to Britain. The U.S. Navy also served to warn British convoys of enemy submarines. The Germans retaliated by attacking American naval vessels. A German torpedo struck the U.S. destroyer Kearny on October 17, 1941, killing eleven men. Ten days later the President delivered the following Navy Day Address to the nation. For the first time he explicitly declared that no effort would be spared to destroy the Nazi regime in Germany.*

Source: *Record, App.*, 77 Cong., 1 Sess., pp. A4877-A4878.

FIVE MONTHS AGO TONIGHT [May 27, 1941] I proclaimed to the American people the existence of a state of unlimited emergency.

Since then much has happened. Our Army and Navy are temporarily in Iceland in the defense of the Western Hemisphere. Hitler has attacked shipping in areas close to the Americas in the North and South Atlantic. Many American-owned mer-

chant ships have been sunk on the high seas. One American destroyer was attacked on September 4. Another destroyer was attacked and hit on October 17. Eleven brave and loyal men of our Navy were killed by the Nazis.

We have wished to avoid shooting. But the shooting has started. And history has recorded who fired the first shot. In the long run, however, all that will matter is who fired the last shot.

America has been attacked. The U.S.S. *Kearny* is not just a Navy ship. She belongs to every man, woman, and child in this nation.

Illinois, Alabama, California, North Carolina, Ohio, Louisiana, Texas, Pennsylvania, Georgia, Arkansas, New York, Virginia — those are the home states of the honored dead and wounded of the *Kearny*. Hitler's torpedo was directed at every American, whether he lives on our seacoasts or in the innermost part of the nation, far from the seas and far from the guns and tanks of the marching hordes of would-be conquerors of the world.

The purpose of Hitler's attack was to frighten the American people off the high seas — to force us to make a trembling retreat. This is not the first time he has misjudged the American spirit. That spirit is now aroused.

If our national policy were to be dominated by the fear of shooting, then all of our ships and those of our sister republics would have to be tied up in home harbors. Our Navy would have to remain respectfully — abjectly — behind any line which Hitler might decree on any ocean as his own dictated version of his own war zone.

Naturally, we reject that absurd and insulting suggestion. We reject it because of our own self-interest, because of our own self-respect, because, most of all, of our own good faith. Freedom of the seas is now, as it has always been, a fundamental policy of your government and mine.

Hitler has often protested that his plans for conquest do not extend across the Atlantic Ocean. But his submarines and raiders prove otherwise. So does the entire design of his new world order. For example, I have in my possession a secret map made in Germany by Hitler's government — by the planners of the new world order. It is a map of South America and a part of Central America as Hitler proposes to reorganize it. Today in this area there are fourteen separate countries. The geographical experts of Berlin, however, have ruthlessly obliterated all existing boundary lines and have divided South America into five vassal states, bringing the whole continent under their domination. And they have also so arranged it that the territory of one of these new puppet states includes the Republic of Panama and our great lifeline — the Panama Canal.

That is his plan. It will never go into effect.

This map makes clear the Nazi design not only against South America but against the United States itself.

Your government has in its possession another document made in Germany by Hitler's government. It is a detailed plan, which, for obvious reasons, the Nazis did not wish and do not wish to publicize just yet, but which they are ready to impose a little later on a dominated world — if Hitler wins. It is a plan to abolish all existing religions — Protestant, Catholic, Mohammedan, Hindu, Buddhist, and Jewish alike. The property of all churches will be seized by the Reich and its puppets. The cross and all other symbols of religion are to be forbidden. The clergy are to be forever silenced under penalty of the concentration camps, where even now so many fearless men are being tortured because they have placed God above Hitler.

In the place of the churches of our civilization, there is to be set up an international Nazi church — a church which will be served by orators sent out by the Nazi government. In the place of the Bible, the words of *Mein Kampf* will be imposed and enforced as Holy Writ. And in place of the cross of Christ will be put two symbols — the swastika and the naked sword. A god of blood and iron will take the place of the God of love and mercy.

Let us well ponder that statement which

I have made tonight. These grim truths which I have told you of the present and future plans of Hitlerism will, of course, be hotly denied tonight and tomorrow in the controlled press and radio of the Axis Powers. And some Americans — not many — will continue to insist that Hitler's plans need not worry us and that we should not concern ourselves with anything that goes on beyond rifle shot of our own shores.

The protestations of these American citizens — few in number — will, as usual, be paraded with applause through the Axis press and radio during the next few days in an effort to convince the world that the majority of Americans are opposed to their duly chosen government and in reality are only waiting to jump on Hitler's bandwagon when it comes this way.

The motive of such Americans is not the point at issue. The fact is that Nazi propaganda continues in desperation to seize upon such isolated statements as proof of American disunity. The Nazis have made up their own list of modern American heroes. It is, fortunately, a short list. I am glad that it does not contain my name.

All of us Americans, of all opinions, are faced with the choice between the kind of world we want to live in and the kind of world which Hitler and his hordes would impose upon us. None of us wants to burrow under the ground and live in total darkness like a comfortable mole.

The forward march of Hitler and of Hitlerism can be stopped — and it will be stopped. Very simply and very bluntly, we are pledged to pull our own oar in the destruction of Hitlerism. And when we have helped to end the curse of Hitlerism, we shall help to establish a new peace which will give to decent people everywhere a better chance to live and prosper in security and in freedom and in faith.

Each day that passes we are producing and providing more and more arms for the men who are fighting on actual battlefronts. That is our primary task. And it is the nation's will that these vital arms and supplies of all kinds shall neither be locked up in American harbors nor sent to the bottom of the sea. It is the nation's will that America shall deliver the goods. In open defiance of that will, our ships have been sunk and our sailors have been killed.

I say that we do not propose to take this lying down. Our determination not to take it lying down has been expressed in the orders to the American Navy to shoot on sight. Those orders stand.

Furthermore, the House of Representatives has already voted to amend part of the Neutrality Act of 1937, today outmoded by force of violent circumstances. The Senate Committee on Foreign Relations has also recommended elimination of other hamstringing provisions in that act. That is the course of honesty and of realism.

Our American merchant ships must be armed to defend themselves against the rattlesnakes of the sea. Our American merchant ships must be free to carry our American goods into the harbors of our friends. Our American merchant ships must be protected by our American Navy.

It can never be doubted that the goods will be delivered by this nation, whose Navy believes in the tradition of "Damn the torpedoes; full speed ahead!"

Yes; our nation will and must speak from every assembly line. Yes; from every coalmine — the all-inclusive whole of our vast industrial machine. Our factories and our shipyards are constantly expanding. Our output must be multiplied.

It cannot be hampered by the selfish obstruction of any small but dangerous minority of industrial managers who perhaps hold out for extra profits or for "business as usual." It cannot be hampered by the selfish obstruction of a small but dangerous minority of labor leaders who are a menace —

for labor as a whole knows that that small minority is a menace — to the true cause of labor itself, as well as to the nation as a whole.

The lines of our essential defense now cover all the seas; and to meet the extraordinary demands of today and tomorrow our Navy grows to unprecedented size. Our Navy is ready for action. Indeed, units of it in the Atlantic Patrol are in action. Its officers and men need no praise from me.

Our new army is steadily developing the strength needed to withstand the aggressors. Our soldiers of today are worthy of the proudest traditions of the United States Army. But traditions cannot shoot down dive bombers or destroy tanks. That is why we must and shall provide for every one of our soldiers equipment and weapons — not merely as good but better than that of any other army on earth. And we are doing that right now.

For this — and all of this — is what we mean by total national defense.

The first objective of that defense is to stop Hitler. He can be stopped and can be compelled to dig in. And that will be the beginning of the end of his downfall, because dictatorship of the Hitler type can live only through continuing victories — increasing conquests. The facts of 1918 are proof that a mighty German Army and a tired German people can crumble rapidly and go to pieces when they are faced with successful resistance.

Nobody who admires qualities of courage and endurance can fail to be stirred by the full-fledged resistance of the Russian people. The Russians are fighting for their own soil and their own homes. Russia needs all kinds of help — planes, tanks, guns, medical supplies, and other aids — toward the successful defense against the invaders. From the United States and from Britain, she is getting great quantities of those essential supplies. But the needs of her huge Army will

continue — and our help and British help will have to continue.

The other day the secretary of state of the United States was asked by a senator to justify our giving aid to Russia. His reply was: "The answer to that, Senator, depends on how anxious a person is to stop and destroy the march of Hitler in his conquest of the world. If he were anxious enough to defeat Hitler, he would not worry about who was helping to defeat him."

Upon our American production falls the colossal task of equipping our own armed forces and helping to supply the British, the Russians, and the Chinese. In the performance of that task we dare not fail. And we will not fail.

It has not been easy for us Americans to adjust ourselves to the shocking realities of a world in which the principles of common humanity and common decency are being mowed down by the firing squads of the Gestapo. We have enjoyed many of God's blessings. We have lived in a broad and abundant land, and by our industry and productivity we have made it flourish.

There are those who say that our great good fortune has betrayed us; that we are now no match for the regimented masses who have been trained in the Spartan ways of ruthless brutality. They say that we have grown fat and flabby and lazy, and that we are doomed. But those who say that know nothing of America or of American life. They do not know that this land is great because it is a land of endless challenge.

Our country was first populated, and it has been steadily developed, by men and women in whom there burned the spirit of adventure and restlessness and individual independence which will not tolerate oppression. Ours has been a story of vigorous challenges which have been accepted and overcome; challenges of uncharted seas, of wild forests and desert plains, of raging floods and withering drought, of foreign tyrants and domestic strife, of staggering problems, social, economic, and physical; and we have come out of them the most powerful nation, and the freest, in all of history.

Today, in the face of this newest and greatest challenge of them all, we Americans have cleared our decks and taken our battle stations. We stand ready in the defense of our nation and the faith of our fathers to do what God has given us the power to see as our full duty.

---

24.

## Robert A. Taft: Opposition to the Roosevelt War Policies

*Following the German U-642 attack on the U.S.S. Greer on September 4, 1941, President Roosevelt had ordered the Navy to "shoot on sight" upon any encounter with a German submarine. He asked Congress to revise the neutrality laws to permit the arming of merchant vessels; and on October 27 he had called for a total defense effort against Germany. Congressional debate was intense; the leading opponent of the President's program was Senator Robert A. Taft, who delivered a speech in the Senate on October 28, from which the following selection is taken. On November 7, in spite of the opposition, the Senate complied with the President's request for a change in the neutrality laws, and six days later the House also concurred.*

Source: *Record,* 77 Cong., 1 Sess., pp. 8278-8284.

Mr. President, the adoption of the joint resolution now before the Senate would be direct authority from the Congress to the President to carry on an undeclared war against Germany, Italy, and Japan on all the oceans of the world and in all the ports into which seagoing ships may sail. If the members of the Senate intend to keep their pledges to the people of the United States, pledges made by themselves, by their leaders, and by their parties, they can only vote "No" on the pending measure.

I intend today to present only one proposition, that the adoption of the resolution is equivalent to authorizing war. I recognize that there are many who feel that war is justified. There is every reason why they should support the resolution. I, myself, am convinced that the entry of the United States into the present war would be unwise and useless and destructive in the end to our own people and our own government.

The time given to the opponents of the pending measure, particularly those not on the Committee on Foreign Relations, has been so short that I have been unable to prepare my remarks on the general question, which is the real issue before us today, whether we should go to war; but there still seem to remain some remnants of the argument which was advanced when the Lease-Lend Bill was before Congress, that this is in fact a move for peace. There are still in the President's statement, the message proposing the legislation, these words:

> The revisions which I suggest do not call for a declaration of war any more than the Lend-Lease Act called for a declaration of war.

Technically, the President is correct. They do not call for a declaration of war. But the suggestion given to the people that we may remain at peace and still adopt this resolution is one which apparently has impressed some members of the public, and apparently is going to be a reason given by some of those who vote for the pending resolution for their support of it.

Mr. President, I cannot understand the position of those senators. Those who have read the President's speeches, and those who heard his speech last night, can hardly doubt that he is proposing that the United States carry on an undeclared naval war, and that in the passage of this resolution he is asking Congress for authority for him to carry on such a war.

The repeal of Sections 2 and 3 of the Neutrality Act would mean the dispatch of American ships into British ports through the submarine blockade of the Germans. It cannot be doubted that many of those ships would be sunk and that many Americans would be drowned. It cannot be doubted that that would be the first result of our vote here to repeal the Neutrality Act and authorize Americans and American ships, not only authorize them but perhaps order them, to proceed into the battlefields of Europe.

It was just such sinkings and such deaths which took us into the World War. It is an almost inevitable cause of complete war. It is probably more likely to be so now than it was in the World War, because now these ships would be invariably carrying contraband manufactured by the United States and shipped by us to the British in order to enable them to carry on war

against Germany. There could hardly be any doubt in the mind of any German commander as to any such ship that it would be carrying contraband.

It is only because of the provisions of the Neutrality Act which we are asked to repeal that we are not at war today.

As the senator from Michigan [Mr. Vandenberg] pointed out, that is not really a neutrality act but an act to keep the United States out of war, and it has up to this time accomplished its purpose. If it had been carried out in good faith, there would be little danger of war today instead of great danger of war.

After all, it is common sense. Regardless of international law, regardless of history two great nations today are at war, and the actual battlefields of that war are the waters which surround Great Britain. There is no other battlefield between the English and the Germans except that battlefield into which we now are going to send our ships and our men. No neutral can venture into a battlefield without danger to its property and its citizens and danger of becoming involved in war. Human nature being what it is, incidents involving American ships and American citizens are likely to lead to war, and because of the death of 11 men, or of 100 men, millions may be sent to slaughter.

It seems common sense to say that in the interest of all of us, Americans shall keep away from battlefields far from our own land. But more than anything else, the actual experience of the World War, the inevitable result of shipping contraband to a belligerent nation through such a zone, is conclusive proof of what will happen if we repeal this law.

Mr. President, I wish to review briefly the various foreign policies that this country has adopted since I have been a member of the Senate. When I came here in 1939 the arms embargo was in effect. It prohibited the shipment of munitions of any kind to any belligerent nation. It was an extreme measure. Personally, I did not favor it and I voted for its repeal because I felt that a policy of arms embargo — absolute refusal to permit anybody to come here and buy arms — was for the benefit of the strong nation, the nation which built up a great warlike force, and against the weak nation. But I voted for repeal of the measure principally because it was accompanied by provisions which reinstated in the law the cash-and-carry provisions of the former act which had then expired and which were no longer in effect. If we had not enacted that law, American ships could have gone through the war zone to Great Britain, unless they were actually carrying contraband.

We adopted then the policy No. 2, the cash-and-carry policy. That was just two years ago, and there are few senators here who did not vote for that measure, or at least of the senators who are likely to vote for the pending measure there are very few who did not vote for the establishment of that cash-and-carry policy. I myself believe it was a sound policy. I believe it was the policy which has kept us out of war. I believe that the policy of saying that any persons may come here if they please and purchase goods, provided the title is transferred to them before the goods leave here, provided they pay for the goods, and provided they carry them away in their own ships, is the policy which is sound and is the only policy which ever will keep the United States out of European wars.

Mr. President, I should like to call attention to the fact that by the pending joint resolution nearly all the senators are being asked to reverse the position which they took at that time, for those who voted for the repeal of the arms embargo and those who voted against it were unanimous in the belief that the establishment of the cash-and-carry policy was the best method of keeping the United States out of war. The record is full of statements which bear out that conclusion.

I should like to read what the President himself said in the campaign of 1940 about the Neutrality Law, in which he took credit for setting up this cash-and-carry system. He said at Madison Square Garden:

By the Neutrality Act of 1935, and by other steps, we made it possible to prohibit American citizens from traveling on vessels belonging to countries at war. Was that right? We made it clear that American investors who put their money into enterprises in foreign nations could not call on American warships or soldiers to bail out their investments. Was that right?

The President went on:

We made it clear that ships flying the American flag could not carry munitions to a belligerent and that they must stay out of war zones. Was that right?

In all these ways —

The President said:

we made it clear to every American, and to every foreign nation that we would avoid becoming entangled through some episode beyond our borders. These were measures to keep us at peace. And through all the years of war since 1935, there has been no entanglement, and there will be no entanglement.

That was the statement of the President of the United States just about a year ago. That certainly was a pledge to the people of the United States that he intended to pursue the policy for which he was claiming credit.

The President today, by asking for the repeal of this law, is repudiating his promise made to the American people, and no future historian will question my statement. . . .

Cash-and-carry was policy No. 2. Then we gradually adopted a third policy — perhaps only a modification of the second. For purposes of convenience I shall call it policy

United Press International

Republicans in the Senate opposed to Roosevelt's Lend-Lease Bill included (left to right) Robert A. Taft, Alexander R. Wiley, and Gerald P. Nye

No. 3. After the downfall of France and the disaster at Dunkerque, we added to the cash-and-carry policy the theory of aid to Britain short of war. That was the policy that prevailed during the entire election campaign of 1940. I do not know exactly what that aid to Britain implied. It was necessarily vague; but at the time it seemed to me very clearly to imply that we would organize our industry so that we could build tanks, airplanes, and every other kind of war material and make it available to be bought by the British.

Let me say that we could have done nothing at that time or since that would have been of more aid to the British than that one thing. That was the thing which Mr. Willkie emphasized in his campaign. That the thing to help the British was production of materials. Yet during that whole period we took practically no steps toward efficient organization of American industry. There was a Council of National Defense, made up of seven men, each one independent, without a chairman, each one reporting to the President. The machinery was so cumbersome that the moment the election was over it was changed and another form of organization was attempted. Production of materials was the meaning of aid to Britain; and I think it is fairly clear that that is what aid to Britain meant to the candidates and to the parties.

The Democratic platform said this about aid to Britain:

In self-defense and in good conscience, the world's greatest democracy cannot afford heartlessly or in a spirit of appeasement to ignore the peace-loving and liberty-loving peoples wantonly attacked by ruthless aggressors. We pledge to extend to these peoples all the material aid at our command consistent with law and not inconsistent with the interests of our own national self-defense, all to the end that peace and international good faith may yet emerge triumphant.

"Consistent with law," I suppose, meant the Neutrality Law. There was not the slightest suggestion that that law was to be repealed, and presumably the pledge meant that aid must be consistent with the Neutrality Law.

The Republican platform was approximately the same. With respect to aid to Britain it said:

> We favor the extension to all peoples fighting for liberty, or whose liberty is threatened, of such aid as shall not be in violation of international law or inconsistent with the requirements of our own national defense.

There never was a suggestion at any time during that campaign that the policy of aid to Britain short of war meant anything but what it said — aid to Britain short of war. There was nothing that indicated or in any way implied an intention to repeal the Neutrality Law. In fact, Mr. Roosevelt and Mr. Willkie went far to make it clear that they were going to keep away from Europe altogether. Those were the pledges they gave to the American people. Those pledges have been frequently quoted here. President Roosevelt said:

> To every man, woman, and child in the nation I say this: Your President and your secretary of state are following the road to peace. We are arming ourselves not for any foreign war. We are arming ourselves not for any purpose of conquest or intervention in foreign disputes. I repeat again that I stand on the platform of our party.

Mr. Willkie went a little further. At Cleveland on Oct. 2, 1940, he said:

> The American people do not want war. They have no idea whatever of joining in any conflict, whether on the Atlantic or the Pacific. They are determined to keep America at peace. In this determination I stand with them. I am for keeping out of war. I am for peace for America. We must not rashly move. Any man who involves us in the risk of war betrays his country.

Policy No. 3 was the policy of aid to Britain short of war. If either of those gentlemen had advocated the repeal of the Neutrality Act he would have signed his own political death warrant. The other man would have won in that election because the people wanted the pledge of peace. They would have repudiated any man who had said, "We will repeal the Neutrality Act and take our chance of war." I am afraid they would even have repudiated any man who had said, "In this aid to Britain I intend to remove the cash provisions of the Neutrality Act and give Britain $13 billion." I do not think any candidate could have made such a statement and carried the suffrage of the American people. Such action was not part of that policy.

If that policy had been administered with fairness and in good faith and if we had in fact tried to aid Britain short of war, the policy would have worked. We could have kept out of the difficulty in which we now find ourselves. We could have built up our production much faster. We could have gone on. We certainly could have been six months or perhaps a year ahead of where we are now, and Britain and Russia might have had the material which they need and which they do not now have. That kind of aid to Britain would have been more effective than the repeal of the Neutrality Act and the substitution of American ships going to Britain for British ships going to Britain.

That policy was an effective and reasonable policy and one that could have been successfully carried out. But the President was determined to go on, and so he came to foreign policy No. 4. Each policy was a step closer to war. He proposed the Lease-Lend Bill. The Lease-Lend Bill, of course, repealed the cash provisions of the Neutrality Act. It had not been mentioned before the campaign or during the campaign. There was not even a proposal to extend credits to Britain. I do not say that we should not have changed our policy and extended credits to Britain; but the lease-lend policy was still a policy that might have been administered without taking us into war. When that bill passed I said — and I now believe — that we gave authority to the President to take us into war if he should see fit to do so. But it was a policy that did not necessarily involve us in war.

There has been much talk to the effect that we must pass the pending measure to carry out the policy of the Lease-Lend Act, but the policy of the Lease-Lend Act never involved the idea of delivery of materials to England.

It is true that the Lease-Lend Act repealed the "cash" end of the cash-and-carry policy, but it did not repeal the "carry" end of that policy; and, after all, it was the "carry" end of the policy that was primarily dangerous in respect to involving us in war. That was the point on which practically everyone spoke. That was the thing which practically got us into the World War, and that was the important end of the cash-and-carry policy.

The President himself, even in his message asking for the passage of the Lease-Lend Bill, simply said:

> I also ask this Congress for authority and for funds sufficient to manufacture additional munitions and war supplies of many kinds to be turned over to those nations which are now in actual war with aggressor nations. . . . I recommend that we make it possible for those nations to continue to obtain war materials in the United States. . . .

He did not say anything about delivering materials.

The lease-lend policy is a perfectly understandable policy. It is a policy of standing on the line of the Atlantic and Pacific oceans, of defending ourselves, of building up a defense sufficiently strong so that no one will attack us, and then saying to the rest of the world, "We are not going to be concerned with your problems; but if any man is attacked unjustly, if any man is attacked by an aggressor, he may come here and get all the arms he needs with which to defend himself against that aggression." . . .

Mr. President, that was the lease-lend policy. That was the policy upon which the President has tried to justify all his more recent warlike acts. That was the policy which does not in fact justify in any way any of those warlike acts. The Lease-Lend Act stepped beyond neutrality. We did abandon real neutrality when we passed the Lease-Lend Bill; but we still avoided any physical contact with Germany. The important part of the Lease-Lend Act was that, while it extended credit in this country, it did not in any way authorize sending American vessels or anything else into the war zones of Europe, and it continued in effect the existing prohibitions.

If that policy had been administered in good faith, we would not today be in danger of war. It could have been so administered. It gave cause for war; but under the circumstances that exist in the world there is no reason to suppose that what we are doing under the Lease-Lend Act could finally have involved us in the European war unless the President chose to exercise to a greater extent than he actually has the powers contained in that act. . . .

Mr. President, the next step, policy No. 5, is that of undeclared naval war. That is a step beyond the Lease-Lend Act. It is a step which we have partially taken. I think we have taken it without authority of law, but the President has certainly moved toward an undeclared naval war. The incident of the *Kearny* is to some extent war. Today, however, we have the opportunity of passing on the question whether we are going to step from the lease-lend policy, under which other nations come to this country, to a policy of undeclared naval war on the two oceans of the world and in every port into which a seagoing ship may go. If we refuse to repeal the Neutrality Act, there is a probability that the President will withdraw from that policy, but if we pass the pending measure, if we repeal the Neutrality Law, we confirm, ratify, and approve everything the President has done and everything he has said. We approve the occupation of Iceland; we approve the orders to shoot on sight; we approve the patrolling and convoying American vessels, not only in the somewhat restricted areas where they have been patrolling and convoying but all the way to the ports of Great Britain; for the only reason that the convoy has not extended to the ports of Great Britain is the fact that the American merchant ships, even if convoyed, cannot go into the war zones of Europe. We do not know that that step itself has not been taken.

The policy of undeclared naval war, it seems to me, is not a very effective policy of aiding Britain. There has not been any destruction of any great percentage of leaselend goods or any other goods; there is not any evidence that the British have not got enough ships of their own. They have something like, so far as I can figure, three times as many ships as the Americans have; and there is plenty of neutral shipping. It is a little difficult to see how they are going to be benefited by American merchant ships sailing to England instead of neutral or British merchant ships sailing to England.

The senator from Michigan yesterday pointed out that arming ships is of no great assistance to the ships. It is very doubtful, indeed, whether it will save any merchant ships or whether it will do any good to the British.

But there is not any question that the adoption of policy No. 5 is a policy of war, a policy of war which every party in this country has denied that it wishes to adopt, and which every senator has denied that he wishes to adopt. It cannot be long, in my opinion, after that policy is adopted, before we have policy No. 6, the policy of complete war, including the sending of troops to Europe or to Africa or to Asia. It is almost impossible to engage in a partial war. If there is actual shooting; if every day there are engagements between American war vessels and German war vessels; if

American sailors are killed day by day, certainly the American people are going to feel that they are fully at war; that it is our war.

They had thought up to now that it was a question of aiding Britain, but once it is our own war there is no stopping short of anything which may be necessary to defeat the enemy; and that necessarily includes an A. E. F. It happened in the World War. The record of President Wilson shows without question that when we went into that war he expected to fight a naval war; he did not intend to send any troops to Europe. It was about three months before he was persuaded to change his mind; before he saw, as we can now see, that a nation cannot engage in an undeclared naval war unless it is prepared to do everything in the world to win that war. That means necessarily the sending of an A. E. F. to Europe. We are getting there. In the World War we first sent a detachment of engineers. They were the first units. Just as President Wilson was persuaded to send a token unit to Europe, and they were reviewed by the King, so this week we read that the King and Queen reviewed 100 Americans who are in the C. T. C., and about 12 naval lieutenants, officers of the American Navy, who were standing up in parade before the King of England.

We have seen this week a demand for doubling the tank program and doubling the airplane program. What possible use is that going to have except for an American expeditionary force? We have the demand now from the British generals for such a force. Such a force probably is not contemplated for a year or more, but what else can be the purpose of this tank program? We have ordered tanks for 3 million men already. Why double the tank program unless we are looking forward to an A. E. F.? If we pass this joint resolution, we should look forward to an A. E. F., and will have to prepare to win the war which we would vote if we adopted this resolution.

If we go ahead now and abandon the

policy of cash-and-carry, if we proceed to vote to authorize American vessels to carry on this war all the way over to the shores of Germany, then I say that the next step, which is the last step of complete war, is on our threshold.

A naval war is bound to be indecisive. It may be that the President hopes that we may win the war against Hitler without sending our troops; but even he cannot feel confident of any such result, and when for six months or twelve months there has been a completely indecisive result, the cry will grow louder and louder that we must finish this war; and the way the war can be finished is by sending perhaps a million men to Africa and later on two or three million men to Europe. There is no other way by which Hitler can be crushed. . . .

Mr. President, I would feel less confident of the inevitable result if it had not been true that all the steps which have been taken seem to have tended so steadily toward war that any reasonable man must conclude that they were intended to tend toward war. I have pointed out how one policy after another could have been administered without taking us into war, without taking the next step. There was no popular pressure for any such step, and yet every step was followed by one more step, by one more evidence that the administration itself is really desiring a policy of complete war with Germany. Otherwise, how could the President permit the remarks which have been made by members of his Cabinet? We have had Mr. Knox declaring war not only on Hitler but also on Japan, we have had Mr. Stimson declaring war, and Mr. Ickes declaring war. Certainly no responsible President could permit members of his Cabinet to make speeches advocating war unless he was, at least, contemplating such a policy or unless, at least, that policy was agreeable to him. To my mind, if he does not repudiate these statements, it is impossible for him to avoid the just charge that he himself is stimulating the policy of war.

We had an eight-point declaration by which the United States and Great Britain, or, at least, the President of the United States and His Majesty's government in Great Britain, entered into an agreement which was somewhat vague in its terms but which was interpreted by Mr. Churchill shortly afterward; and the President has never in any way modified or repudiated the statement of Mr. Churchill. Mr. Churchill said this in his speech:

> You will, perhaps, have noticed that the President of the United States and the British representative, in what is aptly called the Atlantic Charter, have jointly pledged their countries to the final destruction of the Nazi tyranny. That is a solemn and grave undertaking. It must be made good. It will be made good. And, of course, many practical arrangements to fulfill that purpose have been and are being organized and set in motion.

Mr. Churchill says that the President has pledged his country "to the final destruction of the Nazi tyranny." No reasonable man can interpret those words to mean anything except an intention to go to war. There is no other way to crush the Nazi tyranny. Mr. Churchill further said:

> The United States and Great Britain do not now assume that there will never be any more war again. On the contrary, we —

that is, the United States and Great Britain —

> intend to take ample precaution to prevent its renewal in any period we can foresee, by effectively disarming the guilty nations while remaining suitably protected ourselves.

"While effectively disarming the guilty nations" — Germany, Italy, and Japan. I do not see how those words can be interpreted in any way except as an intention to go to war. . . .

Mr. President, the whole approach of the administration today seems to be one of war. I think it is fair to say — at least, the impression given from the newspapers is — that the administration welcomes every incident which may possibly lead to war. Those incidents are not reported in the usual way. They are announced by the President at a press conference. They are sent out to the world as something by which, on the whole, the government is delighted. The story of the *Greer* was told by the President, it seems to me, in such a way as deliberately to incite more feeling than was justified by the actual event which occurred. He said, for instance:

> Our destroyer at the time was in waters which the government of the United States had declared to be waters of self-defense, surrounding outposts of American protection in the Atlantic. The United States destroyer, when attacked, was proceeding on a legitimate mission.

As a matter of fact, the facts which came out much later before a committee, when the public had forgotten the *Greer*, show that it was in the neighborhood of a submarine of which it was told by a British destroyer which was also there; that after it had located the submarine a British plane came and dropped four depth bombs; and that the *Greer* then turned off its course and chased the submarine for three hours and twenty minutes, zigzagging in the way that a vessel would zigzag if it were going to attack a submarine. Whether or not the submarine was justified in finally shooting a torpedo, whether or not it thought this was a joint British-American attack, certainly the President's report of the incident was made in such a way as deliberately to incite the American people. No man who sincerely desired peace would have failed to state the actual circumstances.

I do not know what happened to the *Kearny*. We still do not know for certain; but it seems almost certain that the *Kearny* was engaged in convoying, not American ships but British and neutral ships, from this country. But the President did not so advise the American people. . . .

Mr. President, I may say that convoying was proposed last spring, but there was so much opposition to convoys that authority to convoy never was specifically presented to Congress. Apparently without such presentation we now have the United States engaged in convoying. But the point I wanted to make is that the whole intention of the administration, every indication that a reasonable man can draw from its acts, is that it intends to go into war; and certainly, if we pass this resolution, and the administration has such an intention, we are going very shortly to become involved in war.

There is no argument made today that, after all, we are already at war, and therefore we should not hesitate to go on and vote authority to conduct war. The power to declare war rests solely in the United States Congress. If the President can declare or create an undeclared naval war beyond our power to act upon, the Constitution might just as well be abolished. The Constitution deliberately gave to the representatives of the people the power to declare war, to pass on the question of war and peace, because that was something which kings had always done, which they had done against the interests of the people themselves, and which the founders of the Constitution thought the people ought to determine. It is true there have been one or two acts of war; but if Congress will refuse to repeal the Neutrality Act, I do not believe those acts of war can be continued.

I do not believe the President is prepared to defy the express action of the Congress. Up to date he has not purported to do so. He has only claimed a power which I do not think he has. I stated on the floor of the Senate that I did not think he had the power to send American troops to Iceland because Iceland was not in the Western

Hemisphere, and it was already in the war zone. There was already there a British garrison. We have undertaken a joint defense of Iceland together with the British, who are actually at war with Germany. We can withdraw from Iceland. If we are sending convoys — as we are sending them — we can stop the policy of convoying vessels to Great Britain.

I do not think we are at war. I think the people who say we are at war now will find that when war actually comes it will be something very different. There will be long casualty lists, a constant series of battles, constant incitement of the people to war, gradually building up a bigger and bigger Army, until it is big enough to undertake a trip to Europe.

## 25.

## FRANKLIN D. ROOSEVELT: Request for a Declaration of War

*On September 27, 1940, Germany, Italy, and Japan signed the Tripartite Pact, thus bringing Japan's "Greater East Asia Co-Prosperity Sphere" within the Axis coalition. From that time on, American resistance to Japanese expansionism increased. Negotiations between Japan and the United States toward a peaceful solution of Far Eastern problems were still under way when, on December 7, 1941, Japan attacked Pearl Harbor in Hawaii. The next day, President Roosevelt went before Congress to ask for a declaration of war against Japan. On December 9 he spoke to the nation by radio, describing the events that had led to war. The message of December 8 and portions of the radio address are reprinted below. The United States formally entered the war against Germany and Italy on December 11.*

Source: *Record,* 77 Cong., 1 Sess., pp. 9519-9520.
    *Record, App.,* 77 Cong., 1 Sess., pp. A5509-A5511.

## I.

### Message to Congress

YESTERDAY, DECEMBER 7, 1941 — a date which will live in infamy — the United States of America was suddenly and deliberately attacked by naval and air forces of the Empire of Japan.

The United States was at peace with that nation, and, at the solicitation of Japan, was still in conversation with its government and its emperor looking toward the mainte-

nance of peace in the Pacific. Indeed, one hour after Japanese air squadrons had commenced bombing in Oahu, the Japanese ambassador to the United States and his colleague delivered to the secretary of state a formal reply to a recent American message. While this reply stated that it seemed useless to continue the existing diplomatic negotiations, it contained no threat or hint of war or armed attack.

It will be recorded that the distance of Hawaii from Japan makes it obvious that the attack was deliberately planned many

United Press International

President Roosevelt appearing before a joint session of Congress calling for a declaration of war against Japan, Dec. 8, 1941

days or even weeks ago. During the intervening time the Japanese government has deliberately sought to deceive the United States by false statements and expressions of hope for continued peace.

The attack yesterday on the Hawaiian Islands has caused severe damage to American naval and military forces. Very many American lives have been lost. In addition, American ships have been reported torpedoed on the high seas between San Francisco and Honolulu.

Yesterday the Japanese government also launched an attack against Malaya.

Last night Japanese forces attacked Hong Kong.

Last night Japanese forces attacked Guam.

Last night Japanese forces attacked the Philippine Islands.

Last night the Japanese attacked Wake Island.

This morning the Japanese attacked Midway Island.

Japan has, therefore, undertaken a sur-

prise offensive extending throughout the Pacific area. The facts of yesterday speak for themselves. The people of the United States have already formed their opinions and well understand the implications to the very life and safety of our nation.

As commander in chief of the Army and Navy I have directed that all measures be taken for our defense.

Always will we remember the character of the onslaught against us. No matter how long it may take us to overcome this premeditated invasion, the American people, in their righteous might, will win through to absolute victory. I believe I interpret the will of the Congress and of the people when I assert that we will not only defend ourselves to the uttermost but will make very certain that this form of treachery shall never endanger us again.

Hostilities exist. There is no blinking at the fact that our people, our territory, and our interests are in grave danger.

With confidence in our armed forces — with the unbounded determination of our people — we will gain the inevitable triumph — so help us God.

I ask that the Congress declare that since the unprovoked and dastardly attack by Japan on Sunday, December 7, a state of war has existed between the United States and the Japanese Empire.

## II.

### Fireside Chat

THE SUDDEN CRIMINAL ATTACKS perpetrated by the Japanese in the Pacific provide the climax of a decade of international immorality.

Powerful and resourceful gangsters have banded together to make war upon the whole human race. Their challenge has now been flung at the United States of America. The Japanese have treacherously violated the long-standing peace between us. Many American soldiers and sailors have been killed by enemy action. American ships have been sunk, American airplanes have been destroyed.

The Congress and the people of the United States have accepted that challenge.

Together with other free peoples, we are now fighting to maintain our right to live among our world neighbors in freedom and in common decency, without fear of assault. . . .

We are now in this war. We are all in it — all the way. Every single man, woman, and child is a partner in the most tremendous undertaking of our American history. We must share together the bad news and the good news, the defeats and the victories — the changing fortunes of war.

So far, the news has all been bad. We have suffered a serious setback in Hawaii. Our forces in the Philippines, which include the brave people of that commonwealth, are taking punishment, but are defending themselves vigorously. The reports from Guam and Wake and Midway islands are still confused, but we must be prepared for the announcement that all these three outposts have been seized.

The casualty lists of these first few days will undoubtedly be large. I deeply feel the anxiety of all families of the men in our armed forces and the relatives of people in cities which have been bombed. I can only give them my solemn promise that they will get news just as quickly as possible.

This government will put its trust in the stamina of the American people and will give the facts to the public as soon as two conditions have been fulfilled: first, that the information has been definitely and officially confirmed; and, second, that the release of the information at the time it is received will not prove valuable to the enemy, directly or indirectly.

Most earnestly I urge my countrymen to reject all rumors. These ugly little hints of complete disaster fly thick and fast in wartime. They have to be examined and appraised. As an example, I can tell you frankly that until further surveys are made, I have not sufficient information to state the exact damage which has been done to our naval vessels at Pearl Harbor. Admittedly the damage is serious. But no one can say how serious until we know how much of this damage can be repaired and how quickly the necessary repairs can be made.

I cite as another example a statement made on Sunday night that a Japanese carrier had been located and sunk off the Canal Zone. And when you hear statements that are attributed to what they call "an authoritative source," you can be reasonably sure that under these war circumstances the "authoritative source" was not any person in authority.

Many rumors and reports which we now hear originate with enemy sources. For instance, today the Japanese are claiming that as a result of their one action against Hawaii they have gained naval supremacy in the Pacific. This is an old trick of propaganda which has been used innumerable times by the Nazis. The purposes of such fantastic claims are, of course, to spread fear and confusion among us and to goad us into revealing military information which our enemies are desperately anxious to obtain. Our government will not be caught in this obvious trap — and neither will our people.

It must be remembered by each and every one of us that our free and rapid communication must be greatly restricted in wartime. It is not possible to receive full, speedy, accurate reports from distant areas of combat. This is particularly true where naval operations are concerned. For in these days of the marvels of radio it is often impossible for the commanders of various units to report their activities by radio, for the very simple reason that this information would become available to the enemy, and would disclose their position and their plan of defense or attack.

Of necessity there will be delays in officially confirming or denying reports of operations, but we will not hide facts from the country if we know the facts and if the enemy will not be aided by their disclosure.

To all newspapers and radio stations — all those who reach the eyes and ears of the American people — I say this: You have a most grave responsibility to the nation now and for the duration of this war. If you feel that your government is not disclosing enough of the truth, you have every right to say so. But — in the absence of all the facts, as revealed by official sources — you have no right to deal out unconfirmed reports in such a way as to make people believe they are gospel truth.

Every citizen, in every walk of life, shares this same responsibility. The lives of our soldiers and sailors — the whole future of this nation — depend upon the manner in which each and every one of us fulfills his obligation to our country.

Now a word about the recent past — and the future. A year and a half has elapsed since the fall of France, when the whole world first realized the mechanized might which the Axis nations had been building for so many years. America has used that year and a half to great advantage. Knowing that the attack might reach us in all too short a time, we immediately began greatly to increase our industrial strength and our capacity to meet the demands of modern warfare.

Precious months were gained by sending vast quantities of our war materials to the nations of the world still able to resist Axis aggression. Our policy rested on the fundamental truth that the defense of any country resisting Hitler or Japan was in the long run the defense of our own country. That policy has been justified. It has given us time, invaluable time, to build our American assembly lines of production. Assembly lines are now in operation. Others are being rushed to completion. A steady stream of tanks and planes, of guns and ships, of shells and equipment — that is what these eighteen months have given us.

But it is all only a beginning of what has to be done. We must be set to face a long war against crafty and powerful bandits. The attack at Pearl Harbor can be repeated at any one of many points in both oceans and along both our coastlines and against all the rest of the hemisphere.

It will not only be a long war, it will be a hard war. That is the basis on which we now lay all our plans. That is the yardstick by which we measure what we shall need and demand — money, materials, doubled and quadrupled production, ever increasing. The production must be not only for our own Army and Navy and air forces. It must reinforce the other armies and navies and air forces fighting the Nazis and the war lords of Japan throughout the Americas and the world.

I have been working today on the subject of production. Your government has decided on two broad policies. The first is to speed up all existing production by working on a seven-day-week basis in every war industry, including the production of essential raw materials. The second policy, now being put into form, is to rush additions to the capacity of production by building more new plants, by adding to old plants, and by using the many smaller plants for war needs.

Over the hard road of the past months we have at times met obstacles and difficulties, divisions and disputes, indifference and callousness. That is now all past and, I am sure, forgotten. The fact is that the country now has an organization in Washington built around men and women who are recognized experts in their own fields. I think the country knows that the people who are actually responsible in each and every one of these many fields are pulling together with a teamwork that has never before been excelled.

On the road ahead there lies hard work — gruelling work — day and night, every hour and every minute. I was about to add that ahead there lies sacrifice for all of us. But it is not correct to use that word. The United States does not consider it a sacrifice to do all one can, to give one's best to our nation when the nation is fighting for its existence and its future life.

It is not a sacrifice for any man, old or young, to be in the Army or the Navy of the United States. Rather is it a privilege. It is not a sacrifice for the industrialist or the wage earner, the farmer or the shopkeeper, the trainman or the doctor to pay more taxes, to buy more bonds, to forego extra profits, to work longer or harder at the task for which he is best fitted. Rather is it a privilege. It is not a sacrifice to do without many things to which we are accustomed if the national defense calls for doing without.

A review this morning leads me to the conclusion that at present we shall not have to curtail the normal articles of food. There enough food for all of us and enough left over to send to those who are fighting on the same side with us. There will be a clear and definite shortage of metals of many kinds for civilian use for the very good reason that in our increased program we shall need for war purposes more than half of that portion of the principal metals which during the past year have gone into articles for civilian use. We shall have to give up many things entirely.

I am sure that the people in every part of the nation are prepared in their individual living to win this war. I am sure they will cheerfully help to pay a large part of its financial cost while it goes on. I am sure they will cheerfully give up those material things they are asked to give up. I am sure that they will retain all those great spiritual things without which we cannot win through.

I repeat that the United States can accept no result save victory, final and complete. Not only must the shame of Japanese treachery be wiped out but the sources of international brutality, wherever they exist, must be absolutely and finally broken.

In my message to the Congress yesterday I said that we "will make very certain that this form of treachery shall never endanger us again." In order to achieve that certainty, we must begin the great task that is before us by abandoning once and for all the illusion that we can ever again isolate ourselves from the rest of humanity.

In these past few years — and, most violently, in the past few days — we have learned a terrible lesson. It is our obligation to our dead — it is our sacred obligation to their children and our children — that we must never forget what we have learned.

And what we all have learned is this: There is no such thing as security for any nation — or any individual — in a world ruled by the principles of gangsterism. There is no such thing as impregnable defense against powerful aggressors who sneak up in the dark and strike without warning. We have learned that our ocean-girt hemisphere is not immune from severe attack — that we cannot measure our safety in terms of miles on any map.

We may acknowledge that our enemies have performed a brilliant feat of deception, perfectly timed and executed with great skill. It was a thoroughly dishonorable deed, but we must face the fact that modern warfare as conducted in the Nazi manner is a dirty business. We don't like it — we didn't want to get in it — but we are in it and we're going to fight it with everything we've got.

I do not think any American has any doubt of our ability to administer proper punishment to the perpetrators of these crimes. Your government knows that for weeks Germany has been telling Japan that if Japan did not attack the United States, Japan would not share in dividing the spoils with Germany when peace came. She was promised by Germany that if she came in she would receive the complete and perpetual control of the whole of the Pacific area — and that means not only the Far East, not only all of the islands in the Pacific but also a stranglehold on the west coast of North, Central, and South America. We also know that Germany and Japan are conducting their military and naval operation in accordance with a joint plan. That plan considers all peoples and nations which are not helping the Axis Powers as common enemies of each and every one of the Axis Powers.

That is their simple and obvious grand strategy. That is why the American people must realize that it can be matched only with similar grand strategy. We must realize, for example, that Japanese successes against the United States in the Pacific are helpful to German operations in Libya; that any German success against the Caucasus is inevitably an assistance to Japan in her operations against the Dutch East Indies; that

a German attack against Algiers or Morocco opens the way to a German attack against South America. On the other side of the picture, we must learn to know that guerrilla warfare against the Germans in Serbia helps us; that a successful Russian offensive against the Germans helps us; and that British successes on land or sea in any part of the world strengthen our hands.

Remember always that Germany and Italy, regardless of any formal declaration of war, consider themselves at war with the United States at this moment just as much as they consider themselves at war with Britain and Russia. And Germany puts all the other republics of the Americas into the category of enemies. The people of the hemisphere can be honored by that.

The true goal we seek is far above and beyond the ugly field of battle. When we resort to force, as now we must, we are determined that this force shall be directed toward ultimate good as well as against immediate evil. We Americans are not destroyers; we are builders.

We are now in the midst of a war, not for conquest, not for vengeance, but for a world in which this nation and all that this nation represents will be safe for our children. We expect to eliminate the danger from Japan, but it would serve us ill if we accomplished that and found that the rest of the world was dominated by Hitler and Mussolini.

We are going to win the war, and we are going to win the peace that follows.

And in the dark hours of this day — and through dark days that may be yet to come — we will know that the vast majority of the members of the human race are on our side. Many of them are fighting with us. All of them are praying for us. For, in representing our cause, we represent theirs as well — our hope and their hope for liberty under God.

# 1942

26.

## ROBERT FROST: "The Gift Outright"

*The land, the way of life, and the people of New England inspired Robert Frost to write
much of his finest poetry. However, it was not New England alone but rather the whole of
America that inspired "The Gift Outright." It was an attempt to express the relationship
between the American land and the people who, being given it as a gift, found that
they were called upon to give themselves in return. The poem was first read before
the Phi Beta Kappa Society at William and Mary College on December 5, 1941, and
published in* A Witness Tree *in 1942. Millions of his countrymen remember Frost as
an old man reading the poem at John F. Kennedy's inauguration in January 1961 — or
reciting it from memory, rather, for the sun was so bright on that cold snowy day that
he could not see the words on the paper before him.*

Source: *A Witness Tree*, New York, 1942.

### THE GIFT OUTRIGHT

The land was ours before we were the land's.
She was our land more than a hundred years
Before we were her people. She was ours
In Massachusetts, in Virginia,
But we were England's, still colonials,
Possessing what we still were unpossessed by,
Possessed by what we now no more possessed.
Something we were withholding made us weak
Until we found out that it was ourselves
We were withholding from our land of living,
And forthwith found salvation in surrender.
Such as we were we gave ourselves outright
(The deed of gift was many deeds of war)
To the land vaguely realizing westward,
But still unstoried, artless, unenhanced,
Such as she was, such as she would become.

27.

## BEARDSLEY RUML: The Pay-As-You-Go Income Tax Plan

*In December 1941, when America entered World War II, the federal income tax was
still a "rich man's tax" that was paid by only a .relative handful of citizens. It was
obvious to all not only that taxes on large incomes would increase but also that many
millions of people would have to pay income taxes who had never paid them before.
The question uppermost in the minds of economists and tax experts was how to arrange
the payment of taxes so that the government would be assured of income, on the one
hand, and citizens would not be unduly pressed financially, on the other. A solution
of the problem was proposed by Beardsley Ruml, who suggested a pay-as-you-go
plan whereby wage earners would pay their income taxes, through payroll deductions,
as they earned, rather than paying this year's tax next year, when they might not have
the necessary funds. Congress debated Ruml's suggestion, along with other plans,
throughout much of 1942, finally adopting a Current Tax Payment Act that was signed
into law on June 9, 1943. The following article by Ruml, then chairman of the
Federal Reserve Bank of New York, was introduced into the Congressional Record
by Senator Francis Case of South Dakota on October 15, 1942.*

Source: *Record, App.*, 77 Cong., 2 Sess., pp. A3709-A3710.

THE PAY-AS-YOU-GO INCOME TAX plan has had from the very beginning the hearty support of many officials of state and local governments. These officials see in no uncertain terms the danger that will exist to the financing of their own communities if a load of federal income tax debt is permitted to carry on through the war and into the period beyond the war.

Few people realize how much money they owe the government for income tax. They seem to feel that since they have just paid an installment on September 15, and since the next payment isn't due until December 15, for the time being at least they are not in debt for income tax. They are wrong. They are in debt now for the installment still due this year, and, worse, they are, in addition, in debt for income tax on what they have already earned this year. Under our present system this debt will have to be paid next year whether they then have any income or not.

If they die, this amount will be take from whatever estate they leave. If they los their jobs, there will be a charge again: what they have saved. If their earnings a less, the full tax has to be met out of th lower earnings. Nothing can stop the mar of the days, and when the due date com they must pay the tax they owe on the i come they have already had. It is a re debt, and practically all income-tax paye are actually in debt for about one year's fu income tax.

The present system is a bad system. It a dangerous system for all of us, and should and can be corrected.

Income-tax debt is the meanest kind debt there is because it only hurts peop when they are in trouble. As long as o incomes are the same, or better than th were last year, we can keep on paying that income-tax debt. But if anything happens to this year's income, the income-tax debt remains and there is trouble. Men are called into the armed services; others go into government work at lower pay; men and women are displaced from peacetime industry by wartime dislocation — some suffer sickness and accident; others must retire because of advancing years. All of these find that now, with the new high tax rate, their income-tax debt is an intolerable problem, wiping out savings that have been accumulated over the years, and for tens of thousands that have already been injured, millions of us are in danger because we are each subject to the same hazards and the same inevitable loss of income.

The sooner the problem is solved, the easier it will be to solve. In 1940 there were 4,048,619 income-tax payers; in 1941 there were 7,645,473; in 1942, 17,688,219. On the 1st of January, 1943, under the revenue bill of 1942, there will be 26,900,000 taxpayers in debt to the federal government for tax on their 1942 income — an increase of 22,850,000 since 1940. It is clear that the government cannot continue for long to be the creditor of some 27 million taxpayers and their families in debt for income tax, particularly when there is no substantial question of revenue involved in skipping a year and getting the whole country on a current pay-as-you-go basis.

Not only are the numbers of taxpayers much larger than they were but the amount of debt for each taxpayer is much greater than is commonly understood. Here are the figures now in the new tax bill. Unless we get the pay-as-you-go plan, a man with a taxable net income, after exemptions, of $4,000 in 1942 will owe the government $820 on New Year's Day 1943. If his income as above was $5,000, his debt will be $1,030; and if $10,000, the government will claim $2,620 from him, even though his earnings are lower in 1943, or com-

pletely disappear. If he dies, these sums will be taken from whatever remains of his estate.

The income-tax debt on smaller incomes is likewise startling. For example, a taxable net income, after exemptions, of $2,500 leaves a debt for next year of $490 and even $1,000 means $190 still to be paid. A stenographer who has been making $30 a week during 1942 and who gets married in the early part of next year will carry to the altar an income-tax bill for $192.04; and if she happened to be a secretary getting $50 a week, the happy couple will start off being in debt to Uncle Sam for $386.40 on her account.

If the pay-as-you-go plan is adopted, all these taxpayers will be income-tax-debt free, except for any necessary year-end adjustment. And they will stay on a current paid-up basis, since they will be paying income taxes on what they earn as they earn it.

The pay-as-you-go income-tax plan is a three-way plan; it applies only to individuals and not to corporations. First of all, it is a plan that will relieve thousands of citizens from hardship and distress arising from income-tax debt, and that will bring peace of mind to millions more who are in income-tax-debt danger.

Second, it is a method for clearing the decks for an all-out war-financing program. If we can all be free of income-tax debt on the first of next year, we can start on a pay-as-you-go basis and stay there. If we need high withholding taxes, we can have them; if we need to supplement voluntary savings with compulsory savings, we can do that, too. But whatever is called for, it would be paid out of the current year's income as an assessment on the same year's income. We would not be paying for dead horses while we are fighting a war.

In the third place, the pay-as-you-go income-tax plan is the best kind of financial planning for the postwar period. Our policies can then be forward looking, not backward looking. We will not be trying to collect income taxes from people who are unemployed; we will not be debating whether we should collect taxes on 1941 incomes from men recently demobilized from the armed forces. We will not have a spending spree in the first little boomlet, financed on unpaid taxes, and then a tax-debt headache if incomes should drop off for a year or so.

The answer to the problem is to pay as we go, but the practical question arises — how can we pay our taxes on current income at the same time we are paying our taxes on last year's income? The answer is as simple as daylight saving. When we decided that it was in the national interest to save fuel and power by going to work an hour earlier in the morning, we simply turned all of our clocks ahead and went on with our business.

This is what has been suggested to Congress as the answer to the personal income-tax problem: that we turn our tax clocks ahead 1 year.

The income taxes which we are paying this year are taxes on our 1941 incomes, so what the plan means is that this year the taxes which we are paying out of our 1942 income would be taxes on our 1942 income, and that at the end of the year we would be paid up, or practically so. Then next year in 1943 we would be paying on 1943, and so on.

If at the end of 1942 we have paid too much tax, we will get a credit. If we have not paid enough, we will make up the difference. This adjustment will be made in March of 1943 when we file our new income-tax return. So we shall be out of debt to the federal government on our income tax, and instead be on a continuing cash basis.

In view of the lateness in adopting a tax program, I have suggested that for those taxpayers who have never filed an income-tax return the year 1942 should be skipped for them as a matter of practical necessity.

You may ask how the government can cancel the 1941 income tax without losing a lot of money that is badly needed for the war effort. The answer is this: Since we all go along paying our income tax on our current income, the government will receive in 1943 just as much and perhaps even more revenue than under the present system. The government will ultimately lose the 1941 tax, but this loss will not occur until we either die or stop earning money, which means that the loss will be spread over the lifetime of the present income-tax-paying generation.

The Treasury has never considered taxes receivable as an asset, and so these taxes can be written off the balance sheet of the government without the change of a single penny. The Treasury has made the point that the plan would involve the cancellation of several billions of taxes and that this is no time to cancel taxes; but as the Treasury itself admits, the plan would not reduce tax receipts except over a period of many years, and so since actual revenue is the thing that counts now, mere bookkeeping entries are not important.

The Treasury feels that a withholding tax is highly important in keeping taxpayers current. I, too, favor a withholding tax, because it makes it easier for people to keep on a pay-as-you-go basis. But if we want a withholding tax, the pay-as-you-go plan is the only way to solve the problem of having a withholding tax without having some amount of double taxation, that is, of paying two years' taxes in one. If a withholding-tax provision turns out to be either undesirable or impractical, the pay-as-you-go plan stands on its own feet as a sound method of getting the country free of income-tax debt.

The difficulty with the plan that seems to loom largest in the minds of some is the so-called windfall problem. I pointed out in my original statement that under any plan that gives equal treatment to all taxpayers there will be a certain number of windfall cases, cases of individuals who will benefit unduly because of the fact that for them 1941, or whatever year is skipped, happened to be a year of unusually large income, larger than that of the years that preceded or that followed. Consequently, whatever year is selected, these persons would receive unintended benefits.

In answer, I have pointed out that no tax program will cut with the precision of a surgeon's knife. Furthermore, these few individuals could not have foreseen that this plan would be suggested or adopted, and therefore no deliberate manipulation of income for this purpose is involved.

So far as there is inequity, it resides in being too beneficial to some few taxpayers, but since the plan is beneficial to all and harmful to none, inequity of this kind, though regrettable, is an imperfection of a minor order as compared with the great good that will be achieved.

I have no doubt that once a clear idea has been formed as to what windfall cases under the plan should be taken to be, that provisions can be drawn to catch many of them. I shall suggest certain provisions a little later on. But at best it might not be possible to catch them all — what then?

There are some things that are worse than a few windfall cases. One would be not to adopt any pay-as-you-go plan at all. Another would be to adopt a plan so complicated or so uncertain in its effect that the great good of pay-as-you-go would not be achieved. Another would be not to give equal treatment to all taxpayers under the plan lest the windfall cases receive undue benefits.

Much as I dislike windfalls, even if they cannot be entirely eliminated, I am still for the plan. I cannot bring myself to the point of refusing to do good for millions simply because I will be doing too much good for few that don't deserve it.

I have made the following three suggestions for minimizing the problem of "windfall" cases:

1. Do not cancel the 1941 income tax on capital gains. A large part of the true "windfall" problem comes from capital gains because the year in which the gain is taxed is the year in which the transaction happens to be closed. Capital gains are not like ordinary recurring income and can be properly separated out in the plan.

2. Provide a special death tax to recover what may be considered "windfalls" arising because of death in 1942 or during some appropriate transition period. This tax should be steeply graduated and should take most of the higher-bracket income tax that would be otherwise cancelled, but it should leave some balance of the cancelled tax in the estate subject to ordinary estate taxes only.

3. Take an average of 1940, 1941, and 1942 in all cases where claim for credit exceeds $10,000, or some other suitable amount. The average of the three years will be a practical way of determining a fair normal income for 1941 instead of "windfall" income. The cancellation of 1941 tax would apply to this average income only, and the balance of tax on actual 1941 income to the extent that it exceeded $10,000 would not be credited or refunded.

The Treasury has proposed a modified plan which would apply to the full tax debt of some taxpayers and to only a part of the tax debt of the rest. Concretely, the Treasury proposed that the tax year of 1942 rather than 1941 be skipped, and then for only the lowest two brackets — that is 10 percent — and that the balance of the tax debt remaining should be paid over the next two or three years, this, in addition to current income taxes that will be payable in those years. The Treasury concedes that this would leave between 10 and 20 percent of our taxpayers still owing the government for taxes on their last year's income. This group of 10 to 20 percent includes practically all of administrative, technical, and professional men and women who need freedom from income-tax debt danger as much as anyone else. The Treasury's proposal to change the year from 1941 to 1942 would eliminate from benefits of the plan the millions of men who have gone into the armed services and into the government this year.

Quite apart from the question as to who is included or excluded, or for how much, I personally favor as a matter of principle the overall application of the pay-as-you-go plan for eliminating tax debt, giving all taxpayers equal treatment under the plan. These are my reasons:

For those in the lower brackets the plan will obviously have far-reaching beneficial results, since unfortunate circumstances of loss of income will not be doubly unfortunate because of last year's debt.

For those in the middle brackets, it will eliminate countless personal and family tragedies, free many able citizens for ·public service, and step up the efficiency of American industry by making possible the retirement and pensioning of executives who are holding on, largely to pay their income tax, and never catching up.

For those in the upper brackets, it will make much less practical difference than might appear. First, because, like anybody else, as long as they have their income they continue to pay their taxes; and, second, when they die, what otherwise would have been paid by an individual as income tax on the previous year's income is subject to estate taxes in the highest brackets.

But apart from the practical considerations, the reason I favor overall application of the principle is because it gives equal treatment to all taxpayers under the plan. In adopting pay-as-you-go, by skipping 1941, I believe we should treat all citizens alike; as we turn the tax clock ahead for some, we should turn it ahead for all and get the whole nation out of income-tax debt by the beginning of 1943.

Insofar as we want more equality of income and of wealth, we can have these through the progressive income tax and the progressive inheritance tax, but we should not use this general income-tax reform — pay-as-you-go — unequally to accelerate indirectly the impact of progressive taxation.

The lack of force in the objections which have been made to the plan has been apparent to press and public alike and has been the subject of nationwide comment. The dislike of windfall cases was felt by some, but I have suggested above three methods that would eliminate all of the most objectionable windfall cases. The principle of equal treatment to all taxpayers under the plan has been questioned, but by surprisingly few. I have pointed out that, even if Congress desires to limit the application of this principle, we can still have a pay-as-you-go income-tax plan, but it will leave part of our citizens with a remaining income-tax debt. The specific modified plans suggested by the Treasury have been grossly inadequate so far as eliminating income-tax debt is concerned.

The pay-as-you-go plan was recommended unanimously by a subcommittee of the Senate Finance Committee and was later rejected by the full committee. The plan may be rejected over and over again but these rejections solve no problems. If the plan is killed in committee, it will be introduced on the floor of Congress. If it is killed on the floor before elections, it will reappear after elections. If it is killed in 1942, it will be revived in 1943. The plan stands on its own feet as a legislative measure, and can be enacted to start all of us on a pay-as-you-go basis for 1943 any time up until March 15, 1943, the day the next income-tax declaration has to be made.

I feel that the pay-as-you-go income-tax plan in a form acceptable to Congress will certainly be adopted, because income-taxpayers want to be free of income-tax debt and they know it can be done without hurting the Treasury and without paying two years' taxes in one. The taxpayers know that pay as you go solves the prob lem simply and fairly by skipping an in-come-tax year. They know the whole trou-ble was caused by a basic defect in our in-come-tax law, which has existed from the beginning — that of paying a tax on last year's income out of this year's receipts. The defect was not their fault, and they know it. They want it corrected this year and they want to be on a pay-as-you-go ba-sis by the beginning of 1943.

As a nation of individuals we will be bet-ter able to meet the present and to attack whatever the future has in store for us if we are paid up in our income tax, and, being out of income-tax debt we can pay as we go out of what we earn.

## 28.

# Harold J. Ockenga: Evangelical Christianity

*One of the recurring problems of the Fundamentalists in twentieth-century America was the lack of concerted action in spite of common beliefs and goals. The fault seemed to lie in the excessive individualism of the churches themselves, with their passion for local autonomy and fear of centralized hierarchies. By 1941, it was apparent to many that some cohesion was necessary, especially in view of the influence of the powerful, and liberal, Federal Council of Churches. Evangelicals from all over America convened in St. Louis on April 7, 1942, for a National Conference for United Action Among Evangelicals. The keynote speaker was Dr. Harold Ockenga of Park Street Church in Boston, whose message, "The Unvoiced Multitudes," is reprinted in part below. Out of the convention came a new association, the loosely organized National Association of Evangelicals.*

Source: *Evangelical Action!*, edited by the Executive Committee of the National
Association of Evangelicals for United Action, Boston, 1942, pp. 19-39.

Evangelical Christianity has suffered nothing but a series of defeats for decades. The programs of few major denominations today are controlled by evangelicals. Evan-lical testimony has sometimes been re-duced to the witness of individual churches. New England is an example of this sad situ-ation. Evangelicals, one after another, have been so frozen out that the territory is al-most a mission field. We thank God that certain evidences of revival are now coming, but for more than one hundred years New England was evangelically an arid waste. The enemy has won his victories in over-whelming fashion in Russia, in Germany and Japan, and now he is knocking at our very door. At present our position is very much like that of the small countries sur-rounding Germany or those in the path of Japan. Germany simply isolated one coun-try after another, gave a sense of security to the other countries while it dismembered and conquered the one country, both from without and within. Then it attacked anoth-er. Take one at a time and no combination will be formed sufficiently strong to offset the unified power of Germany.

Thus it is with our evangelicals. One by one various forces have discredited or at-tacked them, or even forced them out of positions of leadership, until today many of them are on the defensive or even the decline. The hour calls for united front for evangelical action. Perhaps you are afraid of that word, but I am not.

Let us learn something from the Soviets and the Nazis. If the children of this world are wiser than the children of light, then it is time for the children of light to open their eyes and learn how to carry on God's work. This is the time, the day for the offensive. Personally, I am just as tired of defensive tactics in ecclesiastical matters as the Americans are tired of defensive tactics on the part of the democracies of the United Nations. In fact, our defensive tactics threaten to be as fatal to us as they have been disastrous to nearly a score of nations of the world. One by one we shall be overwhelmed. Do not be so foolish as to think that though your own personal work is thriving at the present time you will escape.

Analyze this business of the kingdom, if you will, and see wherein any evidence of strength or power exists in America today. I will tell you where I see an evidence of power. It is in Roman Catholicism. There was a day when Boston was a stronghold of evangelical Christianity. Today Roman Catholicism has a practical monopoly. Eighty percent of our citizens are adherents of that faith. It has grown in the 150 years since the first mass was celebrated, until the Roman Catholic cardinal now exercises the dominant and determining political influence, both in the city and in the state legislature. Theirs is a power which cannot be successfully resisted. This is not confined to Boston alone. Check in any major center of the United States today. In fact, the Roman Catholic hierarchy has claimed an increase in membership from 20 million to 35 million in the last decade. If their claims are even half true, it is an amazing growth and a rebuke to the Protestant evangelical forces. Roman Catholicism today is going into the rural areas, into the broadcasting field, into the national magazine field, and into every possible area to reach the masses of the people, and they are reaching them too.

Alongside of Roman Catholicism is that terrible octopus of liberalism, which spreads itself throughout our Protestant Church dominating innumerable organizations, pulpits, and publications, as well as seminaries and other schools. Because of our divided condition, the Federal Council of Churches bids fair to control all government relationships for Protestantism. . . .

Likewise, you need not be told that the Federal Council of Churches has a monopoly on religious broadcasting through the National Broadcasting Company and the Columbia Broadcasting System, although there is yet some leeway in this latter company. I am personally acquainted with several of the officials in the RCA, and I took it upon myself, after corresponding with some of the leading broadcasters, to confer several years ago with the president of the National Broadcasting Company and with the New England manager. As a result, a six-hour conference was held between Mr. Holman, the manager of WBZ and WBZA, Dr. Durham, representative of NBC, and myself, in the Parker House, in Boston. This conference proved to me that, unless there is some such evangelical organization as this movement projected here at St. Louis, we shall have absolutely no opportunity of sharing equally in the broadcasting facilities of that great company. We are a very large minority, perhaps a majority, in America, which is discriminated against because of the folly of our divided condition.

With reference to education. Any evangelical pastor will tell you that materialistic education is the great poison which is spoiling the testimony and message of the majority of our young preachers today. They may go from certain conservative institutions to other institutions and, in many cases, become definitely ruined for Christian faith and action.

The third great influence which is defening evangelical Christianity today is secularism. Floods of iniquity have flowed over America since the great war in a tidal wave of drunkenness, immorality, corruption, dishonesty, and utter atheism. For some reason evangelical Christianity has not been able to cope with this tremendous flood of iniquity; the church simply has not made an impact upon our day, such as it should make if it is in the apostolic succession.

Perhaps I could illustrate this to you in the figure of a river. Grant to me, for the sake of illustration, that man is divided into body, soul, and spirit. From that admission, let us enlarge it to reach society as a whole. There, also, we might speak of body, soul, and spirit; body being the economic structure of society, soul being the political form of society, spirit being the religion dominant in society. In America, using this figure of speech, we should have, first of all, capitalism as the economic form; second, democracy as the political form; third, Christianity as our religious form. Suppose that the economic form is compared to the river, the political form to one bank, and the religious form to the other bank. Within the last few decades we have had what is called the power revolution. Capitalism has gone wild. As a result of the increase of the river the banks should have been diked or reinforced. But what happened simultaneously with this great increase? If we understand it at all, we believe that there has been a disintegration of Christianity; in fact the same thing has been taking place in America which Rauschning described as taking place in Germany before the rise of the Hitler party. He declared flatly that the Christian Church failed Germany in that hour.

With this disintegration of Christianity came the breakup of the moral fiber of the American people. As a result, one bank of the river began to deteriorate while the river rose. In order to offset this the governmental form, namely democracy, attempted, by the increase of bureaus, by "the manage-

rial revolution," and other devices, to overbalance that which was broken down in democracy, namely religion. What was the result? Because our religion failed we have had a revolution in our political form and we have had utter confusion in the whole social state of man. Secularism, in other words, has flooded America. Unless we can have a true revival of evangelical Christianity, able to change the character of men and build up a new moral fiber, we believe Christianity, capitalism, and democracy, likewise, to be imperiled.

Look about you at individuals in our churches. They are defeated, reticent, retiring, and seemingly in despair. Lyman Powell was able to say, in his book on Mary Baker Eddy, that he observed that every time members of the orthodox churches came under the power and influence of Christian Science they became converted to that movement, I might use the word apostatized. Brethren, this ought not to be; this is not evangelical and apostolic Christianity. This sense of isolation and impotency on the part of individuals has driven them into corporate organizations with a strong central governing power, such as the hierarchy of Romanism and into movements such as Christian Science.

It is the same with the missionary movement. There is not a major denominational board of missions in the United States which has not retracted and withdrawn a large percentage of its support in recent years. This is not due to depression or the lack of money, as the laymen's missionary report analyzed it, but it is due to the fundamental change in outlook and thinking of Protestant Christians concerning the nature and purpose of missions. We have found in our own church that when we expressed the true purpose of missions, we increased our gifts 1,000 percent.

To whom are young ministers to look in this day for leadership? To whom am I going to look? I have scanned the horizon of this country for leaders in evangelical Christianity, for men who might blaze a trail of leadership that I might follow, but have found none. This is the condition with innumerable pastors, and it has resulted in dreadful weakness on the part of us all. As a result, Protestantism has turned away from its great preaching mission, the exaltation of the gospel of the cross, to the ceremonialism of an empty cross; the formalism of sacramental religion has been substituted for preaching. You hear men talking about reinstating five or six sacraments in the church instead of two.

In the face of this, we are standing in the most tremendous danger of all. Already a revolution has taken place in our nation. Few people realize this, but it is a fact. Whenever the major part of the business of the nation is being done by the government rather than by private interest, capitalism ceases in its functioning; a new order of society begins. We have seen this take place in America. The crisis is greater than any of us realize. Now, if ever, we need some organ to speak for the evangelical interests, to represent men who, like myself, are "lone wolves" in the church. . . .

Therefore, I believe we must first of all seek unity. This means that this millstone of rugged independency which has held back innumerable movements before, in which individual leaders must be the whole hog or none, must be utterly repudiated by everyone of us. A terrible indictment may be laid against fundamentalism because of its failures, divisions, and controversies. This must be admitted by those of us who believe in the fundamentals and who also seek a new outlook. . . .

Satan's greatest stronghold is the division of Christians into denominations as they are today. In many old churches where Christ was preached for centuries, atheistic philosophy is now presented; in some churches there is no message at all. The division is no longer between denominations; the division is between those who believe in Christ and the Bible, and those who reject Christ — the Christ of the cross and the Bible. Now is the time to forget all of these differences and join together as one with the Crucified One. Calvary should be not only the dividing place between us and the world but it should be our meeting place, where we may jointly bow our heads in praise and thanksgiving for that which has been done for us.

Therefore, I summon you to unity. If the prayer of Jesus on Solomon's porch, that they may be one, was actually answered at Pentecost, then let us demonstrate our unity instead of our division. It is folly to speak of the union of the true Church and then declare that those who profess to believe in the doctrines of the true Church can never work in unity.

The second tradition, I believe, that God would have us hold forth is that of purity. Unless we can have the cardinal evangelical doctrines of Christianity as the fundamental basis of such a program, it is impossible for us to unite; but with these essentials guaranteed to us, even if they are the five major points of the Presbyterian struggle, we can have a basis upon which to unite. This leads me to say that I am of the hearty conviction that our program must not be negative but it must be positive. We cannot adequately organize and launch a movement which in itself is founded merely to attack some already existing movement. Unquestionably there will be times when we must make statements which will attack other nonevangelical movements. If we are to guard our testimony and our purity, our great need is not for something which is negative but something which is positive, something which will launch a program, something which will marshal the enthusiasm and the resources and the strength of the people of Christian conviction throughout America. I am convinced that if the positive attitude is taken, the clear, concise, definite view, we shall receive the response which is necessary. God will add His blessing in a marvelous way.

Lastly, I believe that God intends that we shall have, as a condition of His power, consecrated love. Let me repeat, "consecrated love." This, my friends, is an element which is almost unknown in evangelical circles today. I have read articles in magazines, copies of correspondence, and have listened to conversations, and I must say that I deplore the absence of consecrated love and tolerance among men of mutual convictions. This Conference at the very beginning needs a baptism of love. Remember that Paul pled with the Romans that by the love of the Spirit they should pray for him. If we have the baptism of the Holy Ghost we will have a baptism of love, and if love is absent the Holy Spirit is absent from our midst.

There must be a technic for our purposes. That technic ought to be the launching of an organization which will be the vanguard of a movement. I am thoroughly convinced that our generation is waiting for some movement which will be truly adequate to challenge the average layman to action along Christian lines. Personally, I have accepted many engagements of recent date to speak to men's organizations for the purpose of reaching the men with the Gospel. Invariably, after these meetings, we have had conversations and discussions which these men have called for someone to launch a movement to which they could cling in an hour like this — something which they could back up, something which would have its repercussions in every phase of the life of the nation. I am positive that the hour has come for such a movement. This is corroborated by the fact that in other nations there have been movements which have been social and political, but have taken on something of a religious form. . . .

It is time for us to reach into the rural areas of America with a unified evangelistic program. It is time to have magazines with 2 million circulation instead of a 40,000 or 50,000 as the largest evangelical publications have today. We should have an organization for our colleges and Bible schools which is adequate and representative of the evangelical institutions of America. We should have a clearinghouse for missions sufficient to correlate the work of all of our faith and fundamental denominational missions. We should have a means of broadcasting whereby we can reach the entire population of the United States with the Gospel. We should have an evangelistic committee that will be able to carry on evangelism in any area according to the need. We should be organized to reach our government with a unified pronouncement and our soldiers with a united effort. At present we can do none of these because . . . we are fragmentized.

I call your attention to the fact that we actually have the equipment and the resources for this work. We have at this very meeting, today, the brain trust of the evangelicals which could put this on. I hold that, already in the evangelical movement, there are Gospel broadcasters who have demonstrated that they can bring in enough money to support their program over national hookups, and who could immediately take over worthwhile broadcasting under such a movement. We have editors of papers who could do a superb job of propagandizing our nation for evangelical Christianity, workers who could deal with every phase of Christian doctrine, evangelists who could bring literally millions of converts into the kingdom of God. We have educators of no mean ability. Why must we condemn these men to work individually in the raising of their money, in the getting of subscribers to magazines, in running colleges, or in trying to carry four or five jobs at once, thereby doing nothing well? Yes, we have the brain trust that could be used if we had someone, some good man with enough courage and vision to call these men together and use them. Moreover, the resources have been proved adequate for broadcasting, for our missionary program and numerous other things, if only we will let the people know the need. . . .

Can such an organization be launched here which will be the vanguard of the movement? I answer unqualifiedly, it can. It can if we are representative and we know that we represent many of the evangelical elements of the country. Are we in earnest? Surely, you reply, we are. Are we teachable, or are we determined only to have our own way? Are we clean? Have we put aside our prejudices, our differences, our controversies, even, if I may say it, our hates, that we may be of one mind? Are we willing to dissolve any organizational connection which we may have in order that we, as a group, may adequately represent evangelical Christianity to this nation? If we are, the day has dawned and the hour has struck inaugurating a new era in evangelical Christianity. If we are not, we may well turn our faces homeward with the conviction that as long as this present body constitutes a sizable portion in evangelical leadership, organizational unity among Bible believers is impossible.

God help us to humble ourselves; God help us to be sane; God help us to seek to do His will. God bless you, my brethren in the Lord. We stand together, under the shadow of the cross and cleansed by the blood of the Lamb. There let us unite for His glory.

Today our people may be without God, tomorrow they may turn against God. Woe to him who bears the responsibility of that terrible tragedy.

---

29.

## David Low: Leonardo Da Disney

*Walt Disney's animated cartoon films were immensely popular in the United States from the beginning, and his characters, preeminently Mickey Mouse and Donald Duck, had world reputations in the 1930s. But few Americans thought of Disney as an artist, with a capital "A," seeing him instead as an ingenious craftsman and entertainer whose productions were delightful but not profound. However, Europeans recognized Disney for the great innovator that he was and wrote serious criticism of his films. An example is the following article by David Low, who went so far as to compare Disney to Leonardo Da Vinci and to assert that Disney was the most significant figure in graphic art in five hundred years. Low was the leading British cartoonist of his time and enjoyed a reputation as a political satirist that was second to none.*

Source: *New Republic*, January 5, 1942.

ARTISTS ARE COMMONLY supposed to work by inspiration rather than by the conscious use of their intelligence. It is not always profitable to refute this insulting assumption, for the subtleties of a creative process are hard to communicate; and the tendency of the ignorant to surround the arts with the dignity of mystery has its advantages. But if it were necessary to prove that occasionally artists use their brains one could always produce Leonardo da Vinci and Walt Disney.

The man Leonardo was an adventurous mind, fond of wheels, an engineer. As a artist he was an innovator constantly experimenting to widen the domain of art. He was (so far as I can make out) the first to go after painting round instead of flat, so that he produced an effect, new in his time, of the figures standing out from the background. Before that, artists, judging color and outline more important than light and shade, had been satisfied with figures that seemed merely to be superimposed. Leonardo added to the capacity of expression the power to give depth of atmosphere. ("La Gioconda," by the way, is not a good example of the point, for it has been tinkered with too often. Perhaps the "Virgin and Child" in the Louvre is a better one.)

Leonardo's philosophy was that will was the energy of life. He was all for energy. Muscular movement and the dynamics of anatomy were favorite studies of his. The sketches for his famous equestrian bronze of Francisco Sforza show that he worked out that horse in a whole range of movement, galloping, rearing up, and still. Just like the drafts for what we call a "film cartoon." Incidentally, though Leonardo, by an unaccountable oversight, neglected to invent the cinema for himself and therefore had not its possibilities to play with, he was more than a bit of a cartoonist in our modern sense. Ordinary shapes bored him. He liked strange blobs and angles and burlesque outlines; he often drew allegorical sketches, moral and social satires and fables.

As to the other one: Disney, I think, has the grave disadvantage of not having been dead five hundred years. His generation appreciates his works, of course, but not, I fear, in the right way. Cinema audiences can hardly be expected to perceive his true significance. They are too preoccupied with sound accompaniment and idea content. Put on one side, please, the music and noise. Throw out Donald Duck. Forget "film cartoons." Consider moving drawings.

The first moving drawings made for screen projection by that old Frenchman (whose name I forget) in 1877 (or was it 1885?) were elementary. The drawing was poor. They moved. That was as much as you could say. There followed a procession, mostly of Americans, including Winsor McKay, with his delightful but crudely moving *Trained Dinosaur, Gertie;* J. R. Bray and the magnificent *Colonel Heeza Liar.* Earl Hurd and *Bobby Bump;* Bud Fisher, who animated his newspaper comic strip *Mutt and Jeff;* Sidney Smith; Wallace Carlson and *Dreamy Dud;* Paul Terry and *Farmer Al Falfa;* and Paul Felton and *Hodge Podge.* Not all of these black-and-white comics crossed the Atlantic for British inspection.

About fifteen years ago, so far as Britain was concerned, film-cartooning was topped by Max Fleischer's *Koko, the Clown* and Pat Sullivan's *Felix the Cat,* both of which had regular runs in our cinemas. With Fleischer the animation was too conventional to be artistically interesting, obviously just a trick of drawing over photographs. With Sullivan, it was evident that collective fertility in original tricks of draftsmanship and novel mechanical devices had enabled the whole art form to be advanced a couple of miles or so.

The movement, improving slowly, had up till then been confined to the simplest actions from the easiest angles, in profile mostly, tiresome in repetition. Sullivan's animation was not yet subtle, but it was "all-round." His figures moved from all angles, sometimes a bit painfully, and they had the beginnings of perspective and individual character. Then along comes Disney.

Pat Sullivan and his predecessors were, so to speak, penny-comic. Disney organized the experts and with specialized animators, better draftsmanship, color, and multiplication of the number of drawings per foot soon pushed the art first to tuppenny-comic, and then to three-penny. Now, by gosh! he has made it sixpenny, no, shilling! His last three features, *Snow White, Pinocchio,* and *Fantasia,* have been each an advance upon the last in artistry and extension of range. They reveal a growing understanding of the meaning of observed movement and therefore greatly increased powers of creating imagined movement. Compare the play of human expression in the face of Snow White with that in the faces of the Centaurettes in *Fantasia* and mark the striking improvement. Subtlety is now possible.

Now here's the point. It was perfectly clear donkeys' years ago that graphic Art (with a capital *A*), hit by the mechanical age, needed a new idea. Heaven knows, it hasn't had one since somebody two thousand years ago thought of painting pictures to frame and hang on the wall as a change from carpets. The improving quality of facsimile reproduction probably means sooner or later a consequent reassertion of *real* values in art as opposed to rarity and other artificial commercial values. The painting of pictures to hang on walls threatens to become an increasingly precarious profession except for the few best artists. Admire the new "schools" and "movements" as much as you like or as much as they deserve; their merits are irrelevant here. All the cubes, abstracts, and surrealists' ironmongery haven't really saved the situation.

It was perfectly clear also that as the machinery for representing movement improved, some intelligent lad would drop to it that the new idea was here, that the means were present for opening a new and exciting vista of possibility in graphic Art (with a capital *A*). At present your conventional artist who wishes to represent the beauty and character of, say, a woman or a landscape discovers the emotional elements of shape and color in the subject, and, following principles of selection and emphasis, puts them down in clarified form. But the woman moves with charm, the trees bend in the breeze. There are also emotional elements in the movements to be discovered, selected, emphasized, and represented in heightened form. Why not?

National Galleries and Historical Museums are at present stuffed with portraits of the Great Men of the Past, painted looking out of their frames frozen in moments of time. It is obvious that, as records at least, these portraits are sadly deficient, for true character is not displayed in a man's physical shell but in his individual *use* of it. A row of dead men don't look so very unlike one another; but Roosevelt has his characteristically restless eye and sudden smile; Churchill, his jutting forward of chin. We have many portraits which are great pieces of paint, so far as they go; but if, without losing their present excellent qualities, they gave us also with equal artistry in actual animation characteristic movements of the originals, a shrug of shoulder, curl of nostril, turn of head, they would be great, both as art and as truth. Yes? No?

I do not know precisely how much Disney has to do with the making of his own films. Much of the modern technique of making animated drawings is not, of course, his creation. (Bray and Earl Hurd, I am told, had most to do with that.) I do not know whether he draws a line himself. hear that at his studios he employs hundreds of artists to do the work. But I assume that his is the direction, the constant aiming after improvement in the new expression, the tackling of its problems in an ascending scale and seemingly with aspirations over and above mere commercial success. It is the direction of a real artist. It makes Disney, not as a draftsman but as an artist who uses his brains, the most significant figure in graphic art since Leonardo. In *Fantasia* he lifts the art of drawing movement right out of the "comic" and essays for the first time serious studies of a higher plane. Walpurgis Night (*Night on Bald Mountain*) and the prehistoric sequence (*Rite of Spring*) drive right to the foothills of the New Art of the Future.

Your stick-in-the-muds will scoff, no doubt. But I know what Leonardo would be up to if he were alive today. He would be in his back room inventing simplifications of animating processes and projection devices.

30.

## Karl Shapiro: "University"

*"Any discussion of American poetry resolves itself," Karl Shapiro once declared, "into a search for the meaning of 'American.' This quest for self-definition may be said to be the main theme of all American literature." Shapiro's poem "University," published in* Person, Place and Thing *in 1942 (when its author was serving in the armed forces in the South Pacific), is such a search for self-definition. Reflecting Shapiro's early bitter experiences as a Jewish student at the University of Virginia, where narrow, white, Anglo-Saxon prejudices predominated, the poem also reflects his inability — implied in many other poems — to reconcile America's lofty aims in the war with what he perceived to be smug complacency toward injustice at home. Thus for Shapiro the university epitomized all of American society.*

Source: *Person, Place and Thing,* New York, 1942.

### ❧ UNIVERSITY

To hurt the Negro and avoid the Jew
Is the curriculum. In mid-September
The entering boys, identified by hats,
Wander in a maze of mannered brick
    Where boxwood and magnolia brood
    And columns with imperious stance
    Like rows of ante-bellum girls
        Eye them, outlanders.

In whited cells, on lawns equipped for peace,
Under the arch, and lofty banister,
Equals shake hands, unequals blankly pass;
The exemplary weather whispers, "Quiet, quiet"
    And visitors on tiptoe leave
    For the raw North, the unfinished West,
    As the young, detecting an advantage,
        Practice a face.

Where, on their separate hill, the colleges,
Like manor houses of an older law,
Gaze down embankments on a land in fee,
The Deans, dry spinsters over family plate,
    Ring out the English name like coin,
    Humor the snob and lure the lout.
    Within the precincts of this world
        Poise is a club.

But on the neighboring range, misty and high,
The past is absolute: some luckless race
Dull with inbreeding and conformity
Wears out its heart, and comes barefoot and bad
    For charity or jail. The scholar
    Sanctions their obsolete disease;
    The gentleman revolts with shame
        At his ancestor.

And the true nobleman, once a democrat,
Sleeps on his private mountain. He was one
Whose thought was shapely and whose dream was broad;
This school he held his art and epitaph.
    But now it takes from him his name,
    Falls open like a dishonest look,
    And shows us, rotted and endowed,
        Its senile pleasure.

---

31.

# Negro March on Washington

*Asa Philip Randolph was one of the most active and effective twentieth-century leaders in the Negro's fight to improve his conditions in America. Prominent in the labor movement since 1925, when he organized the Brotherhood of Sleeping Car Porters, he was elected vice-president of the AFL-CIO in 1957. One of his most significant efforts in behalf of the Negro was during the campaign undertaken in 1941 to eliminate segregation in the armed forces and discrimination in employment. A march on Washington planned for July 1941 had been averted after Randolph had conferred with President Roosevelt, who then issued an executive order against discrimination in war industries. The following selection includes an article by Randolph, "Why Should We March?" published in November 1942, and the program of the organizers of the March on Washington Movement.*

Source: *Survey Graphic*, November 1942.

I.

A. PHILIP RANDOLPH:
## Why Should We March?

THOUGH I HAVE FOUND NO NEGROES who want to see the United Nations lose this war, I have found many who, before the war ends, want to see the stuffing knocke out of white supremacy and of empire ove subject peoples. American Negroes, involve as we are in the general issues of the con flict, are confronted not with a choice bu with the challenge both to win democrac for ourselves at home and to help win th war for democracy the world over.

There is no escape from the horns of this dilemma. There ought not to be escape. For if the war for democracy is not won abroad, the fight for democracy cannot be won at home. If this war cannot be won for the white peoples, it will not be won for the darker races.

Conversely, if freedom and equality are not vouchsafed the peoples of color, the war for democracy will not be won. Unless this double-barreled thesis is accepted and applied, the darker races will never wholeheartedly fight for the victory of the United Nations. That is why those familiar with the thinking of the American Negro have sensed his lack of enthusiasm, whether among the educated or uneducated, rich or poor, professional or nonprofessional, religious or secular, rural or urban, North, South, East, or West.

That is why questions are being raised by Negroes in church, labor union, and fraternal society; in poolroom, barbershop, schoolroom, hospital, hairdressing parlor, on college campus, railroad, and bus. One can hear such questions asked as these: What have Negroes to fight for? What's the difference between Hitler and that "cracker" Talmadge of Georgia? Why has a man got to be Jim-Crowed to die for democracy? If you haven't got democracy yourself, how can you carry it to somebody else?

What are the reasons for this state of mind? The answer is: discrimination, segregation, Jim Crow. Witness the Navy, the Army, the Air Corps; and also government services at Washington. In many parts of the South, Negroes in Uncle Sam's uniform are being put upon, mobbed, sometimes even shot down by civilian and military police, and, on occasion, lynched. Vested political interests in race prejudice are so deeply entrenched that to them winning the war against Hitler is secondary to preventing Negroes from winning democracy for themselves. This is worth many divisions to Hitler and Hirohito. While labor, business, and farm are subjected to ceilings and floors and not allowed to carry on as usual, these interests trade in the dangerous business of race hate as usual.

When the defense program began and billions of the taxpayers' money were appropriated for guns, ships, tanks, and bombs, Negroes presented themselves for work only to be given the cold shoulder. North as well as South, and despite their qualifications, Negroes were denied skilled employment. Not until their wrath and indignation took the form of a proposed protest march on Washington, scheduled for July 1, 1941, did things begin to move in the form of defense jobs for Negroes. The march was postponed by the timely issuance (June 25, 1941) of the famous Executive Order No. 8802 by President Roosevelt. But this order and the President's Committee on Fair Employment Practice, established thereunder, have as yet only scratched the surface by way of eliminating discriminations on account of race or color in war industry. Both management and labor unions in too many places and in too many ways are still drawing the color line.

It is to meet this situation squarely with direct action that the March on Washington Movement launched its present program of protest mass meetings. Twenty thousand were in attendance at Madison Square Garden, June 16; 16,000 in the Coliseum in Chicago, June 26; 9,000 in the City Auditorium of St. Louis, August 14. Meetings of such magnitude were unprecedented among Negroes. The vast throngs were drawn from all walks and levels of Negro life — businessmen, teachers, laundry workers, Pullman porters, waiters, and red caps; preachers, crapshooters, and social workers; jitterbugs and Ph.D's. They came and sat in silence, thinking, applauding only when they considered the truth was told, when they felt strongly that something was going to be done about it.

The March on Washington Movement is essentially a movement of the people. It is all Negro and pro-Negro, but not for that reason antiwhite or anti-Semitic, or anti-Catholic, or antiforeign, or antilabor. Its major weapon is the nonviolent demonstration of Negro mass power. Negro leadership has united back of its drive for jobs and justice. "Whether Negroes should march on Washington, and if so, when?" will be the focus of a forthcoming national conference. For the plan of a protest march has not been abandoned. Its purpose would be to demonstrate that American Negroes are in deadly earnest and all out for their full rights. No power on earth can cause them today to abandon their fight to wipe out every vestige of second-class citizenship and the dual standards that plague them.

A community is democratic only when the humblest and weakest person can enjoy the highest civil, economic, and social rights that the biggest and most powerful possess. To trample on these rights of both Negroes and poor whites is such a commonplace in the South that it takes readily to antisocial, antilabor, anti-Semitic, and anti-Catholic propaganda. It was because of laxness in enforcing the Weimar Constitution in republican Germany that Nazism made headway. Oppression of the Negroes in the United States, like suppression of the Jews in Germany, may open the way for a fascist dictatorship.

By fighting for their rights now, American Negroes are helping to make America a moral and spiritual arsenal of democracy. Their fight against the poll tax, against lynch law, segregation, and Jim Crow, their fight for economic, political, and social equality, thus becomes part of the global war for freedom.

## II.

## Program of the March on Washington Movement

1. We demand, in the interest of national unity, the abrogation of every law which makes a distinction in treatment between citizens based on religion, creed, color, or national origin. This means an end to Jim Crow in education, in housing, in transportation, and in every other social, economic, and political privilege; and, especially, we demand, in the capital of the nation, an end to all segregation in public places and in public institutions.

2. We demand legislation to enforce the Fifth and Fourteenth Amendments guaranteeing that no person shall be deprived of life, liberty, or property without due process of law, so that the full weight of the national government may be used for the protection of life and thereby may end the disgrace of lynching.

3. We demand the enforcement of the Fourteenth and Fifteenth Amendments and the enactment of the Pepper Poll Tax Bill so that all barriers in the exercise of the suffrage are eliminated.

4. We demand the abolition of segregation and discrimination in the Army, Navy, Marine Corps, Air Corps, and all other branches of national defense.

5. We demand an end to discrimination in jobs and job training. Further, we demand that the FEPC be made a permanent administrative agency of the U.S. government and that it be given power to enforce its decisions based on its findings.

6. We demand that federal funds be withheld from any agency which practises discrimination in the use of such funds.

7. We demand colored and minority group representation on all administrative agencies so that these groups may have recognition of their democratic right to participate in formulating policies.

8. We demand representation for the colored and minority racial groups on all missions, political and technical, which will be sent to the peace conference so that the interests of all people everywhere may be fully recognized and justly provided for in the postwar settlement.

32.

# War Songs

*World War II, like other wars in which Americans have been engaged, produced its quota of songs expressing the feelings of the participants. Four such songs are reprinted here. "I Got My Questionnairy" is a Negro Blues song that was transcribed by a collector during the war. Not everyone who received a draft summons was so ignorant of what service would mean, but all felt the wrench of being taken away from home and loved ones. "Gee, But I Want to Go Home" is a typical soldier's song about the discomforts of army life. It has its analogues in all wars, and Caesar's Roman legions probably had many of the same complaints. "Don't Sit Under the Apple Tree (With Anyone Else But Me)" reflects the soldier's fear that someone will steal his girl while he is off serving his country. This, too, is a perennial subject of war songs. "Praise the Lord and Pass the Ammunition" was the first major song hit of World War II; it was written by Frank Loesser shortly after Pearl Harbor. The words of the title have been attributed to a U.S. Navy chaplain who is supposed to have spoken them during the Japanese attack on the Hawaii base.*

Source: *Negro Folk Music, U.S.A.*, New York, 1963.
"Praise the Lord and Pass the Ammunition," Famous Music Corporation, New York, 1942.

## ❁ I GOT MY QUESTIONNAIRY

Well I got my questionnairy,
And it leads me to the war.
Well I got my questionnairy,
And it leads me to the war.
Well I'm leavin', pretty baby,
Child, can't do anything at all.

Uncle Sam aint no woman,
But he sure can take your man.
Uncle Sam aint no woman,
But he sure can take your man.
Boys, they got 'em in the service
Doin' something I can't understand.

## GEE, BUT I WANT TO GO HOME

The coffee that they give us,
They say is mighty fine,
It's good for cuts and bruises
And it tastes like iodine.

*Chorus:*
I don't want no more of army life,
Gee, but I want to go,
Gee, but I want to go,
Gee, but I want to go home.

The biscuits that they give us,
They say are mighty fine,
One fell off a table
And killed a pal of mine.

The clothes that they give us,
They say are mighty fine,
Me and my buddy
Can both fit into mine.

They treat us all like monkeys
And make us stand in line,
They give you fifty dollars
And take back forty-nine.

The girls at the service club
They say are mighty fine,
Most are over eighty
And the rest are under nine.


## DON'T SIT UNDER THE APPLE TREE
## (WITH ANYONE ELSE BUT ME)

I just got word from a guy who heard from the guy next door to me.
The girl he met just loves to pet and it fits you to a "T."
So, don't sit under the apple tree with anyone else but me
     Till I come marching home.

*Chorus:*
Don't sit under the apple tree with anyone else but me,
     Anyone else but me,
     Anyone else but me, No! No! No!
Don't sit under the apple tree with anyone else but me
     Till I come marching home.
Don't go walkin' down lover's lane with anyone else but me,
     Anyone else but me,
     Anyone else but me, No! No! No!
Don't go walkin' down lover's lane with anyone else but me
     Till I come marching home.

I told the gang the whole shebang that you were sweet and true;
They ran right out and came right back with a photograph of you.
So, don't sit under the apple tree with anyone else but me
     Till I come marching home.

LEW BROWN, CHARLIE TOBIAS, AND SAM H. STEPT

## PRAISE THE LORD AND PASS THE AMMUNITION

Down went the gunner, a bullet was his fate,
Down went the gunner, and then the gunner's mate.
Up jumped the sky pilot, gave the boys a look,
And manned the gun himself as he laid aside The Book,
Shouting

*Chorus:*
"Praise the Lord, and pass the ammunition!
Praise the Lord, and pass the ammunition!
Praise the Lord, and pass the ammunition
   And we'll all stay free!
Praise the Lord, and swing into position.
Can't afford to sit around a-wishin'.
Praise the Lord, we're all between perdition
   And the deep blue sea!"

   Yes, the sky pilot said it,
   You've got to give him credit
   For a son-of-a-gun of a gunner was he,
Shouting

"Praise the Lord, we're on a mighty mission!
All aboard! We're not a-goin' fishin'.
Praise the Lord, and pass the ammunition
   And we'll all stay free!"

FRANK LOESSER

# 1943

33.

## Franklin D. Roosevelt: The Casablanca Conference

*Two months after the successful Allied landings in North Africa, President Roosevelt and Prime Minister Churchill met at Casablanca to plan future strategy. Stalin was invited to attend the meetings that were held January 12-23, 1943, but sent word that he found it necessary to remain at home to direct the Russian campaign. The major issues of the conference were submarine warfare and the next Allied thrust after victory in Africa. American military leaders wanted to prepare for a landing in France, an offensive that was desired even before the invasion of Africa, but the British argued for an attack on Sicily and then an invasion of Italy. Churchill's long-cherished plan to strike at what he mistakenly thought to be "the soft underbelly" of Europe prevailed. Following the conference President Roosevelt, borrowing a phrase used by General Grant at Fort Donelson in 1862, said to newsmen that "the democracies' war plans were to compel the unconditional surrender of the Axis." In a broadcast speech before the White House Correspondents' Association on February 12, Roosevelt reported the outcome of the conference. The closing portion of his message is reprinted below.*

Source: *Record, App.,* 78 Cong., 1 Sess., pp. A548-A550.

THE DECISIONS REACHED and the actual plans made at Casablanca were not confined to any one theater of war or to any one continent or ocean or sea. Before this year is out, it will be made known to the world — in actions rather than in words — that the Casablanca Conference produced plenty of news; and it will be bad news for the Germans and Italians — and the Japanese.

We have lately concluded a long, hard battle in the southwest Pacific and we have made notable gains. That battle started in the Solomons and New Guinea last summer. It has demonstrated our superior pow-er in planes and, most importantly, in the fighting qualities of our individual soldiers and sailors.

American armed forces in the southwest Pacific are receiving powerful aid from Australia and New Zealand and also directly from the British themselves.

We do not expect to spend the time it would take to bring Japan to final defeat merely by inching our way forward from island to island across the vast expanse of the Pacific. Great and decisive actions against the Japanese will be taken to drive the invader from the soil of China. Important actions will be taken in the skies over China — and over Japan itself. The discussions at Casablanca have been continued in Chungking with the Generalissimo by General Arnold and have resulted in definite plans for offensive operations.

There are many roads which lead right to Tokyo. We shall neglect none of them.

In an attempt to ward off the inevitable disaster, the Axis propagandists are trying all of their old tricks in order to divide the United Nations. They seek to create the idea that if we win this war, Russia, England, China, and the United States are going to get into a cat-and-dog fight. This is their final effort to turn one nation against another in the vain hope that they may settle with one or two at a time — that any of us may be so gullible and so forgetful as to be duped into making "deals" at the expense of our allies.

To these panicky attempts to escape the consequences of their crimes we say — all the United Nations say — that the only terms on which we shall deal with any Axis government or any Axis factions are the terms proclaimed at Casablanca: "Unconditional surrender." In our uncompromising policy we mean no harm to the common people of the Axis nations. But we do mean to impose punishment and retribution in full upon their guilty, barbaric leaders.

The Nazis must be frantic indeed if they believe that they can devise any propaganda which would turn the British and American and Chinese governments and peoples against Russia — or Russia against the rest of us. The overwhelming courage and endurance of the Russian people in withstanding and hurling back the invaders — and the genius with which their great armies have been directed and led by Mr. Stalin and their military commanders — all speak for themselves.

The tragedy of the war has sharpened the vision of the leadership and peoples of all the United Nations, and I can say to you from my own full knowledge that they see the utter necessity of our standing together after the war to secure a peace based on principles of permanence.

You can be quite sure that if Japan should be the first of the Axis partners to fall, the total efforts and resources of all the United Nations would be concentrated on the job of crushing Germany.

And, on the other hand, lest there be any question in Nazi or Japanese minds that we are wholly one in the prosecution of the war to a complete victory all over the world, the Prime Minister wished to make a formal agreement that if Germany should be conquered before Japan, all British Empire resources and manpower would, of course, join with China and us in an out-and-out final attack on Japan. I told him that no formal statement or agreement along these lines was in the least bit necessary — that the American people accept the word of a great English gentleman — and that it was obvious and clear that all of us are completely in accord in our determination to destroy the forces of barbarism in Asia and in Europe and in Africa. In other words, our policy toward our Japanese enemies is precisely the same as our policy toward our Nazi enemies: it is a policy of fighting hard on all fronts and ending the war as quickly as we can on the uncompromising terms of unconditional surrender.

Today is the anniversary of the birth of a great, plain American. The living memory of Abraham Lincoln is now honored and cherished by all of our people, wherever they may be, and by men and women and children throughout the British Commonwealth, and the Soviet Union, and the Republic of China, and in every land on earth where people love freedom and will give their lives for freedom.

President Lincoln said in 1862, "Fellow citizens, we cannot escape history. We of this Congress and this administration will be remembered in spite of ourselves. No personal significance or insignificance can spare one or another of us. The fiery trial through which we pass will light us . . . in honor or dishonor, to the latest generation."

Today, eighty years after Lincoln delivered that message, the fires of war are blazing across the whole horizon of mankind — from Kharkov to Kunming — from the Mediterranean to the Coral Sea — from Berlin to Tokyo.

Again — we cannot escape history. We have supreme confidence that, with the help of God, honor will prevail. We have faith that future generations will know that here, in the middle of the 20th century, there came the time when men of goodwill found a way to unite and produce and fight to destroy the forces of ignorance, intolerance, slavery, and war.

---

34.

## Frederick C. Crawford: Jobs, Freedom, and Opportunity

*When war broke out in Europe and the American government undertook the obligation of being the "arsenal of democracy," the unemployment and searing poverty of the Great Depression all but came to an end. Wages — including double pay for overtime — and profits increased, and with prices on many necessities kept down by government controls, almost everyone felt more prosperous than he had in years. But there were controls on civilian consumption, too; a tremendous backlog of savings as well as consumer desire for goods was building up and becoming more and more something to plan for as the Allied victory seemed imminent after 1943. As president of the National Association of Manufacturers and a director of the U.S. Chamber of Commerce, Frederick C. Crawford was an influential member of the American business community. His speech of April 13, 1943, before the Northern California Industrial Conference held in San Francisco, reflected the anticipation of the business community of an unparalleled prosperity.*

Source: VSD, June 1, 1943: "Jobs, Freedom, Opportunity."

---

THE END OF WORLD AGGRESSION is rolling off the assembly lines of American industry. In the last two months I have seen victory in the making in the bomber plants of the South, the shipyards of New Orleans bayous, the steel mills of Birmingham, the tank factories of busy Detroit, and the aircraft industry of southern California.

War production in February, according to the War Production Board, jumped 8 percent over the January figure, and is going higher and higher everyday — already four times as great as in November just before Pearl Harbor.

This year we will launch the equivalent in tonnage of all the merchant marine in the world. Our plane production, still not big enough to assure victory, is nearly as great as the rest of the world.

The fires of industry blazed so blindingly white in the swift conversion to war production that Mr. Roosevelt and other eloquent phrasemakers called the achievement a "miracle." Industry has been called many things in the last ten years but this is the nicest name we've ever been called — "Miracle Men."

But you and I who do not believe in miracles, know that it did not happen suddenly and inexplicably. It was a natural outgrowth of long effort, the prime fruit of a plant that had been carefully developed for a century and a half. By nurturing ingenuity, protecting inventive genius, rewarding individual initiative, and encouraging the investment of savings in enterprises, we established American industry as the healthiest and most vigorous in the world and American standards of living the highest.

But industry is not resting on its laurels. This year industry — labor and management working together — will produce more than $57 billion worth of arms, ammunition, and supplies — 300 percent over 1942's record — the floodgates of production are wide open to sweep aggression into oblivion.

Industry will meet its 1943 war production obligations. Industry has confidence in its ability to deliver. Industry knew its own strength just after Pearl Harbor when it pledged to the President and the country that industry's production "will be limited only by the human endurance of the men who man and manage its facilities." Industry is keeping that promise, and will keep that promise until the last Nazi has cried "Kamerad" and the last yellow son of Nippon has hissed "Banzai."

Fighter and bomber planes to blast the enemies of democracy from the face of the north, and ships to supply the twenty-seven battlefronts of the world must come from out the magic industrial area of this Pacific Coast. Ships and planes, more ships and planes is the American battle cry of 1943. "Give us the tools for quick victory." That's the patriotic challenge to management and worker alike.

It is going to take better teamwork to get such production. Not compulsory teamwork but the highest degree of national unity based on patriotism and common welfare and not on group-grabbing interests.

Last year, raw material was the key to better production; this year, manpower is the fatal bottleneck. We have enough workers if we employ them correctly. Fullest utilization of that manpower does not mean we must take the liberty of choice from the workingman and woman and make dumb driven slaves of them.

This is a battle of freemen against the slavery of totalitarianism and freemen will win every time, just as free industry has in two years caught up with the great war machinery of the Axis, which was years in the building.

Government, labor, and industry working together instead of publicly exchanging indictments can cut down absenteeism, turnover, labor pirating, job shopping, slow downs, strikes, featherbed rules — paying for work never performed — and other restrictions on production. Above all, we can institute the encouragement of incentive for maximum war production — more pay for more production. If production is the gauge of victory, why hook the rate of that production to the low level of the average worker, why not get better performance by rewarding more production?

Yes! Victory is in the making — if not yet won. But, what of the peace? What of the hopes and aspirations of those millions of young Americans fighting for you and me? Can we face our sons, fresh from filthy foxholes and the screaming hell of war, and say to them: "You've given blood and guts to save the American way. But we've scuttled it while you were fighting for it. Hope you don't mind too much!" Or shall we welcome them home to an America of jobs, freedom, and opportunity — the America they fight for.

What do we mean — *jobs, freedom,* and *opportunity? Jobs* under good working conditions for fair wages. Jobs selected of our own free will and which we are free to change. *Freedom* to live without fear that a dictator or his henchmen will control us, watch our every action, listen to our words, tell us what to read, where to live, what to buy and where to work. We want *freedom* under laws and institutions which are fair, equitably administered, and imposing only minimum restraints necessary for the protection of the rights of individuals and minorities. Such *freedom* is the birthright of our nation — a nation dedicated to tolerance, to the protection of the individual, to the grand old American principle of "live and let live." *Opportunity* to work and get ahead under our own steam, the chance to plan our own future, to raise our children so they may grow and learn and live with that self-respect which is the right of free men.

*Jobs* — *freedom* — *opportunity* — these three, together, can provide for Americans the only security which comes when free citizens can look to the future with confidence. Of the three — *jobs* — *freedom* — *opportunity* — *jobs* will be the keystone of postwar prosperity.

Now management can and must do many things to make more postwar jobs possible, but it cannot guarantee jobs. Government alone can't guarantee jobs for very long. The only guarantee of jobs lies in a free, competitive enterprise system that is both free and competitive, and ever expanding with the growing nation — that is where the future jobs are to be found. To do this enterprise must be free of restraint and government regulation other than that necessary to the public welfare and fully competitive within itself, but not with government or government subsidized enterprise.

The answer to jobs, and more jobs, lies in the multiplication of wealth — not in mere division. In producing more to make more jobs, not in dividing up the jobs in a dwindling controlled economy. It might be a bit too realistic for the times to believe that we must have more horses for more people to go horseback riding instead of cutting up a few horses for distribution — even as popular as horsemeat is becoming. But ever since old man Euclid, or some other ancient, discovered arithmetic, we have been horribly embarrassed by the fact that we cannot divide more when we have less.

America, of all nations, has made the cherished discovery that producing more to have more lies at the very heart of the more abundant life. Free competitive enterprise is not a concoction of a few cussed capitalists bent on plundering the gentlefolk, but a method devised by human beings to care for their exchange of labor and the building of their lives and future through an economy of their own making. It is the best means we or any other nation have devised to produce and distribute wealth to all.

Let me illustrate this national triangle of plenty through production, which is only another name for free competitive enterprise. Industry, under competitive free enterprise, is an unusually vital triangle of interdependence, a triangle with four elements. Industry is an unusual triangle in that it has four, instead of only three elements: (1) *workers;* (2) *investors* or stockholders (for in industry $6,000 of capital is required for each job supplied); (3) most important of all, the consumers or *Market;* and (4) *Management.* Management belongs in the center of the triangle, with a corner each for workers, stockholders, and consumers.

Let's examine our triangle: At the top corner is really the most important of all, the consumers — let's call them *Market.* The American *Market* alone is 130 million people. Americans will always want *more* good things, and their demand will *always* be, as it has been, "Better things at cheaper prices." Americans are bargain buyers. They buy objects not policies at the lowest possible price. Note that their demand upon business and industry is a fundamental demand — a natural demand of human nature — of self-interest.

Over in the second corner of the triangle of industry is *Capital*. And, looking closely, we see that *Capital* is also 130 — and the same 130 — millions of Americans. *Capital* is anyone who has a life insurance policy, a bank account, an automobile, or, indeed, a pair of shoes — for even a pair of shoes represents an investment of capital. Note that the demand of *Capital* on industry is a basic human demand, "How can I get the most of my investment?"

In the third corner of the triangle is *Labor*. And again, this element is the same 130 millions of Americans we found in the other corners. *Labor's* demand on industry is for less work and *more* money. Observe again that this is a natural human reaction — self-interest.

Thus the three demands on industry are just the natural demands of everyday human nature. The buyer wants to pay less money into the triangle of industry; yet capital and labor insist that they each get more out of it. These are three seemingly irreconcilable factors in the triangle.

Now, the fourth element in our unusual triangle is *Management* — in the middle as always. To be successful *Management* must reconcile the three apparently irreconcilable forces. But *Management* is always being pulled or hauled by one or the other of the three corners. When *Market* pulls, it says, "Give me lower prices or I won't buy." *Labor* yanks, saying, "Give me more pay for less work." And at the same time *Capital* hauls, crying "More returns or you'll be fired." That's *Management's* predicament.

Many people follow my picture thus far. Many think at this point that someone tosses in a fixed amount of money and the triangle becomes a poker game in which, if one corner wins, another must lose. This is

not true! Industry is a device for the creation of wealth — a device by which all can share in the new wealth produced.

To illustrate: Imagine a small umbrella factory with a single worker — Joe. Joe stands at an old-fashioned bench running a hand spindle. He makes one umbrella an hour and gets one dollar an hour for his work. After Joe has made the umbrella, *Management* says: "Now, Joe, I haven't any money. I've got to sell this umbrella before I can pay you."

And so *Management* goes to the gate — to the top of our triangle — where the great *American Market* is going by, and he cries, "Umbrellas for sale." Management must get at least $1 for the umbrella to pay Joe's wages. "Too much — won't pay it!" snaps *Market*. But, finally, the umbrella is sold and *Management* returns with the $1 which he pays to Joe.

At the end of the first day, then, we have an unhappy buyer — he wanted a lower price. Joe is unhappy — he wanted a raise. And *Capital* calls up and asks *Management*, "Where is the return on my investment?" There isn't any return — the stockholder is mad and he warns that *Management* will be fired unless the problem is solved and quickly!

*Management*, to save its job, burns midnight oil. *Management* discovers that Joe lost time working by hand and got tired standing at the bench. So *Management* decides to improve the tools of production. A motor is hitched to the spindle, Joe is given a stool, and to save more time Joe's material comes to him on a conveyor.

Joe comes in next morning and somewhat reluctantly tries out the new fangled gadgets. To his amazement, at the end of an hour, he has made two umbrellas with less difficulty than he had making one the day before.

Taking the two umbrellas, *Management* goes back up to the top of the triangle and again calls out to *Market,* "Umbrellas for sale." Yesterday's disgruntled buyer says, "Nothing doing! Your price is too high!" *Management* says, "Not now, I've got just what you want — umbrellas at 75 cents." The buyer is pleased. "Fine," he says, "I'll take two. That's what I want — a bargain."

*Management* returns to the middle of the triangle and says to Joe: "We've discovered the secret of the production of wealth. I've $1.50 where I had only $1 yesterday. I'm giving you a 25 cent raise. Here's $1.25."

Joe is happy and *Management* calls *Capital* to say, "Because there is a quarter left in the cash drawer, some dividends may be possible."

For more than 100 years the triangle of American competitive free enterprise has actually worked. We've produced the best goods at the lowest prices, the greatest accumulation of capital and the highest wages paid anywhere in the world.

There are no classes in American industry. One hundred and thirty million Americans are Market, Capital, and Labor. To prove this, let's go back to Joe and the typical day.

From eight in the morning until four in the afternoon, Joe is labor. He's conscious of it. He's mad at Capital and mad at Market. He wonders why he doesn't get more money. At 4 o'clock Joe goes home and goes shopping with Mrs. Joe. He forgets that during the day he was labor. He's now Market. He's a tough buyer. "Why can't you sell this stuff cheaper." he demands. On the way home, Joe stops to make a deposit in the bank. Now he's Capital. Again, he's a tough guy. "What are you doing with my money? Why can't I get 4 percent instead of only 1 percent. Can't you run a bank any better than this?"

He forgets that he has been Labor, Market, and Capital in the same day.

But Joe, as Labor, picked up a 25-cent raise on the second day because wealth was produced. He picked up a 25 percent increase, as Market, when he purchased umbrellas at the cheaper price and, as Capital, he picked up a better return on his savings or life insurance.

The standard of living rises because, at each corner of the triangle, wealth is distributed. Joe is the American people who go around this triangle, day by day, picking up an ever increasing standard of living.

This might be too simple an explanation for the economist to understand, but I submit that it has done more, and can do more in the future, to bring a better life to all the people than all the edicts, laws, and decrees the government can ever promulgate.

The triangle story shows us that — profits mean increased investment; increased investment means increased wages. Therefore, profits increase wages.

Is this a contradiction, a fantasy?

Dr. Sumner Slichter of Harvard eloquently supports the connection between "larger profits" and "larger payrolls." He says that labor and capital will both discover that the conditions which make it possible to arrive at both larger payrolls and larger profits are the very same conditions. He says that this discovery will lead to cooperation between labor and capital and that this cooperation "will make all previous efforts to raise the standard of living seem feeble."

That's the reason I say the best in America is yet to come. Because all the people in all three corners of the economic triangle — labor, market, investors — are not enemies of one another but the very same people. This kind of an economy is the best for the future, as it has been in the past, and is in present war production.

We had better put all our faith in that triangle of plenty and make it work if we want a postwar world free from want and economic stumbling and experimenting. I believe we can very well throw victory away if we're not prepared for a good peace, and that we should be planning postwar now.

My only objection to the long-distance planner is that those least experienced in making our past and present are hell-bent on blueprinting every detail of a great future. Most of these plans have something very much in common. They are long on high-sounding objectives but short on how to get them.

Reminds me of your late, dearly beloved Will Rogers, who in 1917 had a plan to end submarine warfare.

"Just boil the ocean," Will told an admiral.

"Corking idea," said the admiral, "But how?"

"Oh, that's your job to scheme that out — I've given you the idea," replied Will.

Too many planners who say they believe in private enterprise as a source of postwar jobs do so with their tongue in their cheek. They say yes, free, competitive enterprise must be the source of only a "majority" of the postwar jobs, but then they look to government to provide the rest of the jobs through government spending. To me that is as ridiculous and economically immoral as a part-time wife. Let's all get together to make the right system work instead of combining the worst with the best and then being surprised at its failure.

Combining public and private enterprise is making a hybrid affair of the private enterprise system — half private, half public — half free, half slave. In fact, the big postwar planning decision for the American people is whether they want to continue to emasculate our economic system into a nondescript, unworkable combination of impossibilities, or whether they want to get back to the proven workability of the triangle of free competitive enterprise.

We have rediscovered the efficacy of private enterprise in war production. We have discovered the unworkableness of the promises of substitute schemes. The first step to peacetime plenty is to encourage a public renewal of faith in our American institution of undefiled, undiluted, free enterprise. On this decision as to our American economic policy not only depends our national future but the peaceful welfare of the world. . . .

What we want in an international sense is exactly the same as we want here at home. We want a free world in which the goods produced by agriculture and industry can move easily, not to the advantage of a few or to the injury of a few but to the benefit of all. We have marveled at the facility with which American industry can produce the goods the world wants and needs. Our foremost job in the postwar era will be to develop means of placing in the hands of consumers, abroad as well as at home, the necessities and even the luxuries which we can produce so abundantly.

Critics say we cannot Americanize the world — that forcing the American way down the throats of foreign peoples smacks of dictatorship and power politics. Let me assure you — no force will be needed. Foreign industry envies us our productive capacity and skill — mimics us wherever it can. The people, whenever they've had the opportunity to know American goods, have reached eagerly for more. Denied the American standard of living at home, they have thronged to our shores by the millions.

The American way of life is something concrete, something vital to these people, even if we here at home sometimes forget it. We must not only maintain the American standard; we must lift it higher and higher. We can do it through the medium of production.

We must make certain that production is not stunted by the whimsical restrictions of bureaucrats burdened with the blueprints and designs of economic planners. It must be free to exercise its proper function — to give us more and still more of the good things of life — to lead us ever onward and upward as a free nation and as a world power.

35.

## "Talking Union"

*The model of "Talking Union" was a Negro spiritual that began: "If you want to get to heaven let me tell you what to do." That song, like "Talking Union" itself, was not supposed to be sung but rather to be spoken, in an easy but strong rhythm, to a steady musical accompaniment. Anyone who has not heard the song will discover the rhythm if he reads the words out loud. "Talking Union" was written and popularized in the early 1940s by the Almanac Singers, a group whose personnel changed from time to time but whose best-known members were Pete Seeger, Woody Guthrie, Lee Hays, and Millard Lampell. Although Hays made some suggestions, Seeger and Lampell are credited with most of the lines of "Talking Union."*

Source: *Songs of Work and Freedom*, Edith Fowke and Joe Glazer, eds., New York, 1960.

### ชื TALKING UNION

If you want higher wages, let me tell you what to do,
You've got to talk to the workers in the shop with you.
You've got to build you a union, got to make it strong,
But if you all stick together, boys, 'twon't be long —
You'll get shorter hours . . . better working conditions . . .
Vacations with pay . . . take your kids to the seashore.

It ain't quite this simple, so I'd better explain
Just why you've got to ride on the union train,
'Cause if you wait for the boss to raise your pay
We'll all be a-waiting till the judgment day —
We'll all be buried . . . gone to heaven . . .
St. Peter'll be the foreman then.

Now you know you're underpaid but the boss says you ain't,
He speeds up the work till you're about to faint.
You may be down and out, but you ain't beaten —
You can pass out a leaflet and call a meetin' —
Talk it over . . . speak your mind . . .
Decide to do something about it.

Suppose they're working you so hard it's just outrageous,
And they're paying you all starvation wages.

You go to the boss, and the boss will yell
"Before I raise your pay I'll see you all in hell."

'Course, the boss may persuade some poor damn fool
To go to your meeting and act like a stool,
But you can always tell a stool, boys, that's a fact,
He's got a yellow streak a-running down his back.
He doesn't have to stool . . . he'll always get along . . .
On what he steals out of blind men's cups.

You've got a union now and you're sitting pretty;
Put some of the boys on the bargaining committee.
The boss won't listen when one guy squawks
But he's got to listen when the union talks.
He'd better . . . be mighty lonely . . .
If everybody decided to walk out on him.

He's puffing a big seegar, feeling mighty slick
'Cause he thinks he's got your union licked.
Well, he looks out the window, and what does he see
But a thousand pickets, and they all agree
He's a bastard . . . unfair . . . slave-driver . . .
Bet he beats his wife.

Now, boys, you've come to the hardest time.
The boss will try to bust your picket line.
He'll call out the po-lice and the National Guard;
They'll tell you it's a crime to have a union card;
They'll raid your meetings, they'll hit you on the head —
They'll call every one of you a goddamn Red —
Unpatriotic . . . agitators . . .
Send 'em back where they came from.

But out in De-troit, here's what they found,
And out in Pittsburgh, here's what they found,
And out in Akron, here's what they found,
And up in Toronto, here's what they found:
That if you don't let Red-baiting break you up,
And if you don't let vigilantes break you up,
And if you don't let race hatred break you up,
And if you don't let stool pigeons break you up,
You'll win . . . what I mean . . .
Take it easy . . . but take it!

36.

## Michael Darrock: What Happened to Price Control?

*The threat of inflation posed by the transition to a war economy in the late 1930s was immediately apparent to President Roosevelt. His executive order of April 11, 1941, created the Office of Price Administration and Civilian Supply (later OPA) "to prevent spiraling, rising costs of living, profiteering, and inflation resulting from market conditions." The Emergency Price Control Act, signed January 30, 1942, gave OPA authority to enforce its orders, including consumer rationing, which was handled by means of stamps and certificates. Many Americans grumbled at the restrictions, but the system was generally accepted and ration coupons came to comprise a sort of currency. The OPA was administered by Leon Henderson until December 1942, when political pressures forced his resignation, and after that by Prentiss Brown. An article by Michael Darrock (pseudonym of Waldemar A. Nielsen) in support of Henderson's policies, which seemed in danger of being undermined, is reprinted here in part.*

Source: *Harper's*, July 1943. Copyright © 1943, by Harper's Magazine Inc.
Reprinted from the July 1943 issue by permission of the author.

EIGHT MONTHS AGO OPA was the vigorous leader of the drive against inflation. It was thick in the midst of the contest against the various groups that were trying to loot the nation's treasure of war-swollen rents, wages, and profits. Now the future of price control is in doubt and the collapse of OPA is widely predicted. . . . Upon the successful control of the cost of living depends peace at home, perhaps continued success on the battlefront, and surely stability in the postwar period.

What has happened? What are the causes? Where do we stand? To be complete, any analysis of OPA — its strengths and weaknesses, its successes and failures — properly should wait until we have a greater perspective in time. Despite the extreme complexity of the problem, however, its urgency requires that we seek the nearest approximation of the truth that we can make at this moment. . . .

The story begins with the birth of OPA two years ago. Since then it has grown from a division of a hundred persons in the old Defense Commission to an organization of more than thirty thousand paid workers and countless volunteers, stationed in every section of the land.

The battle against inflation began even before this country was at war with the Axis. Germany invaded Poland in September 1939, and two days later Great Britain and France declared war. Immediately a price boom began in this country. War materials spiraled upward in cost; employment swelled; payrolls reached a new high within three months. As time went on, however, it appeared that prices had jumped the gun; the "blitzkrieg" turned out to be a "sitzkrieg," and the boom abated. Nonetheless the terrible latent threat of inflation had been revealed. Though we were to be caught unprepared at Pearl Harbor two years later, the warning of inflation came in good time and we began then to map our defenses.

The "phony war" period came sharply to

an end, with the invasion of Denmark and Norway in April 1940. France was conquered and the British had been at Dunkirk. The United States hastily launched an expanded defense program; gigantic sums of money were appropriated for war material; the President called for the swift mobilization of our productive plant for defense. To deal with the problems of expanding and redirecting industrial production a Defense Commission was appointed. Significantly it was also charged to check pressures on the price structure. Leon Henderson was appointed to head the Price Division; the appointment was not surprising.

Even though he was not a public figure at that time, Henderson was well known as an economist and was in high favor in the Administration. As early as 1937 he was called the most important fount of new doctrine in Washington, and even then he had a reputation as a crystal-gazer in matters of economics. A year before the great market crash of 1929 he was one of a handful of men who predicted exactly what would happen, and when. Six months in advance he called the slump of 1937; he summarized the figures and outlined his reasoning in a note to the President with the Hendersonian title — "Booms and Busts." "I'm the golfer who made a hole-in-one the first time out," he said afterward. "I had better quit now." But he didn't quit; it was Henderson who sat down with the President after the nervous boom in 1939 and laid out the course of war inflation in this country. He designed the strategy of defense.

Hence when he took charge of the Price Stabilization Division of the Defense Commission he was in his own backyard. The time was early, and pressures on prices were not then great. The Division consulted with industrialists in order to choke off speculative excesses and kept an eye on the general price situation. For several months these weak controls were sufficient and price rises were moderate.

However, as the defense program began to get up steam, shortages spread like a brush fire from one industry to another, and the curve of prices began ominously to creep upward. It became clear that mere advisory controls were not adequate. Early in 1941 the President split the Defense Commission into several major war agencies, and the OPACS emerged as an independent administration. The pressure was on, but several obstacles stood in the way of strong price control.

In the first place the whole price control setup existed only by grace of an executive order. It had no real penalties it could impose. It was not even clear what the powers under the executive order were. In the second place the threat of publicity had little sting because the public was not yet aware of the danger of inflation nor was it aroused against "business as usual" practices which war suddenly had made criminal. The job of price control at that time required, as one dear old Washington lady put it, "A good bluffer with a big bazoo."

Henderson and his "group of bright young men" rushed in where other administrators might have feared to tread. They chose the method of maximum price schedules, backed by consultation, publicity, and voluntary cooperation, as their tool for price control. The first schedule issued covered second-hand machine tools, which at the time were skyrocketing in price. A series of other schedules followed. On a dozen fronts at once they nipped inflationary bulges. . . .

On April 16, 1941, OPACS imposed a ceiling on all iron and steel products at the levels that prevailed on that date. To the average citizen the action might have seemed like just another tedious and technical pronunciamento, but that bold stroke has already saved the government and the people of this country hundreds of millions of dollars.

In the months that followed the steel order the agency brought under its control a larger and larger part of the price structure and developed several formal and informal types of control. Yet it still had no real sanctions it could apply against violators. Toward the middle of 1941 it was again apparent that the inflationary pressures were getting stronger than the makeshift dikes erected to restrain them, and Congress began deliberations on a bill which would give statutory strength to the price-control apparatus. The fundamental cause of the increasing pressures on prices was of course the increasing volume of defense expenditures.

When the Japanese bombed Pearl Harbor the reverberations cracked open the price-control machinery in Washington. Supplies of important raw materials — rubber, tin, chemicals — suddenly were cut off, and all hell was ready to tear loose on prices. What would happen when business opened on that Monday after the first news anybody could guess. All Sunday night Henderson worked with his staff planning the bold, decisive steps which had to be taken. When the sun came up on Monday long-distance calls went out over the country to stop speculative rushes in the important commodity markets. In the remainder of that week additional steps were taken to plug the biggest holes. And on the following Sunday came a sweeping action fixing maximum prices on fats and oils. As a result the back of the threat was broken. Basic commodity prices turned downward; red-eyed officials rubbed out their cigarettes and went to bed.

Within a month after the attack the President presented his "blueprint for victory" to the Congress. His message made it abundantly clear that we were in war up to our ears. One-half of our entire national production was to be devoted to the war effort. Among other things, the program outlined meant the end of selective price control. The turning point had arrived; every part of the national economy would now feel the effects of overwhelming demand and scant supply.

Spurred by war, Congress passed the Emergency Price Control Act and the President signed it at the end of January. For the first time the Office of Price Administration, as the price-control agency was named, had full powers to control prices and rents, and to punish violators. The very existence of price-control legislation was a major victory. In the First World War we had been suckers; in the Second World War we took the lesson of twenty-five years before and put it to work. We caught the danger early and kept our levees just a little higher than the floodwaters, at least during the opening stages. The question was, could we check the much greater pressures that actual all-out war would produce?

At the time, the President said of the Act: ". . . . all in all it is workable. . . . Price-control legislation alone cannot successfully combat inflation. To do that, an adequate tax and fiscal program, a broad savings program, a sound production program, and an effective priorities and rationing program are all needed. Finally, all bulwarks against inflation must fail unless all of us — the business man, the worker, the farmer, and the consumer — are determined to make those bulwarks hold fast." Those remarks are the key to much of what has happened since.

THE ARITHMETIC OF HENDERSON'S JOB of price control was not too difficult to understand. As billions of dollars of war expenditures were poured into the nation's production plant during 1942, wages, farm prices and profits would tumble over one another in their climb upward. At the same time the appetite of the military machine would gobble up a large part of all civilian goods. This wide disparity between the supply of money and the supply of goods would create terrific pressure for prices to rise.

During the time when defense expenditures were moderate, and when there was slack to be taken up in the national economy, persuasion and conciliation if used well could keep prices in line. But when the slack was gone and when unimagined quantities of money were pumped into the machinery, price control changed in its requirements; it no longer was a one-man or one-agency job. As the President explained in his seven-point program to stabilize the cost of living in April 1942, a team of elements had to work together in order to prevent disaster.

According to the seven-point paper program, Henderson's part of the job was to put a lid on prices and to sit on it. Congress was to establish a fiscal program which would suck away inflationary funds; the Treasury was to expand the war-savings program in order to divert money into bonds; the Federal Reserve System was to choke off credit; and Congress and the President together were to limit wages, profits, and farm prices. Without their help Henderson could not stand against the tide indefinitely, for he could control only the symptoms of inflation. It was up to the others to control the causes.

To speak in such exact terms however is somewhat artificial and misleading. If Henderson's only power had been to control symptoms, and if the economic system ran like a clock rather than like a Rube Goldberg invention, then his powers would have been nominal indeed. And if the other members of the team which the President named had taken their posts and done their jobs quickly and well, then Henderson would have needed only nominal powers. Inflation would have been stopped, and OPA could have spent its time in routine chores of scheduling and rationing rather than in brawling with every interest across the board.

In real terms however the limitation of wages, profits, and farm prices is not done with a wave of the cigarette holder. A thousand lobbyists and a million arguments must be listened to, and a hundred million Americans must be pinched before such settlements are made. Miles of paper must be typewritten, evidence must be piled up, and data on slow-forming public sentiment must be collected. Meanwhile the floodwaters of inflation continue to rise.

Henderson could either wait for the others or he could with adroitness and courage advance at every opportunity, slice into the fat on certain parts of the system, play one pressure off against another, frighten the timid into line, encourage the patriotic to hold back on profiteering. His record suggested that he would not play a waiting game. Similarly, he could wait for Congress and the President to be pushed into taking action, or he could actively stir up pressure for action, call on the press for help, and use his agency for propagandizing the cause of inflation control. Here too his record suggested what he would do.

As soon as Congress had given him the power the OPA chief proceeded to prepare a general maximum-price regulation to cover all commodities and services. At the same time orders were prepared for controlling rents in all defense areas. Shortly thereafter the "General Max," as the overall price order was called, was issued together with rent orders, and by these measures the OPA extended price control to the limit of its powers. OPA research men published figures on the effects of uncontrolled farm prices on the cost of living. They published figures on the rate at which corporation profits were zooming in comparison with the growth of wage incomes. Henderson held weekly "lessons in economics" for members of the Washington press to show them what was happening and the causes that lay beneath. He tramped the boards at numberless meetings, banquets, conventions, luncheons; he became the Billy Sunday of economics.

He did his job. What did the others do? The Board of Governors of the Federal Reserve System gave a light jerk on the reins of consumer credit; the Treasury launched a gigantic and weak-kneed voluntary campaign to pull purchasing power into war bonds. The results of their actions were pitifully small compared with the magnitude of the task which had to be done. These combined programs dried up only two and one-half billion dollars of purchasing power, while individual incomes in the same period rose about seven billion dollars.

Congress from the beginning of the defense program has been entirely neurotic — insecure, anxious, frustrated, defensive. Despite the imminence of the danger of inflation and despite the plain simplicity of the action which was needed, petty provincial politics have prevailed. All through the summer of 1942 Congress dawdled over certain needed amendments to the price-control legislation. The effort made to stabilize wages was a flat failure. The tax bill was argued and squabbled over in an endless series of dreary debates. The Farm Bloc in the Senate blocked every attempt to control farm prices, and consequently the Congress was never able fairly to impose restrictions needed on wages. Corporation profits in defense industries swelled, but Congressmen could not muster the independence or the starch to do anything about them. By midsummer it was frighteningly apparent that because the critical elements would not fulfill their responsibilities the battle against inflation was being lost; like the Germans in Tunisia, we were "advancing to the rear" and conducting a series of "offensive retreats."

Henderson wrote in a letter to the Congress at this time: "It is an obvious point and one that has been labored, but I wish to make it again: The President's program against inflation will succeed only as its every element is made fully effective. . . . Hesitation on any of the major fronts imperils the entire campaign. It has been a difficult task to hold ceiling prices in the face of this hesitation of each group to take its battle station until assured that the other groups were taking theirs."

The situation continued to grow worse, but the people were waking up to what was wrong. More and more from all sections of the country came demands for the control of farm prices, the stabilization of wages, and the trimming of profits. Surprisingly, important groups were volunteering to accept restrictions. The national farm lobby, headed by voluble Ed O'Neal, began to see the gap widen between its pork-barrel policy and farmers' attitudes; State farm groups disclaimed adherence to the Lobby's program. Labor groups began to ask for a time-out from the referee in the pointless race of group against group for advantage.

On Labor Day, 1942, the President spoke to Congress and urged the passage of a new price bill, and Congress followed his lead. A month later the President established the Office of Economic Stabilization, headed by perhaps as tactful and effective a political warrior as there is in the country — Jimmy Byrnes, at that time an associate justice of the Supreme Court.

For OPA it seemed for a time that these developments were a beginning and an end — the beginning of a chance to work and the end of the necessity to fight. At the year's end it appeared that under the authority of the new price-control act our slipping grip on the cost of living had been made firm. Henderson was cocky about the prospects. There were still some weaknesses — particularly with regard to farm prices — but his powers appeared to be sufficient to handle the situation. Immediately before his ouster early this year he could honestly boast of having held the line. With gusto he wrote to Congress: "It is my profound pleasure to be able to report that the mandate of the Congress and the directive of the President to halt inflation have thus far been carried out. . . . I was directed to stabilize prices. That directive was obeyed. I was directed to establish prices fair alike to buyer and seller. That directive was obeyed. I was directed to stabilize rents. Rents have been reduced and stabilized."

He could point with pride to the fact that as a result of his efforts under the powers given him, he had saved the Federal Government up until that time nearly 26 billion dollars and he had saved American consumers nearly 6 billion dollars. He pointed out that if prices could continue to be held, by the end of the year the Government would have saved nearly 78½ billion dollars as a result of price control, and American consumers would have saved 23 billion dollars. In individual terms, Henderson's work by December 1942, had saved every American family about $140 and by the end of 1943 will have saved every family nearly $500.

It might seem that a record so brilliant would not make a scoundrel out of the person responsible, but as time went on a "Get Henderson" drive began to snowball. Why?

SOME OPPOSITION TO OPA'S PROGRAM was only natural to expect. Hundreds of thousands of American businessmen had grown lean and gaunt during the long depression and slow recovery. Just at the time when business activity picked up and consumers' pockets were filled with spendable dollars, when demand was as large as their wildest dreams, OPA stepped in and snatched the bread right out of their mouths. Businessmen are human, and they felt thwarted and disappointed.

Since it was the business of OPA not only to squeeze certain kinds of business but also certain localities, such as the Northeast in the matter of fuel oil, a certain amount of political opposition could be expected. However the volume and intensity

of the hostility of businessmen and politicians toward OPA was out of all normal proportions. What were the special catalytic factors in the case of OPA which heightened and sharpened the usual troubles which the large war agencies get into? We can put a finger on some of them at least.

Since 1932, Roosevelt has accumulated a not inconsiderable group of political enemies — purple-passionate Roosevelt-haters whose zeal in cursing everything New Dealish will someday be legendary. The OPA for these people was a made-to-order punching bag. Because its program was so vast there were inevitably mistakes which could be seized upon. By the very nature of the program, OPA was a meddlesome third party in every transaction, from the buying of a house to the buying of a button, and it was thus, from one point of view, socialistic, regimenting, boondoggling, impossible!

The evidence is quite clear that the anti-Roosevelt forces have used OPA as the scapegoat and the whipping-boy for their deep anger. Certain sections of the press have played a daily tune on the misdeeds of the agency, making it a symbol of badness. All business interests are not equally patriotic, and those with a greater urge to cash in on the war than to help win it have joined the bloodthirsty pack and taken up the cry. OPA by its vexing and numerous administrative failures made large numbers of average citizens side with the critics. The success of this political tactic of subjecting one part of the Administration line to extreme pressure is admitted by many observers; there are those who feel that the irritation which voters expressed at the polls in the last national election sprang largely from "the matter of OPA." . . .

THE ONE THING upon which Henderson could rely for protection was the active support of those persons whom he was presumably protecting — namely, the consumers, the American people as individual citizens. If they should understand and sympathize with the OPA program, and if they should back it intelligently on critical issues, he would be invulnerable. But if they should be even indifferent, then the forces of opposition would prevail. Henderson's failure to muster and organize public support can be pointed to as the mistake which cleared the way for his ouster. . . .

The Information Division of OPA has been guilty of much stupidity, and it muffed this job as it did most others. To this day people have only a general and fuzzy idea of what inflation is, what causes it, what groups of persons suffer most from it, in what ways they suffer, and what the individual citizen can do to help prevent it. Some define it as being "like in Germany where it took a million marks to buy a loaf of bread," while others say it is "just a terrible thing because everything you own becomes worthless"; to most perhaps it is just a sinister word, a green-eyed bugaboo. Good price control must spring out of a sensible program at the top and an intelligent people at the bottom. Although the war has been a college education in economics and geography for the American people, they still are relatively uninformed on the subject of inflation, and OPA information in a measure is to blame.

Other matters helped to make people feel that the price-control program had bypassed them. The whole thing was run from Washington. For a long time price ceilings were not published in such a way that the public could help in the enforcement of them. Although OPA's enforcement activity was woefully weak, no vigorous program for the recruitment and training of volunteer price wardens was initiated. To the average man everything OPA did sounded gruff and legalistic. He did not object strenuously; he simply felt left out.

About rationing there was more serious complaint, and the complaint has tarred the whole agency. Despite the fact that rationing and price control are two separate programs within the OPA, the sins of either have been visited on both. In OPA it has been the habit to excuse public outbursts about the program by saying that "people have not accepted the necessity of rationing." But the persistence of antagonism suggests that there may be determinable reasons for it.

The idea of rationing is that when shortages of any commodity develop the fairest way to assure everyone a chance to get his proper share is to apportion the supply, regardless of the buying power of different individuals. This means of course that if a program of rationing is to gain acceptance people first have to stand behind the idea of equal sharing; second, they have to be convinced that shortages do actually exist; and third, they must feel that the red tape of the program is not excessive. There is probably a scattering of subversive discontent about the first, but in general it is strongly popular; the second and third are the sources of trouble.

Doubts about the fact of shortages, and therefore about the necessity of rationing certain commodities, derive from two sources. In some cases commodities have been rationed on a nationwide scale though there was a surplus supply in specific areas, and in those areas rationing has on the surface seemed uncalled-for; in other cases OPA either did not make clear that a general shortage existed or did not explain fully the necessity for the actions it took.

The attack on Pearl Harbor was explanation enough to justify tire rationing, and special informational activity was not needed. But the full necessity for sugar rationing was never clearly presented, nor was the logic of nationwide gasoline rationing. Gasoline rationing on the East Coast was readily related to submarine activity along the shipping lanes. However, the extension o rationing to the whole country was not sufficiently explained. Actually it was done to conserve civilian means of transportation so as to prevent the ultimate overloading of public transportation systems. But the smoke of confusion which has risen out of this issue has enveloped it. Many persons still believe that gasoline is rationed because OPA thinks supplies are short, because OPA thinks transportation is inadequate to supply Midwestern and Western motorists, or because the Government expects to confiscate tires and wants them in good shape. The foolishness of such explanations, especially for certain areas, gives rise to disagreement and resentment; a thousand stories about OPA's incompetence are fed and kept alive in the country by the confusion born of misunderstanding. . . .

All the kinks in OPA during Henderson's time are not yet discernible, nor is this analysis complete. For present purposes however er the important fact is that for want of *something* public support was lost, and for want of public support Henderson was lost. . . .

LONG BEFORE HENDERSON left last January the dopesters had picked his logical successor. The man who piloted the two price-control measures through Congress, and who was Henderson's student in the problems of inflation control at that time, ex-senator Prentiss Brown of Upper Michigan, was the natural choice. In due course he was named to head OPA, his appointment being accompanied by a gush of goodwill.

Many persons remembered Brown's courageous stand late in 1942 against the Farm Lobby's attempt to boost farm prices; they were a little disappointed when he was beaten in the November elections; and they had good feeling toward him when he took office as Price Administrator. Because he had been one of them, and because he had always been well-liked personally, Brown

was quite acceptable to the Congress; as soon as he was appointed much of the tension between the agency and the Hill was discharged. Some felt that he would be more conciliatory, and they felt better.

But the great majority of people, noncommittal, just watched with interest for what the first developments would be. A number of issues were on the fire at the time, and how Brown would handle them would be concrete evidence of the turn he would take. Would Brown insist, as Henderson had been doing, that price control had to be more rigorous? Would he support the push for grade-labeling of canned goods in order to prevent quality-cutting, which would defeat price control? Would he continue to resist the political pressures that plagued the agency? What would he do about the problem of "letting consumers in on the program" and giving them a chance to participate? . . .

The new Administrator was most understanding; he made promises; he called in Mr. Herring and told him to clear all major appointments in the future with the Democrats in the House and Senate; furthermore, he told him to begin a housecleaning of all merit appointees in the field organization. Herring leaped to his task and promptly issued his most important manifesto: he intended to fire all OPA executives who (1) had never met a payroll, or (2) had never carried a precinct. He then withdrew to consider the "reorganization" of OPA; his program got underway and ward heelers began moving into influential positions all over the country.

Next on the docket was open house for the lobbyists, literally hundreds of whom have been prowling the halls of OPA. . . .

A close observer of developments in OPA remarked after Brown's first actions that OPA had become the world's greatest jellyfish, formless, sexless, and characterless. However, what had taken place called for more than wit, more than equanimity, and more even than simple anger and outcry. It called for every American, for every member of every group, to sit down quietly and think.

RECENT DEVELOPMENTS MAKE CLEAR that the contestants in the race of group against group are crouched at the starting line, ready to start the dreadful run again. Moreover it is too clear that the starting pistol has a hair-trigger, and the two-point flick of a price index may set it off. . . .

How does it happen that the inflation-control program, which in principle has so tremendous a base of popular support, has constantly been at the mercy of organized pressure groups? Are our democratic processes so ineffective that the key office of the domestic war program can be turned into a political rookery?

New Dealers may wonder what has happened to the cause of the Forgotten Man. Where is the old idealism? . . . Why is there no People's Lobby? If the President is busy with international affairs, does that leave us headless here at home? What comfort is Congress?

---

37.

# R. H. JACKSON, HUGO BLACK, W. O. DOUGLAS, AND FELIX FRANKFURTER: *West Virginia Board of Education et al.* v. *Barnette et al.*

*West Virginia Board of Education v. Barnette, which upheld the right of Jehovah's Witnesses to forbid their children to salute the flag in the public schools, was preceded by two other cases concerning the Witnesses. The first was Minersville School District v. Gobitis (1940), in which the ruling was 8 to 1 in favor of the school district. It was an uncomfortable decision for several of the justices, especially after open hostility developed in many places against the Witnesses. In the second case (1941) over another issue, three of the justices retreated from the Gobitis ruling, which resulted in a renewal of the flag-salute issue in several states. The West Virginia case, dealing with a ruling of the state school board requiring the flag-salute ceremony in all schools, was decided on June 14, 1943 — Flag Day. The following selection contains portions of the Court's opinion by Justice Jackson, concurring opinions by Justices Black and Douglas, and a portion of Justice Frankfurter's dissent. It was Frankfurter who had originally handed down the ruling in the Gobitis case.*

Source: 319 U.S. 624.

*Mr. Justice Jackson.* Following the decision by this Court on June 3, 1940, in *Minersville School District* v. *Gobitis*, 310 U.S. 586, the West Virginia legislature amended its statutes to require all schools therein to conduct courses of instruction in history, civics, and in the constitutions of the United States and of the state "for the purpose of teaching, fostering and perpetuating the ideals, principles, and spirit of Ameri canism, and increasing the knowledge of the organization and machinery of the government." Appellant Board of Education was directed, with advice of the state superintendent of schools, to "prescribe the courses of study covering these subjects" for public schools. The act made it the duty of private, parochial, and denominational schools to prescribe courses of study "similar to those required for the public schools."

The Board of Education on Jan. 9, 1942, adopted a resolution containing recitals taken largely from the Court's *Gobitis* opinion and ordering that the salute to the flag become "a regular part of the program of activities in the public schools," that all teachers and pupils "shall be required to participate in the salute honoring the nation represented by the flag; provided, however, that refusal to salute the flag be regarded as an act of insubordination, and shall be dealt with accordingly." . . .

Failure to conform is "insubordination" dealt with by expulsion. Readmission is denied by statute until compliance. Meanwhile the expelled child is "unlawfully absent" and may be proceeded against as a delinquent. His parents or guardians are liable to prosecution, and if convicted are subject to fine not exceeding $50 and jail term not exceeding thirty days.

Appellees, citizens of the United States and of West Virginia, brought suit in the United States District Court for themselves and others similarly situated asking its injunction to restrain enforcement of these laws and regulations against Jehovah's Witnesses. The Witnesses are an unincorporated body teaching that the obligation imposed by law of God is superior to that of laws enacted by temporal government. Their religious beliefs include a literal version of Exodus, Chapter 20, verses 4 and 5, which says: "Thou shalt not make unto thee any graven image, or any likeness of anything that is in heaven above, or that is in the earth beneath, or that is in the water

under the earth; thou shalt not bow down thyself to them nor serve them." They consider that the flag is an "image" within this command. For this reason they refuse to salute it.

Children of this faith have been expelled from school and are threatened with exclusion for no other cause. Officials threaten to send them to reformatories maintained for criminally inclined juveniles. Parents of such children have been prosecuted and are threatened with prosecutions for causing delinquency.

The Board of Education moved to dismiss the complaint setting forth these facts and alleging that the law and regulations are an unconstitutional denial of religious freedom and of freedom of speech, and are invalid under the "due process" and "equal protection" clauses of the Fourteenth Amendment to the federal Constitution. The cause was submitted on the pleadings to a District Court of three judges. It restrained enforcement as to the plaintiffs and those of that class. The Board of Education brought the case here by direct appeal.

This case calls upon us to reconsider a precedent decision, as the Court throughout its history often has been required to do. Before turning to the *Gobitis* case, however, it is desirable to notice certain characteristics by which this controversy is distinguished.

The freedom asserted by these appellees does not bring them into collision with rights asserted by any other individual. It is such conflicts which most frequently require intervention of the state to determine where the rights of one end and those of another begin. But the refusal of these persons to participate in the ceremony does not interfere with or deny rights of others to do so. Nor is there any question in this case that their behavior is peaceable and orderly. The sole conflict is between authority and rights of the individual. The state asserts power to condition access to public education on making a prescribed sign and profession and at the same time to coerce attendance by punishing both parent and child. The latter stand on a right of self-determination in matters that touch individual opinion and personal attitude. . . .

There is no doubt that, in connection with the pledges, the flag salute is a form of utterance. Symbolism is a primitive but effective way of communicating ideas. The use of an emblem or flag to symbolize some system, idea, institution, or personality is a shortcut from mind to mind. Causes and nations, political parties, lodges, and ecclesiastical groups seek to knit the loyalty of their followings to a flag or banner, a color or design. The state announces rank, function, and authority through crowns and maces, uniforms and black robes; the church speaks through the cross, the crucifix, the altar and shrine, and clerical raiment. Symbols of state often convey political ideas just as religious symbols come to convey the theological ones. Associated with many of these symbols are appropriate gestures of acceptance or respect: a salute, a bowed or bared head, a bended knee. A person gets from a symbol the meaning he puts into it, and what is one man's comfort and inspiration is another's jest and scorn. . . .

It is also to be noted that the compulsory flag salute and pledge requires affirmation of a belief and an attitude of mind. It is not clear whether the regulation contemplates that pupils forego any contrary convictions of their own and become unwilling converts to the prescribed ceremony or whether it will be acceptable if they simulate assent by words without belief and by a gesture barren of meaning. It is now a commonplace that censorship or suppression of expression of opinion is tolerated by our Constitution only when the expression presents a clear and present danger of action of a kind the state is empowered to prevent and punish. It would seem that involuntary affirmation could be commanded only on even more immediate and urgent grounds than silence.

But here the power of compulsion is invoked without any allegation that remaining passive during a flag salute ritual creates a clear and present danger that would justify an effort even to muffle expression. To sustain the compulsory flag salute, we are required to say that a Bill of Rights which guards the individual's right to speak his own mind left it open to public authorities to compel him to utter what is not in his mind.

Whether the First Amendment to the Constitution will permit officials to order observance of ritual of this nature does not depend upon whether as a voluntary exercise we would think it to be good, bad, or merely innocuous. Any credo of nationalism is likely to include what some disapprove or to omit what others think essential, and to give off different overtones as it takes on different accents or interpretations. If official power exists to coerce acceptance of any patriotic creed, what it shall contain cannot be decided by courts, but must be largely discretionary with the ordaining authority, whose power to prescribe would no doubt include power to amend. Hence validity of the asserted power to force an American citizen publicly to profess any statement of belief or to engage in any ceremony of assent to one presents questions of power that must be considered independently of any idea we may have as to the utility of the ceremony in question.

Nor does the issue as we see it turn on one's possession of particular religious views or the sincerity with which they are held. While religion supplies appellees' motive for enduring the discomforts of making the issue in this case, many citizens who do not share these religious views hold such a compulsory rite to infringe constitutional liberty of the individual. It is not necessary to inquire whether nonconformist beliefs will exempt from the duty to salute unless we first find power to make the salute a legal duty. . . .

Free public education, if faithful to the ideal of secular instruction and political neutrality, will not be partisan or enemy of any class, creed, party, or faction. If it is to impose any ideological discipline, however, each party or denomination must seek to control, or failing that, to weaken the influence of the educational system. Observance of the limitations of the Constitution will not weaken government in the field appropriate for its exercise. . . .

The Fourteenth Amendment, as now applied to the states, protects the citizen against the state itself and all of its creatures — boards of education not excepted. These have, of course, important, delicate, and highly discretionary functions, but none that they may not perform within the limits of the Bill of Rights. That they are educating the young for citizenship is reason for scrupulous protection of constitutional freedoms of the individual if we are not to strangle the free mind at its source and teach youth to discount important principles of our government as mere platitudes.

Such boards are numerous and their territorial jurisdiction often small. But small and local authority may feel less sense of responsibility to the Constitution, and agencies of publicity may be less vigilant in calling it to account. The action of Congress in making flag observance voluntary and respecting the conscience of the objector in a matter so vital as raising the Army contrasts sharply with these local regulations in matters relatively trivial to the welfare of the nation. There are village tyrants as well as village Hampdens, but none who acts under color of law is beyond reach of the Constitution. . . .

The very purpose of a Bill of Rights was to withdraw certain subjects from the vicissitudes of political controversy, to place them beyond the reach of majorities and officials, and to establish them as legal principles to be applied by the courts. One's right to life, liberty, and property, to free speech,

a free press, freedom of worship and assembly, and other fundamental rights may not be submitted to vote; they depend on the outcome of no elections.

In weighing arguments of the parties it is important to distinguish between the due process clause of the Fourteenth Amendment as an instrument for transmitting the principles of the First Amendment and those cases in which it is applied for its own sake. The test of legislation which collides with the Fourteenth Amendment, because it also collides with the principles of the First, is much more definite than the test when only the Fourteenth is involved. Much of the vagueness of the due process clause disappears when the specific prohibitions of the First become its standard. The right of a state to regulate, for example, a public utility may well include, so far as the due process test is concerned, power to impose all of the restrictions which a legislature may have a "rational basis" for adopting. But freedoms of speech and of press, of assembly, and of worship may not be infringed on such slender grounds. They are susceptible of restriction only to prevent grave and immediate danger to interests which the state may lawfully protect. It is important to note that while it is the Fourteenth Amendment which bears directly upon the state, it is the more specific limiting principles of the First Amendment that finally govern this case.

Nor does our duty to apply the Bill of Rights to assertions of official authority depend upon our possession of marked competence in the field where the invasion of rights occurs. True, the task of translating the majestic generalities of the Bill of Rights, conceived as part of the pattern of liberal government in the eighteenth century, into concrete restraints on officials dealing with the problems of the twentieth century is one to disturb self-confidence. These principles grew in soil which also produced a philosophy that the individual was the center of society, that his liberty was attainable through mere absence of governmental restraints, and that government should be entrusted with few controls and only the mildest supervision over men's affairs.

We must transplant these rights to a soil in which the laissez faire concept or principle of noninterference has withered at least as to economic affairs, and social advancements are increasingly sought through closer integration of society and through expanded and strengthened governmental controls. These changed conditions often deprive precedents of reliability and cast us more than we would choose upon our own judgment. But we act in these matters not by authority of our competence but by force of our commissions. We cannot, because of modest estimates of our competence in such specialties as public education, withhold the judgment that history authenticates as the function of this Court when liberty is infringed. . . .

National unity as an end which officials may foster by persuasion and example is not in question. The problem is whether under our Constitution compulsion as here employed is a permissible means for its achievement.

Struggles to coerce uniformity of sentiment in support of some end thought essential to their time and country have been waged by many good as well as by evil men. Nationalism is a relatively recent phenomenon, but at other times and places the ends have been racial or territorial security, support of a dynasty or regime, and particular plans for saving souls. As first and moderate methods to attain unity have failed, those bent on its accomplishment must resort to an ever increasing severity. As governmental pressure toward unity becomes greater, so strife becomes more bitter as to whose unity it shall be. Probably no deeper division of our people could proceed from any provocation than from finding it necessary to choose what doctrine and whose

program public educational officials shall compel youth to unite in embracing.

Ultimate futility of such attempts to compel coherence is the lesson of every such effort from the Roman drive to stamp out Christianity as a disturber of its pagan unity; the Inquisition, as a means to religious and dynastic unity; the Siberian exiles, as a means to Russian unity, down to the fast failing efforts of our present totalitarian enemies. Those who begin coercive elimination of dissent soon find themselves exterminating dissenters. Compulsory unification of opinion achieves only the unanimity of the graveyard.

It seems trite but necessary to say that the First Amendment to our Constitution was designed to avoid these ends by avoiding these beginnings. There is no mysticism in the American concept of the state or of the nature or origin of its authority. We set up government by consent of the governed, and the Bill of Rights denies those in power any legal opportunity to coerce that consent. Authority here is to be controlled by public opinion, not public opinion by authority.

The case is made difficult, not because the principles of its decision are obscure but because the flag involved is our own. Nevertheless, we apply the limitations of the Constitution with no fear that freedom to be intellectually and spiritually diverse or even contrary will disintegrate the social organization. To believe that patriotism will not flourish if patriotic ceremonies are voluntary and spontaneous instead of a compulsory routine is to make an unflattering estimate of the appeal of our institutions to free minds. We can have intellectual individualism and the rich cultural diversitie that we owe to exceptional minds only a the price of occasional eccentricity and ab normal attitudes. When they are so harm less to others or to the state as those w deal with here, the price is not too grea But freedom to differ is not limited t things that do not matter much. That would be a mere shadow of freedom. The test of its substance is the right to differ as to things that touch the heart of the existing order.

If there is any fixed star in our constitutional constellation, it is that no official, high or petty, can prescribe what shall be orthodox in politics, nationalism, religion, or other matters of opinion, or force citizens to confess by word or act their faith therein. If there are any circumstances which permit an exception, they do not now occur to us.

We think the action of the local authorities in compelling the flag salute and pledge transcends constitutional limitations on their power and invades the sphere of intellect and spirit which it is the purpose of the First Amendment to our Constitution to reserve from all official control.

The decision of this Court in *Minersville School District* v. *Gobitis* and the holdings of those few *per curiam* decisions which preceded and foreshadowed it are overruled, and the judgment enjoining enforcement of the West Virginia Regulation is *affirmed.*

*Mr. Justice Black* and *Mr. Justice Douglas.* We are substantially in agreement with the opinion just read, but since we originally joined with the Court in the *Gobitis* case, it is appropriate that we make a brief statement of reasons for our change of view.

Reluctance to make the federal Constitution a rigid bar against state regulation of conduct thought inimical to the public welfare was the controlling influence which moved us to consent to the *Gobitis* decision. Long reflection convinced us that although the principle is sound, its application in the particular case was wrong (*Jones* v. *Opelika,* 316 U.S. 584, 623). We believe that the statute before us fails to accord full scope to the freedom of religion secured to the appellees by the First and Fourteenth Amendments.

The statute requires the appellees to participate in a ceremony aimed at inculcating respect for the flag and for this country. The Jehovah's Witnesses, without any desire to show disrespect for either the flag or the country, interpret the Bible as commanding, at the risk of God's displeasure, that they not go through the form of a pledge of allegiance to any flag. The devoutness of their belief is evidenced by their willingness to suffer persecution and punishment rather than make the pledge.

No well-ordered society can leave to the individuals an absolute right to make final decisions, unassailable by the state, as to everything they will or will not do. The First Amendment does not go so far. Religious faiths, honestly held, do not free individuals from responsibility to conduct themselves obediently to laws which are either imperatively necessary to protect society as a whole from grave and pressingly imminent dangers or which, without any general prohibition, merely regulate time, place, or manner of religious activity. Decision as to the constitutionality of particular laws which strike at the substance of religious tenets and practices must be made by this Court. The duty is a solemn one, and in meeting it we cannot say that a failure, because of religious scruples, to assume a particular physical position and to repeat the words of a patriotic formula creates a grave danger to the nation. Such a statutory exaction is a form of test oath, and the test oath has always been abhorrent in the United States.

Words uttered under coercion are proof of loyalty to nothing but self-interest. Love of country must spring from willing hearts and free minds, inspired by a fair administration of wise laws enacted by the people's elected representatives within the bounds of express constitutional prohibitions. These laws must, to be consistent with the First Amendment, permit the widest toleration of conflicting viewpoints consistent with a society of freemen.

Neither our domestic tranquillity in peace nor our martial effort in war depend on compelling little children to participate in a ceremony which ends in nothing for them but a fear of spiritual condemnation. If, as we think, their fears are groundless, time and reason are the proper antidotes for their errors. The ceremonial, when enforced against conscientious objectors, more likely to defeat than to serve its high purpose, is a handy implement for disguised religious persecution. As such, it is inconsistent with our Constitution's plan and purpose.

*Mr. Justice Frankfurter.* One who belongs to the most vilified and persecuted minority in history is not likely to be insensible to the freedoms guaranteed by our Constitution. Were my purely personal attitude relevant, I should wholeheartedly associate myself with the general libertarian views in the Court's opinion, representing as they do the thought and action of a lifetime. But as judges we are neither Jew nor gentile, neither Catholic nor agnostic. We owe equal attachment to the Constitution and are equally bound by our judicial obligations, whether we derive our citizenship from the earliest or the latest immigrants to these shores.

As a member of this Court I am not justified in writing my private notions of policy into the Constitution, no matter how deeply I may cherish them or how mischievous I may deem their disregard. The duty of a judge who must decide which of two claims before the Court shall prevail, that of a state to enact and enforce laws within its general competence or that of an individual to refuse obedience because of the demands of his conscience, is not that of the ordinary person. It can never be emphasized too much that one's own opinion about the wisdom or evil of a law should be excluded altogether when one is doing one's duty on the bench. The only opinion of our own even looking in that direction that is mate-

rial is our opinion whether legislators could in reason have enacted such a law.

In the light of all the circumstances, including the history of this question in this Court, it would require more daring than I possess to deny that reasonable legislators could have taken the action which is before us for review. Most unwillingly, therefore, I must differ from my brethren with regard to legislation like this. I cannot bring my mind to believe that the "liberty" secured by the due process clause gives this Court authority to deny to the state of West Virginia the attainment of that which we all recognize as a legitimate legislative end, namely, the promotion of good citizenship by employment of the means here chosen. . . .

Conscientious scruples, all would admit, cannot stand against every legislative compulsion to do positive acts in conflict with such scruples. We have been told that such compulsions override religious scruples only as to major concerns of the state. But the determination of what is major and what is minor itself raises questions of policy. For the way in which men equally guided by reason appraise importance goes to the very heart of policy. Judges should be very diffident in setting their judgment against that of a state in determining what is and what is not a major concern, what means are appropriate to proper ends, and what is the total social cost in striking the balance of imponderables.

What one can say with assurance is that the history out of which grew constitutional provisions for religious equality and the writings of the great exponents of religious freedom — Jefferson, Madison, John Adams, Benjamin Franklin — are totally wanting in justification for a claim by dissidents of exceptional immunity from civil measures of general applicability, measures not in fact disguised assaults upon such dissident views. The great leaders of the American Revolution were determined to remove political support from every religious establishment. They put on an equality the different religious sects — Episcopalians, Presbyterians, Catholics, Baptists, Methodists, Quakers, Huguenots — which, as dissenters, had been under the heel of the various orthodoxies that prevailed in different colonies. So far as the state was concerned, there was to be neither orthodoxy nor heterodoxy. And so Jefferson and those who followed him wrote guarantees of religious freedom into our constitutions. Religious minorities as well as religious majorities were to be equal in the eyes of the political state. But Jefferson and the others also knew that minorities may disrupt society. It never would have occurred to them to write into the Constitution the subordination of the general civil authority of the state to sectarian scruples.

The constitutional protection of religious freedom terminated disabilities; it did not create new privileges. It gave religious equality, not civil immunity. Its essence is freedom from conformity to religious dogma, not freedom from conformity to law because of religious dogma. Religious loyalties may be exercised without hindrance from the state, but the state may not exercise that which except by leave of religious loyalties is within the domain of temporal power. Otherwise each individual could set up his own censor against obedience to laws conscientiously deemed for the public good by those whose business it is to make laws.

The prohibition against any religious establishment by the government placed denominations on an equal footing — it assured freedom from support by the government to any mode of worship and the freedom of individuals to support any mode of worship. Any person may therefore believe or disbelieve what he pleases. He may practise what he will in his own house of worship or publicly within the limits of public order. But the lawmaking authority is not circumscribed by the variety of religious beliefs, otherwise the constitutional guarantee would be not a protection of the free exercise of religion but a denial of the exercise of legislation.

The essence of the religious freedom guaranteed by our Constitution is therefore this: No religion shall either receive the state's support or incur its hostility. Religion is outside the sphere of political government. This does not mean that all matters on which religious organizations or beliefs may pronounce are outside the sphere of government. Were this so, instead of the separation of church and state, there would be the subordination of the state on any matter deemed within the sovereignty of the religious conscience. Much that is the concern of temporal authority affects the spiritual interests of men. But it is not enough to strike down a nondiscriminatory law that it may hurt or offend some dissident view. It would be too easy to cite numerous prohibitions and injunctions to which laws run counter if the variant interpretations of the Bible were made the tests of obedience to law. The validity of secular laws cannot be measured by their conformity to religious doctrines. It is only in a theocratic state that ecclesiastical doctrines measure legal right or wrong.

An act compelling profession of allegiance to a religion, no matter how subtly or tenuously promoted, is bad. But an act promoting good citizenship and national allegiance is within the domain of governmental authority and is therefore to be judged by the same considerations of power and of constitutionality as those involved in the many claims of immunity from civil obedience because of religious scruples.

That claims are pressed on behalf of sincere religious convictions does not of itself establish their constitutional validity. Nor does waving the banner of religious freedom relieve us from examining into the power we are asked to deny the states.

Otherwise the doctrine of separation of church and state, so cardinal in the history of this nation and for the liberty of our people, would mean not the disestablishment of a state church but the establishment of all churches and of all religious groups. . . .

Parents have the privilege of choosing which schools they wish their children to attend. And the question here is whether the state may make certain requirements that seem to it desirable or important for the proper education of those future citizens who go to schools maintained by the states, or whether the pupils in those schools may be relieved from those requirements if they run counter to the consciences of their parents. Not only have parents the right to send children to schools of their own choosing but the state has no right to bring such schools "under a strict governmental control" or give "affirmative direction concerning the intimate and essential details of such schools, entrust their control to public officers, and deny both owners and patrons reasonable choice and discretion in respect of teachers, curriculum, and textbooks." . . . Why should not the state likewise have constitutional power to make reasonable provisions for the proper instruction of children in schools maintained by it?

When dealing with religious scruples we are dealing with an almost numberless variety of doctrines and beliefs entertained with equal sincerity by the particular groups for which they satisfy man's needs in his relation to the mysteries of the universe. There are in the United States more than 250 distinctive established religious denominations. In the state of Pennsylvania there are 120 of these, and in West Virginia as many as 65. But if religious scruples afford immunity from civic obedience to laws, they may be invoked by the religious beliefs of any individual even though he holds no membership in any sect or organized denomination. Certainly this Court cannot be called upon to determine what claims of conscience should be recognized and what should be rejected as satisfying the "religion" which the Constitution protects. That would indeed resurrect the very discriminatory treatment of religion which the Constitution sought forever to forbid. . . .

We are told that a flag salute is a doubtful substitute for adequate understanding of our institutions. The states that require such a school exercise do not have to justify it as the only means for promoting good citizenship in children but merely as one of diverse means for accomplishing a worthy end. We may deem it a foolish measure, but the point is that this Court is not the organ of government to resolve doubts as to whether it will fulfill its purpose. Only if there be no doubt that any reasonable mind could entertain can we deny to the states the right to resolve doubts their way and not ours.

That which to the majority may seem essential for the welfare of the state may offend the consciences of a minority. But, so long as no inroads are made upon the actual exercise of religion by the minority, to deny the political power of the majority to enact laws concerned with civil matters simply because they may offend the consciences of a minority really means that the consciences of a minority are more sacred and more enshrined in the Constitution than the consciences of a majority.

We are told that symbolism is a dramatic but primitive way of communicating ideas. Symbolism is inescapable. Even the most sophisticated live by symbols. But it is not for this Court to make psychological judgments as to the effectiveness of a particular symbol in inculcating concededly indispensable feelings, particularly if the state happens to see fit to utilize the symbol that represents our heritage and our hopes. And surely only flippancy could be responsible for the suggestion that constitutional validity of a requirement to salute our flag implies equal validity of a requirement to salute a dictator. The significance of a symbol lies in what it represents. To reject the swastika does not imply rejection of the cross. And so it bears repetition to say that it mocks reason and denies our whole history to find in the allowance of a requirement to salute our flag on fitting occasions the seeds of sanction for obeisance to a leader. To deny the power to employ educational symbols is to say that the state's educational system may not stimulate the imagination because this may lead to unwise stimulation. . . .

The flag salute exercise has no kinship whatever to the oath tests so odious in history. For the oath test was one of the instruments for suppressing heretical beliefs. Saluting the flag suppresses no belief nor curbs it. Children and their parents may believe what they please, avow their belief and practise it. It is not even remotely suggested that the requirement for saluting the flag involves the slightest restriction against the fullest opportunity on the part both of the children and of their parents to disavow as publicly as they choose to do so the meaning that others attach to the gesture of salute. All channels of affirmative free expression are open to both children and parents. Had we before us any act of the state putting the slightest curbs upon such free expression, I should not lag behind any member of this Court in striking down such an invasion of the right to freedom of thought and freedom of speech protected by the Constitution.

I am fortified in my view of this case by the history of the flag salute controversy in this Court. Five times has the precise question now before us been adjudicated. Four times the Court unanimously found that the requirement of such a school exercise was not beyond the powers of the states. Indeed, in the first three cases to come before the Court, the constitutional claim now sustained was deemed so clearly unmeritorious

that this Court dismissed the appeals for want of a substantial federal question. . . .

What may be even more significant than this uniform recognition of state authority is the fact that every justice — thirteen in all — who has hitherto participated in judging this matter has at one or more times found no constitutional infirmity in what is now condemned. Only the two justices sitting for the first time on this matter have not heretofore found this legislation inoffensive to the "liberty" guaranteed by the Constitution. And among the justices who sustained this measure were outstanding judicial leaders in the zealous enforcement of constitutional safeguards of civil liberties — men like Chief Justice Hughes, Mr. Justice Brandeis, and Mr. Justice Cardozo, to mention only those no longer on the Court.

One's conception of the Constitution cannot be served from one's conception of a judge's function in applying it. The Court has no reason for existence if it merely reflects the pressures of the day. Our system is built on the faith that men set apart for this special function, freed from the influences of immediacy and from the deflections of worldly ambition, will become able to take a view of longer range than the period of responsibility entrusted to Congress and legislatures. We are dealing with matters as to which legislators and voters have conflicting views. Are we as judges to impose our strong convictions on where wisdom lies?

That which three years ago had seemed to five successive Courts to lie within permissible areas of legislation is now outlawed by the deciding shift of opinion of two justices. What reason is there to believe that they or their successors may not have another view a few years hence? Is that which was deemed to be of so fundamental a nature as to be written into the Constitution to endure for all times to be the sport of shifting winds of doctrine? Of course, judicial opinions, even as to questions of constitutionality, are not immutable. As has been true in the past, the Court will from time to time reverse its position. But I believe that never before these Jehovah's Witnesses' cases (except for minor deviations subsequently retracted) has this Court overruled decisions so as to restrict the powers of democratic government. Always, heretofore, it has withdrawn narrow views of legislative authority so as to authorize what formerly it had denied.

In view of this history it must be plain that what thirteen justices found to be within the constitutional authority of a state, legislators cannot be deemed unreasonable in enacting. Therefore, in denying to the states what heretofore has received such impressive judicial sanction, some other tests of unconstitutionality must surely be guiding the Court than the absence of a rational justification for the legislation. But I know of no other test which this Court is authorized to apply in nullifying legislation.

In the past this Court has from time to time set its views of policy against that embodied in legislation by finding laws in conflict with what was called the "spirit of the Constitution." Such undefined destructive power was not conferred on this Court by the Constitution. Before a duly enacted law can be judicially nullified, it must be forbidden by some explicit restriction upon political authority in the Constitution. Equally inadmissible is the claim to strike down legislation because to us as individuals it seems opposed to the "plan and purpose" of the Constitution. That is too tempting a basis for finding in one's personal views the purposes of the founders.

The uncontrollable power wielded by this Court brings it very close to the most sensitive areas of public affairs. As appeal from legislation to adjudication becomes more frequent, and its consequences more far-reaching, judicial self-restraint becomes more and not less important, lest we unwarrantably enter social and political domains wholly outside our concern. I think I appreciate fully the objections to the law before us. But to deny that it presents a question upon which men might reasonably differ appears to me to be intolerance. And since men may so reasonably differ, I deem it beyond my constitutional power to assert my view of the wisdom of this law against the view of the state of West Virginia.

Jefferson's opposition to judicial review has not been accepted by history, but it still serves as an admonition against confusion between judicial and political functions. As a rule of judicial self-restraint, it is still as valid as Lincoln's admonition. For those who pass laws not only are under duty to pass laws; they are also under duty to observe the Constitution. And even though legislation relates to civil liberties, our duty of deference to those who have the responsibility for making the laws is no less relevant or less exacting. And this is so especially when we consider the accidental contingencies by which one man may determine constitutionality and thereby confine the political power of the Congress of the United States and the legislatures of forty-eight states. The attitude of judicial humility which these considerations enjoin is not an abdication of the judicial function. It is a due observance of its limits. Moreover, it is to be borne in mind that in a question like this we are not passing on the proper distribution of political power as between the states and the central government. We are not discharging the basic function of this Court as the mediator of powers within the federal system. To strike down a law like this is to deny a power to all government.

---

*Kilroy was here.*
Army saying, World War II

**Explosions rock American base at Pearl Harbor following surprise Japanese attack, Dec. 7, 1941**

# THE WAR: 1941-1944

To Japan, an eventual attack on the United States, specifically on the island outpost of Hawaii, was an inevitable beginning of military action against a nation committed in policy to the support of Japan's enemies. To the American nation, wrestling with the implications and responsibilities of neutrality, the attack on Pearl Harbor was a profound shock. The immediate effect domestically was the silencing of isolationist argument and the hardening of public sentiment against the Axis powers. In the few days following December 7, Italy and Germany upheld the Tripartite Pact by declaring war on the United States; Congress replied in kind, and Britain declared war with Japan. With the enemy in possession of Europe and of Southeast Asia, and with the fall of Russia, China, and the Middle East apparently imminent, the structure of the war of the Allies and the Axis was complete and global.

Churchill, on the "Prince of Wales," watches Roosevelt depart from their shipboard meeting, 1941

Investigations by a presidential commission, by a joint congressional committee, and by Army and Navy boards in the years following Pearl Harbor revealed that ineptitude and incompetence both in Washington and Hawaii were responsible for the complete success of the Japanese attack. Intelligence reports on Japanese ship movements were discounted, security measures were ignored, and there prevailed a general lassitude that was shaken only by bombs and torpedoes. The Pacific Fleet was severely damaged and America was forced into a defensive strategy in the Pacific that was to last for more than six months.

(Left) Cordell Hull with Japanese peace envoys Nomura and Kurusu, who were conferring as the Japanese force prepared to attack Pearl Harbor (below)

(Above) Sailors at the Naval Air Station on Ford Island watch the explosion of the battleship "Arizona" in Pearl Harbor, 1941

(Left) President Roosevelt signs the declaration of war passed by Congress in a special session the day after the attack on Pearl Harbor; (below) U.S. battleship sinks into the harbor after being hit by Japanese torpedoes and dive bombers

(Above) Ammunition dumps in Singapore set afire by Japanese artillery in 1942. The city surrendered to the Japanese after a week of fighting. (Below) Japanese soldiers capture the American forces defending Corregidor after a 28-day siege of the fortress

**(Above) Japanese carrier "Shoho" sinking in the Coral Sea after an attack by a U.S. bomber in May 1942**

By May 1942 the Japanese had overrun most of eastern Asia, from Indochina in the East to New Guinea in the South. Australia was the obvious next step. Seeking air and naval bases for the attack, Japanese forces attempted to take Tulagi and Port Moresby in the southern Solomon Islands. The Allies were alert and the ensuing Battle of the Coral Sea (May 3-8), though a tactical loss for the Allies, was the first successful opposition to Japanese expansion.

**Battle of Coral Sea: (Right) Bomber takes off from the carrier "Lexington" in an aerial attack on the Japanese carriers "Zuikaku" and "Shokaku"; (below) carrier "Yorktown" under fire**

(Above) Nazi soldiers view the destruction of bridges over the Dnieper River from the Citadel of Kiev; (below) Nevsky Prospect under artillery fire in blockaded Leningrad, 1942

After miscalculations and indecision had prolonged the Russian campaign into the winter of 1941-1942, the Soviet Army was more prepared to resist. The German Army was caught between a strong counteroffensive, the Russian winter, and Hitler's refusal to retreat. The German drive was resumed in the summer but with lessened momentum. The Germans hesitated at Stalingrad; the campaign there dragged on and on until the Russians were able to launch a counterattack in November that broke the invasion completely.

**Nazi invasion of Russia: (Top) Russian tanks and ski troops in a counterattack outside Moscow; (center) German infantry approach suburb of Stalingrad; (bottom) Stalingrad under attack**

With the Pacific Fleet unable to carry on more than a delaying strategy against the Japanese, the decision was made to concentrate the major American efforts in the European war. Despite the steps toward economic and military mobilization taken during the non-neutrality period, however, a year of war passed before American forces were ready to take combat action. In the meanwhile, the most pressing problem was the virtual dominance of Atlantic shipping by German submarines.

**(Top) American convoy crossing the North Atlantic in 1942; (center) British ship deploys depth charges to protect convoy from German U-boats; (bottom) sinking of the H.M.S. "Barham," November 1941**

(Above) Allied bombs set fire to Danzig harbor; (below) an R.A.F. Halifax dropping bombs on target in Pas-de-Calais area during a daylight mission in 1944

**Australian troops wait to enter burning Tobruk as Allies gain control of the city in early 1941**

By November 1942 the Allies had begun to secure the Atlantic. Stalin was demanding the opening of a second front against Germany to relieve the pressure on Russia. Britain and America were not yet prepared for a major continental invasion, so a compromise was reached in the North Africa campaign. Landing on November 8, Allied forces forced the capitulation of the Vichy regimes in Morocco and Algeria and drove eastward against Rommel.

**(Left) Knightsbridge in the Libyan desert, scene of a great tank battle between the German and British forces; (below) British cruiser tank passes a burning German tank**

U.S. Army Photo

U.S. troops landing with Higgins assault boats on a beach in French Morocco, November 1942

Imperial War Museum

U.S. Army Photo

(Above) Prisoners captured by the British 1st Household Cavalry Regiment during the North African campaign, late 1942; (left) delegates to the Casablanca Conference, held January 1943: (left to right) General Giraud, President Roosevelt, General de Gaulle, and Winston Churchill

(Above) Allied troops landing on Sicilian beach, July 1943, in preparation for the invasion of Italy; (below) foxholes along the beach outside Salerno protect Allies from German attacks

(Above) British infantrymen rout remaining Germans in the Battle of Cassino, May 1944; (below) Italians cheer Allied forces arriving in Rome to liberate the city, June 1944

Battle of Stalingrad: (Above) German tanks storm city; (below) Soviets fight to control a house

North Africa was cleared of German forces by May 1943. In June the landings began in Sicily; Mussolini was deposed and Italy surrendered in September. German troops, however, remained to fight a bitter defense until April 1945. The Italian campaign, while a sign of progress and a successful application of the joint Allied command system, was neither the second front demanded by Russia nor a real threat to Germany. It did serve to weaken German strength in the East, where Russian troops had regained virtually all their previous losses, and in the Balkans. Meanwhile, planning proceeded for the long-awaited full-scale invasion of Europe, Operation "Overlord." During 1943 the U-boat threat was mastered in the Atlantic, and the Italian campaign had opened the Mediterranean for Allied supply lines; the Allies were in position for the final move against Germany.

(Top) Soviet Army fighting
the Germans in the shops
of the Krasny Oktyabr
Works, January 1943;
(center) Russian infantry
attacks under the cover of
a smoke screen and a
snowstorm; (bottom)
Stalin, Roosevelt, and
Churchill confer at Teheran
in 1943

(Above) Men and materials arrive at Lunga Point to reinforce the U.S. position on Guadalcanal prior to the six-month battle with the Japanese; (below) dead Marines on Buna, New Guinea; one of the first photographs of American dead released for publication in the U.S., late 1942

(Above) Aftermath of the bloody invasion of Tarawa by American Marines, November 1943

After the Navy had turned back Japanese attempts on Port Moresby and Midway Island, inflicting heavy damage on the Japanese fleet, the United States assumed the offensive in the Pacific for the first time. Although still in a position of inferior strength, American forces immediately began a series of island landings designed to isolate Japanese forces and territory and to establish strategic bases for attacks against Japan itself.

(Right) Marines shell Japanese defenses on Cape Gloucester; (below) U.S. troops advance on Tarawa

Marines campaign against Japanese defenses in the Pacific islands. (Left) Exhausted private moves machine gun into position in the front line on Cape Gloucester; (center left) capturing a Japanese prisoner in the Marshall Islands; (center right) crawling to positions along the beach on Saipan under enemy fire, 1944

U.S. Defense Dept.

U.S. Defense Dept.

U.S. Defense Dept.

**Marine infantrymen move into new positions in Garapan, major city on Saipan**

U.S. Defense Dept.

**(Above) U.S. C-46 flying supplies into China**

The Chinese-Japanese war merged into the global war as the Nationalist government under Gen. Chiang Kai-shek formally declared war after Pearl Harbor. A Japanese blockade had cut off supplies to the Nationalist forces, so an Allied airlift from India was begun, flying munitions and equipment "over the hump." Small as it was, Allied assistance was largely negated by the increasing corruption and inefficiency and the decreasing popularity of the Chiang regime; by contrast, the Chinese Communists concentrated in the North won wide popular support in their cooperative campaign against the Japanese.

**(Center) U.S. Ambassador Patrick Hurley meets with Communist Chinese leader Mao Tse-tung and party secretary Yang Shang Kun in an attempt to bring Mao to meet with Nationalist leader Chiang Kai-hek; (right) American General Stillwell (seated center) confers with Liao Yau Siang on the Chinese offensive in Burma, 1944**

**(Above) Sherman tanks and half-tracks amassed in Britain for the D-Day invasion of Europe**

The Italian campaign relieved some of the military and political pressure on the united Allied command while the planning for the major invasion of Europe proceeded. After the Casablanca Conference the massive military build-up in England continued and the intensive bombing of German industrial and military plants was stepped up. In December 1943 Gen. Eisenhower was appointed supreme commander of the invasion forces, with a tentative date set for May 1944.

**(Right) On the eve of invasion, Gen. Eisenhower visits the Allied troops; (below) Rommel inspects western German defenses, early 1944**

38.

## Bill Steele: What Should You Bring Overseas?

*Yank came close to being the GI's Bible during World War II. Published from 1942
to 1945, it was a weekly magazine written by and for enlisted men of the Army and was
the most widely circulated service periodical during the war. Its most popular features
were cartoons, notably George Baker's "Sad Sack," pin-ups, letters from soldiers, and
editorials on subjects of concern to enlisted men. Early in 1943 the magazine published
the following article by Private Bill Steele, a* Yank *field correspondent, giving advice
to servicemen about to be sent overseas to the South Pacific.*

Source: *Yank*, March 26, 1943.

*Somewhere in the South Pacific* — As
soon as they land down here, nine out of
10 GIs say, "I wish to hell I could get back
to the States — long enough to buy a
knife." Nor is it only knives we need —
every Johnny Jeep among us could make
out a long list of items he wishes he had
thought to remember to ship into his barracks bag when he left that port of embarkation. The moral is: Whatever you're going to need, you'd better bring with you.

Chances are that down here there won't
be any civilian outlets where you can get a
shaving mirror or a flashlight. And though
the PXs — if you are lucky enough to be
near one — try hard to supply such items,
they're usually just out when *you* get there.

The foreign-bound soldier should not
load himself with patented worksavers and
fancy gadgets. Your GI equipment, usually
the best, is sufficient. But extra items have
proved practical and useful. They'll add to
your pleasures and do away with some of
the woes of soldiering overseas.

Probably the handiest item to bring along
is a hunting knife. One with a good stout
blade. You'll use it in a dozen ways just

while converting your pyramidal into a
place you can call home, cutting branches
to hang as a clothes rack in the peak of the
tent, and cutting out brush roots for a floor.
The ideal possession would be a miniature
kit containing a saw, pliers, hammer, and
knife — but they're difficult to obtain in
kits even in the States.

When you embark, you'll be completely
outfitted with proper clothing — but you
are probably well stocked with extra socks,
shorts, and handkerchiefs. Okay, stick them
in your barracks bag. Never too many pairs
of clean socks.

Swim trunks — don't forget 'em! It's
awkward to want a swim at a convenient
seashore and not be able to for fear some
nurse with a lieutenant's commission or a
local maid might make a visit to the beach.
You'll wear the trunks en route too — for
a sun bath on deck.

There isn't much need for military ox-
fords over here. Far better types of foot-
wear to bring are rubber soled sneaks or
moccasin slippers. Something to wear when
you're boxing, playing baseball, or just hit-

ting the sack for a few minutes' rest before chow. Something you can slip on for hurry-up nocturnal trips too.

Before you leave, get a small mirror. This mirror will henceforth lead a very rugged life, so it had better be a metal one. Bring plenty of razor blades too. They don't take up much space, and you never know when you won't be able to buy any.

Flashlights are swell to have and impossible to buy around here. So it's a good idea to bring one. You'll have to surrender it while aboard ship, but it's worth the trouble.

There's many a man who'd hock his PFC stripe for a bottle of anti-mosquito dope. The numerous mosquitoes here are active little fellows. They'll drain a fellow of his last corpuscles at night and appear at the Red Cross station as blood donors the next morning. Oil of citronella is effective in repelling them.

Make sure that you or somebody else brings a washboard — one of the small ones that you can buy at a five-and-ten-cent store. You'll be doing most of your laundry yourself and fatigues can be cleaned much more easily with a washboard.

The same tip goes for a camera. Films are difficult to get, and exposures are developed GI, a very slow proposition. Nevertheless, the few cameras we have here are kept very busy indeed taking snapshots of old buddies and new scenery.

Old-timers (anyone who has been here more than a month is an old-timer) will undoubtedly try to buy some of your "luxury" items such as watches, cigarette lighters, fountain pens and pencil sets. Sometimes local civilian shops carry them, but at fantastic prices. Since the opportunities for spending cash are limited, only too often dog-faces will part with the good green for a fancy bauble. You'll be better off, though, to hang onto your fountain pen and wristwatch than to sell them, even at black market prices.

Speaking of watches — the waterproof, shockproof timepiece is easily best if you want to invest a sizeable amount of money. But an inexpensive, Mickey Mouse-type wristwatch will do almost as well.

Here's a final tip to act on when the time comes for you to trade your mainland address for an APO in the Pacific. Have plenty of pictures of the girl back home with you. You'll understand the reason the first day after you arrive.

———◆———

*If it moves, salute it.*
*If it doesn't move, pick it up.*
*If you can't pick it up, paint it.*
    "The Sad Sack's Catechism," World War II

39.

# Ernie Pyle: Americans at War

*The Indiana journalist Ernest Taylor Pyle — Ernie Pyle to the millions who read him*
*and to the soldiers that he liked so well — was probably the most popular and best*
*known of all the American newspapermen who came to the fore during World War II.*
*A correspondent in England, North Africa, Europe, and the Pacific from 1941 to 1945,*
*his columns about "your boys" were devoured on the home front, and his books —*
*Ernie Pyle in England (1941), Here Is Your War (1943), and Brave Men (1944) —*
*were runaway best sellers. His sympathy for and understanding of the ordinary*
*American foot soldier was evident to all, and the fact that he was himself a victim of*
*the war — he was killed by a Japanese machine gun bullet on Ie Shima in 1945 — made*
*him a national hero after it. The last chapter of Here Is Your War is reprinted here.*

Source: *Here Is Your War*, Peoples Book Club Edition, Chicago, 1944: "Aftermath."

THE TUNISIAN CAMPAIGN WAS ENDED. Our air forces moved on farther into Tunisia, to the very edge of the chasm of sea that separated them only so little from Sicily and Sardinia and then from Europe itself. We and the British leaped upon the demolished ports we had captured, cleared out enough wreckage for a foothold for ships, and as the ports grew and grew in usefulness they swarmed with thousands of men, and ships, and trucks. Our combat troops moved back — out of range of enemy strafers — to be cheered and acclaimed momentarily by the cities in the rear, to take a few days of wild and hell-roaring rest, and then to go into an invasion practice that was in every respect, except the one of actually getting shot, as rigorous as a real invasion.

Surely before autumn we of Tunisia would be deep into something new. Most of us realized and admitted to ourselves that horrible days lay ahead. The holocaust that at times seemed so big to us in Tunisia would pale in our memories beside the things we would see and do before another year ran out.

Tunisia for us was not only an end in itself, but without the War of Tunisia we would have been ill-prepared to go on into the bigger wars ahead. Tunisia has been called a warm-up ground. That is a proper word for it, I suppose. We found through actual test which of our weapons and planes and vehicles were good, and which were bad, and which could be made good with a little changing. We seasoned our men in battle, and we found the defects that needed to be found in our communications systems, our supply lines, our methods of organization.

It is hard for you at home to realize what an immense, complicated, sprawling institution a theater of war actually is. As it appears to you in the newspapers, war is a clear-cut matter of landing so many men overseas, moving them from the port to the battlefield, advancing them against the enemy with guns firing, and they win or lose.

To look at war that way is like seeing a trailer of a movie, and saying you've seen the whole picture. I actually don't know what percentage of our troops in Africa were in the battle lines, but I believe it safe to say that only comparatively few ever saw the enemy, ever shot at him, or were shot at by him. All the rest of those hundreds of thousands of men were churning the highways for two thousand miles behind the lines with their endless supply trucks, they were unloading the ships, cooking the meals, pounding the typewriters, fixing the roads, making the maps, repairing the engines, decoding the messages, training the reserves, pondering the plans.

To get all that colossal writhing chaos shaped into something that intermeshed and moved forward with efficiency was a task closely akin to weaving a cloth out of a tubful of spaghetti. It was all right to have wonderful plans ahead of time, but we really learn such things only by doing. Now, after our forces have had more than six months' experience in North Africa, I for one feel that we have washed out the bulk of our miscomprehensions, have abandoned most of our fallacies, and have hardened down into a work-weary ·and battle-dirtied machine of great effect, capable of assimilating and directing aright those greener men who are to follow by the hundreds of thousands and maybe millions.

What I have seen in North Africa has altered my own feelings in one respect. There were days when I sat in my tent alone and gloomed with the desperate belief that it was actually possible for us to lose this war. I don't feel that way any more. Despite our strikes and bickering and confusion back home, America is producing and no one can deny that. Even here at the far end of just one line the trickle has grown into an impressive stream. We are producing at home and we are hardening overseas. Apparently it takes a country like America about two years to become wholly at war. We had to go through that transition period of letting loose of life as it was, and then live the new war life so long that it finally became the normal life to us. It was a form of growth, and we couldn't press it. Only time can produce that change. We have survived that

long passage of time, and if I am at all correct we have about changed our character and become a war nation. I can't yet see when we shall win, or over what route geographically, or by which of the many means of warfare. But no longer do I have any doubts at all that we shall win.

The men over here have changed too. They are too close to themselves to sense the change, perhaps. And I am too close to them to grasp it fully. But since I am older and a little apart, I have been able to notice it more.

For a year, everywhere I went, soldiers inevitably asked me two questions: "When do you think we'll get to go home?" and "When will the war be over?" The homegoing desire was once so dominant that I believe our soldiers over here would have voted — if the question had been put — to go home immediately, even if it meant peace on terms of something less than unconditional surrender by the enemy.

That isn't true now. Sure, they all still want to go home. So do I. But there is something deeper than that, which didn't exist six months ago. I can't quite put it into words — it isn't any theatrical proclamation that the enemy must be destroyed in the name of freedom; it's just a vague but growing individual acceptance of the bitter fact that we must win the war or else, and that it can't be won by running excursion boats back and forth across the Atlantic carrying homesick vacationers.

A year is a long time to be away from home, especially if a person has never been away before, as was true of the bulk of our troops. At first homesickness can almost kill a man. But time takes care of that. It isn't normal to moon in the past forever. Home gradually grows less vivid; the separation from it less agonizing. There finally comes a day — not suddenly but gradually, as a sunset-touched cloud changes its color — when a man is living almost wholly wherever he is. His life has caught up with his body, and his days become full war days, instead of American days simply transplanted to Africa.

That's the stage our soldiers are in now — the ones who have been over since the beginning, I mean. It seems to take about that long. It's only in the last few weeks that I've begun to hear frequent remarks, said enthusiastically and sincerely, about the thrill it will be to see Paris and to march down the streets of Berlin. The immediate goal used to be the Statue of Liberty; more and more it is becoming Unter den Linden. When all of our army has bridged that gap we shall be in the home stretch.

Our men can't make this change from normal civilians into warriors and remain the same people. Even if they were away from you this long under normal circumstances, the mere process of maturing would change them, and they would not come home just as you knew them. Add to that the abnormal world they have been plunged into, the new philosophies they have had to assume or perish inwardly, the horrors and delights and strange wonderful things they have experienced, and they are bound to be different people from those you sent away.

They are rougher than when you knew them. Killing is a rough business. Their basic language has changed from mere profanity to obscenity. More than anything else, they miss women. Their expressed longings, their conversation, their whole conduct show their need for female companionship, and the gentling effect of femininity upon man is conspicuous here where it has been so long absent.

Our men have less regard for property than you raised them to have. Money value means nothing to them, either personally or in the aggregate; they are fundamentally generous, with strangers and with each other. They give or throw away their own money, and it is natural that they are even less thoughtful of bulk property than of their own hard-earned possessions. It is often necessary to abandon equipment they can't take with them; the urgency of war prohibits normal caution in the handling of vehicles and supplies. One of the most striking things to me about war is the appalling waste that is necessary. At the front there just isn't time to be economical. Also, in war areas where things are scarce and red tape still rears its delaying head, a man learns to get what he needs simply by "requisitioning." It isn't stealing, it's the only way to acquire certain things. The stress of war puts old virtues in a changed light. We shall have to relearn a simple fundamental or two when things get back to normal. But what's wrong with a small case of "requisitioning" when murder is the classic goal?

Our men, still thinking of home, are impatient with the strange peoples and customs of the countries they now inhabit. They say that if they ever get home they never want to see another foreign country. But I know how it will be. The day will come when they'll look back and brag about how they learned a little Arabic, and how swell the girls were in England, and how pretty the hills of Germany were. Every day their scope is broadening despite themselves, and once they all get back with their global yarns and their foreign-tinged views, I cannot conceive of our nation ever being isolationist again. The men don't feel very international right now, but the influences are at work and the time will come.

I couldn't say truthfully that they are very much interested in foreign affairs right now, outside of battle affairs. Awhile back a friend of mine in Washington wrote me an enthusiastic letter, telling of the Ball Resolution in the Senate calling for the formation of a United Nations organization to coordinate the prosecution of the war, administer reoccupied countries, feed and economically reestablish liberated nations, and to assemble a United Nations military force to suppress any future military aggression.

My friend told of the enthusiasm the bill had created at home, hailed it as the first definite step in winning the peace as well as the war, and asked me almost pleadingly to send back a report on what the men at the front thought of the bill.

I didn't send any report, because the men at the front thought very little about it one way or the other. I doubt that one out of ten of them remembered the thing two days, even though they may have read about it in *Stars and Stripes.* There wasn't anything specific to get their teeth into and argue about. It sounded too much like another Atlantic Charter or committee meeting.

Of course, by digging, a person could find plenty of politically and internationally minded men in our army — all the way from generals to privates — who do spend considerable time thinking of what is to come after the victory, and how we are to handle it. But what I'm trying to get over is that the bulk of our army in Africa, the run-of-the-mine mass of soldiers, didn't think twice about this bill if they heard of it at all. Their thoughts on the peace can be summed up, I believe, in a general statement that after this war is won they want it fixed so it can't happen again and they want a hand in fixing it, but our average guy has no more conception of how it should be done than to say he supposes some kind of world police force is the answer. There is a great deal more talk along the line of, "Those bluenoses back home better not try to put prohibition over on us while we're away this time," than you hear about bills and resolutions looking toward the postwar world.

Your men have been well cared for in this war. I suppose no soldiers in any other war in history have had such excellent attention as our men overseas. The food is good. Of course we're always yapping about how wonderful a steak would taste on Broadway, but when a soldier is pinned right down he'll admit ungrudgingly that it's Broadway he's thinking about more than the steak, and that he really can't kick on the food. Furthermore, cooking is good in this war. Last time good food was spoiled by lousy cooking, but that is the exception this time. Of course, there were times in battle when the men lived for days on nothing but those deadly cold C rations out of tin cans, and even went without food for a day or two, but those were the crises, the exceptions. On the whole, we figure by the letters from home that we're probably eating better than you are.

A good diet and excellent medical care have made our army a healthy one. Statistics show the men in the mass healthier today than they were in civil life back home.

Our men are well provided with clothing, transportation, mail, and army newspapers. Back of the lines they had Post Exchanges where they could buy cigarettes, candy, toilet articles, and all such things. If they were in the combat zone, all those things were issued to them free.

Our fighting equipment was the only thing that didn't stand head and shoulders above everything issued to soldiers of any other country, and that was only because we weren't ready for war at first, and for two years we have been learning what was good and what was bad. Already many of our weapons are unmatched by any other country. Give us another year and surely it can be said that our men are furnished better weapons, along with better food, health and clothing, than any other army.

Here it is June of 1943 and it seems a long time since we landed at Oran in November of 1942. Of course there were thousands of us even in those first days in Africa, and yet it seemed like a little family then. And especially so when we went on to Tunisia — in those bitter January days we were so small that I knew almost every officer on the staff of every unit, in addition to hundreds of the soldiers. Nothing was very official in our lives then; there was almost no red tape; we correspondents at the front were few and were considered by the army rather like partners in the firm. We made deep friendships that have endured.

During the winter I dropped in frequently at Corps Headquarters, buried deep in a gulch beyond Tebessa. They put up a little tent for me, and I tried to work and sleep in it, but was never very successful at either because of being constantly, paralyzingly cold throughout the twenty-four hours of the day. We ate in a tent with a crushed-stone floor and an iron-bellied stove in the center. It was the only warm place I knew, and so informal was the war in those first days that often I sat around the stove after supper and just gabbed country-storelike with Lieutenant General Lloyd Fredendall, then commander of our armies in Tunisia. I was very fond of General Fredendall, and I admired and respected him. For some unknown reason I always thought of him to myself as "Papa" Fredendall, although I don't think anybody else ever did. I still wear the Armored Corps combat jacket he gave me.

The first pioneering days of anything are always the best days. Everything is new and animating, and acquaintanceships are easy and everyone is knit closely together. In the latter part of the Tunisian war things were just as good for us correspondents — we had better facilities and the fighting army continued to be grand to us — and yet toward the end it became so big that I felt like a spectator instead of a participant. Which is, of course, all that a correspondent is or ever should be. But the old intimacy was gone.

And then finally the Tunisian campaign was over, spectacularly collapsed after the bitterest fighting we had known in our theater. It was only in those last days that I came to know what war really is. I don't know how any of the men who went through the thick of that hill-by-hill butch-

ery could ever be the same again. The end of the Tunisian war brought an exhilaration, then a letdown, and later a restlessness from anticlimax that I can see multiplied a thousand times when the last surrender comes. That transition back to normal days will be as difficult for many as was the change into war, and some will never be able to accomplish it.

Now we are in a lull and many of us are having a short rest period. I tried the city and couldn't stand it. Two days drove me back to the country, where everything seemed cleaner and more decent. I am in my tent, sitting on a newly acquired cot, writing on a German folding table we picked up the day of the big surrender. The days here are so peaceful and perfect they almost give us a sense of infidelity to those we left behind beneath the Tunisian crosses, those whose final awareness was a bedlam of fire and noise and uproar.

Here the Mediterranean surf caresses the sandy beach not a hundred yards away, and it is a lullaby for sleeping. The water is incredibly blue, just as we always heard it was. The sky is a cloudless blue infinity, and the only sounds are the birds singing in the scrub bushes that grow out of the sand and lean precisely away from the sea. Little land terrapins waddle around, and I snared one by the hind leg with a piece of string and tied it in Photographer Chuck Corte's tent while he was out, just for a joke. Then I found myself peeking in every few minutes to see how the captive was getting along, and he was straining so hard to get away that I got to feeling sorry for the poor little devil, so I turned him loose and ruined my joke.

An occasional black beetle strolls innocently across the sandy floor. For two hours I've been watching one of them struggling with a cigarette butt on the ground, trying to move it. Yesterday a sand snake crawled by just outside my tent door, and for the first time in my life I looked upon a snake not with a creeping phobia but with a sudden and surprising feeling of compassion. Somehow I pitied him, because he was a snake instead of a man. And I don't know why I felt that way, for I feel pity for all men too, because they are men.

It may be that the war has changed me, along with the rest. It is hard for anyone to analyze himself. I know that I find more and more that I wish to be alone, and yet contradictorily I believe I have a new patience with humanity that I've never had before. When you've lived with the unnatural mass cruelty that mankind is capable of inflicting upon itself, you find yourself dispossessed of the faculty for blaming one poor man for the triviality of his faults. I don't see how any survivor of war can ever be cruel to anything, ever again.

Yes, I want the war to be over, just as keenly as any soldier in North Africa wants it. This little interlude of passive contentment here on the Mediterranean shore is a mean temptation. It is a beckoning into somnolence. This is the kind of day I think I want my life to be composed of, endlessly. But pretty soon we shall strike our tents and traipse again after the clanking tanks, sleep again to the incessant lullaby of the big rolling guns. It has to be that way, and wishing doesn't change it.

It may be I have unconsciously made war seem more awful than it really is. It would be wrong to say that war is all grim; if it were, the human spirit could not survive two and three and four years of it. There is a good deal of gaiety in wartime. Some of us, even over here, are having the time of our lives. Humor and exuberance still exist. As some soldier once said, the army is good for one ridiculous laugh per minute. Our soldiers are still just as roughly good-humored as they always were, and they laugh easily, although there isn't as much to laugh about as there used to be.

And I don't attempt to deny that war is vastly exhilarating. The whole tempo of life steps up, both at home and on the front.

There is an intoxication about battle, and ordinary men can sometimes soar clear out of themselves on the wine of danger-emotion. And yet it is false. When we leave here to go on into the next battleground, I know that I for one shall go with the greatest reluctance.

On the day of final peace, the last stroke of what we call the "Big Picture" will be drawn. I haven't written anything about the "Big Picture," because I don't know anything about it. I only know what we see from our worm's-eye view, and our segment of the picture consists only of tired and dirty soldiers who are alive and don't want to die; of long darkened convoys in the middle of the night; of shocked silent men wandering back down the hill from battle; of chow lines and Atabrine tablets and foxholes and burning tanks and Arabs holding up eggs and the rustle of high-flown shells; of jeeps and petrol dumps and smelly bedding rolls and C rations and cactus patches and blown bridges and dead mules and hospital tents and shirt collars greasy-black from months of wearing; and of laughter too, and anger and wine and lovely flowers and constant cussing. All these it is composed of; and of graves and graves and graves.

That is our war, and we will carry it with us as we go on from one battleground to another until it is all over, leaving some of us behind on every beach, in every field. We are just beginning with the ones who lie back of us here in Tunisia. I don't know whether it was their good fortune or their misfortune to get out of it so early in the game. I guess it doesn't make any difference, once a man has gone. Medals and speeches and victories are nothing to them any more. They died and others lived and nobody knows why it is so. They died and thereby the rest of us can go on and on. When we leave here for the next shore, there is nothing we can do for the ones beneath the wooden crosses, except perhaps to pause and murmur, "Thanks, pal."

40.

# WILLIAM L. SHIRER: American Radio Traitors

*Probably no war in U.S. history produced such widespread support among America's citizens as World War II — at least after Pearl Harbor, which brought Americans together in a common cause and made them forget the old arguments about isolationism and "America First." The country was fighting, so it seemed to almost everyone, not for an abstract principle — to "save democracy" — but for its own life and against ideas of government that the country had immemorially opposed. Nevertheless, there were a few who did not agree with the great majority, traitors who in one way or another gave "aid and comfort" to the Nazis of Germany and the Fascists of Italy, and to the Japanese. Eight American citizens were indicted by the U.S. government in July 1943 for broadcasting treasonable statements back to their native land. William L. Shirer wrote an article on the subject that was published the following fall. Shirer had spent most of the years between the wars in Europe, and his reports, especially those collected in* Berlin Diary *(1941), were avidly read by his countrymen at home. His article was all the more interesting because never for a moment was there any question about his own loyalty to the country of his birth. The article is reprinted here in part.*

Source: *Harper's*, October 1943: "The American Radio Traitors."

WHEN LAST JULY a federal grand jury returned indictments charging treason against eight American citizens who had been broadcasting Nazi and Fascist propaganda from Berlin and Rome, it set me to wondering again why they had sold out to the enemy. For I had known some of them, and another convert to Nazism who did not appear in the government list — Charles Flicksteger, alias Flick — during my fifteen-year assignment abroad.

These Americans,[1] most of them native-born, did, in the stilted words of the indictments, "knowingly, intentionally, feloniously, traitorously, and treasonably adhere to the enemies of the United States . . . giving to the said enemies aid and comfort" by repeated broadcasts of propaganda designed to "persuade citizens of the United States to decline to support the United States in the conduct of the war."

Why did they do it? For money? Most men turn traitors for money. But from what I know of these citizens, material gain was not the motive, or at least not the main one. . . . It wasn't money, primarily, which turned these Americans into traitors. And it wasn't love, for which sometimes a man or a woman will betray his country. . . .

What was it then? Of all the American turncoats, I knew Best the most intimately. I had met him first in January 1929, in Vienna, to which I had repaired for a long newspaper assignment. I saw him off and on during the next ten turbulent years, the last time being in June 1938, after the An-

1. Frederick Wilhelm Kaltenbach, Dubuque, Iowa; Robert H. Best, Sumter, South Carolina; Ezra Pound, New York City; Douglas Chandler, Baltimore; Edward Leo Delaney, Olney, Illinois; Constance Drexel, Philadelphia; Jane Anderson, Atlanta; Max Otto Koischwitz, New York City. Flicksteger, who was brought up in Saylesville, Rhode Island, and attended Brown University, was not included in the indictment.

schluss, when I left Vienna for good. Frankly, over the years, I liked him as did all the other American correspondents whose fortunes took them to the baroque Austrian capital. . . .

As the years went by he grew a little strange. "Eccentric," we used to call it. But everyone liked him for his generous heart. He would do the slightest acquaintance any favor asked or hinted. He would lend you his last Austrian schilling. Best had no deep political beliefs. He didn't like the Socialists, who controlled the city government of Vienna until Dollfuss massacred them in 1934, but this was because he thought they taxed him too much, and not for any ideological reasons. . . .

That fantastic night of the Anschluss when Austria perished, Best held out hopes to the last minute that Schuschnigg somehow would master the situation and keep the Nazis out. About 10 o'clock that night I found him at his table in the Café Louvre scribbling dispatches. He was called away to the phone and when he returned he announced proudly to the half-hysterical newsmen that Schuschnigg had come back as chancellor and that the Nazis were out. This was typical of his reporting but there was no doubt that he was happy about his "tip." "Things are not over yet," he kept saying to me. At that time, he was not Nazi.

By his side that evening, I remember, was one Major Goldschmidt, a Legitimist follower of Otto and a Jew. About 11 o'clock the Major rose quietly and said, "I will go home and get my revolver." Best did his best to dissuade him. And Best's closest friend in Vienna, as everyone knew, was a Jew.

And yet this is the man who today out-Goebbelses the Propaganda Doktor in the very violence of his attacks on the Jews. He has become Berlin's star American Jew-baiter. . . .

The trouble with Bob Best was that he stayed in Europe too long. Born in Sumter,

South Carolina, April 16, 1896, the son of a Methodist minister, he had graduated from Wofford College in 1917, served as a lieutenant in the Coast Artillery during the war, and had then enrolled as a graduate student in the Columbia School of Journalism. In 1922 he went to Europe on a year's Pulitzer traveling fellowship. He never saw his native land again. . . .

Pretty soon he began to fear that life in America had passed him by, that probably he could never make a go of it here, that he would only be a misfit. A few other correspondents who had gone home for good had found the readjustment difficult. Bob heard of their difficulties. And not unnaturally, and perhaps at first quite unconsciously, he began to share the stirrings that were going on in the breasts of the not-very-well-paid middle class in Europe. Fascism of the clerical brand such as Austria first produced or of the Mussolini-Hitler brand began to attract them. Best, his native American roots decayed, was impressed. It was not difficult for him to drift toward Fascism. It was difficult for him to retain any sense of duty or even loyalty to his own country. America began to loom to him as a land which he no longer knew or belonged to and to which he would never return. . . .

Just how and why Best became so violently anti-Semitic remains a mystery to his former friends and acquaintances. As we have seen, his closest friend was a Jew and a good half of his European newspaper friends who gathered at the Café Louvre were Jews. One of the last things he did before the war was to lend a month's salary to an Austrian editor who was a Jew and then help him escape over the Nazi frontier. This editor happened to be listening to the Berlin short-wave radio in the New York Listening Post of CBS one spring evening of 1942. Suddenly he dashed into my office, a few steps away. He was in tears. "There's someone talking from Berlin who calls himself 'Guess Who,' " he cried. "It sounds like Bob Best. Come and see." I did and there was no doubt that it was Best. He was thundering away at the Jews. . . .

Bob Best's case obviously is a special one but it has this in common with those of the other radio traitors: all of them had a sense of frustration about their role, however small, in the American scene. All of them had come to be conscious of being misfits in their native land. . . .

Between the two wars, Fascism and Nazism attracted human derelicts as a flame attracts a moth. Most of the Nazi hierarchy consisted of derelicts from the first war, men who could not find a place in the Germany of the Republic. Nazism offered them, as it offered our American traitors, a chance to become somebody. It offered them a career. And it gave them something ready-made on which to vent their hates. I happen to know that some of these Americans who were to become traitors made half-hearted attempts in the thirties to "make good" in the land of their birth. Having failed, as they lazily thought, they returned to Europe and threw themselves into the arms of the two Axis nations. . . .

Two Americans who had thus made a last attempt to adjust themselves at home told me about it when they came back to Europe. They were Charles Flicksteger, who wrote under the name of "Flick," and George Nelson Page, nephew of our former ambassador in Rome. . . .

To earn his living, Flicksteger had worked for an American press association in Berlin, but his chief interest lay in music. Married at that time to a retired Munich opera singer, he composed operas, and, naturally, Germany, which had a state-subsidized opera house going full blast in every provincial city as well as two in Berlin, gave him more of an outlet than he could find in America, where there was little opera outside of New York and a half-dozen of our largest cities. . . .

When I saw him next . . . it was June 1940, and the Germans were in Paris. I came home one night sick in the stomach from the nauseating spectacle of Hitler prancing about the little clearing in Compiègne Forest where the Armistice was being signed. I slipped into a seat at a large table in the dining room of the Hotel Scribe. It was full of arrogant, half-drunk German officers. One of them, a first lieutenant, looked familiar. He was grinning at me. "Guess you didn't expect to see me here in this," he said sheepishly, pointing at his uniform. Flicksteger had been making front-line recordings which were being played to America on the German short wave. Today he manages the German-owned radio station XGRS, which pours out anti-American propaganda from Shanghai.

George Nelson Page was an introspective American youngster who had spent most of his life with his relatives in Italy. Unfortunately, he elected to return home at the height of the Depression and after going jobless for a few months and, according to him, being snubbed for his poverty, he returned to Rome, took out his citizenship papers, did his military service, and became an Italian citizen. One night in Rome he poured out to me his bitterness against America for treating him so badly. Through his friendship with Ciano, he got a high post in the Italian Propaganda Ministry (Ministry of Popular Culture, as it was called) but I imagine he has not fared so well since the departure of his friend and his friend's father-in-law.

I did not know Douglas Chandler, who broadcasts from Berlin as "Paul Revere." He was a bit of a mystery man among the American correspondents there, for, though he was constantly being quoted in the German press as "an American correspondent," none of us had ever seen him in the flesh. In fact we thought for a time he was a fictional character. In the end he proved to be real enough, and later on I learned something about the man.

Life in this country proved a little too

tough for him, too, it seems. Born in Chicago, May 26, 1889, he grew up in Baltimore, where, after the war, in which he served for a short time in the Navy, he worked as a reporter and columnist on the Sunday *American*. After his marriage in 1924 . . . to a descendant of John Jay, he went into the brokerage business and, like a great many others who had chosen this particular line of business activity, he was wiped out in the crash of 1929. . . .

In the spring of 1941, as it happened, Dr. Goebbels was trying desperately to find an American radio personality who could build up in the United States a vast listening audience, if only by being amusing, as had Lord Haw-Haw in Britain. Kaltenbach, the former Iowa boy, had not been quite good enough and Delaney, alias Ward, had been a positive failure.

So, if in April 1941 you had listened to the German short-wave programs, you would have heard a tremendous build-up for a new American voice. On April 18, the 166th anniversary of Paul Revere's famous ride, that famous horseman and patriot, Berlin said, would gallop again. April 18 came and nothing happened, but a week later, preceded by the thumping of horses' hoofs and the tune of "Yankee Doodle," "Paul Revere" rode. "Paul Revere" also spoke, trying to incite his fellow Americans to throw off the terrible tyranny of "Roosevelt and his Jews." Before he had finished speaking, he was the flop of the year. He was even worse on the air than the aging Delaney-Ward. A few weeks afterward, "Paul Revere" revealed that he was really Douglas Chandler. His standard beginning for his broadcasts is: "Misinformed, misgoverned friends and compatriots."

Jane Anderson, the Countess de Cienfuegos, born in Atlanta on January 6, 1893, turned traitor, I suppose, because she was bitten by the bug that has smitten a few other of our citizens. Like them she got it into her head that the "Bolshevist hordes" were about to engulf our world and she

thought Hitler and men like Franco could save us. She had been sentenced to death as a spy by the Spanish Loyalists, but the sentence was quelled at the request of the State Department and she was released. After that her tongue never ceased wagging — and always on the same tiresome subject. "I had not been twenty-four hours upon American soil," she reported in a Berlin broadcast, "before I had confirmed . . . that from the pulpits of the land of the Star-Spangled Banner, no word of the God-fearing had been lifted against the hordes from Moscow which had descended upon Madrid to unleash upon a Christian land rivers of blood as the first stride forward in world revolution. . . ."

Miss Anderson's "ranting, melodramatic voice," as one British official described it, ceased abruptly to come off the Berlin air waves in April 1942. She had broadcast to America a tall tale about the wonderful food and champagne in the capital's night clubs. OWI transmitters rebroadcast her glowing account to the German people. She was never heard on the air from Berlin again.

Of all this motley group of Americans, Fred Kaltenbach, of Dubuque, Iowa, probably was the most sincere in his conversion to Nazism. He really believed in it. Born in Dubuque in 1895 of German immigrant parents, he remained essentially German in outlook and, like so many other Germans, was early attracted to the mysticism — or whatever it was — of Nazism.

His American education was considerable. He studied at Grinnell College, took a B.A. from Iowa State Teachers College in 1920 (after serving a short time as a second lieutenant in the Coast Artillery during the war) and an M.A. in history at the University of Chicago. But by 1933, while teaching at the Dubuque High School, he was organizing a group of high school boys into a "hiking club," which he called the "Militant Order of Spartan Knights" and which he modeled on the pattern of the Hitler

Youth, the members sporting brown-shirted uniforms. I am glad to report that Iowa, my own state, had more sense than Germany. The school authorities disbanded the "Knights" and fired Kaltenbach.

He left shortly thereafter for Germany, where, studious fellow that he is, he took a Ph.D. at the University of Berlin and zealously embraced Hitlerism and all its foul works. I will never forget him standing by my side outside the little railway carriage at Compiègne. Through the car windows you could see Hitler sitting proudly at a table while General Keitel read the French the armistice terms. Kaltenbach, as if in a trance, gazed longingly at his Fuehrer as other men might gaze toward their god. It was no surprise, then, when he elected to remain in Germany and betray his country. He was a born Nazi.

So was Max Otto Koischwitz, who did not come to this country until 1925, where he found employment on the faculties of Columbia University and Hunter College. He became a naturalized citizen in 1935, when he had already been converted to Nazism. A former pupil has described him as "thin, dark, Mephistophelean," and his lectures, in which he did not fail to get in his Nazi propaganda, especially on the racial issue, seem to have been very popular. At least his classrooms were always crowded. He turned out to be a versatile fellow on the air and in his broadcasts appears sometimes as "Dr. Anders," a scholarly rogue, sometimes as "Mr. O.K.," a glib talker in the American vernacular, and sometimes just as himself, Dr. Koischwitz. The only wonder about him is that his Nazi loyalties were not discovered before he departed for the Fatherland in 1939.

Ezra Pound, the only one of the traitors to sell out to Italy, was already obsessed by the "decadence of democracy" when as a youth just out of college I used to listen to him prattle on the terrace of the Café Sélect in Paris in the middle twenties. He was a talented poet but had no political sense and

Mussolinism already at that time seemed to attract his flamboyant nature. I suspect also that he became embittered at what he thought was the lack of appreciation of his poetry in his native America. He used to lecture us, if I remember rightly, about "our cultural backwoods we left behind us." His broadcasts from Rome were curiously incoherent for a writer so much interested in language. But he loved the sound of his own words, as when he shouted hoarsely from Rome one day to his former compatriots: "You have been hugger-muggered and scarum-shouted into a war and you know nothing about it."

I heard his last broadcast. It was on the evening of July 25, about three hours after his radio station in Rome had announced the "resignation" of the Duce, whom he had always praised as a god. It was obvious that poor Pound knew nothing about it. But he was not heard from again.

Two of the traitors, Best and Kaltenbach, broadcast replies to their indictments. Best was truculent; Kaltenbach sounded as though he were hurt.

Said Best on the evening of July 28: "The decision not only to indict but to execute most of us was taken by Washington's Jews and Judocrats already in 1942. . . . When I packed my bags and walked out of the internment hotel at Bad Nauheim seventeen months ago, I knew quite well what I was doing. . . . I knew . . . that I was crossing a Rubicon and at the same time burning my bridges behind me. I knew, in other words, that it meant the beginning of a battle to the death between me and the clique of Jewish reptiles which are today running America. . . . In reality, America's Jews have all intended from the first to shoot or to hang every one of us who exposes their game of world enslavement. . . ."

Kaltenbach, replying in his broadcast of July 30, was more wistful. Said he: "Technically, I suppose I am guilty of treason — of treason to Roosevelt and his warmongers, but not to the American people. . . . To have deserted the German people would have been an act of treason against my conscience. On December 8, 1941, I was suddenly confronted with the choice of committing a possible act of treason against my native America or of deserting the German people in their hour of need. I could have returned to the United States. . . . That would have been the easy way out. . . . Don't think the choice was easy. It was not easy to turn my back perhaps forever on my friends in the United States, never to see the land of my birth again. . . . Nevertheless I made then my choice, and I have never regretted that choice for an instant. . . . If that be treason, make the most of it."

Were the words of Patrick Henry ever turned to a more ironical use?

---

41.

# WALTER LIPPMANN: Foreign Policy and Vital Interests

*By 1943 Walter Lippmann was the dean of American newspaper columnists and enjoyed a substantial reputation as a political thinker as well. His U.S. Foreign Policy: Shield of the Republic (1943) provoked widespread discussion, particularly among Lippmann's critics who accused him of advocating power politics. The chapter reprinted here is titled "The General Order of the Nations."*

Source: *U.S. Foreign Policy: Shield of the Republic*, Boston, 1943, Ch. 10.

## 1. THE NUCLEAR ALLIANCE

THE PRESENT association of the United States with Britain, Russia, and China is not a new departure. We have seen how for more than a century, whenever our vital interests were at stake, American foreign relations have always been primarily our relations with Britain, with Russia, and with China. Our relations with all other states have followed upon and have been governed by our relations with those three. In the conduct of American foreign policy our position has been solvent, our power adequate to our commitments, insofar as we were in essential agreement with these three states.

None of them, we may observe, is a European state. We must ponder this fact. For it may throw light upon the famous statement in Washington's Farewell Address that:

> Europe has a set of primary interests which to us have none or a very remote relation. Hence she must be engaged in frequent controversies, the causes of which are essentially foreign to our concerns.

When these words were spoken on September 17, 1796, Napoleon was conducting his first campaign of aggression, the invasion of Italy. His conquest of the continent was still in the future, as was his threat to invade England and his actual invasion of Russia. The war which Washington knew about had all the appearance of being a purely *European* war, which to us had none or a very remote relation. Sixteen years later, however, Napoleon was the master of Europe, and had struck outside of Europe into Russia. The United States had become involved in a local war with England. Yet while America was at war, we find Jefferson, the author of the phrase "no entangling alliances," writing on January 1, 1814, that "surely none of us wish to see Bonaparte conquer Russia, and lay thus at his feet the whole continent of Europe. This done, England would be but a breakfast. . . . Put all Europe into his hands, and he might spare such a force, to be sent in British ships, as I would as leave not have to encounter." Jefferson was writing a private letter in wartime and he added: "I have gone into this explanation, my friend, because I know you will not carry my letter to the newspapers, and because I am willing to trust to your discretion the explaining me to our honest fellow laborers and the bringing them to pause and reflect . . . on the extent of the success we ought to wish to Bonaparte, and with a view to our own interests only."

We see here how the very men who laid down the rule of nonparticipation in European politics really thought about our foreign relations. They were aware that when there was a power in Europe which threatened to *come out of Europe* and conquer Britain, which is at one of the limits of Europe, or to conquer Russia, which is at the other limit, our interests were vitally involved. If we read our history, not as the conventional historians have written it, and not as our lesser statesmen have talked about it, but as in fact Americans have enacted it, we find, I submit, that while our concern has not been with *European* affairs, we have always been concerned with *world* affairs. Our primary relations have been, and are, with the extra-European powers, and with Europe itself only as some power inside of Europe threatens to disrupt the order of things outside of Europe. Thus, if we think as clearly and exactly about American interests as Jefferson, even in the midst of a jingoistic war, was able to think, we shall see that the traditional American policy against being involved in European affairs is not in the last analysis inconsistent with the consolidation of America's vital interest in the world.

Our primary interest in Europe, as shown during the Napoleonic and the two German Wars, is that no European power should emerge which is capable of aggression outside of the European continent. Therefore our two natural and permanent allies have been and are Britain and Russia. For they have the same fundamental interest — to each of them a matter of national life or death — in preventing the rise of such a conquering power in Europe. And that is why Britain and Russia, though they have been at odds on the Near East, the Middle East, and in Asia, have been allies against Napoleon, against William II, and against Hitler.

Here then, founded on vital interest which has been tested and proved in the course of generations, is the nuclear alliance upon which depends the maintenance of the world order in which America lives. Combined action by America, Britain, and Russia is the irreducible minimum guarantee of the security of each of them, and the only condition under which it is possible even to begin to establish any wider order of security.

The formation of this nuclear alliance must in our thinking and in our action take precedence over all other considerations. For without it we cannot make good our existing commitments in the Atlantic and in the Pacific. Without it, our commitment in the Philippines remains a salient, exceedingly difficult to defend against a resurgent Japan or against a combination of powers in Eastern Asia. Without this nuclear alliance, our commitment in South America is open to challenge, if not by direct conquest from Europe and Africa, then by infiltration and conspiracy. Without it, the two oceans and the airways to the north and the south are perilously open and uncertain, since the ports and landing fields beyond would be in uncertain hands.

Only by the formation of this nuclear alliance — whatever we choose to call it, no matter how we choose to seal it — can American foreign policy be said to have balanced our commitments with a safe margin in reserve. We need make no apologies then because we put this first thing first. American foreign relations must be made solvent before the United States can afford to issue any more promissory notes.

Furthermore, we should not have learned the lessons of our failures in the past, especially the lesson of the failure of the League of Nations, if in our projects for organizing world peace we did not fix our attention first of all upon the powers capable of organizing it. Blueprints, covenants, contracts, charters, and declarations do not create living associations. They merely formulate, regulate, ratify, develop, and guide the action of men or groups of men who already have the will to associate themselves. It is not, for example, the marriage laws which make the family, but the union of a man and a woman who in accordance with these laws then found a family. It was not the Constitution which made the American union, but the constituent states which adopted it in order to form a more perfect union.

The will of the most powerful states to remain allied is the only possible creator of a general international order.

## 2. The Justification of Insisting Upon It

There will be many, I realize full well, who will feel that this insistence upon the security of the vital interests of the most powerful states involves an illiberal and even a brutal neglect of the rights of the weaker nations and of their intrinsic importance to civilization itself. I ask their indulgence until the argument is concluded. We shall see why the nuclear alliance must be liberal in its policy if it is to endure.

But if we are to prove this convincingly, and not merely to state it rhetorically, there must be no doubt in our minds why as Americans we must insist upon beginning with the security of the vital interests of the United States. It is that for half a century the United States has so neglected its vital interests that it was incapable of defending them adequately, or of carrying through any measures whatsoever to maintain the peace of the world. For fifty years no nation has been more liberal in its words than has been the United States; none neglected its own interests so dangerously, or contributed less to realizing the ideals it so assiduously preached.

So I make no apology for seeking to define the American foreign policy on which the American people could again become united because it conforms rigorously to American interests. I see no way of our being able to contribute anything to anybody else until we have become fully conscious again of our own interests and feel prepared to maintain them. . . . And I do not doubt that our allies and our friendly neighbors will, as they consider the matter, greatly prefer an American foreign policy founded on an enlightened conception of our own national interest to the ambiguous platitudes with which we have regaled them for the past fifty years.

Nor need we shrink from insisting that the precondition of a better world order is a nuclear alliance of the three powerful military states which will emerge victorious from the present war. They are the states upon which depends the deliverance of Europe from the Nazi despotism, and of the Far East from the empire of Japan. It has needed the combined force of all three of these states, and the utmost exertion of their power, to make the deliverance possible. No one of them, no two of them, could have done it. Why, then, should we hesitate to say that anything less than this combination of great powers is insufficient to preserve order against aggression in the world? Will anyone presume to argue that to dissolve this combination again would promote the liberty of the peoples who have been conquered, or would make secure the order which has been shattered by two devastating world wars?

It is only around this strong nuclear alliance that a wider association of many nations can constitute itself. If that condition is accepted, and once it is accepted, it will become evident that the combination of the great powers cannot, despite their common vital interests, be made to hold together except as they respect the liberties of the other peoples and promote them by the maintenance of law.

I believe it can be demonstrated as conclusively as anything can be demonstrated in human affairs that Britain, Russia, America, and China, as she becomes a great state, cannot remain allies and partners unless they use their power, separately and in combination, to maintain liberty through law.

## 3. The Binding Condition of Unity

WE MUST BEGIN by remembering that Britain, Russia, and America are allies, not by conscious choice but under the compulsion of their common enemies. They have been compelled, as I have tried to show, to become allies whenever a really formidable aggressive power emerged which threatened to break out of Europe into the outer world. Nevertheless, when there is no such enemy which threatens their national existence, the need for their alliance becomes submerged. Their lesser, their separate and conflicting, interests are then free to assert themselves. The greater the peril from the outside, the closer is their union: the greater their security, the more their differences come to the surface.

The unconditional surrender of Germany and of Japan is bound, therefore, to leave all the Allies with an immediate sense of mortal peril averted; and this will reduce the compulsion that binds the alliance together. There will then be opened up disputable secondary questions which push apart the members of the alliance. This has always happened in wars won by a coalition. It happened at the Congress of Vienna, and because of it Talleyrand's diplomacy was so successful. It happened at the Peace Conference in 1919, when the victorious alliance had in fact become dissolved even before peace had been made with the enemy. It can and it may happen again, as we have seen in the winter of 1943, when the first prospects of victory have already opened up fissures among the Allies.

These fissures will tend to become wider and deeper the more any one of the great powers seeks to aggrandize itself either at the expense of one of the other great powers, or at the expense of their smaller allies.

Thus an American policy of imperialist aggrandizement at the expense of the British Empire would impair profoundly, if it did not destroy, the Atlantic Community. It would become necessary for Britain to look for her security in some combination which thwarted American aggrandizement.

By the same token, a British policy which rested on the refusal to recognize the necessary changes in the colonial and imperial system of the nineteenth century would raise up against Britain insurgent forces in Asia, the Middle East, and Africa. Britain could not count upon American support in resisting these forces, and almost certainly she would have to count upon Russian and Chinese encouragement of these forces.

By the same token again, a Russian policy of aggrandizement in Europe, one which threatened the national liberties of her neighbors, would inexorably be regarded as such a threat to Britain and America that they would begin to encourage the nations which resisted Russia. In Asia, a Russian policy of aggrandizement against China would disrupt Russian-American relations in the North Pacific and, in the coming air age, across the top of the globe. On the other hand, an anti-Russian policy in which Britain, America, and the European states sought, as they did in 1919, to blockade and even to disrupt Russia would provoke Russian communist intervention to counteract it.

And by the same token, also, a Chinese policy of aggrandizement in India, Malaya, Indo-China, and the Netherlands Indies would encounter opposition from Britain, from America, from Australia and New Zealand, from France and the Netherlands.

The fissures opened by any one or all of these tendencies to aggrandizement would soon become a breach. This would be followed inevitably and immediately by competition among the Allies to win over to their side the vanquished nations. This would be done by restoring their power. In Europe the separated Allies would bid against one another for the favor of Germany. In Asia, they would bid for the favor of Japan. Thus because aggrandizement had made them rivals, they would restore the aggressor powers which had threatened them. The postwar era would thus be transformed, as the late Frank Simonds observed of the early thirties, into a prewar era.

For these reasons it is evident that a nuclear alliance of Britain, Russia, America, and, if possible, China, cannot hold together if it does not operate within the limitations of an international order that preserves the national liberties of other peoples. The three, or the four, great powers will not remain united against the revival of German and Japanese military power if they become rivals in the domination of Central and Eastern Europe or of the dependent and colonial regions of Asia and Africa.

Nor could the nuclear allies, as some may fear, combine to oppress and exploit the rest of mankind. For, in the last analysis, the resistance of the rest of mankind would disrupt the alliance: one or the other of the great powers would find that its interests and its sympathies lay with the peoples resisting oppression.

Nor could the nuclear allies divide the globe into spheres of influence which each was free to dominate and exploit separately. For no spheres of influence can be defined which do not overlap, which would not therefore bring the great powers into conflict. Where in Europe, for example, could a sphere of influence be fixed which separated Britain and Russia into convenient imperialist compartments? On which side of the line would the Scandinavian countries lie? If on the Russian, then the sea and air approaches to Britain are insecure; if on the British, then the sea and air approaches to Russia are insecure. Where in Africa could a line of demarcation be drawn when, in fact, the defense of South America is dependent upon the presence of friendly powers in North and West Africa, when in fact the security of the Mediterranean is also dependent upon the control of North and West Africa? Where can a sphere of influence be defined in the East which makes secure China, the British nations in Australasia, and the American commitment in the Philippines?

Thus it is as impossible for the Allied great powers to divide up the world and then rule it as it is for them to combine in order to dominate the world. The inexorable logic of their alliance demands that they recognize the liberties of the peoples outside the alliance. For in no other way can they avoid becoming rivals and then enemies for the domination of these other peoples. In no other way but by supporting a worldwide system of liberty under law can they win the consent, earn the confidence, and insure the support of the rest of the world in the continuation of their alliance.

The order which they originate because it is necessary to their own vital security can, therefore, be perpetuated only if they act so as to gain and to hold the goodwill of the other peoples. Delivering the weaker states from the Nazi and Japanese conquest will not in itself hold their goodwill. For the memory of the deliverance will become obscured by what happens afterwards. Their own concept of their own interest, rather than gratitude, is for all masses of peoples the motive which determines their actions. The gratitude of the liberated to the victorious powers will, therefore, continue only if the great powers remain united enough to keep the peace of the world against aggressors and at the same time become liberal enough so that there is no good reason for rebellion against the order which they maintain.

The experience of history supports the conclusion that power can endure only if it gives and maintains laws within which men enjoy the liberties they regard as more important than life. Not all peoples everywhere and always have had the same conception of their essential liberties. But whatever they regard as their essential liberties, be they the liberties of the Christian West or of the Moslem world, or of the Hindus, or of the Chinese, it is these liberties which must be respected under the law if the power behind the law is to endure. Though the world is shrunken, we must not imagine that any system of identical laws can prevail everywhere. The East and the West have been formed in widely different cultural traditions. But what can prevail everywhere, if the alliance holds together, is the universal law that force must not be arbitrary, but must be exercised in accordance with laws that are open to discussion and are subject to orderly revision.

An order of this kind can endure, not forever in a changing world but for a long and beneficent period of time. Security and liberty are the benefits which such an order can provide. They are such great benefits that whenever men have enjoyed them at all they have rallied to the authority which provided them. It was because the Roman legions brought with them the Roman law

that the Roman Empire lived on so long, and, when it fell, lived on in men's memories for a thousand years as an ideal to which they longed to return. It has been Britain's devotion to law which, despite all the rebellion against British rule, has brought so many nations to Britain's side whenever Britain has been really threatened. And I think Americans may without false pride believe that in the last analysis it is our own preference for liberty under law, and not our material power only, which has made the neighbor republics of this hemisphere believe that their vital interests and ours are the same.

## 4. Conclusion as to the Organization of a New Order

FOR THESE REASONS it is self-evident that in a fully enlightened view of the vital interests of the great powers and of the smaller we may conclude that:

To establish and maintain order the nuclear alliance must be consolidated and perpetuated.

To perpetuate their alliance the great powers must become the organizers of an order in which the other peoples find that their liberties are recognized by laws that the great powers respect and that all peoples are compelled to observe.

If this is done, the new order will rest not on sentiment but on enlightened interest. Then only will it be strong enough to have authority. Then only will it be liberal enough to have its authority persist.

## 5. Finale

THE STRUCTURE of the order which the nuclear allies could or should institute, the laws and covenants they could or should subscribe to, the procedures they could or should agree upon — these matters lie outside the province of this inquiry. We have been concerned with finding the American foreign policy which will most adequately and surely make this republic solvent in its foreign relations. We have, therefore, dwelt upon those measures which are indispensable to America if it is to fulfill the commitments it has, if it is to be able to make commitments at all. We have found, I believe, that the measures which will most securely maintain the vital interests of the United States are measures which will no less securely maintain the vital interests of our neighbors, the great ones and the smaller ones alike.

Guided by this principle, and determined to apply it, we shall be capable again of forming an American foreign policy. We shall no longer be, as we have been for nearly fifty years, without a foreign policy which takes account of our interests. We need no longer be divided because the national interest upon which we must unite will have been made evident to us. We shall no longer exhort mankind to build castles in the air while we build our own defenses on sand.

Then, when we know what we ourselves need and how we must achieve it, we shall be not only a great power. We shall have become at last a mature power. We shall know our interests and what they require of us. We shall know our limitations and our place in the scheme of things.

Then "we may choose peace or war, as our interest, guided by justice, shall counsel"; then the duty which Washington laid upon us will be done.

---

42.

# WENDELL L. WILLKIE: Toward One World

*Throughout the war Wendell Willkie, the defeated Republican candidate in 1940, was a staunch supporter of President Roosevelt. When Willkie indicated a desire to be of service to him and to the nation, Roosevelt commissioned Willkie to make a world tour to demonstrate to the Allies America's nonpartisan determination to carry the war through to victory. Roosevelt had also hoped that Willkie's influence would bolster support for the war effort in America. Willkie went to England in 1941, and on August 26, 1942, began a journey that took him to the Middle East, the Soviet Union, and China. When he returned Willkie gave his impressions of his journey on a radio broadcast that was so well received that he decided to write a book. One of the most significant books about the war,* One World, *from which a selection is reprinted here, helped strengthen Allied morale and convince the American people of their responsibility to build a peaceful world after the war.*

Source: *One World,* New York, 1943, pp. 180-206.

### THIS IS A WAR OF LIBERATION

THIS WAR that I saw going on all around the world is, in Mr. Stalin's phrase, a war of liberation. It is to liberate some nations from the Nazi or the Japanese Army, and to liberate others from the threat of those armies. On this much we are all agreed. Are we yet agreed that liberation means more than this? Specifically, are the thirty-one

United Nations now fighting together agreed that our common job of liberation includes giving to *all* peoples freedom to govern themselves as soon as they are able, and the economic freedom on which all lasting self-government inevitably rests?

It is these two aspects of freedom, I believe, which form the touchstone of our good faith in this war. I believe we must include them both in our idea of the freedom we are fighting for. Otherwise, I am certain we shall not win the peace, and I am not sure we can win the war.

In Chungking, on October 7, 1942, I made a statement to the Chinese and foreign press in which I tried to state some of the conclusions I had reached on my trip around the world. In part, this is what I said:

I have traveled through thirteen countries. I have seen kingdoms, soviets, republics, mandated areas, colonies, and dependencies. I have seen an almost bewildering variety of ways of living and ways of ruling and of being ruled. But I have found certain things common to all the countries I have visited and to all the ordinary people in those countries with whom I have talked:

They all want the United Nations to win the war.

They all want a chance at the end of the war to live in liberty and independence.

They all doubt, in varying degree, the readiness of the leading democracies of the world to stand up and be counted for freedom for others after the war is over. This doubt kills their enthusiastic participation on our side.

Now, without the real support of these common people, the winning of the war will be enormously difficult. The winning of the peace will be nearly impossible. This war is not a simple, technical problem for task forces. It is also a war for men's minds. We must organize on our side not simply the sympathies but the active, aggressive, offensive spirit of nearly three-fourths of the people of the world who live in South America, Africa, eastern Europe, and Asia. We have not done this, and at present are not doing this. We have got to do it. . . .

Men need more than arms with which to fight and win this kind of war. They need enthusiasm for the future and a conviction that the flags they fight under are in bright, clean colors. The truth is that we as a nation have not made up our minds what kind of world we want to speak for when victory comes.

Especially here in Asia the common people feel that we have asked them to join us for no better reason than that Japanese rule would be even worse than Western imperialism. This is a continent where the record of the Western democracies has been long and mixed, but where people — and remember there are a billion of them — are determined no longer to live under foreign control. Freedom and opportunity are the words which have modern magic for the people of Asia, and we have let the Japanese — the most cruel imperialists the modern world has known — steal these words from us and corrupt them to their own uses.

Most of the people in Asia have never known democracy. They may or may not want *our* type of democracy. Obviously, all of them are not ready to have democracy handed to them next Tuesday on a silver platter. But they are determined to work out their own destiny under governments selected by themselves.

Even the name of the Atlantic Charter disturbs thoughtful men and women I have been talking to. Do all of those who signed it, these people ask, agree that it applies to the Pacific? We must answer this question with a clear and simple statement of where we stand. And we must begin to sweat over our common problem of translating such a statement into plans which will be concrete and meaningful to the lives of these millions of people who are our allies.

Some of the plans to which such a state-

Wendell Willkie, Republican candidate for President during the 1940 campaign

ment would lead are already clear, I deeply believe, to most Americans:

We believe this war must mean an end to the empire of nations over other nations. No foot of Chinese soil, for example, should be or can be ruled from now on except by the people who live on it. And we must say so *now*, not after the war.

We believe it is the world's job to find some system for helping colonial peoples who join the United Nations' cause to become free and independent nations. We must set up firm timetables under which they can work out and train governments of their own choosing, and we must establish ironclad guarantees, administered by all the United Nations jointly, that they shall not slip back into colonial status.

Some say these subjects should be hushed until victory is won. Exactly the reverse is true. Sincere efforts to find progressive solutions now will bring strength to our cause. Remember, opponents of social change always urge delay because of some present crisis. After the war, the changes may be too little and too late.

We must develop between nations trade and trade routes strong enough to give all peoples the same vested interest in peace which we in America have had.

In the United States, we are being asked to give up temporarily our individual freedom and economic liberty in order to crush the Axis. We must recover this freedom and this liberty after the war. The way to make certain we do recover our traditional American way of life with a rising standard of living for all is to create a world in which all men everywhere can be free.

This statement caused a good deal of comment. Some of it was angry, but for the most part the reaction cheered me greatly. For it confirmed my feeling that the deep drift of public opinion, which works quietly but powerfully, has already moved ahead of many of our leaders on these questions and that it will, before long, push us into the open acknowledgment, before the world, of the beliefs we hold most firmly.

The temptation is great, in all of us, to limit the objectives of a war. Cynically, we may hope that the big words we have used will become smaller at the peace table, that we can avoid the costly and difficult readjustments which will be required to establish and defend real freedom for all peoples.

Many men and women I have talked with from Africa to Alaska asked me the question which has become almost a symbol all through Asia: what about India? Now I did not go to India. I do not propose to discuss that tangled question. But it has one aspect, in the East, which I should report. From Cairo on, it confronted me at every turn. The wisest man in China said to me: "When the aspiration of India for freedom was put aside to some future date, it was not Great Britain that suffered in public esteem in the Far East. It was the United States."

This wise man was not quarreling with British imperialism in India when he said this — a benevolent imperialism, if you like. He does not happen to believe in it but he was not even talking about it. H was telling me that by our silence on India we have already drawn heavily on our reservoir of goodwill in the East. People of the East who would like to count on us are doubtful. They cannot ascertain from our attitude toward the problem of India what we are likely to feel at the end of the war about all the other hundreds of millions of Eastern peoples. They cannot tell from our vague and vacillating talk whether or not we really do stand for freedom, or what we mean by freedom.

In China, students who were refugees a thousand miles from their homes asked me if we were going to try to take back Shanghai after the war. In Beirut, Lebanese asked me if their relatives in Brooklyn — one-third of all the Lebanese in the world live in the United States — would help to persuade the British and French occupying forces to leave Syria and the Lebanon after the war and let them run their own country.

In Africa, in the Middle East, throughout the Arab world, as well as in China and the whole Far East, freedom means the orderly but scheduled abolition of the colonial system. Whether we like it or not, this is true.

The British Commonwealth of Free Nations is the world's most spectacular example of such an orderly process. And the success of that great experiment should be immensely encouraging to the United Nations in working out the problems of self-government that lie ahead. For large sections of the world are still governed by the colonial system. Despite the Commonwealth, Great Britain still has numerous colonies, remnants of empire, with little or no self-rule, though the English people, millions of them, at home and throughout the Commonwealth, are working selflessly and with great skill toward reducing these remnants, toward extending the Commonwealth in place of the colonial system.

The English are by no means the only colonial rulers. The French still claim empire in Africa, in Indo-China, in South America, and in islands throughout the world. The Dutch still regard themselves as rulers of large parts of the East Indies and of territories in the West. The Portuguese, the Belgians, and other nations have colonial possessions. And we ourselves have not yet promised complete freedom to all the peoples in the West Indies for whom we have assumed responsibility. Furthermore, we have our domestic imperialisms.

But the world is awake, at last, to the knowledge that the rule of people by other peoples is not freedom, and not what we must fight to preserve.

There will be lots of tough problems ahead. And they will differ in different mandates and different colonies. Not all the peoples of the world are ready for freedom, or can defend it, the day after tomorrow. But today they all want some date to work toward, some assurance that the date will be kept. For the future, they do not ask that we solve their problems for them. They are neither so foolish nor so faint-hearted. They ask only for the chance to solve their own problems with economic as well as political cooperation. For the peoples of the world intend to be free not only for their political satisfaction, but also for their economic advancement.

## OUR IMPERIALISMS AT HOME

I MENTIONED among the imperialisms of the world our own domestic imperialisms. This war has opened for us new horizons — new geographical horizons, new mental horizons. We have been a people devoted largely to home enterprise. We have become a people whose first interests are beyond the seas. The names of Russian, Burmese, Tunisian, or Chinese towns command primary attention in our newspapers. The most eagerly seized letters coming into our homes are from our young men in Australia, New Guinea, Guadalcanal, Ireland, or North Africa. Our interests go with their interests, and we may feel certain that when they have battled over the world, they will not return home as provincial Americans. Nor will they find us so. What does all this mean? It means that though we began to grow up with the earlier World War, we are only now changing completely from a young nation of domestic concerns to an adult nation of international interests and world outlook.

A true world outlook is incompatible with a foreign imperialism, no matter how high-minded the governing country. It is equally incompatible with the kind of imperialism which can develop inside any nation. Freedom is an indivisible word. If we want to enjoy it, and fight for it, we must be prepared to extend it to everyone, whether they are rich or poor, whether they agree with us or not, no matter what their race or the color of their skin. We cannot, with good conscience, expect the British to set up an orderly schedule for the liberation of India before we have decided for ourselves to make all who live in America free. . . .

It has been a long while since the United States had any imperialistic designs toward the outside world. But we have practised within our own boundaries something that amounts to race imperialism. The attitude of the white citizens of this country toward the Negroes has undeniably had some of the unlovely characteristics of an alien imperialism — a smug racial superiority, a willingness to exploit an unprotected people. We have justified it by telling ourselves that its end is benevolent. And sometimes it has been. But so sometimes have been the ends of imperialism. And the moral atmosphere in which it has existed is identical with that in which men — well-meaning men — talk of "the white man's burden."

But that atmosphere is changing. Today it is becoming increasingly apparent to thoughtful Americans that we cannot fight the forces and ideas of imperialism abroad and maintain any form of imperialism at home. The war has done this to our thinking.

Emancipation came to the colored race in America as a war measure. It was an act of military necessity. Manifestly it would have come without war, in the slower process of humanitarian reform and social enlightenment. But it required a disastrous, internecine war to bring this question of human freedom to a crisis, and the process of striking the shackles from the slave was accomplished in a single hour. We are finding under the pressures of this present conflict that long-standing barriers and prejudices are breaking down. The defense of our democracy against the forces that threaten it from without has made some of its failures to function at home glaringly apparent.

Our very proclamations of what we are fighting for have rendered our own inequities self-evident. When we talk of freedom and opportunity for all nations, the mocking paradoxes in our own society become so clear they can no longer be ignored. If we want to talk about freedom, we must mean freedom for others as well as ourselves, and we must mean freedom for everyone inside our frontiers as well as outside. During a war, this is especially important.

The threat to racial and religious, even to political, minority groups springs in wartime from two things — an overzealous mass insistence upon general conformity to majority standards, and the revival under emotional strains of age-old racial and religious distrusts. Minorities then are apt to be charged with responsibility for the war itself, and all the dislocations and discomforts arising from it. They are jealously subjected to scrutiny to determine if they are the recipients of special advantages. . . .

Our nation is composed of no one race, faith, or cultural heritage. It is a grouping of some thirty peoples possessing varying religious concepts, philosophies, and historical backgrounds. They are linked together by their confidence in our democratic institutions as expressed in the Declaration of Independence and guaranteed by the Constitution for themselves and for their children.

The keystone of our union of states is freedom — freedom for the individual to worship as he chooses, to work as he chooses, and to live and rear his children as he chooses. Liberty, if it is to be for all, must be protected by basic safeguards intended to give it the most general diffusion attainable, and none can expect privileges which encroach upon the rights of others. Despite the functionings of our mischievous bureaucracies and our sometimes excessively enterprising legislatures, and — in deplorable but fortunately isolated instances — the flaring of mob law, we have obtained here in America, in the course of little more than a century and a half of experience and adjustment, the most reasonable expression of freedom that has yet existed in history.

Our success thus far as a nation is not because we have built great cities and big factories and cultivated vast areas, but because we have promoted this fundamental assurance of freedom upon which all our material development has depended, and have tolerated, and learned to use, our diversities.

We remain a relatively new nation. As recently as fifty years ago, more than half our mining and a third of our total manufacturing were carried on by immigrants. More than half of the farm population of some of our leading agricultural states was alien-born. In the formative period of the nation, between 1820 and 1890, more than 5,000,000 newcomers reached our shores, and a still greater number were yet to arrive in the twenty-four years preceding the outbreak of the last war. In other words, we have had two hundred years of reinvigorating immigration which has brought us new blood, new experiences, new ideas. Here was a vast assembly of minority groups which have gone into the welding of a nation. We have created a strong nation because these new arrivals did not have the distractions, under our form of government, of continually opposing and battling one another, but entered as partners into the general upbuilding and consolidation. The height of our civilization, it seems to me, has been reached not by our assembly lines, our inventions, or any of our great factitious development, but by the ability of peoples of varying beliefs and of different racial extractions to live side by side here in the United States with common understanding, respect, and helpfulness.

If we want to see the opposite of this American system, we have merely to look at the military despotism of Hitler and the autocracy of Japan, and the fading dictatorship of Fascist Italy. The story of Germany for the last ten years has been one of racial and religious intolerance that provided a mask behind which a peace-professing dictator lured the people first to minority persecution, then to war. This intolerance gave the German nation the momentary strength of complete regimentation. Actually, it has undermined and weakened the social structure so that when the tide of war turns, collapse is likely to be sudden and complete.

It has always impressed me that, quite apart from any reasons of humanitarianism or justice or any sentiment regarding the protection of the weak by the strong, it is only common sense to safeguard jealously the rights of minorities. For minorities are rich assets of a democracy, assets which no totalitarian government can afford. Dictatorships must, of necessity, fear and suppress them. But within the tolerance of a democracy, minorities are the constant spring of new ideas, stimulating new thought and action, the constant source of new vigor.

To suppress minority thinking and minority expression would tend to freeze society and prevent progress. For the majority itself is stimulated by the existence of minority groups. The human mind requires contrary expressions against which to test itself.

For now more than ever, we must keep in the forefront of our minds the fact that whenever we take away the liberties of those whom we hate, we are opening the way to loss of liberty for those we love.

Our way of living together in America is a strong but delicate fabric. It is made up of many threads. It has been woven over many centuries by the patience and sacrifice of countless liberty-loving men and women. It serves as a cloak for the protection of poor and rich, of black and white, of Jew and gentile, of foreign- and native-born.

Let us not tear it asunder. For no man knows, once it is destroyed, where or when man will find its protective warmth again.

## ONE WORLD

AMERICA MUST CHOOSE one of three courses after this war: narrow nationalism, which inevitably means the ultimate loss of our own liberty; international imperialism, which means the sacrifice of some other nation's liberty; or the creation of a world in which there shall be an equality of opportunity for every race and every nation. I am convinced the American people will choose, by overwhelming majority, the last of these courses. To make this choice effective, we must win not only the war but also the peace, and we must start winning it now.

To win this peace three things seem to me necessary — first, we must plan now for peace on a world basis; second, the world must be free, politically and economically, for nations and for men, that peace may exist in it; third, America must play an active, constructive part in freeing it and keeping its peace.

When I say that peace must be planned on a world basis, I mean quite literally that it must embrace the earth. Continents and oceans are plainly only parts of a whole, seen, as I have seen them, from the air. England and America are parts. Russia and China, Egypt, Syria and Turkey, Iraq and Iran are also parts. And it is inescapable that there can be no peace for any part of the world unless the foundations of peace are made secure throughout all parts of the world.

This cannot be accomplished by mere declarations of our leaders, as in an Atlantic Charter. Its accomplishment depends primarily upon acceptance by the peoples of the world. For if the failure to reach international understanding after the last war taught us anything it taught us this: even if war leaders apparently agree upon generalized principles and slogans while the war is being fought, when they come to the peace table they make their own interpretations of their previous declarations. So unless today while the war is being fought, the people of the United States and of Great Britain, of Russia and of China, and of all the other United Nations, fundamentally agree on their purposes, fine and idealistic expressions of hope such as those of the Atlantic Charter will live merely to mock us as have Mr Wilson's Fourteen Points. The Four Freedoms will not be accomplished by the declarations of those momentarily in power. They will become real only if the people of the world forge them into actuality.

When I say that in order to have peace this world must be free, I am only reporting that a great process has started which no man — certainly not Hitler — can stop. Men and women all over the world are on the march, physically, intellectually, and spiritually. After centuries of ignorant and dull compliance, hundreds of millions of people in eastern Europe and Asia have opened the books. Old fears no longer frighten them. They are no longer willing to be Eastern slaves for Western profit. They are beginning to know that men's welfare throughout the world is interdependent. They are resolved, as we must be, that there is no more place for imperialism within their own society than in the society of nations. The big house on the hill surrounded by mud huts has lost its awesome charm.

Our Western world and our presumed supremacy are now on trial. Our boasting and our big talk leave Asia cold. Men and women in Russia and China and in the Middle East are conscious now of their own potential strength. They are coming to know that many of the decisions about the future of the world lie in their hands. And they intend that these decisions shall leave the peoples of each nation free from foreign domination, free for economic, social, and spiritual growth.

Economic freedom is as important as political freedom. Not only must people have access to what other peoples produce, but their own products must in turn have some chance of reaching men all over the world. There will be no peace, there will be no real development, there will be no economic stability, unless we find the method by which we can begin to break down the unnecessary trade barriers hampering the flow of goods. Obviously, the sudden and uncompromising abolition of tariffs after the war could only result in disaster. But obviously, also, one of the freedoms we are fighting for is freedom to trade. I know there are many men, particularly in America, where our standard of living exceeds the standard of living in the rest of the world, who are genuinely alarmed at such a prospect, who believe that any such process will only lessen our own standard of living. The reverse of this is true.

Many reasons may be assigned for the amazing economic development of the United States. The abundance of our national resources, the freedom of our political institutions, and the character of our population have all undoubtedly contributed. But in my judgment the greatest factor has been the fact that by the happenstance of good fortune there was created here in America the largest area in the world in which there were no barriers to the exchange of goods and ideas.

And I should like to point out to those who are fearful one inescapable fact. In view of the astronomical figures our national debt will assume by the end of this war, and in a world reduced in size by industrial and transportation developments, even our present standard of living in America cannot be maintained unless the exchange of goods flows more freely over the whole world. It is also inescapably true that to raise the standard of living of any man anywhere in the world is to raise the standard of living by some slight degree of every man everywhere in the world.

Finally, when I say that this world demands the full participation of a self-confident America, I am only passing on an invitation which the peoples of the East have given us. They would like the United States and the other United Nations to be partners with them in this grand adventure. They want us to join them in creating a new society of independent nations, free alike of the economic injustices of the West and the political malpractices of the East. But as partners in that great new combination they want us neither hesitant, incompetent, nor afraid. They want partners who will not hesitate to speak out for the correction of injustice anywhere in the world.

Our allies in the East know that we intend to pour out our resources in this war. But they expect us now — not after the war — to use the enormous power of our giving to promote liberty and justice. Other peoples, not yet fighting, are waiting no less eagerly for us to accept the most challenging opportunity of all history — the chance to help create a new society in which men and women the world around can live and grow invigorated by independence and freedom.

# 1943 - 1944

43.

## Modern Painting in America

*The following selections reflect the artistic outlook of four of America's leading twentieth-century artists. Stuart Davis, noted for his adaptation of European modernist techniques in his interpretation of the American landscape, emphasizes the dynamism of modern American painting. Adolph Gottlieb and Mark Rothko, exponents of the postwar abstractionist school, present one of the few manifestos of American art, calling for the depiction of universal themes in the Western, not just the American, tradition. Jackson Pollock, a leader of the Abstract Expressionist school, discusses the influence of European modernists on American painting.*

Source: *Art News*, February 1-14, 1943: "The Cube Root."
*New York Times*, June 13, 1943.
*Arts and Architecture*, February 1944.

I.

### STUART DAVIS: The Dynamic American Scene

MY PICTURES fall into the category commonly called Modern Art, and more specifically into a pigeonhole which the professors have labeled Abstract Art. I have long opposed this "typing" for reasons that seem sensible to me, although time has shown that my arguments do not impress the professors. When I get a part, it is always as an abstract artist. But, nevertheless, modern art is a real entity despite the Surreal nature of many of the things said about it by professors and artists alike. It consists of a body of work produced in the last six or seven decades by men whose names are sufficiently known to preclude the need for particularization.

It would be an error to omit mention that Paris was the geographical center of this movement, because, while unimportant in itself, this place of origin has been used as the basis for various attacks on the validity of the movement as a whole. In America for example, it has often been asserted that virtue in our artists could only be found by complete repudiation of the School of Paris as they called it. The results of these campaigns have not been beneficial for American art, to give it the maximum understatement. But it is the simple truth that the modern art movement was, and in its influence remains, the only objective proof that free expression of the human spirit in art is possible in our epoch.

In my own case, I first saw a comprehensive showing of these pictures at the Armory Show in New York City in 1913. My enthusiasm was aroused by what they had to say, and the fact that they were European in origin in no way inhibited it. I found nothing incompatible between this art and the things I had seen and felt in my own environment. On the contrary, I found an elucidation of those things and an enlarging of my understanding of them.

To many people a picture is a replica of a thing or a story about some kind of a situation. To an artist, on the other hand, it is an object which has been formed by an individual in response to emotional and intellectual needs. His purpose is never to counterfeit a subject but to develop a new subject. His purpose is also to live in giving importance to certain qualities in himself, which everyone presumably possesses, but which relatively few cultivate. Art is a denial of the utilitarian considerations of everyday activity. It does not give directives or convey information. Other people, usually at a much later date, extol it as a marvelous achievement, presumably because it is.

Of course the artist doesn't dream his work into existence; he has the often arduous task of transposing his dream into the dimensional materials of painting. Thus he not only cultivates his soul, as the saying goes, but wrestles with the obstinate physical laws of three-dimensional Color-Space Design on a two-dimensional surface. Necessary theorization on these laws may come under the heading of abstract thought, but the artist does not paint his theories. His picture is shaped by his desire and there is nothing abstract about that. Proof: direct emotional response to it by people who have no knowledge or interest in his theories.

What the people respond to is the new subject the artist has found — his picture. And if the question be asked why they should be interested in that, it is because they find here a new example of the kind of things that have delighted them many times before, in nature and in art. It must be admitted that it generally takes new people to respond to new subjects. But at any rate let's have done with the academic term "abstraction" and call my pictures by the titles I give them as a means of identification. And if a generic term still be called for, just say Color-Space Composition, which they are. What they really are, of course, should only be seen and not heard.

Modern art rediscovered humanity in painting, an essential social service unrestricted by racial or national boundaries. I refer to the discovery that an artist had the power to see the world with a fresh eye. Whether he painted people, still-life, landscape, or invented subjects, every picture was an objective proof of that power to see beyond the traditional. Man's senses were restored to him. It is natural, of course, that people who had forgotten they owned any found no reflection of themselves in these pictures. They attacked them as the vicious jokes of dissolute Bohemians.

It has been often said, even by proponents of those pictures known in aesthetic slang as Cubist and Abstract, that they have no subject matter. Such a statement is equivalent to saying that life has no subject matter. On the contrary, modern pictures deal with contemporary subject matter in terms of art. The artist does not exercise his freedom in a nonmaterial world. Science has created a new environment in which new forms, lights, speeds, and spaces are a reality. The perspectives and chiaroscuro of the Renaissance are no longer physically with us, even though their ghosts linger in many of the best modern work.

In my own case, I have enjoyed the dynamic American scene for many years past, and all of my pictures (including the ones I painted in Paris) are referential to it. They all have their originating impulse in the impact of the contemporary American environment. And it is certainly a fact that the relevant art, literature, and music of other

"Garage Lights" by Stuart Davis

times and places are among the most cherished realities of that environment. I mention this last point only because there is a continuing trend by strong groups in American art who, in this way or that, have sought to deny it.

Some of the things which have made me want to paint, outside of other paintings, are: American wood and ironwork of the past; Civil War and skyscraper architecture; the brilliant colors on gasoline stations, chain-store fronts, and taxicabs; the music of Bach; synthetic chemistry; the poetry of Rimbeau [Rimbaud]; fast travel by train, auto, and aeroplane which brought new and multiple perspectives; electric signs; the landscape and boats of Gloucester, Mass.; 5 & 10 cent store kitchen utensils; movies and radio; Earl Hines' hot piano and Negro jazz music in general, etc. In one way or another the quality of these things plays a role in determining the character of my paintings. Not in the sense of describing them in graphic images, but by predetermining an analogous dynamics in the design, which becomes a new part of the American environment. Paris School, Abstraction, Escapism? Nope, just Color-Space Compositions celebrating the resolution in art of stresses set up by some aspects of the American scene.

The development of modern art in Europe is probably at an end. Indeed it strength seems to have been sapped for some years past. During its regime it broke down traditional concepts of composition unsuited to contemporary expression. It brought new light, color, and perspective to art, suited to its new subject matter. It clarified the prevalent confusion which identified a graphic image with the word "art." It proved once for all that art is a dimensional language and that its subject matter moves us in terms of an objective dimensional coherence. But enormous changes are taking place which demand new forms, and it is up to artists living in America to find them. New environments present themselves. As far as creating art is concerned, is no solution to represent them in illustr tion. If new forms are found, it will be by artists who believe in their right to find them, and in that belief have the courage to look.

## II.

## Adolph Gottlieb and Mark Rothko: Aesthetic Credo

To the artist the workings of the critical mind is one of life's mysteries. That is why, we suppose, the artist's complaint that he is misunderstood, especially by the critic, has become a noisy commonplace. It is therefore an event when the worm turns and the critic quietly, yet publicly, confesses his "befuddlement," that he is "nonplussed" before our pictures at the federation show. We salute this honest, we might say cordial, reaction toward our "obscure" paintings, for in other critical quarters we seem to have created a bedlam of hysteria. And we appreciate the gracious opportunity that is being offered us to present our views.

We do not intend to defend our pictures. They make their own defense. We consider them clear statements. Your failure to dismiss or disparage them is *prima facie* evidence that they carry some communicative power.

We refuse to defend them not because we cannot. It is an easy matter to explain to the befuddled that [Gottlieb's] "The Rape of Persephone" is a poetic expression of the essence of the myth; the presentation of the concept of seed and its earth with all its brutal implications; the impact of elemental truth. Would you have us present this abstract concept, with all its complicated feelings, by means of a boy and girl lightly tipping?

It is just as easy to explain [Rothko's] "The Syrian Bull" as a new interpretation an archaic image, involving unprecedented distortions. Since art is timeless, the significant rendition of a symbol, no matter how archaic, has as full validity today as the archaic symbol had then. Or is the one 3,000 years old truer? . . .

These easy program notes can help only the simple-minded. No possible set of notes can explain our paintings. Their explanation must come out of a consummated experience between picture and onlooker. The point at issue, it seems to us, is not an "explanation" of the paintings but whether the intrinsic ideas carried within the frames of these pictures have significance. We feel that our pictures demonstrate our aesthetic beliefs, some of which we, therefore, list:

1. To us art is an adventure into an unknown world, which can be explored only by those willing to take the risks.

2. This world of the imagination is fancy-free and violently opposed to common sense.

3. It is our function as artists to make the spectator see the world our way — not his way.

4. We favor the simple expression of the complex thought. We are for the large shape because it has the impact of the unequivocal. We wish to reassert the picture plane. We are for flat forms because they destroy illusion and reveal truth.

5. It is a widely accepted notion among painters that it does not matter what one paints as long as it is well painted. This is the essence of academism. There is no such thing as good painting about nothing. We assert that the subject is crucial and only that subject matter is valid which is tragic and timeless. That is why we profess spiritual kinship with primitive and archaic art.

Consequently, if our work embodies these beliefs, it must insult anyone who is spiritually attuned to interior decoration; pictures for the home; pictures for over the mantel; pictures of the American scene; social pictures; purity in art; prizewinning potboilers; the National Academy, the Whitney Academy, the Corn Belt Academy; buckeyes; trite tripe, etc.

III.

## JACKSON POLLOCK:
## Universal Art

*Where were you born?*
Cody, Wyoming, in January, 1912. My ancestors were Scotch and Irish.

*Have you traveled any?*
I've knocked around some in California, some in Arizona. Never been to Europe.

*Would you like to go abroad?*
No. I don't see why the problems of modern painting can't be solved as well here as elsewhere.

*Where did you study?*
At the Art Student's League, here in New York. I began when I was seventeen. Studied with Benton, at the League, for two years.

*How did your study with Thomas Benton affect your work, which differs so radically from his?*
My work with Benton was important as something against which to react very strongly, later on; in this, it was better to have worked with him than with a less resistant personality who would have provided a much less strong opposition. At the same time, Benton introduced me to Renaissance art.

*Why do you prefer living here in New York to your native West?*
Living is keener, more demanding, more intense and expansive in New York than in the West; the stimulating influences are more numerous and rewarding. At the same time, I have a definite feeling for the West: the vast horizontality of the land, for instance; here only the Atlantic Ocean gives you that.

*Has being a Westerner affected your work?*
I have always been very impressed with the plastic qualities of American Indian art. The Indians have the true painter's approach in their capacity to get hold of appropriate images, and in their understanding of what constitutes painterly subject-matter. Their color is essentially Western, their vision has the basic universality of all real art. Some people find references to American Indian art and calligraphy in parts of my pictures. That wasn't intentional; probably was the result of early memories and enthusiasms.

*Do you consider technique to be important in art?*
Yes and no. Craftsmanship is essential to the artist. He needs it just as he needs brushes, pigments, and a surface to paint on.

*Do you find it important that many famous modern European artists are living in this country?*
Yes. I accept the fact that the important painting of the last hundred years was done in France. American painters have generally missed the point of modern painting from beginning to end. (The only American master who interests me is Ryder.) Thus the fact that good European Moderns are now here is very important, for they bring with them an understanding of the problems of Modern painting. I am particularly impressed with their concept of the source of art being the unconscious. This idea interests me more than these specific painters do, for the two artists I admire most, Picasso and Miro, are still abroad.

*Do you think there can be a purely American art?*
The idea of an isolated American painting, so popular in this country during the 'thirties, seems absurd to me, just as the idea of creating a purely American mathematics or physics would seem absurd. . . . And in another sense, the problem doesn't exist at all; or, if it did, would solve itself: An American is an American and his painting would naturally be qualified by that fact, whether he wills it or not. But the basic problems of contemporary painting are independent of any one country.

# 1944

44.

## Franklin D. Roosevelt: A New Bill of Rights

*Perhaps the most lasting result of the domestic New Deal was the general acceptance of the idea that the federal government is a positive instrument to promote the general welfare. "Democracy can thrive only when it enlists the devotion of . . . the common people," Roosevelt had said in 1940. "Democracy can hold that devotion only when it adequately respects their dignity by so ordering society as to assure to the masses of men and women reasonable security and hope for themselves and for their children." In his annual message to Congress on January 11, 1944, reprinted in part below, Roosevelt introduced his Economic Bill of Rights, adding to Jefferson's political ideals of liberty, equality, and self-government that of economic security.*

Source: *Record,* 78 Cong., 2 Sess., pp. 55-57,

N THIS WAR we have been compelled to learn how interdependent upon each other are all groups and sections of the population of America.

Increased food costs, for example, will bring new demands for wage increases from all war workers, which will in turn raise all prices of all things, including those things which the farmers themselves have to buy. Increased wages or prices will each in turn produce the same results. They all have a particularly disastrous result on all fixed income groups.

And I hope you will remember that all of us in this government represent the fixed-income group just as much as we represent business owners, workers, and farmers. This group of fixed-income people includes teachers, clergy, policemen, firemen, widows, and minors on fixed incomes, wives and dependents of our soldiers and sailors, and old-age pensioners. They and their families add up to one-quarter of our 130 million people. They have few or no high-pressure representatives at the Capitol. In a period of gross inflation they would be the worst sufferers.

If ever there was a time to subordinate individual or group selfishness to the national good that time is now. Disunity at home — bickerings, self-seeking partisanship, stoppages of work, inflation, business as usual, politics as usual, luxury as usual — these are the influences which can undermine the morale of the brave men ready to die at the front for us here.

Those who are doing most of the complaining are not deliberately striving to sabotage the national war effort. They are laboring under the delusion that the time is past when we must make prodigious sacrifices — that the war is already won and we can begin to slacken off. But the dangerous folly of that point of view can be measured by the distance that separates our troops from their ultimate objectives in Berlin and Tokyo — and by the sum of all the perils that lie along the way.

Overconfidence and complacency are among our deadliest enemies. Last spring — after notable victories at Stalingrad and in Tunisia and against the U-boats on the high seas — overconfidence became so pronounced that war production fell off. In two months, June and July 1943, more than a thousand airplanes that could have been made and should have been made were not made. Those who failed to make them were not on strike. They were merely saying, "The war's in the bag — so let's relax." That attitude on the part of anyone — government or management or labor — can lengthen this war. It can kill American boys.

Let us remember the lessons of 1918. In the summer of that year the tide turned in favor of the Allies. But this government did not relax. In fact, our national effort was stepped up. In August 1918, the draft-age limits were broadened from 21-31 to 18-45. The President called for "force to the utmost," and his call was heeded. And in November, only three months later, Germany surrendered.

That is the way to fight and win a war — all-out — and not with half-an-eye on the battlefronts abroad and the other eye-and-a-half on personal, selfish, or political interests here at home.

Therefore, in order to concentrate all our energies and resources on winning the war, and to maintain a fair and stable economy at home, I recommend that the Congress adopt:

1. A realistic tax law — which will tax all unreasonable profits, both individual and corporate, and reduce the ultimate cost of the war to our sons and daughters. The tax bill now under consideration by the Congress does not begin to meet this test.

2. A continuation of the law for the renegotiation of war contracts — which will prevent exorbitant profits and assure fair prices to the government. For two long years I have pleaded with the Congress to take undue profits out of war.

3. A cost-of-food law — which will enable the government (a) to place a reasonable floor under the prices the farmer may expect for his production; and (b) to place a ceiling on the prices a consumer will have to pay for the food he buys. This should apply to necessities only, and will require public funds to carry out. It will cost in appropriations about 1 percent of the present annual cost of the war.

4. Early reenactment of the stabilization statute of October 1942. This expires June 30, 1944, and if it is not extended well in advance, the country might just as well expect price chaos by summer. We cannot have stabilization by wishful thinking. We must take positive action to maintain the integrity of the American dollar.

5. A national service law — which, for the duration of the war, will prevent strikes and, with certain appropriate exceptions, will make available for war production or for any other essential services every able-bodied adult in this nation.

These five measures together form a just and equitable whole. I would not recommend a national service law unless the other laws were passed to keep down the cost of living, to share equitably the burdens of taxation, to hold the stabilization line, and to prevent undue profits. The federal government already has the basic power to draft capital and property of all kinds for war purposes on a basis of just compensation.

As you know, I have for three years hesitated to recommend a national service act. Today, however, I am convinced of its necessity. Although I believe that we and our allies can win the war without such a measure, I am certain that nothing less than total mobilization of all our resources of manpower and capital will guarantee an earlier victory and reduce the toll of suffering and sorrow and blood.

I have received a joint recommendation for this law from the heads of the War Department, the Navy Department, and the Maritime Commission. These are the men who bear responsibility for the procurement of the necessary arms and equipment, and for the successful prosecution of the war in the field. They say:

> When the very life of the nation is in peril the responsibility for service is common to all men and women. In such a time there can be no discrimination between the men and women who are assigned by the government to its defense at the battlefront and the men and women assigned to producing the vital materials essential to successful military operations. A prompt enactment of a national service law would be merely an expression of the universality of this responsibility.

I believe the country will agree that those statements are the solemn truth.

National service is the most democratic way to wage a war. Like selective service for the armed forces, it rests on the obligation of each citizen to serve his nation to his utmost where he is best qualified. It does not mean reduction in wages. It does not mean loss of retirement and seniority rights and benefits. It does not mean that any substantial numbers of war workers will be disturbed in their present jobs. Let these facts be wholly clear. . . .

Our soldiers and sailors and marines know that the overwhelming majority of them will be deprived of the opportunity to vote if the voting machinery is left exclusively to the states under existing state laws — and that there is no likelihood of these laws being changed in time to enable them to vote at the next election. The Army and Navy have reported that it will be impossible effectively to administer forty-eight different soldier-voting laws. It is the duty of the Congress to remove this unjustifiable discrimination against the men and women in our armed forces — and to do it as quickly as possible.

It is our duty now to begin to lay the plans and determine the strategy for the winning of a lasting peace and the establishment of an American standard of living higher than ever before known. We cannot be content, no matter how high that general standard of living may be, if some fraction of our people — whether it be one-third or one-fifth or one-tenth — is ill-fed, ill-clothed, ill-housed, and insecure.

This republic had its beginning, and grew to its present strength, under the protection of certain inalienable political rights — among them the right of free speech, free press, free worship, trial by jury, freedom from unreasonable searches and seizures. They were our rights to life and liberty. As our nation has grown in size and stature, however — as our industrial economy expanded — these political rights proved inadequate to assure us equality in the pursuit of happiness.

We have come to a clear realization of the fact that true individual freedom cannot exist without economic security and independence. "Necessitous men are not freemen." People who are hungry and out of a job are the stuff of which dictatorships are made. In our day these economic truths have become accepted as self-evident. We have accepted, so to speak, a second Bill of Rights under which a new basis of security

and prosperity can be established for all —
regardless of station, race, or creed.

Among these are:

The right to a useful and remunerative
job in the industries or shops or farms or
mines of the nation;

The right to earn enough to provide adequate food and clothing and recreation;

The right of every farmer to raise and sell
his products at a return which will give him
and his family a decent living;

The right of every businessman, large and
small, to trade in an atmosphere of freedom
from unfair competition and domination by
monopolies at home or abroad;

The right of every family to a decent
home;

The right to adequate medical care and
the opportunity to achieve and enjoy good
health;

The right to adequate protection from
the economic fears of old age, sickness, accident, and unemployment;

The right to a good education.

All of these rights spell security. And after this war is won, we must be prepared to
move forward, in the implementation of
these rights, to new goals of human happiness and well-being. America's own rightful
place in the world depends in large part
upon how fully these and similar rights
have been carried into practice for our citizens. For unless there is security here at
home there cannot be lasting peace in the
world. . . .

I ask the Congress to explore the means
for implementing this economic bill of
rights — for it is definitely the responsibility of the Congress so to do. Many of these
problems are already before committees of
the Congress in the form of proposed legislation. I shall from time to time communicate with the Congress with respect to these
and further proposals. In the event that no
adequate program of progress is evolved, I
am certain that the nation will be conscious
of the fact.

Our fighting men abroad — and their
families at home — expect such a program
and have the right to insist upon it. It is to
their demands that this government should
pay heed rather than to the whining demands of selfish pressure groups who seek
to feather their nests while young Americans are dying. . . .

Each and every one of us has a solemn
obligation under God to serve this nation in
its most critical hour — to keep this nation
great — to make this nation greater in a
better world.

---

*Politics is the science of how who gets what, when, and why.*
SIDNEY HILLMAN, *Political Primer for All Americans,* 1944

45.

# Frank T. Hines: The G.I. Bill of Rights

*Public Law 346, 78th Congress, otherwise and universally known as the G.I. Bill of Rights, was the most far-reaching item of veteran's legislation in the country's history up to the last third of the twentieth century. Passed on June 22, 1944, the bill benefited millions of returning G.I.'s in their effort to readjust to civilian life by making available temporary unemployment relief, guaranteeing insured loans for homes, farms, and businesses, and paying for education. The educational benefit in the bill probably had the widest effect: more than half the nation's World War II veterans, or 7,800,000, availed themselves of its opportunities during the twelve years it was in operation. The program cost upwards of $14 billion, but few if any have ever doubted that this vast sum was an excellent investment. The following address (reprinted here in part) was delivered to the 26th Annual National Convention of the American Legion, at Chicago, on September 19, 1944, by Brigadier General Hines, administrator of Veterans' Affairs and director of Retraining and Reemployment.*

Source: VSD, November 1, 1944.

One of the finest and most unselfish things which the Legion has ever done, in my judgment, was to conceive, formulate, and take a leading part in the enactment of the GI Bill of Rights. This is a measure not for the benefit of yourselves but for the benefit of your sons, nephews, and other young relatives and those of your neighbors who are fighting World War II.

The GI Bill of Rights also incorporated many other excellent provisions, including that of declaring the Veterans Administration to be an essential war agency and entitled, second only to the War and Navy departments, to priorities in personnel, equipment, supplies, and material under any laws, executive orders, and regulations pertaining to priorities. The act further declared that in appointments of personnel from civil service registers the administrator of veterans affairs granted the same authority and discretion as the War and Navy departments and the United States Public Health Service.

The general eligibility requirements for the three new benefits under the GI Bill (which are educational opportunities, loans, guarantee of loans and employment or readjustment allowances) are service in the active military service on or after Sept. 16, 1940, and prior to the end of the war, discharge or release therefrom under conditions other than dishonorable after ninety days' service, or if sooner discharged for disability incurred in line of duty.

Any such eligible person shall be entitled to education or training, or a refresher or retraining course, at an approved educational or training institution, for a period of one year (or the equivalent thereof in continuous, part-time study), or for such lesser time as may be required for the course of instruction chosen by him.

Upon satisfactory completion of such course of education or training, according to the regularly prescribed standards and practices of the institutions, except a refresher or retraining course, such person shall be entitled to an additional period or periods of education or training, not to exceed the time such person was in the active service on or after Sept. 16, 1940, and before the termination of the war, exclusive of any period he was assigned for a course of education or training under the Army specialized training program or the Navy college training program, which course was a continuation of his civilian course and was pursued to completion, or as a cadet or midshipman at one of the service academies, but in no event shall the total period of education or training exceed four years:

*Provided,* that his work continues to be satisfactory throughout the period, according to the regularly prescribed standards and practices of the institution: *Provided, however,* that wherever the additional period of instruction ends during a quarter or semester and after a major part of such quarter or semester has expired, such period of instruction shall be extended to the termination of such unexpired quarter or semester.

Such person shall be eligible for and entitled to such course of education or training as he may elect, and at any approved educational or training institution at which he chooses to enroll, whether or not located in the state in which he resides, which will accept or retain him as a student or trainee in any field or branch of knowledge which such institution finds him qualified to undertake or pursue:

*Provided,* that, for reasons satisfactory to the administrator, he may change a course of instruction: *And provided further,* that any such course of education or training may be discontinued at any time if it is found by the administrator that, according to the regularly prescribed standards and practices of the institution, the conduct or progress of such person is unsatisfactory.

The law further provides that any person who was not over twenty-five years of age at the time he entered the service shall be deemed to have had his education or training impeded, delayed, interrupted, or interferred with.

The Veterans Administration shall use those educational and training institutions which are approved by the appropriate agency of each state and will not be disposed to approve any other institution except under extraordinary conditions.

Recently I appointed a special committee of consultant specialists composed of outstanding educators in this country to consider the problems affecting the vocational rehabilitation and the education and training of veterans. In their recent deliberations in Washington this committee recommended that the Veterans Administration pay the charges for tuition, laboratory, library, health, infirmary, and other similar fees customarily made by the approved institution for any student who pursues the particular course of training, except that the charge for the tuition fee of a full-time veteran trainee shall not be less than $10 per month, $30 per quarter, or $40 per semester.

This committee also recommended that in the case of state and municipal colleges or universities the charges for tuition, laboratory, library, health, infirmary, and other similar fees should be determined for all veteran trainees as the charges customarily made to nonresident students which were in effect prior to June 22, 1944, except that the charge for the tuition fee of a full-time veteran trainee shall not be less than $10 per month, $30 per quarter, or $40 per semester, provided that the charges are not in conflict with existing laws or other legal requirements.

I approved these recommendations, and

the necessary instructions have been issued to our regional offices effective Sept. 11, 1944. Of course, all payments are subject to the provision of the law which requires that they may not be in excess of $500 for an ordinary school year in respect to any person.

While the veteran is enrolled in and pursuing a course of training under this law, upon his application, the Veterans Administration will pay him a subsistence allowance of $50 per month if without a dependent or dependents or $75 per month if he has a dependent or dependents.

On July 1, 1944, eight days after the passage of the law, there were issued preliminary instructions for instituting the program for education and training.

Approximately 10,000 veterans have applied for training under this law and about 5,600 of them have been determined eligible, and they are now perhaps waiting for schools to open this month and October. There are 442 now taking educational benefits.

The educational and training benefits under the GI Bill were designed for the purpose of aiding non-disabled veterans and should not be confused with the vocational rehabilitation benefits for disabled veterans. . . .

As you know, the GI Bill of Rights provides that private or governmental (state or federal) lending agencies, or individuals, may make loans to qualified veterans and that the United States will guarantee not to exceed 50 percent of the loan but not to exceed $2,000. The loan must not bear interest in excess of the rate of 4 percent per annum. Loans may be made if the proceeds are to be used for the construction or purchase or repair of a home for the veteran, the purchase or improvement of a farm or building or equipment to be used by the veteran in farming, or for the purchase or establishment of a business, or for equip-

ment, machinery, or tools to be used by the veteran in pursuing a gainful occupation. . . .

What we desire to work out, and hope to accomplish, is that a qualified veteran may go to his bank, or federal or other lending agency, or even an individual, and, with the government guarantee, make a loan for any one or more of the purposes authorized by the act, and with the minimum of delay or red tape. Such, I am confident, was the intention of Congress, and it is our purpose to exert every effort to see that this intention is fulfilled.

The unemployment feature of the bill is known as readjustment allowances. The allowance provided is $20 for any week of unemployment or such amount less any wages received in excess of $3 for any week of partial employment, which week occurs not later than two years after discharge or release from active service or the termination of the war, whichever is the later date. The total number of weeks of eligibility of a veteran for readjustment allowances is dependent upon his length of service. . . . The maximum number of weeks to which an eligible veteran may be entitled under the law is fifty-two. . . .

In the enactment of the provisions of Title IV of the GI Bill, the Congress declares as its intent and purpose that there shall be an effective job counseling and employment placement service for veterans, and that to this end policies shall be promulgated and administered so as to provide for them the maximum of job opportunity in the field of gainful employment. . . .

You probably realize that the great demand for workers in war industries, and the relatively high wages paid, has resulted in only a comparatively few eligible veterans taking advantage of our vocational rehabilitation training program for the disabled. When a disabled man's clinical papers are reviewed in connection with a claim for pension, if it is found that his service-connected disability has resulted in a vocational handicap, he is forwarded an application blank so that he may make a claim for vocational rehabilitation.

Up to the present time these application blanks have been mailed to 149,600 eligibles, but only 26,204 of the application blanks have been returned to us in the form of claims. We now have 3,590 men in training and 76 have completed their training courses, most of those having been trained on the job. About two-thirds of those in training are taking the institutional training and about one-third taking job training.

After the war is over and the intense demand for workers no longer exists, we expect that many thousands of eligible young men will apply for vocational rehabilitation training.

The courses may last as long as four years. While the man is in training, his pension is increased to $92 a month if single and $103.50 a month if married, with additional payments for dependents.

We are preparing against the time when many disabled men may apply for training in many parts of the United States. As you know, we have the definite responsibility of counseling and guiding these men into the courses best adapted to their abilities and in which they would be most likely to attain success. . . .

The Veterans Administration is now conducting the largest insurance company in the world under the National Service Life Insurance Act of Oct. 8, 1940. This authorizes life insurance for each person in the armed forces who applies therefor in an amount not to exceed $10,000. Some 16 million applications have been received, some of them duplicates in that they apply for increased insurance on the same person, and the total insurance coverage under such applications is in excess of $121 billion. . . .

You are naturally aware that our men in the armed forces receive their initial hospitalization in Army and Navy hospitals. Last March the War Department announced that more than 850 hospitals with nearly half a million beds were being operated by the Army Service Forces in the continental United States and overseas, excluding some 35,000 beds in overseas mobile units and roughly 85,000 beds at overseas fixed hospitals which could be used for emergencies. The Navy has not announced the number of its hospital beds, but I feel confident that, like the Army, the number available is sufficient to the needs of the Navy, Coast Guard, and Marine Corps.

The medical services provided by our Armed Forces are of the highest type and superior to those furnished during the last war. As a consequence of this, a greater percent of battle casualties are cured and returned to active duty with the armed forces and the percentage of those who die of battle wounds is also much less than in the last war. Blood plasma, sulpha drugs, and combat medical units up in the lines with the troops are in a great measure responsible for this great saving of life of our wounded.

Where members of the armed forces are disabled to such an extent that they cannot be returned to duty, Army and Navy hospitals retain them and give them the most careful and scientific treatment until they are sufficiently cured to receive medical discharges and be returned to their homes or transferred to veterans hospitals. Our veteran hospitals up to date have received only comparatively few battle casualties from Army and Navy hospitals. However, it should be kept in mind that should these men require further care, they can enter our hospitals immediately or receive outpatient treatment for their disabilities, whichever seems advisable for particular cases.

Different situations confront those who develop tuberculosis or neuropsychiatric disease in the armed forces. Neither the Army nor the Navy is prepared to retain large numbers of these men, and, in consequence, we are hospitalizing more of these two groups for service-connected disabilities than for battle casualties.

At the present time, we have 94 hospitals with 89,000 beds, some of which are for domiciliary patients. On June 30, 1941, approximately six months before Pearl Harbor, there were available in facilities operated by the Veterans Administration a total of 61,849 hospital beds, as compared with 74,168 hospital beds on July 31, 1944. This total includes 8,774 emergency beds. . . . We estimate that our peak requirements for beds will not be reached until 1975. Between the end of the war and that date, we estimate that we shall construct or acquire gradually another 100,000 beds, which would give us a grand total of 300,000 beds of all types.

I think most of you are aware that the chief demand for our beds over the past twenty years has been for the nonservice-connected cases, and the program which I have just outlined to you is designed to meet the need for nonservice-connected cases as well as service-connected cases. Since veteran hospitalization without regard to service-connection was authorized in 1924, we have hospitalized 2.9 million cases, 900,000 of which were for service-connected disabilities and 2 million for non-service-connected disabilities. So far as the veterans of the present war are concerned, the ratio of service-connected cases to non-service-connected cases hospitalized has been about one to two and one-half. As to our present sufficiency of hospital beds, I will make this statement to you: none of the managers of any of our hospitals has reported to me that they have refused hospitalization to any veterans on account of a shortage of hospital beds. Some cases are in state hospitals, which we hope will soon be transferred to government hospitals.

Thanks to our gallant troops — Air Force and Navy — our superb leadership, efficient supply lines, and matchless production — plus the efforts of our gallant allies — victory in Europe would seem to be within our grasp in the not-too-distant future. We have confidence this time the mistakes of a quarter of a century ago will not be repeated. *Our terms are unconditional surrender.* This time American doughboys will march down the streets of Berlin.

With victory just ahead of us, we must give serious thoughts to gaining a lasting peace, both on the home front and in the continent of Europe — a peace which because of its justice and its common sense will endure throughout the lives of our sons and other young relatives, whose spirit of intrepidity and self-sacrifice will make the victory and peace possible and secure.

No postwar conditions will satisfy Americans — and especially our returning war veterans — which do not provide full employment and a maximum of job opportunities on our home front — for all who are willing and able to work. This will require the active cooperation of government, industry, labor, and management. The efforts of these four partners in prosperity must be integrated and coordinated, to the end that our country will embark upon the greatest era of peacetime prosperity and happiness which this fruitful land of ours has ever known. All of us must give and take to ensure that this is accomplished.

As Justice Byrnes has said, our present high level of employment and national income, and the maintenance of a sound economy, should be our goal. I am confident you will find that your government is doing and will do its full part toward accomplishing this most desirable end.

When victory has been attained, there will be much to be done to make sure that the peace that follows victory will be a lasting peace and that the United States is prepared to make sure that it lasts. The veterans who have served in this war, with their fathers and grandfathers who served in World War I, will undoubtedly take a leading part in the future of America.

We will have problems at home — readjustment problems of great magnitude that will reach down into the smallest communities. Because of the great interest the Legion has taken in community affairs and the work you have already done in mapping future benefits for veterans of World War II, your members will be in a position to take a leading part in bringing to the United States a stronger and better disciplined citizenship. In other words, Legionnaires will be in a position to influence for good the construction of strong communities, truly American homes, and to fight for the ideals which your forefathers intended should be the basis of our government and of the welfare of our country.

For the first time in five years, the lights in London went on night before last. Let us hope that this will be the harbinger of a new era for all of us — and that the permanent lights of peace, happiness, and prosperity will soon go on throughout the world.

---

46.

## John Desmond: Entertainers at the Front

*U.S. soldiers fought World War II in every quarter of the world — in Europe and Africa, in India and China, in the North, Central, and South Pacific, in the Arctic. They suffered from the heat in the jungles of New Guinea and from the cold in the Aleutians; they suffered from thirst in the Sahara and from the humidity in Burma; they huddled in the rain in foxholes in Normandy and sought vainly for shade in the hot sun of northern Australia. Nowhere that they went and fought was too far or too difficult for the entertainers who were sent out from New York and Hollywood by the Camp Shows branch of the United Service Organizations (USO). Some of the experiences of such traveling shows are described in the following article, written by John Desmond for the* New York Times *and published in 1944.*

Source: *New York Times Magazine*, April 2, 1944.

---

THE STAGE is a rough board affair, supported by freshly hewn logs. On it a girl, dressed in a simple cotton dress like those you see on the boardwalk at Jones Beach on a summer afternoon, is singing. Behind her two other entertainers are sitting on camp stools and to the right an accordionist pumps his arms. His instrument pours out a volume of sound that somehow manages to approximate the tune of "Shoo-Shoo Baby."

The scene is in New Guinea. It is hot —

115 degress in back of the stage, 130 plus under the arc lights that are powered by a mobile Army generator standing nearby. The generator hums softly as if it were a monotonic accompaniment to the accordion's chords. But the accordionist is unaware of the competition. He is visibly sweating as he works — sweating both because of the heat and because his accordion isn't the responsive instrument that it was a few weeks earlier in New York. The jungle does things to accordions. In the heat of day the

wood dries out and the tone becomes sharp and cracked. Then in the sultry night the moisture seeps into the sound box, sticks up the keys, and makes the tone heavy.

Now the accordion's tones swell to a crescendo for the closing phrases. The singer's last note is cut short by a roar that breaks across the jungle stillness. A thousand pairs of hands are clapping. Men are shouting and whistling. Out of the din an occasional shout comes clear, "How about some more, baby?" or "Let's have 'Take It Easy'," or "Give us 'Don't Sweetheart Me.'" The girl looks at the musician and nods. Then the roar suddenly ceases and the strains of another song float over the vast and almost unseen audience of United States servicemen.

The singer and the performers with her on New Guinea make up an overseas company of the Camp Shows branch of the United Service Organizations. At the present time, eighty such companies are out of the country, giving shows in bomb-damaged opera houses in Italy, in rickety Nissen huts in North Africa, in storage barns in Alaska and the Aleutians, in jungles, deserts, mountain hideouts — in fact, wherever American boys are stationed.

In the simplest terms, Camp Shows' job is to bring Hollywood and Broadway to the serviceman. In doing this, Camp Shows over the past two and a half years has built up a far-flung global circuit that makes the famed Keith-Orpheum swings of another day seem by comparison like a New York subway run. During that time camp shows have been given before audiences totaling 37,000,000 servicemen in the United States and an uncalculated number abroad.

The headquarters of this worldwide vaudeville circuit covers half-dozen floors in a building at 8 West Fortieth Street, New York City. Its funds come from the National War Fund and its audience is provided by the armed services. Camp Shows' job — with the help of the Hollywood Victory Committee, which makes available the services of motion-picture stars — is primarily one of finding talent and molding it into variety-type shows that won't be laughed off the boards.

The talent falls into two classifications. First there are the paid USO Camp Show performers, hired from theaters, vaudeville companies, night clubs, and shows, as permanent troupers. They form the backbone of the entertainment for our soldiers and sailors. In the second class are Broadway, Hollywood, and radio volunteers who offer their services for a minimum of six weeks. Hollywood stars, unused as many of them are to personal appearances before large audiences, were at first reluctant to give camp performances because, as Gary Cooper put it, "What can I give them?" But Cooper and many others have been fitted into the variety-show pattern and they have made a tremendous hit.

Once the talent is gathered and a script prepared, the Army takes over. It does this with exemplary military terseness. Special Services orders up entertainment much in the same fashion as it orders tanks or planes or other essentials of war. A typical requisition will read like this: "Immediately, five people, mixed, including personality. Musician essential. Tropical climate. Six weeks."

Two weeks later Camp Shows will have the company collected, briefed, inoculated, and installed in a hotel to await embarkation. Marching orders may come at any time and when they do the entertainers become, for all practical purposes, Army property. Their food, transportation, sleeping accommodations, and audiences are provided by the Army and they follow the route the Army dictates.

One such unit, which was billeted in luxury in a Hollywood hotel a few months ago, made history for USO-Camp Shows. It was made up of Gary Cooper, Una Merkel, Phyllis Brooks, and Andy Arcari. It was to be the first troupe to bring women performers into the Southwest Pacific fighting zone. The front in the Pacific is tough. Accommodations are rude, transport is at a premium, distances are great, and the dangers of enemy action and tropical disease are ever present. But Adolphe Menjou had come back from an extended tour to report that what was wanted was "Girls, Girls, Girls!"

Camp Shows and the Army aimed to please. Miss Brooks, envisaging weeks of short rations, used her last two weeks in the United States to indulge her taste for foods that a Hollywood diet denied her. Then for two months she toured the war zone. She came back sixteen pounds heavier and anxious to go again, even at the risk of gaining another sixteen. Since then women have been going out to the Pacific in increasing numbers. Paulette Goddard has just played China, following Joe E. Brown over "the hump" from India, flying the world's most dangerous air route.

Perhaps the hardest part of an overseas tour is the first week. The company elegantly housed in its Hollywood hotel will leave in the early morning for an unannounced destination. The same evening they will put in at Hawaii, snatch a few hours sleep, and push off before dawn the next day. The bomber is relatively comfortable. In its electrically controlled cabin the players are unaware of the changing temperature outside. Then the plane circles in for a landing. As it drops, the occupants pick out a landing field, and as the ground comes closer, they can identify a landing strip and, finally, the hangars and troops' quarters. The plane taxis to a stop and the opening doors let in a swift rush of hot tropical air. The field is on the northern top of Australia.

It was at such a field that the young conductor Edwin McArthur and the Metropolitan Opera singer Lansing Hatfield landed for a recently concluded tour. They found the officers gathered to meet them and as they moved away from the plane, a major asked, "Where shall we put them up, the Shoreham or the Mayflower?" Hopefully the entertainers followed a guide through the scrubby trees and brush until they came to two pup tents with the inevitable mosquito netting replacing the usual canvas sides. One was placarded "The Shoreham" and the other "The Mayflower." They elected the Mayflower and that was their headquarters for their stay.

After a couple of days in Australia, with trips by jeep or truck over rutted roads to nearby camps, the company will move northward into the islands. The closer to the front, the greater the hardships.

Almost any place in the Pacific theater, the stage performances are given under the worst possible conditions. Usually the stage is a hastily thrown together board affair, or it may be the back of an Army truck with the sides dismantled for the occasion. Often the temperature runs up around 120 to 130 degrees. Intermittent rain squalls — coming as often as two or three times in a single performance — add to the discomfort. The arc lights, powered by mobile generators, draw myriads of winged ants to the stage and they are a source of constant trouble.

"I remember one night on New Guinea," Miss Brooks said. "Ten minutes after the performance started it began to rain. That washed away all our makeup and soaked Andy's accordion. Then the rain stopped and the air was heavy and sultry. A million flying ants swarmed over the stage. Every time I opened my mouth to sing or speak, they would swarm in and I would be blowing them out for five minutes thereafter. Once we switched off the stage lights and lighted a decoy beam at the rim of the amphitheater. The bugs flew to the decoy in a great swarm and we had a couple of unmolested minutes after the lights were switched on."

Rain seldom halts a performance, but there are many interruptions that do. Gen-

United Press International

Martha Raye performing for soldiers at a heavy bomber base in North Africa, 1943

erator failure is a constant source of trouble. But when that happens the soldiers come quickly to the rescue. There is scarcely a trouper who cannot report at least one instance in which a power shortage was solved by a thousand flashlights trained on the stage by as many soldiers in all parts of the audience. In China, Joe E. Brown gave one performance with only the headlights of jeeps to illuminate the stage. "It's a thrill you never get at home," he said, and everyone else echoes his comment.

Enemy action frequently brings a show to a halt in the middle of its most dramatic scene. This happens in Italy more often than elsewhere, because in that theater the players are frequently close behind the front lines. George Raft was giving a performance south of Naples early this year when enemy planes came in overhead, and the audience and performers sat in the darkness until the alarm passed and the show could resume.

There is even an instance where the abrupt embarkation of the audience stopped a show. It happened where a transport heading from the States to the Aleutians put in briefly to await instructions. The troops aboard were hungry for shore leave, but sailing orders were expected momentarily and no one was allowed to leave ship. Two Camp Show outfits happened to be in port and they quickly started a show on an improvised stage on the dock. The men crowded every inch of available space on the dockside, lining up six deep at the rail. An hour later, sailing orders came. Amid the clank of chains, the slamming of hatches, the creak of gangways, the chugging of tugs, as the transport nudged out into the harbor, the show went on.

A wind was blowing cold off the mountain and the water between ship and shore was flecked with white-capped, restless waves. On the dock three USO-Camp Show girls, in flimsy stage costumes, sang into a public-address-system microphone some verses of a popular GI song and the men aboard ship took up the tune. Then, as night stole in, the transport disappeared in the gloom, but the voices of the singing soldiers could still be heard out of the night.

Experiences like that one wipe away the

memory of a thousand hardships for overseas entertainers. The spontaneous response of the servicemen is so swift and heartfelt that there is scarcely an actor who has been overseas who does not fear the day when he will again face a city audience. Overseas these players find that the soldiers like to laugh. Even the oldest jokes will virtually "roll 'em in the aisles." Joe E. Brown's oft-repeated one-man baseball team pantomime was a command performance everywhere he appeared. A joke that never failed him was to single out a GI and shout, "Hey, soldier, where do you come from?" The reply "Cincinnati" would come, and Brown would use the ancient rejoinder. "And you admit it!"

Instantly all over the audience boys would begin pointing at other Cincinnatians and repeating, "And you admit it!"

Old stuff! So was the joke that Phyllis Brooks used over and over again in Australia. She would say, "I met a soldier with a black eye yesterday. I said, 'Where did you get it?' He answered, 'I was out with an Australian girl last night and I asked her to kiss me. She said 'No' (the Australians pronounce it n-o-w) and I did.'"

And Bob Hope, in his whirlwind circuit of the European and Mediterranean theaters late last year, would cheer up a couple of thousand weary men back from battle with gags like this: "I led such a sheltered life I didn't go out with girls till I was almost four," or "Fellas, the folks at home are having a terrible time about eggs. They can't get any powdered eggs at all. They've got to use the old-fashioned kind you break open."

It is the kind of broad humor, with some GI variations, that the boys heard for years in America. It reminds them of home. They like almost anything that smacks of home. One of Gary Cooper's best performances was a recitation of Lou Gehrig's speech in "Pride of the Yankees," and George Raft won many an audience reenacting scenes from some of his better-known films.

But because the men overseas like "old stuff" doesn't mean that military service has dulled their sense of humor. Raft can testify to that, too. On one of his first performances in the Mediterranean theater Raft asked the men at the conclusion of his program if they wanted to ask questions about home. The answer came quickly, "How's Betty Grable?" Raft answered, "You know, fellows, I've backed race horses and they lost; I've backed boxers and they lost; this time I lost." Thereafter, he was careful to work in a reference to Miss Grable and Harry James earlier in his program.

Letters from all theaters flood into the USO-Camp Shows from soldiers and sailors in the fighting zones and from their parents at home attesting the gratitude of the servicemen for the "live shows." There is not an actor who has returned who has not had mail and telephone calls from parents in all parts of the United States to tell how much their sons liked the performances. If the trouper happened to have spoken personally to the soldier in a hospital or at mess, the boy's parents are sure to have heard about it and they call and write, grateful for any scrap of information about a son's whereabouts, his looks, his food. Such letters are a source of deep pleasure to the performers, but their greatest thrill comes from the spontaneous response of men in the fighting zones. Take this one:

Ella Logan, along with two other performers, was giving a show before several hundred men, half of them Negro, in a huge Nissen hut in North Africa. The program had lasted for about two hours and Miss Logan had been on the stage for more than one hour singing dozens of popular songs. After an encore she shouted to the audience, "Fellas, am I keeping you from anything?" And a young kid in the back of the room called back, "Yeh, sufferin'."

47.

# WILLIAM BENTON: What a Free-Enterprise System Is and Is Not

*William Benton, publisher of* Encyclopaedia Britannica *since 1943, has had an extremely varied and successful business, educational, and political career. Founder, with Chester Bowles, of the well-known advertising firm of Benton and Bowles, he sold his interest in 1935 and in 1937 became vice-president of the University of Chicago. He resigned from the university in 1945 to become assistant secretary of state under Truman, in which position he inaugurated the Voice of America broadcasts and promoted international visits of professors and students. While still at the University of Chicago, in 1944, he wrote a pamphlet, originally titled "The Economics of a Free Society," for the Committee for Economic Development, of which he was a member. Part of the pamphlet, which was published in October 1944, is reprinted here.*

Source: *The Economics of a Free Society,* Committee for Economic Development Supplementary Paper No. 1, New York, 1944.

IN A FREE SOCIETY all men are *common* in their rights and opportunities. They are frequently *uncommon* in their individual capacities to contribute to the common good.

The free-enterprise system is a way of economic life open to hope — an economy open to new ideas, new products, new jobs, new men. It stimulates men of all talents and capacities to serve to the best of their abilities. It promotes the capacity of men for bold and independent action. The opportunity to compete in a free and open market encourages men to study the actions of others critically — not passively to accept them — and then resourcefully to act for themselves or for their companies in supplying goods or services to the public. . . .

When we speak of a free-enterprise system, we use a term that has been widely misunderstood, as much because of the practices of its professed friends as because of the professions of its actual enemies. It is of vital importance to the future of the country that the term be properly understood.

## *What A Free-Enterprise System Is Not*

THE FREE-ENTERPRISE SYSTEM is not, never has been, and never should be, a system of complete laissez-faire. For instance, it is:

— not the freedom to seek profit by any and all means;
— not the right to profit at the expense of the welfare of the community;
— not the freedom of any man to exploit any other;
— not the freedom to waste the natural resources of the country;

— not the right to monopolize (which impedes or prevents the establishment of new business, creates scarcity, and imperils the spirit of enterprise);

— not the opposition to necessary and appropriate government regulation or operation (often for no other reason than that it is governmental);

— not the appeal to government for subsidy or protection whenever adversity appears.

These distortions have never belonged in a properly functioning system of free enterprise. They tend to pull down private enterprise. They can pull democratic government down on top of them. Indeed the amazing fact is that a system so much abused and so little understood has functioned as well as it has. Past deficiencies, however, do not demonstrate that a free-enterprise system will not work. They merely demonstrate that we have not yet made a concerted and deliberate effort to make it work with full effectiveness. We must learn how to outlaw its perversions and how to preserve and expand those beneficial features essential to a free society.

### What A Free-Enterprise System Is

THE FREE-ENTERPRISE SYSTEM is a system of production, investment, and consumption under which private individuals and business firms, largely by their own initiative and responsibility, combine the community's labor skills, managerial skills, and capital to produce the bulk of the goods and services men want. Its most characteristic features as compared with other economic systems are: maximum dependence upon competition and the free play of prices to determine who shall produce what, maximum dependence on profit as an incentive rather than on compulsion or prestige, and maximum emphasis on free personal choice among the economic opportunities — be

they goods or jobs — that are available to men.

Under a free-enterprise system, men risk their resources in private venture in the hope of personal gain. A free enterpriser is a young man going to night school to train himself for a profession, a lawyer moving to another locality in the hope of developing a better practice, a worker taking special training to achieve a skilled status, a man shifting from one job to another in search of a better opportunity. In a system of free enterprise, private assets, whether of money, talent, ambition, or energy, are risked in the hope of gain — whether by a businessman seeking profit at the risk of loss, by a tenant buying his own farm at the risk of a mortgage debt, or by a young man starting his own small business at the risk of losing his savings and the steady job he held. A true system of free enterprise thus encourages venture and risk taking, whether by an individual worker or by a group of individuals in the form of a cooperative or a big corporation.

In the U.S. there are 4 million or more farm enterprisers, more than 1 million self-employed who work as their own bosses, more than 2 million private businesses with one or more employees. These provide enormous opportunities for innovation and experimentation. After the war, America must create an economic climate that will develop millions more. Can any centrally controlled economy hope to maintain the dynamic drive, the ingenuity, or the diversity of creative impulse of these millions of enterprises? Their persistent search for improvement results in progress: better products and services adapted more closely to the desires of the buyers at ever lower prices. The driving energy of private incentive thus serves the economic good of the nation as a whole.

The effect of this drive for improvement is clearly visible in the history of the last forty years. Since 1900, new and better ma chines and better methods have more than tripled manufacturing output per man-hour of work. For the economy as a whole, output per man-hour in recent decades has been increasing at the rate of 2½ percent per year.

Much of this increased production, moreover, has reached the consumer in the form of new and improved products — the radio, the automobile, the airplane, electrical household equipment, vitamins, and a thousand other things that have enhanced enjoyment and opened up new vistas of good living.

Nor is there indication that the upward trend of production per man-hour is slackening or is likely soon to slacken. If it is merely maintained at 2½ percent per year, the production per hour of work will be doubled in the course of the next twenty-eight years. That will give us twice as large a volume of goods and services per capita if we maintain high employment or, if it seems preferable, we may have an equivalent combination of more production and more leisure. This is no fantastic dream. It can be achieved. It will be achieved if we maintain the essential features of our system of free enterprise and successfully prevent mass unemployment.

Further, a free market open to the development of new, independent enterprises will continue to provide an economic basis for political freedom. Such a market breeds the millions of rival producers and sellers who do not need to cater to private or public overlords. They help keep the balance on the side of freedom and against the arbitrary exercise of economic power. They provide the competition that minimizes the need for government regulation and operation. They provide an element of balance that counteracts potential dangers to our democratic institutions.

Lack of competition stifles the free market. So-called monopoly practices of business, labor, and government, which remove the necessity of trying to undersell a competitor or to match or improve on his quality, induce complacency. Such practices have no place in a free-enterprise system designed to serve the common good. They require government action either to remove their source or, where monopoly is essential to public service, to regulate them in the public interest.

The American people have continued up to now to tolerate abuses that have developed in our economic system because of their conviction that the free-enterprise system, however they may have abused it, has achieved a net gain substantially greater than that to be expected from any other system. They believe it can be made to work for the good of all. They want it to work with the maximum possible effectiveness. They see in it a chance for a better life for themselves. Almost unanimously, they want it for their sons and daughters. They see in it an economic tool that properly used will reinforce and not endanger constitutional democracy.

### The U.S. In The World Economy

AFTER THE WAR, the U.S. must decide on how best it can aid in the maintenance of world peace. It must decide on the part it will play in the world economy. Under its bylaws the Committee for Economic Development dedicates itself to the problems of the domestic economy. However, its members recognize the imperative necessity of a world climate favorable to enterprise and believe that high levels of employment and productivity can be most readily achieved and maintained in America in a world environment providing a maximum opportunity for private enterprise in international trade.

Questions pertaining to our international obligations and our international economic opportunities involve matters of military and political, as well as economic, strategy.

They are not ours in the U.S. alone to decide. Decisions of other countries will inevitably affect ours and will do so in ways that are hard to foretell.

One thing is certain: the maintenance of high levels of production and employment in the U.S. will be one of the most important influences contributing to prosperity and peace throughout the world. Depression here will breed depression if not fascism abroad. Prosperity here will beget prosperity and stability in other countries.

After the war, the U.S. must learn to import, as well as export, if we are not to disrupt the economies of other countries and if we want to be paid for what we sell. We must buy goods and services from others to give them the means to buy from us.

Whatever America's future role in world trade and commerce, it has the strength and must develop the ability to work out its economic destiny within the framework of a system of free enterprise for itself. Within this framework, it must learn how to deal with those countries that have other economic systems.

### Government And Business

IF PRIVATE ENTERPRISE is to fulfill its promise and its obligations, the people through their government must police it without obstructing it, must encourage it without pampering it, and must help provide it with a balance wheel in times of business boom or depression.

We are at a crucial point in the development of free enterprise in America and in the world. From the founding of America to the closing of the Western frontier, American enterprise kept pace with the expanding population that penetrated the empty or thinly inhabited acres of the West. Since then the development of American enterprise has been based on the boundless opportunities offered by the ever accelerating wants of the ever more populated centers of the U.S. and the globe. The present social and scientific frontier offers greater opportunities than did the thinly populated geographic frontier for high production, consumption, and employment. In the development of this new frontier, great economic organizations have been created that present new problems in the relations of government and business. Before we can take full advantage of the internal frontier, we must develop greater insight into the responsibilities of both government and business and into the rules upon which a free-enterprise system must rest.

Much past government regulation has been necessary and in the interest of preserving free enterprise. All wartime regulations, when hostilities cease, cannot be immediately removed on the fallacious principle of "a return to normalcy." After the war, the role of "government-in-business" will and must be lessened in many areas of the economy, transferred in others, and increased in still others.

A high degree of imagination, goodwill, and inventiveness will be required in the new world after the war to work out improved rules of the game. We shall require improved forms of administrative organization for carrying out those rules, in the enforcement of which a large measure of human discretion is required. The more skillfully we handle the role of government in the economy, the less the role that government may have to play. More adequate government skills must be devised, for example, to help stabilize the economy against the effects of the "business cycle."

We must rid the economy of injurious or unnecessary governmental regulation, as well as administration that is hostile or harmful. Moreover, businessmen must rid themselves of hostility to evolution and change in the responsibilities of government in the discharge of its proper functions. Without government, business cannot do the job after this war that must be done. Wherein is government regulation in the public interest? Wherein is it restrictive and harmful? The answer to these questions is imperative to the future of our economy. . . .

After the war, the American people must insist that their government pursue constructive fiscal, monetary, and other policies that provide a climate in which a private-enterprise system can flourish. The failure to insist on this may lead to some form of dictatorship or fascism. Thus far the appeal of totalitarianism has fallen on deaf ears in the U.S. community. But totalitarianism thrives on fear bred by war and want. If, after the war, millions of men cannot find work that gives a man human dignity, our democratic community may turn to it in desperation.

## Opportunity And Security

"OPPORTUNITY" AND "SECURITY" are not conflicting alternatives. Opportunity is an indispensable part of true security — the opportunity to earn an adequate income through work, the opportunity to risk one's energy and savings for profit, the opportunity to live decently, to aspire to live better, to educate one's children, and to develop the highest powers inherent in every man.

Throughout all history, men have not been able to grow enough food for all the people, or to build them all homes, or to provide them all with adequate clothing. The technological advances already achieved by industry demonstrate the possibility of creating high levels of food and shelter and clothing for all our people. No artificial restrictions should be allowed to stand in the way of further technological advances and their full utilization. Labor, agriculture, and government, as well as business, must divest themselves of all practices that check expansion of production or that restrict output. They must all make appropriate adjustments to the age of abundance which today's technical advances have made possible. In so doing, they can find their own opportunities and at the same time fulfill their

obligations. Thus they can play their part in a free-enterprise system that makes possible genuine security.

While it is obvious that real security lies in the availability of good jobs, men should and will seek security against the hazards of unemployment and the inability to work. The goods and services required to supply security against unemployment and old age are, however, derived from the total production of the economic system. A bookkeeping credit to an old-age pension in 1944 must be paid out of the country's total production when the credit falls due. To achieve high production, so that such credits can be paid without hardship, our system requires rewards for energy and initiative. A balance must be struck between the output going to provide security and the output going to provide rewards for work, i.e., wages, salaries, fees, royalties, profits, etc. Only if opportunity for reward is provided will the economic system develop the high level of production required to provide social security. Real security depends on the abundance to be shared. Only through providing opportunity for the individual can abundance be secured.

Men want the security that includes opportunity. It is discouragement that has germinated the "security psychosis" that in some countries has induced men to take a defeatist view of human life and abandon human freedom. . . .

New products and services that only wait for development — they are everywhere around us — will beckon men on to renewed exertion. America stands at the gate of an age of plenty. The key is in our hand. A system of free enterprise, based upon the principles herein set forth, can act as the provider as well as the safeguard of democracy.

Most Americans would agree on the economic goals for America: a community permanently rich in opportunity and security. We can secure both if we work together. We can work together only if we understand one another. The people of America can build an America — and help build a world — that is in fact the land of the free.

We in America have always had a dream. We have never lost it. We have it now.

With the enterprise, initiative, and goodwill of man urged on to the common good, we can make that dream come alive — not in the millennium but in the America of the approaching tomorrow.

---

48.

# David E. Lilienthal: The Tennessee Valley Authority

*The TVA, incorporated by Congress in 1933, implemented a recovery program for the entire Tennessee River Valley, an area of 40,000 square miles supporting (at the time) 3 million people. The undertaking, which affected the economics of seven states, was opposed by private power companies and by many who felt that any government corporation was unconstitutional. Despite TVA's success and a Supreme Court decision upholding its constitutionality (Ashwander et al. v. Tennessee Valley Authority, 1936), it still had many critics in the 1940s. In a book published in 1944, David Lilienthal, the first director of TVA, defended the project. Excerpts from the chapter entitled "Democracy at the Grass Roots: For the People and by the People" are reprinted here.*

Source: *TVA: Democracy on the March*, 3rd edition, New York, 1944, pp. 75-89.

> *It is not the earth, it is not America who is so great,*
> *It is I who am great or to be great, it is You up there, or any one,*
> *It is to walk rapidly through civilizations, governments, theories,*
> *Through poems, pageants, shows, to form individuals.*
>
> *Underneath all, individuals, I swear nothing is good to me now*
> *that ignores individuals. . . .*
>
> — Walt Whitman

People are the most important fact in resource development. Not only is the welfare and happiness of individuals its true purpose, but they are the means by which that development is accomplished; their genius, their energies and spirit are the instruments; it is not only "for the people" but "by the people." . . .

From the outset of the TVA undertaking it has been evident to me, as to many others, that a valley development envisioned in its entirety could become a reality if and only if the people of the region did much of the planning and participated in most of the decisions. To a considerable degree this is what is happening. Each year, almost each month, one can see the participation of the people, as a fundamental practice, grow more vigorous, and, although it suffers occasional setbacks, it is becoming part of the thinking and the mechanics of the development of the Tennessee Valley. . . .

I shall illustrate how TVA has undertaken its job of region-building at the grass roots, and how regional decentralization is at work in almost every side of the valley's life — among farmers, workmen, businessmen, local officials, and in TVA's relations with state and local governments. In telling how these ideas have been put in practice, I have chosen to begin with the story of how TVA has applied grass-roots democracy to the job of rebuilding the land.

The farmers — there are about 225,000 farms in the watershed of the Tennessee River, with 1,350,000 people living on them — have long seen that their lands were in trouble. They knew, almost all of them, what they wanted. They knew that what was needed was to increase the productivity of their lands, to heal the gullies, to keep water on the land, and to prevent the soil from washing away. Like almost everyone else they were reluctant to change their habits of doing things. They wanted to have a say-so about changes, they had to be "shown"; but when their confidence had been earned they were enthusiastic, and they were generous of spirit.

The farm experts, both in the Department of Agriculture's scientific bureaus in Washington and in the state agencies of the Tennessee Valley, had known most of the technical answers to the *separate* problems of soils, of fertilizer, of terracing, and had known them for a good many years. They were competent in their special fields and devoted to their work. Nevertheless farm income in the valley as in the whole Southeast continued at a low ebb; in some counties the average cash income for a farm *family* was less than $150 a year. Soil losses were appalling. Farm tenantry increased. Changes in farming favored by the technicians, away from cotton and corn, for example, did occur, but the pace was so slow that the direction on the whole continued downward. Entire rural counties, the towns included, were without a single telephone, a mile of farm electric line, a public library, a newspaper, a hospital, a single public health officer.

The technical knowledge of farming problems in the agricultural agencies, state and federal, was extensive, but it was largely generalized. It was not based on the needs of a particular farm or farming community. When this knowledge did reach the farmer, through reports of scientific results on experimental plots, in pamphlets, or by word of mouth through one of many agencies, it was usually a succession of separate bits of knowledge, and it was often remote from the farmer's individual problems. He was likely to be confused by the multiplicity of "remedies" and the more than a score of different governmental agencies with which he must deal on agricultural problems.

What was needed was not alone more technical information, but that *on the farm itself* there should be a unification of all the available knowledge and skills. The technical knowledge of all kinds available at the various state university agricultural experiment farms had somehow to be moved to thousands of valley farms, actual farms. What happened at a beautifully equipped experiment station or in a laboratory was one thing; what would happen on a man's farm was quite another. The laboratory had to be taken to the farm; the whole farm as a business was the farmer's problem.

Furthermore, as TVA saw it, and as the agricultural colleges were quick to confirm, the individual farmer was the only one who could *apply* all this available expertness. He must therefore become the center of the scheme of education in new methods. We did not want a method of restoring soil whereby the farmer would be ordered; he would learn *by doing,* on his own place; his neighbors would learn by watching him and adapting what "worked out." Nor did we want a mere false front, using the outward form of voluntary and educational methods to disguise actual coercion, or "uplift," or narrow political purposes.

After some searching the method that was worked out, with state, local, and federal agencies as cooperating parties, centered about "whole farm demonstrations" on tens of thousands of dirt farms. . . . On the land of these demonstration farmers two ideas met and were combined in action: the idea of unity and the democratic idea that much of the planning and execution of resource development must be in the hands of the people.

These thousands of typical working farms are the schoolrooms of the valley. Here farmers, their wives and children, with their neighbors learn and demonstrate the unity of resources, learn and demonstrate the principles of grass-roots democracy. Here there is brought to them the fruits of the technical man's skills. In each of the valley's counties there are one or more Farm Improvement Associations, with a total membership of more than 32,000 farmers. These associations are organized by the farmers and operated entirely by boards of trustees elected by them. . . .

Once selected, the first step was to map and inventory this farm schoolroom. These maps and inventories are not "documents," built up by questionnaires from a distance, nor are they "professional." They are made by the farmer and the committee of his neighbors. Then the farmer, the technicians, and the county agent and his demonstration assistant "talk over" that map. They walk over the place, map and inventory in hand, often several times, still talking it over. A new management plan for the farm is the result, reduced to writing. In return for the use of his farm as a schoolroom and for his promise to keep detailed records so that others may profit by his experience, the demonstrator is supplied without cost (except freight) with TVA concentrated phosphate minerals sufficient to carry out the "new plan." He agrees with his neighbors to use these minerals on crops that will further the building of the soil and store more water in it, and not otherwise. For all the other adjustments he must pay his own way: the needed lime, terracing, cattle for

the pasture that takes the place of the cotton field, and fencing for that pasture; the sheds and barns and necessary machinery. Most of these farmers had depended for their cash upon the soil-costly crops: cotton, corn, tobacco. They embarked upon a change that would rebuild the soil. Most of them had little if any working capital. What they put in, out of meager resources, was "venture capital," and too they risked the loss of their source of cash income to carry the family through the winter. But they tried it voluntarily, more than 20,000 of them in the states of the Tennessee Valley alone, and succeeded.

Most demonstration farmers have succeeded in increasing their capital resources, many have increased their income in cash received or in a rising family living standard; at the same time they have conserved and revitalized their soil. This is important because this method, being voluntary with no powers of enforcement in anyone, depends upon hitching together the farmer's self-interest and the general public interest in the basic resource of the soil. The individual has made himself one with the common purpose which the TVA idea holds for all individuals, the development of the resources upon which all stand. Self-interest here has served that public interest.

For a time these new ways of doing things were viewed with some suspicion. All kinds of rumors spread through the countryside. One story was that, once a farmer put this TVA phosphate on his land, the land would thenceforth belong to the "gov'ment." But when on one side of a line fence there grew little but worthless sedge grass, and on the other the field was heavy with crimson clover and alfalfa, a change in attitude and interest took place. The demonstration farms became places to visit, to study, to emulate. The greatest effect in spreading new farming practices has been among those who have never been selected as demonstrators at all. . . .

First of course the farmer thought about

his own land, his own family, then about his neighborhood. He began to work with his neighbors. First they concerned themselves with farming, then community forest-fire protection, then the school, the community's health problems, the church. Thus what begins as "soil building" or "better farming," by the inevitable force of unity of resources and men, soon "touches and gives life to all forms of human concerns," to use language of the President's original message concerning the TVA.

Farmers began working together, concentrating their efforts upon a matter far more important than any one man but in which each individual was deemed an essential part. The single farm demonstration developed into area demonstrations, these into countywide associations, with trustees elected from all parts of the county. From phosphate and lime other common interests grew, such as livestock and its improvement, since without cattle and sheep no farmer could utilize the forage of his pastures and meadows. . . .

In the Tennessee Valley the effect of working together, building a fertile soil, and finding ways to protect it and keep it strong is not merely a matter of men's livelihood. Revitalizing the soil has done things to the people and their institutions quite as much as to the land. Schools have been painted, lighted, or rebuilt, church and community activities stimulated; the effect is felt in a score of people's activities which they share in common. Only cynics will find this surprising. To those with faith in humankind it is natural enough that when men adopt a common purpose so deep and broad as that of working with nature to build a region's resources there ensue inevitable consequences to the spirit of men. These indeed may be the most important result of all.

Similar consequences in the rural life of this valley have followed upon another fruit of technology: electricity. Here again farmers worked together, organizing their own

electric cooperatives, sometimes against the opposition of private agencies. Electricity became a fulcrum, as did phosphate, for many changes. Electricity induced changes in farm management practices; soil conservation was encouraged. The portable electric motor, the refrigerator, electric cooling of milk, and soil heating by electricity meant increased farm income, and so the farmer could afford to buy more phosphate at the store, bid in more cattle at the auction, put in more grass, winter grain, and legumes, less corn and cotton.

And, as in the case of the technical lever of phosphate, electricity's part in furthering unified development of resources through human understanding went far beyond the business of making a living. The coming of electricity has had an important effect upon standards in rural schools, for example. Similarly in farm homes. When an electric range or refrigerator comes into a farm kitchen the effect is always much the same: the kitchen gets a coat of paint, is furbished up; not long after, the rest of the house spruces up; a new room is built on, pride begins to remake the place — pride supported by the added income that comes from "smart" use of electricity for farm purposes. You can follow the trail of new electric lines in many sections by observing the houses that have been thus tidied up.

When the principles of grass-roots democracy are followed, electricity, like soil minerals, provides men with a stimulus in their own lives, as well as an opportunity to work together with others toward a purpose bigger than any individual. By that act of joint effort, of citizen participation, the individual's essential freedom is strengthened and his satisfactions increased.

A common purpose furthered by grass-roots methods not only draws neighbors together in a community, then in a county and a group of counties; as time goes on the whole region, from one end to another, has felt the effect. The North Carolina farmers in the high mountains of Watauga or Jackson counties are brought closer to the Virginians and to the Alabama and western Kentucky farmers of the red clay flatlands. A common purpose is making us one valley.

Nor is this cohesive effect confined even to the Tennessee Valley. In twenty-one states outside the valley, seventeen of them outside the South, similar demonstration farms using TVA phosphate, now numbering 5,000, have been organized by the farmers and the institutions of those states and are operating along similar lines, though on a less extensive scale.

Not long ago two busloads of farmers from the great dairy state of Wisconsin came to the valley "to see for ourselves." Something had gone wrong with their own lands. They spent days walking over Ten-

nessee and Alabama demonstration farms. Today, in Wisconsin, TVA phosphate is being used in the same kind of demonstrations in twenty-seven counties of that state. For me one of the pleasantest experiences of these years was the sight of a Wisconsin farmer sitting on an automobile running board with an Alabama cotton farmer, both completely absorbed, talking over together their experiences with their land. Their grandfathers may have fought against each other at Shiloh. These citizens, however, would never think of Alabama and Wisconsin in the same way again. Not even the visits to the valley of hundreds of earnest "learners" from Mexico, China, Brazil, Australia, and a dozen other foreign lands has more meaning than the meeting of those two men on that Alabama farm.

---

49.

# H. Black, F. Frankfurter, F. Murphy, and R. H. Jackson: *Korematsu v. United States*

*After Pearl Harbor government officials began to fear a Japanese invasion of the West Coast and, short of that, the possibility of sabotage and subversion by Japanese-Americans living in the area. Though most of the Japanese immigrants were by now American citizens, and though some of them had been born in the United States, the War Department prevailed on President Roosevelt to relocate the Japanese-Americans in special detention camps, where they stayed throughout the war. In 1943 the Supreme Court upheld the constitutionality of the government's policy, and in* Korematsu v. United States, *a case decided in 1944, it reaffirmed its earlier decision. Parts of the Court's ruling, a concurring opinion, and two strong dissents are reprinted here.*

Source: 323 U.S. 214.

*Mr. Justice Black* delivered the opinion of the Court.

The petitioner, an American citizen of Japanese descent, was convicted in a Federal District Court for remaining in San Leandro, California, a "Military Area," contrary

to Civilian Exclusion Order No. 34 of the Commanding General of the Western Command, U. S. Army, which directed that after May 9, 1942, all persons of Japanese ancestry should be excluded from that area. No question was raised as to petitioner's loyalty to the United States. The Circuit Court of Appeals affirmed, and the importance of the constitutional question involved caused us to grant certiorari.

It should be noted, to begin with, that all legal restrictions which curtail the civil rights of a single racial group are immediately suspect. That is not to say that all such restrictions are unconstitutional. It is to say that courts must subject them to the most rigid scrutiny. Pressing public necessity may sometimes justify the existence of such restrictions; racial antagonism never can.

In the instant case, prosecution of the petitioner was begun by information charging violation of an Act of Congress, of March 21, 1942, 56 Stat. 173, which provides that:

> Whoever shall enter, remain in, leave, or commit any act in any military area or military zone prescribed, under the authority of an executive order of the President, by the secretary of war, or by any military commander designated by the secretary of war, contrary to the restrictions applicable to any such area or zone or contrary to the order of the secretary of war or any such military commander, shall, if it appears that he knew or should have known of the existence and extent of the restrictions or order and that his act was in violation thereof, be guilty of a misdemeanor and upon conviction shall be liable to a fine of not to exceed $5,000 or to imprisonment for not more than one year, or both, for each offense.

Exclusion Order No. 34, which the petitioner knowingly and admittedly violated, was one of a number of military orders and proclamations, all of which were substantially based upon Executive Order No. 9066, 7 Fed. Reg. 1407. That order, issued after we were at war with Japan, declared that "the successful prosecution of the war requires every possible protection against espionage and against sabotage to national-defense material, national-defense premises, and national-defense utilities. . . ."

One of the series of orders and proclamations, a curfew order, which, like the exclusion order here was promulgated pursuant to Executive Order 9066, subjected all persons of Japanese ancestry in prescribed West Coast military areas to remain in their residences from 8 P.M. to 6 A.M. As is the case with the exclusion order here, that prior curfew order was designed as a "protection against espionage and against sabotage." In *Hirabayashi* v. *United States*, 320 U.S. 81, we sustained a conviction obtained for violation of the curfew order. The *Hirabayashi* conviction and this one thus rest on the same 1942 congressional act and the same basic executive and military orders, all of which orders were aimed at the twin dangers of espionage and sabotage.

The 1942 act was attacked in the *Hirabayashi* case as an unconstitutional delegation of power; it was contended that the curfew order and other orders on which it rested were beyond the war powers of the Congress, the military authorities, and of the President, as commander in chief of the Army; and, finally, that to apply the curfew order against none but citizens of Japanese ancestry amounted to a constitutionally prohibited discrimination solely on account of race. To these questions, we gave the serious consideration which their importance justified. We upheld the curfew order as an exercise of the power of the government to take steps necessary to prevent espionage and sabotage in an area threatened by Japanese attack.

In the light of the principles we announced in the *Hirabayashi* case, we are unable to conclude that it was beyond the war power of Congress and the executive to exclude those of Japanese ancestry from the West Coast war area at the time they did. True, exclusion from the area in which one's home is located is a far greater deprivation than constant confinement to the home from 8 P.M. to 6 A.M. Nothing short of apprehension by the proper military authorities of the gravest imminent danger to

Camp for Japanese-Americans set up by the government in California, 1942. In the foreground is baggage of incoming inhabitants

the public safety can constitutionally justify either. But exclusion from a threatened area, no less than curfew, has a definite and close relationship to the prevention of espionage and sabotage. The military authorities, charged with the primary responsibility of defending our shores, concluded that curfew provided inadequate protection and ordered exclusion. They did so, as pointed out in our *Hirabayashi* opinion, in accordance with congressional authority to the military to say who should and who should not remain in the threatened areas.

In this case the petitioner challenges the assumptions upon which we rested our conclusions in the *Hirabayashi* case. He also urges that by May 1942, when Order No. 34 was promulgated, all danger of Japanese invasion of the West Coast had disappeared. After careful consideration of these contentions, we are compelled to reject them.

Here, as in the *Hirabayashi* case, *supra,* at p. 99,

> We cannot reject as unfounded the judgment of the military authorities and of Congress that there were disloyal members of that population, whose number and strength could not be precisely and quickly ascertained. We cannot say that the warmaking branches of the government did not have ground for believing that in a critical hour such persons could not readily be isolated and separately dealt with, and constituted a menace to the national defense and safety, which demanded that prompt and adequate measures be taken to guard against it. . . .

It is said that we are dealing here with the case of imprisonment of a citizen in a concentration camp solely because of his ancestry, without evidence or inquiry concerning his loyalty and good disposition toward the United States. Our task would be simple, our duty clear, were this a case involving the imprisonment of a loyal citizen in a concentration camp because of racial prejudice. Regardless of the true nature of the assembly and relocation centers — and we deem it unjustifiable to call them concentration camps with all the ugly connotation that term implies — we are dealing specifically with nothing but an exclusion order

To cast this case into outlines of racial prejudice, without reference to the real military dangers which were presented, merely confuses the issue.

Korematsu was not excluded from the Military Area because of hostility to him or his race. He *was* excluded because we are at war with the Japanese Empire, because the properly constituted military authorities feared an invasion of our West Coast and felt constrained to take proper security measures, because they decided that the military urgency of the situation demanded that all citizens of Japanese ancestry be segregated from the West Coast temporarily, and, finally, because Congress, reposing its confidence in this time of war in our military leaders — as inevitably it must — determined that they should have the power to do just this.

There was evidence of disloyalty on the part of some, the military authorities considered that the need for action was great, and time was short. We cannot by availing ourselves of the calm perspective of hindsight — now say that at that time these actions were unjustified.

*Mr. Justice Frankfurter*, concurring.

According to my reading of Civilian Exclusion Order No. 34, it was an offense for Korematsu to be found in Military Area No. 1, the territory wherein he was previously living, except within the bounds of the established Assembly Center of that area. Even though the various orders issued by General DeWitt be deemed a comprehensive code of instructions, their tenor is clear and not contradictory. They put upon Korematsu the obligation to leave Military Area No. 1, but only by the method prescribed in the instructions, *i.e.*, by reporting to the Assembly Center. I am unable to see how the legal considerations that led to the decision in *Hirabayashi* v. *United States*, 320 U.S. 81, fail to sustain the military order

which made the conduct now in controversy a crime. And so I join in the opinion of the Court, but should like to add a few words of my own.

The provisions of the Constitution which confer on the Congress and the President powers to enable this country to wage war are as much part of the Constitution as provisions looking to a nation at peace. And we have had recent occasion to quote approvingly the statement of former Chief Justice Hughes that the war power of the government is "the power to wage war successfully." *Hirabayashi* v. *United States*, *supra* at 93; and see *Home Bldg. & L. Assn.* v. *Blaisdell*, 290 U.S. 398, 426. Therefore, the validity of action under the war power must be judged wholly in the context of war. That action is not to be stigmatized as lawless because like action in times of peace would be lawless. To talk about a military order that expresses an allowable judgment of war needs by those entrusted with the duty of conducting war as "an unconstitutional order" is to suffuse a part of the Constitution with an atmosphere of unconstitutionality.

The respective spheres of action of military authorities and of judges are of course very different. But within their sphere, military authorities are no more outside the bounds of obedience to the Constitution than are judges within theirs. "The war power of the United States, like its other powers . . . is subject to applicable constitutional limitations," *Hamilton* v. *Kentucky Distilleries Co.*, 251 U.S. 146, 156. To recognize that military orders are "reasonably expedient military precautions" in time of war and yet to deny them constitutional legitimacy makes of the Constitution an instrument for dialectic subtleties not reasonably to be attributed to the hard-headed framers, of whom a majority had had actual participation in war.

If a military order such as that under review does not transcend the means appropriate for conducting war, such action by the military is as constitutional as would be any authorized action by the Interstate Commerce Commission within the limits of the constitutional power to regulate commerce. And being an exercise of the war power explicitly granted by the Constitution for safeguarding the national life by prosecuting war effectively, I find nothing in the Constitution which denies to Congress the power to enforce such a valid military order by making its violation an offense triable in the civil courts. Compare *Interstate Commerce Commission* v. *Brimson,* 154 U.S. 447; 155 U.S. 3, and *Monongahela Bridge Co.* v. *United States,* 216 U.S. 177. To find that the Constitution does not forbid the military measures now complained of does not carry with it approval of that which Congress and the executive did. That is their business, not ours.

*Mr. Justice Murphy,* dissenting.

It must be conceded that the military and naval situation in the spring of 1942 was such as to generate a very real fear of invasion of the Pacific Coast, accompanied by fears of sabotage and espionage in that area. The military command was therefore justified in adopting all reasonable means necessary to combat these dangers. In adjudging the military action taken in light of the then apparent dangers, we must not erect too high or too meticulous standards; it is necessary only that the action have some reasonable relation to the removal of the dangers of invasion, sabotage, and espionage. But the exclusion, either temporarily or permanently, of all persons with Japanese blood in their veins has no such reasonable relation. And that relation is lacking because the exclusion order necessarily must rely for its reasonableness upon the assumption that *all* persons of Japanese ancestry may have a dangerous tendency to commit sabotage

and espionage and to aid our Japanese enemy in other ways. It is difficult to believe that reason, logic, or experience could be marshaled in support of such an assumption.

That this forced exclusion was the result in good measure of this erroneous assumption of racial guilt rather than bona fide military necessity is evidenced by the Commanding General's Final Report on the evacuation from the Pacific Coast area. In it he refers to all individuals of Japanese descent as "subversive," as belonging to "an enemy race" whose "racial strains are undiluted," and as constituting "over 112,000 potential enemies . . . at large today" along the Pacific Coast. In support of this blanket condemnation of all persons of Japanese descent, however, no reliable evidence is cited to show that such individuals were generally disloyal, or had generally so conducted themselves in this area as to constitute a special menace to defense installations or war industries, or had otherwise by their behavior furnished reasonable ground for their exclusion as a group.

Justification for the exclusion is sought instead, mainly upon questionable racial and sociological grounds not ordinarily within the realm of expert military judgment, supplemented by certain semi-military conclusions drawn from an unwarranted use of circumstantial evidence. Individuals of Japanese ancestry are condemned because they are said to be "a large, unassimilated, tightly knit racial group, bound to an enemy nation by strong ties of race, culture, custom and religion." They are claimed to be given to "emperor-worshiping ceremonies" and t "dual citizenship." Japanese languag schools and allegedly pro-Japanese organiza tions are cited as evidence of possible grou disloyalty, together with facts as to certai persons being educated and residing a length in Japan. It is intimated that man of these individuals deliberately resided "a jacent to strategic points," thus enabling them "to carry into execution a tremendous program of sabotage on a mass scale should any considerable number of them have been inclined to do so."

The need for protective custody is also asserted. The report refers without identity to "numerous incidents of violence" as well as to other admittedly unverified or cumulative incidents. From this, plus certain other events not shown to have been connected with the Japanese Americans, it is concluded that the "situation was fraught with danger to the Japanese population itself" and that the general public "was ready to take matters into its own hands." Finally, it is intimated, though not directly charged or proved, that persons of Japanese ancestry were responsible for three minor isolated shellings and bombings of the Pacific Coast area, as well as for unidentified radio transmissions and night signaling.

The main reasons relied upon by those responsible for the forced evacuation, therefore, do not prove a reasonable relation between the group characteristics of Japanese Americans and the dangers of invasion, sabotage, and espionage. The reasons appear, instead, to be largely an accumulation of much of the misinformation, half-truths, and insinuations that for years have been directed against Japanese Americans by people with racial and economic prejudices — the same people who have been among the foremost advocates of the evacuation. A military judgment based upon such racial and sociological considerations is not entitled to the great weight ordinarily given the judgments based upon strictly military considerations. Especially is this so when every charge relative to race, religion, culture, geographical location, and legal and economic status has been substantially discredited by independent studies made by experts in these matters.

The military necessity which is essential to the validity of the evacuation order thus resolves itself into a few intimations that certain individuals actively aided the enemy, from which it is inferred that the entire group of Japanese Americans could not be trusted to be or remain loyal to the United States. . . .

No adequate reason is given for the failure to treat these Japanese Americans on an individual basis by holding investigations and hearings to separate the loyal from the disloyal, as was done in the case of persons of German and Italian ancestry. See House Report No. 2124 (77th Cong., 2d Sess.) 247-52. It is asserted merely that the loyalties of this group "were unknown and time was of the essence." Yet nearly four months elapsed after Pearl Harbor before the first exclusion order was issued; nearly eight months went by until the last order was issued; and the last of these "subversive" persons was not actually removed until almost eleven months had elapsed. Leisure and deliberation seem to have been more of the essence than speed. And the fact that conditions were not such as to warrant a declaration of martial law adds strength to the belief that the factors of time and military necessity were not as urgent as they have been represented to be.

Moreover, there was no adequate proof that the Federal Bureau of Investigation and the military and naval intelligence services did not have the espionage and sabotage situation well in hand during this long period. Nor is there any denial of the fact that not one person of Japanese ancestry was accused or convicted of espionage or sabotage after Pearl Harbor while they were still free, a fact which is some evidence of the loyalty of the vast majority of these individuals and of the effectiveness of the established methods of combatting these evils. It seems incredible that under these circumstances it would have been impossible to hold loyalty hearings for the mere

112,000 persons involved — or at least for the 70,000 American citizens — especially when a large part of this number represented children and elderly men and women. Any inconvenience that may have accompanied an attempt to conform to procedural due process cannot be said to justify violations of constitutional rights of individuals.

I dissent, therefore, from this legalization of racism. Racial discrimination in any form and in any degree has no justifiable part whatever in our democratic way of life. It is unattractive in any setting but it is utterly revolting among a free people who have embraced the principles set forth in the Constitution of the United States. All residents of this nation are kin in some way by blood or culture to a foreign land. Yet they are primarily and necessarily a part of the new and distinct civilization of the United States. They must accordingly be treated at all times as the heirs of the American experiment and as entitled to all the rights and freedoms guaranteed by the Constitution.

*Mr. Justice Jackson,* dissenting.

Korematsu was born on our soil, of parents born in Japan. The Constitution makes him a citizen of the United States by nativity and a citizen of California by residence. No claim is made that he is not loyal to this country. There is no suggestion that apart from the matter involved here he is not law-abiding and well disposed. Korematsu, however, has been convicted of an act not commonly a crime. It consists merely of being present in the state whereof he is a citizen, near the place where he was born, and where all his life he has lived.

Even more unusual is the series of military orders which made this conduct a crime. They forbid such a one to remain, and they also forbid him to leave. They were so drawn that the only way Korematsu could avoid violation was to give himself up to the military authority. This meant submission to custody, examination, and transportation out of the territory, to be followed by indeterminate confinement in detention camps.

A citizen's presence in the locality, however, was made a crime only if his parents were of Japanese birth. Had Korematsu been one of four — the others being, say, a German alien enemy, an Italian alien enemy, and a citizen of American-born ancestors convicted of treason but out on parole — only Korematsu's presence would have violated the order. The difference between their innocence and his crime would result, not from anything he did, said, or thought different than they but only in that he was born of different racial stock.

Now, if any fundamental assumption underlies our system, it is that guilt is personal and not inheritable. Even if all of one's antecedents had been convicted of treason, the Constitution forbids its penalties to be visited upon him, for it provides that "no attainder of treason shall work corruption of blood or forfeiture except during the life of the person attainted." But here is an attempt to make an otherwise innocent act a crime merely because this prisoner is the son of parents as to whom he had no choice and belongs to a race from which there is no way to resign. If Congress in peacetime legislation should enact such a criminal law, I should suppose this Court would refuse to enforce it.

But the "law" which this prisoner is convicted of disregarding is not found in an act of Congress but in a military order. Neither the act of Congress nor the executive order of the President, nor both together, would afford a basis for this conviction. It rests on the orders of General DeWitt. And it is said that if the military commander had reasonable military grounds for promulgating the orders, they are constitutional and be come law, and the Court is required to enforce them. There are several reasons why I cannot subscribe to this doctrine.

It would be impracticable and dangerous idealism to expect or insist that each specific military command in an area of probable operations will conform to conventional tests of constitutionality. When an area is so beset that it must be put under military control at all, the paramount consideration is that its measures be successful rather than legal. The armed services must protect a society, not merely its Constitution. The very essence of the military job is to marshal physical force, to remove every obstacle to its effectiveness, to give it every strategic advantage. Defense measures will not, and often should not, be held within the limits that bind civil authority in peace. No court can require such a commander in such circumstances to act as a reasonable man; he may be unreasonably cautious and exacting. Perhaps he should be. But a commander in temporarily focusing the life of a community on defense is carrying out a military program; he is not making law in the sense the courts know the term. He issues orders, and they may have a certain authority as military commands, although they may be very bad as constitutional law.

But if we cannot confine military expedients by the Constitution, neither would I distort the Constitution to approve all that the military may deem expedient. That is what the Court appears to be doing, whether consciously or not. I cannot say, from any evidence before me, that the orders of General DeWitt were not reasonably expedient military precautions, nor could I say that they were. But even if they were permissible military procedures, I deny that it follows that they are constitutional. If, as the Court holds, it does follow, then we may as well say that any military order will be constitutional and have done with it. . . .

A military order, however unconstitutional, is not apt to last longer than the military emergency. Even during that period a succeeding commander may revoke it all. But once a judicial opinion rationalizes such an order to show that it conforms to the Constitution, or rather rationalizes the Constitution to show that the Constitution sanctions such an order, the Court for all time has validated the principle of racial discrimination in criminal procedure and of transplanting American citizens. The principle then lies about like a loaded weapon ready for the hand of any authority that can bring forward a plausible claim of an urgent need. Every repetition imbeds that principle more deeply in our law and thinking and expands it to new purposes. All who observe the work of courts are familiar with what Judge Cardozo described as "the tendency of a principle to expand itself to the limit of its logic." A military commander may overstep the bounds of constitutionality and it is an incident. But if we review and approve, that passing incident becomes the doctrine of the Constitution. There it has a generative power of its own, and all that it creates will be in its own image. Nothing better illustrates this danger than does the Court's opinion in this case. . . .

I should hold that a civil court cannot be made to enforce an order which violates constitutional limitations even if it is a reasonable exercise of military authority. The courts can exercise only the judicial power, can apply only law, and must abide by the Constitution, or they cease to be civil courts and become instruments of military policy.

---

*Go to Hell, Babe Ruth — American, you die.*
Japanese war cry, Pacific, 1942

50.

# Denis W. Brogan: American Schooling

*Denis Brogan, professor of political science at Cambridge University, is generally recognized as the leading foreign analyst of American society in recent times. In his numerous writings Brogan has attempted to define the unique qualities of Americans. "It is the main thesis of this book," he wrote in the Introduction to the 1956 Vintage Edition of* The American Character, *". . . that the society, climate, geography, history, political institutions have produced a 'new man, this American'. . . . American institutions, habits of life and thought had better be studied, at first, as things in themselves, that we should note what marks the American off from the European rather than what unites the two kindred stocks." Brogan's analysis of the American educational system reprinted here is taken from Chapter Five.*

Source: *The American Character,* New York, 1944, pp. 135-148.

THE WORD "SCHOOL" IN AMERICA covers every type of educational institution. Being "at school" may mean being at a kindergarten or at Harvard. School, too, has kept much of its Greek meaning. It is a system of organization and training for leisure as well as work. And it has become more and more adjusted to its environment, undertaking to do more than it can (which is very American) and doing much more than it seems to do (which is also very American).

The social and political role of American education cannot be understood if it is thought of as being primarily a means of formal instruction. If it is so thought of, it will be overrated and underrated. It will be overrated because the figures of two million college students, of seven million high-school students, will dazzle the visitor used to seeing opportunities for higher education doled out (except in Soviet Russia) on a combined class-and-intellectual basis. It will be underrated if, at any stage below the highest (that is, below the great universi-

ties), the academic standards are compared with those of a good English, French, or pre-Hitler German school. If these millions of boys and girls are to be judged by their academic accomplishments, they will be judged harshly. But they are not to be so judged, for their schools are doing far more than instruct them: they are letting them instruct each other in how to live in America.

Of those millions, a large section will be the children of immigrants to whom English is still largely a foreign tongue. Of these millions, a very large proportion will be the children of migrants from different parts of the United States. Others will be the children of rural-bred parents, forced to adjust themselves to the new urban world. They have to learn a common language, common habits, common tolerances, a common political and national faith. And they do. It is this aim and this success that justifies the lavish buildings of the local high school; not merely the classrooms and the laboratories but the gymnasium, the field-house where basketball can be played in comfort in the depth of the bitter winter, the swimming pools in which the summer heat can be endured.

It is true that the teachers are relatively badly paid and have an inferior social as well as economic standing, insecure tenure and politics making their condition worse. More money spent on men might get better results than more money spent on buildings. But it is easier to get the materials for buildings than the materials for teachers. As long as American society remains individualistic, competitive, confident that the answers to the present are in the future, not in the past, it is going to take more than money to seduce the right men and women in adequate numbers away from the life of action. And, a point too seldom remembered, the necessity for providing teachers for the two million college students hampers recruiting for high schools. In many cases, the colleges are doing what is really high school work and it matters comparatively little where the good teachers are, as long as they are teaching.

The political function of the schools is to teach Americanism, meaning not merely political and patriotic dogma but the habits necessary to American life. This justifies the most extravagant items in the curriculum. Since the ability to play bridge is one of the marks of Americanism in a suburb, it is reasonable that there should be bridge clubs in schools. The main political achievement of the high schools and grammar schools is to bring together the young of all classes and all origins, to provide, artificially, the common background that in an old, rural society is provided by tradition, by the necessary collaboration of village life. The elementary schools — the "grade" schools — do this, too, but as far as an American town is broken up into racial blocs, the Ethan Allen Public School may have mainly Polish pupils, the Zachary Chandler, mainly

Welsh. Only in the Warren G. Harding High School is a big enough common pool formed in which Americans can be made.

Some of that Americanization is, of course, done deliberately and formally. Mr. Carlton Hayes pointed out long ago that the ritual of flag worship and oath-taking in an American school is a religious observance. Little boys and girls, in a school from which religion in the old sense is barred, solemnly rising each morning and reciting together the "American's Creed" are performing a religious exercise as truly as if they began the day with "I believe in God the Father Almighty" or asserted that "There is no God but God."

And that these daily rituals are religious has been at last affirmed by the Supreme Court in a series of cases in which the children of a fanatical sect, Jehovah's Witnesses, had been excluded from schools for refusing to give to the flag honors that, so their parents had taught them, were due to God alone. In 1940, all the Court except Chief Justice Stone held that flag worship was among the things that were Caesar's. Since that year, however, they have decided by a majority that the religious rights of the children were being infringed. What is significant in the cases is not the Court's reversal of itself but the reality of the issue presented to it. For to the Court, and to the overwhelming majority of the American people, the objections of the Witnesses were as unintelligible as the objections of the Christians to making a formal sacrifice to the Divine Emperor were to Trajan and Pliny. The school board of Minersville, Pennsylvania, was faced with a real problem when it was asked to admit that children refusing to take part in the most sacred rite of the day should be allowed to associate with the believing children of the formally unestablished national church of the United States. So, too, was the state of Oregon when it found Catholic and Lutheran children refusing to go to the schools it provided. But in both cases the Supreme Court held, finally, that compulsory Americanism was not Americanism at all, that coerced belief was not what the American people needed to stay united. This was not Germany or Russia but the country of Jefferson and Justice Holmes. . . .

Thus Americanization by ritual is an important and necessary part of the function of the American school. And because it is best carried out in schools, it matters little that the high-school curriculum has been so widened that it no longer means a great deal that this boy or that girl has graduated from it — if we are looking for proof of academic achievement. But graduation from high school is reasonable proof that a great deal has been learned about American ways of life, that lessons in practical politics, in organization, in social ease have been learned that could not have been learned in factory or office. . . .

Most American parents do not want, or are not able, to send their children to anything but public high schools, and the life in such a school is a training in life for America. It may be and often is a training in life *against* Europe. For Europe is the background from which many of the children are reacting and from which they must be delivered if they are to be Americanized. For nearly all immigrants, America is promotion, and this promotion is more clearly felt by their children. The old people may hanker after the old country, but the children — whatever sentimental feelings for their ancestral homes they may have, especially when provoked — are, above all else, anxious to be Americans. . . .

Study is not the only way up to Americanization, to acceptation. Sport is another — and one that does the job more dramatically for the newcomers gifted with what it takes to excel in competitive contests, with what is needed to win personal and community and institutional glory. . . . And sport is rigorously democratic. The sons of

Czechs and Poles can score there, can break through the barriers that stand in the way of the children of "Bohunks" and "Polacks." And although Harvard may secretly rejoice when it can put a winning team on to Soldiers' Field whose names suggest the *Mayflower*, it would rather put on a team that can beat Yale, even though it is not a "Yankee" team, than go down to defeat with the descendants of generations of Brahmins. And in the Middle West, sport is a real means of promotion. The Ohio high school that produced the great Negro runner, Jesse Owens, was prouder of him than if he had made Phi Beta Kappa at Ohio State; and Hitler would have made a less serious mistake if he had snubbed a great American scholar whose race he didn't like than he did by sulking at the Olympic Games when the Herrenvolk were beaten by a Negro.

It is a frontier tradition; Lincoln's great strength gave him a prestige that helped him as a lawyer and politician. The great athlete performing for the glory of the school, college, state, or nation is a less egoistic figure than the great scholar pursuing his own studies with an undemocratic concentration. And the Negroes, whose greatest hero is Joe Louis, not Paul Robeson, are not substantially wrong so far. In American society as it is, a Negro heavyweight champion, like a Negro tapdancer, is a better adjusted figure than a great Negro artist — or America is a less maladjusted society for them. Of course, this will not and should not last. The Irish were rising when their great hero became Governor Al Smith rather than a successor of John L. Sullivan, the "Boston strong boy." But to get assent to a Negro's *right* to be heavyweight champion is something — as those will agree who remember the frenzied search round 1910 for a "white hope" to save the heavyweight championship from the indignity of being held by Jack Johnson. Great Indian athletes like Jim Thorpe, great Negro football heroes like Paul Robeson in his earlier days, the polyglot teams put on the field by the great Swedish coach Knut Rockne for the "Irish" of Notre Dame — these become "All-American" figures in a wider and deeper sense than that in which the Yale of Walter Camp understood the term. . . .

Things have changed a great deal since the ideal of American college education was "Mark Hopkins at one end of a log and a student at the other." Then the college existed to provide a common background for lawyers and doctors and divines; it was small and select, not select in a social or financial sense, but select in that only those who accepted the old intellectual order of things were catered for. It was a decisive moment when President Eliot of Harvard (which had long ceased to concentrate on providing for a "learned ministry") introduced the elective system. The college abandoned any idea of imposing a hierarchy of subjects The student could select what he wanted from the menu provided; à la carte had succeeded table d'hôte. But in newer, less secure, less rich institutions than Harvard, the change went farther than that, for not only was the student free to choose from what was offered — he was entitled to complain if the college did not offer what he wanted to learn, or even what he wanted to learn in the sense that it was all he could hope to learn.

As more and more students came to college with varying school preparation, as life grew more complex and the techniques of life and business more impressive in their results, the unity of college life disappeared. Boys and girls were no longer taken in hand by a successor of Mark Hopkins and given a few general ethical and philosophical ideas suitable to a world still pretty much agreed on fundamentals. They were visitors to an institution that seemed to have more in common with the Mark Hopkins Hotel in San Francisco than with the Williams College of a century ago; and from the glass-walled bar, "The Top of the Mark," they could see the modern world, the bridges and skyscrapers of San Francisco, and across the Bay the lights of Berkeley where the University of California provides for all tastes from addicts of the Greek theater to the most modern biological and physical techniques. . . .

The very success of the school system in Americanizing the American young may result in the killing of natural curiosity. For example, the cult of the Constitution leads to the exclusive identification of a political concept like "liberty" with the American constitutional system. This being so, a Latin-American "republic" with a paper constitution like the American is regarded as "free" while Canada is not. For Canada is part of an "empire" with a monarch at the head of it. Some two-thirds of the American people, accordingly, think that Canada pays taxes to Britain; even in the states bordering on the Dominion about half the Americans think this! In the same way, the word "republic" has an almost magical significance for the Americans. Plutarch, as Mr. Wells once suggested, had a good deal to do with this; but, whatever the origins of the belief, it is now part of the American credo that only citizens of a republic can be free. And no matter what romantic interest Americans may display in the human side of monarchy, it should never be forgotten that, politically, they regard it as a childish institution. Mark Twain, a very pro-English American, refused for that very reason to write one of his amusing, critical travel books about England. But he did write two books about England, all the same: *The Prince and the Pauper* and *A Connecticut Yankee at the Court of King Arthur*. How deeply antimonarchical, anticlerical, antitraditional those books are!

And in *Huckleberry Finn*, the traditional American view of royalty as expensive foolishness is admirably set forth in Huck's remark to Nigger Jim: "Sometimes I wish we could hear of a country that's out of kings."

A great many Americans still think like Huck Finn. And it must be remembered that for Americans the great event of their own and of world history was the destruction of the royal power of George III and the establishment of a Constitution guaranteeing to each State "a republican form of government." It is in that light that the modern world is seen by nearly all Americans.

Nothing is more natural and understandable than the American assumption that all modern historical events are either American or unimportant. The Pole who wrote a book on *The Elephant and the Polish Question* was not merely a typical Pole but a typical human being. There are remote academic subjects that we study, and real, living subjects that concern us. "Listen to my bomb story and I'll listen to yours," as they said in London in 1940. Therefore the American conviction that the First World War really began in 1917, and that this one began on December 7, 1941, is simply an American example of a general illusion.

We know that the Chinese were fighting the Japanese long before we were, but we don't *feel* it. We could remember, if we tried, that the Poles were fighting the Germans a little before the British and long before the Russians or the Americans, but we don't feel any urgency to recall it. The Americans who, in March 1944, learned that their countrymen had bombed Berlin for the first time were astonished. The "We" who bombed Berlin in 1943 included Americans psychologically, but the "We" who bombed Tokyo didn't include British either factually or psychologically. This is all part of human nature. . . .

Such an attitude can be very irritating, yet the assumption that world history is part of American history is healthier than any belief that the two are completely separate and that the one is real while the other is merely interesting. It is only when the heads and hearts of the American people are touched that they can be induced to listen to a call from the outer world for leadership. And that leadership will be given only if moral as well as material interests are involved. The only appeal that will be listened to will be the appeal to come over to Macedonia and help.

"It will be no cool process of mere science. . . . The feelings with which we face this new age of right and opportunity sweep across our heartstrings like some air out of God's own presence, where justice and mercy are reconciled and the judge and the brother are one. . . . Men's hearts wait upon us; men's lives hang in the balance; men's hopes call upon us to say what we will do. Who shall live up to the great trust? Who dare fail to try? I summon all honest men, all patriotic forward-looking men, to my side. God helping me, I will not fail them, if they will but counsel and sustain me." Till that note is struck again no answer can be expected from the plain people.

But in the meantime, millions of young Americans, serving their country, if not as yet any general cause, are exiled in a foreign world for which their training in a sense has unfitted them. For that training was based on the theory that there is an answer available to every question; all you have got to do is to find the right authority, whether the question relates to the technique of football, of spot welding, or of love. There is a charming optimism in this view, an optimism that, in America, is justified most of the time. It creates a world in which, as a wise American friend of mine said, there are known Plimsoll lines in most fields of conduct. It is a world in which formal good manners and comradeship are both happily cultivated between the sexes.

It is true that the hearty camaraderi

which is so charming at twenty palls a little at thirty and may give a superficial justification for the sour remark of a European critic that "what the American woman suffers from is too much poor-quality attention." It may even justify another view — that American men and American women are better company apart than together, and that the men are better company than the women. But these illusions of solutions attained, in politics and in life, are a tribute to the success with which American life has been made attractive to Americans, to the vast majority of Americans who feel at home in America and are consequently swept away from their moorings in a strange world whose standards they cannot understand and from whose apparent moral and political anarchy they long to escape by going home.

---

## 51.

# Gunnar Myrdal: Negro Leadership in North and South

*Gunnar Myrdal, a Swedish economist and sociologist, was commissioned by the Carnegie Corporation in 1938 to investigate the conditions of the Negro in the United States. In 1944 the results of his study were published in* An American Dilemma: The Negro Problem and Modern Democracy, *which has been acclaimed as one of the most thorough and perceptive analyses of the Negro in America. "Our task in this inquiry," Myrdal wrote in 1944, "is to ascertain social reality as it is. We shall seek to depict the actual life conditions of the American Negro people and their manifold relations to the larger American society . . . to discover and dissect the doctrines and ideologies, valuations and beliefs, embedded in the minds of white and Negro Americans." The following is a portion of the chapter entitled "Compromise Leadership."*

Source: *An American Dilemma*, New York, 1944, pp. 768-780.

### 1. THE DAILY COMPROMISE

IN DISCUSSING the accommodating Negro leader . . . we assumed for the purposes of abstract analysis that the protest motive was absent. This assumption, however, has some real truth in it. . . . The accommodation motive has predominant importance in the daily life of the American Negroes. But it is true that the protest motive is ever present. In some degree it has reached practically all American Negroes. To many individuals it is a major interest. And the Negro protest is bound to rise even higher. But the influence of the protest motive is limited mainly to the propagation of certain ideas about how things *should* be. In any case, but few Negro individuals are in a position to do anything practical about it. Everyone, however, has to get on with his own life from day to day, *now and here*. Even when the individual plans for future employment, for business, or for schooling, he has to reckon with the world as it is. He has to accommodate.

The Negro protest is thus mainly suppressed and turned inward. But it has effects upon Negro personality, upon the relations between the classes in the Negro community, and also upon caste relations. The whites, on their side, are accustomed to a certain amount of Negro unreliability, dishonesty, laziness, secretiveness, and even insolence and impudence. They shut their eyes to its explanation in Negro dissatisfaction and the other results of the caste system. The average white man, in the South, actually gets enjoyment out of observing and joking about Negro inefficiency and slyness. He knows that he gets the services of Negroes for a cheap price, and so he can afford to joke about this. But, apparently, he also wants to convince himself that the Negroes are well satisfied. Now and then, however, he reveals to the observer, more or less incidentally, that he knows about and understands the Negro protest.

The Southerner keeps watching all the time for germs of unrest and dissatisfaction in the Negro community. He preserves the machinery of caste controls in a state of perpetual preparedness and applies it occasionally as an exercise or a demonstration. In this system, the Negroes *have* to accommodate individually and as a group. This is the situation in the South. . . . The Northern situation is considerably different.

### 2. The Vulnerability of the Negro Leader

In the protective Negro community much goes on which the white man does not know about. The reality of this reserve is well known to Negroes, and it is coming to effective use in the Negro church, the Negro school, and the Negro press. But the Negro leader has stepped out of the anonymity, and the eyes of influential white people are focused on him. He has to watch his moves carefully in order not to fall out with them. This would end his usefulness to the Negro community as a go-between. And it would spell his own ruin, as the whites have a close control on his income and his status.

In the South practically all Negro teachers — from the lonely teacher in a dilapidated one-room schoolhouse isolated off somewhere in a rural county, to the president of a Negro college — are appointed by white leaders and they hold their position under the threat of being dismissed if they become troublesome. The Negro church is often claimed to be the one independent Negro institution founded entirely upon the organizational efforts and the economic contributions of the Negro people themselves. But the observer finds that to an amazing extent there are ties of small mortgage loans and petty contributions from whites which restrict the freedom of the preachers. Negro professionals and Negro businessmen, operating in the tight areas behind the caste wall, are also dependent on the goodwill, the indulgence, and sometimes the assistance of whites. The same is even more true of the successful Negro landowner, who in most Southern areas meets the envy of poor whites, and so needs the protection of the substantial white people in the community. And for all local Negro leaders, it is perhaps not the economic sanction that is most important, but the sanction of physical punishment, destruction of property, and banishment.

In a sense, every ambitious and successful Negro is more dependent upon the whites than is his caste fellow in the lower class. He is more conspicuous. He has more to lose and he has more to gain. If he becomes aggressive, he is adding to all the odds he labors under, the risk of losing the goodwill and protection of the influential whites. The Southern whites have many ways of keeping this prospect constantly before his mind. He knows he has to "go slow."

### 3. Impersonal Motives

This should not be construed to imply that there is a crude self-seeking opportunism on the part of Negro leaders or a cynical despotism on the part of the whites. The power situation is conducive to the creation of both, and the standards of power morals are low. But even the most right-minded, ambitious Negro would be foolish not to realize that he has to keep in line if he wants to do something for his own people. Accommodation on his part can be, and often is, altruistically motivated. He can view it as a sacrifice of personal dignity and conviction which he undergoes to further, not only his own aspirations but also those of his whole group. He can point out, rightly, that reckless opposition on his part might endanger Negro welfare.

There is much bitterness among Southern Negro leaders because they are criticized for being "Uncle Toms," especially by Northern Negro intellectuals. They will tell the observer that it takes little courage to stay in the safety of the North and to keep on protesting against Negro sufferings in the South. "They should come down here and feel the fears, uncertainties, and utter dependence of one of us in their own bones," said one prominent Negro banker in the Upper South. And he added: "If they then continued their outbursts, we would know that they are crazy, and we would have to try to get rid of them as a public danger. But, sure, they would come along. They would be cautious and pussy-footing as we are."

On the white side, the motives are usually neither base nor crude. Often a Southern school board will try to appoint the best Negro they can get for teacher, school principal, or college president. When they look for a "cautious," "sane," "sober," "safe," "restrained," and "temperate" Negro, they have in view a person who they honestly think will be good for "racial harmony." The same is true when they help a Negro preacher whom they consider a well-intentioned person. Mortgage loans and contributions to Negro churches are most of the time not given with the conscious intent to fabricate caste controls but to help religious work among Negroes by ministers who

have their respect. But they operate within the framework of the Southern white philosophy of race relations.

According to this philosophy, the whites should "look after their Negroes." Negroes should not protest but accommodate. They should not demand their rights but beg for help and assistance. Everything then works out for the good of both groups. When they dismiss a "radical" professor from a Southern Negro college or put the screws on an incautious preacher, doctor, or businessman or do not listen to his requests any longer, they act "in the best interest of the Negro group." Even whites who personally would prefer to be more broad-minded, even Northern philanthropists who would help the South, have to take into account "the public opinion among whites," what "people will stand for down here."

*The selection and the behavior of Negro leaders in the South is an outcome of this fact, that practically all the economic and political powers are concentrated in the white caste while the small amount of influence, status, and wealth that there is in the Negro community is derivative and dependent.* The Negro masses are well aware of this situation. They need Negro leaders who can get things from the whites. They know that a Negro leader who starts to act aggressively is not only losing his own power and often his livelihood but might endanger the welfare of the whole Negro community.

In Southern Negro communities there is apparently much suspicion against "radical," "hot-headed," and "outspoken" Negroes. Negroes do not want to be observed associating with such persons, because they might "get in trouble." A barricade will often be thrown up around them by a common consent that they are "queer." The Negro community itself will thus often, before there is any white interference, advise individual Negroes who show signs of aggression that they had better trim their sails.

### 4. The Protest Motive

Nevertheless, the protest motive is not without influence on Negro leadership in the South. For one thing, some protest is almost a necessary ingredient in the leadership appeal to Negroes. The furthering of race pride and racial solidarity is the means of diminishing internal strivings in the Negro community and of lining up the community into a working unity. Whites sometimes understand this, and there is, therefore, also a certain amount of "tolerated impudence" which a trusted and influential Negro leader can get away with even in the presence of whites. If the Negro community feels sure that he, nevertheless, retains the ear of whites, such a guarded outspokenness will increase his prestige. Negro leaders are often keenly aware of just how far they can go with white people — just what they can afford to say, how they should say it, and when they should say it. Often a protest will be produced under the cover of a joke, or in a similar form, so that the whites do not quite get the full meaning or, anyhow, can pretend that they have not got it. There is a whole technique for how to "tell it right in the face of the whites" without being caught. The stories about such successful protests under cover form a mythology around a Negro leader who has the admiration and allegiance of his community.

But much more generally the Negro community enjoys the demonstration of the Negro protest — as long as it does not become too dangerous for racial harmony. The vicarious satisfaction taken in the victories of Negro athletes who have beaten white competitors has long been observed. The esteem in the Negro community for the "bad nigger" is another point. The "bad nigger" is one who will deliberately run the risks involved in ignoring the caste etiquette, behaving impudently and threateningly toward whites and actually committing crimes of violence against them. Because he often creates fear in the white community, and because he sometimes acts the role of "Robin Hood" for lesser Negroes in trouble with whites, he is accorded a fearful respect by other Negroes. He certainly does not become a Negro "leader." But, particularly in the lower classes, he is a race hero and will be protected by them by means of pretended ignorance as to his doings and whereabouts.

Whenever a Negro leader can afford — without endangering his own status or the peace of the Negro community — to speak up against, or behave slightingly toward, members of the superior caste, this will increase his prestige.

### 5. The Double Role

More generally, the presence of the protest motive in the Negro community tends to induce the Negro leader to take on two different appearances: one toward the whites and another toward the Negro followership. Toward the Negroes he will pretend that he has dared to say things and to take positions much in exaggeration of what actually has happened. The present author, when comparing notes from interviews in the Negro community with what the white community leaders have told him about their "good Negroes," has frequently observed this discrepancy.

A dual standard of behavior is not unnatural for a Southern Negro. It is rather to be expected of anybody in the lower layer of the Southern caste system. But the Negro leaders especially are pressed into such a pattern as they are more regularly, and in a sense professionally, in contact with whites and have a more considerable stake in the game.

They play two roles and must wear two fronts. . . . The adjustments and adaptations of the Negro leader are apt to be more pronounced and in bolder relief than those of the common Negro fol-

the reason that the Negro leader clearly has much more to lose. He has two worlds to please and to seek his status in.

There is a limit, though, to what an accommodating Negro leader can pretend in the Negro community of what he has been bold enough to say or do. What he says to the Negroes, if it is really startling, will most of the time be reported by servants and other stool pigeons to the whites, and might make them suspicious of him.

The Negro community gets a revenge against the whites, not only out of the Negro leaders' cautious aggressions but also out of the whites' being deceived. The satisfaction when some member of the community has succeeded in "pulling the wool" over the eyes of trusting white men is apparent. If deception is achieved, the Negroes seem to enjoy their leaders' spreading the flattery thick when approaching the whites. This is the most concealed, the almost perverted, form of the Negro protest

## 6. NEGRO LEADERSHIP TECHNIQUES

THIS SITUATION is likely to make the Negro leader sophisticated and "wise." He becomes intensely conscious of all his moves. One Southern Negro leader outlined the most effective technique to use when approaching influential white people to get them to do something for the Negro community, in the following words:

> Don't emphasize the Negro's "right" . . . don't *press* for anything . . . make him feel he's a big man, get to other white men to make him want to avoid seeming small, and you can make him jump through the barrel. You can make him a friend or a rattlesnake, depending on your approach.

Another Negro leader told us:

> I'm a respectable citizen, but when I try to get my rights I do so in a way that will not be obnoxious, and not in a radical way. I don't believe in radicalism.

> We *ask* for things, but never *demand*. When I'm in Rome, I burn Roman candles . . . but I don't "Uncle Tom."

A Negro editor in another Southern city explained:

> If a Negro goes so far as to make an enemy of the white man who has the power he is foolish. You can't hit a man in the mouth and expect him to loan you money. By all means keep in with the man who hires and pays you. A man wouldn't be head of a big concern if he weren't a smart man, and a smart man will always react to facts. My approach is to the fellow on top because he is going to have to take care of me and I must work with him — he has the stick.

The successful Negro leader becomes a consummate manipulator. Getting the white man to do what he wants becomes a fine art. This is what is called "playing 'possum." The Negro leader gets satisfaction out of his performance and feels pride in his skill in flattering, beguiling, and outwitting the white man. The South is full of folklore and legend on this aspect of Negro leadership. And the stories are told among whites too, just as are stories about clever children or animals.

Every person in this game has a double standard of understanding and behavior. The white leaders know that they are supposed to be outwitted by the subservient but sly Negro leaders. In the Southern aristocratic tradition they are supposed not only to permit and to enjoy the flattery of the Negro leaders but also to let them get away with something for themselves and for their group. It is the price due the Negro leaders for their adaptive skills and for their tactful abstention from raising the Negro protest. The Negro leaders also know their double role.

The Negro community is thus, on the one hand, filled by the Negro protest and it demands to be appealed to in terms of Negro solidarity. It also wants to feel that the protest is getting over to the whites. On the other hand, the Negro community knows the caste situation, is afraid of radical leaders and troublemakers, and wants its go-betweens to be able to make some real deliveries.

### 7. Moral Consequences

THIS SITUATION is pregnant with all sorts of double-dealing, cynicism, and low morals in the Negro community. The leaders are under constant suspicion from the Negro community that they are dishonest, venal, and self-seeking. One observing Negro citizen expressed a common view when he told us: "You give a few Negroes a break, hand them a job, and all problems are solved." The complaints about "bad leadership" — "incompetent," "selfish," "treacherous," "corrupt" — were raised in every single Negro community the present author has visited. These complaints may, indeed, be said to constitute one of the unifying popular theories in the Negro world, a point upon which everybody can agree. "There are few Negro leaders," Ralph Bunche confirms, "who are not suspect immediately they attain any eminence. The racial situation has created a vicious circle in Negro reasoning on leadership, and the Negro leader is caught in it."

The Negro community in the South cannot expect — and does not want — its leaders to act out the protest the common Negroes actually feel. There is, indeed, little reason to believe that the leaders are less militant than the community seriously wants them to be. But the common Negroes do feel humiliated and frustrated. And they can afford to take it out on their leaders by defaming them for their "kowtowing," "pussyfooting," and "Uncle Tomming"; by calling them "handkerchief heads" and "hats in hand"; and particularly by suspecting them for being prepared to barter away their own honor and the interests of the group for a job or a hand-out.

*The Negro hates the Negro role in American society, and the Negro leader, who acts out this role in public life, becomes the symbol of what the Negro hates.*

The Southern Negro leader — not being allowed to state and follow a clear ideological line but doomed to opportunism, having constantly to compromise with his pride and dignity, and never being allowed to speak upon the authority of the strength of an organized group behind him but appearing as an individual person trusted by the adversary group before him — does not have the sanctions ordinarily operating to preserve the honor and loyalty of a representative leader. The temptation to sell out the group and to look out for his own petty interest is great. He thus easily comes to justify the common suspicions around him by becoming a self-seeker and opportunist. The anger in the Negro community against unscrupulous leaders is often directed against the fact that they do not get more for themselves out of their unscrupulousness in sacrificing the common interest:

> That [leadership] which can be bought . . . is usually purchaseable for "peanut money." The scorn for the practice among Negroes, frequently expressed is often less due to the fact that Negro leaders "sell out" than because they do so so cheaply.

### 8. Leadership Rivalry

SINCE POWER AND PRESTIGE are scarce commodities in the Negro community, the struggle for leadership often becomes ruthless. Such is the situation even in those fields where there is little white interference. White influence is likely to increase bitter personal rivalry, as the leader comes to operate as a single individual, trusted by the whites but generally without any organized backing or control in the Negro community and without a cause or an issue.

For the same reasons this rivalry does not

provide a check on dishonesty. It rather loosens still more the loyalty of the Negro community. It also provides the influential whites with increased possibilities to "divide and rule." And it defiles still more the atmosphere around Negro leadership. The rivalry, the envy, and the disunity in the Negro community, and the destructive effects, are felt by even the poorest Negro, who will everywhere tell the inquirer that "Negroes just can't stick together." "Lambasting our leaders is quite a popular pastime," observes James Weldon Johnson. Under those circumstances the attainment of Negro leadership also tends to "do something" to the individual Negro:

> For when a value is scarce its possession tends to inflate the possessor. The Negro leader often quickly puffs up when given power. He "struts" and puts up a big front, or puts on "airs," often indulges in exhibitionism. It is often truly said that the Negro leader "can't stand power." Actually, there is a sort of ambivalence which characterizes the attitudes of Negro leaders. The leader will pay lip-service to the concepts of democracy for he understands their significance and appeal to the Negro as a group. But in his personal views and relationship the Negro leader is ordinarily very allergic to democracy — he prefers to play the role of the aristocrat, or the dictator or tyrant. *For leadership itself is a form of escape.*

## 9. QUALIFICATIONS

IT SHOULD BE OBSERVED that *these detrimental effects upon public confidence and morals in the Negro community are derivative from the basic lack of democracy inherent in the Southern caste situation,* and, further, that *they become increased by the rising Negro protest as long as it is denied free outlet.* They have close parallels in all other subordinate groups.

In this situation it is understandable why so many well-equipped upper-class Negroes in the South withdraw voluntarily from attempting to play a leadership role. . . . But many cannot afford to withdraw entirely. So many of the vocations and positions which mean an economic and social career in the Negro community are under white control, directly or indirectly. And the influential whites reckon on their Negro college presidents, their Negro high-school principals, their favored Negro ministers, farmers, and businessmen to shepherd the Negro community.

This may, indeed, be a blessing to the Negro community as so many of the most devoted and capable Negro leaders in the South actually are persons who would prefer to stay away and mind their own business, if their position, and, especially, white expectations, did not draw them out as Negro leaders. It must never be forgotten — in spite of what many Negro interlocutors in their dismay and pessimism tell the interviewer to the contrary — that there are *in the South many honest and diligent Negro leaders* who unselfishly forward Negro interests by a slow, patient, but determined, plodding along against odds and difficulties. And an important aspect of the changing South is that — as the general educational level is raised, racial liberalism progresses, and federal agencies become important — *they are the Negro leaders to become increasingly trusted by the whites in power.*

---

*Paint him black and bring him over here.*
A young Negro girl when asked how she would punish Hitler. Quoted by Walter Winchell, March 26, 1945

52.

# Reinhold Niebuhr: Democracy and the Children of Light

*Reinhold Niebuhr, one of America's most influential Protestant theologians and social critics, was a pioneer in developing a theology that reinterpreted Christian teaching for the modern world. His writings of the 1930s leaned toward socialism, but World War II convinced him that the democracies of the world, though imperfect, were still the best equipped for "finding proximate solutions for insoluble problems."* The Children of Light and the Children of Darkness *(1944), excerpts of which are reprinted below, examined the nature and problems of democracy.*

Source: *The Children of Light and the Children of Darkness,* New York, 1944, pp. ix-xiii, 10-41, 86-118.

THE THESIS of this volume grew out of my conviction that democracy has a more compelling justification and requires a more realistic vindication than is given it by the liberal culture with which it has been associated in modern history. The excessively optimistic estimates of human nature and of human history with which the democratic credo has been historically associated are a source of peril to democratic society; for contemporary experience is refuting this optimism and there is danger that it will seem to refute the democratic ideal as well.

A free society requires some confidence in the ability of men to reach tentative and tolerable adjustments between their competing interests and to arrive at some common notions of justice which transcend all partial interests. A consistent pessimism in regard to man's rational capacity for justice invariably leads to absolutistic political theories; for they prompt the conviction that only preponderant power can coerce the various vitalities of a community into a working harmony. But a too consistent optimism in regard to man's ability and inclination to grant justice to his fellows obscures the perils of chaos which perennially confront every society, including a free society. In

one sense a democratic society is particularly exposed to the dangers of confusion. If these perils are not appreciated they may overtake a free society and invite the alternative evil of tyranny.

But modern democracy requires a more realistic philosophical and religious basis, not only in order to anticipate and understand the perils to which it is exposed but also to give it a more persuasive justification. Man's capacity for justice makes democracy possible; but man's inclination to injustice makes democracy necessary. In all nondemocratic political theories the state or the ruler is invested with uncontrolled power for the sake of achieving order and unity in the community. But the pessimism which prompts and justifies this policy is not consistent; for it is not applied, as it should be, to the ruler. If men are inclined to deal unjustly with their fellows, the possession of power aggravates this inclination. That is why irresponsible and uncontrolled power is the greatest source of injustice.

The democratic techniques of a free society place checks upon the power of the ruler and administrator and thus prevent it from becoming vexatious. The perils of uncontrolled power are perennial reminders of the virtues of a democratic society; particularly if a society should become inclined to impatience with the dangers of freedom and should be tempted to choose the advantages of coerced unity at the price of freedom.

The consistent optimism of our liberal culture has prevented modern democratic societies both from gauging the perils of freedom accurately and from appreciating democracy fully as the only alternative to injustice and oppression. When this optimism is not qualified to accord with the real and complex facts of human nature and history, there is always a danger that sentimentality will give way to despair and that a too consistent optimism will alternate with a too consistent pessimism. . . .

ACCORDING TO THE SCRIPTURE "the children of this world are in their generation wiser than the children of light." This observation fits the modern situation. Our democratic civilization has been built, not by children of darkness but by foolish children of light. It has been under attack by the children of darkness, by the moral cynics, who declare that a strong nation need acknowledge no law beyond its strength. It has come close to complete disaster under this attack, not because it accepted the same creed as the cynics; but because it underestimated the power of self-interest, both individual and collective, in modern society. The children of light have not been as wise as the children of darkness.

The children of darkness are evil because they know no law beyond the self. They are wise, though evil, because they understand the power of self-interest. The children of light are virtuous because they have some conception of a higher law than their own will. They are usually foolish because they do not know the power of self-will. They underestimate the peril of anarchy in both the national and the international community. Modern democratic civilization is, in short, sentimental rather than cynical. It has an easy solution for the problem of

United Press International

Reinhold Niebuhr with the president of Radcliffe College following his appearance at the college's baccalaureate services, 1938

anarchy and chaos on both the national and international level of community because of its fatuous and superficial view of man. It does not know that the same man who is ostensibly devoted to the "common good" may have desires and ambitions, hopes and fears, which set him at variance with his neighbor.

It must be understood that the children of light are foolish not merely because they underestimate the power of self-interest among the children of darkness. They underestimate this power among themselves. The democratic world came so close to disaster not merely because it never believed that Nazism possessed the demonic fury which it avowed. Civilization refused to recognize the power of class interest in its own communities. It also spoke glibly of an international conscience; but the children of darkness meanwhile skilfully set nation against nation. They were thereby enabled to despoil one nation after another, without every civilized nation coming to the defense of each. Moral cynicism had a provisional advantage over moral sentimentality. Its advantage lay not merely in its own lack of moral scruple but also in its shrewd assessment of the power of self-interest, individual and national, among the children of light, despite their moral protestations. . . .

Our modern civilization . . . was ushered in on a wave of boundless social optimism. Modern secularism is divided into many schools. But all the various schools agreed in rejecting the Christian doctrine of original sin. It is not possible to explain the subtleties or to measure the profundity of this doctrine in this connection. But it is necessary to point out that the doctrine makes an important contribution to any adequate social and political theory the lack of which has robbed bourgeois theory of real wisdom; for it emphasizes a fact which every page of human history attests. Through it one may understand that no matter how wide the perspectives which the human mind may reach, how broad the loyalties which the human imagination may conceive, how universal the community which human statecraft may organize, or how pure the aspirations of the saintliest idealists may be, there is no level of human moral or social achievement in which there is not some corruption of inordinate self-love.

This sober and true view of the human situation was neatly rejected by modern culture. That is why it conceived so many fatuous and futile plans for resolving the conflict between the self and the community; and between the national and the world community. Whenever modern idealists are confronted with the divisive and corrosive effects of man's self-love, they look for some immediate cause of this perennial tendency, usually in some specific form of social organization. One school holds that men would be good if only political institutions would not corrupt them; another believes that they would be good if the prior evil of a faulty economic organization could be eliminated. Or another school thinks of this evil as no more than ignorance, and therefore waits for a more perfect educational process to redeem man from his partial and particular loyalties. But no school asks how it is that an essentially good man could have produced corrupting and tyrannical political organizations or exploiting economic organizations, or fanatical and superstitious religious organizations.

The result of this persistent blindness to the obvious and tragic facts of man's social history is that democracy has had to maintain itself precariously against the guile and the malice of the children of darkness, while its statesmen and guides conjured up all sorts of abstract and abortive plans for the creation of perfect national and international communities. . . .

The preservation of a democratic civilization requires the wisdom of the serpent and the harmlessness of the dove. The children of light must be armed with the wisdom of the children of darkness but remain free from their malice. They must know the power of self-interest in human society without giving it moral justification. They must have this wisdom in order that they may beguile, deflect, harness and restrain self-interest, individual and collective, for the sake of the community. . . .

EVERY RELATION BETWEEN PERSONS ultimately involves the questions of possessions. The "I" is so intimately related to the "mine" and the "thou" to the "thine" that relations of accord or conflict between individuals usually imply questions of property. When life is very intimately related to life, as for instance in the family, questions of mine and thine are resolved in a sense of common possessions. Tension between persons, on the other hand, usually expresses itself in a sharpening of the sense of unique and distinctive possessions, which are carefully defined in order to discourage the other from taking advantage of the self.

The collective tensions of society may be created by ethnic rivalries and competing power impulses. They are not as universally economic in origin as Marxism assumes. But questions of ownership and economic power are usually involved in them, even when they are not primary. The class conflicts of human history are, on the whole, contests between those who have, and those who lack, economic power, the latter of whom are driven by want, hunger and resentment to challenge the power of the economic overlords. These conflicts may not be overt; but they have not been absent in any society. They have become, however, increasingly overt and acrimonious in modern industrial society.

The agrarian societies of the past were not devoid of class conflict. . . . But an added reason for the acrimony of the modern class conflict lies in the fact that the issue between the classes has become something more than the question of an equitable distribution of property. It is the issue about the very legitimacy of the right of property. On this issue there is little, or no, common ground between the middle classes, who regard property as the fruit of virtue and the guarantor of justice, and the industrial classes, who have come to think of the institution of property as the root of all evil in man and of all injustice in society. . . .

The bourgeois notions about property contain two errors, closely related to each other. The one error is the excessive individualism of the bourgeois property concept, which is part and parcel of a general exaggeration of individual freedom in middle-class existence. The other error is contained in the prevailing presupposition of liberal thought that property represents primarily an ordinate and defensive power to be used against the inclination of others to take advantage of the self. The fact is that property, as every other form of power, cannot be limited to the defensive purpose. If it grows strong enough it becomes an instrument of aggression and usurpation. These two errors must be considered more fully.

Bourgeois ideas of property participated in the generally excessive individualism of middle-class life. Just as the individual does not have as discrete an existence as is assumed in liberal thought, so also is it impossible to draw as sharp distinctions between "mine" and "thine" as liberal property ideas imply. One reason for the acrimony of the conflict on property in the modern world is that this individualism was introduced into history at the beginning of the very epoch which would develop highly collective forms of commercial and industrial wealth. There is thus a serious gulf between social function of modern property and the emphasis upon its "private" character in legal tradition and social thought. . . .

Even if a community approached the socialization of property by gradual stages and circumvented the period of revolution and dictatorship, it would still face the question of how to socialize property without creating pools of excessive social power in the hands of those who manage both its economic and political processes. A community which preserved its democratic institutions in the area of politics, while it socialized its large-scale industrial property, would have the advantage of preserving a democratic check upon the power of economic managers. Yet their power might be so great that they could use it to establish control over the political institutions.

A full analysis of these complexities must invalidate any simple solution of the problem of property. Since economic power, as every other form of social power, is a defensive force when possessed in moderation and a temptation to injustice when it is great enough to give the agent power over others, it would seem that its widest and most equitable distribution would make for the highest degree of justice. This gives a provisional justification to the liberal theory. But bourgeois liberalism assumes a natural equilibrium of economic power in the community which historic facts refute. If the economic process is left severely alone either the strong devour the weak, in which case monopoly displaces competition, or competition breeds chaos in the community. The anarchy of competition in a modern situation of technical interdependence sometimes forces the community to encourage rather than destroy the unification of economic process (in public utilities for instance) in order to avoid the competitive waste.

The tendency toward monopoly is obviously a concomitant of the general increase of interdependence in communal relations in a technical society. In so far as the unification of technical process is a service to the community (despite the perils of centralization of power which inhere in it), the effort to destroy the unification in order to avoid its concomitant perils, would seem as unwise and futile as the analogous effort of peasants of a previous age to prevent the use of machinery upon the land. The community must find a way of dealing with the problem of centralized power without destroying the unity and efficiency of the process. The social ownership of the power and wealth, derived from unified process, is certainly more plausible than the effort to maintain its individual character in defiance of inexorable historical developments. Yet it may be wise for the community to sacrifice something to efficiency for the sake of preserving a greater balance of forces and avoiding undue centralization of power.

This is the kind of question which cannot be solved once for all. The contrasting perils of anarchy and injustice, arising from too little and too much equilibrium of economic power, or from too much or too little social control of it, must be considered in the light of each new situation and technical development. The property issue must, in other words, be continually solved within the framework of the democratic process. In attempting proximate solutions certain distinctions in types of property are valuable without being final. It is valuable to remember that some forms of property are by their very nature power over others, while other types are primarily the power to secure the person against the aggrandizement of others or against the caprice of life and nature; and again others represent primarily the power to perform one's social function. Yet modern civilization has developed socialized processes in defiance of these distinctions. A workman's tool is the most obvious form of the extension of personal power. It is an aid for the performance of his function. But the tool has become too big for the worker to own. The home is the most obvious form of property as individual security; and yet the multiple dwellings of urban communities have placed the home beyond the reach of individual ownership.

Property in land is both individual security and an instrument for the performance of function. Individual ownership in land, therefore, has a moral justification which dogmatic collectivists have never understood. Yet landlordism is the most ancient form of oppression and the effects of a technical civilization have not left agriculture unaffected. Mechanization tends toward large-scale agricultural production; and large-scale production tends to destroy the small owner unless he learns to develop voluntary cooperation in the use of large-scale machinery. Many solutions depend upon the degree of resourcefulness with which new situations are met and cannot be determined abstractly.

While the intensity and extent of technical interdependence have invalidated bourgeois conceptions of property and have placed the logic of history behind proposals for socialization, the logic is not unambiguous. Since there are no forms of the socialization of property which do not contain some peril of compounding economic and political power, a wise community will walk warily and test the effect of each new adventure before further adventures.

There must, in other words, be a continuous debate on the property question in democratic society and a continuous adjustment to new developments. Such a debate is possible, however, only if there is some common denominator between opposing factions.

The contradictory dogmas about property can be most easily dissolved if the utopianism which underlies both of them, is dispelled. In communities, such as America, where the Marxist dogma has never developed the power to challenge the bourgeois one, the primary requirement of justice is that the dominant dogma be discredited. The obvious facts about property which both liberal and Marxist theories have obscured are: that all property is power; that some forms of economic power are intrinsically more ordinate than others and therefore more defensive, but that no sharp line can be drawn between what is ordinate and what is inordinate; that property is not the only form of economic power and that the destruction of private property does not therefore guarantee the equalization of economic power in a community; that inordinate power tempts its holders to abuse it, which means to use it for their own ends; that the economic, as well as the political, process requires the best possible distribution of power for the sake of justice and the best possible management of this equilibrium for the sake of order.

None of these propositions solves any specific issue of property in a given instance. But together they set the property issue within the framework of democratic procedure. For democracy is a method of finding proximate solutions for insoluble problems.

---

53.

# E. E. Cummings: Poetical Reflections on America

*The bitterness of the Depression years, forgotten by most Americans in the excitement and prosperity of the war, continued to be expressed by a group of leading poets among whom was E. E. Cummings. His "plato told" reflects the anguish of those who throughout the 1930s had warned of the coming war and of war's inevitable miseries. (The Sixth Avenue "El" in New York City had been torn down and the scrap sold to Japan, which forged it into guns and bullets to use against American soldiers after 1941.) "a salesman is an it that stinks excuse" expresses another common complaint of the 1930s — the dislike of the commercialism of American civilization.*

Source: *Poems: 1923-1954*, New York, 1954.

### ✥ PLATO TOLD

plato told

him:he couldn't
believe it(jesus

told him;he
wouldn't believe
it)lao

tsze
certainly told
him,and general
(yes

mam)
sherman;
and even
(believe it
or

not)you
told him:i told
him;we told him
(he didn't believe it,no

sir)it took
a nipponized bit of
the old sixth

avenue
el;in the top of his head:to tell

him


## ❧ A SALESMAN IS AN IT THAT STINKS EXCUSE

a salesman is an it that stinks Excuse

Me whether it's president of the you were say
or a jennelman name misder finger isn't
important whether it's millions of other punks
or just a handful absolutely doesn't
matter and whether it's in lonjewray

or shrouds is immaterial it stinks

a salesman is an it that stinks to please

but whether to please itself or someone else
makes no more difference than if it sells
hate condoms education snakeoil vac
uumcleaners terror strawberries democ
ra(caveat emptor)cy superfluous hair

or Think We've Met subhuman rights Before

54.

# E. B. White: Christmas 1944

*E. B. White wrote the following selection for the 1944 Christmas issue of the*
*New Yorker and later reprinted it in* The Wild Flag *(1946). The piece is of course*
*an extended metaphor: the successes of our armed forces throughout the year are*
*treated as if they were presents from America's soldiers, sailors, and airmen to*
*their country. Nineteen forty-four was a year of triumph, during which the Axis*
*powers were turned back both in Europe and the Pacific and forced to give up most*
*of the islands, cities, and countries that they had won in the first years of the war.*
*Nevertheless, the cost of the American victories, in lives and in material, was high,*
*a fact that White emphasizes when he speaks of the "price tags" of these precious*
*"gifts" under the Christmas tree.*

Source: This editorial was first published in *The New Yorker*, December 23, 1944,
and later in *The Wild Flag*, by E. B. White, Houghton Mifflin, 1946
© E. B. White, December, 1944. By permission of the author.

## December 23, 1944

THEY ARE NOT WRAPPED as gifts (there was no time to wrap them), but you will find them under the lighted tree with the other presents. They are the extra gifts, the ones with the hard names. Certain towns and villages. Certain docks and installations. Atolls in a sea. Assorted airstrips, beachheads, supply dumps, rail junctions. Here is a gift to hold in your hand — Hill 660. Vital from a strategic standpoint. "From the Marines," the card says. Here is a small strip of the Italian coast. Merry Christmas from the members of the American Fifth (who waded ashore). This is Kwajalein, Maloelap, Wotje. This is Eniwetok. Place them with your other atolls, over by the knitted scarf from Aunt Lucy. Here is Gea. If the size isn't right, remember it was selected at night, in darkness. Roi, Mellu, Boggerlapp, Ennugarret, Ennumennet, Ennubirr. Amphibious forces send season's greetings. How pretty! A little reef-fringed islet in a coral sea. Kwajalein! A remembrance at

Christmas from the Seventh Division. Los Negros Island. Put it with the others of the Admiralty group. Elements of the First Cavalry Division (dismounted) have sent Momote airfield, a very useful present. Manus, largest of the Admiralties. Lorengau, taken from the Japanese garrison in the underground bunkers. Talasea airdrome. Wortho Atoll (a gift from the 22nd Marine Regiment). Emirau Island, and ten more atolls in the Marshalls to make your Christmas bright in 1944: Ujae, Lae, Lib, Namu, Ailinglapalap (never mind the names), together with a hundred-and-fifty-mile strip of the northern New Guinea coast, Tanahmera Bay and Humboldt Bay, together with Hollandia. "From some American troops covered with red mud."

Here is a novel gift — a monastery on a hill. It seems to have been damaged. A bridge on Highway 6. A mountain stronghold, Castelforte (Little Cassino, they used to call it). And over here the roads — Via Casilina and the Appian Way. Valleys, plains, hills, roads, and the towns and villages. Santa Maria Infante, San Pietro, Monte Cerri, and Monte Bracchi. One reads the names on the cards with affection. Best wishes from the Fifth. Gaeta, Cisterna, Terracina, the heights behind Velletri, the Alban Hills, Mount Peschio, and the fortress of Lazio. Velletri and Valmontone. Best wishes from the Fifth. The suburbs of Rome, and Rome. The Eternal City! Holiday greetings from the American Fifth.

Who wouldn't love the Norman coast for Christmas? Who hasn't hoped for the Atlantic Wall, the impregnable? Here is the whole thing under the lighted tree. First the beaches (greetings from the Navy and the Coast Guard), then the cliffs, the fields behind the cliffs, the inland villages and towns, the key places, the hedgerows, the lanes, the houses, and the barns. Ste. Mère Eglise (with greetings from Omar Bradley and foot soldiers). This Norman cliff (best from the Rangers). St. Jacques de Nehou (from the 82nd Airborne Division, with its best). Cherbourg — street by street, and house by house. St. Remy des Landes, La Broquière, Baudreville, Neufmesnil, La Poterie, the railroad station at La Haye du Puits. And then St. Lô, and the whole vista of France. When have we received such presents? Saipan in the Marianas — only they forgot to take the price tag off. Saipan cost 9,752 in dead, wounded, and missing, but that includes a mountain called Tapotchau. Guam. "Merry Christmas from Conolly, Geiger, and the boys." Tinian, across the way. Avranches, Gavray, Torigny-sur-Vire, a German army in full retreat under your tree. A bridge at Pontorson, a bridge at Ducey, with regards from those who take

bridges. Rennes, capital of Brittany (our columns fan out). Merry Christmas, all! Brest, Nantes, St. Malo, a strategic fortress defended for two weeks by a madman. Toulon, Nice, St. Tropez, Cannes (it is very gay, the Riviera, very fashionable). And now (but you must close your eyes for this one) . . . Paris.

Still the gifts come. You haven't even noticed the gift of the rivers Marne and Aisne: Château-Thierry, Soissons (this is where you came in). Verdun, Sedan (greetings from the American First Army, greetings from the sons of the fathers). Here is a most unusual gift, a bit of German soil. Priceless. A German village, Roetgen. A forest south of Aachen. Liége, the Belfort Gap. Geilenkirchen, Crucifix Hill, Uebach. Morotai Island in the Halmaheras. An airport on Peleliu. Angaur (from the Wildcats). Nijmegen Bridge, across the Rhine. Cecina, Monteverdi, more towns, more villages on the Tyrrhenian coast. Leghorn. And, as a special remembrance, sixty-two ships of the Japanese Navy, all yours. Tacloban, Dulag, San Pablo . . . Ormoc, Valleys and villages in the Burmese jungle. Gifts in incredible profusion and all unwrapped, from old and new friends: gifts with a made-in-China label, gifts from Russians, Poles, British, French, gifts from Eisenhower, de Gaulle, Montgomery, Malinovsky, an umbrella from the Air Forces, gifts from engineers, rear gunners, privates first class . . . there isn't time to look at them all. It will take years. This is a Christmas you will never forget, people have been so generous.

----

*Austin White — Chicago, Ill. — 1918*
*Austin White — Chicago, Ill. — 1945*
*This is the last time I want to write my name here.*
Inscription discovered by a *Yank* reporter on a wall of the fortress of Verdun

# 1945

55.

## Robert A. Taft: Should the Government Guarantee Employment?

*Robert A. Taft of Ohio, who spent most of his years in the Senate (1939-1953) as leader of the "loyal opposition," was unalterably opposed to legislation that he believed weakened private initiative and the free enterprise system. President Roosevelt's Economic Bill of Rights of 1944 and the Full Employment Bill of 1945 were regarded by Taft as unwarranted expansion of the government's power over the economy. In a speech delivered before the National Industrial Conference Board of New York on January 18, 1945, and reprinted here in part, Taft expressed his objections to the President's idea of an "economics of full employment."*

Source: *Record, App.*, 79 Cong., 1 Sess., pp. A218-A220.

It is a great pleasure to appear again before your Board which for so many years has conducted a sound, impartial survey of economic problems and set an example now followed by many organizations. I am sure that none has investigated questions with a more realistic and impartial approach, and that none has more successfully assembled the basic facts on which every sound economic policy must be based.

In the last year or two we have seen the announcement of a new theory of government or economics that every man and every woman is entitled to a full-time job at good wages, just as he or she is entitled to police protection and the possession of his own home. The necessary corollary has followed that the government must guarantee him a full-time job at good wages. This is an attractive and plausible theory and it has made substantial headway throughout the United States with very little critical examination of its soundness. Your purpose here this evening is to examine the basis for this new theory. . . .

Just what is this theory of a government guarantee of employment? My attention was first called to it in the National Resources Planning Board Report of Jan. 1, 1943, in which that Board stated its belief that it should be the declared policy of the United States government "to underwrite full employment for the unemployed and guarantee a job for every man released from the armed forces or the war industries with fair pay and working conditions." The whole report of that Board was based on that theory, without the slightest consideration of cost or taxation. It proposed a vast spending program for the United States government as a means of producing prosperity. The government was not only to underwrite full employment but it was to "underwrite effective demand for goods and services" and "underwrite the attainment of high production."

President Roosevelt adopted the so-called economic bill of rights of the Board in his address to Congress in January 1944, and reaffirmed his position this year, saying that "of these rights the most fundamental, and one on which the fulfillment of the others in large degree depends, is the right to a useful and remunerative job in the industries or shops or farms or mines of the nation." He adds that the full employment means not only jobs but productive jobs at standard wages.

The CIO-PAC platform of January 1944 commends the President's new bill of rights and says that the full employment program must "be guaranteed by the government with a prepared program of jobs at useful work, with standard wages and working conditions, if and to the extent that private industry falls short of the guarantee."

The Kilgore subcommittee of the Senate Military Affairs Committee, largely dominated by the Political Action Committee thinking, proposed the enactment of this theory into law. Their bill would require the President each year to inform Congress as to the prospects of employment and national production and, if his estimate falls short of full employment, to recommend a specific program of federal expenditure to fill the gap. The policy crystallizes into the proposal that the United States government shall guarantee 60 million jobs at $2,500 a year.

The whole policy sounds so easy and attractive that it has been thoughtlessly accepted by many without analysis. Even the Committee of Economic Development, made up of hard-headed businessmen, at first rather undertook to assume for industry the responsibility of guaranteeing from 53 million to 57 million jobs. A guarantee of employment by private enterprise of course is even more difficult than one by government, because there are millions of employers wholly unable to employ more men than economic conditions permit, and wholly without the power to combat nationwide economic forces. The danger is that if employers undertake the responsibility and fail in any degree because of conditions beyond their control, it would open the door for the claim that the government must step into the breach with the complete guarantee.

The first question that arises is whether it is necessary or wise to provide, or try to provide, 60 million or even 50 million full-time jobs. There are only 35 million families in the United States, and this would provide two jobs for many million families. Should there be an obligation to provide a full-time job for every woman who wants to work when perhaps her husband or other member of the family is perfectly able and willing to support her? Is it perhaps not better to keep boys and girls longer in school and retire the aged at a lower age? How can we say that there must be 60 million jobs when perhaps 50 million workers can do all the work of the nation? Doesn't a nation have a higher standard of living if the work can be done by a fewer number of people in fewer hours? . . .

It is clear to me that any direct guarantee of full-time jobs at good wages would involve the government in the placement of every man and woman in the country, and ultimately the assignment by the government of every man and woman to the job selected by the government. This is exactly the system pursued in Russia today, as anyone can see by reading the recent articles in the Readers' Digest by William L. White. It is in contradiction of the whole American tradition and is bound to destroy the very freedom for which our armies fight throughout the world. It is obvious to me that the proponents of the theory would very quickly back away from any literal interpretation of the supposed guarantee. They must quickly disown the theory that the right to work is one which can be ordered by the government and protected by court decree.

How then is this guarantee to be carried out? The Political Action Committee suggests that it is to be done by direct government employment of all those not employed by private industry. The unthinking popular view is that the jobs are to be guaranteed by the planning and execution of public works. . . .

We found in the Great Depression that the employment of a man on public works cost three to five times the amount expended on work relief programs per man, and six to ten times the cost of direct relief. Furthermore, public works are only a stopgap, because most such works cost money to maintain after they are constructed. The construction of a factory may give employment to many men year after year. But a courthouse or a new road or a new school costs more to maintain and more taxes than before. Of course, there are some productive public works, but most of them produce no permanent jobs.

The lack of public works available to meet mass unemployment suggests to those who advocate direct government employment that the government would have to go into many fields of nongovernment activity. Most employment in any nation must be in the making of goods and the furnishing of service. The government could take over factories and make clothing, food, and other necessities to be given away to the low-income groups. We saw a start in that direction in the 30s. The difficulty is that the moment the government enters such a field, private capital is afraid to go ahead. You hamper and discourage the re-

covery of the very economic machine on which you are relying to produce prosperity. No individual can successfully compete with the government. Constant government experimentation and interference in the 30s delayed recovery far beyond the time required in foreign countries or in past depressions in this country. The expenditure by the government of $30 billion or $40 billion a year to give direct employment on a full-time basis and good wages to, say, 15 million men would add that sum to the public debt and certainly discourage any attempt at real recovery. . . .

It is said that we have had full employment during the war because of vast government spending and the only way we can fulfill the new guarantee is to continue this government spending in time of peace. In this form the supposed guarantee of employment merges into the same old government-spending theory advocated by Keynes and Hansen — the theory that a nation can spend itself into prosperity, that deficits are a blessing in disguise, that we need have no concern about our public debt because we owe it to ourselves. We tried this theory in the thirties, and it left us with a large debt and 10 million unemployed. Any huge spending, whether for direct employment or to prime the pump for indirect employment, leads to the same result.

The postwar budget of the government will be at least $20 billion for expenses that we cannot escape — four times our prewar budget. It may be just possible to find a tax system that will produce this much income in time of peace without discouraging all initiative. If we add the additional government spending proposed by the guarantee theory, we will run the budget up to $40 billion or $50 billion. Either a tax system must be imposed at even higher rates than the war system now in force, or we must increase the debt by somewhere between $15 billion and $30 billion a year. Either of these alternatives would destroy the economic machine upon which our prosperity has been based. Either would destroy the system of private enterprise to which the advocates of this new theory, even Earl Browder, give lip service.

If the present tax rates on business are continued, there will be no incentive to anyone either to put his money into new business or to expand old business. If the present rates on individual incomes are continued, there will be little incentive to any man to exert himself to build up his income with the hope of providing a better living for himself and a better education for his children, or a better provision for his family after death. The incentive created by the American system of rewards for genius, initiative, and daring will disappear, and it is vain to hope that the expansion of private industry will continue. One industry after another will become unprofitable, just as the railroads became unprofitable before the war. The government will have to finance necessary expansion and will gradually absorb one industry after another.

The advocates of the theory, however, do not really contemplate any such tax system. They are disciples of the Keynesian theory that the public debt can be indefinitely increased.

To me it is obvious that this can only end in extreme inflation. Because of government deficits, we have had an increase in the cost of living of approximately 30 percent during the war, in spite of the most rigid price and wage controls. In my opinion, while controls of this kind can be enforced to some extent in wartime, in peacetime in America they would suffer the fate of prohibition. A steady increase in prices would force increases of wages and a cycle of rising costs which could not be checked while government deficits continued.

Such an inflation would lead to more attempted government regulation of everything and everybody and more government expense and finally a complete breakdown of the financial and banking structure upon which our commerce, business, and currency are based. It would mean the destruction of the private-industry system. We could point out that it had been sabotaged by its enemies, but I am afraid it would be like Humpty Dumpty, and, once fallen, all the king's horses and all the king's men could not put it together again. We would have to reconstruct our business and price system completely and that would only be done on the basis of 100 percent government control and operation. In my opinion the more radical wing of those who advocate the spending theory, and this government guarantee of full employment, really look forward with pleasure to that result. It is the best and surest method of destroying the system which they detest.

One interesting phase of the full employment program and the spending theory is the plan to lend money abroad in large sums. It is frequently said, and generally accepted without analysis of any kind, that we cannot provide full employment without a tremendous increase in our export trade. We are exporting about $12 billion worth of goods a year, about 80 percent under lease-lend. It is said that that volume must continue even though we have to lend all the money to continue it.

Of course, in the immediate postwar period it will be necessary to lend money for humanitarian reasons, and perhaps in an amount sufficient to enable the foreign countries to set their own economic machinery in motion, but continued government lending can only have the same effect which we saw in the twenties with private lending. Sooner or later it becomes glaringly apparent that the loans will never be repaid. Thereupon the lending stops and the employment created thereby comes to a sudden and disastrous end, producing or accentuating a depression; and the debt is added to our own debt and our citizens pay the interest on it. Obviously, it can be of no advantage to our workers to produce goods and give them away, and that is what foreign trade means if it is created only by large loans which cannot be repaid. Like the other forms of spending, it will produce employment at the cost of ultimately destroying all employment and all freedom with it.

The sounder advocates of a stimulated foreign trade realize that we must import goods if the trade is to give us any permanent increase in employment. But if those imports reduce employment in our home industries, why is there any net increase in employment, except a very small advantage comparatively in buying the imports cheaper? The theory is that by manufacturing goods to be shipped abroad we create an additional purchasing power in the workers who produce those exports, which can be used to pay for imported goods without interfering with our own industries. Since, however, it is admitted that exports are of no use unless paid for by imports, and that an American market must be created for those imports, why isn't it just as easy to create an additional home market for home goods as it is to create an American market for imported goods?

The truth probably lies between the two extremes. Some additional market can be created for imported goods which is not available for domestic production. But the idea that foreign trade can produce any tremendous increase in employment, unless we are going to give away our products at the expense of the taxpayer, is a mirage. And one thing is certainly clear. There can be no sound expansion of employment by the government guaranteeing expanded exports, but only by the gradual building up by hard work of a foreign trade based on mutual advantage in the exchange of certain types of goods. Tariffs can be lower, but they cannot be so reduced as to destroy established industries in this country.

So also the path to prosperity and happiness at home cannot be solved by any panacea of public spending or a government guarantee of full employment. It can only be achieved by the gradual speeding up of the great private economic machinery upon which our prosperity depends. That is indeed a difficult task because the economic machine is infinitely delicate. To secure the best results, prices must bear the right relation to wages and wages to prices. There must be an accurate adjustment between the production of capital goods and consumer goods. There must be incentive to save and invest and work and open up new fields. There must be a continued reward for hard work and ability and the willingness to take a chance. There must be a free choice of employment so that every man may choose that profession or calling to which he is best suited. These results can only be brought about by sound fiscal policies, proper encouragement of spending, and the maintenance of individual freedom.

The progress which we have achieved under the American system in the last 150 years at least suggests that we had better rely on it a while longer. It has the advantage of being based on freedom of the individual as no other economic system is based. Let us not give up our guarantee of freedom for a spurious guarantee of employment.

For the spending theory on which the legal guarantee of full employment is based is a false god. It is fatal to the very prosperity which it seeks to attain. It is fatal to sound government because the spending of money becomes its own justification regardless of the soundness of the project for which it is spent. It teaches the people that they can obtain something for nothing and that every man is entitled to the same living from the government whether his ability and his willingness to produce justify it or not; and therefore it is fatal to the character of the people who fall down and worship it.

56.

# Henry A. Wallace: An Economic Bill of Rights

*As World War II drew to a close and production dropped off, the question of full employment once again came to the fore. President Roosevelt's program for individual economic security, promised in his message to Congress in January 1944, was presented in the Full Employment Bill of 1945. It provided that the federal government would gear its investments and expenditures to providing jobs for everyone. Congress devoted intensive study to the bill throughout 1945. On January 25, Henry Wallace, secretary of commerce and former vice-president, delivered the following testimony before a Senate committee in behalf of the President's program.*

Source: *New York Times*, January 26, 1945.

In the President's message to Congress last year and this year he set forth eight self-evident economic truths as representing a second Bill of Rights under which a new basis of security and prosperity can be established for all — regardless of station, race, or creed.

America led the world in establishing political democracy. It must lead the world once more in strengthening and extending political democracy by firmly establishing economic democracy. Let us not forget the painful lessons of the rise of Fascism. Let us remember that political democracy is at best insecure and unstable without economic democracy. Fascism thrives on domestic economic insecurity, as well as on lack of or divided resistance to external aggression. Fascism is not only an enemy from without, it is also potentially an enemy from within.

We now must establish an economic bill of rights, not only out of common decency but also to insure the preservation of our political freedoms. We must accord to this economic bill of rights the same dignity — the same stature — in our American tradition as that we have accorded to the original Bill of Rights.

Let us therefore affirm this economic bill of rights — and keep affirming it — until it is as familiar and real to us as our political bill of rights.

The economic bill of rights as embodied in the President's message to Congress last January is:

The right to a useful and remunerative job in the industries or shops or farms or mines of the nation;

The right to earn enough to provide adequate food and clothing and recreation;

The right of every farmer to raise and sell his products at a return which will give him and his family a decent living;

The right of every businessman, large and small, to trade in an atmosphere of freedom from unfair competition and domination by monopolies at home or abroad;

The right of every family to a decent home;

The right to adequate medical care and the opportunity to achieve and enjoy good health;

The right to adequate protection from the economic fears of old age, sickness, accident, and unemployment;

The right to a good education.

But the achievement of this American

economic bill of rights will not come of itself. These rights will not come to those
who merely sit and wait. Nor will they
come through merely pious repetition. Our
forefathers had to struggle for our political
Bill of Rights, we will have to struggle for
our economic bill of rights. If we are going
to make those rights a living reality, we
must map out a vigorous and concerted
course. We must set as our goal the implementation and fulfillment of the eight self-
evident truths which together constitute our
economic bill of rights.

The key to making this economic bill of
rights a part of the American way of life is
as self-evident as are the rights themselves.
The key is the wholehearted recognition by
all our people of the simple fact that in
America the future of the American worker
lies in the well-being of American private
enterprise; and the future of American private enterprise lies in the well-being of the
American worker. The greatest single thing
that this war has demonstrated on the home
front is that when the American worker and
the American businessman and the American farmer work together as one team,
there are no limits on what America can
accomplish.

But to work together as a team, however,
there must be a common goal. In this war
that goal has been the defeat of our enemies
in the shortest possible period of time. In
the peace to come the goal must be the
well-being of America.

I am now going to outline to you the
type of program which I think would make
each of these economic rights a part of our
way of life.

In your consideration of this program
you will note this striking fact, namely, that
to the extent that private enterprise grows
in strength, the economic bill of rights
grows in reality — and to the extent that
the economic bill of rights grows in reality,
American private enterprise grows in
strength. Thus, all the measures which are
suggested in this program for the imple-

mentation of the economic bill of rights are
at the same time designed to make American capitalism and private enterprise work
in the same great manner in peace as it has
worked in war.

And I also want to emphasize what the
implementation of these rights will mean to
our service men and women. They have
given America the opportunity to work out
its destiny as a free nation in a free world.
The America to which they return must be
a land of economic opportunity in which
they will find not only jobs but a chance
for economic advancement and independent
enterprise in industry, commerce, agriculture, and the professions.

A grateful nation can do no less for her
returning service men and women. The GI
Bill of Rights, which became law in June of
last year following a series of recommendations which the President made to the Congress, is only designed to fulfill the special
needs of our men and women in the service. The economic bill of rights is designed
to fulfill the needs which they value most
— yes, the needs which they value more
than life itself — the needs of America.

The first economic right is the right to a
useful and remunerative job in the industries or shops or farms or mines of the nation.

To assure the full realization of this right
to a useful and remunerative job, an adequate program must provide America with
60 million productive jobs. We must have
more jobs than workers, not more workers
than jobs. Only with more jobs than workers can every man be guaranteed a job with
good wages and decent working conditions.
This requires private enterprise working at
expanded capacity.

This necessary expansion of our peacetime productive capacity will require new
facilities, new plants and new equipment. It
will require large outlays of money which
should be raised through normal investment
channels. But while private capital should
finance this expansion program, the govern-

ment should recognize its responsibility for sharing part of any special or abnormal risk of loss attached to such financing.

Therefore, I propose that the government guarantee the lender against the special and abnormal risks which may be involved in achieving our objective. This will provide new and expanding industry with plenty of private credit at reasonable interest rates. Through this program we shall merely be extending to the financing of old and new business the principles which have proved so successful in our experience with the V loans, T loans and the Federal Housing Administration loans.

A comprehensive investment program dedicated to expanding the peacetime productive capacity of America is the very essence of the American way of raising our standard of living. We build the plants for greater production so that all of us may share in their greater output. But greater output is not our only benefit from this plant expansion. In fact, our benefits also include the wages paid to the labor employed in building these plants, in constructing the machinery to be used in the plants, and in operating the plants after they are erected. These payments as wages all contribute to the nation's buying power, so that as a nation we shall have more money with which to buy the goods produced by these expanded plants.

As a matter of fact, a comprehensive investment program of this character could make possible $20 billion of new private investment each year. Why, just the job of building these plants and the machinery for them would give America 5 million more jobs a year than we had in this work before the war. And this does not include the workers who would be needed to operate these plants after they are built.

In a nutshell, then, if we are going to have remunerative jobs for all, we must have an expanded private industry capable of hiring millions more men. I propose that the government do its part in helping private enterprise finance this expansion of our industrial plant. It will be privately owned, privately operated, and privately financed; but the government will share with the private investor the unusual and abnormal financial risks which may be involved in getting started.

But, in providing jobs for everyone, we shall not only have to increase demand for our industrial and agricultural production here at home but also abroad. Some parts of our industrial and agricultural production demand a high level of foreign trade to be efficient and prosperous. This is particularly true in our heavy-equipment industries whose output will be needed. The foreign demand for such farm commodities as cotton, tobacco, and wheat will also be great if other countries have the opportunity to buy. We therefore must take steps, in cooperation with other countries, to see that international trade and investment is resumed promptly on a sound basis.

This administration has pioneered in the direction of international economic collaboration with its reciprocal trade program and the establishment of the Export-Import Bank. It has again taken the lead in suggesting international monetary stabilization and sound international investment measures — measures that are a fundamental prerequisite to healthy foreign trade and commerce. . . .

But America will not be merely a seller of goods abroad. A truly prosperous America — an America with jobs for all — will be a tremendous buyer of raw materials and products abroad. It will be an America constantly enlarging the scope of our reciprocal trade agreements. It will be an America with the time and money to spend on tourist travel, abroad as well as at home. It will be an America from which other countries can afford to buy more because they are selling more.

With congressional approval of this program and with our program of jobs for all in this country, the foreign trade of the

United States can be trebled after the war. This increase in our foreign trade should mean 3 million more jobs after the war than we had before the war. Nor are the benefits of increased foreign trade and investment confined to increasing our prosperity. I want to emphasize that such cooperative measures for expanding international trade and investment are at the same time the economic foundation for a lasting peace. A prosperous world will be a world free of both economic and political aggression.

There is one further phase of this program of providing jobs for all which must be made an integral part of any long-range program. That is the task of seeing to it that there are not just jobs for all next year — or for the year after that. No, we are talking about jobs for all as a permanent part of our American way of life.

But it is inevitable, however, that an economy of free enterprise like ours will have some fluctuation in the number of jobs it can provide. Adjustments in employment are an essential part of an expanding free economy, and for these minor fluctuations, we provide unemployment insurance. But we must not allow such fluctuations ever to deteriorate into panic or depression. We cannot again be caught in that vicious downward spiral of unemployment, wage cuts, and stagnated business. Whenever the number of gainfully employed in this country falls below 57 million, our government should take prompt steps to see that new jobs are made available to keep the total from falling significantly below that figure. This is the floor below which we must not allow employment to fall.

The basic function of your government in taking care of any such slack in jobs is to see to it that private enterprise is assisted until it can absorb this slack. This is entirely possible. During the war the federal, state, and local governments have found it necessary to put aside the construction of roads, buildings, and public facilities to the value of many billions of dollars. We have a need,

too, for vast programs of the type exemplified by TVA.

Some of this construction will have to be undertaken immediately after the war. A good deal of it, however, can be postponed so that its construction could be timed with periods when the volume of employment that industry, commerce, and agriculture can offer begins to fall. We must have a reservoir of planned and approved federal, state, and local projects ready to be tapped. And when employment falls below this floor of 57 million jobs, this reservoir of planned and approved public works should be opened up to provide more jobs and take up the slack.

Such useful and essential public works should not produce government or "relief" jobs, however. No, they should produce private jobs. This is possible if we insist that this construction be done by private firms under contract with the government; private firms employing labor at the prevailing rate of wages and under standard labor conditions.

This assurance of a reserve of private jobs through constructive public works when needed to take up the slack will have a profound effect on the whole direction of our economy. In fact, the knowledge that government accepts this responsibility of maintaining a floor under jobs will act as an immense stabilizing force on the whole economy.

The second economic right is the right to earn enough to provide food and clothing and recreation.

America must remain preeminently the land of high wages and efficient production. Every job in America must provide enough for a decent living.

During the war we have been compelled to hold down wage increases that might have provoked runaway inflation. With all the arms and war materials we were producing, there was only a limited amount of consumption goods available. Increasing wages without increasing the amount of goods available to the consumer would have been an open invitation to inflation. However, the end of the war, even the end of the war in Europe, will change this picture. Then there will be more goods available for America to buy, and it is only good common sense to see that the workman is paid enough to buy these goods.

The gains made by labor during the war must be retained in full. After the last war, as part of the process of returning to "normalcy," the slogan "Labor must be deflated" was adopted. This must not happen again. This time we must make sure that wage rates are not reduced when the wartime demand for labor is diverted into peacetime channels. We must make sure that the labor market is not broken by unemployment and wage slashes. American labor should be assured that there are not going to be any wage cuts after this war. What is even more important — when the worker's hours are cut back to peacetime levels, a real attempt must be made to adjust wage rates upward.

And wages should be constantly increased as the productivity of industry is increased. An expanding American economy can continue to expand only if the increased productivity is divided equitably between business and the worker. In fact, you know and I know that unless the worker does get his share of America's increased production in the form of increased wages and unless business gets its share in the form of increased profits, neither will prosper and all — businessmen, wage earners, and farmers — will lose.

But an increase in wages is not the only benefit the American worker should secure from increased productivity. He should also benefit in the form of shorter hours of work, in the form of increased leisure and opportunities for healthful recreation. Thus increased wages and shorter hours go hand-in-hand in solving the prosperity problem the American way.

There is one further aspect of the wage-earner's problem that I would like to comment on. That is his aspiration for an annual wage or guaranteed annual income from his job. It is a terribly important part of any real attempt to implement America's economic bill of rights. The size of the wage-earner's pay envelope is important — vitally important to American prosperity. But we all know that it is equally important to know how many pay envelopes he gets during a year. I would like to see him get a guaranteed minimum annual wage and I think the time has come for America to begin tackling this most difficult problem.

Now this goal cannot be attained overnight. It cannot be achieved in a manner to harm business. Nor can it be achieved with the same speed in every business. But we can start on the job of giving labor an annual wage. We can do a lot if we all will only agree that it is a problem business and labor must solve and if we all approach the problem with a genuine desire to succeed. And government must do its part too. It must aid business in stabilizing its labor needs so that the burden of an annual wage will not be uneconomical. This, in my opinion, is the American way to bring about the annual wage, and I have confidence in the American way of doing things.

The third economic right is the right of every farmer to raise and sell his products at a rate which will give him and his family a decent living.

American farmers now have by far the largest farm income in history. This is their due reward for the greatest agricultural production in history. We must assure the farmers that there will always be a market for all their output at good prices. Concretely, we should maintain an adequate floor on farm prices and thereby assure the farmer against the dangers of falling prices for his products. Our farm program must be one of expansion rather than curtailment. With jobs for all at good wages and with foreign markets greatly expanded, the farmer will be able to sell at good prices all that he can raise.

But this is not all. The farmer's income must have stability. To that end there should be established a comprehensive federal crop-insurance program which will secure the farmer against the hazards of crop failure. To this must be added concrete steps to raise the standards of living on the farm and in the rural areas. We need a complete program of new and modernized homes and farm buildings. We must press forward with rural electrification and improvement. Only in this way can we bring to the rural communities modern facilities for decent and healthful living.

The fourth economic right is the right of every businessman, large and small, to trade in an atmosphere of freedom from unfair competition and domination by monopolies at home and abroad.

Our economic bill of rights, like our political Bill of Rights, is based on freedom of enterprise — freedom of enterprise not merely and exclusively for the few but broadly and inclusively for the many. The political Bill of Rights insured the destruction of special prerogatives and privileges. The economic bill of rights will insure the destruction of special economic prerogatives and privileges.

No special class of business deserves to be the spoiled darling of government. The American people have no interest in preserving the vested interests and monopolistic privileges of greedy big business. The interest of the American people lies in using the resources of the country to achieve a prosperous America, prosperous for all business, large and small, and for all the people. . . .

The fifth economic right is the right of every family to a decent home.

Concretely, we should adopt a housing program looking toward the construction, through private enterprise of 2 million

housing units a year and ridding this country of its urban and rural slums. We need to build at least 15 million new housing units if we are to eliminate all our slums and substandard dwellings. The right to a home is meaningless when that home is a hovel. We cannot afford slums.

A well-housed America must have modern homes — homes with all the latest electrical and mechanical equipment which will eliminate the drudgery of household work. To the fullest extent possible we must be a land of homeowners, and to that end we must assure every family an opportunity for homeownership by making certain that there is available private credit on terms which will reduce the down payment and cut by one-third the monthly cost of buying homes.

New residential construction and the modernization of America's homes alone can provide jobs for 4 million people a year. This is 2 million more than the maximum amount engaged in such work prior to the war.

The sixth economic right is the right to adequate medical care and the opportunity to achieve and enjoy good health.

As Selective Service has revealed, too large a proportion of our younger men now fall below reasonable health standards. This is a warning signal to America with respect to that state of health of all segments of our population. This condition calls for immediate and drastic action.

We cannot permit the health of our people to be impaired by poverty or lack of medical and hospital facilities. I say to you that your federal and state governments have just as much responsibility for the health of their people as they have for providing them with education and police and fire protection. Health and adequate medical and hospital care are not luxuries. They are basic necessities to which all are entitled.

We must see that medical attention is

available to all the people. But this health program must be achieved in the American way. Every person should have the right to go to the doctor and hospital of their own choosing. The federal and state governments should work hand-in-hand in making health insurance an integral part of our Social Security program just as old-age and unemployment benefits are today. We need more hospitals and doctors. We should make sure that such facilities are available and that we build hospitals in every community, rural and urban, that does not now have such facilities for all of its people.

Never again can we afford the waste of poor health in America because of poverty or inadequate facilities. And I say to you now that this program will prove in the long run to be a saving to America.

We must not be content to provide medical attention for people after they become sick. We must implement and extend our knowledge of maximum health as well as preventions of sickness. The government should appropriate needed funds to finance a greatly expanded program of medical research in private and public institutions.

The seventh economic right is the right to adequate protection from the economic fears of old age, sickness, accident, and unemployment.

We must assure people who are disabled and temporarily unemployed that they will be taken care of adequately. We must assure them that they will not be in want because of loss of income during this period of compulsory unemployment. We cannot neglect these groups without incurring serious dangers to the stability of our whole economy.

A broader Social Security program will be needed after the war. Old-Age Insurance should be adequate to provide all of our older men and women with the means for decent living. Our present old-age benefits are definitely inadequate. A decent, self-respecting old-age Social Security program should be deemed to be a right, not a chari-

ty, a right springing from the years of service each person delivers to the sum total of a better America. An adequate Social Security program will, of itself, by adding to the spendable purchasing power available to the people and by placing a floor on consumption, add more than 2 million jobs a year.

The eighth economic right is the right to a good education.

We must have an educated and informed America. Even now most of our rural areas and some of our urban areas are poorly provided with schools. Our teachers are underpaid. Our schools are badly understaffed. We need more schools and at least 500,000 more teachers.

Through federal aid to poorer communities for the development of locally controlled educational programs we propose to equalize and extend educational opportunities through the land. We propose to provide facilities for technical and higher education for all qualified young men and women without regard to their financial means. In this America, the pioneer of free education, the right to technical and higher education should be as universal as the right to a secondary school education. This is the kind of program that can provide jobs, economic security, and rising standards of living for all Americans regardless of race, color, or creed. Our democracy can be a living force only if it means the good life for all the people.

The millions of productive jobs that this program will bring are jobs in private enterprise. They are jobs based on the expanded demand for the output of our economy for consumption and investment. And this program need place no real burden on the federal budget, notwithstanding the reduction in taxes which must come after the war. On the contrary, a program of this character can provide America with a national income of such a size that it will be possible to reduce the tax rates still further on personal incomes, on business profits, and on consumption, and still collect enough tax revenues to meet the needs of the government, including orderly retirement of the national debt.

These should be our immediate goals once final victory over our enemies has been achieved.

Now there are those who say that these goals are the dream of a "man willing to jeopardize the country's future with untried ideas and idealistic schemes." These people think they are the realists. Actually, these are the persons of limited vision and stunted imagination. These people are of the same breed as these "sound businessmen" who haggled over pennies in the purchase of strategic stockpiles before the war, only to leave the materials for the Japs to use against us. Those are people who will fight against enemies, waging total war, by pinching pennies. These people think the same as those who said the President was

dreaming when he declared in 1940 that the American people would produce 50,000 planes in one year. Do these Monday-morning quarterbacks have that great faith in the American people and in their way of life which is required in order to understand the meaning of America?

I am confident, however, that the great majority of the American people share the same great faith in America and in the American way of doing things which I have expressed here. We know our way and the road ahead is straight and broad, although there are many hills which we must climb. The program which I have set forth is only the first milestone, for the capacity of the American way of life in the years to come is beyond the vision of man. The American system of free enterprise is the best the world has ever known, and through it we can obtain, God willing, the best that this world has to offer.

---

## 57.

## John Fischer: The Defects of Civil Service

*The Pendleton Act, which established the first Civil Service Commission in 1883, was the culmination of a long struggle against the spoils system that had flourished since the days of Andrew Jackson. Since its inception the Civil Service system has undergone several reforms and expansions, most notably by Theodore Roosevelt in 1903 (Civil Service Rules and Orders) and by Franklin D. Roosevelt between 1936 and 1940. By the middle of the twentieth century, three and a half million federal employees came under its auspices. The system has never been without its critics. An attack by John Fischer, "Let's Go Back to the Spoils System," was published in 1945 and is reprinted here in part.*

Source: *Harper's*, October 1945.

WHAT'S GONE WRONG with Civil Service is easy enough to find out. You can get the story, in almost identical terms, from anybody who has ever held an executive job in Washington.

First of all, it's too slow. If you were an administrator in urgent need of a new assistant, you might hope to get somebody on the job — with luck and infinite finagling — in six or eight weeks. (He wouldn't be the man you want, of course.) In wartime the pace was a little faster — there were even cases in which a man was hired within a week — but even then par for the course was at least a month. If you wanted to beat that, you had to "hand process" the appointment, personally carrying the sheaf of papers through the maze of the agency personnel office and the Civil Service Commission, and mobilizing all the pressure you could, including telephone calls from the applicant's congressman.

When you want to fire a man, the procedure naturally is more tedious. In theory, it is as easy to get rid of an incompetent in the government service as it is in private industry; in practice, the ordeal may drag on for six or eight painful months. If you are an experienced administrator, you will never try to fire anybody — you will foist him off on some unsuspecting colleague in another bureau, or transfer him to the South Dakota field office, or reorganize your section to abolish his position. . . .

Even worse than the Civil Service Commission's leisurely gait is its delight in harassing the operating officials who are responsible for running the government. The typical administrator may spend as much as a third of his time placating the commission and the hordes of minor personnel specialists who infest Washington. He draws organization charts, argues with classification experts, fills out efficiency ratings, justifies the allocation of vacancies, and listens to inspiring lectures on personnel management until he has little energy left for his real job. He may search for hours for those magic words which, properly recited in a job description, will enable him to pay a subordinate $4,600 instead of $3,800. (The phrase "with wide latitude for exercise of individual initiative and responsibility" is nearly always worth $800 of the taxpayers' money; but it took me two years to find that out.)

No bureaucrat can avoid this boondoggling. If he fails to initial a Green Sheet or to attach the duplicate copy of Form 57, the whole machinery of his office grinds to a halt. If he deliberately flouts the established ritual, or neglects to show due respect for the personnel priesthood, his career may be ruined and his program along with it. In a thousand subtle ways the personnel boys can throw sand in the gears. They can freeze appointments and promotions, block transfers, lose papers, and generally bedevil any official who refuses to "cooperate." If they bog down a government project in the process, that is no skin off their backs — nobody can ever hold them responsible.

Nor can the administrator escape the Civil Service investigators, who drop in once or twice a week to question him about the morals, drinking habits, and possibly treasonable opinions of some poor wretch who has applied for a federal job. These investigators often are amusing fellows. I got well acquainted with one who formerly had been a small-town private detective; he had an uncommonly prurient mind, which led him to handle every case as if he were working up adultery charges for a divorce suit. Nearly all of them operate on the theory that anybody willing to work for the government must be a scoundrel, probably with Communist tendencies, who could never hold a job anywhere else. They have a boundless appetite for gossip, and they waste a lot of other people's time. What purpose they serve is obscure, because their investigations often are not completed until five or six months after the new employee starts work. If he actually were as villainous as they seem to suspect, he would have plenty of time to sell the country's secrets to a sinister foreign power before the investigators caught up with him.

These are minor indictments, however. The really serious charge against the Civil Service system is that it violates the most fundamental rule of sound management. That rule is familiar to every businessman.

when you hold a man responsible for doing a job, you must give him the authority he needs to carry it out. Above all, he must be free to hire his own staff, assign them to tasks they can do best, and replace them if they don't make good.

In peacetime, at least, no agency operating under the trammels of Civil Service has this authority. Suppose, for example, that Congress sets up a special Flood Control Agency, with urgent orders to harness the rampaging Ohio River. The new FCA administrator, full of zeal, asks the Civil Service Commission to give him the best chief engineer the merit system can supply.

After some argument whether a first-class engineer — capable of earning $30,000 a year in private practice — is worth $6,500 to the government, the commission finally tells the administrator to take his choice of three men. They head its list of people who once took a Civil Service engineering examination. All the best men on the list have already been snapped up by other agencies, of course, because the last examination was held five years ago. And it wasn't a very good list in the first place, because few people in the profession knew that such an examination was being held. (It had been announced in a bulletin, printed in the kind of type used for Bible footnotes and displayed on post office notice boards between the Marine recruiting posters and the FBI photos of escaped kidnappers.)

Of the three "referrals," one turns out to be a professor at Freshwater Academy who never poured a yard of concrete in his life. The second is afflicted with a personality which makes it impossible for him to work in any organization. The third actually has had some practical experience — he once designed a garbage disposal plant — but he has no sympathy with the flood control program; he is a firm believer in Free Enterprise and noninterference with acts of God. The administrator has to take him anyway, although he personally knows a

dozen better-qualified men who are eager to tackle the job.

During the next six months, while the administrator tries desperately to recruit the rest of his staff from Civil Service registers, the chief engineer surveys the Ohio River. He reports that flood control is neither practical nor desirable, and that in any case it should be left to private industry. Meanwhile, a flood wipes out Cincinnati, Louisville, and Paducah. With one voice the press denounces the administrator as a bungling bureaucrat, and a Senate investigating committee demands his head.

The Civil Service Commission, of course, is unperturbed. It has done its duty in preserving the merit system free from all taint of patronage. The sacred regulations have been kept intact. If a few thousand unfortunates have been drowned in the Ohio Valley, that is none of its concern.

Fantastic? Not in the least. In the past twelve years a number of government programs have been hobbled in precisely this fashion.

Although the defects of Civil Service are plain enough, the reasons for them are not so easy to find.

By no means all the blame rests on the Civil Service Commissioners. They are three earnest, well-meaning people, who grieve sincerely over the flaws in their organization. . . .

These veteran bureaucrats know that their bosses come and go, while they endure forever. They are skilled in the art of passive resistance, and they have no intention of letting any upstart commissioner tamper unduly with their time-hallowed procedures. Their idol is Theodore Roosevelt, the only Civil Service commissioner who ever attained national prominence — his desk is enshrined in the central hall of their F Street lair — and they look with grave suspicion on any ideas which he did not sanction in 1895.

The tight inner circle of the permanent

staff is made up of men who started with the commission as messengers or clerks some twenty years ago, and rose to positions of power on the seniority escalator. Few of them have had any experience in private business or other government departments; they have little conception of the problems of an operating agency.

They have two guiding principles. The first is Keep the Rascals Out. Civil Service, in their view, is a kind of police force designed to keep political patronage appointees from creeping into federal jobs. This they do well — but they rarely feel any responsibility for positive action to make the government work, or to persuade the best possible men to enter the federal service.

The second aim of the commission bureaucracy is to increase the dignity and power of the personnel profession. To this end, they have developed a special jargon which no outsider can understand, plus an elaborate structure of regulations, red tape, and ritual which can be mastered only after years of study. They demand of the whole government what Dr. Floyd W. Reeves, professor of administration at the University of Chicago, has described as "an almost idolatrous worship" of the commission's "detailed and antiquated rules."

It is hard to blame them for this — after all, they are only doing what the legal and medical professions did centuries ago. The result, however, is a vested interest in complexity and formalism which is largely responsible for the ill-repute of the Civil Service system.

But the greatest share of guilt falls on Congress. Lacking any real enthusiasm for the Civil Service idea, it has never bothered to work out comprehensive legislation for a modern, effective system of personnel administration. Instead, over the course of years it has encrusted the original act of 1883 with scores of piecemeal amendments and special statutes. This has resulted in a legal patchwork which would baffle even the ablest and most aggressive commissioners. One law, for example, sets up special qualifications for coal mine inspectors; another provides that employees of the Farmers' Home Corporation must be residents of the states where they work; a third specifies that superintendents of national cemeteries must be disabled Army veterans — no sailors or Marines need apply. All of these laws, and many more like them, undermine the principle that the best man ought to get the job; each one is intended to confer special preference on some particular group of job-hunters. They are simply devices for legalizing favoritism and patronage on a large scale.

In addition, Congress has steadfastly refused to give the commission enough money to hire a proper staff or to run its business efficiently. (Until a few years ago, one of the field offices got along with a single telephone and borrowed chairs from the federal jail whenever it had to hold an examination.) Nor have there ever been funds to develop scientific testing methods, or to keep the registers fresh with frequent examinations.

It is true, of course, that the commission seldom fights aggressively for the money it needs, and that it sometimes has actually encouraged Congress to pass bad legislation. Only a few months ago, for example, the commission managed to have written into law one of its most hampering regulations — the so-called "Rule of Three," which limits choice in appointments to the three names at the top of the register. Dr. Reeves, a leading authority in the field of public administration, characterized this step as "a major disaster."

Nevertheless, such blunders would be impossible if Congress took an intelligent interest in the problems of federal employment. Of all the present congressmen, only one — Robert Ramspeck of Georgia — has shown such an interest. The attitudes of the rest range from indifference to frank contempt. As a result, government pay scales are notoriously low, and any bill designed to harass or discriminate against government workers is almost sure to pass with whoops of glee.

Worst of all, Congress has perpetuated the basic flaw in the original Civil Service Act. The commission is still an independent agency, entirely divorced from the normal structure of government. Although it wields great power it is responsible to no one. It serves only as a kind of decrepit watchdog, which growls at the regular departments, but seldom tries to help them get their job done.

It can be argued, in all seriousness, that Congress would do well to wipe out Civil Service, hide, horns, and tallow, and go back to the old-fashioned spoils system.

Any political party which believes intensely in its program presumably would choose the ablest men in its ranks to put that program into effect. Each administrator would be in sympathy with the project he is assigned to run, and he could expect loyal support from every subordinate. Moreover, he could count on fast action; no ward heeler could survive unless he handled appointments more promptly than the present Civil Service machinery.

Naturally every congressman would slip a few of his maiden aunts and broken-down henchmen onto the public payroll. But they could hardly be more useless or expensive than the thousands of personnel men now roosting in Washington. Indeed, the treasury might well save a few millions, since most political hacks are harmless creatures, who merely draw their pay and don't bother anybody, while personnel experts take great zest in pestering the working officials.

And if the party in power should ever load the payroll with too many thieves and incompetents, then a healthy democracy would throw out the whole gang at the next election. The constant threat of a change in administration would help keep all government employees on their toes; they would never dare sink into the smug mediocrity which now afflicts so many civil servants who are sure of indefinite tenure.

Such a forthright return to the patronage system would, however, be a pretty drastic step — probably more drastic than is actually necessary. Before junking Civil Service entirely, maybe Congress should consider replacing the 1883 jalopy with a 1945 model.

The blueprint for a modern and workable Civil Service is already at hand. It was drawn up in 1937, after months of careful study, by a group of experts from outside the government known as the Committee on Administrative Management. The committee's suggestions were warmly endorsed by most of the recognized authorities in this field, and the President urged Congress to put them into effect immediately. As usual, Congress wasn't interested, and nothing happened.

These proposals are still as sensible as they were eight years ago and even more urgently needed. They call for four major reforms:

1. The present commission should be abolished, along with its whole collection of red tape and the senescent bureaucrats who weave it. (These gentlemen should be permitted to leave Washington quietly, in spite of a widespread demand among other government workers that they be tarred, feathered, and ridden out of town on their own filing cabinets.)

2. Each agency should be permitted to hire its own help. They should be chosen strictly on merit, with all political influence ruled out, on the same basis which TVA now is using so successfully. Every department would then be able to get a competent personnel staff to replace its present herd of second-raters — it could attract good men because it could give them real responsibility.

3. A single Federal Personnel Administrator, responsible directly to the President, would lay down overall policies for the various agencies, and see to it that they are carried out. (He would *not* try to enforce a multitude of petty rules.) His office also could carry on the few functions of the present commission which really need to be centralized — such as handling retirement funds, arranging transfers, and pooling the recruitment of minor employees.

4. A part-time, unpaid, nonpolitical board should be set up to keep a wary eye on the administrator and on the personnel operations of the agencies. From time to time it might suggest general policies or standards. Its main job, however, would be to look out for the public interest, and make sure that the new, decentralized merit system actually worked with a minimum of political interference. (It would of course be impossible, and probably undesirable, to get a scheme which would be entirely free of politics. The present setup certainly is not — the whims of a senator now are treated with religious deference by nearly all Washington personnel men, from the commission down.)

---

58.

# General and Special Education in a Free Society

*That there was a basic corpus of knowledge that every educated person ought to have, aside from the knowledge necessary for a "specialist," was the assumption underlying the experiments with a general undergraduate curriculum at a number of American colleges and universities during the 1930s and 1940s. The attempt to establish a "general education" curriculum involved restoring as much as possible of the common heritage of Western civilization after its alleged fragmentation by the elective system, which had been enthusiastically adopted in the previous decades. In 1945 a Harvard committee composed of faculty members in the arts and sciences issued a report that was both widely acclaimed and fiercely attacked. The following selection is drawn from the chapter entitled "General and Special Education."*

Source: *General Education in a Free Society*, Cambridge, 1945, pp. 51-58.

EDUCATION IS BROADLY DIVIDED into general and special education; our topic . . . is the difference and the relationship between the two. The term "general education" is somewhat vague and colorless; it does not mean some airy education in knowledge in general (if there be such knowledge), nor does it mean education for all in the sense of universal education. It is used to indicate that part of a student's whole education which looks first of all to his life as a responsible human being and citizen; while the term "special education" indicates that part which looks to the student's competence in some occupation.

These two sides of life are not entirely separable, and it would be false to imagine education for the one as quite distinct from education for the other — more will be said on this point presently. Clearly, general education has somewhat the meaning of liberal education, except that, by applying to high school as well as to college, it envisages immensely greater numbers of students and thus escapes the invidium which, rightly or wrongly, attaches to liberal education in the minds of some people. But if one clings to the root meaning of liberal as that which befits or helps to make free men, then general and liberal education have identical goals. The one may be thought of as an earlier stage of the other, similar in nature but less advanced in degree.

The opposition to liberal education — both to the phrase and to the fact — stems largely from historical causes. The concept of liberal education first appeared in a slave-owning society, like that of Athens, in which the community was divided into freemen and slaves, rulers and subjects. While the slaves carried on the specialized occupations of menial work, the freemen were primarily concerned with the rights and duties of citizenship. The training of the former was purely vocational; but as the freemen were not only a ruling but also a leisure class, their education was exclusively in the liberal arts, without any utilitarian tinge. The freemen were trained in the reflective pursuit of the good life; their education was unspecialized as well as unvocational; its aim was to produce a rounded person with a full understanding of himself and of his place in society and in the cosmos.

Modern democratic society clearly does not regard labor as odious or disgraceful; on the contrary, in this country at least, it regards leisure with suspicion and expects its "gentlemen" to engage in work. Thus we attach no odium to vocational instruction. Moreover, insofar as we surely reject the idea of freemen who are free insofar as they have slaves or subjects, we are apt wrongly to deprecate the liberal education

which went with the structure of the aristocratic ideal. Herein our society runs the risk of committing a serious fallacy.

Democracy is the view that not only the few but that all are free, in that everyone governs his own life and shares in the responsibility for the management of the community. This being the case, it follows that all human beings stand in need of an ampler and rounded education. The task of modern democracy is to preserve the ancient ideal of liberal education and to extend it as far as possible to all the members of the community. In short, we have been apt to confuse accidental with fundamental factors, in our suspicion of the classical ideal. To believe in the equality of human beings is to believe that the good life, and the education which trains the citizen for the good life, are equally the privilege of all.

And these are the touchstones of the liberated man: first, is he free? That is to say, is he able to judge and plan for himself so that he can truly govern himself? In order to do this, his must be a mind capable of self-criticism; he must lead that self-examined life which according to Socrates is alone worthy of a free man. Thus he will possess inner freedom, as well as social freedom. Second, is he universal in his motives and sympathies? For the civilized man is a citizen of the entire universe; he has overcome provincialism, he is objective, and is a "spectator of all time and all existence." Surely these two are the very aims of democracy itself.

But the opposition to general education does not stem from causes located in the past alone. We are living in an age of specialism, in which the avenue to success for the student often lies in his choice of a specialized career, whether as a chemist, or an engineer, or a doctor, or a specialist in some form of business or of manual or technical work. Each of these specialties makes an increasing demand on the time and on the interest of the student. Specialism is the means for advancement in our mobile social structure; yet we must envisage the fact that a society controlled wholly by specialists is not a wisely ordered society. We cannot, however, turn away from specialism. The problem is how to save general education and its values within a system where specialism is necessary.

The very prevalence and power of the demand for special training makes doubly clear the need for a concurrent, balancing force in general education. Specialism enhances the centrifugal forces in society. The business of providing for the needs of society breeds a great diversity of special occupations; and a given specialist does not speak the language of the other specialists. In order to discharge his duties as a citizen adequately, a person must somehow be able to grasp the complexities of life as a whole. Even from the point of view of economic success, specialism has its peculiar limitations. Specializing in a vocation makes for inflexibility in a world of fluid possibilities. Business demands minds capable of adjusting themselves to varying situations and of managing complex human institutions.

Given the pace of economic progress, techniques alter speedily; and even the work in which the student has been trained may no longer be useful when he is ready to earn a living or soon after. Our conclusion, then, is that the aim of education should be to prepare an individual to become an expert both in some particular vocation or art and in the general art of the freeman and the citizen. Thus the two kinds of education once given separately to different social classes must be given together to all alike.

In this epoch in which almost all of us must be experts in some field in order to make a living, general education therefore assumes a peculiar importance. Since no one can become an expert in all fields, everyone is compelled to trust the judgment of other people pretty thoroughly in most areas of activity. I must trust the advice of my doctor, my plumber, my lawyer, my radio repairman, and so on. Therefore I am in peculiar need of a kind of sagacity by which to distinguish the expert from the quack, and the better from the worse expert.

From this point of view, the aim of general education may be defined as that of providing the broad critical sense by which to recognize competence in any field. William James said that an educated person knows a good man when he sees one. There are standards and a style for every type of activity — manual, athletic, intellectual, or artistic; and the educated man should be one who can tell sound from shoddy work in a field outside his own. General education is especially required in a democracy where the public elects its leaders and officials; the ordinary citizen must be discerning enough so that he will not be deceived by appearances and will elect the candidate who is wise in his field.

Both kinds of education — special as well as general — contribute to the task of implementing the pervasive forces of our culture. Here we revert to what was said at the start . . . on the aims of education in our society. It was argued there that two complementary forces are at the root of our culture: on the one hand, an ideal of man and society distilled from the past but at the same time transcending the past as a standard of judgment valid in itself, and, on the other hand, the belief that no existent expressions of this ideal are final but that all alike call for perpetual scrutiny and change in the light of new knowledge. Specialism is usually the vehicle of this second force. It fosters the open-mindedness and love of investigation which are the wellspring of change, and it devotes itself to the means by which change is brought about. The fact may not always be obvious. There is a sterile specialism which hugs accepted knowledge and ends in the bleakest conservatism.

Modern life also calls for many skills which, though specialized, are repetitive and certainly do not conduce to inquiry. These minister to change but unconsciously. Nevertheless, the previous statement is true in the sense that specialism is concerned primarily with knowledge in action, as it advances into new fields and into further applications.

Special education comprises a wider field than vocationalism; and correspondingly, general education extends beyond the limits of merely literary preoccupation. An example will make our point clearer. A scholar — let us say a scientist (whether student or teacher) — will, in the laudable aim of saving himself from narrowness, take a course in English literature, or perhaps read poetry and novels, or perhaps listen to good music and generally occupy himself with the fine arts. All this, while eminently fine and good, reveals a misapprehension. In his altogether unjustified humility, the scientist wrongly interprets the distinction between liberal and illiberal in terms of the distinction between the humanities and the sciences.

Plato and Cicero would have been very much surprised to hear that geometry, astronomy, and the sciences of nature in general, are excluded from the humanities. There is also implied a more serious contempt for the liberal arts, harking back to the fallacy which identifies liberal education with the aristocratic ideal. The implication is that liberal education is something only genteel. A similar error is evident in the student's attitude toward his required courses outside his major field as something to "get over with," so that he may engage in the business of serious education, identified in his mind with the field of concentration.

Now, a general education is distinguished from special education, not by subject matter, but in terms of method and outlook, no matter what the field. Literature, when studied in a technical fashion, gives rise to the special science of philology; there is also the highly specialized historical approach to painting. Specialism is interchangeable, not with natural science but with the method of science, the method which abstracts material from its context and handles it in complete isolation. The reward of scientific method is the utmost degree of precision and exactness. But, as we have seen, specialism as an educational force has its own limitations; it does not usually provide an insight into general relationships.

A further point is worth noting. The impact of specialism has been felt not only in those phases of education which are necessarily and rightly specialistic; it has affected also the whole structure of higher and even of secondary education. Teachers, themselves products of highly technical disciplines, tend to reproduce their knowledge in class. The result is that each subject, being taught by an expert, tends to be so presented as to attract potential experts. This complaint is perhaps more keenly felt in colleges and universities, which naturally look to scholarship. The undergraduate in a college receives his teaching from professors who, in their turn, have been trained in graduate schools. And the latter are dominated by the ideal of specialization.

Learning now is diversified and parceled into a myriad of specialties. Correspondingly, colleges and universities are divided into large numbers of departments, with further specialization within the departments. As a result, a student in search of a general course is commonly frustrated. Even an elementary course is devised as an introduction to a specialism within a department; it is significant only as the beginning of a series of courses of advancing complexity. In short, such introductory courses are planned for the specialist, not for the student seeking a general education. The young chemist in the course in literature and the young writer in the course in chemistry find themselves in thoroughly uncomfortable positions so long as the purpose of these courses is primarily to train experts who will go on to higher courses rather than to give some basic understanding of science as it is revealed in chemistry or of the arts as they are revealed in literature.

It is most unfortunate if we envisage general education as something formless — that is to say, the taking of one course after another; and as something negative, namely, the study of what is not in a field of concentration. Just as we regard the courses in concentration as having definite relations to one another, so should we envisage general education as an organic whole whose parts join in expounding a ruling idea and in serving a common aim. And to do so means to abandon the view that all fields and all departments are equally valuable vehicles of general education. It also implies some prescription. At the least it means abandoning the usual attitude of regarding "distribution" as a sphere in which the student exercises a virtually untrammeled freedom of choice.

It may be objected that we are proposing to limit the liberty of the student in the very name of liberal education. Such an objection would only indicate an ambiguity in the conception of liberal education. We must distinguish between liberalism in education and education in liberalism. The former, based as it is on the doctrine of individualism, expresses the view that the student should be free in his choice of courses. But education in liberalism is an altogether different matter; it is education which has a pattern of its own, namely, the pattern associated with the liberal outlook. In this view, there are truths which none can be free to ignore, if one is to have that wisdom through which life can become useful. These are the truths concerning the structure of the good life and concerning the factual conditions by which it may be achieved, truths comprising the goals of the free society.

Finally, the problem of general education is one of combining fixity of aim with diversity in application. It is not a question of providing a general education which will be uniform through the same classes of all schools and colleges all over the country, even were such a thing possible in our decentralized system. It is rather to adapt general education to the needs and intentions of different groups and, so far as possible, to carry its spirit into special education. The effectiveness of teaching has always largely depended on this willingness to adapt a central unvarying purpose to varying outlooks. Such adaptation is as much in the interest of the quick as of the slow, of the bookish as of the unbookish, and is the necessary protection of each. What is wanted, then, is a general education capable at once of taking on many different forms and yet of representing in all its forms the common knowledge and the common values on which a free society depends.

---

*A despot doesn't fear eloquent writers preaching freedom — he fears a drunken poet who may crack a joke that will take hold.*

E. B. WHITE

59.

# Ralph B. Wagner: Public Relations

*Until World War II probably the best-known American public relations man was Ivy Ledbetter Lee, who, starting in 1914, developed the "art" of public relations in a series of famous campaigns in behalf of such persons and corporations as John D. Rockefeller, the Bethlehem Steel Corporation, and the Pennsylvania Railroad. But Lee's fame — or notoriety — is partly accounted for by the fact that he was one of the very few American "public relations counsels" in the years between the wars. By the 1940s many persons and companies had come to see the desirability of engaging an expert to put their name or the name of their product before the public in the best possible light, and the breed proliferated. The following speech by Ralph B. Wagner, professor of speech at St. Louis University, delivered to the Paint, Varnish, and Lacquer Association of that city, reveals the attitude toward their "image" of forward-looking businessmen at the beginning of the postwar period.*

Source: VSD, January 1, 1946: "Don't Neglect Your Relations!"

IN THE CONFUSION of fears for their futures, alert business executives are beginning to attach as much importance to "relations" as they are to the technical and merchandising needs of their enterprises. With the present psychological and economic insecurity, forward-looking business leaders are aware of the fact that much of their future success depends upon an understanding public opinion. They realize that they must convert, modify, and strengthen public attitude if they hope to stave off corporate losses in this period of readjustments and hoped-for return to normalcy.

Fully conscious of the seriousness of the situation, you progressive businessmen are trying to solve the pressing problems that confront your respective businesses. But, do your plans include a definite and concerted program of enlightened publicity, propaganda, and promotion? Whatever else you may be doing by way of constructive ground-

work for the future, *don't neglect your relations — your public relations.* What do I mean by that? I mean: your *contacts* — direct and indirect — with anybody whose opinions and actions in any way can affect your business.

The sum total of all such contacts is what "public relations" consists of. It includes the entire gamut of activities that go to make up impressions. It comprises every phase of endeavor that touches public interest. It must be an "operating philosophy" applied to everything your organization does — as that includes your broad program for creating goodwill — to the end that it will restore faith in industry. This means that, as an applied institutional activity, public relations is essentially and primarily a matter of shaping and carrying out policies which eventually reflect themselves in favorable public attitude toward a service or product. All of which suggests that everything an establishment does and says that influences the opinion and reaction of people — whether favorably or unfavorably — is "public relations" and must, therefore, be based on an understanding of, and adaptation to, the psychology of the mass mind to be reached.

To live and to prosper, each of us — as an individual — must constantly try to express himself to others. He must impress upon them what he feels, thinks, knows, and can do. Almost from birth, each of us is faced with the problem of doing this in such a way as to be understood and accepted. We communicate — whether favorably or unfavorably — largely by the way we look, act, and sound when we speak. It is chiefly through this medium of expression that we register our aims, ambitions, attitudes, ideas, and services.

If we succeed in arresting the satisfactory attention of those we contact, arousing their interests, gaining their confidence, and securing their support as a result of our speaking activities, we can be said to have established good relations. To the extent that we fail — by our appearance, manners, actions, and words — to create the impressions that make for acceptance of ourselves, what we stand for, and what we have to offer, we "muff" our relations with those we contact. Whether we hit or miss the mark, progress or retrograde, stand or fall, is largely determined by the reactions we provoke in the minds and hearts of others when we talk. If we please and satisfy our listening "public," we "go places"; if we displease or irritate that public, we "stay at home." It all depends on what people think of us, in reaction to our address. The power of opinion is that potent!

Now, just as the prosperity of an individual is so indisputably contingent on the extent to which his speech is pleasing, so the success of a business is conditioned by the ability of its spokesman to project the worth of its services into the public mind.

Unless an institution — whether industrial, commercial, or, for that matter, educational — favorably impresses itself and its services on the consciousness of its public through effective communication, its existence is imperiled. Make no mistake about this — public relations is a real "selling" job today. The force of opinion is "the sovereign mistress of effects" when translated into action. The pressure of that opinion is like the pressure of the atmosphere. "You can't see it," as James Russell Lowell once said, "but all the same it is sixteen pounds to the square inch."

Since public opinion, then, is the raw material with which we must work, our key question is: Can we fashion it, and how?

It is true that public opinion changes "with the wind," because it is subject to so many influences and factors that tend to sway the people. What do people believe? Well, beliefs are largely determined by desires and needs. Most people are inclined to believe what they like or want to believe rather than what they deduce through a process of reasoning on the strength of evidence. They evaluate what they hear and read in the light of many personal prejudices that are hard to explain. Does it follow, therefore, that there is no sure way to control opinion or belief? Frankly, there is no absolute and infallible pattern for positively dominating opinion. Nevertheless, there are certain psychological principles of prevailing upon individual opinion that constitute a basis for fairly successful control of public opinion. These principles are based on scientific research findings that are sufficiently representative to enable us to accomplish rather startling results in molding mass mind.

Chief among the more significant discoveries about fundamental human nature that can be utilized to shape public opinion is the fact that normal human beings, generally, are still rather primitively selfish, inquisitive, imitative, and emotional. They are almost as interested as children in conflicts, mysteries, pictures, success stories, and secrets. Don't most people like to believe what appeals to them because it holds out a promise of profit, advantage, or some other personal satisfaction? Don't they want to know? Aren't they intrigued by the new and the novel? And, if their feelings are stirred, don't they often do things that their reason would never sanction? Such basic "drives" lie at the very roots of public judgments. If I'm wrong, then why do we seal confidential letters? Why do we go to ball games? Why do we jam the movie theaters and boxing arenas?

And if people, by and large, are not inclined to be followers, why do they congregate — go with crowds and prevailing currents? Probably one of the greatest stimuli to the average mind is the apparent popularity of an idea or movement. Have you ever observed how applause "picks up" at a public gathering, or what a strong influence it exerts on the mob? When "everybody seems to be doing it," as the saying goes, more and more "hop on the bandwagon." That's probably why phrases that suggest universal acceptance of an idea are hard to resist. There's "authority" in numbers!

Now, I don't mean to imply that a human being is solely and utterly influenced by unreasoned instincts and emotions. I do submit, however, that most judgments of the average person are controlled less by logic than by suggestibility and unreasoned "drives." So long as something is plausible — seems "sensible" — it is usually adopted by the average individual. It is a well-known psychological fact that most opinions, attitudes, decisions, and actions are the result of "feeling" or some other nonlogical factors. No matter how sincere we may be or how impersonally we try to think, we are for or against persons, products, programs, and propositions without much "reason."

Oh yes, we like to use that word. We want to appear reasonable. We like to give our opinions, attitudes, and actions the cloak of sanity. We may say, "I'll give you my reason." But, what does that generally amount to? Simply a semblance of sound reasoning. When we are not on the alert, we seldom say more than, "That's how I *feel* about it." Then, if we are challenged to justify a sentiment or stand, we are at a loss to do more than rationalize. Feelings certainly influence responses. The average person, for the most part, *feels* first; he *reasons* next — if at all. He starts with a predisposition or prepossession and follows with an opinion; then he may search for so-called "reasons" to justify himself. Yes, we *rationalize* much, but we "reason" precious little.

In this connection, it is illuminating to recall that, as Mark Twain — I believe it was — once remarked: "It is astounding to what lengths people will go to avoid thinking." The average person almost instinctively resents the challenge to think things out for himself. If he can't "make sense" out of words — can't relate an unfamiliar idea to one he already knows — he quickly tosses it aside. He is bored when he has to exert himself to understand.

Which observation leads us to a point that is of particular importance. It concerns the characteristic response-tendency by the mass mind to language. Reliable surveys reveal that verbalization — the form in which an idea is phrased — makes a tremendous difference in acceptance-probability of ideas. Notice how differently you yourselves react when a statement addressed to you is couched in conciliatory and apparently fair-minded and "reasoned" language than when that same thought is phrased in curt, dogmatic, and seemingly intolerant terms. Who would not be more susceptible to "Lend me your ears" than to "Be silent that you may hear"? Yes, words can work wonders!

And while we are on this topic — the

power of words — you all have observed, no doubt, how susceptible people are to intriguing catchwords and fanciful phrases that seem to epitomize the motif or dominant idea that constitutes the gist of a message. History is replete with mass responses to slogans, many of which "defy definition." Nations have rallied to a cause, men have been elected to high office, and armies have conquered formidable foes because of the dynamic power of some striking, concrete, specific, vivid, and pithy slogan.

What does this frank examination lead us to? Well, it certainly establishes a background against which endeavor in the direction of profitable control of public opinion can be made. It points the way, at least, to a resultful pattern of approach in the important process of molding the mass mind. It indicates a fundamental procedure that can be formulized as follows:

1. Since prejudices, prepossessions, and predilections largely control attention and favorable response: *Line up with attitudes.*

2. Since human beings are inclined to be selfish: *Satisfy self-interests.*

3. Since people are interested in action: *Dramatize facts.*

4. Since most people are indolent but take pride in their "good sense": *Make things plain and reasonable.*

5. Since the average person likes to be "on the popular side": *Challenge the imitative instinct.*

6. Since people enjoy the compliment of deference and suggestive slogans: *Use impelling language.*

This is the fundamental formula that applies as a guiding principle to all segments of a public. It is the basic in every channel of expression and communication. Couple this formula with newly created, sparkling idea-symbols that register deeply upon the public consciousness, and with frankness, honesty, temperance, sincerity, accuracy, and dignity of statement, and you have a resultful technique that is bound to eventuate in the desired control of mass-mind reaction needed to revive old accounts and to establish new business. People will endorse and support almost anything if they understand it and if it serves their own ends, gives them some satisfactory emotional experience, and is put to them the right way.

So, your problem is plain and the challenge clear: *Don't neglect your relations* with old and new publics if you want to capitalize on a future that is fraught with undreamed-of opportunities in markets. With realistic vision, courage, resolve, and perseverance, take advantage of every chance you have to establish general public confidence that is built upon public understanding. If you *don't neglect your relations now,* you will reap the fruits of your labors when "business as usual" is once again the spirit of the times.

---

*The difficult we do immediately. The impossible takes a little longer.*

*Hurry up and wait.*

Army sayings, World War II

**Production line in a Boeing aircraft plant manufacturing B-17 heavy bombers, 1942**

# WAR MOBILIZATION

The methods of governmental influence and control developed within the New Deal proved well suited to the problem of controlled mobilization of capital, labor, and the whole machinery of production and distribution for the war effort. Economic mobilization had been directed but not controlled during World War I when, for example, prices rose 100 percent from 1914 to 1920. The administration took a total view of the economic situation in 1940-1941; the aim was war production without inflation, followed by peace without depression. The heavy demands of war ended the last traces of depression; full employment and full production were quickly attained as the nation's economic output far surpassed that of the peak year 1929. War mobilization was not without its problems, however; beyond the expected disagreements over economic measures, particularly the balancing of price and wage controls, the suspension of civil liberties came into painful contrast with proclaimed war aims.

(Above) Officers of the Industrial Union of Marine and Shipbuilding Workers attending the national convention; (below) workmen marching in a New York parade backing the war mobilization

Soon after Pearl Harbor representatives of major labor organizations and industries met with Roosevelt and agreed on a no-strike policy. The War Labor Board was established to handle disputes and stabilize wages. Slow to respond to inflation, the WLB forwarded the "Little Steel" formula of 15 percent wage increases in July 1942. Cost-of-living indices rose beyond this level and friction developed, particularly in the United Mine Workers, who forced the government to take over 3,000 bituminous mines until satisfactory increases were approved.

**(Top) New Orleans shipyard workers protest the cancellation of a defense contract; (center) striking shipbuilders attack car; (bottom) signs asking labor-management harmony for war effort**

Brown Brothers

Library of Congress

(Above) Sign on Japanese-American store in Oakland, Calif., 1942; (below) evacuation of Japanese-American families from Los Angeles, Calif., 1942, photo by Russell Lee

In 1942 the West Coast was swept by a wave of what approached hysteria over the presence of large numbers of Japanese-Americans. Gen. De Witt, responsible for the defense of the region, added to the agitation for removal of the danger with his claim that "The very fact that no sabotage has taken place to date is a disturbing and confirming indication that such action will be taken." Forced to leave homes and jobs, selling property at a loss, 117,000 Japanese-Americans were transferred to 10 inland resettlement areas.

(Top) Nisei Restaurant "under new management" as a result of the federal government's relocation order; (center) children sitting with possessions during relocation process; (bottom) reception center at a camp near Salinas, Calif.

Bomb racks paraded before a civilian audience in a New York war parade

Victor De Palma from Black Star

UPI — Compix

TOUGH AMERICAN YOUTH OF TODAY

TOJO'S PRIDE

YESTERDAY'S JITTERBUG

Courtesy, Hugh Hutton and "The Philadelphia Inquirer"

(Left) Frank Sinatra surrounded by some of his female admirers at a New York concert appearance in 1943; (right) cartoon by Hugh Hutton in "The Philadelphia Inquirer" in 1943; (below) Ernie Pyle, the war's most popular correspondent, rests with a Marine patrol while covering the Pacific campaign

Defense Dept. Photo

**Loose Talk can cost Lives !**

## Keep it under your STETSON

John B. Stetson Company

**Could you tell him you're tired of buying WAR BONDS?**

General Tire and Rubber Company

To pay for the war, the direct cost of which was about 330 billion dollars, both taxation and bonding were used. While taxes were both raised and broadened, bonds were the preferred source of revenue for they served other purposes: they held down inflation by absorbing excess income and they spread the war costs over a wide period of time. Employing the facilities of advertising and Hollywood, the bond drives were all oversubscribed.

(Top) Two national advertisements designed to stimulate popular support for the war effort; (center) Cabinet member Harold Ickes places sticker on his car window indicating support of gasoline rationing; (bottom) New Yorkers line up for sugar rationing cards in 1942

UPI — Compix

Wide World

(Above) Craftsmen pass security check at war-plane factory; (below) shipment of military tanks

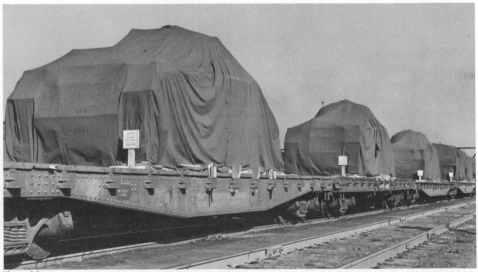

Douglas Aircraft and other defense plants employed women to fill manpower shortages

(Above) Ship sliding off the shipways into the harbor at Baltimore, Md., 1943; (below) view of the Baltimore shipyards; both photographs by Siegel

(Right) Gary Cooper joins other celebrities in a war bond rally in Los Angeles; (center left) popular bandleader Glenn Miller and his Air Force band; (center right) recruiting poster on a parade float; (bottom) farmers attending a "Food for Victory" meeting in North Dakota

Wide World

Wide World

Uncle Sam needs You! JOIN THE WAAC

Burkhart from Black Star

Library of Congress

# HOW TO SHOP WITH WAR RATION BOOK TWO
## ... to Buy Canned, Bottled and Frozen Fruits and Vegetables; Dried Fruits, Juices and all Canned Soups

(Right) Poster distributed by the Office of Price Administration explaining the new point rationing system introduced in 1943; (center left) cartoon by Lewis in the "Milwaukee Journal" reflecting new rationing, 1942; (center right) children working in victory gardens; (bottom) scrap pile in Tulare, Calif., 1942

**1. USE THIS RATION BOOK.** You may use one or all of your family's ration books when you shop. You may not shop with loose ration stamps.

**2. USE BLUE STAMPS ONLY.** All blue point stamps marked A, B, and C are good during the first ration period. They add up to 48 points for each member of the family.

**3. THE NUMBERS SHOW POINTS.** You will not be able to get "change" in point stamps, so save your low-value stamps for buying low-point foods.

**4. LOOK AT THE POINT VALUES** before you buy. Points have nothing to do with prices or quality. Point values will be the same in all stores.

**5. GIVE THE STAMPS TO YOUR GROCER.** Tear out stamps in the presence of your grocer — or tear them out in the presence of the delivery boy.

**6. FRESH FRUITS AND VEGETABLES** are not rationed. Use them instead of rationed foods whenever possible. Try out recipes that make your rations go further.

## YOUR POINT ALLOWANCE MUST LAST FOR THE FULL RATION PERIOD
### Plan How Many Points You Will Use Each Time Before You Shop

**BUY EARLY IN THE WEEK** — Foods are going to our fighting men. They come first! Your ration gives you your fair share of the foods that are left. — **BUY EARLY IN THE DAY**

Wide World

*'The Shape of Things to Come?'*
Courtesy, Ross Lewis and the "Milwaukee Journal"

Library of Congress

Victor De Palma from Black Star

(Above) Funeral cortege for Franklin Roosevelt passing in front of the White House; (below) crowds line Constitution Avenue as the flag-draped coffin passes on a horse-drawn caisson

60.

# Frank Lloyd Wright: Architecture of Democracy

*Frank Lloyd Wright's conception of architecture as the creation of structures that harmonize with their natural setting guided much of his work. "Organic Architecture," as he called it, "knows that all architectural values are true human values. . . . Architecture may again be the true shield for whatever aspiration, glory, or privacy humanity desires or most needs." The following selection, taken from a book published by Wright in 1945, attempts to define the architecture of a democracy.*

Source: *When Democracy Builds*, Chicago, 1945, pp. 48-53, 58-65.

Call Organic Architecture the architecture of and for the Individual, as distinguished from the pseudo-classic order of the schools which was only derived from survivals of the military and monarchic order. Or that later attempt at elimination and reclassification grafted upon it and called the 'International style." Or, as distinguished from any preconceived, pertinent, or impertinent formula for mere appearances whatsoever. Organic Architecture is architecture in the reflex: Architecture that seeks to serve Man rather than those forces that try to rule over him. That is another reason why we can say Organic Architecture is the Architecture of Democracy.

In any concept of Organic Architecture, Style is the expression of Character; there is no longer any question of "styles." Essential style is in all and of all building provided only that it be naturally achieved from within the nature of the building problem and be in the very means by which the building is built. Character is only the expression of principle at work from within. It is in this interior sense only that the Free City will have Style. But it will have great Style all the while as something Natural not something exterior forced either in its structure or its people by any of the old exterior disciplines whatever or ruled by any academic attempt at reclassification and establishment according to the classic externals of the antique. Architecture and acreage will again be seen together as Landscape, as has the best of the architecture of the world been seen: that is to say, the great architectures formed within the lifetime of the civilizations which they actually did express.

If as a people we understood the eternal principles of our own human nature and were to use our current industrial means — machines and vast stores of new materials — to good advantage, use them according to a faithful sense of their fitness to purpose, we should universally arrive at forms and a Life that had true Style. And perhaps (though we need not bother much about that) arrive at what, looked back upon in distance of time, might be the twentieth-century Usonian Style. But if that should come to pass, it would not be by calculated intention but by honest production and long-continued honest experiment. Style is a desirable circumstance but a style is, always, a danger.

Perhaps because it is chiefly concerned with integrity of structure, Organic Architecture first grasps the integrity of this modern demand of modern life for a new and higher Spiritual Order of all things and living persons. Perhaps only the Mind imbued with a deep sense of structure can perceive this fine Integrity as a fundamental necessity demanding and creating the more livable and gracious human simplicities. These Simples were never necessary to such substitutes-for-culture as bear the authorized hallmark of these United States. . . .

For us today, Organic Architecture does reinterpret and can construct an eternal Idea of human Freedom. So, today, Architecture naturally seeks the spaciousness, openness, lightness, and strength that is so completely logical that it is bound to scatter this servile imitation that disgraces us, takes all urban stricture and depravity first into the regional field and then — as all inadvertent disease is absorbed — absorb superfluous urbanism into the circulation of the healthy body politic that is bound to be the whole country properly circumstanced and integrated as one great Free City of Cities: Usonia. . . .

All individual Free City features naturally harmonize with those of immediate nature environment. Therefore no two districts could ever be precisely alike except as the New City might spread to some featureless plain which, too, has a certain natural beauty of its own and might well bear repetition of appropriate patterns of tillage and forestation. Broadacres would be so built in sympathy with Nature that a deep feeling for the beauty of the terrain would be a fundamental qualification in the new city-builders. They would be seeking for beauty of feature in the landscape not to build *upon* that beauty so much as to build *with* it. Endless unity-in-variety thus becomes inevitable. Indigenous character is as inevitable. Both endless variety and indigenous character would be the inevitable effect of Terrain and Individuality together, and a naturally varied topography would naturally

vary all forms of Organic Architecture wherever they might naturally arise. . . .

It is the Good Ground that should determine the fundamental shape, even the style, of every building, road, or institution in the Free City. To see where the ground leaves off and building begins would require careful attention. With this proper "ground motive" established in practice, variety in unity would be infinite. The ideal of Organic unity thus held firmly in mind, the Architect would himself gradually become more equal to vast opportunities. . . .

Imagine, now, spacious landscaped highways, grade crossings eliminated by a new kind of integrated "bypassing," over- or underpassing all cultivated or living areas: all these great highways devoid of the ugly scaffolding of telegraph and telephone poles and wires, free of glaring billboards and especially free from ugly fencing; ditching and hedging now taking its place. Imagine these great highways of generous safe width and always easy grade, bright with wayside flowers or cool with shade trees, joined at intervals with modern aer-rotor fields from which self-contained mechanical units — safe, noiseless transport planes, radio controlled, carrying neither engines nor fuel — take off from convenient stations and land anywhere. Giant roads, themselves great architecture, pass public service stations now no longer eyesores but expanded as good architecture to include all kinds of roadside service for the traveler, with charm and comfort throughout.

These great roads unite and separate — separate and unite in endless series of diversified units passing by farm units; roadside markets, garden schools, dwelling places each on its acres of individually adorned and cultivated ground and developed homes, all places for pleasure in work or leisure. And imagine these man units so arranged and integrated each to the other that every citizen may have as he chooses all forms of production, distribution, self-improvement, enjoyment, within the radius of say, ten to twenty miles of his own home, speedily available by means of his private car or plane or public conveyance. This integrated harmonious distribution of Living related to Ground composes this great City that I see embracing all this country. This would be the Broadacre City of Tomorrow that is the Nation: Democracy realized?

Then, when every man, woman, and child may put foot on their own acre and every unborn child finds his acre waiting for him when he is born, then does an Organic Architecture become the greatest servant of Man. Great architects will then create appropriate beauty in buildings, not only in harmony with greenery and the ground but intimate with the pattern of the personal life of the individual owner of the ground. No two homes, no two gardens, none of the one- to three- to ten-acre, or more acres, farm units, no two farmsteads or factory buildings or markets need be alike nor any of them be ugly. And, because absurd "styles" were no longer fashionable, Style would flourish everywhere: be Indigenous — Integral.

Light, strong appropriate houses and the spacious convenient workplaces to which all would be tributary, each item would be solidly and sympathetically built out of materials native to the Time, the Place, and the Man. All building construction would be so designed as to take full advantage of the Nature of the Ground. Farmers and factory workers in the New City, then, work in environment no less harmonious than they live in in their homes. All live within walking distance of work or pleasures and live a short ride, in Time, away from the now interesting, attractive factories, smokeless of course and noiseless of course. No longer will the farmer envy the urban dweller his mechanical improvements while the latter in turn covets the farmer's green pastures.

Each factory unit, farm, or dwelling will normally be within a ten-mile radius, say, of vast, variegated wayside fresh-food and manufacturers' markets so that each unit can serve the other units simply and effectively all together serving directly the population living and working in its particular neighborhood. No longer any need exists for futile racing to and from a common center, tired out but racing back and forth again. No more stalling of Time and crucifying of Life just to keep things congested and "big" for the pacing of some moneymaker's patent Moneymaking System.

Without fresh air, fresh food, sunlight, good, green land underfoot, and appropriate spaciousness everywhere, human life cannot further develop. No, nor even go on living! Recognizing these facts as we all are beginning to do except the Banker and the University, Usonian home life will not eliminate the gadgetry of modern comforts. Yet, it will all come back and keep to the ageless health-giving comforts due to ground. Modern steel, glass, and the plastic will be sensibly called upon to rationally fulfill their natural uses, steel for strength, durability, and lightness; translucent glass inclosing interior space to give privacy and yet make of living in any Usonian house a delightful association with sun, sky, surrounding gardens, and the neighbors. The Home an outdoor garden; the Garden an outdoor house.

Tall buildings would seldom be barred. But leaving forever all interior walled courts, they would be impelled to stand free of neighbors in small green parks or in the countryside in natural parks where desirable. "Cooperative" apartment houses might be erected for immured but untrained urbanites desiring the beauty of the country but unable yet to use it. Apartment houses, say, eighteen stories tall, tier on tier of glass screen-walls golden with sun on the shining steel of copper-sheathed frames, each tier with its flower and vine-festooned balcony terraces. The tall building would stand in iridescence of vivid color in the landscape, set up in spacious blossoming grounds in the midst of a neighborhood of varied activities all similarly independent — each, *presentable to all!* . . .

Everywhere I see the warm upsurging Love-of-Life that should be our heritage in a country truly Free. Great woods, fields, streams, mountains, ranges of hills, the windblown sweep of plains, all brought into the service of Man without doing violence to them, Man reconciled to their service, proud of preserving their Beauty. Citizens now, who understand, revere, and conserve all natural resources whether of Materials or Men. This — to me — is Organic Architecture! Architecture the cultivator of acreage, the lover of man and wife and their children, the conservator of flocks and herds no less. Organic Architecture looks and sees these all together as Usonian Landscape.

---

## 61.

# The Yalta Agreement

*The scene of the famous Yalta Conference of February 4-11, 1945, was the summer palace of Czar Nicholas II on the Black Sea coast of the ravaged Crimea, only recently liberated from the Nazis. The last meeting of the "Big Three" Allied leaders — Roosevelt, Churchill, and Stalin — opened as victory in Europe was imminent. Roosevelt had been advised by the Joint Chiefs of Staff that Japan was capable of continued resistance and that Russian participation in the Pacific war would save a million American casualties. The major questions to be resolved were, besides Russian aid in the war against Japan, the partition of Germany, the future of the liberated nations of Eastern Europe, and the establishment of an international organization to keep the peace. The most heated discussion revolved around the future of Poland, by then almost wholly occupied by the Red Army, but the question uppermost in Roosevelt's mind was probably the creation of a peace-keeping organization. Both Roosevelt and Churchill came to the conference firmly convinced that Russian cooperation was essential, not only for ending the war quickly but also for the future success of the United Nations. The Yalta Agreement was signed on February 11.*

Source: PRFA, Department of State Publication 6199: "The Conferences at Malta and Yalta 1945."

---

THE CRIMEA CONFERENCE of the heads of the governments of the United States of America, the United Kingdom, and the Union of Soviet Socialist Republics which took place from February 4 to 11 came to the following conclusions.

I. WORLD ORGANIZATION

It was decided:
1. That a United Nations Conference on the proposed world organization should be summoned for Wednesday, 25 April, 1945, and should be held in the United States of America.

2. The nations to be invited to this conference should be:

(*a*) the United Nations as they existed on the 8 February, 1945, and

(*b*) such of the Associated Nations as have declared war on the common enemy by 1 March, 1945. (For this purpose by the term "Associated Nation" was meant the eight Associated Nations and Turkey.) When the Conference on World Organization is held, the delegates of the United

Kingdom and United States of America will support a proposal to admit to original membership two Soviet Socialist republics, *i.e.*, the Ukraine and White Russia.

3. That the United States government on behalf of the Three Powers should consult the government of China and the French Provisional Government in regard to the decisions taken at the present conference concerning the proposed world organization.

4. That the text of the invitation to be issued to all the nations which would take part in the United Nations Conference should be as follows:

### Invitation

The government of the United States of America, on behalf of itself and of the governments of the United Kingdom, the Union of Soviet Socialist Republics, and the Republic of China and of the Provisional Government of the French Republic, invite the government of ——— to send representatives to a Conference of the United Nations to be held on 25 April, 1945, or soon thereafter, at San Francisco in the United States of America to prepare a charter for a general international organization for the maintenance of international peace and security.

The above-named governments suggest that the conference consider as affording a basis for such a charter the proposals for the establishment of a general international organization which were made public last October as a result of the Dumbarton Oaks Conference, and which have now been supplemented by the following provisions for Section C of Chapter VI:

### C. Voting

1. Each member of the Security Council should have one vote.
2. Decisions of the Security Council on procedural matters should be made by an affirmative vote of seven members.

3. Decisions of the Security Council on all other matters should be made by an affirmative vote of seven members, including the concurring votes of the permanent members; provided that, in decisions under Chapter VIII, Section A, and under the second sentence of paragraph 1 of Chapter VIII, Section C, a party to a dispute should abstain from voting.

Further information as to arrangements will be transmitted subsequently.

In the event that the government of ——— desires in advance of the conference to present views or comments concerning the proposals, the government of the United States of America will be pleased to transmit such views and comments to the other participating governments.

### Territorial Trusteeship

It was agreed that the five nations which will have permanent seats on the Security Council should consult each other prior to the United Nations Conference on the question of territorial trusteeship.

The acceptance of this recommendation is subject to its being made clear that territorial trusteeship will only apply to (*a*) existing mandates of the League of Nations; (*b*) territories detached from the enemy as a result of the present war; (*c*) any other territory which might voluntarily be placed under trusteeship; and (*d*) no discussion of actual territories is contemplated at the forthcoming United Nations Conference or in the preliminary consultations, and it will be a matter for subsequent agreement which territories within the above categories will be placed under trusteeship.

### II. DECLARATION ON LIBERATED EUROPE

The following declaration has been approved:

The Premier of the Union of Soviet Socialist Republics, the Prime Minister of the

United Press International

Working session at the conference of the "Big Three" in Yalta. Joseph Stalin and the
Russian delegation, upper left; President Roosevelt with George Marshall, Admiral
Leahy and other members of the United States delegation, right; Winston Churchill
and the British delegates, left foreground with backs to camera

United Kingdom, and the President of the
United States of America have consulted
with each other in the common interests of
the peoples of their countries and those of
liberated Europe. They jointly declare their
mutual agreement to concert during the
temporary period of instability in liberated
Europe the policies of their three governments in assisting the peoples liberated from
the domination of Nazi Germany and the
peoples of the former Axis satellite states of
Europe to solve by democratic means their
pressing political and economic problems.

The establishment of order in Europe and
the rebuilding of national economic life
must be achieved by processes which will
enable the liberated peoples to destroy the
last vestiges of Nazism and Fascism and to
create democratic institutions of their own
choice. This is a principle of the Atlantic
Charter — the right of all peoples to

choose the form of government under
which they will live — the restoration of
sovereign rights and self-government to
those peoples who have been forcibly deprived of them by the aggressor nations.

To foster the conditions in which the liberated peoples may exercise these rights, the
three governments will jointly assist the
people in any European liberated state or
former Axis satellite state in Europe where
in their judgment conditions require (a) to
establish conditions of internal peace; (b) to
carry out emergency measures for the relief
of distressed peoples; (c) to form interim
governmental authorities broadly representative of all democratic elements in the population and pledged to the earliest possible
establishment through free elections of governments responsive to the will of the
people; and (d) to facilitate where necessary
the holding of such elections.

The three governments will consult the other United Nations and provisional authorities or other governments in Europe when matters of direct interest to them are under consideration.

When, in the opinion of the three governments, conditions in any European liberated state or any former Axis satellite state in Europe make such action necessary, they will immediately consult together on the measures necessary to discharge the joint responsibilities set forth in this declaration.

By this declaration we reaffirm our faith in the principles of the Atlantic Charter, our pledge in the Declaration by the United Nations, and our determination to build in cooperation with other peace-loving nations world order under law, dedicated to peace, security, freedom, and general well-being of all mankind.

In issuing this declaration, the Three Powers express the hope that the Provisional Government of the French Republic may be associated with them in the procedure suggested.

## III. DISMEMBERMENT OF GERMANY

It was agreed that Article 12 (a) of the Surrender Terms for Germany should be amended to read as follows:

> The United Kingdom, the United States of America, and the Union of Soviet Socialist Republics shall possess supreme authority with respect to Germany. In the exercise of such authority they will take such steps, including the complete disarmament, demilitarization, and the dismemberment of Germany as they deem requisite for future peace and security.

The study of the procedure for the dismemberment of Germany was referred to a committee consisting of Mr. Eden (chairman), Mr. Winant, and Mr. Gousev. This body would consider the desirability of associating with it a French representative.

## IV. ZONE OF OCCUPATION FOR THE FRENCH AND CONTROL COUNCIL FOR GERMANY

It was agreed that a zone in Germany, to be occupied by the French forces, should be allocated to France. This zone would be formed out of the British and American zones and its extent would be settled by the British and Americans in consultation with the French Provisional Government.

It was also agreed that the French Provisional Government should be invited to become a member of the Allied Control Council for Germany.

## V. REPARATION

The following protocol has been approved:

1. Germany must pay in kind for the losses caused by her to the Allied Nations in the course of the war. Reparations are to be received in the first instance by those countries which have borne the main burden of the war, have suffered the heaviest losses, and have organized victory over the enemy.

2. Reparation in kind is to be exacted from Germany in three following forms:

(a) Removals within two years from the surrender of Germany or the cessation of organized resistance from the national wealth of Germany located on the territory of Germany herself, as well as outside her territory (equipment, machine tools, ships, rolling stock, German investments abroad, shares of industrial, transport, and other enterprises in Germany, etc.), these removals to be carried out chiefly for purpose of destroying the war potential of Germany.

(b) Annual deliveries of goods from current production for a period to be fixed.

(c) Use of German labor.

3. For the working out on the above principles of a detailed plan for exaction of reparation from Germany, an Allied Reparation Commission will be set up in Mos-

cow. It will consist of three representatives
— one from the Union of Soviet Socialist
Republics, one from the United Kingdom,
and one from the United States of America.

4. With regard to the fixing of the total
sum of the reparation as well as the distribution of it among the countries which suffered from the German aggression, the Soviet and American delegations agreed as follows:

> The Moscow Reparation Commission
> should take in its initial studies as a basis
> for discussion the suggestion of the Sovi-
> et government that the total sum of the
> reparation in accordance with the points
> (a) and (b) of the paragraph 2 should be
> $20 billion and that 50 percent of it
> should go to the Union of Soviet Social-
> ist Republics.

The British delegation was of the opinion
that pending consideration of the reparation
question by the Moscow Reparation Commission no figures of reparation should be
mentioned.

The above Soviet-American proposal has
been passed to the Moscow Reparation
Commission as one of the proposals to be
considered by the Commission.

## VI. MAJOR WAR CRIMINALS

The Conference agreed that the question
of the major war criminals should be the
subject of inquiry by the three foreign secretaries for report in due course after the
close of the conference.

## VII. POLAND

The following Declaration on Poland was
agreed by the conference:

A new situation has been created in Poland as a result of her complete liberation
by the Red Army. This calls for the establishment of a Polish Provisional Government which can be more broadly based
than was possible before the recent libera-

tion of the western part of Poland. The
Provisional Government which is now functioning in Poland should therefore be reorganized on a broader democratic basis with
the inclusion of democratic leaders from
Poland itself and from Poles abroad. This
new government should then be called the
Polish Provisional Government of National
Unity.

M. Molotov, Mr. Harriman, and Sir A.
Clark Kerr are authorized as a commission
to consult in the first instance in Moscow
with members of the present Provisional
Government and with other Polish democratic leaders from within Poland and from
abroad, with a view to the reorganization of
the present government along the above
lines. This Polish Provisional Government
of National Unity shall be pledged to the
holding of free and unfettered elections as
soon as possible on the basis of universal
suffrage and secret ballot. In these elections
all democratic and anti-Nazi parties shall
have the right to take part and to put forward candidates.

When a Polish Provisional Government
of National Unity has been properly formed
in conformity with the above, the government of the U.S.S.R., which now maintain
diplomatic relations with the present Provisional Government of Poland, and the gov
ernment of the United Kingdom and the
government of the U.S.A. will establish
diplomatic relations with the new Polish
Provisional Government of National Unity
and will exchange ambassadors by whose
reports the respective governments will b
kept informed about the situation in Po
land.

The three heads of government conside
that the eastern frontier of Poland shoul
follow the Curzon Line, with digression
from it in some regions of five to eight k
lometers in favor of Poland. They recogniz
that Poland must receive substantial acce
sions of territory in the north and wes
They feel that the opinion of the new Po
ish Provisional Government of Nation

Unity should be sought in due course on the extent of these accessions and that the final delimitation of the western frontier of Poland should thereafter await the Peace Conference.

## VIII. YUGOSLAVIA

It was agreed to recommend to Marshal Tito and to Dr. Subasic:

1. That the Tito-Subasic Agreement should immediately be put into effect and a new government formed on the basis of the agreement.

2. That as soon as the new government has been formed it should declare:

(a) that the Anti-Fascist Assembly of National Liberation (AUNOJ) will be extended to include members of the last Yugoslav Skupstina who have not compromised themselves by collaboration with the enemy, thus forming a body to be known as a temporary parliament and

(b) that legislative acts passed by the Anti-Fascist Assembly of National Liberation (AUNOJ) will be subject to subsequent ratification by a constituent assembly. And that this statement should be published in the communique of the conference.

## IX. ITALO-YUGOSLAV FRONTIER; ITALO-AUSTRIA FRONTIER

Notes on these subjects were put in by the British delegation and the American and Soviet delegations agreed to consider them and give their views later.

## X. YUGOSLAV-BULGARIAN RELATIONS

There was an exchange of views between the foreign secretaries on the question of the desirability of a Yugoslav-Bulgarian pact of alliance. The question at issue was whether a state still under an armistice regime could be allowed to enter into a treaty with another state. Mr. Eden suggested that the Bulgarian and Yugoslav governments

should be informed that this could not be approved. Mr. Stettinius suggested that the British and American ambassadors should discuss the matter further with M. Molotov in Moscow. M. Molotov agreed with the proposal of Mr. Stettinius.

## XI. SOUTHEASTERN EUROPE

The British delegation put in notes for the consideration of their colleagues on the following subjects:

(a) the Control Commission in Bulgaria

(b) Greek claims upon Bulgaria, more particularly with reference to reparations.

(c) Oil equipment in Rumania.

## XII. IRAN

Mr. Eden, Mr. Stettinius, and M. Molotov exchanged views on the situation in Iran. It was agreed that this matter should be pursued through the diplomatic channel.

## XIII. MEETINGS OF THE THREE FOREIGN SECRETARIES

The conference agreed that the permanent machinery should be set up for consultation between the three foreign secretaries; they should meet as often as necessary, probably about every three or four months. These meetings will be held in rotation in the three capitals, the first meeting being held in London.

## XIV. THE MONTREUX CONVENTION AND THE STRAITS

It was agreed that at the next meeting of the three foreign secretaries to be held in London they should consider proposals which it was understood the Soviet government would put forward in relation to the Montreux Convention and report to their governments. The Turkish government should be informed at the appropriate moment.

62.

# The Act of Chapultepec

*Latin-American countries on the whole reciprocated the Good Neighbor policy of President Roosevelt by supporting the United States during World War II. Only Argentina and, to a lesser extent, Chile withheld full aid, mostly because of the presence of large numbers of Axis sympathizers in these countries. Cooperation in the war effort reached a peak at the Inter-American Conference in Mexico City in February and March 1945. The conference reaffirmed the unity of the American nations and reached broad agreements on social and economic problems. The most important outcome of the conference was the Act of Chapultepec, adopted on March 3, which established the first multilateral collective security system in the Western Hemisphere. The main provisions of the Act are reprinted below.*

Source: *Record,* 79 Cong., 1 Sess., pp. 2021-2022.

## PART I

THE GOVERNMENTS represented at the Inter-American Conference on War and Peace declare:

1. That all sovereign states are juridically equal amongst themselves.

2. That every state has the right to the respect of its individuality and independence on the part of the other members of the international community.

3. That every attack of a state against the integrity or the inviolability of the territory, or against the sovereignty or political independence of an American state, shall, conformably to Part III hereof, be considered as an act of aggression against the other states which sign this act. In any case, invasion by armed forces of one state into the territory of another, trespassing boundaries established by treaty and demarcated in accordance therewith, shall constitute an act of aggression.

4. That in case acts of aggression occur or there may be reasons to believe that an aggression is being prepared by any other state against the integrity and inviolability of the territory, or against the sovereignty or political independence of an American state, the states signatory to this act will consult amongst themselves in order to agree upon the measures it may be advisable to take.

5. That during the war, and until the treaty recommended in Part II hereof is concluded, the signatories of this act recognize that such threats and acts of aggression, as indicated in paragraphs 3 and 4 above, constitute an interference with the war effort of the United Nations, calling for such procedures, within the scope of their constitutional powers of a general nature and for war, as may be found necessary, including recall of chiefs of diplomatic missions; breaking of diplomatic relations; breaking of consular relations; breaking of postal, telegraphic, telephonic, radiotelephonic relations; interruption of economic, commercial

and financial relations; use of armed force to prevent or repel aggression.

6. That the principles and procedure contained in this declaration shall become effective immediately, inasmuch as any act of aggression or threat of aggression during the present state of war interferes with the war effort of the United Nations to obtain victory. Henceforth, and to the end that the principles and procedures herein stipulated shall conform with the constitutional processes of each republic, the respective governments shall take the necessary steps to perfect this instrument in order that it shall be in force at all times.

## PART II

THE INTER-AMERICAN Conference on Problems of War and Peace recommends that, for the purpose of meeting threats or acts of aggression against any American republic following the establishment of peace, the governments of the American republics should consider the conclusion, in accordance with their constitutional processes, of a treaty establishing procedures whereby such threats or acts may be met by the use, by all or some of the signatories of said treaty of any one or more of the following measures: Recall of chiefs of diplomatic missions; breaking of diplomatic relations; breaking of consular relations; breaking of postal, telegraphic, telephonic, radiotelephonic relations; interruption of economic, commercial, and financial relations; use of armed force to prevent or repel aggression.

## PART III

THE ABOVE DECLARATION and recommendation constitute a regional arrangement for dealing with such matters relating to the maintenance of international peace and security as are appropriate for regional action in this hemisphere. The said arrangement, and the pertinent activities and procedures, shall be consistent with the purposes and principles of the general international organization, when established.

This agreement shall be known as the Act of Chapultepec.

———◆———

REBECCA: *I never told you about that letter Jane Crofut got from her minister when she was sick. The minister of her church in the town she was in before she came here. He wrote Jane a letter and on the envelope the address was like this: It said: Jane Crofut, The Crofut Farm; Grover's Corners; Sutton County; New Hampshire; United States of America.*
GEORGE: *What's funny about that?*
REBECCA: *But listen, it's not finished: the United States of America; Continent of North America; Western Hemisphere; the Earth; the Solar System; the universe; the Mind of God — that's what it said on the envelope.*
GEORGE: *What do you know!*
REBECCA: *And the postman brought it just the same.*
GEORGE: *What do you know!*

THORNTON WILDER, *Our Town*

63.

# Luis Muñoz-Marín: The Future of Puerto Rico

*Puerto Rico was one of the fruits of the American victory in the Spanish-American War.*
*By the Treaty of Paris (1898) the island was ceded by Spain to the United States, and*
*by the Jones Act (1917) its people became U.S. citizens. Puerto Rico was hit hard by*
*the Depression of the 1930s, and the migration to the States — mainly to New York*
*and other large cities — began then; but the really significant numbers of Puerto Ricans*
*arrived in the 1940s and '50s (during the latter decade at the rate of about 50,000 a year)*
*living, as had so many immigrants before them, in enclaves or ghettos that were social*
*and economic problems. All was not problems, however; for life on the shining little*
*Caribbean island, even for the very poor, was better than in many other South and*
*Central American countries, and the United States could point with pride to its colonial*
*policies after 1917. Such success as Puerto Rico achieved in the postwar period*
*was largely owing to one of the great democrats of the Western Hemisphere, Luis*
*Muñoz-Marín, who served Puerto Rico as its governor from 1949 to 1964. Governor*
*Muñoz, then president of the Puerto Rican Senate, broadcast the following speech over*
*the CBS network on May 26, 1945.*

Source: VSD, August 1, 1945.

THE FUTURE PEACE of the world depends to an important degree on the solution or solutions that may be found to the colonial problem. It also depends, to a still greater degree, on the prestige of the United States among the peoples of the world — on the confidence that the common man everywhere shall continue to have in the human understanding and the democratic sincerity of the American people.

It is of the utmost importance to democracy that the United States shall not cease to be the champion of democratic rights in the minds of men and women everywhere. It is clear that our great ally Russia is making a bid for the confidence and that trust which have been the traditional heritage of the United States. Of course, Russia's attitude in this respect should not be unwel-come. There is no such thing as too much goodwill, as too much recognition of rights and liberties. The world certainly needs as much of that as it can get from all possible sources. But certainly Russia's attitude should not be allowed to displace and substitute the traditional American attitude, but only to complement it and support it. Russia's developing international liberalism would appear best in its proper place, that is, as a follower of the tradition that the United States has made its own these many years.

In the treatment of colonies and of otherwise dependent peoples, the United States has an eminent field for sustaining, strengthening, and developing its policy for a good, for a confidence-inspiring, for a lasting peace under the principles that have

Don Luis Muñoz-Marín photographed in 1948 with his two daughters shortly before assuming the office of first native governor of Puerto Rico.

reared the national greatness of the American people.

I am proud to say that in this respect my own country, Puerto Rico, which has contributed without stint to the war effort, is now making what is perhaps a still more important contribution to the peace effort. Puerto Rico is a Caribbean island country of 2 million people which came under the jurisdiction of the United States as a result of the Spanish-American War almost half a century ago. Puerto Rico is a colony of the United States. It is a colony, it is true, that has been administered in a mild, though not always intelligible, way, by the United States government. But it is a colony. It is what each of the original thirteen states were before 1776; basically its government does not derive its powers from the consent of the governed. That is, by the time-honored definition written by Jefferson, what colonialism means to the American mind; and by that definition, Puerto Rico is a colony of the United States.

Puerto Rico is also a very poor country in its economic geography. It has but 3,500 square miles of territory. Half of its land is not arable, much of the rest is not of very good quality; there is not much mineral wealth under that land, and 2 million people, that is 560 persons per square mile, must make their living from the top of that land. In order for so many people to subsist on such a scarcity of resources, the bulk of production must be of intensive cash crops that can be sold in extensive markets at reasonably good prices.

It is this same people of Puerto Rico, to whom nature has been so harsh, who have reached their political maturity, according to a message of the late President Roosevelt to the Congress. They have given proof of this maturity. Eighty-five percent of the registered voters vote on the basis of universal adult suffrage. Although political passions frequently run high, elections are absolutely peaceful and orderly. Defeated candidates recognize their defeat and the fairness of the electoral process. The buying of votes has been unheard of for quite some time. The people vote on the clear understanding that they are giving a mandate for certain laws to be enacted and certain policies to be carried out insofar as their elected legislators have the legal authority to do so, and they are vigilant as to whether their clear-cut democratic mandates are carried out or not. The Puerto Rican people, in fact, are more than just a politically mature people. I sincerely and proudly believe that in their hinterland of the world they constitute the best rural school of democracy in America today, and that there is profit in looking to its poverty-stricken electorate as an example of sound democratic practice.

It is these people, so politically sound and so economically harassed, that are now contributing to the peace effort, as they are contributing to the war effort. They are now proposing to the Congress and the government of the United States a plan for self-determination. This plan may well serve as a basis for dealing with the colonial problem in many other parts of the world as well as in Puerto Rico. It should also help the United States in clarifying, maintaining, strengthening, and developing that leadership of hard-pressed mankind everywhere which is of such decisive importance to world justice and world peace.

The legislature of Puerto Rico has unanimously proposed to the Congress of the United States a clear-cut, straightforward method of solving the colonial problem, on the basis of self-determination, in democratic terms, and in the fiber of American policy and tradition. The Puerto Rican proposal is as follows:

At the request, the unanimous request, of the legislature of Puerto Rico, all political parties concurring, a bill has been introduced in the Senate by United States Senator Millard E. Tydings, of Maryland, and in the United States House of Representatives by Resident Commissioner Pinero, of Puerto Rico. This bill contains four titles and offers three alternative forms of government to the people of Puerto Rico. Title 1 provides that there shall be a referendum in which the people of Puerto Rico shall decide whether they want independence under

certain economic conditions necessary for their survival, or statehood, or dominion status similar to that of Australia or Canada in the British Commonwealth of Nations. Title 2 describes independence. Title 3 describes statehood. Title 4 describes dominion status. If a majority of the people of Puerto Rico vote for independence, then Title 2 shall go into effect. If they vote for statehood, then Title 3 shall go into effect. If they vote for dominion status, then Title 4 shall go into effect. In this manner, if the bill is approved, the people of Puerto Rico themselves will choose their own future, on the basis of an offer by the American Congress, and in choosing it they will have before them the fullest possible picture of what they are voting about.

It is worthy of note that the proposal provides that the United States shall have in perpetuity all the military and naval bases and rights that they may need in Puerto Rico for the defense of the United States and the Western Hemisphere. This is of very great importance, as Puerto Rico constitutes one of the chief military protections of the Panama Canal and has been called by military authorities "the Gibraltar of the Caribbean." Parallel with these perpetual rights of the United States, under any form of government that the people of Puerto Rico may choose, certain minimum economic conditions are established, also under any form of government that the people of Puerto Rico may choose. These minimum economic conditions are considered necessary if the people are to survive in the face of the difficult economic circumstances that confront them.

I should call attention to the fact that these minimum economic conditions do not represent any increase in economic facilities. Therefore the granting of them would not in any way increase the commitments of the United States, but would rather decrease them. What is, therefore, proposed is to wipe out political discontent without intol erably increasing economic suffering and discontent. This is of importance, not only as a matter of justice and of American leadership in democracy but also as a means of surrounding important military defenses with the greatest possible democratic goodwill.

Let us look at what the colonial problem means in broad terms. Obviously, the United States will have need of military and naval establishments in many parts of the world. But just as obviously these establishments are a second line of defense. The need for military establishments is predicated upon the sensible provision that all goodwill means of keeping the peace may fail. The first line of defense is the maintenance of peace, the creation of conditions that, so far as human understanding and good sense can make it so, will tend to keep the world at peace with itself. For that reason, the need for military establishments — the second line of defense — should not contradict the need for democratic procedure in the maintenance of world confidence in American leadership. Neither, of course, should the need to maintain this leadership weaken in any way America's maximum ability to defend itself if peace should fail. The Puerto Rican proposal is made in the clear recognition of these two paramount factors.

Military and naval establishments may be needed in two broadly different kinds of places. They may be needed in small places scantily populated, and they may be needed, as they are in Puerto Rico, for instance, among large populations with a developed civilization, with a recognized political ma-

turity, and an acute consciousness that the principles of freedom are applicable to them also. The United States is making this distinction clear at the San Francisco Conference. Military and naval bases and establishments, of course, must be where strategy says they must be, whether on small rocks of the sea where the problems of the population are at a minimum or in developed communities where the problems of the people are of great significance and importance with relation to the general democratic principles and policies at stake.

In offering its proposal for self-determination, Puerto Rico is bearing in mind these considerations. The United States, at San Francisco, are standing for self-government to colonies, which may include independence. The Puerto Rican proposal is a specific proposal for self-government on the basis of an alternative offer by Congress of different forms of self-government, which may include independence, and an acceptance by the people of Puerto Rico, in referendum, of one of the forms of self-government offered by Congress.

The proposal that the legislature of Puerto Rico has unanimously presented to the Congress of the United States is a self-determination proposal as embodied in Senate Bill 1002 and in House Bill 3237. We make this proposal both as a claim of justice for Puerto Rico and as a contribution to American leadership — a leadership so completely necessary for the prevention of future wars — in the minds and hearts of average men and women the world over. For both reasons we hope to receive for our proposal the support of the American people.

---

*The Italian navigator has landed; the natives are friendly.*

ANON., code message, telegraphed to scientists on Dec. 2, 1942, to indicate that the first self-sustaining nuclear chain reaction had been made to work by Enrico Fermi and a group of researchers at the University of Chicago

64.

# Second Thoughts About Atomic Power

*Even before the United States entered World War II, a number of physicists, aware of German advances in nuclear research, had taken an active role in persuading the American government to develop an atomic bomb. In June 1945 the climate had changed: Germany was defeated, and much more was known about the destructive power of atomic energy. As a result, many of the same physicists who had earlier urged government research in the nuclear field began to reconsider their views. A bomb had been assembled at Los Alamos, New Mexico, and the government was preparing for its first test of the weapon, which took place on July 16. Secretary of War Stimson had appointed a group of physicists, including Glenn Seaborg and Leo Szilard, to explore the uses of the new source of power, and in June the group issued the following report.*

Source: *The Atomic Age*, Morton Grodzins and Eugene Rabinowitch, eds., New York, 1963, pp. 19-27.

IT COULD BE SUGGESTED that the danger of destruction by nuclear weapons can be avoided — at least as far as this country is concerned — either by keeping our discoveries secret for an indefinite time, or else by developing our nuclear armaments at such a pace that no other nation would think of attacking us from fear of overwhelming retaliation.

The answer to the first suggestion is that although we undoubtedly are at present ahead of the rest of the world in this field, the fundamental facts of nuclear power are a subject of common knowledge. British scientists know as much as we do about the basic wartime progress of nucleonics — if not of the specific processes used in our engineering developments — and the role which French nuclear physicists have played in the prewar development of this field, plus their occasional contact with our projects, will enable them to catch up rapidly, at least as far as basic scientific discoveries are concerned. German scientists, in whose discoveries the whole development of this field originated, apparently did not develop it during the war to the same extent to which this has been done in America, but to the last day of the European war we were living in constant apprehension as to their possible achievements.

The certainty that German scientists were working on this weapon and that their government would certainly have no scruples against using it when available was the main motivation of the initiative which American scientists took in urging the development of nuclear power for military purposes on a large scale in this country. In Russia, too, the basic facts and implications of nuclear power were well understood in 1940, and the experience of Russian scientists in nuclear research is entirely sufficient to enable them to retrace our steps within a few years, even if we should make every attempt to conceal them. Even if we can retain our leadership in basic knowledge of nucleonics for a certain time by maintaining secrecy as to all results achieved on this and associated projects, it would be foolish to hope that this can protect us for more than a few years.

It may be asked whether we cannot prevent the development of military nucleonics in other countries by a monopoly on the raw materials of nuclear power. The answer is that even though the largest now known deposits of uranium ores are under the control of powers which belong to the "Western" group (Canada, Belgium, and British India), the old deposits in Czechoslovakia are outside this sphere. Russia is known to be mining radium on its own territory, and even if we do not know the size of the deposits discovered so far in the U.S.S.R., the probability that no large reserves of uranium will be found in a country which covers one-fifth of the land area of the earth (and whose sphere of influence takes in additional territory), is too small to serve as a basis for security. *Thus, we cannot hope to avoid a nuclear armament race either by keeping secret from the competing nations the basic scientific facts of nuclear power or by cornering the raw materials required for such a race.*

We now . . . ask whether we could not feel ourselves safe in a race of nuclear armaments by virtue of our greater industrial potential, including greater diffusion of scientific and technical knowledge, greater volume and efficiency of our skilled labor corps, and greater experience of our management — all the factors whose importance has been so strikingly demonstrated in the conversion of this country into an arsenal of the Allied Nations in the present war. The answer is that all that these advantages can give us is the accumulation of a larger number of bigger and better atomic bombs.

However, such a quantitative advantage in reserves of bottled destructive power will not make us safe from sudden attack. Just because a potential enemy will be afraid of being "outnumbered and outgunned," the temptation for him may be overwhelming to attempt a sudden unprovoked blow, particularly if he should suspect us of harboring aggressive intentions against his security or his sphere of influence. In no other type of warfare does the advantage lie so heavily with the aggressor. He can place his "infernal machines" in advance in all our major cities and explode them simultaneously, thus destroying a major part of our industry and a large part of our population aggregated in densely populated metropolitan districts. Our possibilities of retaliation — even if retaliation should be considered adequate compensation for the loss of millions of lives and destruction of our largest cities — will be greatly handicapped because we must rely on aerial transportation of the bombs, and also because we may have to deal with an enemy whose industry and population are dispersed over a large territory.

In fact, if the race for nuclear armaments is allowed to develop, the only apparent way in which our country can be protected from the paralyzing effects of a sudden attack is by dispersal of those industries which are essential for our war efforts and dispersal of the populations of our major metropolitan cities. As long as nuclear bombs remain scarce (*i.e.,* as long as uranium remains the only basic material for their fabrication), efficient dispersal of our industry and the scattering of our metropolitan population will considerably decrease the temptation to attack us by nuclear weapons.

At present, it may be that atomic bombs can be detonated with an effect equal to that of 20,000 tons of TNT. One of these bombs could then destroy something like 3 square miles of an urban area. Atomic bombs containing a larger quantity of active material but still weighing less than one ton may be expected to be available within ten years which could destroy over 10 square miles of a city. A nation able to assign ten tons of atomic explosives for a sneak attack on this country can then hope to achieve the destruction of all industry and most of the population in an area from 500 square miles upwards. If no choice of targets, with a total area of 500 square miles of American territory, contains a large enough fraction of the nation's industry and population to make their destruction a crippling blow to the nation's war potential and its ability to defend itself, then the attack will not pay and may not be undertaken. At present, one could easily select in this country a hundred areas of 5 square miles each whose simultaneous destruction would be a staggering blow to the nation. Since the area of the United States is about 3 million square miles, it should be possible to scatter its industrial and human resources in such a way as to leave no 500 square miles important enough to serve as a target for nuclear attack.

We are fully aware of the staggering difficulties involved in such a radical change in the social and economic structure of our nation. We felt, however, that the dilemma had to be stated to show what kind of alternative methods of protection will have to be considered if no successful international agreement is reached. It must be pointed out that in this field we are in a less favorable position than nations which are either now more diffusely populated and whose industries are more scattered, or whose governments have unlimited power over the movement of population and the location of industrial plants.

If no efficient international agreement is achieved, the race for nuclear armaments will be on in earnest not later than the morning after our first demonstration of the existence of nuclear weapons. After this, it might take other nations three or four years to overcome our present head start, and eight or ten years to draw even with us if we continue to do intensive work in this field. This might be all the time we would have to bring about the relocation of our population and industry. Obviously, no time should be lost in inaugurating a study of this problem by experts.

The consequences of nuclear warfare and the type of measures which would have to be taken to protect a country from total destruction by nuclear bombing must be as abhorrent to other nations as to the United States. England, France, and the smaller nations of the European continent, with their congeries of people and industries, would be in a particularly desperate situation in the face of such a threat. Russia and China are the only great nations at present which could survive a nuclear attack. However, even though these countries may value human life less than the peoples of Western Europe and America, and even though Russia, in particular, has an immense space over which its vital industries could be dispersed and a government which can order this dispersion the day it is convinced that such a measure is necessary, there is no doubt that Russia, too, will shudder at the possibility of a sudden disintegration of Moscow and Leningrad, almost miraculously preserved in the present war, and of its new industrial cities in the Urals and Siberia. Therefore, only lack of mutual *trust* and not lack of *desire* for agreement can stand in the path of an efficient agreement for the prevention of nuclear warfare. The achievement of such an agreement will thus essentially depend on the integrity of intentions and readiness to sacrifice the necessary fraction of one's own sovereignty by all the parties to the agreement.

One possible way to introduce nuclear weapons to one world — which may particularly appeal to those who consider nuclear bombs primarily as a secret weapon developed to help win the present war — is to use them without warning on appropriately selected objects in Japan.

Although important tactical results undoubtedly can be achieved by a sudden introduction of nuclear weapons, we nevertheless think that the question of the use of the very first available atomic bombs in the Japanese war should be weighed very carefully, not only by military authorities but by the highest political leadership of this country.

Russia, and even allied countries which bear less mistrust of our ways and intentions, as well as neutral countries may be deeply shocked by this step. It may be very difficult to persuade the world that a nation which was capable of secretly preparing and suddenly releasing a new weapon as indiscriminate as the rocket bomb and a thousand times more destructive is to be trusted in its proclaimed desire of having such weapons abolished by international agreement. We have large accumulations of poison gas but do not use them, and recent polls have shown that public opinion in this country would disapprove of such a use even if it would accelerate the winning of the Far Eastern war. It is true that some irrational element in mass psychology makes gas poisoning more revolting than blasting by explosives, even though gas warfare is in no way more "inhuman" than the war of bombs and bullets. Nevertheless, it is not at all certain that American public opinion, if it could be enlightened as to the effect of atomic explosives, would approve of our own country being the first to introduce such an indiscriminate method of wholesale destruction of civilian life.

Thus, from the "optimistic" point of view — looking forward to an international agreement on the prevention of nuclear warfare — the military advantages and the saving of American lives achieved by the sudden use of atomic bombs against Japan may be outweighed by the ensuing loss of confidence and by a wave of horror and repulsion sweeping over the rest of the world and perhaps even dividing public opinion at home.

*From this point of view, a demonstration of the new weapon might best be made, before the eyes of representatives of all the United Nations, on the desert or a barren island.* The best possible atmosphere for the achievement of an international agreement could be achieved if America could say to the world, "You see what sort of a weapon we had but did not use. We are ready to renounce its use in the future if other nations join us in this renunciation and agree to the establishment of an efficient international control."

After such a demonstration the weapon might perhaps be used against Japan if the sanction of the United Nations (and of public opinion at home) were obtained, perhaps after a preliminary ultimatum to Japan to surrender or at least to evacuate certain regions as an alternative to their total destruction. This may sound fantastic, but in nuclear weapons we have something entirely new in order of magnitude of destructive power, and if we want to capitalize fully on the advantage their possession gives us, we must use new and imaginative methods.

It must be stressed that if one takes the pessimistic point of view and discounts the possibility of an effective international control over nuclear weapons at the present time, then the advisability of an early use of nuclear bombs against Japan becomes even more doubtful — quite independent of any humanitarian considerations. If an international agreement is not concluded immediately after the first demonstration, this will mean a flying start toward an unlimited armaments race. If this race is inevitable, we have every reason to delay its beginning as long as possible in order to increase our head start still further.

The benefit to the nation and the saving of American lives in the future achieved by renouncing an early demonstration of nuclear bombs and letting the other nations come into the race only reluctantly, on the basis of guesswork and without definite knowledge that the "thing does work," may far outweigh the advantages to be gained by the immediate use of the first and comparatively inefficient bombs in the war against Japan. On the other hand, it may be argued that without an early demonstration it may prove difficult to obtain adequate support for further intensive development of nucleonics in this country and that thus the time gained by the postponement of an open armaments race will not be properly used. Furthermore one may suggest that other nations are now or will soon be not entirely unaware of our present achievements, and that consequently the postponement of a demonstration may serve no useful purpose as far as the avoidance of an armaments race is concerned and may only create additional mistrust, thus worsening rather than improving the chances of an ultimate accord on the international control of nuclear explosives.

Thus, if the prospects of an agreement will be considered poor in the immediate future, the pros and cons of an early revelation of our possession of nuclear weapons to the world — not only by their actual use against Japan but also by a prearranged demonstration — must be carefully weighed by the supreme political and military leadership of the country, and the decision should not be left to the considerations of military tactics alone.

One may point out that scientists themselves have initiated the development of this "secret weapon" and it is therefore strange that they should be reluctant to try it out on the enemy as soon as it is available. . . . The compelling reason for creating this weapon with such speed was our fear that Germany had the technical skill necessary to develop such a weapon, and that the German government had no moral restraints regarding its use.

Another argument which could be quoted in favor of using atomic bombs as soon as they are available is that so much taxpayers' money has been invested in these projects that the Congress and the American public will demand a return for their money. The attitude of American public opinion, mentioned earlier in the matter of the use of poison gas against Japan, shows that one can expect the American public to understand that it is sometimes desirable to keep a weapon in readiness for use only in extreme emergency; and as soon as the potentialities of nuclear weapons are revealed to the American people, one can be sure that they will support all attempts to make the use of such weapons impossible.

Once this is achieved, the large installations and the accumulation of explosive material at present earmarked for potential military use will become available for important peacetime developments, including power production, large engineering undertakings, and mass production of radioactive materials. In this way, the money spent on wartime development of nucleonics may become a boon for the peacetime development of national economy.

We now consider the question of how an effective international control of nuclear armaments can be achieved. This is a difficult problem, but we think it soluble. It requires study by statesmen and international lawyers, and we can offer only some preliminary suggestions for such a study.

Given mutual trust and willingness on all sides to give up a certain part of their sovereign rights by admitting international control of certain phases of national economy, the control could be exercised (alternatively or simultaneously) on two different levels.

The first and perhaps simplest way is to ration the raw materials — primarily the uranium ores. Production of nuclear explosives begins with the processing of large quantities of uranium in large isotope separation plants or huge production piles. The amounts of ore taken out of the ground at different locations could be controlled by resident agents of the international control board, and each nation could be allotted only an amount which would make large scale separation of fissionable isotopes impossible.

Such a limitation would have the drawback of making impossible also the develop ment of nuclear power for peacetime purposes. However, it need not prevent the production of radioactive elements on a scale sufficient to revolutionize the industrial, scientific, and technical use of these materials, and would thus not eliminate the main benefits which nucleonics promises to bring to mankind.

An agreement on a higher level, involving more mutual trust and understanding, would be to allow unlimited production but keep exact bookkeeping on the fate of each pound of uranium mined. If, in this way, check is kept on the conversion of uranium and thorium ore into pure fissionable materials, the question arises as to how to prevent accumulation of large quantities of such materials in the hands of one or several nations. Accumulations of this kind could be rapidly converted into atomic bombs if a nation should break away from international control. It has been suggested that a compulsory denaturation of pure fissionable isotopes may be agreed upon by diluting them after production with suitable isotopes to make them useless for military purposes, while retaining their usefulness for power engines.

---

65.

# Charter of the United Nations

*At the Moscow Conference in October 1943 the foreign ministers of the United States, Great Britain, and the Soviet Union reached an agreement to establish "a general international organization, based on the sovereign equality of all peace-loving states," after the war ended. The United States invited the Great Powers, along with China, to a conference held in August-October 1944 at Dumbarton Oaks, near Washington, where it was proposed to draw up a tentative charter for the organization, a substitute for the League of Nations. The Dumbarton Oaks proposals, published in October 1944, were the basis for the future United Nations Charter. At the Yalta Conference in February 1945 it was decided to hold the planning conference for the world organization in San Francisco, beginning on April 25 of the same year. The United Nations Charter was adopted by fifty nations on June 26 and ratified by the U.S. Senate, after relatively little debate (compared to the lengthy debate on the League of Nations), on July 28. The Charter, which in some ways is a lineal descendant of the American Declaration of Independence and of the U.S. Constitution, is reprinted here in part.*

WE THE PEOPLES
OF THE UNITED NATIONS
DETERMINED

to save succeeding generations from the scourge of war, which twice in our lifetime has brought untold sorrow to mankind, and

to reaffirm faith in fundamental human rights, in the dignity and worth of the human person, in the equal rights of men and women and of nations large and small, and

to establish conditions under which justice and respect for the obligations arising from treaties and other sources of international law can be maintained, and

to promote social progress and better standards of life in larger freedom,

AND FOR THESE ENDS

to practice tolerance and live together in peace with one another as good neighbors, and

to unite our strength to maintain international peace and security, and

to ensure, by the acceptance of principles and the institution of methods, that armed force shall not be used, save in the common interest, and

to employ international machinery for the promotion of the economic and social advancement of all peoples,

HAVE RESOLVED TO
COMBINE OUR EFFORTS TO
ACCOMPLISH THESE AIMS.

Accordingly, our respective Governments, through representatives assembled in the city of San Francisco, who have exhibited their full powers found to be in good and due form, have agreed to the present Charter of the United Nations and do hereby establish an international organization to be known as the United Nations.

## Chapter I
### PURPOSES AND PRINCIPLES
#### ARTICLE 1

The Purposes of the United Nations are:

1. To maintain international peace and security, and to that end: to take effective collective measures for the prevention and removal of threats to the peace, and for the suppression of acts of aggression or other breaches of the peace, and to bring about by peaceful means, and in conformity with the principles of justice and international law, adjustment or settlement of international disputes or situations which might lead to a breach of the peace;

2. To develop friendly relations among nations based on respect for the principle of equal rights and self-determination of peoples, and to take other appropriate measures to strengthen universal peace;

3. To achieve international cooperation in solving international problems of an economic, social, cultural, or humanitarian character, and in promoting and encouraging respect for human rights and for fundamental freedoms for all without distinction as to race, sex, language, or religion; and

4. To be a center for harmonizing the actions of nations in the attainment of these common ends.

#### ARTICLE 2

The Organization and its Members, in pursuit of the Purposes stated in Article 1, shall act in accordance with the following Principles.

1. The Organization is based on the principle of the sovereign equality of all its Members.

2. All Members, in order to ensure to all of them the rights and benefits resulting from membership, shall fulfill in good faith the obligations assumed by them in accordance with the present Charter.

3. All Members shall settle their international disputes by peaceful means in such a manner that international peace and security, and justice, are not endangered.

4. All Members shall refrain in their international relations from the threat or use of force against the territorial integrity or political independence of any state, or in any other manner inconsistent with the Purposes of the United Nations.

5. All Members shall give the United Nations every assistance in any action it takes in accordance with the present Charter, and shall refrain from giving assistance to any state against which the United Nations is taking preventive or enforcement action.

6. The Organization shall ensure that states which are not Members of the United Nations act in accordance with these Principles so far as may be necessary for the maintenance of international peace and security.

7. Nothing contained in the present Charter shall authorize the United Nations to intervene in matters which are essentially within the domestic jurisdiction of any state or shall require the Members to submit such matters to settlement under the present Charter; but this principle shall not prejudice the application of enforcement measures under Chapter VII.

## Chapter II
## MEMBERSHIP
### Article 3

The original Members of the United Nations shall be the states which, having participated in the United Nations Conference on International Organization at San Francisco, or having previously signed the Declaration by United Nations of January 1, 1942, sign the present Charter and ratify it in accordance with Article 110.

### Article 4

1. Membership in the United Nations is open to all other peace-loving states which accept the obligations contained in the present Charter and, in the judgment of the Organization, are able and willing to carry out these obligations.

2. The admission of any such state to membership in the United Nations will be effected by a decision of the General Assembly upon the recommendation of the Security Council.

### Article 5

A Member of the United Nations against which preventive or enforcement action has been taken by the Security Council may be suspended from the exercise of the rights and privileges of membership by the General Assembly upon the recommendation of the Security Council. The exercise of these rights and privileges may be restored by the Security Council.

### Article 6

A Member of the United Nations which has persistently violated the Principles contained in the present Charter may be expelled from the Organization by the General Assembly upon the recommendation of the Security Council.

## Chapter III
## ORGANS
### Article 7

1. There are established as the principal organs of the United Nations: a General Assembly, a Security Council, an Economic and Social Council, a Trusteeship Council, an International Court of Justice, and a Secretariat.

2. Such subsidiary organs as may be found necessary may be established in accordance with the present Charter.

### Article 8

The United Nations shall place no restrictions on the eligibility of men and women to participate in any capacity and under conditions of equality in its principal and subsidiary organs.

## Chapter IV
## THE GENERAL ASSEMBLY

*Composition*

### ARTICLE 9

1. The General Assembly shall consist of all the Members of the United Nations.

2. Each Member shall have not more than five representatives in the General Assembly.

*Functions and Powers*

### ARTICLE 10

The General Assembly may discuss any questions or any matters within the scope of the present Charter or relating to the powers and functions of any organs provided for in the present Charter, and, except as provided in Article 12, may make recommendations to the Members of the United Nations or to the Security Council or to both on any such questions or matters.

### ARTICLE 11

1. The General Assembly may consider the general principles of cooperation in the maintenance of international peace and security, including the principles governing disarmament and the regulation of armaments, and may make recommendations with regard to such principles to the Members or to the Security Council or to both.

2. The General Assembly may discuss any questions relating to the maintenance of international peace and security brought before it by any Member of the United Nations, or by the Security Council, or by a state which is not a Member of the United Nations in accordance with Article 35, paragraph 2, and, except as provided in Article 12, may make recommendations with regard to any such question to the state or

states concerned or to the Security Council or to both. Any such question on which action is necessary shall be referred to the Security Council by the General Assembly either before or after discussion.

3. The General Assembly may call the attention of the Security Council to situations which are likely to endanger international peace and security. . . .

*Voting*

### ARTICLE 18

1. Each member of the General Assembly shall have one vote.

2. Decisions of the General Assembly on important questions shall be made by a two-thirds majority of the members present and voting. These questions shall include: recommendations with respect to the maintenance of international peace and security, the election of the non-permanent members of the Security Council, the election of the members of the Economic and Social Council, the election of members of the Trusteeship Council in accordance with paragraph 1(c) of Article 86, the admission of new Members to the United Nations, the suspension of the rights and privileges of membership, the expulsion of Members, questions relating to the operation of the trusteeship system, and budgetary questions.

3. Decisions on other questions, including the determination of additional categories of questions to be decided by a two-thirds majority, shall be made by a majority of the members present and voting.

### ARTICLE 19

A Member of the United Nations which is in arrears in the payment of its financial contributions to the Organization shall have no vote in the General Assembly if the amount of its arrears equals or exceeds the amount of the contributions due from it for the preceding two full years. The General Assembly may, nevertheless, permit such a Member to vote if it is satisfied that the failure to pay is due to conditions beyond the control of the Member. . . .

## Chapter V
## THE SECURITY COUNCIL

*Composition*

### ARTICLE 23

1. The Security Council shall consist of eleven Members of the United Nations. The Republic of China, France, the Union of Soviet Socialist Republics, the United Kingdom of Great Britain and Northern Ireland, and the United States of America shall be permanent members of the Security Council. The General Assembly shall elect six other Members of the United Nations to be non-permanent members of the Security Council, due regard being specially paid, in the first instance to the contribution of Members of the United Nations to the maintenance of international peace and security and to the other purposes of the Organization, and also to equitable geographical distribution.

2. The non-permanent members of the Security Council shall be elected for a term of two years. In the first election of the non-permanent members, however, three shall be chosen for a term of one year. A retiring member shall not be eligible for immediate re-election.

3. Each member of the Security Council shall have one representative.

*Functions and Powers*

### ARTICLE 24

1. In order to ensure prompt and effective action by the United Nations, its Members confer on the Security Council primary responsibility for the maintenance of international peace and security, and agree that in carrying out its duties under this responsibility the Security Council acts on their behalf.

2. In discharging these duties the Security Council shall act in accordance with the Purposes and Principles of the United Nations. The specific powers granted to the Security Council for the discharge of these duties are laid down in Chapters VI, VII, VIII, and XII.

3. The Security Council shall submit annual and, when necessary, special reports to the General Assembly for its consideration.

### ARTICLE 25

The Members of the United Nations agree to accept and carry out the decisions of the Security Council in accordance with the present Charter.

### ARTICLE 26

In order to promote the establishment and maintenance of international peace and security with the least diversion for armaments of the world's human and economic resources, the Security Council shall be responsible for formulating, with the assistance of the Military Staff Committee referred to in Article 47, plans to be submitted to the Members of the United Nations for the establishment of a system for the regulation of armaments.

*Voting*

### ARTICLE 27

1. Each member of the Security Council shall have one vote.

2. Decisions of the Security Council on procedural matters shall be made by an affirmative vote of seven members.

3. Decisions of the Security Council on all other matters shall be made by an affirmative vote of seven members including the concurring votes of the permanent members; provided that, in decisions under Chapter VI, and under paragraph 3 of Article 52, a party to a dispute shall abstain from voting. . . .

## Chapter VI
## PACIFIC SETTLEMENT OF DISPUTES

### ARTICLE 33

1. The parties to any dispute, the continuance of which is likely to endanger the maintenance of international peace and security, shall, first of all, seek a solution by negotiation, enquiry, mediation, conciliation, arbitration, judicial settlement, resort to regional agencies or arrangements, or other peaceful means of their own choice.

2. The Security Council shall, when it deems necessary, call upon the parties to settle their dispute by such means.

### ARTICLE 34

The Security Council may investigate any dispute, or any situation which might lead to international friction or give rise to a dispute, in order to determine whether the continuance of the dispute or situation is likely to endanger the maintenance of international peace and security.

### ARTICLE 35

1. Any Member of the United Nations may bring any dispute, or any situation of the nature referred to in Article 34, to the attention of the Security Council or of the General Assembly.

2. A state which is not a Member of the United Nations may bring to the attention of the Security Council or of the General Assembly any dispute to which it is a party if it accepts in advance, for the purposes of the dispute, the obligations of pacific settlement provided in the present Charter. . . .

## Chapter VII
## ACTION WITH RESPECT TO THREATS TO THE PEACE, BREACHES OF THE PEACE, AND ACTS OF AGGRESSION

### ARTICLE 39

The Security Council shall determine the existence of any threat to the peace, breach of the peace, or act of aggression and shall make recommendations, or decide what measures shall be taken in accordance with Articles 41 and 42, to maintain or restore international peace and security.

### ARTICLE 40

In order to prevent an aggravation of the situation, the Security Council may, before making the recommendations or deciding upon the measures provided for in Article 39, call upon the parties concerned to comply with such provisional measures as it deems necessary or desirable. Such provisional measures shall be without prejudice to the rights, claims, or position of the parties concerned. The Security Council shall duly take account of failure to comply with such provisional measures.

### ARTICLE 41

The Security Council may decide what measures not involving the use of armed force are to be employed to give effect to its decisions, and it may call upon the Members of the United Nations to apply such measures. These may include complete or partial interruption of economic relation and of rail, sea, air, postal, telegraphic, radio, and other means of communication, and the severance of diplomatic relations.

## ARTICLE 42

Should the Security Council consider that measures provided for in Article 41 would be inadequate or have proved to be inadequate, it may take such action by air, sea, or land forces as may be necessary to maintain or restore international peace and security. Such action may include demonstrations, blockade, and other operations by air, sea, or land forces of Members of the United Nations.

## ARTICLE 43

1. All Members of the United Nations, in order to contribute to the maintenance of international peace and security, undertake to make available to the Security Council, on its call and in accordance with a special agreement or agreements, armed forces, assistance, and facilities, including rights of passage, necessary for the purpose of maintaining international peace and security. . . .

## ARTICLE 51

Nothing in the present Charter shall impair the inherent right of individual or collective self-defense if an armed attack occurs against a Member of the United Nations, until the Security Council has taken measures necessary to maintain international peace and security. Measures taken by Members in the exercise of this right of self-defense shall be immediately reported to the Security Council and shall not in any way affect the authority and responsibility of the Security Council under the present Charter to take at any time such action as it deems necessary in order to maintain or restore international peace and security.

## Chapter VIII
## REGIONAL ARRANGEMENTS

### ARTICLE 52

1. Nothing in the present Charter precludes the existence of regional arrangements or agencies for dealing with such matters relating to the maintenance of international peace and security as are appropriate for regional action, provided that such arrangements or agencies and their activities are consistent with the Purposes and Principles of the United Nations.
2. The Members of the United Nations entering into such arrangements or constituting such agencies shall make every effort to achieve pacific settlement of local disputes through such regional arrangements or by such regional agencies before referring them to the Security Council. . . .

### ARTICLE 54

The Security Council shall at all times be kept fully informed of activities undertaken or in contemplation under regional arrangements or by regional agencies for the maintenance of international peace and security.

## Chapter IX
## INTERNATIONAL ECONOMIC AND SOCIAL COOPERATION

### ARTICLE 55

With a view to the creation of conditions of stability and well-being which are necessary for peaceful and friendly relations among nations based on respect for the principle of equal rights and self-determination of peoples, the United Nations shall promote:
a. higher standards of living, full employment, and conditions of economic and social progress and development;

b. solutions of international economic, social, health, and related problems; and international cultural and educational cooperation; and

c. universal respect for, and observance of, human rights and fundamental freedoms for all without distinction as to race, sex, language, or religion. . . .

## Chapter XI
## DECLARATION REGARDING NON-SELF-GOVERNING TERRITORIES

### Article 73

Members of the United Nations which have or assume responsibilities for the administration of territories whose peoples have not yet attained a full measure of self-government recognize the principle that the interests of the inhabitants of these territories are paramount, and accept as a sacred trust the obligation to promote to the utmost, within the system of international peace and security established by the present Charter, the well-being of the inhabitants of these territories, and, to this end:

a. to ensure, with due respect for the culture of the peoples concerned, their political, economic, social, and educational advancement, their just treatment, and their protection against abuses;

b. to develop self-government, to take due account of the political aspirations of the peoples, and to assist them in the progressive development of their free political institutions, according to the particular circumstances of each territory and its peoples and their varying stages of advancement;

c. to further international peace and security;

d. to promote constructive measures of development, to encourage research, and to cooperate with one another and, when and where appropriate, with specialized international bodies with a view to the practical achievement of the social, economic, and scientific purposes set forth in this Article; and

e. to transmit regularly to the Secretary-General for information purposes, subject to such limitation as security and constitutional considerations may require, statistical and other information of a technical nature relating to economic, social, and educational conditions in the territories for which they are respectively responsible other than those territories to which Chapters XII and XIII apply.

### Article 74

Members of the United Nations also agree that their policy in respect of the territories to which this Chapter applies, no less than in respect of their metropolitan areas, must be based on the general principle of good-neighborliness, due account being taken of the interests and well-being of the rest of the world, in social, economic, and commercial matters.

## Chapter XII
## INTERNATIONAL TRUSTEESHIP SYSTEM

### Article 75

The United Nations shall establish under its authority an international trusteeship system for the administration and supervision of such territories as may be placed thereunder by subsequent individual agreements. These territories are hereinafter referred to as trust territories.

### Article 76

The basic objectives of the trusteeship system, in accordance with the Purposes of the United Nations laid down in Article I of the present Charter, shall be:

a. to further international peace and security;

b. to promote the political, economic, social, and educational advancement of the inhabitants of the trust territories, and their progressive development towards self-government or independence as may be appropriate to the particular circumstances of each territory and its peoples and the freely expressed wishes of the peoples concerned, and as may be provided by the terms of each trusteeship agreement;

c. to encourage respect for human rights and for fundamental freedoms for all without distinction as to race, sex, language, or religion, and to encourage recognition of the interdependence of the peoples of the world; and

d. to ensure equal treatment in social, economic, and commercial matters for all Members of the United Nations and their nationals, and also equal treatment for the latter in the administration of justice, without prejudice to the attainment of the foregoing objectives and, subject to the provisions of Article 80.

### ARTICLE 77

1. The trusteeship system shall apply to such territories in the following categories as may be placed thereunder by means of trusteeship agreements:

a. territories now held under mandate;

b. territories which may be detached from enemy states as a result of the Second World War; and

c. territories voluntarily placed under the system by states responsible for their administration.

2. It will be a matter for subsequent agreement as to which territories in the foregoing categories will be brought under the trusteeship system and upon what terms. . . .

### Chapter XIV
### THE INTERNATIONAL COURT OF JUSTICE

### ARTICLE 92

The International Court of Justice shall be the principal judicial organ of the United Nations. It shall function in accordance with the annexed Statute, which is based upon the Statute of the Permanent Court of International Justice and forms an integral part of the present Charter.

### ARTICLE 93

1. All Members of the United Nations are *ipso facto* parties to the Statute of the International Court of Justice.

2. A state which is not a Member of the United Nations may become a party to the Statute of the International Court of Justice on condition to be determined in each case by the General Assembly upon the recommendation of the Security Council.

### ARTICLE 94

1. Each Member of the United Nations undertakes to comply with the decision of the International Court of Justice in any case to which it is a party.

2. If any party to a case fails to perform the obligations incumbent upon it under a judgment rendered by the Court, the other party may have recourse to the Security Council, which may, if it deems necessary, make recommendations. . . .

### Chapter XV
### THE SECRETARIAT

### ARTICLE 97

The Secretariat shall comprise a Secretary-General and such staff as the Organization may require. The Secretary-General shall be appointed by the General Assembly upon the recommendation of the Security Council. He shall be the chief administrative officer of the Organization.

### ARTICLE 98

The Secretary-General shall act in that capacity in all meetings of the General Assembly, of the Security Council, of the Economic and Social Council, and of the Trusteeship Council, and shall perform such other functions as are entrusted to him by these organs. The Secretary-General shall make an annual report to the General Assembly on the work of the Organization.

### ARTICLE 99

The Secretary-General may bring to the attention of the Security Council any matter which in his opinion may threaten the maintenance of international peace. . . .

### ARTICLE 100

1. In the performance of their duties the Secretary-General and the staff shall not seek to receive instruction from any government or from any other authority external to the Organization. They shall refrain from any action which might reflect on their position as international officials responsible only to the Organization.

2. Each Member of the United Nations undertakes to respect the exclusively international character of the responsibilities of the Secretary-General and the staff. . . .

### Chapter XVII
### TRANSITIONAL SECURITY ARRANGEMENTS

### ARTICLE 106

Pending the coming into force of such special agreements referred to in Article 43

as in the opinion of the Security Council enable it to begin the exercise of its responsibilities under Article 42, the parties to the Four-Nation Declaration, signed at Moscow, October 30, 1943, and France, shall, in accordance with the provisions of paragraph 5 of that Declaration, consult with one another and as occasion requires with other Members of the United Nations with a view to such joint action on behalf of the Organization as may be necessary for the purpose of maintaining international peace and security. . . .

### Chapter XIX
### RATIFICATION AND SIGNATURE

### ARTICLE 110

1. The present Charter shall be ratified by the signatory states in accordance with their respective constitutional processes.

2. The ratifications shall be deposited with the Government of the United States of America, which shall notify all the signatory states of each deposit as well as the Secretary-General of the Organization when he has been appointed.

3. The present Charter shall come into force upon the deposit of ratifications by the Republic of China, France, the Union of Soviet Socialist Republics, the United Kingdom of Great Britain and Northern Ireland, and the United States of America, and by a majority of the other signatory states. A protocol of the ratifications deposited shall thereupon be drawn up by the Government of the United States of America which shall communicate copies thereof to all the signatory states. . . .

### ARTICLE 111

The present Charter, of which the Chinese, French, Russian, English, and Spanish texts are equally authentic, shall remain deposited in the archives of the Government of the United States of America. Duly certified copies thereof shall be transmitted by that Government to the Governments of the other signatory states.

*In faith whereof,* the representatives of the Governments of the United Nations have signed the present Charter.

Done at the city of San Francisco the twenty-sixth day of June, one thousand nine hundred and forty-five.

---

66.

## Arthur H. Vandenberg: Sovereignty and the United Nations

*Anticipating some congressional opposition to American participation in the United Nations, President Roosevelt chose a bipartisan delegation, including distinguished members of Congress, to attend the San Francisco Conference. The selection of Senator Arthur Vandenberg of Michigan was particularly important because of his influence in the Republican Party. Though, in the late 1930s, Vandenberg had led the isolationists in opposing American participation in the war, by 1945 he had become the most internationally minded of Republican leaders. His effective work at the conference exerted a powerful influence in quelling Republican opposition to the United Nations Charter when it was brought before the Senate for ratification. Vandenberg delivered a speech, reprinted here in part, in support of the Charter during the Senate debate of July 23.*

Source: *Record,* 79 Cong., 1 Sess., pp. 7956-7957.

The San Francisco Charter may not succeed in its God-blessed purposes. Personally, I think it will. World War No. 3 is too horrible to contemplate. It clearly threatens the end of civilization. Here is our chance to try to stop this disaster before it starts; and here is a formula which, in its initial operation at the San Francisco Conference, has proved that it can work in harmonizing controversies among fifty nations of this world.

In the event, Mr. President, of the unexpected failure of this experiment, I should prefer to have been associated with its hopeful trial than with a refusal to permit it to prove its expected success. For the sake of the mothers of men, I think this Charter deserves the overwhelming ratification which seems imminent in the Senate of the United States. . . .

It occurs to me that perhaps the chief service I might briefly render today would be frankly to face what seem to be some of the misgivings which still linger in some minds. Therefore, without any thought of complaining against the free expression of anybody's opinion, I want most respectfully to turn my attention very briefly to what it seemed to me was a rather complete adverse summary which recently appeared in a two-column editorial in certain important metropolitan newspapers which seemed to symbolize what I believe to be these misconceptions. I use this as my brief text be-

United Press International

Sen. Arthur Vandenberg, foreground, at a Senate committee hearing with Sen. Millard Tydings

cause the editorial in essence seemed to be a personal challenge addressed to me. I quote from the editorial in its final summary:

This United Nations Charter embodies Roosevelt's dream of a postwar superstate. It entails the destruction of parts of the written Constitution, without a by-your-leave to the American people. That apparently is O.K. with Vandenberg and his cohorts.

Mr. President, I wish to say for the *Record*, and with elementary consideration for my own status as, I believe, a loyal American, that this is a totally unjustified, unwarranted, and insupportable indictment of the Charter. The greatest respect for the opinions of those who differ with me, I deny every factual word of it. This would be of no importance except as I am using the editorial to illustrate what I believe to be these remaining misconceptions so far as they still linger in a very small minority of our public opinion.

Mr. President, if the "United Nations Charter embodies Roosevelt's dreams of a postwar superstate," then our late President was guiltless of "dreaming" about any "superstate" at all. There is no "superstate," even remotely or by the widest indirection, in this Charter. If we have taken care of anything in writing this Charter we have scrupulously taken care of that. Such a fantastic charge defies support by any rational bill of particulars.

Now, listen. The United States retains every basic attribute of its sovereignty. We cannot be called to participate in any sort of sanctions, military or otherwise, without our own free and untrammeled consent. We cannot be taken into the World Court except at our own free option. The ultimate disposition of enemy territory which we have captured in this war is dependent solely upon our own will so far as this Charter is concerned. Our domestic questions are eliminated from the new organization's jurisdiction. Our inter-American system and the Monroe Doctrine are unimpaired in their realities. Our right of withdrawal from the new organization is absolute and is dependent solely upon our own discretion. In a word, Mr. President, the flag stays on the dome of the Capitol.

These things, quoting the editorial, I confess are "O.K. with Vandenberg and his cohorts." These things we toiled at San Francisco to preserve. We can effectively cooperate for peace without the loss of these things. To cooperate is not to lose our sovereignty. It is to use our sovereignty in quest of the dearest boon which the prayer of humankind pursue. I respectfully suggest that those who voice a superlative attachment to these elements of sovereignty should be the last to invite the wholly unjustified interpretation that we have surrendered the very things we have so scrupulously preserved.

So it is also with the equally irresponsibl

charge that the Charter "entails the destruction of parts of the written Constitution." What parts, I beg to inquire? Certainly the fact that we propose to cooperate to prevent World War III, if we can, destroys no part of our Constitution. Our Constitution is not allergic to peace. It is not yet treason to abhor the ugly implications of war and to attempt to do something realistic about it.

Where, I ask again, do we invade our "written Constitution"? If it is meant that we "destroy" the exclusive congressional right to declare war, I answer that the control of our American voice on the new Security Council is entirely and exclusively within our own congressional jurisdiction when we create this voice. The Charter does not even pretend to invade our own domestic control over this purely domestic matter. If it did it would be promptly and rightly pilloried for any such invasion.

The Charter gives us a veto on war and on any steps leading to war. The Charter could do no more. It says that our agreement covering the contribution of troops to any joint action must be approved by our own constitutional process. Does that destroy our constitutional process? To ask the question is to answer it. The Charter actually confirms our constitutional process. We shall decide for ourselves where we wish to draw the line, if any, between the constitutional authority of the President to use our armed forces in preliminary national defense action and the constitutional authority of Congress to declare war. Both constitutional rights have existed, Mr. President, and have stood unchallenged for 150 years. We have never thought it necessary or desirable to try to set metes and bounds for each. I doubt if it is necessary or desirable now. We have but to continue the constitutional practice of a century and a half.

In our domestic statute, however, which is none of the Charter's business whatsoever — in our domestic statute creating our American delegateship to the Security Council, we can appropriately require that he shall vote for sanctions only upon instruction from the President, and that the President shall simultaneously notify the Congress. In the presence of this constant information, Congress can act in any way it pleases. I repeat that this is our business, and if there be any doubt, Mr. President, that in addition to the exclusive congressional power to declare war there is this basic constitutional military authority resident in the first instances in the President of the United States, I quote just one authority and pass on. I quote the man who is probably the favorite congressional authority upon subjects of this nature, Professor Borchard, of Yale, discussing the right and the duty of the President to protect American life, American property, and American interests anywhere in the world:

> Inasmuch as the Constitution vests in Congress the authority to declare war and does not empower Congress to direct the President to perform his constitutional duty of protecting American citizens on foreign soil, it is believed that the Executive has unlimited authority to use the armed forces of the United States for protective purposes abroad in any manner and on any occasion he considers expedient.

I believe that when the President concludes to use preliminary force, in cooperation with the Security Council, to stop a dispute before it graduates into war, he is most emphatically protecting American welfare.

So far as the Charter is concerned, it does not destroy, it does not threaten, it does not even remotely approach so much as an indirect impingement upon any portion of our written Constitution. That, too, Mr. President, if I may refer again to the personal element in the editorial from which I quote, is "O.K. with Vandenberg and his cohorts."

67.

# Harry S. Truman: Announcement of the Dropping of an Atomic Bomb on Hiroshima

*The leaders of the Allied powers met at Potsdam, Germany, from July 17 to August 2, 1945, to consider the fate of defeated Germany and to plan the final campaign against Japan. The U.S. representative was President Truman, who had succeeded to the presidency on Roosevelt's death three months before; and Clement Attlee replaced Winston Churchill as British prime minister during the course of the conference. The first declaration issued by the conferees was the "unconditional surrender" ultimatum presented to Japan on July 26. Earlier in the conference Truman had informed Churchill that the United States had successfully tested an atomic device on July 16, to which Churchill is supposed to have responded: "This is the Second Coming, in wrath." On July 25, a day before the ultimatum, Truman ordered the 20th Air Force at Saipan to use one of the two atomic bombs in their possession at the first opportunity after August 3 if Japan had not yet surrendered. On July 29 the Japanese cabinet decided to make no immediate comment on the ultimatum, but press reports of their decision indicated to Truman and the Joint Chiefs of Staff that they had "ignored" it. This note of defiance, which may actually have been unintended, led to the decision in Washington to use the bombs. The first was dropped on Hiroshima on the morning of August 6, destroying over four square miles of the city and killing or injuring more than 135,000 people. The President's address to the nation on August 6 is reprinted here.*

Source: *Public Papers of the Presidents of the United States: Harry S. Truman, Containing the Public Messages, Speeches, and Statements of the President, April 12 to December 31, 1945,* Washington, 1961, pp. 197-200.

Sixteen hours ago an American airplane dropped one bomb on Hiroshima, an important Japanese Army base. That bomb had more power than 20,000 tons of TNT. It had more than 2,000 times the blast power of the British "Grand Slam," which is the largest bomb ever yet used in the history of warfare.

The Japanese began the war from the air at Pearl Harbor. They have been repaid manyfold. And the end is not yet. With this bomb we have now added a new and revolutionary increase in destruction to supplement the growing power of our armed forces. In their present form these bombs are now in production, and even more powerful forms are in development.

It is an atomic bomb. It is a harnessing of the basic power of the universe. The force from which the sun draws its power has been loosed against those who brought war to the Far East.

Before 1939, it was the accepted belief of scientists that it was theoretically possible to release atomic energy. But no one knew any practical method of doing it. By 1942 however, we knew that the Germans were working feverishly to find a way to add atomic energy to the other engines of war with which they hoped to enslave the world. But they failed. We may be grateful to Providence that the Germans got the V-1's and V-2's late and in limited quantities and even more grateful that they did not get the atomic bomb at all.

The battle of the laboratories held fateful risks for us as well as the battles of the air, land, and sea, and we have now won the battle of the laboratories as we have won the other battles.

Beginning in 1940, before Pearl Harbor, scientific knowledge useful in war was pooled between the United States and Great Britain, and many priceless helps to our victories have come from that arrangement. Under that general policy the research on the atomic bomb was begun. With American and British scientists working together we entered the race of discovery against the Germans.

The United States had available the large number of scientists of distinction in the many needed areas of knowledge. It had the tremendous industrial and financial resources necessary for the project, and they could be devoted to it without undue impairment of other vital war work. In the United States the laboratory work and the production plants, on which a substantial start had already been made, would be out of reach of enemy bombing, while at that time Britain was exposed to constant air attack and was still threatened with the possibility of invasion. For these reasons Prime Minister Churchill and President Roosevelt agreed that it was wise to carry on the project here.

We now have two great plants and many lesser works devoted to the production of atomic power. Employment during peak construction numbered 125,000 and over 65,000 individuals are even now engaged in operating the plants. Many have worked

Wide World

Smoke rising from the explosion of the atomic bomb at Hiroshima; photo taken from Yoshiura on the other side of the mountain to the north. Spots on film were caused by radiation from the explosion

there for two and a half years. Few know what they have been producing. They see great quantities of material going in and they see nothing coming out of these plants, for the physical size of the explosive charge is exceedingly small. We have spent $2 billion on the greatest scientific gamble in history — and won.

But the greatest marvel is not the size of the enterprise, its secrecy, nor its cost, but the achievement of scientific brains in putting together infinitely complex pieces of knowledge held by many men in different fields of science into a workable plan. And hardly less marvelous has been the capacity of industry to design, and of labor to operate, the machines and methods to do things never done before so that the brainchild of many minds came forth in physical shape and performed as it was supposed to do. Both science and industry worked under the direction of the United States Army, which achieved a unique success in managing so diverse a problem in the advancement of knowledge in an amazingly short time. It is doubtful if such another combination could be got together in the world. What has been done is the greatest achievement of organized science in history. It was done under high pressure and without failure.

We are now prepared to obliterate more rapidly and completely every productive enterprise the Japanese have above ground in any city. We shall destroy their docks, their factories, and their communications. Let there be no mistake; we shall completely destroy Japan's power to make war.

It was to spare the Japanese people from utter destruction that the ultimatum of July 26 was issued at Potsdam. Their leaders promptly rejected that ultimatum. If they do not now accept our terms they may expect a rain of ruin from the air, the like of which has never been seen on this earth. Behind this air attack will follow sea and land forces in such numbers and power as they have not yet seen and with the fighting skill of which they are already well aware.

The secretary of war, who has kept in personal touch with all phases of the project, will immediately make public a statement giving further details.

His statement will give facts concerning the sites at Oak Ridge near Knoxville, Tennessee, and at Richland near Pasco, Washington, and an installation near Santa Fe, New Mexico. Although the workers at the sites have been making materials to be used in producing the greatest destructive force in history, they have not themselves been in danger beyond that of many other occupations, for the utmost care has been taken of their safety.

The fact that we can release atomic energy ushers in a new era in man's understanding of nature's forces. Atomic energy may in the future supplement the power that now comes from coal, oil, and falling water, but at present it cannot be produced on a basis to compete with them commercially. Before that comes there must be a long period of intensive research.

It has never been the habit of the scientists of this country or the policy of this government to withhold from the world scientific knowledge. Normally, therefore, everything about the work with atomic energy would be made public.

But under present circumstances it is not intended to divulge the technical processes of production or all the military applications, pending further examination of possible methods of protecting us and the rest of the world from the danger of sudden destruction.

I shall recommend that the Congress of the United States consider promptly the establishment of an appropriate commission to control the production and use of atomic power within the United States. I shall give further consideration and make further recommendations to the Congress as to how atomic power can become a powerful and forceful influence towards the maintenance of world peace.

---

*Soldiers who wish to be a hero*
*Are practically zero,*
*But those who wish to be civilians,*
*Jesus, they run into the millions.*

Army latrine inscription,
quoted by Norman Rosten,
*The Big Road,* 1945

68.

# William L. Laurence: Atomic Bomb on Nagasaki

*On August 9, 1945, the United States dropped a second atomic bomb, this time on Nagasaki, a highly populous provincial capital and naval base near the southern tip of Japan. The bomb destroyed 40 percent of the buildings, completely razing the center of the city, killed 39,000 persons, and injured an additional 25,000. William L. Laurence, a science writer for the* New York Times *who was also a witness at Alamogordo, accompanied the plane that dropped the bomb. His account is reprinted here. Premier Suzuki accepted the terms of the Potsdam ultimatum, on condition that Emperor Hirohito keep his throne, on August 10; and Japan surrendered unconditionally on August 14. V-J Day, ending the war, was August 15.*

Source: *New York Times*, September 9, 1945.

THE FIRST SIGNS OF DAWN came shortly after 5 o'clock. Sergeant Curry, who had been listening steadily on his earphones for radio reports, while maintaining a strict radio silence himself, greeted it by rising to his feet and gazing out the window.

"It's good to see the day," he told me. "I get a feeling of claustrophobia hemmed in in this cabin at night."

He is a typical American youth, looking even younger than his twenty years. It takes no mind reader to read his thoughts.

"It's a long way from Hoopeston, Ill.," I find myself remarking.

"Yep," he replies, as he busies himself decoding a message from outer space.

"Think this atomic bomb will end the war?" he asks hopefully.

"There is a very good chance that this one may do the trick," I assure him, "but if not, then the next one or two surely will. Its power is such that no nation can stand up against it very long."

This was not my own view. I had heard it expressed all around a few hours earlier, before we took off. To anyone who had seen this man-made fireball in action, as I had less than a month ago in the desert of New Mexico, this view did not sound over-optimistic.

By 5:50 it was real light outside. We had lost our lead ship, but Lieutenant Godfrey, our navigator, informs me that we had arranged for that contingency. We have an assembly point in the sky above the little island of Yakoshima, southeast of Kyushu, at 9:10. We are to circle there and wait for the rest of our formation.

Our genial bombardier, Lieutenant Levy, comes over to invite me to take his front-row seat in the transparent nose of the ship and I accept eagerly. . . .

Somewhere beyond these vast mountains of white clouds ahead of me there lies Japan, the land of our enemy. In about four hours from now one of its cities, making weapons of war for use against us, will be wiped off the map by the greatest weapon ever made by man. In one-tenth of a millionth of a second, a fraction of time immeasurable by any clock, a whirlwind from the skies will pulverize thousands of its buildings and tens of thousands of its inhabitants.

Our weather planes ahead of us are on their way to find out where the wind blows. Half an hour before target time we will know what the winds have decided.

Does one feel any pity or compassion for the poor devils about to die? Not when one thinks of Pearl Harbor and of the Death March on Bataan.

Captain Bock informs me that we are about to start our climb to bombing altitude. . . .

It was 9:56 when we began heading for the coastline. Our weather scouts had sent us code messages, deciphered by Sergeant Curry, informing us that both the primary target as well as the secondary were clearly visible.

The winds of destiny seemed to favor certain Japanese cities that must remain nameless. We circled about them again and again and found no opening in the thick umbrellas of clouds that covered them. Destiny chose Nagasaki as the ultimate target.

We had been circling for some time when we noticed black puffs of smoke coming through the white clouds directly at us. There were fifteen bursts of flak in rapid succession, all too low. Captain Bock changed his course. There soon followed eight more bursts of flak, right up to our altitude, but by this time were too far to the left.

We flew southward down the channel and at 11:33 crossed the coastline and headed straight for Nagasaki about 100 miles to the west. Here again we circled until we found an opening in the clouds. It was 12:01 and the goal of our mission had arrived.

We heard the prearranged signal on our radio, put on our arc-welder's glasses and watched tensely the maneuverings of the strike ship about half a mile in front of us.

"There she goes!" someone said.

Out of the belly of *The Great Artiste* what looked like a black object went downward.

Captain Bock swung around to get out of range; but even though we were turning away in the opposite direction, and despite the fact that it was broad daylight in our cabin, all of us became aware of a giant flash that broke through the dark barrier of our arc-welder's lenses and flooded our cabin with intense light.

We removed our glasses after the first flash, but the light still lingered on, a bluish-green that illuminated the entire sky all around. A tremendous blast wave struck our ship and made it tremble from nose to tail. This was followed by four more blasts in rapid succession, each resounding like the boom of cannon fire hitting our plane from all directions.

Observers in the tail of our ship saw a giant ball of fire rise as though from the bowels of the earth, belching forth enormous white smoke rings. Next they saw a gigantic pillar of purple fire, 10,000 feet high, shooting skyward with enormous speed.

By the time our ship had made another turn in the direction of the atomic explosion, the pillar of purple fire had reached the level of our altitude. Only about forty-five seconds had passed. Awestruck, we watched it shoot upward like a meteor coming from the earth instead of from outer space, becoming ever more alive as it climbed skyward through the white clouds. It was no longer smoke, or dust, or even a cloud of fire. It was a living thing, a new species of being born before our incredulous eyes.

At one stage of its evolution, covering millions of years in terms of seconds, the entity assumed the form of a giant square totem pole, with its base about three miles long, tapering off to about a mile at the top. Its bottom was brown, its center was amber, its top, white. But it was a living totem pole, carved with many grotesque masks grimacing at the earth.

Then, just when it appeared as though the thing had settled down into a state of permanence, there came shooting out of the top a giant mushroom that increased the height of the pillar to a total of 45,000 feet

The mushroom top was even more alive than the pillar, seething and boiling in a white fury of creamy foam, sizzling upward and then descending earthward, a thousand Old Faithful geysers rolled into one.

It kept struggling in an elemental fury, like a creature in the act of breaking the bonds that held it down. In a few seconds it had freed itself from its gigantic stem and floated upward with tremendous speed, its momentum carrying it into the stratosphere to a height of about 60,000 feet.

But no sooner did this happen when another mushroom, smaller in size than the first, began emerging out of the pillar. It was as though the decapitated monster was growing a new head.

As the first mushroom floated off into the blue, it changed its shape into a flower-like form, its giant petal curving downward, creamy white outside, rose-colored inside. It still retained that shape when we last gazed at it from a distance of about 200 miles.

---

69.

## DOUGLAS MACARTHUR: Today the Guns Are Silent

*The formal surrender documents ending hostilities with Japan were signed on September 2, 1945, on board the U.S.S.* Missouri, *one of numerous ships of the Pacific Fleet that had entered Tokyo Bay after preliminary arrangements for the surrender had been made in Manila. The ceremony, which took place only a few miles from where Commodore Perry had signed the treaty with Japan in March 1854, closed shortly before 9:30 A.M., and the sky was darkened by an overflight of several hundred aircraft. General MacArthur then broadcast the following address to the people of the United States. MacArthur was subsequently appointed supreme commander Allied powers during the military occupation of Japan that lasted until 1952. "If the historian of the future should deem my service worthy of some slight reference," he wrote later, "it would be my hope that he mention me not as a commander engaged in . . . battles, even though victorious to American arms, but rather as that one whose sacred duty it became, once the guns were silenced, to carry to the land of our vanquished foe the solace and hope and faith of Christian morals."*

Source: VSD, September 15, 1945, pp. 707-708.

TODAY THE GUNS ARE SILENT. A great tragedy has ended. A great victory has been won. The skies no longer rain death — the seas bear only commerce — men everywhere walk upright in the sunlight. The entire world lies quietly at peace. The holy mission has been completed. And in reporting this to you, the people, I speak for the thousands of silent lips, forever stilled among the jungles and the beaches and in the deep waters of the Pacific which marked the way. I speak for the unnamed brave millions homeward bound to take up the challenge of that future which they did so much to salvage from the brink of disaster.

As I look back on the long, tortuous trail from those grim days of Bataan and Corregidor, when an entire world lived in fear, when democracy was on the defensive everywhere, when modern civilization trembled in the balance, I thank a merciful God that He has given us the faith, the courage, and the power from which to mold victory. We have known the bitterness of defeat and the exultation of triumph, and from both we have learned there can be no turning back. We must go forward to preserve in peace what we won in war.

A new era is upon us. Even the lesson of victory itself brings with it profound concern, both for our future security and the survival of civilization. The destructiveness of the war potential, through progressive advances in scientific discovery, has in fact now reached a point which revises the traditional concept of war.

Men since the beginning of time have sought peace. Various methods through the ages have been attempted to devise an international process to prevent or settle disputes between nations. From the very start workable methods were found insofar as individual citizens were concerned, but the mechanics of an instrumentality of larger international scope have never been successful. Military alliances, balance of power, Leagues of Nations all in turn failed, leaving the only path to be by way of the crucible of war. The utter destructiveness of war now blots out this alternative. We have had our last chance. If we do not devise some greater and more equitable system, Armageddon will be at our door. The problem basically is theological and involves a spiritual recrudescence and improvement of human character that will synchronize with our almost matchless advance in science, art, literature, and all material and cultural developments of the past 2,000 years. It must be of the spirit if we are to save the flesh.

We stand in Tokyo today reminiscent of our countryman Commodore Perry ninety-two years ago. His purpose was to bring to Japan an era of enlightenment and progress by lifting the veil of isolation to the friendship, trade, and commerce of the world. But, alas, the knowledge thereby gained of Western science was forged into an instrument of oppression and human enslavement. Freedom of expression, freedom of action, even freedom of thought were denied through suppression of liberal education, through appeal to superstition, and through the application of force. We are committed by the Potsdam Declaration of Principles to see that the Japanese people are liberated from this condition of slavery. It is my purpose to implement this commitment just as rapidly as the armed forces are demobilized and other essential steps taken to neutralize the war potential. The energy of the Japanese race, if properly directed, will enable expansion vertically rather than horizontally. If the talents of the race are turned into constructive channels, the country can lift itself from its present deplorable state into a position of dignity.

To the Pacific basin has come the vista of a new emancipated world. Today, freedom is on the offensive, democracy is on the march. Today, in Asia as well as in Europe, unshackled peoples are tasting the full sweetness of liberty, the relief from fear.

In the Philippines, America has evolved a model for this new free world of Asia. In the Philippines, America has demonstrated that peoples of the East and peoples of the West may walk side by side in mutual respect and with mutual benefit. The history of our sovereignty there has now the full confidence of the East.

And so, my fellow countrymen, today I report to you that your sons and daughters have served you well and faithfully with the calm, deliberate, determined fighting spirit of the American soldier and sailor based upon a tradition of historical truth, as against the fanaticism of an enemy supported only by mythological fiction. Their spiritual strength and power has brought us through to victory. They are homeward bound — take care of them.

70.

# The Control of Atomic Energy

*The immediate need for international cooperation in the control of atomic energy was recognized by the United States, Canada, and Great Britain (the three countries whose scientists developed the atomic bomb) despite what appeared to be at the time at least a ten-year lead over the rest of the world. The following declaration on atomic energy agreed on by the President of the United States, the Prime Minister of the United Kingdom, and the Prime Minister of Canada, was issued on November 15, 1945, and outlined the policy that the United States was to follow until the Anglo-American test-ban treaty with the Soviet Union in July 1963. Until that time the Soviet Union rejected all American proposals, principally on the grounds that inspection was a violation of their national sovereignty.*

Source: 79 Congress, 2 Session, Senate Committee Monograph No. 1.

THE PRESIDENT of the United States, the Prime Minister of the United Kingdom, and the Prime Minister of Canada have issued the following statement.

1. We recognize that the application of recent scientific discoveries to the methods and practice of war has placed at the disposal of mankind means of destruction hitherto unknown, against which there can be no adequate military defense and in the employment of which no single nation can in fact have a monopoly.

2. We desire to emphasize that the responsibility for devising means to insure that the new discoveries shall be used for the benefit of mankind, instead of as a means of destruction, rests, not on our nations alone but upon the whole civilized world. Nevertheless, the progress that we have made in the development and use of atomic energy demands that we take an initiative in the matter, and we have accordngly met together to consider the possibili-y of international action —

(*a*) to prevent the use of atomic energy or destructive purposes;

(*b*) to promote the use of recent and fu-

ture advances in scientific knowledge, particularly in the utilization of atomic energy, for peaceful and humanitarian ends.

3. We are aware that the only complete protection for the civilized world from the destructive use of scientific knowledge lies in the prevention of war. No system of safeguards that can be devised will of itself provide an effective guarantee against production of atomic weapons by a nation bent on aggression. Nor can we ignore the possibility of the development of other weapons or of new methods of warfare which may constitute as great a threat to civilization as the military use of atomic energy.

4. Representing, as we do, the three countries which possess the knowledge essential to the use of atomic energy, we declare at the outset our willingness, as a first contribution, to proceed with the exchange of fundamental scientific information and the interchange of scientists and scientific literature for peaceful ends with any nation that will fully reciprocate.

5. We believe that the fruits of scientific research should be made available to all nations, and that freedom of investigation and

free interchange of ideas are essential to the progress of knowledge. In pursuance of this policy, the basic scientific information essential to the development of atomic energy for peaceful purposes has already been made available to the world. It is our intention that all further information of this character that may become available from time to time shall be similarly treated. We trust that other nations will adopt the same policy, thereby creating an atmosphere of reciprocal confidence in which political agreement and cooperation will flourish.

6. We have considered the question of the disclosure of detailed information concerning the practical industrial application of atomic energy. The military exploitation of atomic energy depends, in large part, upon the same methods and processes as would be required for industrial uses.

We are not convinced that the spreading of the specialized information regarding the practical application of atomic energy, before it is possible to devise effective, reciprocal, and enforceable safeguards acceptable to all nations, would contribute to a constructive solution of the problem of the atomic bomb. On the contrary, we think it might have the opposite effect. We are, however, prepared to share, on a reciprocal basis with others of the United Nations, detailed information concerning the practical industrial application of atomic energy just as soon as effective, enforceable safeguards against its use for destructive purposes can be devised.

7. In order to attain the most effective means of entirely eliminating the use of atomic energy for destructive purposes and promoting its widest use for industrial and humanitarian purposes, we are of the opinion that at the earliest practicable date a commission should be set up under the United Nations Organization to prepare recommendations for submission to the organization.

The commission should be instructed to proceed with the utmost dispatch and should be authorized to submit recommendations from time to time dealing with separate phases of its work.

In particular, the commission should make specific proposals —

(a) for extending between all nations the exchange of basic scientific information for peaceful ends;

(b) for control of atomic energy to the extent necessary to insure its use only for peaceful purposes;

(c) for the elimination from national armaments of atomic weapons and of all other major weapons adaptable to mass destruction;

(d) for effective safeguards by way of inspection and other means to protect complying states against the hazards of violations and evasions.

8. The work of the commission should proceed by separate stages, the successful completion of each one of which will develop the necessary confidence of the world before the next stage is undertaken. Specifically, it is considered that the commission might well devote its attention, first, to the wide exchange of scientists and scientific information; and, as a second stage, to the development of full knowledge concerning natural resources of raw materials.

9. Faced with the terrible realities of the application of science to destruction, every nation will realize more urgently than before the overwhelming need to maintain the rule of law among nations and to banish the scourge of war from the earth. This can only be brought about by giving wholehearted support to the United Nations Organization and by consolidating and extending its authority, thus creating conditions of mutual trust in which all peoples will be free to devote themselves to the arts of peace. It is our firm resolve to work without reservation to achieve these ends.

71.

# Harry S. Truman: Postwar Foreign Policy

*When Harry S. Truman became President on Roosevelt's death on April 12, 1945, he was little known to the country as a whole. As vice-president he had been left largely uninformed about general war policy, and the shock of Roosevelt's death left him momentarily bewildered. "Did you ever have a bull or a load of hay fall on you?" he remarked. "If you ever did, you know how I felt last night." But he quickly found his bearings and moved to bring the war to a speedy conclusion, deciding with what was apparently little hesitation to use the atomic bomb against Japan. His real troubles began after the Japanese surrender when, the wartime alliance between the U.S.S.R. and the Western democracies on the verge of dissolution, he encountered strong partisan opposition, combined with public indifference, to his attempt to carry on with Roosevelt's foreign policy. On October 27, 1945, in New York City, Truman delivered an address, part of which is reprinted here, in which he stated his views concerning the nation's foreign policy in the postwar era.*

Source: VSD, November 15, 1945: "Fundamentals of U.S. Foreign Policy."

1. We seek no territorial expansion or selfish advantage. We have no plans for aggression against any other state, large or small. We have no objective which need clash with the peaceful aims of any other nations.

2. We believe in the eventual return of sovereign rights and self-government to all peoples who have been deprived of them by force.

3. We shall approve no territorial changes in any friendly part of the world unless they accord with the freely expressed wishes of the people concerned.

4. We believe that all peoples who are prepared for self-government should be permitted to choose their own form of government by their own freely expressed choice, without interference from any foreign source. That is true in Europe, in Asia, in Africa, as well as in the Western Hemisphere.

5. By the combined and cooperative action of our war allies, we shall help the de-feated enemy states establish peaceful democratic governments of their own free choice. And we shall try to attain a world in which Nazism, Fascism, and military aggression cannot exist.

6. We shall refuse to recognize any government imposed upon any nation by the force of any foreign power. In some cases it may be impossible to prevent forceful imposition of such a government. But the United States will not recognize any such government.

7. We believe that all nations should have the freedom of the seas and equal rights to the navigation of boundary rivers and waterways and of rivers and waterways which pass through more than one country.

8. We believe that all states which are accepted in the society of nations should have access on equal terms to the trade and the raw materials of the world.

9. We believe that the sovereign states of the Western Hemisphere, without interference from outside the Western Hemisphere,

must work together as good neighbors in the solution of their common problems.

10. We believe that full economic collaboration between all nations, great and small, is essential to the improvement of living conditions all over the world, and to the establishment of freedom from fear and freedom from want.

11. We shall continue to strive to promote freedom of expression and freedom of religion throughout the peace-loving areas of the world.

12. We are convinced that the preservation of peace between nations requires a united nations organization composed of all the peace-loving nations of the world who are willing jointly to use force if necessary to insure peace.

---

72.

## Eugene V. Rostow: Our Worst Wartime Mistake

*The government's decision to confine 117,000 Japanese-Americans, most of whom were citizens, in relocation centers during World War II aroused the indignation of many distinguished Americans who regarded the action as a gross infringement on the rights of American citizens. Critics of the action argued that there was no evidence of disloyalty on the part of the group as a whole, that treating them as a group was tantamount to racism, and that the Japanese-Americans were forced to abandon their work and dispose of their property. Professor Eugene Rostow published an article, entitled "Our Worst Wartime Mistake," in September 1945, analyzing the Japanese removal and the Supreme Court's justificatory decision in* Korematsu v. United States *of 1944. His article is reprinted in part below.*

Source: *Harper's,* September 1945.

As TIME PASSES, it becomes more and more plain that our wartime treatment of the Japanese and the Japanese-Americans on the West Coast was a tragic and dangerous mistake. That mistake is a threat to society, and to all men. Its motivation and its impact on our system of law deny every value of democracy.

In the perspective of our legal tradition, the facts are almost incredible.

During the bleak spring of 1942, the Japanese and the Japanese-Americans who lived on the West Coast of the United States were taken into custody and removed to camps in the interior. More than 100,000 men, women, and children were thus exiled and imprisoned. More than two-thirds of them were American citizens.

These people were taken into custody as a military measure on the ground that espionage and sabotage were especially to be feared from persons of Japanese blood. The whole group was removed from the West Coast because the military authorities thought it would take too long to conduct individual investigations on the spot. They were arrested without warrants and were held without indictment or a statement of charges, although the courts were open and freely functioning. They were transported to camps far from their homes, and kept there under prison conditions, pending investigations of their "loyalty." Despite the good intentions of the chief relocation officers the centers were little better than concentration camps.

If the evacuees were found "loyal," they were released only if they could find a job and a place to live, in a community where no hoodlums would come out at night to chalk up anti-Japanese slogans, break windows, or threaten riot. If found "disloyal" in their attitude to the war, they were kept in the camps indefinitely — although sympathy with the enemy is no crime in the United States (for white people at least) so long as it is not translated into deeds or the visible threat of deeds. On May 1, 1945, three years after the program was begun, about 70,000 persons were still in camps. While it is hoped to have all these people either free, or in more orthodox confinement, by January 1, 1946, what is euphemistically called the Japanese "relocation" program will not be a closed book for many years.

The original program of "relocation" was an injustice, in no way required or justified by the circumstances of the war. But the Supreme Court, in three extraordinary decisions, has upheld its main features as constitutional. This fact converts a piece of wartime folly into national policy — a permanent part of the law — a doctrine enlarging the power of the military in relation to civil authority. It is having a sinister impact on the minority problem in every part of the country. It is giving aid to reactionary politicians who use social division and racial prejudice as their tools. The precedent is being used to encourage attacks on the civil rights of both citizens and aliens. As Mr. Justice Jackson has said, the principle of these decisions "lies about like a loaded weapon ready for the hand of any authority that can bring forward a plausible claim of an urgent need." All in all, the case of the Japanese-Americans is the worst blow our liberties have sustained in many years. Unless repudiated, it may support devastating and unforeseen social and political conflicts. . . .

Immediately after Pearl Harbor there were no special regulations for persons of Japanese extraction. Known enemy sympathizers among the Japanese, like white traitors and enemy agents, were arrested. There was no sabotage by persons of Japanese ancestry. There was no reason to suppose that the 112,000 persons of Japanese descent on the West Coast, less than 2 per cent of the population, constituted a greater menace than such persons in Hawaii, where they were 32 percent of the population.

After a month's silence, the organized minority whose business it has been to exploit racial tensions on the West Coast went to work. They had strong support in the Hearst press and its equivalents. Politicians, fearful of an unknown public opinion, spoke out for white supremacy. West Coast Congressional delegations led by Senator Hiram Johnson, urged the administration to exclude all persons of Japanese blood from the coast states. Anti-Oriental spokesmen appeared before special hearings of the Tolan Committee, and explained the situation as they conceived it to Lieutenant General J. L. DeWitt, commanding the Western Defense Command. Tension was intensified, and doubters, worried about the risks of another Pearl Harbor, remained silent, preferring too much caution to too little. An opinion crystallized in favor of evacuating the Japanese.

After some hesitation, General DeWitt proposed the policy of exclusion on grounds of military need. The War Department backed him up. No one in the government took the responsibility for opposing or overruling him.

Despite the nature of the emergency, the Army's lawyers wanted more legal authority before action was taken. The President issued an Executive Order in February 1942, and in March Congress passed a statute, authorizing military commanders to designate "military areas" and to prescribe the terms on which any persons could enter, leave, or remain in such areas. A policy of encouraging the Japanese to move away individually had shown signs of producing confusion. It was therefore decided to establish a compulsory system of detention in camps, to simplify the process of resettlement, and to afford the fullest measure of security.

The history of law affords nothing more fantastic than the evidence which is supposed to justify this program. General DeWitt's final recommendation to the Secretary of War, dated February 14, 1942, but not made public until early in 1944, explains the basis of his decision.

"In the war in which we are now engaged," he said, "racial affinities are not severed by migration. The Japanese race is an enemy race and while many second and third generation Japanese born on United States soil, possessed of United States citizenship, have become 'Americanized,' the racial strains are undiluted." From the premise of a war of "races," the general had no difficulty reaching his conclusion. There is "no ground for assuming," he said, that Japanese-Americans will not turn against the United States. So much for the idea that men are presumed innocent until proved guilty, and that American citizens stand on an equal footing before the law without regard for race, color, or previous condition of servitude! "It therefore follows," the general added, "that along the vital Pacific Coast over 112,000 potential enemies, of Japanese extraction, are at large today. There are disturbing indications that these are organized and ready for concerted action at a favorable opportunity. The very fact that no sabotage has taken place to date is a disturbing and confirming indication that such action will be taken." . . .

The most striking comment on the quality of the evidence produced by General DeWitt to support his proposal was made by Solicitor General Fahy, whose job it was to defend the general's plan before the Supreme Court. He relied upon the general's report "only to the extent that it relates"

statistics and other details concerning the actual evacuation and the events which took place after it. But the briefs that he himself presented were identical in the substance of their argument. The Japanese-Americans were an unknown, unknowable, foreign group, living together, and moving in mysterious ways, inscrutable to puzzled white men. Therefore, let them be imprisoned; let their property be taken into custody, sold off at bargain prices, dissipated, and lost; let their roots be torn up, let their children suffer the irreparable shock of life in a concentration camp; let their relation to society be distorted by the searing memory of humiliation, rejection, and punishment.

The evidence supports one conclusion only: the dominant element in the development of our relocation policy was race prejudice, not a military estimate of a military problem. . . .

In a bewildering and unimpressive series of opinions, relieved only by the dissents of Justice Roberts and Justice Murphy in one of the three cases — *Korematsu* v. *United States* — the court chose to assume that the main issues did not exist. In avoiding the risks of overruling the government on an issue of war policy, it weakened society's control over military power — one of the controls on which the whole organization of our society depends. It failed to uphold the most ordinary rights of citizenship, making Japanese-Americans into second-class citizens, who stand before the courts on a different legal footing from other Americans. It accepted and gave the prestige of its support to dangerous racial myths about a minority group, in arguments which can easily be applied to any other minority in our society. . . .

The conception of the war power under the American Constitution rests on the experience of the Revolution and the Civil War. It rests on basic political principle which men who had endured those times of trouble had fully discussed and carefully set forth. The chief architects of the conception were men of affairs who had participated in war, and had definite and well-founded ideas about the role of the professional military mind in the conduct of war.

The first and dominating principle of the war power under the Constitution is that the commander in chief of the armed forces must be a civilian, elected and not promoted to his office. In no other way can the subordination of the military to the civil power be assured. And in every democracy, the relationship between civil and military power is the crucial issue — the issue on which its capacity to survive in time of crisis ultimately depends.

The second principle governing the war power in a democracy is that of responsibility. Like every other officer of government, soldiers must answer for their decisions to the nation's system of law, and not to the chief of staff alone. Where military decisions lead to conflicts between individuals and authority — as in the Japanese exclusion program — the courts must adjudicate them. It is essential to every democratic value in society that official action, taken in the name of the war power, should be held to standards of responsibility under such circumstances. The courts have not in the past, and should not now, declare such problems to be beyond the reach of judicial review. The present Supreme Court is dominated by the conviction that in the past judicial review has unduly limited the freedom of administrative action. But surely the right answer to bad law is good law, rather than no law at all. The court must review the exercise of military power in a way which permits ample freedom to the executive, yet assures society as a whole that appropriate standards of responsibility have been met.

The issue for judicial decision in these cases is not lessened or changed by saying that the war power includes any steps required to win the war. The problem is still one of judgment as to what helps win a war. Who is to decide whether there was a sensible reason for doing what was done? Is it enough for the general to say that when he acted, he honestly thought it was a good idea to do what he did?

Unless the courts require a showing, in cases like these, of an intelligible relationship between means and ends, society has lost its basic protection against the abuse of military power. The general's good intentions must be irrelevant. There should be evidence in court that his military judgment had a suitable basis in fact.

The history of this question in the Supreme Court is unmistakable. The earlier decisions of the court had vigorously asserted that "what are the allowable limits of military discretion, and whether or not they have been overstepped in a particular case, are judicial questions"; and that there must be evidence enough to satisfy the court as to the need for the action taken. They had made it clear that the law is not neutral in such issues, but has a positive preference for protecting civil rights where possible, and a long-standing suspicion of the military mind when acting outside its own sphere.

Yet in the Japanese-American cases there was literally no evidence whatever by which the court might test the responsibility of General DeWitt's action. Dozens of Supreme Court decisions had said that the court would not pass on serious constitutional questions without a record before it, establishing the essential facts. Those cases were all ignored. One hundred thousand persons were sent to concentration camps on a record which wouldn't support a conviction for stealing a dog.

The earlier cases not only established the rule that there must be an independent judicial examination of the justification for a military act. They went much further. They declared a simple rule-of-thumb as a guide in handling cases involving military discretion, in which the military undertook to arrest, hold, or try people. So long as the civil courts were open and functioning, the Supreme Court had previously held, there could be no military necessity for allowing generals to hold, try, or punish people. The safety of the country could be thoroughly protected against treason, sabotage, and like crimes by ordinary arrest and trial in the civil courts, unless the courts were shut by riot, invasion, or insurrection.

That was the moral of the great case of *Ex Parte Milligan*, decided in 1866. *Ex Parte Milligan* is a monument in the democratic tradition, and until now it has been the animating force in this branch of our law. To be sure, there is a tendency nowadays to treat *Ex Parte Milligan* as outmoded, as if new methods of "total" warfare made the case an anachronism; but those who take this view have forgotten the circumstances of the Civil War, when fifth columns, propaganda, sabotage, and espionage were rife.

*Ex Parte Milligan* illustrates the point. Milligan was convincingly charged with active participation in a fifth column plot worthy of Hitler. A group of armed and determined men planned to seize federal arsenals at Columbus, Indianapolis, and at three points in Illinois, and then to release Confederate prisoners of war held in those states. Thus they would create a Confederate army behind the Union lines in Tennessee. Milligan and his alleged co-conspirators acted in Indiana, Missouri, Illinois, and in other border states. Their strategy had a political arm. The Union was to be split politically, and a Northwest Confederation was to be declared, friendly to the South, and embracing six states. This was not an idle dream. It was sponsored by a well-financed society, the Sons of Liberty, thought to have 300,000 members, many of them rich and respectable, and the planned uprising would coincide with the Chicago convention of the Democratic Party, which was then sympathetic to abandoning the war and recognizing the Confederacy.

The unanimous court which freed Milligan for civil trial was a court of fire-eating Unionists. Mr. Justice Davis, who wrote for the majority, was one of President Lincoln's closest friends. The chief justice, who wrote for the concurring minority, was a valiant supporter of the war, whatever his shortcomings in other respects. Yet the court had no difficulty in freeing Milligan, and facing down the outcry provoked by the decision.

The court held in Milligan's case that it was unconstitutional to try him before a military commission, rather than a court of law. There was little doubt of his guilt. But it was beyond the powers of the military to measure or punish it. . . .

Yet in the cases of the Japanese-Americans, the Supreme Court held the precedent of *Ex Parte Milligan* inapplicable. The reasoning is extraordinarily dangerous. The Japanese-Americans, the court said, were detained by a civilian agency, not by the Army. The program was not exclusively a matter for military administration, and it was enforceable under a statute by ordinary criminal remedies. Therefore, it did not present the question of the power of military tribunals to conduct trials under the laws of war.

But the Japanese-Americans were ordered detained by a general, purporting to act on military grounds. The military order was enforceable, on pain of imprisonment. While a United States marshal, rather than a military policeman, assured obedience to the order, the ultimate sanction behind the marshal's writ is the same as that of the military police: the bayonets of United States troops. It is hardly a ground for distinction that the general's command was backed by the penalty of civil imprisonment, or that he obtained civilian aid in running the relocation camps. The starting point for the entire program was a military order, which had to be obeyed.

In *Ex Parte Milligan*, the Supreme Court had said that the military could not constitutionally arrest, nor could a military tribunal constitutionally try, civilians charged with treason and conspiracy to destroy the state by force, at a time when the civil courts were open and functioning. Yet under the plan considered in the Japanese-American cases, people not charged with crime are imprisoned without even a military trial, on the ground that they have the taint of Japanese blood. It would seem clear that if it is illegal to arrest and confine people after an unwarranted military trial, it is surely even more illegal to arrest and confine them without any trial at all. But the Supreme Court says that the issues of the *Milligan* case were not involved in this case because the evacuees were committed to camps by military orders, not by military tribunals, and because their jailers did not wear uniforms!

There are, then, two basic constitutional problems concealed in the court's easy dismissal of *Ex Parte Milligan:* the arrest, removal, and confinement of persons without trial, pending examination of their loyalty; and the indefinite confinement of persons found to be disloyal. On both counts, at least as to citizens, the moral of *Ex Parte Milligan* is plain.

As for the Japanese *aliens* involved in the evacuation program, the constitutional problem is different. In time of war, the government possesses great powers over enemy aliens, which are to be exercised, the courts say, for the "single purpose" of preventing enemy aliens from aiding the enemy. They may be interned if dangerous and their property in the United States may be taken into custody. Yet they are entitled to our general constitutional protections of individual liberty — to trial by jury, the writ of habeas corpus, and the other basic rights of the person. Is it permissible to intern all the Japanese who live on the West Coast, but to allow German and Italian aliens, and Japanese who live elsewhere, general freedom? Surely the control and custody of enemy aliens in wartime should be reasonably equal and evenhanded.

The Japanese exclusion program rests on five propositions of the utmost potential menace:

1. Protective custody, extending over three or four years, is a permitted form of imprisonment in the United States.

2. Political opinions, not criminal acts, may contain enough danger to justify such imprisonment.

3. Men, women, and children of a given racial group, both Americans and resident aliens, can be presumed to possess the kind of dangerous ideas which require their imprisonment.

4. In time of war or emergency the military — perhaps without even the concurrence of the legislature — can decide what political opinions require imprisonment, and which groups are infected with them.

5. The decision of the military can be carried out without indictment, trial, examination, jury, the confrontation of witnesses, counsel for the defense, the privilege against self-incrimination, or any of the other safeguards of the Bill of Rights.

The idea of punishment only for individual criminal behavior is basic to all systems of civilized law. A great principle was never lost so casually. Mr. Justice Black's comment was weak to the point of impotence: "Hardships are a part of war, and war is an aggregation of hardships." It was an answer in the spirit of cliché: "Don't you know there's a war going on?" It ignores the rights of citizenship, and the safeguards of trial practice which have been the historical attributes of liberty.

We believe that the German people bear a common political responsibility for outrages secretly committed by the Gestapo and the SS. What are we to think of our own part in a program which violates every principle of our common life, yet has been approved by the President, Congress, and the Supreme Court?

73.

## Allan Nevins: The Pearl Harbor Controversy

*The nation had gone into World War II probably more unified than during any conflict in its history. But as the war went on, and ultimate success became more and more certain, the unity brought about by the emergency of 1941 began to dissolve. As early as 1944 public discussion began to be heard regarding President Roosevelt's role in the attack on Pearl Harbor, and it began to be suggested — first by "professional" Roosevelt-haters and then by a number of others — that the President and Secretary of State Hull "manufactured" the attack in order to get the country into the war. After the victory in 1945 the criticism swelled to a chorus, perhaps in large part because Roosevelt was now dead, and charges were leveled from all sides. The distinguished historian Allan Nevins discussed what he called this "challenge to historic truth" in an article published in the* New York Times *at the end of 1945, and in so doing summed up the attack on the government's policy before Pearl Harbor and indicated the arguments opposing it.*

Source: *New York Times Magazine,* December 16, 1945.

IN DUE COURSE this country will have expert reviews of the systematic, malignant, and all-too-successful attempt in the 1930s to blacken the motives of the Wilson administration in entering the First World War. Meanwhile, a far more urgent issue presents itself. The American people have to rouse themselves to the real nature of the attack on government policy just before Pearl Harbor — an attack that is a challenge not only to historic truth but to certain fundamental moral and political tenets of our democracy.

This attack, which has inspired Secretary Hull to denounce "false and flimsy pretexts," emanates from two principal groups. One is a body of partisan critics of the Roosevelt administration, attempting to make political capital out of allegations that the President and secretary of state deliberately provoked a Japanese declaration of war; provoked it by a harsh ultimatum and by threatening naval movements. The other is a body of diehard isolationists who seek to prove that we were betrayed into a needless war by administration leaders who flouted the first principles of neutrality and set their own passions above the nation's welfare.

The whole attempt, if not resented, confuted, and rendered despicable, may have the most lamentable consequences. It may distort the truth, not only about *how* we went to war but about *why* we went to war. It may confuse and delude millions of Americans, not merely as to American purposes in the fateful negotiations of August-November 1941 but as to the much larger question of American policy in facing the fundamental issues of the world upheaval of 1939-45. . . .

The partisan half of the attack on the government's acts before Pearl Harbor has at least the merits of a barefaced candor. Representative Gearhart put the indictment bluntly. The Japanese, he said, "were doing everything in their power to get an acceptable agreement." Making these friendly, peaceable approaches, they "got slapped in the face on Nov. 26" (1941) by Mr. Hull's note of that date. That "precipitated the war."

The isolationist attack is not so explicit. It is more often couched in innuendo. The thesis is that our government, hoodwinked once more by Allied propaganda, home profiteers, and a President's unneutral bias, deliberately courted hostilities. One isolationist historian quotes without dissent Tokyo's complaints "that the United States was violating Japan's rights as a belligerent by giving financial aid to the government of China and by sending munitions to that government." Some innuendos suggest a treasonable suppression of information by the President.

Several issues are presented by these attempts to defile the national record just before Pearl Harbor. Of these, the first, which raises the question whether Tokyo or Washington was guilty of provocation, is the simplest. It is neither more nor less than the issue whether a brazen undertaking to call white black, and black white, shall succeed. It is an issue of fact and subject to a demonstration as clear as Euclid.

The attempt to fasten the "provocation" upon Mr. Roosevelt or Mr. Hull can be made plausible only by an essential misrepresentation of the meaning of the Japanese program in the Pacific. What was that program? The Japanese committed the first overt act in the assault of aggressor states upon peaceful nations when they launched their Manchurian attack in 1931. This was a flat violation of treaty obligations. Having seized Manchuria, they waited until Britain and France were paralyzed by fear of Germany, and then delivered their second stroke. Their design embraced the conquest of all China. Having partly succeeded in this, they undertook a third great movement in 1940-41 when Europe was reduced to impotence by war.

This movement carried Japan southward into a huge area controlled politically by three nations helpless to make any effective resistance. One sector comprised the rich islands under Dutch control. Another sector, inadequately protected by the Singapore base, was under British government. The third sector, Indo-China, was French.

By seizing this area, Japan would hold a great empire extending from Sakhalin to Java and New Guinea, rich in oil, rubber, tin, and other vital materials of conquest. Once entrenched there, Japan could complete the subjugation of China, drive westward against India, and dominate a full half of the Pacific. A totalitarian, warlike, and aggressive regime, its purposes extending to conquest of half the world, could seal off all the wealth, markets, and hopeful democratic impulses of the Orient, while Hitler sealed off the most important parts of the Occident.

Any American government which regarded this threat passively would have betrayed the vital interests of the Republic. It would have betrayed mankind, for the semi-paralysis of the Netherlands, France, and Britain made us a trustee for those democracies. Action to persuade Japan to halt was imperative. Such action had to be taken when Japan, by agreement with Hitler, occupied northern Indo-China. Powerful Japanese armaments at that point, far beyond any defensive line, plainly had but one purpose — aggression against the Dutch, the British, the Australasian states, and inevitably the Philippines.

The American government never threatened to fight Japan. It asked only that the plainly indicated program of conquest be given up. For its own future and that of the globe, it could not see a sinister, pitiless conqueror reducing the Far East to serfdom, extinguishing all political liberty and cutting off all commercial and intellectual intercourse.

To say that the Japanese "were doing everything in their power to get an acceptable agreement" is to give the Japanese note of Nov. 20, 1941, an interpretation grotesque enough to amuse an insane asylum. This note asked the United States to desist from giving any assistance to China so that China might collapse and lie at Tokyo's feet. It demanded that the United States supply Japan with "a required quantity of oil" until military operations in China were completed. It asked for cooperation in inducing the Netherlands Indies to supply both oil and rubber. It demanded restoration of the old commercial relations prior to the freezing of assets. Far from offering any guarantees of cessation from aggression, it insisted upon maintenance of the threatening army in northern Indo-China — with the right to augment that army.

Although Mr. Hull did not know it, these Japanese demands were linked with a timed program of military action; failing of assent by a given date, Japan would strike.

The idea that Mr. Hull's note of November 26 was an ultimatum or "slap" cannot survive one reading of the document. Far from contemplating a break, its whole object — as the State Department long ago said — was to "keep alive conversations looking toward inducing Japan to choose the pathway of self-restraint." It asked a withdrawal of Japanese forces from China and Indo-China — and what right had they there? We were a signatory of a solemn treaty for preserving China's integrity.

The note proposed a multilateral nonaggression pact. It then envisaged a removal of all freezing orders and embargoes and a restoration of trade on the most-favored-nation principle. It was to be interpreted in the light of Mr. Hull's statement to Ambassador Nomura on November 22 that if Japan was seen pursuing a peaceful course there would be no question about supplying her with all the materials she desired. It was to be further interpreted in the light of Mr. Roosevelt's statement to Nomura on November 27 that as soon as Japan gave clear manifestation of peaceful intent, the United States would take practical steps designed to improve the economic position of Japan.

Of course the government could have taken a different course. As Mr. Hull says, it could have surrendered all its principles and let Japan push on with the conquest of half the globe. So in 1917 it could have abandoned all our rights as neutrals. So in 1861 it could have given up the cause of Union and freedom. But it would not have been an American government had it taken the poltroon's policy; it would have been the most un-American government in our history.

One isolationist historian, trying to make it appear that surrender was feasible, quotes a report that late in November "a kind of truce with Japan was reached in Washington, with the approval of the British and Australians and reluctantly of the Dutch," and that "the Chinese ambassador protested to President Roosevelt against the proposed truce, and the plan for avoiding an immediate conflict with Japan was dropped." On this suggestion that we paltered with principle, Secretary Hull gave explicit testimony. A three months' *modus vivendi* agreement was considered, but Hull and Roosevelt rejected it from conviction, and because it was manifest that there would be widespread opposition from American opinion to the *modus vivendi* aspect of the proposal, especially to the supplying to Japan of even limited quantities of oil. The Chinese government violently opposed the idea. The other interested governments were sympathetic to the Chinese view and fundamentally were unfavorable or lukewarm.

But indissolubly linked with this issue of "provocation" is another. The provocation was all Japanese. But what encouraged it? Was it the unyielding adherence of the administration to principle? Or was it the course pursued by our isolationists — a course calculated to make Japanese leaders believe that America was faction-torn, too deeply divided to react vigorously against aggression, too complacently sure of her safety to face any peril?

On this highly important question it is to

be noted that the Japanese government from 1931 onward nicely coordinated its aggressive program with every display of weakness and timidity on the part of its opponents. Each step was linked with events in Europe and America. The Japanese sense of timing was remarkably apt; it resembled Hitler's.

Japan acted in Manchuria in October 1931, when Britain and the United States were plunged in a sea of economic depression; when Mr. Hoover was notoriously against any action that might lead to war, and Sir John Simon was spokesman for the appeasement element in London finance and trade. The main Japanese drive against China in July 1937 coincided with the great initial successes of Mussolini and Hitler in Europe and Africa, and the passage of the Neutrality Acts in America. In 1940-41 the Japanese drive southward took place when France and the Netherlands lay conquered, and Britain and China were standing alone against the aggressor powers. When, in September 1940, Tokyo landed its troops in northern French Indo-China, it expected to see Britain fall before a German invasion within six months.

Did the Japanese not look both east and west when they enlarged their aggressive measures in 1941? The war lords were highly encouraged by the support which Hitler promised Foreign Minister Matsuoka when the two conferred in Berlin on March 27. They were still more elated when Matsuoka obtained Molotov's signature on April 13 to a treaty providing that if either nation became involved in war "the other contracting party will observe neutrality throughout the conflict."

With support from Hitler, and a hands-off course promised by Russia, it was only America that Japan had to fear as in mid-June it angrily recalled the economic mission it had sent to Batavia and prepared to take stronger measures; as in July, with Vichy encouragement, it occupied all of Indo-China. Japanese eyes were fixed on American opinion; Japanese ears eager for American comment.

And what encouragement did Japanese aggressors receive from America? It came in two different ways. It came, first, from men who loudly proclaimed that whatever Japan did in Asia was no affair of ours; that we should concern ourselves with nothing outside our own borders. It came, in the second place, from men who asserted that the United States need never fear any attack from any power whatever; that war with Japan was (as Oswald Garrison Villard wrote) "impossible"; that Japan could never hurt us and we could never hurt Japan.

"We have been asked," Colonel Lindbergh scornfully remarked on July 1, 1941, "to defend the English way of life and the Chinese way of life." It would be silly, he argued, to support either. "We believe that the best way to defend America," he said in a Minneapolis speech, "is to keep our armies on our own soil." Hiram Johnson, speaking in the National Radio Forum program on Feb. 24, 1941, declared that the conflict raging in China and Europe had no conceivable relation to our interests. "Thus far there has been no attempt in any way to interfere with us," he asserted.

Hamilton Fish, denouncing Lend-Lease, declared that he knew from a personal poll that 90 percent of Americans wanted nothing whatever to do, under any circumstances, with "Europe's and Asia's wars." Some went so far as to suggest that the Japanese co-prosperity sphere might well have favorable implications for America.

Meanwhile, with Japan already laying plans for a blow, others derided the idea of any foreign attack as preposterous. Hanford MacNider, who described the struggles raging in Europe and Asia as the "Old World's everlasting quarrels," said in January 1941 that he knew of no authority who thought we were in imminent danger of attack from any source. "No foreign power or group of powers will ever attack a prepared America."

Even the destruction of the British Navy, declared Lindbergh in the Lend-Lease hearings, would not affect America adversely. Hiram Johnson exultantly told the country that in these hearings "practically every witness who pretended to be expert at all held that the invasion of our country was impossible." The Military Service Act of 1940 and the Military Service Extension Act of 1941 met embittered opposition in isolationist quarters.

We have direct evidence that such utterances were well noted in Japan. The *Japan Times-Advertiser* of May 5, 1941, carried a news story on the subject. "These evidences of disunity and interior strife in the United States," it said, "at this critical time, complemented by evidences of labor unrest, will go far to reinforce those states that are consolidating behind their governments and where open criticism or interference with state policy would never be tolerated."

Its editorial of the same date was headed: "American Disunity Undermines Democracies and Strengthens Axis Cause." American isolationists, it commented, "are likely to arouse a bitter feud throughout the United States which can seriously undermine the drive" to aid China and Britain. Senator Nye, who was against the most important preparedness measure thus far taken, gloried in this feud. "There is bound to be disunity," he said in a New York speech in September, "when our government borrows the ways of dictators and disrupts millions of young men's lives in a program of peacetime conscription."

It was with the belief that Germany would soon win a sweeping victory in Europe that Japan in July of 1941 consolidated its grip upon Indo-China as a springboard for attacks upon British Malaya and the Netherlands East Indies. It was also with the knowledge that a large section of American opinion was being roused by Senator Tobey, Rush Holt, and others already quoted, to a demand that, whatever happened in Asia, America must never interfere.

But a still larger issue is comprehended in this attempt to blacken the record of the American government in making a firm stand in principle against Japan. The effort is essentially an attempt to create and capitalize upon an utter rejection of the grander objects of the war. So, sneer the critics, we fought to get Japan out of Indo-China; we fought to halt Germany in another European power contest. This moral obtuseness had plenty of exponents in 1941. There were numerous isolationists who said with Lindbergh that they did not wish either Germany or Britain to win — which meant they did not wish Germany defeated.

There were many who nodded approvingly when Senator Wheeler said that what Europe needed was a conference to agree on a fixed peace; and then defined that peace as one in which Germany should have her 1914 boundaries, with all her colonial empire, and with a measure of autonomy for the Poles and Czechs under her dominion. But that after the tremendous struggle of the past four years, and after the clear revelation of just what Japanese and German triumph would have meant, such moral myopia should persist — this is disheartening indeed.

It was for the future of America and of all civilization that we fought this mightiest of wars, and this future would have been sacrificed had we not taken precisely the stand we did. By cowardice, by evasion, by a surrender of the principles dearest to thoughtful Americans, we might indeed have purchased, in that momentous autumn of 1941, a little temporary safety. But we would have sacrificed not only our national dignity and honor but all future security for ourselves and for nations of kindred standards and ideals. We would have been reduced in the end not only to the basest but to the most abjectly helpless position ever held by a great civilized nation professing exalted virtues and aims.

# 1946

74.

## Louis N. Ridenour: Pilot Lights of the Apocalypse

*The postwar world faced a potentially greater danger than the war itself — the proliferation of atomic weapons. The scientists who had helped develop the atomic bomb were among the first to call for international control of the new weapon, for they were certain that other industrial nations, especially the Soviet Union, would soon develop their own supply. By January 1946, when atomic physicist Louis Ridenour published the following one-act play dramatizing the consequences of failure to control the awesome new power, the nuclear arms race had already begun.*

Source: *Fortune*, January 1946.

*The curtain rises to disclose the operations room of the Western Defense Command, somewhere in the San Francisco area and a hundred feet underground. Two sergeants, RIGHT, are tending a row of teletype machines that connect the room with the world's principal cities. Two others, REAR, sit before a sort of telephone switchboard with key switches, lights, and labels representing the world's major cities. Behind them stands a captain. At a large desk, CENTER, sit a brigadier general and two colonels all reading teletype messages. The wall, LEFT, has a sturdy barred door, a world map, and a framed motto: "Remember Pearl Harbor."*

TIME: *Some years after all the industrialized nations have mastered the production and use of atomic power.*

BRIGADIER (*laying down the message he has been reading*): Nothing much tonight, I'd

say. We'd better get tidied up a little. Captain Briggs!

CAPTAIN (*facing about and standing at attention*): Yes, sir.

BRIGADIER: Ready for company?

CAPTAIN: Yes, sir. I think so, sir.

BRIGADIER: See that the men look busy — on their toes and busy.

CAPTAIN: Yes, sir. (*A bell rings.*) Schwartz, you get the door. (*One of the sergeants crosses to the door and opens it. All stand rigidly at attention. A little confused, the sergeant goes through the formality of examining passes. He then admits a group of four: a four-star general, a major, and two civilians.*)

GENERAL: Carry on. (*The men relax. The General leads the two civilians over to the Brigadier and the Colonels. The Major takes up his station by the door. Nobody pays any attention to him.)* Mr. President, this is General Anderson, Watch Officer in charge of the Operations Room.

THE PRESIDENT: How do you do?

BRIGADIER: How do you do, sir? *(They shake hands.)*

GENERAL: Colonel Sparks and Colonel Peabody, Deputy Watch Officers on duty.

THE PRESIDENT: Glad to meet you both. *(They shake hands.)*

GENERAL: Dr. Thompson — General Anderson, Colonel Sparks, and Colonel Peabody. *(All nod and smile.)* Now, Mr. President, this is the nerve center of our counterattack organization for the western area. The teletype machines you see over there *(pointing)* are on radio circuits that connect us with our people in all the principal cities of the world, and with the other continental defense commands. The stations, and their statuses, are marked on the map. *(He gestures toward the map.)* We've just come from the defense center, where the radar plots are kept and the guns and the fighters controlled. That's defense. But this is counterattack. Along that wall *(waving toward the rear)* is our control board. If you'll step over here, sir, I'll show you how it works.

THE PRESIDENT *(moving with the General toward the telephone switchboard against the back wall)*: Defense and counterattack, eh? Why keep them separate?

GENERAL: Well, the defense has to move quickly, or it's no good at all. They don't have time to think. But counterattack — well, counterattack has to move quickly, too. But we want them to have time to decide what they need to do. You can't tell just from the direction of an attack who launched it. An attack might be staged entirely by mines planted inside our borders, so there wouldn't be any direction connected with it. And then again, we have pretty good information that some other countries besides us have got bombs up above the stratosphere, 800 miles above the earth, going round us in

orbits like little moons. We put up 2,000 and we can see about 5,400 on our radar. Any time, somebody can call down that odd 3,400 by radio and send them wherever they want. There's no telling from trajectory which nation controls those bombs. What this all means is that the data these fellows here have to go on is mainly political. Radar doesn't do them any good. What they need is intelligence; and that's what comes in all the time, as complete and up-to-date as we can get it, on the teletypes. In the defense center, you saw scientists and technicians. The officers here are political scientists.

THE PRESIDENT: That's very interesting. Maybe you'll give me a job here if I ever need one. I'm a political scientist.

GENERAL *(laughing just enough)*: Yes, sir!

THE PRESIDENT: General, you haven't told me what all these gadgets are for. *(He waves toward the switchboard.)*

GENERAL: No, sir, I haven't. This is our counterattack control board. You see that every station is marked with the name of a city. And every station has three pilot lights: red, yellow, and green.

THE PRESIDENT: All the green ones are on.

GENERAL: That's right, sir. We have unattended radio transmitters, each with three spares, in stations in every city covered on this board. If one of the transmitters goes on the blink, a spare is automatically switched on. But if all four transmitters in any station are destroyed, well, we lose the signal from that station. When that happens the green light goes out and the yellow light comes on.

THE PRESIDENT: How about the red light?

GENERAL: That comes on instead of the yellow when all our stations in the whole city go off the air. Yellow means partial destruction — red means substantially complete destruction.

THE PRESIDENT: And green means peace.

GENERAL: Yes, sir. But this isn't just a monitoring board. You see this key here.

THE PRESIDENT: Yes.

GENERAL: That sets off our mines. We have them planted in a great many cities, and the radio control circuit can be unlocked from here.

THE PRESIDENT: Is the whole world mined now?

GENERAL: Well, no. We haven't bothered much with Asia. And some countries are so hard to get into that coverage is spotty. Our schedule calls for completion of mine installations in two more years. But we have another card to play. You remember I told you about the satellite bombs — the ones that are circling around, 800 miles up?

THE PRESIDENT: Yes.

GENERAL: Well, this other key here will bring down on the city shown on the marker — we are looking at Calcutta — one of those satellite bombs every time it is pressed.

THE PRESIDENT: Is one of those bombs earmarked for each particular city?

GENERAL: No, sir. The bomb that happens to be in the most favorable location at the time this key is pressed is the one brought down. It might be any one of the whole 2,000.

THE PRESIDENT: This is all damned clever.

GENERAL: We have Dr. Thompson to thank for most of it. His people worked out all the technical stuff. All the Army has to do is man the installations and watch the intelligence as it comes along.

DR. THOMPSON: Good of you to say that, General. But seriously, Mr. President, as people pointed out soon after the first atomic bomb was dropped, there isn't any other nation with the industrial know-how to do a job like this.

THE PRESIDENT: It is very impressive, I must say. Are the other Defense Commands equipped the same way?

GENERAL: Yes, sir. As a matter of fact, to guard against accidents, each Defense Command has two complete operations rooms like this, either one of which can take full control if the other is destroyed.

THE PRESIDENT: We've kept ahead in the armaments race. Who'd dare attack us when we're set up like this?

DR. THOMPSON: Surely nobody would. I don't think you need expect any trouble.

THE PRESIDENT: Well, this has all been very interesting. *(To the Brigadier)* General, have you had any exciting times here you can tell me about?

BRIGADIER: Yes, sir. Every time a meteorite comes down — a shooting star, you know — our radar boys track it, shoot it down, and send us in an alert. We have a few bad moments until we get the spectrographic report. If it's iron and nickel and it always has been so far — we know God sent it, and relax. Someday it'll be uranium, and then we'll have to push a button. Or plutonium.

THE PRESIDENT: How many shooting stars have you shot?

COLONEL SPARKS *(laughing politely)*: We get an average of twelve a month. In August it's the worst, of course. The Perseids, you know

THE PRESIDENT *(puzzled)*: Iran. . . ?

BRIGADIER *(hastily)*: No, sir. The Perseid meteors. Named after Perseus. Astronomers are a classical bunch.

THE PRESIDENT *(recovering)*: Oh, sure. *(Turning to the Colonels)* Gentlemen, how do you like this job?

COLONEL SPARKS: We have a feeling of grave responsibility.

THE PRESIDENT: The fate of nations is in your hands. But always remember that our nation is the most precious.

BOTH COLONELS *(awed)*: Yes, sir.

GENERAL: Well, Mr. President, we've fallen a little behind our schedule. They'll be waiting for us at the mess.

THE PRESIDENT: All right, General, let's get along. General Anderson, Colonel Sparks, Colonel Peabody, I've enjoyed very much seeing your installation. Keep on your toes. We're all depending on you.

GENERAL AND COLONELS *(together)*: Yes, sir. *(Schwartz goes over, opens the door, and stands stiffly at attention as the visitors file out amid a general chorus of "Goodby" and "Goodby, sir." Schwartz closes the door. The Brigadier and Colonels sit at their desks.)*

BRIGADIER: Well, that's that. The Old Man gave him a good story; I couldn't have done better myself.

COLONEL SPARKS *(still in the clouds):* He is depending on us.

BRIGADIER: Don't take it too hard. All we're supposed to do is make the other guy sorry. We can't save any lives or rebuild any cities. Never forget what those buttons do.

COLONEL SPARKS: Just the same, sir, I'm glad I was born an American. We've got the know-how. I'm glad I'm on the side that's ahead in the race.

COLONEL PEABODY *(disgusted):* Sparks, you talk like a damn high-school kid. For this job, you're supposed to have some good sense and detachment. *(Just then, there is a dull rumble. The floor and the walls of the room shake, and a couple of sizable chunks of concrete fall out of the ceiling. The lights go out, except for the green ones on the control board. Emergency lights, dimmer than the regular ones, come on at once. All the men are on their feet.)*

BRIGADIER: Good God! What was that? *(Recollecting himself)* Peabody, get on the phone to headquarters. Sparks, get out the red-line messages for the last twenty-four hours. Captain, anything from the defense center?

CAPTAIN: My line to them seems to be out.

BRIGADIER: What have you got for status? Anybody showing yellow or red?

CAPTAIN: San Francisco is red, sir.

COLONEL SPARKS *(riffling wildly through tele-type messages):* Oh, Jesus. This must be it. San Francisco! *(Screaming)* San Francisco gone!

BRIGADIER: Shut up, Sparks. Take it easy. *(To Peabody)* Can't you get headquarters?

COLONEL PEABODY: The line is dead. I can't get reserve operations, either. Maybe this *is* the real thing.

COLONEL SPARKS *(still half-hysterical):* We better do something. Remember what it says in the book: counterattack must take action before the enemy's destruction of our centers is complete.

BRIGADIER: *First we need an enemy. Who's got the highest negative rating in the latest State Department digest?*

COLONEL PEABODY *(who has quietly taken the messages from in front of Sparks):* Denmark, sir. But it's well below the danger point. All we've got is this: *(reading)* CO-PENHAGEN 1635 HOURS 22 JANUARY. WIDE-SPREAD DISAPPROVAL OF WILLIAMS FOUN-TAIN, STATUARY GROUP PRESENTED THE KING DENMARK BY U.S., BEING SHOWN BY PEOPLE COPENHAGEN. FOUNTAIN BEEN PELT-ED VEGETABLES BY HOODLUM GROUPS THREE OCCASIONS. FORMAL PROTEST STATING STAT-UE INSULTS KING RECEIVED FROM ROYAL ACADEMY ART IN FOLLOWING TERMS QUOTE . . . and so on. Nothing there, I'd say.

COLONEL SPARKS: Nothing there! San Francisco's in ruins, you damn fool, and we're sitting here like three warts on a pickle. All that over a lousy set of statues. I say let 'em have it.

BRIGADIER *(to Peabody):* Is that the hottest you've got?

COLONEL PEABODY: Yes, sir. I don't think it could have been Denmark. Though that sculptor, Williams, does live in San Francisco.

BRIGADIER: We better wait and be sure. Captain, how are your lines now?

COLONEL SPARKS *(with rising hysteria):* What have we got this stuff for if we don't use it? My God, didn't you hear what the President said? He's depending on us; they're all depending on us. If you haven't got the guts, I have. *(Before he can be stopped, he rushes to the control board and shoves a sergeant to the floor. Peabody is after Sparks in a flash. He pulls him around and knocks him to the floor. Spark's head hits hard, and he lies still.)*

COLONEL PEABODY: General, he did it! Co-penhagen shows red!

SERGEANT (*at a teletype*): Sir, here's a message from the defense center. They've got their line working again. (*He tears it off and brings it to the Brigadier.*)

CAPTAIN: Stockholm's gone red, sir.

COLONEL PEABODY: Sure. The Danes thought it was the Swedes. That export-duties row.

BRIGADIER: And the Swedes have got two hot arguments on their hands. They'll take the British, too, just to be sure. the British soak the Russians, and then we're next. (*He reads the message he has been holding, and drops into a chair.*) My God! Peabody, that was an earthquake. Epicenter right smack in San Francisco.

CAPTAIN: London's gone red, sir. And Edinburgh, and Manchester, and Nottingham, and —

COLONEL PEABODY: Dark Ages, here I come. It's a pity the Security Council didn't have time to consider all this.

BRIGADIER: Peabody, you're beginning to sound a little like Sparks. Come to think of it, there was nothing wrong with him but too much patriotism and too little sense. Captain, we probably can't pull this out of the fire but we've got to try. Send a message on all circuits. (*The Captain sits down at a teletype keyboard.*)

CAPTAIN: Ready, sir.

BRIGADIER: To all stations: URGE IMMEDIATE WORLDWIDE BROADCAST THIS MESSAGE: DESTRUCTION COPENHAGEN 1910 HOURS THIS DATE INITIATED BY THIS STATION THROUGH GRIEVOUS ERROR — ATTACKS MADE SINCE BASED ON IDEA DESTRUCTION COPENHAGEN WAS ACT OF WAR, WHICH IT WAS NOT REPEAT NOT — URGE ATTACKS BE STOPPED UNTIL SITUATION CAN BE CLARIFIED — THERE IS NO REPEAT NO WAR. END.

COLONEL PEABODY (*who has been watching board*): The hell there isn't. New York's gone red, and Chicago, and . . . (*The room rocks, the lights go out. With a dull, powerful rumble, the roof caves in.*)

CURTAIN

---

*It is hard to understand why our town must be destroyed to make a bomb that will destroy someone else's town that they love as much as we love ours.*

ANON., sign on the outskirts of Ellenton, South Carolina, when the Atomic Energy Commission decided to make its first H-Bomb plant on the Savannah River near the town, which had to be evacuated.

75.

# Bernard M. Baruch: A Choice Between the Quick and the Dead

*Proposals for the international control of atomic energy were first made by the Allied Powers in November 1945. At the first meeting of the UN General Assembly in January 1946 a United Nations Atomic Energy Commission was established to devise a workable plan. That spring Secretary of State James F. Byrnes appointed a committee to present an American plan for international control. David E. Lilienthal and J. Robert Oppenheimer drafted a proposal in consultation with Undersecretary of State Dean Acheson and Bernard Baruch, the American representative to the UN Atomic Energy Commission. On June 14 Baruch submitted a reworked version of the Acheson-Lilienthal Report to the UN commission. The Russians objected to the idea of international inspection and countered with their own plan, which called for the immediate destruction of existing atomic weapons and an end to further production. The inspection issue kept efforts toward international control of atomic weapons deadlocked until the Nuclear Test-Ban Treaty between the U.S.S.R., Great Britain, and the U.S. was signed in 1963. A portion of Baruch's June 14 address to the commission is reprinted here.*

Source: *Bulletin,* June 23, 1946: "Proposals for an International Atomic Development Authority."

MY FELLOW MEMBERS of the United Nations Atomic Energy Commission and My Fellow Citizens of the World:

We are here to make a choice between the quick and the dead. That is our business.

Behind the black portent of the new atomic age lies a hope which, seized upon with faith, can work our salvation. If we fail, then we have damned every man to be the slave of fear. Let us not deceive ourselves: We must elect world peace or world destruction.

Science has torn from nature a secret so vast in its potentialities that our minds cower from the terror it creates. Yet terror is not enough to inhibit the use of the atomic bomb. The terror created by weapons has never stopped man from employing them, for each new weapon a defense has been produced, in time. But now we face a condition in which adequate defense does not exist.

Science, which gave us this dread power, shows that it *can* be made a giant help to humanity, but science does *not* show us how to prevent its baleful use. So we have been appointed to obviate that peril by finding a meeting of the minds and the hearts of our peoples. Only in the will of mankind lies the answer.

It is to express this will and make it effective that we have been assembled. We must provide the mechanism to assure that atomic energy is used for peaceful purposes and preclude its use in war. To that end, we must provide immediate, swift, and sure punishment of those who violate the agreements that are reached by the nations. Penalization is essential if peace is to be more than a feverish interlude between wars. And, too, the United Nations can prescribe individual responsibility and punishment on the principles applied at Nuremberg by the Union of Soviet Socialist Republics, the United Kingdom, France, and the United States — a formula certain to benefit the world's future.

In this crisis, we represent not only our governments but, in a larger way, we represent the peoples of the world. We must remember that the peoples do not belong to the governments but that the governments belong to the peoples. We must answer their demands; we must answer the world's longing for peace and security.

In that desire, the United States shares ardently and hopefully. The search of science for the absolute weapon has reached fruition in this country. But she stands ready to proscribe and destroy this instrument — to lift its use from death to life — if the world will join in a pact to that end. . . .

The United States proposes the creation of an International Atomic Development Authority, to which should be entrusted all phases of the development and use of atomic energy, starting with the raw material and including:

1. Managerial control or ownership of all atomic energy activities potentially dangerous to world security.

2. Power to control, inspect, and license all other atomic activities.

3. The duty of fostering the beneficial uses of atomic energy.

4. Research and development responsibilities of an affirmative character intended to put the Authority in the forefront of atomic knowledge and thus to enable it to comprehend, and therefore to detect, misuse of atomic energy. To be effective, the Authority must itself be the world's leader in the field of atomic knowledge and development and thus supplement its legal authority with the great power inherent in possession of leadership in knowledge.

I offer this as a basis for beginning our discussion.

But I think the peoples we serve would not believe — and without faith nothing counts — that a treaty merely outlawing possession or use of the atomic bomb constitutes effective fulfillment of the instructions to this commission. Previous failures have been recorded in trying the method of simple renunciation, unsupported by effective guarantees of security and armament limitation. No one would have faith in that approach alone.

Now, if ever, is the time to act for the common good. Public opinion supports the world movement toward security. If I read the sign aright, the peoples want a program not composed merely of pious thoughts but of enforceable sanctions — an international law with teeth in it.

We of this nation, desirous of helping to bring peace to the world and realizing the heavy obligations upon us arising from our possession of the means of producing the bomb and from the fact that it is a part of our armament, are prepared to make our full contribution toward effective control of atomic energy.

When an adequate system for control of atomic energy, including the renunciation of the bomb as a weapon, has been agreed upon and put into effective operation and condign punishments set up for violations of the rules of control which are to be stigmatized as international crimes, we propose that:

1. Manufacture of atomic bombs shall stop;

2. Existing bombs shall be disposed of pursuant to the terms of the treaty; and

3. The authority shall be in possession of full information as to the know-how for the production of atomic knowledge.

Let me repeat, so as to avoid misunderstanding: My country is ready to make its full contribution toward the end we seek, subject, of course, to our constitutional processes and to an adequate system of control becoming fully effective, as we finally work it out.

Now as to violations. In the agreements, penalties of as serious a nature as the nations may wish and as immediate and certain in their execution as possible, should be fixed for:

1. Illegal possession or use of an atomic bomb.

2. Illegal possession, or separation, of atomic material suitable for use in an atomic bomb.

3. Seizure of any plant or other property belonging to or licensed by the authority.

4. Willful interference with the activities of the Authority.

5. Creation or operation of dangerous projects in a manner contrary to, or in the absence of, a license granted by the international control body.

It would be a deception, to which I am unwilling to lend myself, were I not to say to you and to our peoples that the matter of punishment lies at the very heart of our present security system. It might as well be admitted, here and now, that the subject goes straight to the veto power contained in the Charter of the United Nations so far as it relates to the field of atomic energy. The Charter permits penalization only by concurrence of each of the five great powers — the Soviet Union, the United Kingdom, China, France, and the United States.

I want to make very plain that I am concerned here with the veto power only as it affects this particular problem. There must be no veto to protect those who violate their solemn agreements not to develop or use atomic energy for destructive purposes.

The bomb does not wait upon debate. To delay may be to die. The time between violation and preventive action or punishment would be all too short for extended discussion as to the course to be followed.

As matters now stand, several years may be necessary for another country to produce a bomb, *de novo*. However, once the basic information is generally known, and the Authority has established producing plants for peaceful purposes in the several countries, an illegal seizure of such plant might permit a malevolent nation to produce a bomb in twelve months, and if preceded by secret preparation and necessary facilities, perhaps even in a much shorter time. The time required — the advance warning given of the possible use of a bomb — can only be generally estimated but obviously will depend upon many factors, including the success with which the Authority has been able to introduce elements of safety in the design of its plants and the degree to which illegal and secret preparation for the military use of atomic energy will have been eliminated. Presumably no nation would think of starting a war with only one bomb.

This shows how imperative speed is in detecting and penalizing violations.

The process of prevention and penalization — a problem of profound statecraft — is, as I read it, implicit in the Moscow statement, signed by the Union of Soviet Socialist Republics, the United States, and the United Kingdom a few months ago.

But before a country is ready to relinquish any winning weapons, it must have more than words to reassure it. It must have a guarantee of safety, not only against the offenders in the atomic area but against the illegal users of other weapons — bacteriological, biological, gas — perhaps — and why not? — against war itself.

In the elimination of war lies our solution, for only then will nations cease to compete with one another in the production and use of dread "secret" weapons which are evaluated solely by their capacity to kill. This devilish program takes us back, not merely to the Dark Ages but from cosmos to chaos. If we succeed in finding a suitable way to control atomic weapons, it is reasonable to hope that we may also preclude the use of other weapons adaptable to mass destruction. When a man learns to say "A" he can, if he chooses, learn the rest of the alphabet, too.

Let this be anchored in our minds: Peace is never long preserved by weight of metal

Presidential adviser Bernard Baruch (right) conferring with Senators Homer Ferguson and Owen Brewster in 1947

or by an armament race. Peace can be made tranquil and secure only by understanding and agreement fortified by sanctions. We must embrace international cooperation or international disintegration.

Science has taught us how to put the atom to work. But to make it work for good instead of for evil lies in the domain of dealing with the principles of human duty. We are now facing a problem more of ethics than of physics.

The solution will require apparent sacrifice in pride and in position, but better pain as the price of peace than death as the price of war.

I now submit the following measures as representing the fundamental features of a plan which would give effect to certain of the conclusions which I have epitomized.

1. *General* — The Authority should set up a thorough plan for control of the field of atomic energy through various forms of ownership, dominion, licenses, operation, inspection, research, and management by competent personnel. After this is provided

for, there should be as little interference as may be with the economic plans and the present private, corporate, and state relationships in the several countries involved.

2. *Raw Materials* — The Authority should have as one of its earliest purposes to obtain and maintain complete and accurate information on world supplies of uranium and thorium and to bring them under its dominion. The precise pattern of control of deposits of such material will have to depend upon the geological, mining, refining, and economic facts involved in different situations.

The Authority should conduct continuous surveys so that it will have the most complete knowledge of the world geology of uranium and thorium. Only after all current information on world sources of uranium and thorium is known to us all can equitable plans be made for their production, refining, and distribution.

3. *Primary Production Plants* — The Authority should exercise complete managerial control of the production of fissionable ma-

terials. This means that it should control and operate all plants producing fissionable materials in dangerous quantities and must own and control the product of these plants.

4. *Atomic Explosives* — The Authority should be given sole and exclusive right to conduct research in the field of atomic explosives. Research activities in the field of atomic explosives are essential in order that the Authority may keep in the forefront of knowledge in the field of atomic energy and fulfill the objective of preventing illicit manufacture of bombs. Only by maintaining its position as the best-informed agency will the Authority be able to determine the line between intrinsically dangerous and nondangerous activities.

5. *Strategic Distribution of Activities and Materials* — The activities entrusted exclusively to the Authority because they are intrinsically dangerous to security should be distributed throughout the world. Similarly, stockpiles of raw materials and fissionable materials should not be centralized.

6. *Nondangerous Activities* — A function of the Authority should be promotion of the peacetime benefits of atomic energy. Atomic research (except in explosives), the use of research reactors, the production of radioactive tracers by means of nondangerous reactors, the use of such tracers, and to some extent the production of power should be open to nations and their citizens under reasonable licensing arrangements from the Authority. Denatured materials, whose use we know always also requires suitable safeguards, should be furnished for such purposes by the Authority under lease or other arrangement. Denaturing seems to have been overestimated by the public as a safety measure.

7. *Definition of Dangerous and Nondangerous Activities* — Although a reasonable dividing line can be drawn between dangerous and nondangerous activities, it is not hard and fast. Provision should, therefore, be made to assure constant reexamination of the questions and to permit revision of the dividing line as changing conditions and new discoveries may require.

8. *Operations of Dangerous Activities* — Any plant dealing with uranium or thorium after it once reaches the potential of dangerous use must be not only subject to the most rigorous and competent inspection by the Authority but its actual operation shall be under the management, supervision, and control of the Authority.

9. *Inspection* — By assigning intrinsically dangerous activities exclusively to the Authority, the difficulties of inspection are reduced. If the Authority is the only agency which may lawfully conduct dangerous activities, then visible operation by others than the Authority will constitute an unambiguous danger signal. Inspection will also occur in connection with the licensing functions of the Authority.

10. *Freedom of Access* — Adequate ingress and egress for all qualified representatives of the Authority must be assured. Many of the inspection activities of the Authority should grow out of, and be incidental to, its other functions. Important measures of inspection will be associated with the tight control of raw materials, for this is a keystone of the plan. The continuing activities of prospecting, survey, and research in relation to raw materials will be designed not only to serve affirmative development functions of the Authority but also to assure that no surreptitious operations are conducted in the raw materials field by nations or their citizens.

11. *Personnel* — The personnel of the Authority should be recruited on a basis of proven competence but also so far as possible on an international basis.

12. *Progress by Stages* — A primary step in the creation of the system of control is the setting forth, in comprehensive terms of the functions, responsibilities, powers, and limitations of the Authority. Once a charter for the Authority has been adopted, the Authority and the system of control for which

it will be responsible will require time to become fully organized and effective. The plan of control will, therefore, have to come into effect in successive stages. These should be specifically fixed in the charter or means should be otherwise set forth in the charter for transition from one stage to another, as contemplated in the resolution of the United Nations Assembly which created this commission.

13. *Disclosures* — In the deliberations of the United Nations Commission on Atomic Energy, the United States is prepared to make available the information essential to a reasonable understanding of the proposals which it advocates. Further disclosures must be dependent, in the interests of all, upon the effective ratification of the treaty. When the Authority is actually created, the United States will join the other nations in making available the further information essential to that organization for the performance of its functions. As the successive stages of international control are reached, the United States will be prepared to yield, to the extent required by each stage, national control of activities in this field to the Authority.

14. *International Control* — There will be questions about the extent of control to be allowed to national bodies when the Authority is established. Purely national authorities for control and development of atomic energy should to the extent necessary for the effective operation of the Authority be subordinate to it. This is neither an endorsement nor a disapproval of the creation of national authorities. The commission should evolve a clear demarcation of the scope of duties and responsibilities of such national authorities.

---

76.

## WINSTON CHURCHILL: The Iron Curtain

*As early as May 1945, when the war with Germany was hardly over, Prime Minister Churchill had foreseen that most of eastern Europe would be drawn into the Soviet sphere of influence. Russian policies, in Churchill's view, offered little chance for a successful establishment of peace in the years ahead. By 1946 the Cold War between Russia and the West had become a reality, although most Americans were not eager to reckon with such a problem so soon after the war. At President Truman's request, Churchill came to the United States in 1946 and on March 5 at Westminster College in Fulton, Missouri, delivered an address on East-West relations and the prospects for maintaining peace. A portion of the address is reprinted below.*

Source: VSD, March 15, 1946: "Alliance of English-Speaking People."

NEITHER THE SURE PREVENTION of war nor the continuous rise of world organization will be gained without what I have called the fraternal association of the English-speaking peoples. This means a special relationship between the British Commonwealth and Empire and the United States.

This is no time for generalities. I will venture to be precise. Fraternal association requires not only the growing friendship and mutual understanding between our two vast but kindred systems of society but the continuance of the intimate relationships between our military advisers, leading to com-

Winston Churchill speaking at Westminster College
in Fulton, Missouri, March 1946

mon study of potential dangers, similarity
of weapons and manuals of instruction, and
interchange of officers and cadets at colleges. It should carry with it the continuance of the present facilities for mutual security by the joint use of all naval and air-
force bases in the possession of either country all over the world. This would perhaps
double the mobility of the American Navy
and Air Force. It would greatly expand that
of the British Empire forces, and it might
well lead, if and as the world calms down,
to important financial savings. Already we
use together a large number of islands;
many more will be entrusted to our joint
care in the near future.

The United States already has a permanent defense agreement with the Dominion
of Canada, which is so devotedly attached
to the British Commonwealth and Empire.
This agreement is more effective than many
of those which have often been made under
formal alliances. This principle should be
extended to all the British commonwealths
with full reciprocity. Thus, whatever hap-

pens, and thus only we shall be secure ourselves and able to work together for the
high and simple causes that are dear to us
and bode no ill to any. Eventually there
may come the principle of common citizenship, but that we may be content to leave
to destiny, whose outstretched arm so many
of us can clearly see.

There is, however, an important question
we must ask ourselves. Would a special relationship between the United States and
the British Commonwealth be inconsistent
with our overriding loyalties to the world
organization? I reply that, on the contrary,
it is probably the only means by which that
organization will achieve its full stature and
strength. There are already the special
United States relations with Canada and
between the United States and the South
American republics. We also have our
twenty-year treaty of collaboration and mutual assistance with Soviet Russia. I agree
with Mr. Bevin that it might well be a fif-
ty-year treaty. We have an alliance with
Portugal unbroken since 1384. None of
these clash with the general interest of a
world agreement. On the contrary, they
help it. "In my father's house are many
mansions." Special associations between
members of the United Nations which have
no aggressive point against any other country, which harbor no design incompatible
with the Charter of the United Nations, far
from being harmful, are beneficial and, as I
believe, indispensable.

I spoke earlier of the temple of peace.
Workmen from all countries must build
that temple. If two of the workmen know
each other particularly well and are old
friends, if their families are intermingled and
if they have faith in each other's purpose,
hope in each other's future and charity toward each other's shortcomings, to quote
some good words I read here the other day,
why cannot they work together at the common task as friends and partners? Why
cannot they share their tools and thus in

crease each other's working powers? Indeed, they must do so or else the temple may not be built, or, being built, it may collapse, and we shall all be proved unteachable and have to go and try to learn again for a third time, in a school of war, incomparably more rigorous than that from which we have just been released. The Dark Ages may return, the Stone Age may return on the gleaming wings of science, and what might now shower immeasurable material blessings upon mankind may even bring about its total destruction.

Beware, I say; time may be short. Do not let us take the course of letting events drift along till it is too late. If there is to be a fraternal association of the kind I have described, with all the extra strength and security which both our countries can derive from it, let us make sure that that great fact is known to the world, and that it plays its part in steadying and stabilizing the foundations of peace. Prevention is better than cure.

A shadow has fallen upon the scenes so lately lighted by the Allied victory. Nobody knows what Soviet Russia and its Communist international organization intends to do in the immediate future, or what are the limits, if any, to their expansive and proselytizing tendencies. I have a strong admiration and regard for the valiant Russian people and for my wartime comrade Marshal Stalin. There is sympathy and goodwill in Britain — and I doubt not here also — toward the peoples of all the Russias and a resolve to persevere through many differences and rebuffs in establishing lasting friendships.

We understand the Russians need to be secure on her western frontiers from all renewal of German aggression. We welcome her to her rightful place among the leading nations of the world. Above all we welcome constant, frequent, and growing contacts between the Russian people and our own people on both sides of the Atlantic. It is my duty, however, to place before you certain facts about the present position in Europe — I am sure I do not wish to, but it is my duty, I feel, to present them to you.

From Stettin in the Baltic to Trieste in the Adriatic, an iron curtain has descended across the Continent. Behind that line lie all the capitals of the ancient states of central and eastern Europe. Warsaw, Berlin, Prague, Vienna, Budapest, Belgrade, Bucharest, and Sofia, all these famous cities and the populations around them lie in the Soviet sphere and all are subject in one form or another, not only to Soviet influence but to a very high and increasing measure of control from Moscow. Athens alone, with its immortal glories, is free to decide its future at an election under British, American, and French observation. The Russian-dominated Polish government has been encouraged to make enormous and wrongful inroads upon Germany, and mass expulsions of millions of Germans on a scale grievous and undreamed of are now taking place.

The Communist parties, which were very small in all these Eastern states of Europe, have been raised to preeminence and power far beyond their numbers and are seeking everywhere to obtain totalitarian control. Police governments are prevailing in nearly every case, and so far, except in Czechoslovakia, there is no true democracy. Turkey and Persia are both profoundly alarmed and disturbed at the claims which are made upon them and at the pressure being exerted by the Moscow government. An attempt is being made by the Russians in Berlin to build up a quasi-Communist Party in their zone of occupied Germany by showing special favors to groups of left-wing German leaders.

At the end of the fighting last June, the American and British armies withdrew westward in accordance with an earlier agreement to a depth, at some points, 150 miles on a front of nearly 400 miles to allow the Russians to occupy this vast expanse of territory which the Western democracies had conquered. If now the Soviet government tries, by separate action, to build up a pro-Communist Germany in their areas, this will cause new serious difficulties in the British and American zones and will give the defeated Germans the power of putting themselves up to auction between the Soviets and Western democracies. Whatever conclusions may be drawn from these facts — and facts they are — this is certainly not the liberated Europe we fought to build up. Nor is it one which contains the essentials of permanent peace.

The safety of the world, ladies and gentlemen, requires a new unity in Europe from which no nation should be permanently outcast.

It is impossible not to comprehend — twice we have seen them drawn by irresistible forces in time to secure the victory but only after frightful slaughter and devastation have occurred. Twice the United States has had to send millions of its young men to fight a war, but now war can find any nation between dusk and dawn. Surely we should work within the structure of the United Nations and in accordance with our Charter. That is an open course of policy.

In front of the iron curtain which lies across Europe are other causes for anxiety. In Italy the Communist Party is seriously hampered by having to support the Communist-trained Marshal Tito's claims to former Italian territory at the head of the Adriatic. Nevertheless, the future of Italy hangs in the balance. Again one cannot imagine a regenerated Europe without a strong France. All my public life I have worked for a strong France and I never lost faith in her destiny, even in the darkest hours. I will not lose faith now.

However, in a great number of countries, far from the Russian frontiers and throughout the world, Communist fifth columns are established and work in complete unity and absolute obedience to the directions they receive from the Communist center. Except in the British Commonwealth and in this United States, where Communism is in its infancy, the Communist parties or fifth columns constitute a growing challenge and peril to Christian civilization. These are somber facts for anyone to have to recite on the morrow of a victory gained by so much splendid comradeship-in-arms and in the cause of freedom and democracy, and we should be most unwise not to face them squarely while time remains.

The outlook is also anxious in the Far East, and especially in Manchuria. The agreement which was made at Yalta, to which I was a party, was extremely favorable to Soviet Russia, but it was made at a time when no one could say that the German war might not extend all through the summer and autumn of 1945 and when the Japanese war was expected to last for a further eighteen months from the end of the German war. In this country you are all so well informed about the Far East, and such devoted friends of China, that I do not need to expatiate on the situation there.

I have felt bound to portray the shadow which, alike in the West and in the East, falls upon the world. I was a minister at the time of the Versailles Treaty and a close friend of Mr. Lloyd George. I did not myself agree with many things that were done, but I have a very vague impression in my mind of that situation, and I find it painful to contrast it with that which prevails now. In those days there were high hopes and unbounded confidence that the wars were over and that the League of Nations would become all-powerful. I do not see or feel the same confidence or even the same hopes in the haggard world at this time.

On the other hand I repulse the idea that a new war is inevitable; still more that it is imminent. It is because I am so sure that our fortunes are in our own hands and that we hold the power to save the future that I feel the duty to speak out now that I have an occasion to do so. I do not believe that

Soviet Russia desires war. What they desire is the fruits of war and the indefinite expansion of their power and doctrines. But what we have to consider here today, while time remains, is the permanent prevention of war and the establishment of conditions of freedom and democracy as rapidly as possible in all countries.

Our difficulties and dangers will not be removed by closing our eyes to them. They will not be removed by mere waiting to see what happens; nor will they be relieved by a policy of appeasement. What is needed is a settlement, and the longer this is delayed the more difficult it will be and the greater our dangers will become. From what I have seen of our Russian friends and allies during the war, I am convinced that there is nothing they admire so much as strength, and there is nothing for which they have less respect than for military weakness. For that reason the old doctrine of a balance of power is unsound. We cannot afford, if we can help it, to work on narrow margins, offering temptations to a trial of strength.

If the Western democracies stand together in strict adherence to the principles of the United Nations Charter, their influence for furthering these principles will be immense and no one is likely to molest them. If, however, they become divided or falter in their duty, and if these all-important years are allowed to slip away, then indeed catastrophe may overwhelm us all.

Last time I saw it all coming and cried aloud to my fellow countrymen and to the world, but no one paid any attention. Up till the year 1933, or even 1935, Germany might have been saved from the awful fate which has overtaken her and we might all have been spared the miseries Hitler let loose upon mankind. There never was a war in all history easier to prevent by timely action than the one which has just desolated such great areas of the globe. It could have been prevented without the firing of a single shot, and Germany might be power-

ful, prosperous, and honored today, but no one would listen, and one by one we were all sucked into the awful whirlpool.

We surely must not let that happen again. This can only be achieved by reaching now, in 1946, a good understanding on all points with Russia under the general authority of the United Nations Organization and by the maintenance of that good understanding through many peaceful years, by the world instrument, supported by the whole strength of the English-speaking world and all its connections.

Let no man underrate the abiding power of the British Empire and Commonwealth. Because you see the 46 million in our island harassed about their food supply, of which they grew only one-half, even in wartime, or because we have difficulty in restarting our industries and export trade after six years of passionate war effort, do not suppose that we shall not come through these dark years of privation as we have come through the glorious years of agony, or that half a century from now you will not see 70 or 80 million Britons spread about the world and united in defense of our traditions, our way of life, and of the world causes we and you espouse.

If the population of the English-speaking Commonwealth be added to that of the United States, with all that such cooperation implies in the air, on the sea, and in science and industry, there will be no quivering, precarious balance of power to offer its temptation to ambition or adventure. On the contrary, there will be an overwhelming assurance of security. If we adhere faithfully to the Charter of the United Nations and walk forward in sedate and sober strength, seeking no one's land or treasure, or seeking to lay no arbitrary control on the thoughts of men, if all British moral and material forces and convictions are joined with your own in fraternal association, the highroads of the future will be clear, not only for us but for all, not only for our time but for a century to come.

77.

# Henry A. Wallace: The Price of Peace

*Shortly after World War II it became clear that the Soviet Union no longer intended fully to abide by the Yalta and Potsdam agreements. The foreign policy of President Roosevelt, which had emphasized cooperation with the Soviet Union, gave way to the "get tough" policy of President Truman. Secretary of Commerce Henry Wallace, still believing that an alliance with the Soviets was essential to world peace, became an outspoken critic of Truman's policy. His opposition led to an open breach with the administration when, on September 12, 1946, Wallace delivered a highly critical speech at Madison Square Garden in New York City. At the insistence of Secretary of State James F. Byrnes, Truman forced Wallace to resign from the Cabinet, which he did on September 17. We reprint here a shortened version of the Madison Square Garden speech, omitting domestic political references, published by Wallace in October 1946.*

Source: *The Fight for Peace*, New York, 1946, pp. 17-22.

Tonight I want to talk about peace — and how to get peace. Never have the common people of all lands so longed for peace. Yet, never in a time of comparative peace have they feared war so much.

Up till now peace has been negative and unexciting. War has been positive and exciting. Far too often, hatred and fear, intolerance and deceit have had the upper hand over love and confidence, trust and joy. Far too often, the law of nations has been the law of the jungle; and the constructive spiritual forces of the Lord have bowed to the destructive forces of Satan.

During the past year or so, the significance of peace has been increased immeasurably by the atom bomb, guided missiles, and airplanes which soon will travel as fast as sound. Make no mistake about it — another war would hurt the United States many times as much as the last war. We cannot rest in the assurance that we invent-

ed the atom bomb — and therefore that this agent of destruction will work best for us. He who trusts in the atom bomb will sooner or later perish by the atom bomb — or something worse.

I say this as one who steadfastly backed preparedness throughout the Thirties. We have no use for namby-pamby pacifism. But we must realize that modern inventions have now made peace the most exciting thing in the world — and we should be willing to pay a just price for peace. If modern war can cost us $400 billion, we should be willing and happy to pay much more for peace. But certainly, the cost of peace is to be measured not in dollars but in the hearts and minds of men.

The price of peace — for us and for every nation in the world — is the price of giving up prejudice, hatred, fear and ignorance.

Let's get down to cases here at home.

First, we have prejudice, hatred, fear, and ignorance of certain races. The recent mass lynching in Georgia was not merely the most unwarranted, brutal act of mob violence in the United States in recent years; it was also an illustration of the kind of prejudice that makes war inevitable.

Hatred breeds hatred. The doctrine of racial superiority produces a desire to get even on the part of its victims. If we are to work for peace in the rest of the world, we here in the United States must eliminate racism from our unions, our business organizations, our educational institutions, and our employment practices. Merit alone must be the measure of man.

Second, in payment for peace, we must give up prejudice, hatred, fear, and ignorance in the economic world. This means working earnestly, day after day, for a larger volume of world trade. It means helping undeveloped areas of the world to industrialize themselves with the help of American technical assistance and loans.

We should welcome the opportunity to help along the most rapid possible industrialization in Latin America, China, India, and the Near East. For as the productivity of these peoples increases, our exports will increase.

We all remember the time, not so long ago, when the high tariff protectionists blindly opposed any aid to the industrialization of Canada. But look at our exports to Canada today. On a per capita basis our Canadian exports are seven times greater than our exports to Mexico.

I supported the British loan of almost $4 billion because I knew that without this aid in the rehabilitation of its economy the British government would have been forced to adopt totalitarian trade methods and economic warfare of a sort which would have closed the markets of much of the world to American exports.

For the welfare of the American people and the world it is even more important to invest $4 billion in the industrialization of undeveloped areas in the so-called backward nations, thereby promoting the long-term stability that comes from an ever increasing standard of living. This would not only be good politics and good morals. It would be good business.

The United States is the world's great creditor nation. And low tariffs by creditor nations are a part of the price of peace. For when a great creditor demands payment, and at the same time adopts policies which make it impossible for the debtors to pay in goods — the first result is the intensification of depression over large areas of the world; and the final result is the triumph of demagogues who speak only the language of violence and hate.

There are those who have expressed themselves as favoring an alliance of mutual defense with Great Britain as the key to our foreign policy. This may sound attractive because we both speak the same language and many of our customs and traditions have the same historical background. Moreover, to the military men, the British Isles are our advanced air base against Europe.

Certainly we like the British people as individuals. But to make Britain the key to our foreign policy would be, in my opinion, the height of folly. We must not let reactionary leadership force us into that position. We must not let British balance-of-power manipulations determine whether and when the United States gets into war. Make no mistake about it — the British imperialistic policy in the Near East alone, combined with Russian retaliation, would lead the United States straight to war unless we have a clearly defined and realistic policy of our own.

Neither of these two great powers wants war now, but the danger is that whatever their intentions may be, their current policies may eventually lead to war. To prevent war and insure our survival in a stable world, it is essential that we look abroad through our own American eyes and not through the eyes of either the British Foreign Office or a pro-British or anti-Russian press.

In this connection, I want one thing clearly understood. I am neither anti-British nor pro-British — neither anti-Russian nor pro-Russian. And just two days ago, when President Truman read these words, he said that they represented the policy of his administration.

I plead for an America vigorously dedicated to peace — just as I plead for opportunities for the next generation throughout the world to enjoy the abundance which now, more than ever before, is the birthright of man.

To achieve lasting peace, we must study in detail just how the Russian character was formed — by invasions of Tartars, Mongols, Germans, Poles, Swedes, and French; by the czarist rule based on ignorance, fear, and force; by the intervention of the British, French, and Americans in Russian affairs from 1919 to 1921; by the geography of the huge Russian land mass situated strategically between Europe and Asia; and by the vitality derived from the rich Russian soil and the strenuous Russian climate. Add to all this the tremendous emotional power which Marxism and Leninism gives to the Russian leaders — and then we can realize that we are reckoning with a force which cannot be handled successfully by a "get tough with Russia" policy.

"Getting tough" never bought anything real and lasting — whether for schoolyard bullies or businessmen or world powers. The tougher we get, the tougher the Russians will get.

Throughout the world there are numerous reactionary elements which had hoped for Axis victory — and now profess great friendship for the United States. Yet, these enemies of yesterday and false friends of to-day continually try to provoke war between the United States and Russia. They have no real love of the United States. They only long for the day when the United States and Russia will destroy each other. We must not let our Russian policy be guided or influenced by those inside or outside the United States who want war with Russia. This does not mean appeasement.

We most earnestly want peace with Russia — but we want to be met halfway. We want cooperation. And I believe that we can get cooperation once Russia understands that our primary objective is neither saving the British Empire nor purchasing oil in the Near East with the lives of American soldiers. We cannot allow national oil rivalries to force us into war. All of the nations producing oil, whether inside or outside of their own boundaries, must fulfill the provisions of the United Nations Charter and encourage the development of world petroleum reserves so as to make the maximum amount of oil available to all nations of the world on an equitable peaceful basis — and not on the basis of fighting the next war.

For her part, Russia can retain our respect by cooperating with the United Nations in a spirit of open-minded and flexible give-and-take.

The real peace treaty we now need is between the United States and Russia. On our part, we should recognize that we have no more business in the political affairs of Eastern Europe than Russia has in the political affairs of Latin America, Western Europe, and the United States. We may not like what Russia does in Eastern Europe. Her type of land reform, industrial expropriation, and suppression of basic liberties offends the great majority of the people of the United States. But whether we like it or not the Russians will try to socialize their sphere of influence just as we try to democratize our sphere of influence. This applies also to Germany and Japan. We are striving to democratize Japan and our area of control in Germany, while Russia strives to socialize Eastern Germany.

As for Germany, we all must recognize that an equitable settlement, based on a unified German nation, is absolutely essential to any lasting European settlement. This means that Russia must be assured that never again can German industry be converted into military might to be used against her — and Britain, Western Europe, and the United States must be certain that Russia's Germany policy will not become a tool of Russian design against Western Europe.

The Russians have no more business in stirring up native communists to political activity in Western Europe, Latin America, and the United States than we have in interfering in the politics of Eastern Europe and Russia. We know what Russia is up to in Eastern Europe, for example, and Russia knows what we are up to. We cannot permit the door to be closed against our trade in Eastern Europe any more than we can in China. But at the same time we have to recognize that the Balkans are closer to Russia than to us — and that Russia cannot permit either England or the United States to dominate the politics of that area.

China is a special case and although she holds the longest frontier in the world with Russia, the interests of world peace demand that China remain free from any sphere of influence, either politically or economically. We insist that the door to trade and economic development opportunities be left wide open in China as in all the world. However, the open door to trade and opportunities for economic development in China are meaningless unless there is a unified and peaceful China — built on the cooperation of the various groups in that country and based on a hands-off policy of the outside powers.

We are still arming to the hilt. Our excessive expenses for military purposes are the chief cause of our unbalanced budget. If taxes are to be lightened we must have the basis of a real peace with Russia — a peace that cannot be broken by extremist propagandists. We do not want our course determined for us by master minds operating out of London, Moscow, or Nanking.

Russian ideas of social-economic justice are going to govern nearly a third of the world. Our ideas of free-enterprise democracy will govern much of the rest. The two ideas will endeavor to prove which can deliver the most satisfaction to the common man in their respective areas of political dominance. But by mutual agreement, this competition should be put on a friendly basis and the Russians should stop conniving against us in certain areas of the world just as we should stop scheming against them in other parts of the world. Let the results of the two systems speak for themselves.

Meanwhile, the Russians should stop teaching that their form of communism must, by force if necessary, ultimately triumph over democratic capitalism — while we should close our ears to those among us who would have us believe that Russian communism and our free-enterprise system cannot live, one with another, in a profitable and productive peace.

Under friendly, peaceful competition the Russian world and the American world will gradually become more alike. The Russians will be forced to grant more and more of the personal freedoms; and we shall become more and more absorbed with the problems of social-economic justice.

Russia must be convinced that we are not planning for war against her and we must be certain that Russia is not carrying on territorial expansion or world domination through native communists faithfully following every twist and turn in the Moscow party line. But in this competition, we must insist on an open door for trade throughout the world. There will always be an ideological conflict — but that is no reason why diplomats cannot work out a basis for both systems to live safely in the world side by side.

Once the fears of Russia and the United States Senate have been allayed by practical regional political reservations, I am sure that concern over the veto power would be greatly diminished. Then the United Nations would have a really great power in those areas which are truly international and not regional. In the worldwide as distinguished from the regional field, the armed might of the United Nations should be so great as to make opposition useless. Only the United Nations should have atomic bombs, and its military establishment should give special emphasis to air power. It should have control of the strategically located air bases with which the United States and Britain have encircled the world. And not only should individual nations be prohibited from manufacturing atomic bombs, guided missiles, and military aircraft for bombing purposes, but no nation should be allowed to spend on its military establishment more than perhaps 15 percent of its budget.

Practically and immediately, we must recognize that we are not yet ready for world federation. Realistically, the most we can hope for now is a safe reduction in military expense and a long period of peace based on mutual trust between the Big Three.

During this period, every effort should be made to develop as rapidly as possible a body of international law based on moral principles and not on the Machiavellian principles of deceit, force, and distrust — which, if continued, will lead the modern world to rapid disintegration.

In brief, as I see it today, the World Order is bankrupt — and the United States, Russia, and England are the receivers. These are the hard facts of power politics on which we have to build a functioning, powerful United Nations and a body of international law. And as we build, we must develop fully the doctrine of the rights of small peoples as contained in the United Nations Charter. This law should ideally apply as much to Indonesians and Greeks as to Bulgarians and Poles — but practically, the application may be delayed until both British and Russians discover the futility of their methods.

In the full development of the rights of small nations, the British and Russians can learn a lesson from the Good Neighbor Policy of Franklin Roosevelt. For under Roosevelt, we in the Western Hemisphere built a workable system of regional internationalism that fully protected the sovereign rights of every nation — a system of multilateral action that immeasurably strengthened the whole of world order.

In the United States an informed public opinion will be all-powerful. Our people are peace-minded. But they often express themselves too late — for events today move much faster than public opinion. The people here, as everywhere in the world, must be convinced that another war is not inevitable. And through mass meetings such as this and through persistent pamphleteering, the people can be organized for peace — even though a large segment of our press is propagandizing our people for war in the hope of scaring Russia. And we who look on this war-with-Russia talk as criminal foolishness must carry our message direct to the people — even though we may be called communists because we dare to speak out.

I believe that peace — the kind of a peace I have outlined tonight — is the basic issue, both in the congressional campaign this fall and right on through the presidential election in 1948. How we meet this issue will determine whether we live not in "one world" or "two worlds" — but whether we live at all.

British SeaBees search for friends among the dead lying along Normandy Beach, D-Day, 1944

# AN UNCERTAIN VICTORY

Unexpected delays in the Italian campaign that had held up the relay of landing craft to Britain necessitated the postponement of D-Day to early June. The proper combination of tide, weather, and moonlight came on June 6; on that date the Allied force of 5,000 ships, 10,000 aircraft, and 4,000,000 assault and supporting troops mounted the massive invasion of the Normandy coast. Although stubborn resistance was met in a few sectors, the landing forces quickly secured a strong beachhead, and supplies and equipment were rapidly moved in behind the advance waves. The German command had expected the major Allied effort farther north in the Boulogne-Calais area, and the Normandy action was generally regarded as diversionary until late July. By that time the combined armies of the Allies had taken the Cotentin Penin-sula and were moving steadily inland. This major miscalculation by the German General Staff, combined with the brilliant planning of the Allied command, threw the German defenses into confusion and disorganized retreat. Paris was liberated on August 25. A second invasion on the southern coast of France on August 15 had opened Marseilles for supplies, and this force then moved northward to join Eisenhower's command. The German forces finally retreated to the strongly defended Siegfried Line on the German frontier. A period of adjustment and consolidation of fronts and supply lines was followed by the resumption of the Allied drive, past the Siegfried Line to the Rhine River. During this time the Russians had launched a major offensive in the East and had driven deep into Poland and Lithuania.

**First wave of Allied invasion troops going ashore at Normandy under fire from the Germans**

**Ships land supplies and reinforcements along French beaches to support the invasion**

(Top) Germans surrender to the Americans during the fighting on Omaha Beach, June 9, 1944; (center) American soldier runs for cover after setting fire to a house in northern France that was used as an ammunition dump by the Germans; (bottom) American infantrymen supported by British tanks march through Argentan en route to Paris

(Both) Robert Capa from Magnum

(Above) Parisians hit the ground for protection during the fighting to liberate Paris, August 1944; (below) Gen. Charles de Gaulle parades through the city the day after liberation

War in the Pacific: (Above) Allies view damage in Manila after recapturing the Philippine city, February 1945; (below) Marines work their way up a sandy slope of Mt. Suribachi on Iwo Jima

**Strategic bombing of Japan: (Above) Airstrip on Guam; (below) Emperor Hirohito views damage in Tokyo**

**Roosevelt and Churchill in a private meeting at Yalta**

In February 1945 the Big Three leaders, Roosevelt, Churchill, and Stalin, met again for top level policy discussions on the last stages of the war and the structure of the postwar world. The Russian-Allied occupation lines in Germany had been agreed upon earlier; what remained was the stabilization and reorganization of liberated countries and the coordination of the war with Japan. Extensive concessions, political and territorial, were made to Russia in return for a promise of Russian aid against Japan and in the interest of postwar cooperation; it could not be foreseen that the atomic bomb would render such assistance superfluous.

**Churchill, Roosevelt, and Stalin pose with leading Allied officers at the Yalta Conference, 1945**

German officer jokes with American officers while discussing terms for surrender of
20,000 Nazi troops in Romorantin, France, 1944

(Above) Town of Westka-
pelle in ruins following the
invasion of Walcheren Is-
land in the Netherlands,
November 1944; (right)
British commandos rout
out snipers in Wesel

**American tanks enter bomb-damaged Nuremberg after fierce fighting with Nazi forces, April 1945**

The Allied reconquest of Europe had proceeded rapidly through France and the Low Countries in 1944 and brought Allied troops to the threshold of Germany. The dramatic German counteroffensive in December, the Battle of the Bulge, was stopped after a month, and by February the invasion of Germany was imminent. As Allied forces moved into Germany, the incredible inhumanity of the Nazi concentration camps was discovered. Elsewhere, in laboratories in Chicago and New Mexico, something new and frighteningly unpredictable was beginning.

**(Below) Dachau prisoners cheer Yank liberators, 1945**

**(Above) Road near Belsen lined with dead bodies from a concentration camp, April 1945; (below) rows of dead inmates fill the yard of Nordhausen concentration camp**

(Above) Soviet Marshals Meretskov, Malinovski, and Vasilevsky on the Far Eastern front; (below) Pfc. Apt in Pilsen, Czechoslovakia; (bottom) Gen. Montgomery discussing the surrender terms

The Allied armies under Gen. Eisenhower began to cross the Rhine during March 1945 and moved quickly to cut off pockets of German troops in the Ruhr and elsewhere. With the Russians surrounding Berlin, American forces were sent toward Czechoslovakia to cut western Germany in two. On April 30 Hamburg radio announced the suicide of Hitler; Admiral Doenitz assumed the leadership of Germany and immediately sought peace. On May 7 Gen. Alfred Jodl signed the act of surrender at Reims.

In the Pacific: (Above) Coast Guard and Navy vessels land supplies on the Marine beachhead at Iwo Jima, February 1945; (below) injured treated at Iwo Jima aid station

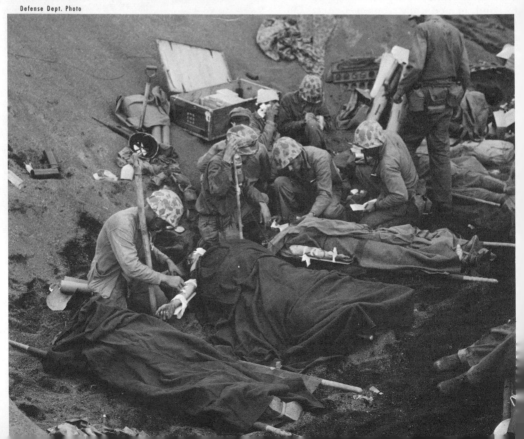

(Above) Chinese line the streets of Kunming as the first supply convoy reaches the city over the Allied-controlled Burma-Ledo road; (below) Chinese recapture Luchow, 1945

(Above) Marines battle for control of a ridge near Naha on Okinawa, May 1945; (below) Japanese soldier flushed from a cave by a smoke grenade surrenders to the Marines on Okinawa

(Above) President Truman addresses the delegates to the charter session of the United Nations in San Francisco, 1945; (below) atom bomb explodes in test in New Mexico, July 16, 1945

**Truman, with a new weapon at his disposal, adopted a hard line at Potsdam; (below) bodies of civilians killed at Nagasaki, August 1945**

The Potsdam Conference was intended to deal with the political questions left unsolved at Yalta, but the principal effect of the meeting was to highlight the distrust among the Allies. Ideological hostility dominated what was essentially an effort to work out the lines of power in the postwar world. Implicit in the positions at the conference was America's new weapon, unleashed on Japan three days after the conference closed. The decision to use the bomb defies rational explanation. An invasion of Japan was not planned until late fall; conventional bombing of Japan had already sent Japanese envoys to Russia seeking mediation; there were strong indications that Japan would accept the Potsdam ultimatum on the condition that the Emperor remain.

78.

# WILLIAM J. DONOVAN: Call for a Central Intelligence Agency

*Espionage is as old as warfare, and the United States has practised it in all of its wars but not very effectively until World War II. Even then, the U.S. depended mainly on British intelligence for information about the enemy in Europe, although it did break the Japanese code before 1939 and had general if not specific knowledge of Japan's hostile intentions prior to Pearl Harbor. The most notable espionage activities performed by Americans during World War II were carried out by the Office of Strategic Services (OSS), under William J. "Wild Bill" Donovan. Formed early in the war, the OSS not only gathered essential information but also saved many American lives, as General Donovan pointed out in the following speech, delivered to the* New York Herald Tribune *High School Forum on April 13, 1946. General Donovan's call for a centralized intelligence organization was answered when the Central Intelligence Agency (CIA) was established in 1947. Working under the direction of the National Security Council, the CIA engaged in many and varied intelligence activities during the subsequent twenty years and obtained great power and influence in the government.*

Source: VSD, May 1, 1946: "A Central Intelligence Agency."

IMAGINE THAT YOU have been called in here today as consultants. Consultants on an important problem. Your government needs a foreign policy. How is it going to go about getting one? What do you have to know, first, to give an opinion?

Well, what are the first things you have to know when you are planning your own future? What kind of policy are you going to have for that future? To determine that policy, you have to know what possibilities there are for you — where you can get a job — what you have to know to get the job, and hold it — where you can learn what you have to know. In other words, you've got to get information. Then you've got to evaluate and interpret that information. When you do this, then you have a decision that you feel confident is an informed decision.

Government is no different. Government policy, too, must be based upon a tested knowledge of the facts. What facts? The capabilities, the intentions, and the policies of other nations. That's what an intelligence service means.

Let's debunk all this loose talk about intelligence. It's not cloak and dagger. It's just the careful gathering and analysis and interpretation of many minute bits of evidence. And it's not easy. It's something you've got to sweat out.

We've never realized this as a nation. We've been the only great power without an intelligence service. It was to meet this lack and to unmask the intentions of our enemies that the Office of Strategic Services was set up.

Intelligence service that counts isn't the kind you read about in spy books. Women agents are less often the sultry blonde or the dazzling duchess than they are girls like the young American with an artificial leg who stayed on in France to operate a clandestine radio station; girls like the thirty-seven who worked for us in China, daughters of missionaries and of businessmen, who had grown up there. I hope that the story of the women in OSS will soon be written.

Our men agents didn't fit the traditional types in spy stories any more than the women we used. Do you know that one of our most notable achievements was the extent to which we found we could use labor unions? Our informer in this war was less often a slick little man with a black moustache than a transport worker, a truck driver, or a freight train conductor.

In war you've got to get two things — your long-range information and your immediate operational information. We did this kind of thing — from bases in Sweden, Spain, Turkey, and Switzerland, we sent agents into the interior of enemy and enemy-occupied territory. We got a man into the German Foreign Office. He had access to cables coming in from the commanding generals in the field and from German ambassadors all over the world. Then we had a man in the Gestapo itself, in a leading position. We even had one of our own men in a Gestapo training school. By such means we were able to get the first information on the V-1 and V-2 weapons, and the use of the island of Peenemunde as a testing area.

We had to know about German tank production. How would you find out about it? Well, we sent some of our young scholar economists in the OSS out on patrols. They examined captured German tanks. Each tank had a factory serial number. We knew that these numbers were consecutive and didn't vary — because we already knew that was the German system. We did the same thing with airplanes. And when we had looked at a sufficient number, we could estimate what production was. When the war was over, we checked. And we found we were only about 4 percent off.

How were German casualties running? That was important to know, not merely to tell us about the forces that could be put into the field but also about available manpower for their internal economy. The names of German dead weren't published in the press. But in every little town we found that the local paper carried obituaries of German officers who had been killed. By various means we got the local papers from all the little towns and villages in Germany. We read these obituaries. As in all armies, we knew that there was a rather fixed proportion of men to officers. We knew that there was also a certain ratio between enlisted men and officers killed. So, in that way, our research men skilled in such techniques were able to make an estimate of the strength of the German Army in 1943 that was found to be curiously exact.

Besides obtaining information this way, we also had to fight for it. We did this by sending in small units to seize radio stations or to work with resistance groups. As far as we were able, we went to the minority groups of different nationalities in this country and trained volunteers for hazardous work. Most of these were American citizens of the racial origin and of the language of the country which we were seeking to liberate. Thus we had units going to Greece, Yugoslavia, France, Italy, China, Indochina, and Siam.

Let me give you three illustrations:

1. In Yugoslavia we had units both with Tito and with Mihajlovic. After the British had withdrawn their units from Mihajlovic, we kept an intelligence team in his area. We did that because it was the best way of

getting into Austria. In addition, we worked with our Air Force in setting up search parties throughout the Balkans to rescue American aviators that were shot down. We aided in the rescue of some 5,000 airmen.

Right here is a young officer, a major of Marines, an American, a lawyer, who was three months with Mihajlovic in Yugoslavia and who was a year and a half behind the Japanese lines in China leading Chinese guerrillas. I'll ask Walter Mansfield to stand up.

2. We had a joint mission to work with the underground in Slovakia. It was made up of British and American OSS men, under the command of Lt. Holt Green of the Navy, who was part of the OSS. The Slovak uprising collapsed in the fall and winter of 1944. The Germans made a very determined and sustained search for this group. As you saw in the *Herald Tribune* yesterday, most of them were captured, taken to Mulhausen, tortured, and shot. Only two British and two Americans were rescued.

They owe their lives to the energy and intelligence of a young Slovak girl interpreter, Maria Gulovich, who helped them escape. Although she had her legs, feet, and fingers badly frozen, the men she saved say she was courageous, uncomplaining, and resourceful. She got them through the German lines by her ability to speak German; and by her knowledge of Russian, Czech, and Hungarian she got them the cooperation of the Russians and the Hungarians. Maria, who is now at Vassar, is here today. I'll ask her to stand up.

3. Now let us tell you what we did in Siam. There were thirty Siamese students studying here who wanted to help, so we took them into OSS, trained them in guerrilla warfare, taught them to parachute, and, with eighteen Americans, we distributed them throughout Siam in 1942. Siam was a most important observation point for us because it was a strategic base for the Japanese. Once, one of our agents was even able to tell us that Tojo's house in Tokyo had been stoned by an angry mob of Japanese following a B-29 raid. Finally, to tie in more closely, we had to send in two more American OSS representatives in 1944 — John Webster, who had lived in Siam before the war, and Dick Greenlee, a major in the Army, a young lawyer from Scarsdale. They landed in the Gulf of Siam in a Catalina seaplane, transferred to a launch, went up the main river into Bangkok, and were able to make a detailed study of Japanese shipbuilding. They spent from January 25 to February 5 in one room in Bangkok getting the details of proposed plans for our cooperation with the people of Siam. Greenlee returned to the United States with those plans, and then went back and stayed in there from April 1 to June 30, 1944.

With Major Webster and Captain Palmer of OSS, he rescued two flyers — Major Kellogg of the Air Force, and William McGary of the Flying Tigers.

He lived in the house right next to the prime minister's, and sent by radio directly to Washington the most valuable information on the steady disintegration of Japanese resistance and morale. And Dick Greenlee is right here, practising law in New York. Stand up, Dick.

These are a few illustrations of the kind of thing you have to do in wartime. They show that America was able to set up a system that could compare and compete with the intelligence systems of the older nations. But, you may say, that's all right for war. But how about peace? Why should we need an intelligence service in peacetime?

Let me explain this. You probably have already seen that in many respects it is much more difficult to prevent war than to wage it. It is even more important in peacetime, in a sense, to know what people are up to and what's going on, so that the peace can be preserved. If you want to have peace in the world, you've got to know the truth of what is happening and not be forced to rely upon rumor. Rumor might make us act in one way, and knowledge would compel us to act in another.

Now all of us want America to be reasonable and just. But only a strong nation can be resolute. And to be effective in her resolution, that nation must have tested knowledge — which is a true definition of intelligence. To obtain that, she must have a real intelligence service. We haven't got one. And now, since all foreign nations know that to be true, it's time our own people knew it too to be the fact.

We had the makings of one during the war, but that has been disbanded. Experience has shown that the only kind of a system for us to have is a centralized, impartial, independent agency reporting directly to the President, or to the same unit to which the operational departments report.

At present we have a director of an intelligence group reporting to a committee called an intelligence authority made up of the secretaries of state, war, and Navy. Now, these men have their own jobs to do, running their own departments. But intelligence is an all-time job. And intelligence must be independent of the people it serves so that the material it obtains will not be slanted or distorted by the views of the people directing operations. At present the director of intelligence is dependent on the departments of state, war, and Navy for his funds, his facilities, and his personnel. To be effective, an intelligence agency should be on a basis of equality with other agencies and responsible to the same ultimate authority as they are.

Our present system still does give us a means of getting facts, but also the danger of getting facts that will conform to the particular prejudices or preconceptions of department heads. We have dissipated the unit of scholars skilled in research and analysis set up under OSS, scholars who could evaluate and interpret the factual material brought in. It's no use to have facts coming in, without interpretations. Without interpretations you have no real intelligence service at all, but just a lot of isolated facts. And that can be very dangerous.

Just think, if we had had such an intelligence service at the time of Pearl Harbor, if we had had such a service to which the reported facts were available and which could have mobilized the very items of intelligence which were disclosed at the hearings, we could have driven out the preconception of the Army and Navy Command, which, as the investigation showed, was obsessed with the idea that the Japs could not do what they did do to us.

It is even more important now, as we plan the peace, that we don't do it on some preconceived notions or half-baked concepts of what other nations are likely to do. We must build on the solid ground of what is actually happening, not on what we would like to see happen.

I know that the world you want is one based on better understanding. And you and I both know that the more we know about the other fellow, the better we shall understand him. Thus, I firmly believe that the world you want will be nearer to realization if we build it upon knowledge that has been tested and found true.

There are many young men and women whose patriotism and skill in this kind of work have been tested and trained in war and who are eager to be used if our government will only have sense enough to use them. These young men and women can well be the saviors of the peace.

79.

## James T. Farrell: Themes in American Realism

*James T. Farrell is best known for his fictional studies of urban social groups, of which the leading example is his Lonigan trilogy (Young Lonigan, 1932; The Young Manhood of Studs Lonigan, 1934; and Judgment Day, 1935). The story told of the career of a boy growing up on the South Side of Chicago during the worst years of the Depression; and it garnered critical acclaim both in America and abroad and established Farrell as one of the foremost contemporary proponents of social realism in fiction. In the essay reprinted here Farrell offered a sociological analysis of American literature, in the process surveying the development of social realism from the 1890s to the 1940s.*

Source: *Literature and Morality,* New York, 1947: "Social Themes in American Realism."

### I

SINCE THE 1890's, American writers of the realistic tradition have been trying to tell the story of the human consequences of the advance of American civilization. As is well known, a pioneer in this tradition was Theodore Dreiser. A significant distinction can be made between his work and that of such writers as Henry James, Stephen Crane, and Harold Frederic. While these writers differ greatly from one another, they were all concerned with the same theme of self-development, of awareness. This theme is even involved in the manner in which James creates suspense. Crane's *The Red Badge of Courage* is not merely a war novel. Using the setting of war, he tells the story of how a boy becomes a man. Frederic's *The Damnation of Theron Ware* also deals with the theme of awareness or development, though negatively. Theron Ware becomes aware of values superior to, and more sophisticated than, those embodied in his ministerial education and in his life as a

minister in a small community in upstate New York. His "damnation" or disintegration is the result of his inability to live by these superior values.

With Dreiser, the conditions of life and the ideals of success in America are thematic: the motif of development or awareness, when treated by him, is secondary to these. His characters usually take on the color of their environment. Failure and tragedy in his novels are to be interpreted as consequences of the pitiless force of circumstances. His heroes and heroines are seeking to rise socially, to change their class status. If they fail, it is because of the circumstances of their lives — a lack of education, a lack of physical magnetism, or a lack of control of the levers of social power, most notably, money. Money provides the means for wielding power and, if it is gained, the individual is in a better position to satisfy desire. Human beings — for instance, Roberta Alden, in *An American Tragedy,* or Jennie Gerhardt — are sacrificed in the interests of success and social prestige in a society dominated by those who control because they are rich or, at least, well off. And only those who are born into the upper classes, or those who are particularly strong-willed, magnetic, shrewd, or lucky, can escape the alternative fates of tragedy and failure or apathetic mediocrity. In the Dreiserian world, the emotional capacities of men and women for affection and the powers of the individual will are weaker than the forces of social circumstance. In this sense, Dreiser wrote realistic novels about the conditions of American life.

## II

IN RECENT YEARS the cultural climate provided by the "New Deal" has had a manifest influence on American writing. In a political speech, the late President Franklin D. Roosevelt said: "Always the heart and soul of our country will be the heart and soul of the common man — the men and women who never have ceased to believe in democracy, who never have ceased to love their families, their homes, and their country." The faith of America, he declared, is the faith of the common man. The New Deal cultural climate which evolved in America during the 1930's, and which was patently exemplified in many motion pictures, radio plays, and novels of the war period, helped to produce a pseudo-populist literature of the common man. This neo-populist art and literature emphasizes the concept of Americanism as the means of unifying all races, creeds, and classes. Instead of a literature which penetratingly describes class differences and which also reveals the consequences of the conditions of life that thwart the boy and girl of plebeian origin in the struggle for success and growth, as Dreiser did, this literature has generally stressed and sentimentalized the theme that the common man is human; it has also used the theme

that the rich are Americans, too, and that they are like the common man.

The cultural influence of populism, like its political influence, cannot be interpreted in the same way for the 1940's as for the nineteenth century. The agrarian populist movement, reaching its political height with the rise of William Jennings Bryan, played a profound role in the shaping of American literature and in influencing American social thinking. It is one of the social, political, economic developments which stand behind twentieth-century American literature. One of the best illustrations of the populist influence can be found in Frank Norris, a major initiator of modern American literature. His books are democratic, popular, anti-snobbish. In his essay "The Responsibilities of the Novelist," he argues that the novelist must accept the responsibility of writing truthfully for the large mass of the people. The Octopus, Volume I of Norris' uncompleted trilogy, An Epic of the Wheat, portrays economic struggle and class relationships on the level of personal experience. It recounts the conflict between independent wheat-growers of the West and the railroad "octopus." Although the former think of themselves as the "people," they are independent capitalists who are producing wheat on a capitalist basis and with the use of the most advanced machinery of the time; thus, while they think they are fighting the battles of the people against the railroad, they are also reducing smaller producers to the status of tenants or of agricultural laborers. A poet character, Pressley, speaks in these pages for the author; he formalizes and generalizes this populist theme by conceiving it in terms of the interests of the people as a whole. In this sense The Octopus can be called "populist." However, populism is not introduced as a vehicle for rhetorical persuasiveness; rather, it is implanted in the novel as a conviction which is integral in the narrative; it is socially rooted and empirically developed as part of the story.

In contrast to this, recent works of a "populist" character are tendentiously organized and rely for conviction on the author's editorializations. A most notable example of this is to be seen in the radio plays of Norman Corwin. This difference is important, both artistically and sociologically. Some recent works that grew out of the New Deal cultural climate present life in America on the level of newspaper editorials, oversimplifying character and situation. Oversimplification of this kind is to be found, for instance, in such books as *The Grapes of Wrath*.

### III

THE AMERICAN REALISTIC NOVEL has treated the American Way of Life in terms of the human costs of American success and expansion. Dreiser's "successful" characters do not find inner harmony. This is exemplified by his financier, Cowperwood, and by Carrie Meeber of *Sister Carrie*. The most notable characters who fail, Hurstwood and Clyde Griffiths, suffer a terrible and tragic end. Sherwood Anderson, influenced by Dreiser, wrote principally of the little man of the lower middle class, the man on the level of the handicraftsman. Many of his characters have already lost their social identity before the stories commence or are in the process of losing it as the stories progress. With capitalist relationships conquering in the small town — in fact, all over the country — types such as those which Anderson describes are declassed. Anderson deals, then, with the consequences of such a development. This is even seen in his emphasis on hands — on working with one's hands. And the feeling of human need in his writings is seen in the need for contacts, for physical contacts. Through con-

tacts, need will be satisfied, and some sense of personal and social identity will be regained. The Andersonian emphasis on sex grows out of this; sex is a way out of confusion, a form of intimate contact which might make more happy the lot of the confused child of a confused world.

Dreiser presents more formally the result of conflict between the need for sexual expression and the repressions imposed by the Puritan moral code. David Graham Phillips also does this in his novel, *Susan Lenox: Her Fall and Rise*. His heroine, Susan, is presented as a superior and attractive girl. However, she is socially ostracized because she was born out of wedlock. She is socially punished because of her mother's "sin." Both Dreiser and Phillips (the latter in a more sentimentally romantic vein) reveal social aspects of class relationships and class differences through their treatment of sex. As a result of social ostracism, Susan is driven out of her class; she is made a victim of the sexual appetites of men of a superior class. This is the essence of her "fall" in the first portions of this work. Dreiser's heroines, Carrie Meeber and Jennie Gerhardt, also have lovers who are of a social class superior to the one from which they come. Jennie is punished for her sin. Here, class injustice is involved in the punishment which society metes out to the girl who "sins." Sex in works of this kind serves as a focus which permits the author to reveal social consequences rooted in class differentiation. At the same time, we are shown the social snobbery, the social hypocrisy, and the double standard prevalent in the upper classes.

### IV

IN THE LITERATURE of the 1920's, leisure and consumption are of growing thematic importance. Also, the commodity and commodity values become either an open or a concealed theme. Babbitt's shallowness, for instance, is related to the fact that his social life and his inner world are controlled by commodities and cash values. Even his pleasures are bought, and a cash value placed on them. His thoughts and his life are governed to a great extent by the fact that he must impress those who are impressing him with cost prices. Childish display and ostentation are dominating factors in his life. Babbitt is living on the other side of the Success Dream. In a small way, he has become a success. But his individuality has been lost. In a time of standardized commodities, he is a standardized man. This suggests the major criticism Sinclair Lewis makes of American civilization. The representative American, Babbitt, does not know how to use and enjoy his leisure, does not, with his success and greater leisure, learn how to *consume* more civilized and more sophisticated cultural values.

Other writers of this period, for instance, F. Scott Fitzgerald, Hemingway, and Ring Lardner, also deal with the theme of leisure. Fitzgerald describes the social disillusionments and ballroom romanticism of the young people of the upper classes and the loneliness of Gatsby, who gives large parties and has an extensive social life; yet he is lonely, and his guests scarcely know him. Hemingway's characters live in a tourist world, and one of their major problems is that of consuming time itself. It is interesting to observe that his works are written from the standpoint of the spectator. His characters are usually people who are looking — looking at bull fights, scenery, and at one another across café tables. Ring Lardner's satire is directed against the snobbery and stupidity of people who are trying to enjoy themselves and do not know how. Most of his characters are seen in their leisure. If we see them at work, it is at some occupation concerned with the amusement or entertainment of others. Thus he shows us baseball players, prize fighters, a golf caddy, and songwriters at work. Leisure as a theme in such works is treated in terms of satire and social disillusionment.

V

AFTER THE DEPRESSION, with the entry of a new generation into literature, we can observe another thematic change in realistic American fiction. By and large, the plebeian classes, the lower class, and special groups of the American population were not centrally treated in American fiction before the end of the Twenties. But suddenly we can observe the change. It is mirrored in the racial backgrounds of writers, in the themes, in the subjects, and in the conditions of life which are treated. The orphan asylum, the streets of the city, poolrooms, lower-class homes and family life, the backward sections of America, such as parts of Georgia or the decaying sections of New England, hobo life — all this is introduced into the American novel and short story, and introduced from the inside rather than the outside. At the same time, first- and second-generation Americans of diverse racial and national backgrounds become characters in the American novel and short story.

With this, the problems of lower-class childhood are carefully and realistically introduced into the American novel. The burden placed on the child in a society which is gradually becoming more stratified is dealt with more painfully and in greater detail than was usually the case in earlier fiction. One of the first books suggesting the new trend was *Bottom Dogs,* by Edward Dahlberg, a novel dealing with the life of a boy in an orphan asylum and his subsequent migratory existence. One could use the title of this novel to suggest the new emphasis. A bottom-dog literature, in the social sense, began to develop.

An important feature of this literature is

that social snobbery — thematically dealt with in earlier realistic novels (like those of Dreiser and Phillips) — is revealed here as ugly racial prejudice. There should be nothing surprising in this fact. Snobbery and prejudice find different outlets on different levels of society. The snobbery of the upper classes is pressed down on the lower classes. The lower classes are undefended in the face of a class educational system which favors the sons and daughters of the upper classes. Possession of money and the sense of security it usually provides can easily give a tone, a veneer, a seeming graciousness to upper-class life. Prejudice in such circles is a matter of excluding others, of not inviting them to one's home or social functions. Toward the bottom of the social ladder there is more interracial contact. The burden of all social problems weighs down most heavily on the areas of lower-class life. The personal psychological frustrations of those in the lower classes are additionally emphasized by economic frustration. Just as life here is less secure, it often happens that the personality, also, is less secure. This lack of security commonly exacerbates tempers. The struggle for place, money, and social position on the upper rungs is often transformed into the naked struggle of individual vanities on the lower plane. This is all revealed in the violence described in some of the realistic writings of American plebeian writers. A clear example can be found in the short stories of Richard Wright, in *Uncle Tom's Children*, where we can see lynch violence breaking out or threatening to break out over seeming coincidences or accidents. Thus, a white woman sees a colored boy naked after he has been swimming. Coincidences such as these, in a society of acute class and racial tensions, flare into the social tragedy of violence.

Two of the dominant notes in the best of this literature are tension and violence — inner tension, expressed in frustration, frequently that of children, and violence on

the physical plane. The class, group, and racial tensions in American society produce frustration and violence when there is a world or society of isolated and more-or-less estranged individuals who express their natures in a savage personal struggle of vanities. When you do not express your vanity through money and social position, you do it by your fists, by your sexual conquests, and by your language of insult and aggression. Even the dialogue of this literature is frequently sharp and violent.

This bottom-dog literature, a literature that is sharply realistic and that depicts conditions of dirt, physical misery, and inner frustration, is also a literature that introduces the plebeian classes on a more human level than was the case (with perhaps a few exceptions) in American writings before the late 1920's and early 1930's. It implicitly asserts the humanity of its characters; this constitutes its most positive value. It boldly introduces men and women and boys and girls of the lowest social stratum as human beings whose problems and whose feelings demand the urgent attention of the serious reading public of America. The boy on the street, the uneducated Negro, the sharecropper, the worker, and many others are here introduced, irrevocably, into the consciousness of America.

And with *Black Boy*, by Richard Wright, the problem of awareness, of development, is shown to be as important among the lower strata of American society as in the world of Henry James. This bottom-dog literature has now begun to combine a treatment of awareness with an account of conditions of life in America.

In this new literature, characterizations are developed without acceptance of prevailing stereotypes. Just as earlier realistic writing turned upside down the attitudes and editorial affirmations of the American dream, so this literature has done away with the stereotypes of the stage Irishman, the stage Negro, the stage Jew of earlier popular writing. One of the social implications or meanings of this work is that it breaks — in fact, it tears to ribbons — the earlier stereotypes associated with the American melting pot. By and large, this literature is one of realistic statement. It states social problems, not in terms of generalizations but rather in terms of direct characterization, of the immediacy of life described on the printed page. If we define social causation as the more deeply influential economic and social forces in a society, which affect all the members in that society, we can then say that, in this literature, social causation is translated into individual motivation and into immediacy of action, thought, dream, and word. This literature deals concretely and directly with the major phases of American life which now seriously interest scores of sociologists, social workers, psychiatrists, criminologists, jurists, and others. It seeks to present in the more humanizing terms of literature much of what the newspapers sensationalize and view with alarm. Often it tells us what the quality of life is really like among "one-third of the nation."

It is easy to confuse such writings with neo-populist works on "the common man" that sentimentalize poverty and point up an editorialized national unity and a verbally formalized affirmation of democracy that exudes snobbery when evidence daily substantiates the conclusion that American class society is torn apart and exacerbated by class, group, and racial tensions. If one sees the pertinence in the obvious point that, in order to make men better, you must first tell them what they are like, it is easier to make distinctions between these two types

of writing. There is always a gap between conventional images of life and life as it is lived. Realistic writing has constantly sought to narrow that gap. Earlier in the present century, American realistic writing had the effect of tearing away conventional images of the American dream, of sex, and of the social snobbery of the upper classes; in the last decade and a half, a major impact of American realistic writing has been the tearing apart of conventional images of life among the lower strata. Thus the realistic writers of America have contributed to social thinking by setting down in fictional form material that can help to create wider consciousness of what life is like in America.

If this literature is appreciated as a fictional account of the quality of many American lives, it may then be a little easier to tear aside conventional false images; it will be possible to make people try to see more directly, more clearly. Literature is not, in itself, a means of solving problems: these can be solved only by action, by social and political action. But realistic literature can and should serve as a means of helping people discover more about themselves and about the conditions of life around them. And the best of American realistic literature can be shown to have contributed toward this effort. This analysis (necessarily sketchy because of the limitation of space) is an attempt to show in what way we should approach the problem of evaluating American literature by seeing it as a body of works that reveal how American realists have struggled to pin down important aspects of the realities of living in America, here and now.

————◆————

*America is a "happy-ending" nation.*
Dore Schary

80.

# Responsibilities of Broadcasting

*The proliferation in the 1920s of commercial radio broadcasting stations led Congress to create a Federal Radio Commission in 1927 to regulate the licensing of stations in the public interest. This Commission was replaced by the Federal Communications Commission (FCC) in 1934. Because the airwaves were considered to be public domain, it was felt that the federal government should be the guardian of broadcasting standards lest these become entirely dictated by commercial and advertising interests. Because the public itself has always held divergent views as to what good programming is, uniform standards have never been established. The following portions of a 1946 report by the FCC deal with the roles of the public and of the Commission in promoting the public interest.*

Source: *Public Service Responsibility of Broadcast Licensees,* Report by the Federal Communications Commission, March 7, 1946, pp. 54-56.

## A. ROLE OF THE PUBLIC

PRIMARY RESPONSIBILITY for the American system of broadcasting rests with the licensee of broadcast stations, including the network organizations. It is to the stations and networks rather than to federal regulation that listeners must primarily turn for improved standards of program service. The Commission, as the licensing agency established by Congress, has a responsibility to consider overall program service in its public-interest determinations, but affirmative improvement of program service must be the result primarily of other forces.

One such force is self-regulation by the industry itself through its trade associations.

Licensees acting individually can also do much to raise program-service standards, and some progress has indeed been made. Here and there across the country some stations have evidenced an increased awareness of the importance of sustaining programs, live programs, and discussion programs.

Other stations have eliminated from their own program service the middle commercial, the transcribed commercial, the piling up of commercials, etc. This trend toward self-improvement, if continued, may further buttress the industry against the rising tide of informed and responsible criticism.

Forces outside the broadcasting industry similarly have a role to play in improved program service. There is need, for example, for professional radio critics, who will play in this field the role which literary and dramatic critics have long assumed in the older forms of artistic expression. It is, indeed, a curious instance of the time lag in our adjustment to changed circumstances that while plays and concerts performed to comparatively small audiences in the "legitimate" theater or concert hall are regularly reviewed in the press, radio's best productions performed before an audience of millions receive only occasional and limited critical consideration.

*Publicity* for radio programs is useful, but

limited in the function it performs. Responsible criticism can do much more than mere promotion; it can raise the standards of public appreciation and stimulate the free and unfettered development of radio as a new medium of artistic expression. The independent radio critic, assuming the same role long occupied by the dramatic critic and the literary critic, can bring to bear an objective judgment on questions of good taste and of artistic merit which lie outside the purview of this Commission. The reviews and critiques published weekly in *Variety* afford an illustration of the role that independent criticism can play; newspapers and periodicals might well consider the institution of similar independent critiques for the general public.

Radio listener councils can also do much to improve the quality of program service. Such councils, notably in Cleveland, Ohio, and Madison, Wisconsin, have already shown the possibilities of independent listener organization. First, they can provide a much-needed channel through which listeners can convey to broadcasters the wishes of the vast but not generally articulate radio audience. Second, listener councils can engage in much-needed research concerning public tastes and attitudes. Third, listener councils can check on the failure of network affiliates to carry outstanding network sustaining programs and on the local programs substituted for outstanding network sustaining programs. Fourth, they can serve to publicize and to promote outstanding programs — especially sustaining programs which at present suffer a serious handicap for lack of the vast promotional enterprise which goes to publicize many commercial programs. Other useful functions would also no doubt result from an increase in the number and an extension of the range of activities of listener councils, cooperating with the broadcasting industry but speaking solely for the interest of listeners themselves.

Colleges and universities, some of them already active in the field, have a like distinctive role to play. Together with the public schools, they have it in their power to raise a new generation of listeners with higher standards and expectations of what radio can offer.

In radio workshops, knowledge may be acquired of the techniques of radio production. There are already many examples of students graduating from such work who have found their way into the industry, carrying with them standards and conceptions of radio's role, as well as talents, by which radio service cannot fail to be enriched.

Even more important, however, is the role of colleges and universities in the field of radio research. There is room for a vast expansion of studies of the commercial, artistic and social aspects of radio. The cultural aspects of radio's influence provide in themselves a vast and fascinating field of research.

It is hoped that the facts emerging from this report and the recommendations which follow will be of interest to the groups mentioned. With them rather than with the Commission rests much of the hope for improved broadcasting quality.

## B. ROLE OF THE COMMISSION

WHILE MUCH OF THE RESPONSIBILITY for improved program service lies with the broadcasting industry and with the public, the Commission has a statutory responsibility for the public interest of which it cannot divest itself. The Commission's experience with the detailed review of broadcast renewal applications since April 1945, together with the facts set forth in this report, indicate some current trends in broadcasting which, with reference to licensing procedure, require its particular attention.

In issuing and in renewing the licenses of broadcast stations, the Commission proposes to give particular consideration to four program-service factors relevant to the public interest. These are: (1) the carrying of sustaining programs, including network sustaining programs, with particular reference to the retention by licensees of a proper discretion and responsibility for maintaining a well-balanced program structure; (2) the carrying of local live programs; (3) the carrying of programs devoted to the discussion of public issues; and (4) the elimination of advertising excesses.

(1) *Sustaining programs.* The carrying of sustaining programs has always been deemed one aspect of broadcast operation in the public interest. Sustaining programs . . . perform a fivefold function in *(a)* maintaining an overall program balance; *(b)* providing time for programs inappropriate for sponsorship; *(c)* providing time for programs serving particular minority tastes and interest; *(d)* providing time for nonprofit organizations — religious, civic, agricultural, labor, educational, etc.; and *(e)* providing time for experiment and for unfettered artistic self-expression.

Accordingly, the Commission concludes that one standard of operation in the public interest is a reasonable proportion of time devoted to sustaining programs.

Moreover, if sustaining programs are to perform their traditional functions in the American system of broadcasting, they must be broadcast at hours when the public is awake and listening. The time devoted to sustaining programs, accordingly, should be reasonably distributed among the various segments of the broadcast day. . . .

The Commission, in considering overall program balance, will also take note of network sustaining programs available to but not carried by a station, and of the programs which the station substitutes therefor.

(2) *Local live programs.* The Commission has always placed a marked emphasis, and in some cases perhaps an undue emphasis, on the carrying of local live programs as a standard of public interest. The development of network, transcription, and wire news services is such that no sound public interest appears to be served by continuing to stress local live programs exclusively at the expense of these other categories. Nevertheless, reasonable provision for local self-expression still remains an essential function of a station's operation . . . and will continue to be so regarded by the Commission. In particular, public interest requires that such programs should not be crowded out of the best listening hours.

(3) *Programs devoted to the discussion of public issues.* The crucial need for discussion programs, at the local, national, and international levels alike, is universally realized. . . . Accordingly, the carrying of such programs in reasonable sufficiency, and during good listening hours, is a factor to be considered in any finding of public interest.

(4) *Advertising excesses.* The evidence set forth . . . warrants the conclusion that some stations during some or many portions of the broadcast day have engaged in advertising excesses which are incompatible with their public responsibilities and which threaten the good name of broadcasting itself.

As the broadcasting industry itself has insisted, the public interest clearly requires that the amount of time devoted to advertising matter shall bear a reasonable relationship to the amount of time devoted to programs. Accordingly, in its application forms, the Commission will request the applicant to state how much time he proposes to devote to advertising matter in any one hour.

This by itself will not, of course, result in the elimination of some of the particular excesses. . . . This is a matter in which self-regulation by the industry may properly be sought and, indeed, expected. The Commission has no desire to concern itself with the particular length, content, or irritating qualities of particular commercial plugs.

81.

## HUGO BLACK: *United States* v. *Lovett, Watson, and Dodd*

*In 1943 the House Un-American Activities Committee, in the course of an ongoing investigation of disloyalty among government officials, charged thirty-nine persons with being members of Communist organizations and recommended that Congress cut off their salaries. Following a special inquiry, the House attached an amendment to the Urgent Deficiency Appropriation Act of 1943 stipulating that the salaries of Robert Morss Lovett, government secretary of the Virgin Islands, and of Goodwin B. Watson and William E. Dodd, Jr., staff members of the Federal Communications Commission, would no longer be paid after November 15. Both the Senate and President Roosevelt protested against the legislation but finally accepted it in order to save a wartime appropriation. The three men continued to work for the government at the request of their superiors and filed suit in the Court of Claims for their unpaid salaries. The court upheld the plaintiffs; and when the government appealed the case to the Supreme Court in 1946, the Court declared the legislation unconstitutional. A portion of Justice Hugo Black's opinion for the majority appears here.*

Source: 328 U.S. 303.

IN 1943 THE RESPONDENTS, Lovett, Watson, and Dodd, were and had been for several years working for the government. The government agencies which had lawfully employed them were fully satisfied with the quality of their work and wished to keep them employed on their jobs. Over the protest of those employing agencies, Congress provided in Section 304 of the Urgent Deficiency Appropriation Act of 1943, by way of an amendment attached to the House bill, that after Nov. 15, 1943, no salary or compensation should be paid respondents out of any monies then or thereafter appropriated except for services as jurors or members of the armed forces, unless they were prior to Nov. 15, 1943, again appointed to jobs by the President with the advice and consent of the Senate. . . .

Notwithstanding the congressional enactment and the failure of the President to reappoint respondents, the agencies kept all the respondents at work on their jobs for varying periods after Nov. 15, 1943; but their compensation was discontinued after that date. To secure compensation for this post-November 15 work, respondents brought these actions in the Court of Claims. They urged that Section 304 is unconstitutional and void on the grounds that (1) The section, properly interpreted, shows a congressional purpose to exercise the power to remove executive employees, a power not entrusted to Congress but to the executive branch of government under Article II, Sections 1, 2, 3, and 4 of the Constitution; (2) the section violates Article I Section 9, Clause 3, of the Constitution which provides that "No Bill of Attainder or ex post facto law shall be passed"; (3) the section violates the Fifth Amendment in that it singles out these three respondents and deprives them of their liberty and property without due process of law. The solicitor general, appearing for the government, joined in the first two of respondents' contentions but took no position on the third. . . .

In the background of the statute here challenged lies the House of Representatives' feeling in the late thirties that many "subversives" were occupying influential positions in the government and elsewhere and that their influence must not remain unchallenged. As part of its program against "subversive" activities the House in May 1938 created a Committee on Un-American Activities, which became known as the Dies Committee, after its chairman, Congressman Martin Dies. . . . This Committee conducted a series of investigations and made lists of people and organizations it thought "subversive." . . .

The creation of the Dies Committee was followed by provisions . . . of the Hatch Act . . . and . . . of the Emergency Relief Appropriation Act of 1941 . . . which forbade the holding of a federal job by anyone who was a member of a political party or organization that advocated the overthrow of our constitutional form of government in the United States. It became the practice to include a similar prohibition in all appropriations acts, together with criminal penalties for its violation. Under these provisions, the Federal Bureau of Investigation began wholesale investigations of federal employees, which investigations were financed by special congressional appropriations. . . . Thousands were investigated.

While all this was happening, Mr. Dies on Feb. 1, 1943, in a long speech on the floor of the House, attacked thirty-nine named government employees as "irrespon-

sible, unrepresentative, crackpot, radical bureaucrats" and affiliates of "Communist-front organizations." Among these named individuals were the three respondents. Congressman Dies told the House that respondents, as well as the other thirty-six individuals he named, were because of their beliefs and past associations unfit to "hold a government position" and urged Congress to refuse "to appropriate money for their salaries." In this connection he proposed that the Committee on Appropriations "take immediate and vigorous steps to eliminate these people from public office." . . . Four days later an amendment was offered to the Treasury-Post Office Appropriation Bill which provided that "no part of any appropriation contained in this act shall be used to pay the compensation of" the thirty-nine individuals Dies had attacked. . . . The *Congressional Record* shows that this amendment precipitated a debate that continued for several days. . . .

All of those participating agreed that the "charges" against the thirty-nine individuals were serious. Some wanted to accept Congressman Dies' statements as sufficient proof of "guilt," while others referred to such proposed action as "legislative lynching" . . . smacking "of the procedure in the French Chamber of Deputies, during the Reign of Terror." . . . The Dies charges were referred to as "indictments," and many claimed this made it necessary that the named federal employees be given a hearing and a chance to prove themselves innocent. . . . Congressman Dies then suggested that the Appropriations Committee "weigh the evidence and . . . take immediate steps to dismiss these people from the federal service." . . . Eventually a resolution was proposed to defer action until the Appropriations Committee could investigate, so that accused federal employees would get a chance to prove themselves "innocent" of communism or disloyalty, and so that each "man would have his day in court," and "There would be no star chamber proceedings."

After the resolution was passed, a special subcommittee of the Appropriations Committee held hearings in secret executive session. Those charged with "subversive" beliefs and "subversive" associations were permitted to testify, but lawyers, including those representing the agencies by which the accused were employed, were not permitted to be present. At the hearings, committee members, the committee staff, and whatever witness was under examination were the only ones present. The evidence, aside from that given by the accused employees, appears to have been largely that of reports made by the Dies Committee, its investigators, and Federal Bureau of Investigation reports, the latter being treated as too confidential to be made public.

After this hearing, the subcommittee's reports and recommendations were submitted to the House as part of the Appropriation Committee's report. The subcommittee stated that it had regarded the investigations "as in the nature of an inquest of office" with the ultimate purpose of purging the public service of anyone found guilty of "subversive activity." The committee, stating that "subversive activity" had not before been defined by Congress or by the courts, formulated its own definition of "subversive activity." . . . Respondents Watson, Dodd, and Lovett were, according to the subcommittee, guilty of having engaged in "subversive activity within the definition adopted by the committee." . . .

Section 304 was submitted to the House along with the Committee Report. Congressman Kerr, who was chairman of the subcommittee, stated that the issue before the House was simply: ". . . whether or not the people of this country want men who are not in sympathy with the institutions of this country to run it." He said further: ". . . these people under investigation

have no property rights in these offices. One Congress can take away their rights given them by another." . . . Other members of the House during several days of debate bitterly attacked the measure as unconstitutional and unwise. . . . Finally, Section 304 was passed by the House.

The Senate Appropriation Committee eliminated Section 304 and its action was sustained by the Senate. . . . After the first conference report, which left the matter still in disagreement, the Senate voted 69 to 0 against the conference report which left Section 304 in the bill. The House, however, insisted on the amendment and indicated that it would not approve any appropriation bill without Section 304. Finally, after the fifth conference report showed that the House would not yield, the Senate adopted Section 304. When the President signed the bill he stated: "The Senate yielded, as I have been forced to yield, to avoid delaying our conduct of the war. But I cannot so yield without placing on record my view that this provision is not only unwise and discriminatory, but unconstitutional." . . .

In view of the facts just set out, we cannot agree with the two judges of the Court of Claims who held that Section 304 required "a mere stoppage of disbursing routine, nothing more," and left the employer governmental agencies free to continue employing respondents and to incur contractual obligations by virtue of such continued work which respondents could enforce in the Court of Claims. Nor can we agree with counsel for Congress that the section did not provide for the dismissal of respondents but merely forbade governmental agencies to compensate respondents for their work or to incur obligations for such compensation at any and all times. We therefore cannot conclude, as he urges, that Section 304 is a mere appropriation measure, and that, since Congress under the Constitution has complete control over appropriations, a challenge to the measure' constitutionality does not present a justiciable question in the courts, but is merely a political issue over which Congress has final say.

We hold that the purpose of Section 304 was not merely to cut off respondents' compensation through regular disbursing channels but permanently to bar them from government service, and that the issue of whether it is constitutional is justiciable. The section's language as well as the circumstances of its passage which we have just described show that no mere question of compensation procedure or of appropriations was involved, but that it was designed to force the employing agencies to discharge respondents and to bar their being hired by any other governmental agency. Cf. *United States v. Dickerson,* 310 U.S. 554. Any other interpretation of the section would completely frustrate the purpose of all who sponsored Section 304, which clearly was to "purge" the then existing and all future lists of government employees of those whom Congress deemed guilty of "subversive activities" and therefore "unfit" to hold a federal job. What was challenged, therefore, is a statute which, because of what Congress thought to be their political beliefs, prohibited respondents from ever engaging in any government work, except as jurors or soldiers.

Respondents claimed that their discharge was unconstitutional; that they consequently rightfully continued to work for the government, and that the government owes them compensation for services performed under contracts of employment. Congress has established the Court of Claims to try just such controversies. What is involved here is a congressional proscription of Lovett, Watson, and Dodd, prohibiting their ever holding a government job. Were this case to be not justiciable, congressional action, aimed at three named individuals, which stigmatized their reputation and seriously impaired their chance to earn a living,

could never be challenged in any court.

Our Constitution did not contemplate such a result. To quote Alexander Hamilton, ". . . a limited constitution . . . [is] one which contains certain specified exceptions to the legislative authority; such, for instance, as that it shall pass no bills of attainder, no ex post facto laws, and the like. Limitations of this kind can be preserved in practice no other way than through the medium of the courts of justice; whose duty it must be to declare all acts contrary to the manifest tenor of the Constitution void. Without this, all the reservations of particular rights or privileges would amount to nothing" (*Federalist* Paper No. 78).

We hold that Section 304 falls precisely within the category of congressional actions which the Constitution barred by providing that "no bill of attainder or ex post facto law shall be passed." In *Cummings v. Missouri,* 4 Wall. 277, 323, this Court said, "A bill of attainder is a legislative act which inflicts punishment without a judicial trial. If the punishment be less than death, the act is termed a bill of pains and penalties. Within the meaning of the Constitution, bills of attainder include bills of pains and penalties." . . .

Section 304 was designed to apply to particular individuals. Just as the statute in the two cases mentioned, it "operates as a legislative decree of perpetual exclusion" from a chosen vocation. . . . This permanent proscription from any opportunity to serve the government is punishment, and of a most severe type. It is a type of punishment which Congress has only invoked for special types of odious and dangerous crimes, such as treason . . . acceptance of bribes by members of Congress . . . or by other government officials . . . and interference with elections by Army and Navy officers. . . .

Section 304 thus clearly accomplishes the punishment of named individuals without a judicial trial. The fact that the punishment is inflicted through the instrumentality of an act specifically cutting off the pay of certain named individuals found guilty of disloyalty makes it no less galling or effective than if it had been done by an act which designated the conduct as criminal. No one would think that Congress could have passed a valid law, stating that after investigation it had found Lovett, Dodd, and Watson "guilty" of the crime of engaging in "subversive activities," defined that term for the first time, and sentenced them to perpetual exclusion from any government employment. Section 304, while it does not use that language, accomplishes that result. The effect was to inflict punishment without the safeguards of a judicial trial and "determined by no previous law or fixed rule." The Constitution declares that that cannot be done either by a state or by the United States.

Those who wrote our Constitution well knew the danger inherent in special legislative acts which take away the life, liberty, or property of particular named persons because the legislature thinks them guilty of conduct which deserves punishment. They intended to safeguard the people of this country from punishment without trial by duly constituted courts. . . . And even the courts to which this important function was entrusted were commanded to stay their hands until and unless certain tested safeguards were observed.

An accused in court must be tried by an impartial jury, has a right to be represented by counsel, he must be clearly informed of the charge against him, the law which he is charged with violating must have been passed before he committed the act charged, he must be confronted by the witnesses against him, he must not be compelled to incriminate himself, he cannot twice be put in jeopardy for the same offense, and even after conviction no cruel and unusual punishment can be inflicted upon him. . . .

When our Constitution and Bill of Rights were written, our ancestors had ample reason to know that legislative trials and punishments were too dangerous to liberty to exist in the nation of free men they envisioned. And so they proscribed bills of attainder. Section 304 is one. Much as we regret to declare that an act of Congress violates the Constitution, we have no alternative here.

Section 304 therefore does not stand as an obstacle to payment of compensation to Lovett, Watson, and Dodd. The judgment in their favor is *affirmed*.

---

*We hear about constitutional rights, free speech and the free press. Every time I hear those words I say to myself, "That man is a Red, that man is a Communist." You never heard a real American talk in that manner.*
FRANK HAGUE, speech before Jersey City Chamber of Commerce, 1946

82.

## "Hallelujah I'm A-Travelin' "

*"Hallelujah I'm A-Travelin' " is said to have been composed by an unknown Negro tenant farmer in Tennessee in 1946 to express his joy at the Supreme Court's decision in the case of* Morgan v. Virginia, *which banned discrimination in interstate travel. Whether or not the song was actually occasioned by the Court's action, it became popular during the ensuing period and was taken up by civil rights marchers a decade later.*

Source: *This Singing Land,* compiled and edited by Irwin Silber,
© 1965, Amsco Music Publishing Co., Used by Permission.

### ❧ HALLELUJAH I'M A-TRAVELIN'

Stand up and rejoice! A great day is here!
We are fighting Jim Crow, and the vict'ry is near!

*Chorus:*
Hallelujah, I'm a-travelin'
Hallelujah, ain't it fine?
Hallelujah, I'm a travelin'
Down freedom's main line!

I read in the news, the Supreme Court has said,
"Listen here, mister Jim Crow, it's time you was dead."

The judges declared in Washington town,
"You white folks must take that old
　　　Jim Crow sign down."

I'm paying my fare on the Greyhound Bus line,
I'm riding the front seat to Nashville this time.

Columbia's the gem of the ocean, they say,
We're fighting Jim Crow in Columbia today.

I hate Jim Crow and Jim Crow hates me,
And that's why I'm fighting for my
　　　liberty.

# 1947

83.

## WALTER B. WEISENBURGER: Objections to Industry-Wide Collective Bargaining

*During the 1930s organized labor increased both its numbers and its power. A series of court decisions that exempted unions from antitrust laws promoted the growth of national labor organizations. With the National Labor Relations Act of 1935 collective bargaining became a powerful weapon, and the national unions attempted to establish industry-wide bargaining whereby wage contracts in an entire industry could be negotiated under a single agreement. After World War II a series of deadlocks in the bargaining process in several major industries aroused the opposition of business leaders to the whole idea of collective bargaining. In the following article of February 1947, Walter Weisenburger, executive vice-president of the National Association of Manufacturers, presented management's objections to industry-wide bargaining.*

Source: *The Sign*, February 1947.

SOME UNION SPOKESMEN go on the assumption that, if it is a good thing for the employees in a plant to organize to bargain collectively, it must be even better for workers in an entire industry to bargain collectively. Aside from the possibility of carrying a good thing too far, these people do not realize that industry-wide collective bargaining is entirely different from collective bargaining at the plant level. It is far more than merely extending collective bargaining to a larger unit. There is a change in the very nature of the resulting negotiations.

### Industry-wide and Plant Level Bargaining Differ

I THINK OF COLLECTIVE BARGAINING as a method of determining wages, hours and working conditions for a given group of employees by a process of discussion, consideration and negotiation, and administration of the resultant agreement. The process is carried on by an employer on one side of the bargaining table and a union on the other — a union which is the freely chosen representative of the employees. Some of the union representatives are usually workers in the plant.

Now what is industry-wide collective bargaining? That is a situation where the employer's side of the table is occupied not only by one employer, but by a representative of all of the employers in the whole industry. He cannot be thoroughly familiar with the conditions and circumstances of any one plant, since he is required to know something about all the plants in the industry. Instead of a specific knowledge of particular facts, he must have a general knowledge of average conditions.

And who represents the union in industry-wide negotiations? Not the local union representative who devotes his major attention to the working conditions, wages and hours in a specific plant or company. The union representative in industry-wide bargaining is a national (or international) union president whose interest is no one specific plant or company, but who presumably knows something about the whole industry, and is concerned primarily about the union's national (or international) interests and policies. National union interests are paramount even if some particular company is thrown out of business and its employees lose their jobs.

Which type of collective bargaining is likely to be most successful in meeting the needs of employers and workers? More important still, which type of bargaining is likely to serve the consumers who, in the final analysis, pay the worker's wage and the manager's salary?

### The Individual Worker, the Forgotten Man of Industry-wide Bargaining

LET'S LOOK AT COLLECTIVE BARGAINING from the viewpoint of an employee. I am not thinking of a nameless clock-number in a theoretical average plant. I am thinking of John H. Brown, who has a wife and two kids at home, and works as a milling machine operator at the C. A. Whyte Mfg. Company. John Brown has some very specific problems. In the first place, he's wondering what are his chances of getting another wage increase. Moreover, he suspects that his foreman showed favoritism in giving someone else the gravy jobs. He'd like to know whether the C. A. Whyte Mfg. Co. is making a 50 percent profit, as he heard at the last union meeting. And he'd like to know just how much chance he stands of being made a group leader, and maybe a foreman.

In other words, John Brown's chief interest lies in his particular job, his foreman, his company. And he joined his union because he believes his union can help him about some of these problems.

But who's worried about John Brown when it comes to industry-wide bargaining? The bargaining is carried on by people whom John Brown doesn't know and may never have heard of. They're discussing industry-wide problems. They may be concerned about tariffs and foreign competition and nationwide conditions. They never heard of John Brown and don't know what his problems are. They get involved in such things as regional differentials, uniform standards, long-range trends in the industry. That doesn't help John Brown one bit.

He reads in the newspapers about the negotiations. Sure, maybe he'll get a wage raise out of it. But is he going to have to go on strike again just because a couple of negotiators in Washington (or Pittsburgh, or New York) couldn't get together? He remembers the steel strike of 1945 when he and hundreds of others were told to "hit the bricks" even though there was no dispute with his employer.

He knows that his local union officers understand his problems, but he is rightly afraid that the international union president never heard of him. Brown knows that he and his local union officers can talk things over with C. A. Whyte, the president of the company, and can usually reach an understanding; but he knows very little about this employer negotiator who represents the whole industry and he fears the worst. Why can't the local union and individual employer or plant manager settle their problems right at home instead of passing the buck to somebody a thousand miles away?

### Industry-wide Bargaining Encourages Union Autocracy

IN THE LONG RUN industry-wide bargaining encourages more and more concentration of union power and authority in a few hands at the top and less and less real autonomy in the membership at the local level. The United Mine Workers offers a shining example of concentrated union power which flourishes under industry-wide bargaining.

There is also the possibility that a union will obtain a closed shop on a national basis. Should this happen, the hierarchy of officials in charge of that union acquires the power to determine whether any individual citizen shall have the right to earn a living in that industry in any part of the nation. Surely it would be tempting fate to take any step which would give any group such power over individuals.

### The Employer Prefers to Deal Directly with the Local Union

AND WHAT ABOUT the employer? Some employers, it is true, have become so fed up with abuses of collective bargaining that they've been quite willing to let someone else handle this problem child. But in general, once employers are convinced that their employees voluntarily elect to bargain collectively, the average employer undertakes his collective bargaining responsibilities as an integral part of his job as an employer, and tries to make it work. But he is confused and mystified by union insistence

on industry-wide bargaining. Except as a competitor, he is not interested in the rest of the industry of which his company is a part. He is ready and willing to bargain collectively with his employees and their representatives. He does not understand why he should become involved in negotiations with other companies having entirely different problems. Nor does he understand why he should be faced with a strike when there is no dispute between him and his employees.

### Industry-wide Bargaining Threatens the Public Welfare

BUT IT IS FROM a viewpoint of the public that industry-wide bargaining looks most suspicious. Here are some points that lead me to the definite conclusion that industry-wide bargaining is a threat to the public welfare.

1. Practical experience shows that the better a labor agreement meets the needs and problems of a particular group of employees and a particular management, the better it promotes stable and satisfactory labor relations. The old adage about fitting square pegs into square holes and round pegs into round holes holds true in labor relations as in other human activities. If it does not meet the needs of employees and employers at the local level, collective bargaining will not result in industrial peace. And industrial peace is what the people of this country demand.

2. If collective bargaining agreements are not negotiated at the plant level, the people in the plants cannot fully understand them. They will have difficulty in administering negotiated agreements. A badly worded agreement that is fully understood is better than a model agreement which labor and management at the plant level cannot understand. Lack of understanding can only lead to industrial strife.

3. If labor and management at the plant level have negotiated an agreement, they

will both do their very best to make it work. But if they have an agreement thrust upon them by national negotiators from Washington or New York, their natural reaction will be to find fault with it and declare that somebody ought to have his head examined. There will be little inducement to try to make it work.

4. The public has a tremendous stake in the maintenance of effective competition. Industry-wide bargaining tends to stifle competition in two ways: (1) collective bargaining on an industry-wide basis may lead to other activities on an industry-wide basis equally inconsistent with free competition; (2) to the extent that industry-wide bargaining results in uniform wages, it drives marginal companies out of business, thereby throwing workers out of jobs.

5. If we endorse collective bargaining, we must accept the right of the employees to strike if good faith bargaining does not give them the kind of agreement which they believe they should have. A strike in a plant is unfortunate, but may be justified as the price we must pay for free collective bargaining in a free economy. But a strike which closes down an entire industry is intolerable, and is bound to bring government intervention. Government intervention prevents free collective bargaining, and may lead to increasing government control of industry and of labor.

Let those who endorse industry-wide collective bargaining consider whether the doubtful advantages and conveniences of industry-wide negotiations are worth the loss of free industry and free labor unions.

6. Aside from industry-wide strikes, bargaining on an industry-wide basis tends to become less and less an economic problem, and assumes a more and more political complexion. The farther from the plant level, the more likely the negotiations are to be based on matters of principle and strategy. Negotiations are much more likely to revolve about ideology rather than about the needs of John H. Brown, the milling

machine operator at the C. A. Whyte Mfg. Co. Do we want to settle our collective bargaining problems by political means? I think not. Moreover, the resulting agreement may actually put the C. A. Whyte Mfg. Co. out of business, since the agreement is based on conditions of the industry rather than those of one company. It is little solace to John H. Brown, as he is laid off, to know that the new agreement is excellent for the industry.

7. Opinion polls have shown that the public is concerned about the excessive powers of national union leaders. That excessive power is strengthened by industry-wide collective bargaining. It puts tremendous power in the hands of a very few. That power is subject to abuse. It has led two labor leaders to defy the government of the United States itself. The examples of John L. Lewis and James Caesar Petrillo may well make the staunchest friends of labor hesitate to encourage the kind of bargaining upon which these men have waxed powerful and arrogant.

8. Industry-wide bargaining may lead to ever greater concentration of industry in fewer hands. Agreement to uniform terms may help the larger, more efficient units in an industry to freeze out the small or less efficient manufacturers. Any practice which tends to encourage ever greater concentration and to discourage newcomers should certainly be avoided.

9. Industry-wide bargaining offers an extremely fertile field for those whose primary interest lies, not in advancing the people's standards of living, but in overthrowing our system of competitive enterprise and political freedom. It offers opportunities for widespread critical strikes, dictatorial control, and government intervention. Plant level collective bargaining gets at the grass roots problems where they can best be handled; industry-wide collective bargaining leads to the rarefied atmosphere of ideological clashes.

10. The American competitive enterprise

system has been marked by diversity, freedom, flexibility and opportunity for individual initiative. That is why it has been able to produce the world's highest standard of living, and goods and services in great abundance. Freedom to experiment, to try the unorthodox, to seek better ways of production is vital to the health of competitive enterprise. Industry-wide bargaining introduces rigidities and encourages deadening uniformity. . . .

There are some union spokesmen who characterize our opposition to industry-wide bargaining as an effort to "divide and conquer." I want to make it clear that I demand no more "division" on the labor side than now exists on the management side. Let the national unions represent their members in the way the NAM, for example, represents its members. We do not and will not bargain collectively for our members. We do not issue instructions for them

to follow. We interpret the views of industry to the public and to the government; and we seek to raise management's sights to ever higher levels of achievement and even higher standards of performance.

But we do not bargain for our members. We do not formulate any common plan of action. And we certainly do not seek to undermine or "fight" labor unions. That is a time honored myth assiduously cultivated by the more vocal labor spokesmen when they need a convenient scapegoat.

A spokesman for the CIO has said that he is looking forward to the day when the presidents of the CIO and AFL can sit down and bargain collectively with appropriate representatives of industry for all the workers of the United States. With all the vehemence at my command, I say that I hope that that day never comes. For when it does, free collective bargaining and free competitive enterprise will both be dead.

---

84.

# Robert A. Taft: Analysis of the Taft-Hartley Act

*A period of industrial strife in 1945, culminating in the nationwide railroad strike of 1946, heightened public opposition toward labor. When the Republican Party gained control of Congress in the election of 1946, it responded to antilabor sentiment by passing legislation curbing the power of unions. President Truman vetoed the measures. As chairman of the Senate Labor Committee, Senator Robert A. Taft then steered through Congress the Labor-Management Relations Act of 1947, popularly known as the Taft-Hartley Act, which was enacted over a presidential veto on June 23. On April 23, during the Senate debate, Senator Taft delivered a detailed speech in defense of the Act, part of which is reprinted here.*

Source: *Record*, 80 Cong., 1 Sess., pp. 3834-3840.

THE GREATER PART of the bill which is now before the Senate is a revision and amendment of the Wagner Labor Relations Act, which is rewritten from the first section to the last, with amendments dealing with par-

ticular injustices which were called to our attention and which we believe can be corrected by an amendment of the law. These various injustices have been frozen into the law by the fact that for eight years since the hearings in 1939 there has been no labor bill, no comprehensive consideration of the problem, and nothing for action by the Senate except the Case Bill of last year, which was only a partial approach to the problem, and which was vetoed by the President.

Mr. President, the interpretations not only of the laws themselves but of the administrative regulations and the administrative rulings, and the decisions of the Supreme Court itself — holding in effect that there was no way in which any court could revise injustices perpetrated by the National Labor Relations Act — resulted in gradually building up the power of the labor leaders, so that today, in my opinion, the weight in collective bargaining negotiations is all on the side of the labor leaders, except perhaps against the very largest companies in the United States. In particular I believe that in dealing with small business, with farmers, and even with the workers themselves, the labor-union leaders have acquired a power which today the people resent and which inevitably has been abused.

Many of our labor leaders are just as judicial and as fair as anyone could wish them to be, but extreme power, unreasonable power, cannot be granted to any group of men without a large number of them being willing to exercise it to accomplish ends which are not reasonable. Polls taken today show that union members themselves resent the power of labor-union leaders. Even on the question of the closed shop, which the union leaders are most vigorously defending, the polls show that more than half their men are actually opposed to the position the leaders are taking, because apparently they feel that today they are at a great disadvantage in dealing with union leaders, and that the power given to the leaders by existing legislation is so great that the individual is unable to exercise their right to free speech, his right to work as he pleases, and their general right to live as he pleases.

As to the proper method of correcting the situation, certainly there is no panacea. I have been interested in talking with employers. A group of employers will say, "This situation must be corrected." When asked, "What is the most important thing?" one man will say one thing, another man will say another thing, and a third man will say something else, because those are the matters that have come to their attention in dealing with labor unions.

The problem is infinitely complicated. I suppose there are at least fifty amendments to the present law in the pending bill. Wherever we found an injustice, we tried to correct it; and, of course, the net result of correcting a number of injustices is incidentally to decrease some of the power of the labor-union leaders. It seems to me that our aim should be to get back to the point where, when an employer meets with his employees, they have substantially equal bargaining power, so that neither side feels that it can make an unreasonable demand and get away with it. If neither side feels that it can get away with certain demands, I do not believe that the demands will ever be made. If there is reasonable equality at the bargaining table, I believe that there is much more hope for labor peace. That is the method pursued by the bill which is now before the Senate. It is not an antilabor bill. It is not a bill inspired by a desire to wreak vengeance on anyone because of what he may have done. It simply proposes to deal with the causes of labor trouble and the injustices and inequities of the present law.

Basically, I believe that the committee feels, almost unanimously, that the solution of our labor problems must rest on a free economy and on free collective bargaining. The bill is certainly based upon that proposition. That means that we recognize freedom to strike when the question involved is the improvement of wages, hours, and working conditions, when a contract has expired and neither side is bound by a contract. We recognize that right in spite of the inconvenience, and in some cases perhaps danger, to the people of the United States which may result from the exercise of such right. In the long run, I do not believe that that right will be abused. In the past, few disputes finally reached the point where there was a direct threat to and defiance of the rights of the people of the United States.

We have considered the question whether the right to strike can be modified. I think it can be modified in cases which do not involve the basic question of wages, prices, and working conditions. But if we impose compulsory arbitration, or if we give the government power to fix wages at which men must work for another year or for two years to come, I do not see how in the end we can escape a collective economy. If we give the government power to fix wages, I do not see how we can take from the government the power to fix prices; and if the government fixes wages and prices, we soon reach the point where all industry is under government control, and finally there is a complete socialization of our economy.

I feel very strongly that so far as possible we should avoid any system which attempts to give to the government this power finally to fix the wages of any man. Can we do so constitutionally? Can we say to all the people of the United States, "You must work at wages fixed by the government"? I think it is a long step from freedom and a long step from a free economy to give the government such a right.

It is suggested that we might do so in the case of public utilities; and I suppose the argument is stronger there, because we fix the rates of public utilities, and we might, I suppose, fix the wages of public-utility workers. Yet we have hesitated to embark even on that course, because if we once begin a process of the government fixing wages, it must end in more and more wage fixing and finally government price fixing. It may be a popular thing to do. Today

people seem to think that all that it is necessary to do is to forbid strikes, fix wages, and compel men to continue working, without consideration of the human and constitutional problems involved in that process.

If we begin with public utilities, it will be said that coal and steel are just as important as public utilities. I do not know where we could draw the line. So far as the bill is concerned, we have proceeded on the theory that there is a right to strike and that labor peace must be based on free collective bargaining. We have done nothing to outlaw strikes for basic wages, hours, and working conditions after proper opportunity for mediation. . . .

We have provided for the delay of national emergency strikes. We have provided that when a threatened or actual strike or lockout affecting substantially an entire industry engaged in trade, commerce, transportation, transmission, or communication among the several states, if permitted to occur or to continue, would imperil the national health or safety, the attorney general may appoint a board of inquiry to inquire into the issues and make a statement of the issues and report back to him as promptly as he may direct. He may then seek from the court an injunction against striking for a period of sixty days, during which time the government has another opportunity through the Mediation Board to try to bring about an agreement between employers and employees which will prevent a nationwide strike.

If such mediation should fail, then at the end of sixty days it is provided that there shall be an election by the employees to determine whether or not they accept the last offer made by the employer. If they vote to accept it, of course the strike is terminated. If they vote not to accept it, the injunction is dissolved and they are free to strike. The bill provides that when that happens the attorney general shall submit to the President a full and comprehensive report of the proceedings, and that the President shall transmit such report, together with such recommendations as he may see fit to make, to the Congress for consideration and appropriate action.

If there finally develops a complete national emergency threatening the safety and health of the people of the United States, Congress can pass an emergency law to cover the particular emergency.

We did not feel that we should put into the law, as a part of the collective-bargaining machinery, an ultimate resort to compulsory arbitration, or to seizure, or to any other action. We feel that it would interfere with the whole process of collective bargaining. If such a remedy is available as a routine remedy, there will always be pressure to resort to it by whichever party thinks it will receive better treatment through such a process than it would receive in collective bargaining, and it will back out of collective bargaining. It will not make a bona fide attempt to settle if it thinks it will receive a better deal under the final arbitration which may be provided.

We have felt that perhaps in the case of a general strike, or in the case of other serious strikes, after the termination of every possible effort to resolve the dispute, the remedy might be an emergency act by Congress for that particular purpose.

I have had in mind drafting such a bill, giving power to seize the plants and other necessary facilities, to seize the unions, their money, and their treasury, and requisition trucks and other equipment; in fact, to do everything that the British did in their general strike of 1926. But while such a bill might be prepared, I should be unwilling to place such a law on the books until we actually face such an emergency, and Congress applies the remedy for the particular emergency only. Eighty days will provide plenty of time within which to consider the possibility of what should be done; and we believe very strongly that there should not

be anything in this law which prohibits finally the right to strike. . . .

But of course the injunctive process does not deal with the main causes of labor trouble, the injustices, and the inequalities of the present law. The bill seeks to restore equality of bargaining power and imposes on the unions the responsibility to balance the power which they have acquired. The bill is not inspired by mere theory or by any hostility to unions. It is based on specific testimony of specific wrongs. . . .

The bill provides that foremen shall not be considered employees under the National Labor Relations Act. They may form unions if they please, or join unions, but they do not have the protection of the National Labor Relations Act. They are subject to discharge for union activity, and they are generally restored to the basis which they enjoyed before the passage of the Wagner Act.

It is felt very strongly by management that foremen are part of management; that it is impossible to manage a plant unless the foremen are wholly loyal to the management. We tried various inbetween steps, but the general conclusion was that they must either be a part of management or a part of the employees. It was proposed that there be separate foremen's unions not affiliated with the men's unions, but it was found that that was almost impossible; that there was always an affiliation of some sort; that foremen, in order to be successful in a strike, must have the support of the employees' union. A plant can promote other men to be foremen if necessary. The tie-up with the employees is inevitable. The committee felt that foremen either had to be a part of management and not have any rights under the Wagner Act, or be treated entirely as employees, and it was felt that the latter course would result in the complete disruption of discipline and productivity in the factories of the United States. . . .

The provisions of the bill regarding the closed shop . . . do not abolish the union shop. They do abolish the so-called closed shop. A closed shop is a shop in which the employer binds himself not to employ anyone unless he is a member of the union at that time. A union shop is defined as a shop in which the employer binds himself not to continue anyone in employment after the first thirty days unless he joins the union. In other words, an employer may employ anyone whom he chooses to employ, but after thirty days such employee has to join the union or else the employer can no longer employ him. . . .

In the first place, Mr. President, the bill does abolish the closed shop. Perhaps that is best exemplified by the so-called hiring halls on the West Coast, where shipowners cannot employ anyone unless the union sends him to them. That has produced a situation, certainly on the ships going to Alaska, as the testimony before our committee showed clearly, where there is no discipline. A man may be discharged one day and may be hired the next day, either for the same ship or for another ship. Such an arrangement gives the union tremendous power over the employees; furthermore, it abolishes a free labor market. A man cannot get a job where he wants to get it. He has to go to the union first; and if the union says that he cannot get in, then he is out of that particular labor field. Under such circumstances there is no freedom of exchange in the labor market, but all labor opportunities are frozen.

As a matter of fact, most of the so-called closed shops in the United States are union shops; there are not very many closed shops. If in a few rare cases the employer wants to use the union as an employment agency, he may do so; there is nothing to prohibit his doing so. But he cannot make a contract in advance that he will only take the men recommended by the union.

There are two conditions which we have imposed even on the union shop. In the first place, the men must vote that they wish to have such a union shop provided for in the contract with the employer, and the vote must carry by a majority of all the men in the unit, not just a majority of those voting, but a majority of all the men in the unit. That follows, in a somewhat reduced form, the bill introduced by the junior senator from Indiana [Mr. Jenner]. Certainly it seems clear to me that unless a majority of the men in the unit want a union shop they should not have to have a union shop imposed upon them by some agreement made by their leaders, thus giving the leaders increased power over their men.

In the second place, we have proposed a proviso in the case where a man is refused admittance to a union, when an employer employs a nonunion man, and during the first thirty days of his employment he goes to the union and says, "I want to join the union," but the union refuses to take him. It is provided that in such case the employer shall not be compelled to discharge the man simply because the union will not let him join the union on the same terms and conditions as any other member. In effect, we say, "If you are going to have a union shop, then you must have an open union. You cannot say to people, 'We have a closed union shop, and we are not going to let you in under any circumstances.'"

The bill further provides that if the man is admitted to the union and subsequently is fired from the union for any reason other than nonpayment of dues, then the employer shall not be required to fire that man. In other words, what we do, in effect, is to say that no one can get a free ride in such a shop. That meets one of the arguments for the union shop. The employee has to pay the union dues. But, on the other hand, if the union discriminates against him and fires him from the union, the employer shall not be required to fire him from the job. . . .

Rep. Fred Hartley and Sen. Robert A. Taft look on as Senate secretary Carl A. Loeffler signs the Taft-Hartley labor bill which the Senate voted into law, over the veto of President Truman, by a margin of 68 to 25

I think the justice of such an arrangement should be clear. As I have said, either we should have an open shop or we should have an open union. I do not believe we should permit the complete exclusion from any industry of a man who wants to work in that industry, and whom the employer wants to employ, and who is perfectly competent to work there, simply because the union says, "We do not want you and we will not let you in," or "We are going to fire you from the union because we do not like the way you act."

Mr. President, I have hesitated to support the complete outlawing of the union shop because the union shop has been in force in many industries for many years, and to upset it today probably would destroy relationships of long standing and probably would bring on more strikes than it would cure. I think there are abuses. I mentioned three or four during the course of the hearings. With respect to abuses of that kind, we have attempted to deal with them by this proviso. . . .

We have completely revised the nature of the National Labor Relations Board. That is required for the reason that we have created a number of unfair labor practices on the part of unions. The Senate is aware that in the past there have only been unfair labor practices on the part of employers. All action taken has been taken against employers. The Board has been given a necessary bias because the Board's only job has been to act against employers and to take action in the case of wrongs which it has been alleged that employers have committed. This bill designates a number of unfair labor practices on the part of employees and labor unions as being unfair. . . . The result is that it changes the nature of the Board; it gives it more work to do, and we have increased the number of the members of the Board from three to seven in order that they may sit in two panels, with three members on each panel, and accordingly may accomplish twice as much in the way of the number of hearings held. Today the Board is behind in its work, and of course this bill will impose a considerably greater volume of work upon the Board.

We have attempted to deal with the obvious fault, in the early days, that the Board not only prosecuted a man, or initiated the prosecution of a man, but also judged the fairness of its own prosecution, almost completely free from any review by the courts. That has offended certainly my sense of justice and it has offended every principle of Anglo-Saxon law. We have tried in various ways to assure that there shall be a separation of those functions. We have not provided for a complete separation, because the Board itself, as time has passed since 1939, has gradually separated those functions in most respects, and a good many of the really serious abuses which occurred previously could not occur today. We have abolished the Review Section, so that this Board will act more as a court; the cases will go directly to the Board, and must be heard by the Board; and each member of the Board is to be given attorneys to work for him, just as each justice of the Supreme Court has attorneys working for him. So the policy of the Board will not be determined by some anonymous Review Section but will be determined by the Board itself.

It is provided that when a trial examiner makes a report he shall not then enter into secret meetings with the Board in an attempt to persuade the Board that he is right after the hearing has been held. His point of view is to be presented in open hearings, and the other side of the matter is to be heard in open hearings. Thereafter, it will not be possible for the trial examiner to have a private or secret meeting with the Board, to argue against a possible reversal of his opinion, just as it is not permissible for a United States district judge to have a private meeting with the judges of a Circuit Court of Appeals after a hearing has been held before that court to determine whether the district judge's opinion shall be reversed.

If exceptions are taken in representation matters, the hearing officer, who is in effect in the prosecuting end of the job, shall make no recommendations; he shall simply pass on the hearing to the Board, and the Board itself shall pass on the question of representation, and shall do so on the basis of the facts that are shown in the hearing.

The general attempt is to separate those functions so that we do not have the confusion which has existed and which has operated unfairly against those prosecuted by the Board.

I think the very fact that we specify unfair labor practices on the part of labor unions as well as on the part of employers will necessarily restore the Board to a more judicial attitude of mind. I think that in itself may eliminate much of the difficulty which has arisen.

What are the new unfair labor practices on the part of unions? . . . First, it is provided that —

> It shall be an unfair labor practice for a labor organization or its agents —
> 1. To interfere with, restrain, or coerce an employer in the selection of his representatives for the purposes of collective bargaining or the adjustment of grievances. . . .

This unfair labor practice referred to is not perhaps of tremendous importance, but employees cannot say to their employer, "We do not like Mr. X, we will not meet Mr. X. You have to send us Mr. Y." That has been done. It would prevent their saying to the employer, "You have to fire Foreman Jones. We do not like Foreman Jones, and therefore you have to fire him or we will not go to work." This is the only section in the bill which has any relation to nationwide bargaining. Under this provision it would be impossible for a union to say to a company, "We will not bargain with you unless you appoint your national employers' association as your agent so that we can bargain nationally." Under the bill the employer has a right to say, "No, I will not join in national bargaining. Here is my representative, and this is the man you have to deal with." I believe the provision is a necessary one, and one which will accomplish substantially wise purposes. . . .

Second, it is made an unfair labor practice for a union to try to get an employer to discharge a man who has been improperly fired from the union. That is supplemental to the provisions I have dealt with relating to the closed shop.

In the third place, it is made an unfair labor practice for a union to refuse to bargain collectively with an employer. Up to this time the obligation to bargain collectively has been solely on the employer. Now it is on both the employer and the employee.

The fourth unfair labor practice is an extremely important one. It is made an unfair labor practice for any union to engage in a secondary boycott. . . .

It is made an unfair labor practice for any union to engage in an indirect organizational strike. That is to say, the teamsters cannot go to a store and say, "Unless you sign up with the clerks' union, we are going to boycott your store," unless the clerks' union has been certified as a bargaining agent by the National Labor Relations Board.

The third type of strike which is made an unfair labor practice is the strike in which one union is certified by the National Labor Relations Board and another union strikes against the decision of the National Labor Relations Board.

The fourth type of unfair labor practice is the ordinary jurisdictional strike, in which two unions compete for work on a particular job.

I think the committee all agreed that those types of strikes are in effect racketeering strikes. They are strikes which are not direct strikes to settle questions of wages or hours or better working conditions. They are strikes which are, in effect, attempts to bring indirect pressure on third parties, to get third parties to work in some way to bring about a result which may ultimately be favorable to the one initiating the pressure, which has no direct relation to the work except perhaps with regard to the question of power. . . .

Finally, violation of a contract by a union or an employer is also made an unfair labor practice which may be enjoined by the Board.

Mr. President, one of the matters which created the greatest complaint in the early days, and still does, is conduct of elections by the National Labor Relations Board. An election under present law may be sought only by a union. In the early days the Board exercised its discretion in favor of particular unions. It would not order an election until the union told it conditions were favorable, and it might win. Many of the greatest abuses on the part of unions occurred in the use of that discretionary power by the Board in the early days.

Today an employer is faced with this situation. A man comes into his office and says, "I represent your employees. Sign this agreement, or we strike tomorrow." Such instances have occurred all over the United States. The employer has no way in which to determine whether this man really does represent his employees or does not. The bill gives him the right to go to the Board under those circumstances, and say, "I want an election. I want to know who is the bargaining agent for my employees." Certainly I do not think anyone can question the fairness of such a proposal.

We provide, further, that there may be an election asked by the men to decertify a particular union. Today if a union is once certified, it is certified forever; there is no machinery by which there can be any decertification of that particular union. An election under this bill may be sought to decertify a union and go back to a nonunion status, if the men so desire.

It is provided that where there is a ballot having three proposals on it, the A.F. of L. union, the CIO union, and no union at all, the two highest shall be certified in the run-off. Under existing conditions if, we will say, the A.F. of L. has the highest number but not a majority, the no-union has next, and the CIO union, third, the Board says that since the A.F. of L. and CIO together had a majority of the total, therefore the men want a union, and they do not put on the ballot the no-union proposal which was second in number of votes cast, they simply put the A.F. of L. and the CIO on it.

This bill requires them to pursue the policy that has been pursued in every run-off election I know of — the two highest have to be certified in the run-off. The bill also provides that elections shall be held only once a year, so that there shall not be a constant stirring up of excitement by continual elections. The men choose a bargaining agent for one year. He remains the bargaining agent until the end of that year.

The bill provides further that in these elections, and otherwise, there shall be equal treatment of independent unions. Today the Board refuses as a rule to certify an independent union. Most of the independent unions had some cloud on their original formation. Originally, perhaps they were a company union, or they had some aid from the company. The Board has taken the position that if those facts are once shown, they never will certify such a union, although it may have purged itself of that connection for the last ten or fifteen years. The telephone union was originally a company union. Now, nobody can question it is bona fide.

If there be an A.F. of L. or CIO affiliate union which is company dominated, but which affiliates itself with the national A.F. of L. union, then the Board will permit it to purge itself promptly and will certify it as bargaining agent. This bill provides that it must give independent unions, under

those circumstances, the same treatment that would be given a union affiliated with the A.F. of L. or the CIO. Numerous representatives of independent unions appeared before the committee who told us how unfairly they had been treated. It was felt that theirs was a good case.

The bill provides that in elections one shall not have the right to vote if he has no right to be reinstated in his employment. In the Redwood case, in California, the men in a particular sawmill company plant struck and walked out. They have been out now for eighteen months, and gradually they have been replaced, mostly by returning veterans, until there is a full force working in the plant, and the men who were formerly employed are out, working on other jobs; and yet, when an election is held, the old men still vote, still select the bargaining agent; and there is no possible way for the employer to stop the strike or stop the picketing that still continues, because he can deal only with the union which is represented by men who are no longer there. The men who are in the plant cannot be strikebreakers, they cannot be men who are given more money than the ordinary employee; but under present decisions if the new men are standard replacements, men willing to work, and taken on for permanent work, then they take the jobs of men who are striking and the former workers are not entitled to have their jobs back. This bill provides in that case that the former employee cannot vote in the election, so that the new men can form a union and can make finally an agreement, an effective legal agreement with their employer.

Mr. President, the bill provides that unions must file financial reports on forms certified by the secretary of labor, and furnish the reports to all their members, and file a copy with the secretary of labor. Such reports are not open to the public, any more than corporation reports are open to the public; but they are open to inspection by the members, and they are also open to proper government officials. There is no special provision, but they are not specifically provided to be open to the public.

The filing of such report is a condition of certification as bargaining agent under the law, and is also a condition of the right to file any charges under the National Labor Relations Act. One of the most important things, I think, that the public feel should be done is to make unions responsible. This bill provides that such reports shall be made. They are made in many unions today. Many unions favored the proposal. No man may longer conduct a union as his private concern and conceal from his members the salary he receives or the methods by which he disposes of their funds.

The bill makes a change in the provision regarding court review of National Labor Relations Board decisions. The present rule in the law is simply that any decision supported by evidence shall be final as to the facts, and the result has been that as a practical matter it is almost impossible for a court to reverse the National Labor Relations Board.

Under this proposal, it is said that the finding of the Board with respect to questions of fact, if supported by substantial evidence on the record considered as a whole, shall be conclusive. In the first place, the evidence must be substantial; in the second place, it must still look substantial when viewed in the light of the entire record. That does not go so far as saying that a decision can be reversed on the weight of the evidence. It does not go quite so far as the power given to a Circuit Court of Appeals to review a District Court decision, but it goes a great deal further than the present law and gives the court greater opportunity to reverse an obviously unjust decision on the part of the National Labor Relations Board.

Mr. President, Title III of the bill . . . makes unions suable in the federal courts

for violation of contract. As a matter of law unions, of course, are liable in theory on their contracts today, but as a practical matter it is difficult to sue them. They are not incorporated; they have many members; in some states all the members must be served; it is difficult to know who is to be served. But the pending bill provides they can be sued as if they were corporations and if a judgment is found against the labor organization, even though it is an unincorporated association, the liability is on the labor union and the labor-union funds, and it is not on the individual members of the union, where it has fallen in some famous cases to the great financial distress of the individual members of labor unions.

Finally, Mr. President, the bill provides for a joint committee to study and report on basic problems affecting friendly labor relations and productivity. We have not had time to study a good many fundamental questions relating to labor relations. There are various subjects which were not covered by the testimony, and we felt that there should be a more fundamental study leading to better relations between employer and employee, leading to better productivity on the part of the individual workman, with his willingness and consent, because, after all, his standard of living depends ultimately on his particular productivity. . . .

The committee is to study, first, a means by which permanent friendly cooperation between employers and employees and stability of labor relations may be secured throughout the United States;

Second, the means by which the individual employee may achieve a greater productivity and higher wages, including plans for guaranteed annual wages, incentive profit-sharing and bonus systems. There are many such plans proposed as solutions of the labor problem, and we believe all of them should have a hearing and that they should be studied by Congress;

Third, the labor relations policies and

practices of employers and associations of employees;

Fourth, the coordination of welfare funds with the social-security system. . . .

Finally, the methods and procedures for best carrying out the collective-bargaining processes, with special attention to the effects of industry-wide or regional bargaining upon the national economy, and such other problems as the committee sees fit to study. That committee is to be composed of seven members of the Senate Committee on Labor and Public Welfare and seven members of the House Committee on Education and Labor, a total of fourteen, which is given the usual power of joint committees. . . .

We have provided in the revision of the collective-bargaining procedure, in connection with the mediation process, that before the end of any contract, whether it contains such a provision or not, either party who wishes to open the contract may give sixty days' notice in order to afford time for free collective bargaining, and then for the intervention of the Mediation Service. If such notice is given, the bill provides for no waiting period except during the life of the contract itself. If, however, either party neglects to give such notice and waits, let us say, until thirty days before the end of the contract to give the notice, then there is a waiting period provided during which the strike is an unlawful labor practice for sixty days from that time, or to the end of the contract and thirty days beyond that time.

In that case there is a so-called waiting period during which a strike is illegal, but it is only brought about by the failure of the union itself to give the notice which the bill requires shall be given. So it seems to me to be no real limitation of the rights of labor unions.

Mr. President, I have covered the bill. I shall be glad to answer any questions dealing with it today or at any other time. I feel that the bill makes an extraordinary reversal along the right lines toward the equalizing of the power of labor unions and employers. It is certainly a substantial step forward. . . . I hope very much that the Senate will proceed to a consideration of the bill and will act upon it promptly.

I do not think that labor can claim that any of its legitimate rights are interfered with, but if anyone can point out language which seems to be broader than the legitimate purposes shown to be necessary by the hearings we have held, certainly we shall be glad to modify such language.

I think I can say that I support wholeheartedly the bill which is here presented, and I believe it will deal with a majority of the serious problems which now exist in the relations between employers and employees; that it will impose upon unions a responsibility more equal to the power which they have acquired, and that it will tend to bring about industrial peace in the United States.

---

*Every day, I have a matutinal indisposition that emanates from the nauseous effluvia of that oppressive slave statute.*
                    JOHN L. LEWIS, of the Taft-Hartley Law, in 1953

85.

# Richard A. Lester: The "Labor Monopoly" Issue

*By the end of World War II labor had made significant gains over the prewar period.*
*Wages and union membership were at new highs, and industry-wide bargaining had*
*become an established fact. But as an era of almost unrelieved strikes, especially*
*in key industries, set in following the war, the public began to fear that labor might*
*gain a degree of control over the whole economy comparable to the control once*
*exerted by the large corporations — the hated trusts. There was talk of a developing*
*labor monopoly; and in an article published in December 1947 and reprinted below in*
*part, Associate Professor Richard A. Lester of Princeton University analyzed the*
*new concept.*

Source: *Journal of Political Economy,* December 1947: "Reflections on the
'Labor Monopoly' Issue."

ESPECIALLY DURING the last two years, the terms "labor monopoly" and "monopolistic unions" have been widely used in the newspapers, in congressional hearings, in periodicals, and in books. Unfortunately, those who employ the terms, although perhaps citing an example or two of what they have in mind, have not been prone to develop precise definitions or criteria for determining the existence and extent of such monopoly. It is not surprising, therefore, to find statements by economists that seem to be based on different conceptions of "labor monopoly," labor markets, and the nature of labor unions. . . .

## MEANING OF "LABOR MONOPOLY"

PERUSAL OF RECENT WRITINGS and statements indicates that the terms "labor monopoly" and "union monopoly" carry a variety of connotations and meanings. Some writers stress the purpose of unions as the controlling factor; some point to means (certain specified union activities or legislative policies) as the test; to others the economic effects are the criterion for judging the existence of "labor monopoly"; while still others emphasize personal power as the prime consideration.

On the basis of purpose alone, unions have been termed "monopolistic." For example, the counsel of the National Association of Manufacturers asserts: "It must be recognized that labor unionism is, by its very nature, essentially monopolistic." . . .

In stressing union action and legislative provisions, some economists point to exclusive bargaining rights or to combined action as the essence of "labor monopoly." Thus, Professors Harley L. Lutz and Leo Wolman criticize as "monopoly" the certification of a union as exclusive bargaining agent under federal legislation.

To other economists, the fact of combined action (and therefore collective bargaining or the strike per se) is "monopolistic," apparently regardless of purpose. Presumably, therefore, the threat to strike, or its execution, to prevent discrimination in wages among employees by race or sex or to protest against arbitrary management action, say, in discharges or layoffs would be as "monopolistic" as a strike for the closed shop. To others, union activities or collective bargaining really become "monopolistic" when they cover jointly two or more employers, and especially when the bargaining or strike includes a whole industry or a whole national union.

"Industry-wide" bargaining per se is often condemned as "patently monopolistic" or "the essence of monopoly in labor relations." . . .

Most frequently labor unions have been condemned as "monopolies" because of restrictive policies and practices that affect labor output, labor supply, and labor demand. . . . The same notion is expressed even more forcefully by John W. Scoville, former economist of the Chrysler Corporation, as follows:

> General Motors must pay the market price for copper, for steel, and for labor. For if it pays less than the market price, it will be short of materials and be short of workmen. But the United Automobile Workers' Union is not willing that its members receive the market price of labor, for workers can secure the market price without any collective action.
>
> The purpose of the labor union monopoly is the same as the purpose of every other monopoly. The monopoly is formed to get a price above the market price.

The preceding discussion of labor markets indicates how unrealistic and erroneous is such commodity-market reasoning as applied to labor markets. Prior to labor organization in General Motors, the company was the dominant or largest employer in a number of the localities where its plants were operating. General Motors quoted the wage scales that it would pay and enjoyed a significant range of discretion in fixing and modifying such wage quotation. With real wage differentials prevailing as a normal condition in the absence of employer cooperation or union organization it is fanciful

to talk of "*the* market price of labor" in a labor-market area. Without unions, labor markets are subject to employer "influence over price," which, by commodity-market reasoning, is considered to be one of the two "essential criteria of monopolistic position" — the other being "control of supply." . . .

"Monopolistic wage determination" and "monopolistic distortions in the wage structure" were widely prevalent in industry prior to unionization. For example, companies like Standard Oil of New Jersey, Goodyear Tire and Rubber Company, Ford Motor Company, International Harvester Company, and Botany Worsted Mills paid wage scales 10-20 percent above their competitors during the 1920s. Many qualified workers would have preferred to work for those concerns but could not do so with limits to the total number of jobs available in such companies. The same has been true for high-paying firms in nonunion areas in the South. . . . Companies do not, in the absence of unions or employer understandings, pay "equal wage rates for identical work" in a locality. Economists indicate their lack of understanding of labor markets and policies when they assert that "different wage rates for the same work in different industries. . . . are economic foolishness." . . .

Although it cannot be conclusively demonstrated by statistics, there can be little doubt that the spread of unionism since 1932 has tended to reduce the amount of "unjustified" differentials in wage rates (a) between occupations within a plant, (b) between plants in the same locality, (c) between manufacturing industries, and (d) between areas and regions. Union insistence on "equal pay for equal work" and the stimulus to job evaluation from labor organization — admittedly with some assistance from wartime scarcity of labor and War Labor Board policies — has resulted in the elimination of many intraplant and interplant "wage inequities." Consequently, the wage structure in American industry now is probably less "distorted" than it was in all nonunion industry during the 1920s. At least that is the opinion of a number of industrialists who are in a good position to make such a comparative judgment.

The application of a uniform wage scale throughout an industry, whether by industry-wide bargaining or union-wide enforcement of standards, has been called "complete monopoly" and "monopoly pure and simple," on the grounds that such a wage scale is not adjusted to "the competitive wage level" in each locality and that it eliminates wage competition in the whole industry.

If uniformity in wage scales throughout the country is monopoly, then a number of multiplant firms — such as Ford and Libbey-Owens-Ford — were guilty of such monopoly prior to union organization in the 1930s, having for decades followed a policy of paying the same wage scale wherever their plants were located. The same has been true for civil service jobs with the United States government.

The analogy to commodities is not usually carried over in this respect. For hundreds of industrial products, companies quote uniform delivered prices on a national basis so that purchasers pay the same price regardless of locality or region. Many other products carry uniform delivered prices by zone or region. Prices of such items have not varied with local demand and supply, with differences in freight costs from the producing plant, or with differences in local operating costs including retail delivery. Through various pricing devices, employers are able to achieve unity with regard to price and practically eliminate price competition.

It is no doubt advantageous to a multiplant company to follow a policy of geographic price uniformity in order to reduce price competition among sellers in its product markets, a policy of paying prevailing local wage scales in order to reduce price competition among buyers in local labor markets, and a policy of stimulating price competition on the seller's side of the labor market, especially intermarket rivalry. The policy of company adherence to local prevailing wage rates permits buyer cooperation to aid in local wage uniformity and to discourage competitive upbidding of local wage scales while encouraging intercommunity rivalry in the selling of labor. By quoting the price in both commodity and labor markets, manufacturing firms have often been able to take advantage of any monopolistic elements in their position in each market.

Critics argue that industry-wide uniformity in wage scales tends to curtail employment expansion in low-wage areas, citing such industries as the rubber-tire and -tube industry. Tires and tubes carrying the well-known brand names have a uniform price all over the United States, yet the cost of production of tires and tubes in Southern plants apparently has, on the average, been lower than in Northern plants, for the large companies report that wage rates for all comparable jobs have been 20-30 percent below the rates in Northern plants, and some companies also report that labor efficiency and actual labor output in their Southern plants has equaled that in their northern plants. Pricing on an f.o.b., plant-by-plant basis (cost plus reasonable profit) would, therefore, be the effective, competitive method of bringing about expansion in production and employment in the rubber-tire industry in the South. Uniform delivered prices with the producer absorbing the varying freight charges to all destinations and with cost and profits calculated on a company-wide basis may serve to confuse and conceal plant production-cost differences and to retard expansion in the South.

Actually, it is extremely difficult to argue that the price of labor should vary from locality to locality when the worker's tools or equipment, the materials he works on, and the products he makes all carry uniform prices regionally or nationally and when many of the goods he purchases (clothes, foods, household equipment, building supplies, etc.) likewise are sold at uniform prices geographically.

Especially is that the case when the reasons given by economists in support of South-North and other geographic wage differentials are found upon investigation to be weak half-truths and even to be, in some respects, erroneous. For example, Professor Simons writes: "Southern labor, on the whole, simply isn't worth much, to enterprisers or to the community. Climate, culture, poverty, and scarcity of complementary resources (especially capital) account for chronically low productivity." Actually, interregional and intraregional wage structures, and the effects of elimination or reduction of wage differentials, are far more complex than such statements would imply. For example, the wage scales of many Southern firms and some Southern industries averaged as high as (or higher than) their Northern counterparts prior to unionization in the South; wage differentials in single labor-market areas in the South are sometimes greater than real South-North industry differentials; and a majority of interregional manufacturing concerns and industrial engineers report labor efficiency and output as high (or higher) in their Southern plants as in their Northern plants. . . .

It is Dr. Florence Peterson's opinion that "those who speak of union monopoly usually think in terms of a strongly entrenched clique of union officers who, because of compulsory membership requirements, are enabled to exercise despotic power over workers and employers alike."

Increasing concentration of economic power in the hands of individual union officials or groups of officials, and the possibilities for arbitrary or imprudent use of such power, raise some real problems for a political democracy and a relatively free, market economy. Involved are such issues as the size and industrial jurisdiction of a national union, the distribution of power and functions within a national union, the extent and operation of the democratic process within the national union, and the possibilities of joint collusion under national or industry-wide bargaining. . . .

## WAGE COMPARISONS

STATEMENTS CONCERNING the effects of unions on wage scales and wage structures have often seemed somewhat contradictory. Some economists have contended that unions, by means of their bargaining power, have pushed wage scales too high in organized firms, occupations, and industries, thus causing "monopolistic distortions" in the wage structure. Other economists have pointed out that, in a number of industries, wage scales in unionized plants have averaged no higher than in nonunion plants; that hourly earnings or wage levels in unionized industries have not increased relative to nonunion industries over periods as long as four or five decades; and that during the last three or four decades wage scales and hourly earnings under national bargaining in manufacturing industries have not been higher, and have not increased more rapidly, than for manufacturing as a whole. . . .

Limitations of the data preclude sweeping generalizations about the effects of unions, or of national and industry-wide bargaining, upon wage scales and wage structures. The available material does not, however, support the assumption that unions act in the labor market as a monopolist would in a commodity market, or that more rivalry between unions would lead to lower rather than to higher wages. One reason that wage rates could remain relatively low for long periods of time under national bargaining in some manufacturing industries is that such bargaining arrangements increase the security of the union and its leaders. Under certain circumstances, industry-wide bargaining or union-wide action might, of course, result in relatively rapid wage increases and comparatively high wage scale. Especially is that likely to be true where rival union centers and dual unions exist, with competition between union officials for leadership, prestige, and personal position.

## SOME PROPOSED REMEDIES

BASICALLY, ONE'S CONCEPTS and objectives determine the character of his remedial proposals. An author who conceives of the labor market as essentially the same as a commodity market and the labor union as essentially analogous to a business enterprise producing and selling commodities will apply commodity-market reasoning to labor unions and attempt to make labor markets conform more closely to organized commodity or security markets. Assuming that labor unions are on all fours with business monopolies, he is likely to propose strict application of commodity-market principles and legislation (such as the antitrust laws) to labor-union activities. On the other hand, one may conceive of the labor market as subject to its own peculiar principles and conditions, which normally and necessarily involve price-fixing and monopolistic elements, and view labor unions as political institutions, striving to survive, expand, and gain certain positions within a labor movement. . . .

One proposal, based on commodity-market reasoning, is that "competitive bidding" by labor unions be substituted for exclusive "monopoly of bargaining" granted under federal legislation to the union gaining majority representation. Professor Harley L. Lutz, for example, would have employers as free to bargain in the purchase of labor as they are in buying commodities, selecting the supplier currently offering the best terms. On the assumption that unions are suppliers of labor, he would arrange it so that "an employer, having failed to reach an agreement with one group of workers as to wages or other matters of employment,

[would] be free to invite some other group to enter into negotiations with a view to arriving at mutually agreeable terms. . . ." With slavery illegal, however, unions are not suppliers of labor in the sense that producers or merchants are suppliers of commodities.

Any such attempt to utilize "competitive bidding" between unions, with the employer free to choose among all offering unions, would stimulate interunion strife and strikes, with the recent evils of union rivalry increased manyfold. Moreover, the proposal overlooks the essential differences between practices in labor and commodity markets and neglects the psychology of employees and employers. Workers value job security and employment stability; either seniority under the proposal would be meaningless and programs for employee advancement disrupted, or workers would have to shift from union to union at the will and interest of the employer. Companies value employee loyalty and employee knowledge of the company's jobs and policies. In encouraging frequent group turnover of labor, the proposal not only disregards company investment in employee training but also the other factors that cause employers to operate in the labor market differently than they do in purchasing and selling commodities.

A proposal that has won support by its superficial plausibility is that the antitrust laws be applied to "labor monopolies" in the same way that they are utilized to curtail "industrial monopolies." Underlying such a recommendation is an assumption that it would be in the public interest to have labor markets conform as closely as possible to the pattern of organized commodity or security markets.

The proposal to subject labor markets and labor unions to the antitrust laws overlooks the fact that the market is not a satisfactory apparatus for solving many labor problems — the optimum hours of work, working conditions, child labor, job security, workers' grievances, and other human aspects of labor relations. Employee and union rivalry and suits at law may be detrimental, rather than helpful, to labor productivity and labor relations. Labor and management are not competitors in the sense that producers of the same commodity are competitors; nor should unions be considered, or be forced, to be rivals in the manner of competing firms.

The antitrust laws do not define "monopoly" or "restraint of trade," nor does the Sherman Act set forth any definite criteria for determining their existence. Do unions restrain trade when they restrict employers by seniority rules, grievance procedures, definitions of normal working hours and holidays, and all the other nonwage provisions of the typical labor agreement? The restriction is not on consumers who, as pointed out above, may enjoy a larger output as a result of union restrictions on management. Do such practices as wage-fixing, domination of a labor market by a single employer, or agreement on labor-market policies by employers constitute "monopoly," which would subject employers to penalties under the proposed extension of the antitrust laws? How would the extent of injury, for which treble damages can be collected under the Sherman Act, be calculated and assessed by the courts if collective bargaining and some of the provisions of typical labor agreements, including wage-fixing, were considered in violation of the antitrust laws? Presumably Senator Robert A. Taft had some of these questions in mind when he stated: "You would practically have to write an antitrust law for labor, because I do not think the Sherman Act is really aimed at it, or that the wording is particularly suitable."

The fact is that the antitrust laws and litigation under them have proved costly, ineffective, and ill-adapted for the determination and solution of monopoly problems. Court cases drag on for as long as ten years. Court victories usually are only moral victories; companies adjudged guilty can try oth-er means, and generally there is no follow-up after the court decision. . . .

The antitrust laws have proved to be impotent to prevent the growth of large industrial empires and increasing concentration of economic power in American industry. Extension of the antitrust laws to labor markets, in the face of their unsuccessful record in the field for which they were designed and in view of the essential differences between labor and commodity markets, would certainly not be sensible.

During the past year or two, a number of special limitations on labor unions have been recommended for congressional action. One type of proposal . . . would restrict collective bargaining to a single operating company or to one local labor-market area and would enforce independence of union policy and decision on a company or community basis. Collective bargaining could encompass the employees of two or more employers only if the firms included had a combined total of no more than, say, one hundred employees and were all located in the same trade area or no more than fifty miles apart.

The stated objectives of such proposals are "to prevent monopolistic concentrations of bargaining power," to eliminate bargaining by national unions, to insure complete freedom of action by local unions, to secure more employer-employee participation in collective bargaining, and to forestall industry-wide shutdowns. Careful consideration indicates, however, that the proposed legislation is not well designed to achieve some of the avowed objectives and would not be in the public interest.

Since the restrictions are to be applied only to labor unions and not to employers or employer organizations, they seem patently unfair. One of the fundamental objectives of labor organization, unity of action on wages over the whole area of competitive production of an article, is forbidden, but no corresponding restriction is proposed with respect to unity of action on the price of the article over the whole competitive area. If "employer" were substituted for labor organization in these proposals, such employer practices as exchange of wage information, use of a common consulting service, discussion at employer meetings, or even casual conversation or correspondence would presumably be considered illegal if they resulted in two or more companies (of any size or in separate communities) adopting any particular wage, hour, or other labor policy.

This type of recommendation is radical in the extent to which it would alter the character and structure of labor unions as they have existed here and abroad for as long as one hundred and fifty years. National unions would presumably become ineffectual federations. . . . Craft unions would be most severely affected, since they are organized by occupation rather than employer; even some existing craft and industrial locals would have to be divided. Without a thoroughgoing breakup of industrial combinations and large companies, this sort of proposal seems neither logical nor defensible. There may be little more reason for unions to be cut up according to the odd conglomeration of activities in many of the multiplant companies than there would be for companies to be confined to the jurisdiction of individual national or local unions. A union limited to the operations of one employer or a few small employers in one community might be too small or distorted for economical and effective operation.

The consequences of such a proposal would not be what proponents indicate. It would foster union rivalry, instability in labor relations, and irresponsibility in organized labor. National unions generally are a restraining influence on local unions, because their officers are farther removed from the scene of conflict, have a broader and longer-run point of view, are more aware of the lessons of past experience, and are more interested in conserving strike funds and re-

taining their union jobs. To destroy the responsibility of the parent organization, to increase the number of independent unions in manufacturing by five hundred to a thousand times, and to have labor negotiations and changes in the terms of employment occurring in an industry all the time would serve to increase the confusion and turmoil, the labor unrest, the amount of industrial conflict, and the time lost from strikes. Also, compulsory independence of policy-determination would retard the spread of labor practices that the experience of one or more companies showed to be beneficial. In addition, there would be the unfavorable effects on labor relations resulting from the disruption of existing relationships and the bitterness engendered by dissolution of national unions and enforced segregation of the pieces.

It is not clear which of the various meanings of "labor monopoly" the proponents of this type of legislation have in mind as their target. Since the labor market is a local market, confining collective bargaining and policy determination to one "labor-market area" would not necessarily prevent monopoly in that market, either on the demand or on the supply side. Limitation of the bargaining and collective action to an individual firm might seem to reduce the possibility of monopoly if the industry is not dominated by one or a few large firms and the number of firms is not decreasing. However, individual-firm bargaining favors the large company and may help to reduce the number of firms in existence. To prevent small companies in an industry from gaining the advantages of joint action in collective bargaining (except when they happen to be located in the same community) is to discourage the existence of small companies by exposing them both to pattern-setting in labor matters by the large concerns without consideration of the interest of the smaller firms and to the threat of strike action against one small company at a time. It has been to avoid such weak and unsatisfactory positions that many employers have resorted to multi-employer bargaining, which has been especially prevalent in industries characterized by a hundred or more small firms, with no one firm having as much as 5 percent of the industry's total output, such as men's and ladies' clothing, women's hosiery, and cotton textiles.

Industry-wide shutdowns have often taken place in industries in the absence of multiple-employer bargaining and can readily occur through the spreading of a strike, regardless of the area included in a single negotiation. Indeed, the manufacturing industries subject to national and regional collective bargaining have been notably free from crippling strikes during the past decade, and some of them have had no authorized strikes since national or regional bargaining was instituted.

The proposal to compel local or company-wide independence of bargaining and union policy raises serious practical problems. The employer unit of organization is especially objectionable where employment is characteristically of short duration, as in the building and maritime industries and in some canning operations.

Even more difficult would be the problems of effective enforcement. To prevent national unions from playing any role in union policy formulation or determination and to compel independence of union policy by company or community, it would presumably be necessary to make it an "unfair labor practice" or illegal for national union officials to make statements on union policy or to print suggestions for union demands, if the granting or withholding of the use of the national union's support, insignia, funds, or favors were implied in any way. Therefore, enforcement would seem to require significant curtailments of freedom of speech and the press as well as a marked degree of government intervention in the internal affairs of unions.

If national officials were trying to bring pressure upon an official or officials of an affiliated local in favor of some policy, the local officials would usually be the only ones directly cognizant of that fact. But they might hesitate to complain, for example, for fear that their progress within the union would be jeopardized thereby. Would the National Labor Relations Board or some other government agency attempt to prevent — for an *indefinite period* through an injunction or cease-and-desist order — the national union from withdrawing its charter to the local, or the national officials from discriminating against a complaining official in promotion? If so, how could the Board assure the complaining official that his opportunities to elective or appointive office in the national union were fully protected at all times? Such questions indicate the real practical difficulties facing any attempt to enforce decentralization of national unions and local autonomy within a political organization that is part of a labor movement, with its own loyalties, traditions, and codes of conduct.

Some union officials have urged enforced "union democracy" and "systematic decentralization of power and devolution of function," reducing the power of top officials of national unions by increasing rank-and-file control. To attempt through legislative enactment and enforcement to control the operation of unions, or even the frequency and nature of elections to union office, would, however, involve governmental interference in the internal affairs of unions that could hardly be justified as an anti-monopoly measure. To promote a broad outlook instead of narrow economic interests and stress on short-run advantages of single unions, Professor Sumner Slichter urges a shift of power and influence from national unions to the two great federations. He does not, however, propose legislation for that purpose.

86.

## Merle Travis: "Sixteen Tons"

*"Sixteen Tons," written by Merle Travis in 1947, became one of the first labor songs to attain success as a "popular" song. It was inspired by the life of Travis' coal-miner father, of whom Travis once remarked: "My Dad never saw real money. He was constantly in debt to the coal company. When shopping was needed, Dad would go to a window and draw little brass tokens against his account. They could only be spent at the company store. He used to say: 'I can't afford to die. I owe my soul to the company store.' " "Tennessee Ernie" Ford introduced the song on his television show, and his recording of it sold over a million copies.*

### SIXTEEN TONS

Now some people say a man's made out of mud,
But a poor man's made out of muscle and blood,
Muscle and blood, skin and bone,
A mind that's weak and a back that's strong.

*Chorus:*
You load sixteen tons and what do you get?
You get another day older and deeper in debt.
Saint Peter, don't you call me 'cause I can't go,
I owe my soul to the company store.

I was born one morning when the sun didn't shine,
I picked up my shovel and I walked to the mine.
I loaded sixteen tons of number nine coal,
And the straw boss hollered, "Well, bless my soul!"

I was born one morning in the drizzling rain;
Fighting and trouble is my middle name.
I was raised in the bottoms by a momma hound —
I'm mean as a dog but I'm gentle as a lamb.

If you see me coming, you better step aside;
A lot of men didn't, and a lot of men died.
I got a fist of iron and a fist of steel,
If the right one don't get you then the left one will.

87.

# Harry S. Truman: The Truman Doctrine

*Throughout 1946 Communist forces, supported by the Soviet satellite states of
Bulgaria, Yugoslavia, and Albania, carried on a full-scale guerrilla war against
the Greek government. At the same time the U.S.S.R. demanded from Turkey
the right to establish bases and the surrender of Turkish territory at the eastern
end of the Black Sea. Soviet expansionism threatened not only the Mediterranean
but the oil-rich Middle East. The civil war in Greece had reached a critical
stage when Great Britain informed the United States on February 24, 1947, that
it could no longer give aid to the Greek government. President Truman was
advised by military experts that Greece might fall to the Communists unless
American aid was immediately forthcoming. Despite anticipated opposition from
Congress, Truman decided to commit the United States to the defense of Greece
and Turkey. On March 12, before a joint session of Congress, he set forth what
has become known as the Truman Doctrine. The doctrine marked the reversal
of American foreign policy, from cooperation with the Soviet Union to "containment"
of Soviet power.*

Source: *Record*, 80 Cong., 1 Sess., pp. 1980-1981.

THE GRAVITY OF THE SITUATION which confronts the world today necessitates my appearance before a joint session of the Congress. The foreign policy and the national security of this country are involved.

One aspect of the present situation which I wish to present to you at this time for your consideration and decision concerns Greece and Turkey. The United States has received from the Greek government an urgent appeal for financial and economic assistance. Preliminary reports from the American economic mission now in Greece and reports from the American ambassador in Greece corroborate the statement of the Greek government that assistance is imperative if Greece is to survive as a free nation.

I do not believe that the American people and the Congress wish to turn a deaf ear to the appeal of the Greek government.

Greece is not a rich country. Lack of sufficient natural resources has always forced the Greek people to work hard to make both ends meet. Since 1940, this industrious and peace-loving country has suffered invasion, four years of cruel enemy occupation, and bitter internal strife.

When forces of liberation entered Greece they found that the retreating Germans had destroyed virtually all the railways, roads, port facilities, communications, and merchant marine. More than a thousand villages had been burned. Eighty-five percent of the children were tubercular. Livestock, poultry, and draft animals had almost disappeared. Inflation had wiped out practically all savings. As a result of these tragic conditions, a militant minority, exploiting human want and misery, was able to create political chaos which, until now, has made economic recovery impossible.

Greece is today without funds to finance

the importation of those goods which are essential to bare subsistence. Under these circumstances the people of Greece cannot make progress in solving their problems of reconstruction. Greece is in desperate need of financial and economic assistance to enable it to resume purchases of food, clothing, fuel, and seeds. These are indispensable for the subsistence of its people and are obtainable only from abroad. Greece must have help to import the goods necessary to restore internal order and security so essential for economic and political recovery.

The Greek government has also asked for the assistance of experienced American administrators, economists, and technicians to insure that the financial and other aid given to Greece shall be used effectively in creating a stable and self-sustaining economy and in improving its public administration.

The very existence of the Greek state is today threatened by the terrorist activities of several thousand armed men, led by Communists, who defy the government's authority at a number of points, particularly along the northern boundaries. A commission appointed by the United Nations Security Council is at present investigating disturbed conditions in northern Greece and alleged border violations along the frontier between Greece, on the one hand, and Albania, Bulgaria, and Yugoslavia, on the other. Meanwhile, the Greek government is unable to cope with the situation. The Greek Army is small and poorly equipped. It needs supplies and equipment if it is to restore the authority of the government throughout Greek territory.

Greece must have assistance if it is to become a self-supporting and self-respecting democracy. The United States must supply this assistance. We have already extended to Greece certain types of relief and economic aid but these are inadequate. There is no other country to which democratic Greece can turn. No other nation is willing and able to provide the necessary support for a democratic Greek government.

The British government, which has been helping Greece, can give no further financial or economic aid after March 31. Great Britain finds itself under the necessity of reducing or liquidating its commitments in several parts of the world, including Greece.

We have considered how the United Nations might assist in this crisis. But the situation is an urgent one requiring immediate action, and the United Nations and its related organizations are not in a position to extend help of the kind that is required.

It is important to note that the Greek government has asked for our aid in utilizing effectively the financial and other assistance we may give to Greece and in improving its public administration. It is of the utmost importance that we supervise the use of any funds made available to Greece in such a manner that each dollar spent will count toward making Greece self-supporting and will help to build an economy in which a healthy democracy can flourish.

No government is perfect. One of the chief virtues of a democracy, however, is that its defects are always visible and under democratic processes can be pointed out and corrected. The government of Greece is not perfect. Nevertheless, it represents 35 percent of the members of the Greek Parliament who were chosen in an election last year. Foreign observers, including 692 Americans, considered this election to be a fair expression of the views of the Greek people.

The Greek government has been operating in an atmosphere of chaos and extremism. It has made mistakes. The extension of aid by this country does not mean that the United States condones everything that the Greek government has done or will do. We have condemned in the past, and we condemn now, extremist measures of the right or the left. We have in the past advised tolerance, and we advise tolerance now.

Greece's neighbor, Turkey, also deserves our attention. The future of Turkey as an independent and economically sound state is clearly no less important to the freedom-loving peoples of the world than the future of Greece. The circumstances in which Turkey finds itself today are considerably different from those of Greece. Turkey has been spared the disasters that have beset Greece. And during the war, the United States and Great Britain furnished Turkey with material aid. Nevertheless, Turkey now needs our support.

Since the war, Turkey has sought financial assistance from Great Britain and the United States for the purpose of effecting that modernization necessary for the maintenance of its national integrity. That integrity is essential to the preservation of order in the Middle East.

The British government has informed us that, owing to its own difficulties, it can no longer extend financial or economic aid to Turkey. As in the case of Greece, if Turkey is to have the assistance it needs, the United States must supply it. We are the only country able to provide that help.

I am fully aware of the broad implications involved if the United States extends assistance to Greece and Turkey, and I shall discuss these implications with you at this time.

One of the primary objectives of the foreign policy of the United States is the creation of conditions in which we and other nations will be able to work out a way of life free from coercion. This was a fundamental issue in the war with Germany and Japan. Our victory was won over countries which sought to impose their will and their way of life upon other nations.

To insure the peaceful development of nations, free from coercion, the United States has taken a leading part in establishing the United Nations. The United Nations is designed to make possible lasting freedom and independence for all its members. We shall not realize our objectives, however, unless we are willing to help free peoples to maintain their free institutions and their national integrity against aggressive movements that seek to impose upon them totalitarian regimes. This is no more than a frank recognition that totalitarian regimes imposed on free peoples, by direct or indirect aggression, undermine the foundations of international peace and hence the security of the United States.

The peoples of a number of countries of the world have recently had totalitarian regimes forced upon them against their will. The government of the United States has made frequent protests against coercion and intimidation, in violation of the Yalta Agreement, in Poland, Rumania, and Bulgaria. I must also state that in a number of other countries there have been similar developments.

At the present moment in world history, nearly every nation must choose between alternative ways of life. The choice is too often not a free one.

One way of life is based upon the will of the majority, and is distinguished by free institutions, representative government, free elections, guarantees of individual liberty, freedom of speech and religion, and freedom from political oppression. The second way of life is based upon the will of a minority forcibly imposed upon the majority. It relies upon terror and oppression, a controlled press and radio, fixed elections, and the suppression of personal freedoms.

I believe that it must be the policy of the United States to support free peoples who are resisting attempted subjugation by armed minorities or by outside pressures. I believe that we must assist free peoples to work out their own destinies in their own way. I believe that our help should be primarily through economic and financial aid which is essential to economic stability and orderly political processes.

The world is not static and the status quo is not sacred. But we cannot allow changes in the status quo in violation of the Charter of the United Nations by such methods as coercion or by such subterfuges as political infiltration. In helping free and independent nations to maintain their freedom, the United States will be giving effect to the principles of the Charter of the United Nations.

It is necessary only to glance at a map to realize that the survival and integrity of the Greek nation are of grave importance in a much wider situation. If Greece should fall under the control of an armed minority, the effect upon its neighbor, Turkey, would be immediate and serious. Confusion and disorder might well spread throughout the entire Middle East. Moreover, the disappearance of Greece as an independent state would have a profound effect upon those countries in Europe whose peoples are struggling against great difficulties to maintain their freedoms and their independence while they repair the damages of war.

It would be an unspeakable tragedy if these countries, which have struggled so long against overwhelming odds, should lose that victory for which they sacrificed so much. Collapse of free institutions and loss of independence would be disastrous not only for them but for the world. Discouragement and possibly failure would quickly be the lot of neighboring peoples striving to maintain their freedom and independence.

Should we fail to aid Greece and Turkey in this fateful hour, the effect will be far-reaching to the West as well as to the East. We must take immediate and resolute action.

I therefore ask the Congress to provide authority for assistance to Greece and Turkey in the amount of $400 million for the period ending June 30, 1948. In requesting these funds, I have taken into consideration the maximum amount of relief assistance which would be furnished to Greece out of the $350 million which I recently requested that the Congress authorize for the prevention of starvation and suffering in countries devastated by the war.

In addition to funds, I ask the Congress to authorize the detail of American civilian and military personnel to Greece and Turkey, at the request of those countries, to assist in the tasks of reconstruction, and for the purpose of supervising the use of such financial and material assistance as may be furnished. I recommend that authority also be provided for the instruction and training of selected Greek and Turkish personnel.

Finally, I ask that the Congress provide authority which will permit the speediest and most effective use, in terms of needed commodities, supplies, and equipment, of such funds as may be authorized.

If further funds, or further authority, should be needed for purposes indicated in this message, I shall not hesitate to bring the situation before the Congress. On this subject the executive and legislative branches of the government must work together.

This is a serious course upon which we embark. I would not recommend it except that the alternative is much more serious.

The United States contributed $341 billion toward winning World War II. This is an investment in world freedom and world peace. The assistance that I am recommending for Greece and Turkey amounts to little more than one-tenth of 1 percent of this investment. It is only common sense that we should safeguard this investment and make sure that it was not in vain.

The seeds of totalitarian regimes are nurtured by misery and want. They spread and grow in the evil soil of poverty and strife. They reach their full growth when the hope of a people for a better life has died. We must keep that hope alive.

The free peoples of the world look to us for support in maintaining their freedoms. If we falter in our leadership, we may endanger the peace of the world — and we shall surely endanger the welfare of our own nation.

Great responsibilities have been placed upon us by the swift movement of events. I am confident that the Congress will face these responsibilities squarely.

88.

## GEORGE C. MARSHALL: The Marshall Plan

*The policy known as the Truman Doctrine successfully checked the spread of Soviet
expansion in the Mediterranean and the Middle East, but the future of Western Europe
remained in jeopardy. The war had devastated its economy and widespread popular
discontent was fomented by Communist propaganda, both from within and without. Of the
four great European powers before the war, only the Soviet Union remained a power
in Europe. As the economic and political situation deteriorated, the United States
deemed it necessary to bolster the economic recovery of Europe in order to check the
further spread of Communism. In a commencement speech at Harvard University on
June 5, 1947, Secretary of State George C. Marshall outlined the principles of what
was to become the European Recovery Program, popularly known as the Marshall Plan.*

Source: *Record, App.,* 80 Cong., 1 Sess., p. A3248.

I NEED NOT TELL YOU gentlemen that the
world situation is very serious. That must
be apparent to all intelligent people. I think
one difficulty is that the problem is one of
such enormous complexity that the very
mass of facts presented to the public by
press and radio make it exceedingly difficult
for the man in the street to reach a clear
appraisement of the situation. Furthermore,
the people of this country are distant from
the troubled areas of the earth and it is
hard for them to comprehend the plight
and consequent reactions of the long-
suffering peoples, and the effect of those reactions on their governments in connection
with our efforts to promote peace in the
world.

In considering the requirements for the
rehabilitation of Europe, the physical loss of
life, the visible destruction of cities, factories, mines, and railroads was correctly estimated; but it has become obvious during
recent months that this visible destruction
was probably less serious than the disloca-

tion of the entire fabric of European economy. For the past ten years conditions have
been highly abnormal. The feverish preparation for war and the more feverish maintenance of the war effort engulfed all aspects
of national economies. Machinery has fallen
into disrepair or is entirely obsolete. Under
the arbitrary and destructive Nazi rule, virtually every possible enterprise was geared
into the German war machine. Long-
standing commercial ties, private institutions, banks, insurance companies, and shipping companies disappeared through loss of
capital, absorption through nationalization, or by simple destruction. In many
countries, confidence in the local currency
has been severely shaken.

The breakdown of the business structure
of Europe during the war was complete.
Recovery has been seriously retarded by the
fact that two years after the close of hostilities a peace settlement with Germany and
Austria has not been agreed upon. But even
given a more prompt solution of these diff-

cult problems, the rehabilitation of the economic structure of Europe quite evidently will require a much longer time and greater effort than had been foreseen.

There is a phase of this matter which is both interesting and serious. The farmer has always produced the foodstuffs to exchange with the city dweller for the other necessities of life. This division of labor is the basis of modern civilization. At the present time it is threatened with breakdown. The town and city industries are not producing adequate goods to exchange with the food-producing farmer. Raw materials and fuel are in short supply. Machinery is lacking or worn out. The farmer or the peasant cannot find the goods for sale which he desires to purchase. So the sale of his farm produce for money which he cannot use seems to him an unprofitable transaction. He, therefore, has withdrawn many fields from crop cultivation and is using them for grazing. He feeds more grain to stock and finds for himself and his family an ample supply of food, however short he may be on clothing and the other ordinary gadgets of civilization.

Meanwhile people in the cities are short of food and fuel. So the governments are forced to use their foreign money and credits to procure these necessities abroad. This process exhausts funds which are urgently needed for reconstruction. Thus a very serious situation is rapidly developing which bodes no good for the world. The modern system of the division of labor upon which the exchange of products is based is in danger of breaking down.

The truth of the matter is that Europe's requirements for the next three or four years of foreign food and other essential products — principally from America — are so much greater than her present ability to pay that she must have substantial additional help or face economic, social, and political deterioration of a very grave character.

The remedy lies in breaking the vicious circle and restoring the confidence of the European people in the economic future of their own countries and of Europe as a whole. The manufacturer and the farmer throughout wide areas must be able and willing to exchange their products for currencies the continuing value of which is not open to question.

Aside from the demoralizing effect on the world at large and the possibilities of disturbances arising as a result of the desperation of the people concerned, the consequences to the economy of the United States should be apparent to all. It is logical that the United States should do whatever it is able to do to assist in the return of normal economic health in the world, without which there can be no political stability and no assured peace. Our policy is directed not against any country or doctrine but against hunger, poverty, desperation, and chaos. Its purpose should be the revival of a working economy in the world so as to permit the emergence of political and social conditions in which free institutions can exist.

Such assistance, I am convinced, must not be on a piecemeal basis as various crises develop. Any assistance that this government may render in the future should provide a cure rather than a mere palliative. Any government that is willing to assist in the task of recovery will find full cooperation, I am sure, on the part of the United States government. Any government which maneuvers to block the recovery of other countries cannot expect help from us. Furthermore, governments, political parties, or groups which seek to perpetuate human misery in order to profit therefrom politically or otherwise will encounter the opposition of the United States.

It is already evident that, before the United States government can proceed much further in its efforts to alleviate the situation and help start the European world on its way to recovery, there must be some agreement among the countries of Europe as to the requirements of the situation and the part those countries themselves will take in order to give proper effect to whatever action might be undertaken by this government. It would be neither fitting nor efficacious for this government to undertake to draw up unilaterally a program designed to place Europe on its feet economically. This is the business of the Europeans. The initiative, I think, must come from Europe. The role of this country should consist of friendly aid in the drafting of a European program and of later support of such a program so far as it may be practical for us to do so. The program should be a joint one, agreed to by a number [of], if not all, European nations.

An essential part of any successful action on the part of the United States is an understanding on the part of the people of America of the character of the problem and the remedies to be applied. Political passion and prejudice should have no part. With foresight, and a willingness on the part of our people to face up to the vast responsibility which history has clearly placed upon our country, the difficulties I have outlined can and will be overcome.

89.

# GEORGE F. KENNAN: Sources of Soviet Conduct

*The forward thrust of Soviet power in the immediate postwar period led to a shift in American foreign policy from one of promoting cooperation with Soviet Russia to one of "containment" of Soviet Communist expansion. The "containment" policy was first formulated by George F. Kennan, counselor of the American Embassy in Moscow in 1945 and later director of the Policy Planning Committee of the State Department. The Truman Doctrine was the first public expression of the "containment" policy, a position that shortly after was elaborated and defined in an unsigned article in* Foreign Affairs. *It was soon learned that the article had been written by Kennan, and it attracted widespread attention as a more or less official statement of American policy toward the Soviet Union. "The Sources of Soviet Conduct" is reprinted here in part.*

Source: Reprinted by special permission from *Foreign Affairs,* July 1947. Copyright by the Council on Foreign Relations, Inc., New York.

THE POLITICAL PERSONALITY of Soviet power as we know it today is the product of ideology and circumstances: ideology inherited by the present Soviet leaders from the movement in which they had their political origin, and circumstances of the power which they now have exercised for nearly three decades in Russia. There can be few tasks of psychological analysis more difficult than to try to trace the interaction of these two forces and the relative role of each in the determination of official Soviet conduct. Yet the attempt must be made if that conduct is to be understood and effectively countered.

It is difficult to summarize the set of ideological concepts with which the Soviet leaders came into power. Marxian ideology, in its Russian-Communist projection, has always been in process of subtle evolution

The materials on which it bases itself are extensive and complex. But the outstanding features of Communist thought as it existed in 1916 may perhaps be summarized as follows: (a) that the central factor in the life of man, the factor which determines the character of public life and the "physiognomy of society," is the system by which material goods are produced and exchanged; (b) that the capitalist system of production is a nefarious one which inevitably leads to the exploitation of the working class by the capital-owning class and is incapable of developing adequately the economic resources of society or of distributing fairly the material goods produced by human labor; (c) that capitalism contains the seeds of its own destruction and must, in view of the inability of the capital-owning class to adjust itself to economic change, result eventually and inescapably in a revolutionary transfer of power to the working class; and (d) that imperialism, the final phase of capitalism, leads directly to war and revolution. . . .

Now it lies in the nature of the mental world of the Soviet leaders, as well as in the character of their ideology, that no opposition to them can be officially recognized as having any merit or justification whatsoever. Such opposition can flow, in theory, only from the hostile and incorrigible forces of dying capitalism. As long as remnants of capitalism were officially recognized as existing in Russia, it was possible to place on them, as an internal element, part of the blame for the maintenance of a dictatorial form of society. But as these remnants were liquidated, little by little, this justification fell away; and when it was indicated officially that they had been finally destroyed, it disappeared altogether. And this fact created one of the most basic of the compulsions which came to act upon the Soviet regime: since capitalism no longer existed in Russia and since it could not be admitted that there could be serious or widespread opposition to the Kremlin springing sponta-neously from the liberated masses under its authority, it became necessary to justify the retention of the dictatorship by stressing the menace of capitalism abroad. . . .

Now the maintenance of this pattern of Soviet power, namely, the pursuit of unlimited authority domestically, accompanied by the cultivation of the semi-myth of implacable foreign hostility, has gone far to shape the actual machinery of Soviet power as we know it today. Internal organs of administration which did not serve this purpose withered on the vine. Organs which did serve this purpose became vastly swollen. The security of Soviet power came to rest on the iron discipline of the Party, on the severity and ubiquity of the secret police, and on the uncompromising economic monopolism of the state. The "organs of suppression," in which the Soviet leaders had sought security from rival forces, became in large measure the masters of those whom they were designed to serve.

Today the major part of the structure of Soviet power is committed to the perfection of the dictatorship and to the maintenance of the concept of Russia as in a state of siege, with the enemy lowering beyond the walls. And the millions of human beings who form that part of the structure of power must defend at all costs this concept of Russia's position, for without it they are themselves superfluous.

As things stand today, the rulers can no longer dream of parting with these organs of suppression. The quest for absolute power, pursued now for nearly three decades with a ruthlessness unparalleled (in scope at least) in modern times, has again produced internally, as it did externally, its own reaction. The excesses of the police apparatus have fanned the potential opposition to the regime into something far greater and more dangerous than it could have been before those excesses began.

But least of all can the rulers dispense with the fiction by which the maintenance of dictatorial power has been defended. For this fiction has been canonized in Soviet philosophy by the excesses already committed in its name; and it is now anchored in the Soviet structure of thought by bonds far greater than those of mere ideology. . . .

Of the original ideology, nothing has been officially junked. Belief is maintained in the basic badness of capitalism, in the inevitability of its destruction, in the obligation of the proletariat to assist in that destruction and to take power into its own hands. But stress has come to be laid primarily on those concepts which relate most specifically to the Soviet regime itself — to its position as the sole truly Socialist regime in a dark and misguided world, and to the relationships of power within it.

The first of these concepts is that of the innate antagonism between capitalism and Socialism. We have seen how deeply that concept has become imbedded in foundations of Soviet power. It has profound implications for Russia's conduct as a member of international society. It means that there can never be on Moscow's side any sincere assumption of a community of aims between the Soviet Union and powers which are regarded as capitalist. It must invariably be assumed in Moscow that the aims of the capitalist world are antagonistic to the Soviet regime, and therefore to the interests of the peoples it controls. If the Soviet government occasionally sets its signature to documents which would indicate the contrary, this is to be regarded as a tactical maneuver permissible in dealing with the enemy (who is without honor) and should be taken in the spirit of *caveat emptor*.

Basically, the antagonism remains. It is postulated. And from it flow many of the phenomena which we find disturbing in the Kremlin's conduct of foreign policy: the secretiveness, the lack of frankness, the duplicity, the wary suspiciousness, and the basic unfriendliness of purpose. These phenomena are there to stay, for the foreseeable future. There can be variations of degree and of emphasis. When there is something the Russians want from us, one or the other of these features of their policy may be thrust temporarily into the background; and when that happens there will always be Americans who will leap forward with gleeful announcements that "the Russians have changed," and some who will even try to take credit for having brought about such "changes." But we should not be misled by tactical maneuvers. These characteristics of Soviet policy, like the postulate from which they flow, are basic to the internal nature of Soviet power, and will be with us, whether in the foreground or the background, until the internal nature of Soviet power is changed.

This means that we are going to continue for a long time to find the Russians difficult to deal with. It does not mean that they should be considered as embarked upon a do-or-die program to overthrow our society by a given date. The theory of the inevitability of the eventual fall of capitalism has the fortunate connotation that there is no hurry about it. The forces of progress can take their time in preparing the final *coup de grâce*. Meanwhile, what is vital is that the "Socialist fatherland" — that oasis of power which has been already won for Socialism in the person of the Soviet Union — should be cherished and defended by all good Communists at home and abroad, its fortunes promoted, its enemies badgered and confounded. The promotion of premature, "adventuristic," revolutionary projects abroad which might embarrass Soviet power in any way would be an inexcusable, even a counterrevolutionary act. The cause of Socialism is the support and promotion of Soviet power, as defined in Moscow.

This brings us to the second of the concepts important to contemporary Soviet outlook. That is the infallibility of the Kremlin. The Soviet concept of power which permits no focal points of organization outside the Party itself, requires that the Party leadership remain in theory the sole repository of truth. For if truth were to be found elsewhere, there would be justification for its expression in organized activity. But it is precisely that which the Kremlin cannot and will not permit.

The leadership of the Communist Party is therefore always right, and has been always right ever since in 1929 Stalin formalized his personal power by announcing that decisions of the Politburo were being taken unanimously.

On the principle of infallibility there rests the iron discipline of the Communist Party. In fact, the two concepts are mutually self-supporting. Perfect discipline requires recognition of infallibility. Infallibility requires the observance of discipline. And the two together go far to determine the behaviorism of the entire Soviet apparatus of power. But their effect cannot be understood unless a third factor be taken into account: namely, the fact that the leadership is at liberty to put forward for tactical purposes any particular thesis which it finds useful to the cause at any particular moment and to require the faithful and unquestioning acceptance of that thesis by the members of the movement as a whole. This means that truth is not a constant but is actually created, for all intents and purposes, by the Soviet leaders themselves. It may vary from week to week, from month to month. It is nothing absolute and immutable — nothing which flows from objective reality. It is only the most recent manifestation of the wisdom of those in whom the ultimate wisdom is supposed to reside, because they represent the logic of history. The accumulative effect of these factors is to give to the whole subordinate apparatus of Soviet power an unshakeable stubbornness and steadfastness in its orientation. This orientation can be changed at will by the Kremlin but by no other power.

Once a given party line has been laid down on a given issue of current policy, the whole Soviet governmental machine, including the mechanism of diplomacy, moves inexorably along the prescribed path, like a persistent toy automobile wound up and headed in a given direction, stopping only when it meets with some unanswerable force. The individuals who are the components of this machine are unamenable to argument or reason which comes to them from outside sources. Their whole training has taught them to mistrust and discount the glib persuasiveness of the outside world. Like the white dog before the phonograph, they hear only the "master's voice." And if they are to be called off from the purposes last dictated to them, it is the master who must call them off.

Thus the foreign representative cannot hope that his words will make any impression on them. The most that he can hope is that they will be transmitted to those at the top, who are capable of changing the party line. But even those are not likely to be swayed by any normal logic in the words of the bourgeois representative. Since there can be no appeal to common purposes, there can be no appeal to common mental approaches. For this reason, facts speak louder than words to the ears of the Kremlin; and words carry the greatest weight when they have the ring of reflecting, or being backed up by, facts of unchallengeable validity.

But we have seen that the Kremlin is under no ideological compulsion to accomplish its purposes in a hurry. Like the church, it is dealing in ideological concepts which are of long-term validity, and it can afford to be patient. It has no right to risk the existing achievements of the revolution for the sake of vain baubles of the future. The very teachings of Lenin himself require great caution and flexibility in the pursuit of Communist purposes. Again, these precepts are fortified by the lessons of Russian history — of centuries of obscure battles between nomadic forces over the stretches of a vast unfortified plain. Here, caution, circumspection, flexibility, and deception are the valuable qualities; and their value finds natural appreciation in the Russian or the Oriental mind.

Thus the Kremlin has no compunction about retreating in the face of superior force. And being under the compulsion of no timetable, it does not get panicky under the necessity for such retreat. Its political action is a fluid stream which moves constantly, wherever it is permitted to move, toward a given goal. Its main concern is to make sure that it has filled every nook and cranny available to it in the basin of world power. But if it finds unassailable barriers in its path, it accepts these philosophically and accommodates itself to them. The main thing is that there should always be pressure, unceasing constant pressure, toward the desired goal. There is no trace of any feeling in Soviet psychology that that goal must be reached at any given time.

These considerations make Soviet diplomacy at once easier and more difficult to deal with than the diplomacy of individual aggressive leaders like Napoleon and Hitler. On the one hand, it is more sensitive to contrary force, more ready to yield on individual sectors of the diplomatic front when that force is felt to be too strong, and thus more rational in the logic and rhetoric of power. On the other hand, it cannot be easily defeated or discouraged by a single victory on the part of its opponents. And the patient persistence by which it is animated means that it can be effectively countered not by sporadic acts which represent the momentary whims of democratic opinion but only by intelligent, long-range policies on the part of Russia's adversaries — policies no less steady in their purpose, and no less variegated and resourceful in their application, than those of the Soviet Union itself.

In these circumstances it is clear that the main element of any United States policy toward the Soviet Union must be that of a long-term, patient but firm and vigilant containment of Russian expansive tenden-

cies. It is important to note, however, that such a policy has nothing to do with outward histrionics — with threats or blustering or superfluous gestures of outward "toughness." While the Kremlin is basically flexible in its reaction to political realities, it is by no means unamenable to considerations of prestige. Like almost any other government, it can be placed by tactless and threatening gestures in a position where it cannot afford to yield even though this might be dictated by its sense of realism. The Russian leaders are keen judges of human psychology, and as such they are highly conscious that loss of temper and of self-control is never a source of strength in political affairs. They are quick to exploit such evidences of weakness. For these reasons, it is a *sine qua non* of successful dealing with Russia that the foreign government in question should remain at all times cool and collected and that its demands on Russian policy should be put forward in such a manner as to leave the way open for a compliance not too detrimental to Russian prestige. . . .

In the light of the above, it will be clearly seen that the Soviet pressure against the free institutions of the Western world is something that can be contained by the adroit and vigilant application of counterforce at a series of constantly shifting geographical and political points, corresponding to the shifts and maneuvers of Soviet policy, but which cannot be charmed or talked out of existence. The Russians look forward to a duel of infinite duration, and they see that already they have scored great successes. It must be borne in mind that there was a time when the Communist Party represented far more of a minority in the sphere of Russian national life than Soviet power today represents in the world community. . . .

It is clear that the United States cannot expect in the foreseeable future to enjoy political intimacy with the Soviet regime.

must continue to regard the Soviet Union as a rival, not a partner, in the political arena. It must continue to expect that Soviet policies will reflect no abstract love of peace and stability, no real faith in the possibility of a permanent happy coexistence of the Socialist and capitalist worlds, but rather a cautious, persistent pressure toward the disruption and weakening of all rival influence and rival power.

Balanced against this are the facts that Russia, as opposed to the Western world in general, is still by far the weaker party, that Soviet policy is highly flexible, and that Soviet society may well contain deficiencies which will eventually weaken its own total potential. This would of itself warrant the United States entering with reasonable confidence upon a policy of firm containment designed to confront the Russians with unalterable counterforce at every point where they show signs of encroaching upon the interests of a peaceful and stable world.

But in actuality the possibilities for American policy are by no means limited to holding the line and hoping for the best. It is entirely possible for the United States to influence by its actions the internal developments, both within Russia and throughout the international Communist movement, by which Russian policy is largely determined. This is not only a question of the modest measure of informational activity which this government can conduct in the Soviet Union and elsewhere, although that, too, is important. It is rather a question of the degree to which the United States can create among the peoples of the world generally the impression of a country which knows what it wants, which is coping successfully with the problems of its internal life and with the responsibilities of a World Power, and which has a spiritual vitality capable of holding its own among the major ideological currents of the time.

To the extent that such an impression can be created and maintained, the aims of Russian Communism must appear sterile and quixotic, the hopes and enthusiasm of Moscow's supporters must wane, and added strain must be imposed on the Kremlin's foreign policies. For the palsied decrepitude of the capitalist world is the keystone of Communist philosophy. Even the failure of the United States to experience the early economic depression which the ravens of the Red Square have been predicting with such complacent confidence since hostilities ceased would have deep and important repercussions throughout the Communist world.

By the same token, exhibitions of indecision, disunity, and internal disintegration within this country have an exhilarating effect on the whole Communist movement. At each evidence of these tendencies, a thrill of hope and excitement goes through the Communist world; a new jauntiness can be noted in the Moscow tread; new groups of foreign supporters climb on to what they can only view as the bandwagon of international politics; and Russian pressure increases . . . in international affairs.

It would be an exaggeration to say that American behavior unassisted and alone could exercise a power of life and death over the Communist movement and bring about the early fall of Soviet power in Russia. But the United States has it in its power to increase enormously the strains under which Soviet policy must operate, to force upon the Kremlin a far greater degree of moderation and circumspection than it has had to observe in recent years, and in this way to promote tendencies which must eventually find their outlet in either the break-up or the gradual mellowing of Soviet power. For no mystical, Messianic movement — and particularly not that of the Kremlin — can face frustration indefinitely without eventually adjusting itself in one way or another to the logic of that state of affairs.

Thus the decision will really fall in large

measure on this country itself. The issue of Soviet-American relations is in essence a test of the overall worth of the United States as a nation among nations. To avoid destruction the United States need only measure up to its own best traditions and prove itself worthy of preservation as a great nation.

Surely, there was never a fairer test of national quality than this. In the light of these circumstances, the thoughtful observer of Russian-American relations will find no cause for complaint in the Kremlin's challenge to American society. He will rather experience a certain gratitude to a Providence which, by providing the American people with this implacable challenge, has made their entire security as a nation dependent on their pulling themselves together and accepting the responsibilities of moral and political leadership that history plainly intended them to bear.

---

90.

# Harry S. Truman: Loyalty Order

*As the joyous peace of 1945 developed into the Cold War of 1946, the American public became concerned over the possible infiltration into government agencies of Communist agents. The close cooperation between the United States and Russia against a common enemy during the war had opened the way for Communist sympathizers and agents to become active in several strategic areas. Mounting political pressures led the Truman administration to undertake an extensive loyalty check of government employees. The executive order reprinted below was issued on March 21, 1947, to inaugurate this security check. By April 1951 a survey had been completed of well over 3,000,000 government workers. Only a little more than 3,000 persons — less than a tenth of one percent — left government employ as a result of the investigations. But unceasing pressure both from Congress and the public kept the administration sensitive to the issue of loyalty.*

Source: *Code of Federal Regulations,* Title 3 — The President, 1943-1948 Compilation, Washington, 1957, pp. 627-631.

### Executive Order 9835

*Prescribing Procedures for the Administration of an Employees Loyalty Program in the Executive Branch of the Government*

*Whereas* each employee of the government of the United States is endowed with a measure of trusteeship over the democratic processes which are the heart and sinew of the United States; and

*Whereas* it is of vital importance that persons employed in the federal service be of complete and unswerving loyalty to the United States; and

*Whereas,* although the loyalty of by far the overwhelming majority of all government employees is beyond question, the presence within the government service of any disloyal or subversive person constitutes a threat to our democratic processes; and

*Whereas* maximum protection must be afforded the United States against infiltration of disloyal persons into the ranks of its employees, and equal protection from unfounded accusations of disloyalty must be afforded the loyal employees of the government:

*Now, therefore,* by virtue of the authority vested in me by the Constitution and statutes of the United States, including the Civil Service Act of 1883 (22 Stat. 403), as amended, and Section 9A of the act approved August 2, 1939 (18 U.S.C. 61i), and as President and chief executive of the United States, it is hereby, in the interest of the internal management of the government, ordered as follows:

PART I — INVESTIGATION OF APPLICANTS

1. There shall be a loyalty investigation of every person entering the civilian employment of any department or agency of the executive branch of the federal government.

a. Investigations of persons entering the competitive service shall be conducted by the Civil Service Commission, except in such cases as are covered by a special agreement between the commission and any given department or agency.

b. Investigations of persons other than those entering the competitive service shall be conducted by the employing department or agency. Departments and agencies without investigative organizations shall utilize the investigative facilities of the Civil Service Commission.

2. The investigations of persons entering the employ of the executive branch may be conducted after any such person enters upon actual employment therein, but in any such case the appointment of such person shall be conditioned upon a favorable determination with respect to his loyalty.

a. Investigations of persons entering the competitive service shall be conducted as expeditiously as possible; provided, however, that if any such investigation is not completed within eighteen months from the

date on which a person enters actual employment, the condition that his employment is subject to investigation shall expire, except in a case in which the Civil Service Commission has made an initial adjudication of disloyalty and the case continues to be active by reason of an appeal, and it shall then be the responsibility of the employing department or agency to conclude such investigation and make a final determination concerning the loyalty of such person.

3. An investigation shall be made of all applicants at all available pertinent sources of information and shall include reference to:

a. Federal Bureau of Investigation files.

b. Civil Service Commission files.

c. Military and naval intelligence files.

d. The files of any other appropriate government investigative or intelligence agency.

e. House Committee on Un-American Activities files.

f. Local law-enforcement files at the place of residence and employment of the applicant, including municipal, county, and state law-enforcement files.

g. Schools and colleges attended by applicant.

h. Former employers of applicant.

i. References given by applicant.

j. Any other appropriate source.

4. Whenever derogatory information with respect to loyalty of an applicant is revealed, a full field investigation shall be conducted. A full field investigation shall also be conducted of those applicants, or of applicants for particular positions, as may be designated by the head of the employing department or agency, such designations to be based on the determination by any such head of the best interests of national security.

PART II — INVESTIGATION OF EMPLOYEES

1. The head of each department and agency in the executive branch of the gov-

ernment shall be personally responsible for an effective program to assure that disloyal civilian officers or employees are not retained in employment in his department or agency.

a. He shall be responsible for prescribing and supervising the loyalty determination procedures of his department or agency, in accordance with the provisions of this order, which shall be considered as providing minimum requirements.

b. The head of a department or agency which does not have an investigative organization shall utilize the investigative facilities of the Civil Service Commission.

2. The head of each department and agency shall appoint one or more loyalty boards, each composed of not less than three representatives of the department or agency concerned, for the purpose of hearing loyalty cases arising within such department or agency and making recommendations with respect to the removal of any officer or employee of such department or agency on grounds relating to loyalty, and he shall prescribe regulations for the conduct of the proceedings before such boards.

a. An officer or employee who is charged with being disloyal shall have a right to an administrative hearing before a loyalty board in the employing department or agency. He may appear before such board personally, accompanied by counsel or representative of his own choosing, and present evidence on his own behalf, through witnesses or by affidavit.

b. The officer or employee shall be served with a written notice of such hearing in sufficient time, and shall be informed therein of the nature of the charges against him in sufficient detail, so that he will be enabled to prepare his defense. The charges shall be stated as specifically and completely as, in the discretion of the employing department or agency, security considerations permit, and the officer or employee shall be informed in the notice (1) of his right to reply to such charges in writing within a specified reasonable period of time; (2) of his right to an administrative hearing on such charges before a loyalty board; and (3) of his right to appear before such board personally, to be accompanied by counsel or representative of his own choosing, and to present evidence on his behalf, through witness or by affidavit.

3. A recommendation of removal by a loyalty board shall be subject to appeal by the officer or employee affected, prior to his removal, to the head of the employing department or agency or to such person or persons as may be designated by such head, under such regulations as may be prescribed by him, and the decision of the department or agency concerned shall be subject to appeal to the Civil Service Commission's Loyalty Review Board, hereinafter provided for, for an advisory recommendation.

4. The rights of hearing, notice thereof, and appeal therefrom shall be accorded to every officer or employee prior to his removal on grounds of disloyalty, irrespective of tenure, or of manner, method, or nature of appointment, but the head of the employing department or agency may suspend any officer or employee at any time pending a determination with respect to loyalty.

5. The loyalty boards of the various departments and agencies shall furnish to the Loyalty Review Board, hereinafter provided for, such reports as may be requested concerning the operation of the loyalty program in any such department or agency.

### PART III — RESPONSIBILITIES OF CIVIL SERVICE COMMISSION

1. There shall be established in the Civil Service Commission a Loyalty Review Board of not less than three impartial persons, the members of which shall be officers or employees of the commission.

a. The board shall have authority to review cases involving persons recommended for dismissal on grounds relating to loyalty by the loyalty board of any department or agency and to make advisory recommendations thereon to the head of the employing department or agency. Such cases may be referred to the board either by the employing department or agency, or by the officer or employee concerned.

b. The board shall make rules and regulations, not inconsistent with the provisions of this order, deemed necessary to implement statutes and executive orders relating to employee loyalty.

c. The Loyalty Review Board shall also:

(1) Advise all departments and agencies on all problems relating to employee loyalty.

(2) Disseminate information pertinent to employee loyalty programs.

(3) Coordinate the employee loyalty policies and procedures of the several departments and agencies.

(4) Make reports and submit recommendations to the Civil Service Commission for transmission to the President from time to time as may be necessary to the maintenance of the employee loyalty program.

2. There shall also be established and maintained in the Civil Service Commission a central master index covering all persons on whom loyalty investigations have been made by any department or agency since September 1, 1939. Such master index shall contain the name of each person investigated, adequate identifying information concerning each such person, and a reference to each department and agency which has conducted a loyalty investigation concerning the person involved.

a. All executive departments and agencies are directed to furnish to the Civil Service Commission all information appropriate for the establishment and maintenance of the central master index.

b. The reports and other investigative material and information developed by the investigating department or agency shall be retained by such department or agency in each case.

3. The Loyalty Review Board shall currently be furnished by the Department of Justice the name of each foreign or domestic organization, association, movement, group, or combination of persons which the attorney general, after appropriate investigation and determination, designates as totalitarian, fascist, communist, or subversive, or as having adopted a policy of advocating or approving the commission of acts of force or violence to deny others their rights under the Constitution of the United States, or as seeking to alter the form of government of the United States by unconstitutional means.

a. The Loyalty Review Board shall disseminate such information to all departments and agencies.

PART IV — SECURITY MEASURES IN INVESTIGATIONS

1. At the request of the head of any department or agency of the executive branch, an investigative agency shall make available to such head, personally, all investigative material and information collected by the investigative agency concerning any employee or prospective employee of the requesting department or agency, or shall make such material and information available to any officer or officers designated by such head and approved by the investigative agency.

2. Notwithstanding the foregoing requirement, however, the investigative agency may refuse to disclose the names of confidential informants, provided it furnishes sufficient information about such informants on the basis of which the requesting department or agency can make an adequate eval-

uation of the information furnished by them, and provided it advises the requesting department or agency in writing that it is essential to the protection of the informants or to the investigation of other cases that the identity of the informants not be revealed. Investigative agencies shall not use this discretion to decline to reveal sources of information where such action is not essential.

3. Each department and agency of the executive branch should develop and maintain, for the collection and analysis of information relating to the loyalty of its employees and prospective employees, a staff specially trained in security techniques, and an effective security control system for protecting such information generally and for protecting confidential sources of such information particularly.

## PART V — STANDARDS

1. The standard for the refusal of employment or the removal from employment in an executive department or agency on grounds relating to loyalty shall be that, on all the evidence, reasonable grounds exist for belief that the person involved is disloyal to the government of the United States.

2. Activities and associations of an applicant or employee which may be considered in connection with the determination of disloyalty may include one or more of the following:

a. Sabotage, espionage, or attempts or preparations therefor, or knowingly associating with spies or saboteurs;

b. Treason or sedition or advocacy thereof;

c. Advocacy of revolution or force or violence to alter the constitutional form of government of the United States;

d. Intentional, unauthorized disclosure to any person, under circumstances which may indicate disloyalty to the United States, of documents or information of a confidential

or nonpublic character obtained by the person making the disclosure as a result of his employment by the government of the United States;

e. Performing or attempting to perform his duties, or otherwise acting, so as to serve the interests of another government in preference to the interests of the United States.

f. Membership in, affiliation with, or sympathetic association with any foreign or domestic organization, association, movement, group, or combination of persons, designated by the attorney general as totalitarian, fascist, communist, or subversive, or as having adopted a policy of advocating or approving the commission of acts of force or violence to deny other persons their rights under the Constitution of the United States, or as seeking to alter the form of government of the United States by unconstitutional means.

## PART VI — MISCELLANEOUS

1. Each department and agency of the executive branch, to the extent that it has not already done so, shall submit, to the Federal Bureau of Investigation of the Department of Justice, either directly or through the Civil Service Commission, the names (and such other necessary identifying material as the Federal Bureau of Investigation may require) of all of its incumbent employees.

a. The Federal Bureau of Investigation shall check such names against its records of persons concerning whom there is substantial evidence of being within the purview of paragraph 2 of Part V hereof, and shall notify each department and agency of such information.

b. Upon receipt of the above-mentioned information from the Federal Bureau of Investigation, each department and agency shall make, or cause to be made by the Civil Service Commission, such investigation of those employees as the head of the department or agency shall deem advisable.

2. The Security Advisory Board of the State-War-Navy Coordinating Committee shall draft rules applicable to the handling and transmission of confidential documents and other documents and information which should not be publicly disclosed, and upon approval by the President such rules shall constitute the minimum standards for the handling and transmission of such documents and information, and shall be applicable to all departments and agencies of the executive branch.

3. The provisions of this order shall not be applicable to persons summarily removed under the provisions of Section 3 of the act of December 17, 1942, 56 Stat. 1053, of the act of July 5, 1946, 60 Stat. 453, or of any other statute conferring the power of summary removal.

4. The secretary of war and the secretary of the navy, and the secretary of the treasury with respect to the Coast Guard, are hereby directed to continue to enforce and maintain the highest standards of loyalty within the armed services, pursuant to the applicable statutes, the Articles of War, and the Articles for the Government of the Navy.

5. This order shall be effective immediately, but compliance with such of its provisions as require the expenditure of funds shall be deferred pending the appropriation of such funds.

6. Executive Order No. 9300 of February 5, 1943, is hereby revoked.

---

91.

# J. EDGAR HOOVER: The Menace of the Communist Party

*Public and congressional concern over Communist influence on American life led the House Un-American Activities Committee to conduct a series of investigations of the feasibility of legislation to outlaw the Communist Party or at least curb its activities. On March 26, 1947, J. Edgar Hoover, director of the Federal Bureau of Investigation, testified concerning the diversity and extent of Communist activity in the United States and discussed measures undertaken by the FBI to safeguard the nation's security. Part of Hoover's testimony is reprinted here.*

Source: *Investigation of Un-American Propaganda Activities in the United States, Hearings Before the Committee on Un-American Activities, House of Representatives,* 80 Congress, 1 Session, Washington, 1947, Pt. 2, pp. 33-50.

MY FEELINGS CONCERNING the Communist Party of the United States are well known. I have not hesitated over the years to express my concern and apprehension. As a consequence its professional smear brigades have conducted a relentless assault against the FBI. You who have been members of this committee also know the fury with which the party, its sympathizers and fellow travelers can launch an assault. I do not mind such attacks. What has been disillusioning is the manner in which they have been able to enlist support often from apparently well-meaning but thoroughly duped persons. . . .

The Communist movement in the United States began to manifest itself in 1919. Since then it has changed its name and its party line whenever expedient and tactical. But always it comes back to fundamentals and bills itself as the party of Marxism-Leninism. As such, it stands for the destruction of our American form of government; it stands for the destruction of American democracy; it stands for the destruction of free enterprise; and it stands for the creation of a "Soviet of the United States" and ultimate world revolution.

The preamble of the latest constitution of the Communist Party of the United States, filled with Marxian "double talk," proclaims that the party "educates the working class, in the course of its day-to-day struggles, for its historic mission, the establishment of socialism." The phrase "historic mission" has a sinister meaning. To the uninformed person it bespeaks tradition, but to the Communist, using his own words, it is "achieving the dictatorship of the proletariat"; "to throw off the yoke of imperialism and establish the proletarian dictatorship"; "to raise these revolutionary forces to the surface and hurl them like a devastating avalanche upon the united forces of bourgeois reaction, frenzied at the presentment of their rapidly approaching doom."

In recent years, the Communists have been very cautious about using such phrases as "force and violence"; nevertheless, it is the subject of much discussion in their schools and in party caucus where they readily admit that the only way in which they can defeat the present ruling class is by world revolution.

The Communist, once he is fully trained and indoctrinated, realizes that he can create his order in the United States only by "bloody revolution."

Their chief textbook, *The History of the Communist Party of the Soviet Union,* is used as a basis for planning their revolution. Their tactics require that to be successful they must have:

1. The will and sympathy of the people.
2. Military aid and assistance.
3. Plenty of guns and ammunition.
4. A program for extermination of the police as they are the most important enemy and are termed "trained Fascists."
5. Seizure of all communications, buses, railroads, radio stations, and other forms of communications and transportation.

They evade the question of force and violence publicly. They hold that when Marxists speak of force and violence they will not be responsible — that force and violence will be the responsibility of their enemies. They adopt the novel premise that they do not advocate force and violence publicly but that when their class resists to defend themselves then they are thus accused of using force and violence. A lot of double talk. . . .

In establishing the party's illegal character in 1942, the then Attorney General Biddle based his findings on the contents of the same Communist publications which today are being sold and circulated in party circles in the United States. The American Communist, like the leopard, cannot change his spots. The Communist Party line changes from day to day. The one cardinal rule that can always be applied to what the party line is or will be is found in the fundamental principle of Communist teachings that the support of Soviet Russia is the duty of Communists of all countries.

One thing is certain. The American progress which all good citizens seek, such as old-age security, houses for veterans, child assistance, and a host of others, is being adopted as window dressing by the Communists to conceal their true aims and entrap gullible followers.

The record of the American Communists conclusively proves their true feelings. In the prewar days, when they were allied with Hitler, they marched on Washington protesting Selective Service, Lend-Lease, shouting "The Yanks are not coming." The American Peace Mobilization picketed the White House until the day before the Nazis marched into Russia and then within less than a month reconverted it into the American People's Mobilization, demanded all-out production, and started the chant for the second front.

We are witnessing the same tactics today. Since Secretary Schwellenbach advocated outlawing the Communist Party, and President Truman called for aid to Greece and Turkey, the Communists have been mobilizing, promoting mass meetings, sending telegrams and letters to exert pressure on Congress. The American Communists fail to realize that already they have outlawed themselves in the minds and hearts of loyal Americans.

The mad march of Red fascism is a cause for concern in America. But the deceit, the trickery, and the lies of the American Communists are catching up with them. Whenever the spotlight of truth is focused upon them they cry, "red-baiting." Now that their aims and objectives are being exposed, they are creating a Committee for the Constitutional Rights of Communists, and are feverishly working to build up what they term a quarter-million-dollar defense fund to place ads in papers, to publish pamphlets, to buy radio time. They know that today it is a fight to the finish and that their backs will soon be to the wall.

A few days ago word leaked out that the annual Communist convention scheduled to be held in Chicago had been shifted from July to September in order that they might carry on their campaign of obstruction to American foreign policy and increase their membership. They have been conducting an active membership campaign, as the leadership is concerned over the manner in which membership has slipped. The numerical strength of the party's enrolled membership is insignificant. But it is well known that there are many actual members who be-

cause of their position are not carried on party rolls. . . .

What is important is the claim of the Communists themselves that for every party member there are ten others ready, willing, and able to do the party's work. Herein lies the greatest menace of communism. For these are the people who infiltrate and corrupt various spheres of American life. So rather than the size of the Communist Party, the way to weigh its true importance is by testing its influence, its ability to infiltrate.

The size of the party is relatively unimportant because of the enthusiasm and iron-clad discipline under which they operate. In this connection it might be of interest to observe that in 1917, when the Communists overthrew the Russian government, there was 1 Communist for every 2,277 persons in Russia. In the United States today there is 1 Communist for every 1,814 persons in the country.

One who accepts the aims, principles, and programs of the party, who attends meetings, who reads the party press and literature, who pays dues and who is active on behalf of the party "shall be considered a member." The open, avowed Communist who carries a card and pays dues is no different, from a security standpoint, than the person who does the party's work but pays no dues, carries no card, and is not on the party rolls. In fact, the latter is a greater menace because of his opportunity to work in stealth.

The burden of proof is placed upon those who consistently follow the ever changing, twisting party line. Fellow travelers and sympathizers can deny party membership but they can never escape the undeniable fact that they have played into the Communist hands, thus furthering the Communist cause by playing the role of innocent, gullible, or willful allies.

The Communists have developed one of the greatest propaganda machines the world has ever known. They have been able to penetrate and infiltrate many respectable and reputable public opinion mediums. They capitalize upon ill-founded charges associating known honest progressive liberals with left-wing causes. I have always entertained the view that there are few appellations more degrading than "Communist" and hence it should be reserved for those justly deserving the degradation.

The Communist propaganda technique is designed to promote emotional response with the hope that the victim will be attracted by what he is told the Communist way of life holds in store for him. The objective, of course, is to develop discontent and hasten the day when the Communists can gather sufficient support and following to overthrow the American way of life.

Communist propaganda is always slanted in the hope that the Communist may be aligned with liberal progressive causes. The honest liberal and progressive should be alert to this, and I believe the Communists' most effective foes can be the real liberals and progressives who understand their devious machinations. . . .

Communists and their followers are prolific letter writers, and some of the more energetic ones follow the practice of directing numerous letters of protest to editors but signing a different name to each. Members of Congress are well aware of Communists starting their pressure campaigns by an avalanche of mail which follows the party line.

The party has departed from depending upon the printed word as its medium of propaganda and has taken to the air. Its members and sympathizers have not only infiltrated the airways but they are now persistently seeking radio channels.

The American Communists launched a furtive attack on Hollywood in 1935 by the issuance of a directive calling for a concentration in Hollywood. The orders called for action on two fronts: (1) an effort to infiltrate the labor unions; (2) infiltrate the so-called intellectual and creative fields.

In movie circles, Communists developed an effective defense a few years ago in meeting criticism. They would counter with the question, "After all, what is the matter with communism?" It was effective because many persons did not possess adequate knowledge of the subject to give an intelligent answer.

Some producers and studio heads realized the possibility that the entire industry faces serious embarrassment because it could become a springboard for Communist activities. Communist activity in Hollywood is effective and is furthered by Communists and sympathizers using the prestige of prominent persons to serve, often unwittingly, the Communist cause. The party is content and highly pleased if it is possible to have inserted in a picture a line, a scene, a sequence conveying the Communist lesson and, more particularly, if they can keep out anti-Communist lessons.

The Communist tactic of infiltrating labor unions stems from the earliest teachings of Marx, which have been reiterated by party spokesmen down through the years. They resort to all means to gain their point and often succeed in penetrating and literally taking over labor unions before the rank and file of members are aware of what has occurred. . . .

I am convinced that the great masses of union men and women are patriotic American citizens interested chiefly in security for their families and themselves. They have no use for the American Communists, but in those instances where Communists have taken control of unions, it has been because too many union men and women have been outwitted, outmaneuvered, and outwaited by Communists.

The Communists have never relied on numerical strength to dominate a labor organization. Through infiltration tactics they have in too many instances captured positions of authority. Communists have boasted that with 5 percent of the membership the Communists, with their military, superior organizational ability and discipline, could control the union. . . .

A few months ago a party functionary said it was imperative that 3,000 party members be infiltrated into the A. F. of L. without publicizing this fact. They say this action is necessary because of the danger of a third world war and the need to fulfill the Communist plan of creating a third party.

If more union members took a more active role and asserted themselves it would become increasingly difficult for Communists to gain control. Patriotic union members can easily spot sympathizers and party members in conventions and union meetings because invariably the latter strive to establish the party line instead of serving the best interests of the union and the country.

The party for the past eighteen months has been giving special attention to foreign-language groups and has called for a sweeping self-critical examination of its work in this field. As long ago as 1945, in urging the importance of penetrating these groups, party leaders said, "We need only mention the Polish, Italian, Yugoslav, and Greek questions," and in characteristic party double talk observed that they occupied an important relationship "to the entire democratic camp and to the broader peoples movements." In other words, the Communists now seek strength from foreign groups who may have relatives in countries which Russia seeks to influence.

The recent Canadian spy trials revealed the necessity of alertness in keeping Communists and sympathizers out of government services. In fact, the high command of the Communist Party regards such assignments of sufficient importance to demand that party members not contact fellow members in the government and if such government employees are carried on party rolls at all they are assigned an alias. Last fall a high-ranking party leader instructed that all party membership cards of government employees be destroyed and that par-

ty organizational meetings in government circles are too obvious to mention. . . .

The united-front program of the Communist Party was launched at the Seventh World Congress of the Communist International in 1935. The Communist Party in the United States immediately took up the program and a systematic plan was worked out of infiltrating existing organizations with Communists.

For the most part, front organizations assumed the character of either a mass or membership organization or a paper organization. Both solicited and used names of prominent persons. Literally hundreds of groups and organizations have either been infiltrated or organized primarily to accomplish the purposes of promoting the interests of the Soviet Union in the United States, the promotion of Soviet war and peace aims, the exploitation of Negroes in the United States, work among foreign-language groups, and to secure a favorable viewpoint toward the Communists in domestic, political, social, and economic issues.

The first requisite for front organizations is an idealistic-sounding title. Hundreds of such organizations have come into being and have gone out of existence when their true purposes have become known or exposed, while others with high-sounding names are continually springing up. . . .

I feel that this committee could render a great service to the nation through its power of exposure in quickly spotlighting existing front organizations and those which will be created in the future. There are easy tests to establish the real character of such organizations:

1. Does the group espouse the cause of Americanism or the cause of Soviet Russia?

2. Does the organization feature as speakers at its meetings known Communists, sympathizers, or fellow travelers?

3. Does the organization shift when the party line shifts?

4. Does the organization sponsor causes, campaigns, literature, petitions, or other ac-

tivities sponsored by the party or other front organizations?

5. Is the organization used as a sounding board by or is it endorsed by Communist-controlled labor unions?

6. Does its literature follow the Communist line or is it printed by the Communist press?

7. Does the organization receive consistent favorable mention in Communist publications?

8. Does the organization present itself to be nonpartisan yet engage in political activities and consistently advocate causes favored by the Communists?

9. Does the organization denounce American and British foreign policy while always lauding Soviet policy?

10. Does the organization utilize Communist "double talk" by referring to Soviet-dominated countries as democracies, complaining that the United States is imperialistic and constantly denouncing monopoly-capital?

11. Have outstanding leaders in public life openly renounced affiliation with the organization?

12. Does the organization, if espousing liberal progressive causes, attract well-known honest patriotic liberals or does it denounce well-known liberals?

13. Does the organization have a consistent record of supporting the American viewpoint over the years?

14. Does the organization consider matters not directly related to its avowed purposes and objectives?

The Communist Party of the United States is a fifth column if there ever was one. It is far better organized than were the Nazis in occupied countries prior to their capitulation. They are seeking to weaken America just as they did in their era of obstruction when they were aligned with the Nazis. Their goal is the overthrow of our government. There is no doubt as to where a real Communist's loyalty rests. Their allegiance is to Russia, not the United States. . . .

What can we do? And what should be our course of action? The best antidote to communism is vigorous, intelligent, old-fashioned Americanism, with eternal vigilance. I do not favor any course of action which would give the Communists cause to portray and pity themselves as martyrs. I do favor unrelenting prosecution wherever they are found to be violating our country's laws.

As Americans, our most effective defense is a workable democracy that guarantees and preserves our cherished freedoms.

I would have no fears if more Americans possessed the zeal, the fervor, the persistence, and the industry to learn about this menace of Red fascism. I do fear for the liberal and progressive who has been hoodwinked and duped into joining hands with the Communists. I confess to a real apprehension so long as Communists are able to secure ministers of the gospel to promote their evil work and espouse a cause that is alien to the religion of Christ and Judaism. I do fear so long as school boards and parents tolerate conditions whereby Communists and fellow travelers, under the guise of academic freedom, can teach our youth a way of life that eventually will destroy the sanctity of the home, that undermines faith in God, that causes them to scorn respect for constituted authority and sabotage our revered Constitution.

I do fear so long as American labor groups are infiltrated, dominated, or saturated with the virus of communism. I do fear the palliation and weasel-worded gestures against communism indulged in by some of our labor leaders who should know better but who have become pawns in the hands of sinister but astute manipulations for the Communist cause.

I fear for ignorance on the part of all our people who may take the poisonous pills of Communist propaganda.

I am deeply concerned whenever I think of the words of an old-time Communist. Disillusioned, disgusted, and frightened, he came to us with his story and concluded:

> God help America or any other country if the Communist Party ever gets strong enough to control labor and politics.
> God help us all!

The Communists have been, still are, and always will be a menace to freedom, to democratic ideals, to the worship of God and to America's way of life.

I feel that once public opinion is thoroughly aroused as it is today, the fight against communism is well on its way. Victory will be assured once Communists are identified and exposed, because the public will take the first step of quarantining them so they can do no harm. Communism, in reality, is not a political party. It is a way of life — an evil and malignant way of life. It reveals a condition akin to disease that spreads like an epidemic, and, like an epidemic, a quarantine is necessary to keep it from infecting the nation.

---

92.

## Henry Steele Commager: Who Is Loyal to America?

*The Cold War climate of the late Forties brought the question of loyalty to the forefront of national attention. Loyalty investigations to ferret out allegedly subversive individuals and groups in the government became commonplace, both in government and without. The Federal Bureau of Investigation instituted security checks on all government employees. The House Un-American Activities Committee conducted intensive investigations of subversion in government. And many private firms established their own "unofficial" loyalty programs. A number of prominent American intellectuals became apprehensive that the loyalty investigations were creating a "police state" that threatened the traditional civil liberties of citizens. Professor Henry Steele Commager, one of the most outspoken critics of loyalty programs, examined the issue of loyalty historically and attempted to establish a sound definition of loyalty in the following essay, published in September 1947.*

Source: *Harper's,* September 1947.

On May 6 a Russian-born girl, Mrs. Shura Lewis, gave a talk to the students of the Western High School of Washington, D.C. She talked about Russia — its school system, its public health program, the position of women, of the aged, of the workers, the farmers, and the professional classes — and compared, superficially and uncritically, some American and Russian social institutions. The most careful examination of the speech — happily reprinted for us in the *Congressional Record* — does not disclose a single disparagement of anything American, unless it is a quasi-humorous reference to the cost of having a baby and of dental treatment in this country. Mrs. Lewis said nothing that had not been said a thousand times, in speeches, in newspapers, magazines, and books. She said nothing that any normal person could find objectionable.

Her speech, however, created a sensation. A few students walked out on it. Others improvised placards proclaiming their devotion to Americanism. Indignant mothers telephoned their protests. Newspapers took a strong stand against the outrage. Congress, rarely concerned for the political or economic welfare of the citizens of the capital city, reacted sharply when its intellectual welfare was at stake. Congressmen Rankin and Dirksen thundered and lightened; the District of Columbia Committee went into a huddle; there were demands for housecleaning in the whole school system, which was obviously shot through and through with Communism.

All this might be ignored, for we have learned not to expect either intelligence or understanding of Americanism from this element in our Congress. More ominous was the reaction of the educators entrusted with the high responsibility of guiding and guarding the intellectual welfare of our boys and girls. Did they stand up for intellectual freedom? Did they insist that high-school children had the right and the duty to learn about other countries? Did they protest that students were to be trusted to use intelligence and common sense? Did they affirm that the Americanism of their students was staunch enough to resist propaganda? Did they perform even the elementary task, expected of educators above all, of analyzing the much-criticized speech?

Not at all. The district superintendent of schools, Dr. Hobart Corning, hastened to agree with the animadversions of Representatives Rankin and Dirksen. The whole thing was, he confessed, "a very unfortunate occurrence," and had "shocked the whole school system." What Mrs. Lewis said, he added gratuitously, was "repugnant to all who are working with youth in the Washington schools," and "the entire affair contrary to the philosophy of education under which we operate." Mr. Danowsky, the hapless principal of the Western High School, was "the most shocked and regret-

ful of all." The District of Columbia Committee would be happy to know that though he was innocent in the matter, he had been properly reprimanded!

It is the reaction of the educators that makes this episode more than a tempest in a teapot. We expect hysteria from Mr. Rankin and some newspapers; we are shocked when we see educators, timid before criticism and confused about first principles, betray their trust. And we wonder what can be that "philosophy of education" which believes that young people can be trained to the duties of citizenship by wrapping their minds in cotton wool.

Merely by talking about Russia, Mrs. Lewis was thought to be attacking Americanism. It is indicative of the seriousness of the situation that during this same week the House found it necessary to take time out from the discussion of the labor bill, the tax bill, the International Trade Organization, and the world famine to meet assaults upon Americanism from a new quarter. This time it was the artists who were undermining the American system, and members of the House spent some hours passing around reproductions of the paintings which the State Department had sent abroad as part of its program for advertising American culture. We need not pause over the exquisite humor which congressmen displayed in their comments on modern art: weary statesmen must have their fun. But we may profitably remark the major criticism which was directed against this unfortunate collection of paintings. What was wrong with these paintings, it shortly appeared, was that they were un-American. "No American drew those crazy pictures," said Mr. Rankin. Perhaps he was right. The copious files of the Committee on Un-American Activities were levied upon to prove that of the forty-five artists represented "no less than twenty were definitely New Deal in various shades of Communism." The damning facts are specified for each of the pernicious twenty; we can content ourselves with the first of them, Ben-Zion. What is the evidence here? "Ben-Zion was one of the signers of a letter sent to President Roosevelt by the United American Artists which urged help to the U.S.S.R. and Britain after Hitler attacked Russia." He was, in short, a fellow traveler of Churchill and Roosevelt.

The same day that Mr. Dirksen was denouncing the Washington school authorities for allowing students to hear about Russia ("In Russia equal right is granted to each nationality. There is no discrimination. Nobody says, you are a Negro, you are a Jew") Representative Williams of Mississippi rose to denounce the *Survey-Graphic* magazine and to add further to our understanding of Americanism. The *Survey-Graphic*, he said, "contained 129 pages of outrageously vile and nauseating anti-Southern, anti-Christian, un-American, and pro-Communist tripe, ostensibly directed toward the elimination of the custom of racial segregation in the South." It was written by "meddling un-American purveyors of hate and indecency."

All in all, a busy week for the House. Yet those who make a practice of reading their *Record* will agree that it was a typical week. For, increasingly, Congress is concerned with the eradication of disloyalty and the defense of Americanism, and scarcely a day passes that some congressman does not treat us to exhortations and admonitions, impassioned appeals and eloquent declamations, similar to those inspired by Mrs. Lewis, Mr. Ben-Zion, and the editors of the *Survey-Graphic*. And scarcely a day passes that the outlines of the new loyalty and the new Americanism are not etched more sharply in public policy.

And this is what is significant — the emergence of new patterns of Americanism and of loyalty, patterns radically different from those which have long been traditional. It is not only the Congress that is busy designing the new patterns. They are outlined in President Truman's recent disloyalty order; in similar orders formulated by the New York City Council and by state and local authorities throughout the country; in the programs of the D.A.R., the American Legion, and similar patriotic organizations; in the editorials of the Hearst and the McCormick-Patterson papers; and in an elaborate series of advertisements sponsored by large corporations and business organizations. In the making is a revival of the red hysteria of the early 1920s, one of the shabbiest chapters in the history of American democracy; and more than a revival, for the new crusade is designed not merely to frustrate Communism but to formulate a positive definition of Americanism, and a positive concept of loyalty.

What is the new loyalty? It is, above all, conformity. It is the uncritical and unquestioning acceptance of America as it is — the political institutions, the social relationships, the economic practices. It rejects inquiry into the race question or socialized medicine, or public housing, or into the wisdom or validity of our foreign policy. It regards as particularly heinous any challenge to what is called "the system of private enterprise," identifying that system with Americanism. It abandons evolution, repudiates the once-popular concept of progress, and regards America as a finished product, perfect and complete.

It is, it must be added, easily satisfied; for it wants not intellectual conviction nor spiritual conquest, but mere outward conformity. In matters of loyalty it takes the word for the deed, the gesture for the principle. It is content with the flag salute, and does not pause to consider the warning of our Supreme Court that "a person gets from a symbol the meaning he puts into it, and what is one man's comfort and inspiration is another's jest and scorn." It is satisfied with membership in respectable organizations and, as it assumes that every member of a liberal organization is a Communist, concludes that every member of a conservative one is a true American. It has not yet learned that not everyone who saith Lord,

Lord, shall enter into the kingdom of heaven. It is designed neither to discover real disloyalty nor to foster true loyalty.


## II

WHAT IS WRONG with this new concept of loyalty? What, fundamentally, is wrong with the pusillanimous retreat of the Washington educators, the barbarous antics of Washington legislators, the hysterical outbursts of the D.A.R., the gross and vulgar appeals of business corporations? It is not merely that these things are offensive. It is rather that they are wrong — morally, socially, and politically.

The concept of loyalty as conformity is a false one. It is narrow and restrictive, denies freedom of thought and of conscience, and is irremediably stained by private and selfish considerations. "Enlightened loyalty," wrote Josiah Royce, who made loyalty the very core of his philosophy,

> means harm to no man's loyalty. It is at war only with disloyalty, and its warfare, unless necessity constrains, is only a spiritual warfare. It does not foster class hatreds; it knows of nothing reasonable about race prejudices; and it regards all races of men as one in their need of loyalty. It ignores mutual misunderstandings. It loves its own wherever upon earth its own, namely, loyalty itself, is to be found.

Justice, charity, wisdom, spirituality, he added, were all definable in terms of loyalty, and we may properly ask which of these qualities our contemporary champions of loyalty display.

Above all, loyalty must be to something larger than oneself, untainted by private purposes or selfish ends. But what are we to say of the attempts by the NAM and by individual corporations to identify loyalty with the system of private enterprise? Is it not as if officeholders should attempt to identify loyalty with their own party, their own political careers? Do not those corporations which pay for full-page advertisements associating Americanism with the competitive system expect, ultimately, to profit from that association? Do not those organizations that deplore, in the name of patriotism, the extension of government operation of hydroelectric power expect to profit from their campaign?

Certainly it is a gross perversion, not only of the concept of loyalty but of the concept of Americanism, to identify it with a particular economic system. This precise question, interestingly enough, came before the Supreme Court in the Schneiderman case not so long ago — and it was Wendell Willkie who was counsel for Schneiderman. Said the Court:

> Throughout our history many sincere people, whose attachment to the general constitutional scheme cannot be doubted, have, for various and even divergent reasons, urged differing degrees of governmental ownership and control of natural resources, basic means of production, and banks and the media of exchange, either with or without compensation. And something once regarded as a species of private property was abolished without compensating the owners when the institution of slavery was forbidden. Can it be said that the author of the Emancipation Proclamation and the supporters of the Thirteenth Amendment were not attached to the Constitution?

There is, it should be added, a further danger in the willful identification of Americanism with a particular body of economic practices. Many learned economists predict for the near future an economic crash similar to that of 1929. If Americanism is equated with competitive capitalism, what happens to it if competitive capitalism comes a cropper? If loyalty and private enterprise are inextricably associated, what is to preserve loyalty if private enterprise fails? Those who associate Americanism with a particular program of economic practices have a grave responsibility, for if their program should fail, they expose Americanism itself to disrepute.

The effort to equate loyalty with conformity is misguided because it assumes that there is a fixed content to loyalty and that this can be determined and defined. But loyalty is a principle and eludes definition except in its own terms. It is devotion to the best interests of the commonwealth, and may require hostility to the particular policies which the government pursues, the particular practices which the economy undertakes, the particular institutions which society maintains. "If there is any fixed star in our constitutional constellation," said the Supreme Court in the Barnette case, "it is that no official, high or petty, can prescribe what shall be orthodox in politics, nationalism, religion, or other matters of opinion, or force citizens to confess by word or act their faith therein. If there are any circumstances which permit an exception, they do not now occur to us."

True loyalty may require, in fact, what appears to the naïve to be disloyalty. It may require hostility to certain provisions of the Constitution itself, and historians have not concluded that those who subscribed to the "Higher Law" were lacking in patriotism. We should not forget that our tradition is one of protest and revolt, and it is stultifying to celebrate the rebels of the past — Jefferson and Paine, Emerson and Thoreau — while we silence the rebels of the present. "We are a rebellious nation," said Theodore Parker, known in his day as the Great American Preacher, and went on:

> Our whole history is treason; our blood was attainted before we were born; our creeds are infidelity to the mother church; our Constitution, treason to our fatherland. What of that? Though all the governors in the world bid us commit treason against man, and set the example, let us never submit.

Those who would impose upon us a new concept of loyalty not only assume that this is possible but have the presumption to believe that they are competent to write the definition. We are reminded of Whitman's defiance of the "never-ending audacity of elected persons." Who are those who would set the standards of loyalty? They are Rankins and Bilbos, officials of the D.A.R. and the Legion and the NAM, Hearsts and McCormicks. May we not say of Rankin's harangues on loyalty what Emerson said of Webster at the time of the Seventh of March speech: "The word honor in the mouth of Mr. Webster is like the word love in the mouth of a whore."

What do men know of loyalty who make a mockery of the Declaration of Independence and the Bill of Rights, whose energies are dedicated to stirring up race and class hatreds, who would straitjacket the American spirit? What indeed do they know of America — the America of Sam Adams and Tom Paine, of Jackson's defiance of the Court and Lincoln's celebration of labor, of Thoreau's essay on Civil Disobedience and Emerson's championship of John Brown, of the America of the Fourierists and the Come-Outers, of cranks and fanatics, of socialists and anarchists? Who among American heroes could meet their tests, who would be cleared by their committees? Not Washington, who was a rebel. Not Jefferson, who wrote that all men are created equal and whose motto was "rebellion to tyrants is obedience to God." Not Garrison, who publicly burned the Constitution; or Wendell Phillips, who spoke for the underprivileged everywhere and counted himself a philosophical anarchist; not Seward of the Higher Law or Sumner of racial equality. Not Lincoln, who admonished us to have malice toward none, charity for all; or Wilson, who warned that our flag was "a flag of liberty of opinion as well as of political liberty"; or Justice Holmes, who said that our Constitution is an experiment and that while that experiment is being made "we should be eternally vigilant against attempts to check the expression of opinions that we loathe and believe to be fraught with death."

### III

THERE ARE FURTHER and more practical objections against the imposition of fixed concepts of loyalty or tests of disloyalty. The effort is itself a confession of fear, a declaration of insolvency. Those who are sure of themselves do not need reassurance, and those who have confidence in the strength and the virtue of America do not need to fear either criticism or competition. The effort is bound to miscarry. It will not apprehend those who are really disloyal, it will not even frighten them; it will affect only those who can be labeled "radical." It is sobering to recall that though the Japanese relocation program, carried through at such incalculable cost in misery and tragedy, was justified to us on the ground that the Japanese were potentially disloyal, the record does not disclose a single case of Japanese disloyalty or sabotage during the whole war. The warning sounded by the Supreme Court in the Barnette flag-salute case is a timely one:

> Ultimate futility of such attempts to compel obedience is the lesson of every such effort from the Roman drive to stamp out Christianity as a disturber of pagan unity, the Inquisition as a means to religious and dynastic unity, the Siberian exiles as a means to Russian unity, down to the fast-failing efforts of our present totalitarian enemies. Those who begin coercive elimination of dissent soon find themselves exterminating dissenters. Compulsory unification of opinion achieves only the unanimity of the graveyard.

Nor are we left to idle conjecture in this matter; we have had experience enough. Let us limit ourselves to a single example, one that is wonderfully relevant. Back in 1943 the House Un-American Activities Committee, deeply disturbed by alleged disloyalty among government employees, wrote a definition of subversive activities and proceeded to apply it. The definition was admirable, and no one could challenge its logic or its symmetry:

> Subversive activity derives from conduct intentionally destructive of or inimical to the government of the United States — that which seeks to undermine its institutions, or to distort its functions, or to impede its projects, or to lessen its efforts, the ultimate end being to overturn it all.

Surely anyone guilty of activities so defined deserved not only dismissal but punishment. But how was the test applied? It was applied to two distinguished scholars, Robert Morss Lovett and Goodwin Watson, and to one able young historian, William E. Dodd, Jr., son of our former ambassador to Germany. Of almost 3 million persons employed by the government, these were the 3 whose subversive activities were deemed the most pernicious, and the House cut them off the payroll. The sequel is familiar. The Senate concurred only to save a wartime appropriation; the President signed the bill under protest for the same reason. The Supreme Court declared the whole business a "bill of attainder" and therefore unconstitutional. Who was it, in the end, who engaged in "subversive activities" — Lovett, Dodd, and Watson, or the Congress which flagrantly violated Article I of the Constitution?

Finally, disloyalty tests are not only futile in application, they are pernicious in their consequences. They distract attention from activities that are really disloyal and silence criticism inspired by true loyalty. That there are disloyal elements in America will not be denied, but there is no reason to suppose that any of the tests now formulated will ever be applied to them. It is relevant to remember that when Rankin was asked why his committee did not investigate the Ku Klux Klan he replied that the Klan was not un-American, it was American!

Who are those who are really disloyal? Those who inflame racial hatreds, who sow religious and class dissensions. Those who subvert the Constitution by violating the freedom of the ballot box. Those who make a mockery of majority rule by the use of the filibuster. Those who impair democracy by denying equal educational facilities. Those who frustrate justice by lynch law or by making a farce of jury trials. Those who deny freedom of speech and of the press and of assembly. Those who press for special favors against the interest of the commonwealth. Those who regard public office as a source of private gain. Those who would exalt the military over the civil. Those who for selfish and private purposes stir up national antagonisms and expose the world to the ruin of war.

Will the House Committee on Un-American Activities interfere with the activities of these? Will Mr. Truman's disloyalty proclamation reach these? Will the current campaigns for Americanism convert these? If past experience is any guide, they will not. What they will do, if they are successful, is to silence criticism, stamp out dissent — or drive it underground. But if our democracy is to flourish, it must have criticism; if our government is to function, it must have dissent. Only totalitarian governments insist upon conformity and they — as we know — do so at their peril. Without criticism, abuses will go unrebuked; without dissent, our dynamic system will become static. The American people have a stake in the maintenance of the most thoroughgoing inquisition into American institutions. They have a stake in nonconformity, for they know that the American genius is nonconformist. They have a stake in experimentation of the most radical character,

for they know that only those who prove all things can hold fast that which is good.

## IV

IT IS EASIER TO SAY what loyalty is not than to say what it is. It is not conformity. It is not passive acquiescence in the status quo. It is not preference for everything American over everything foreign. It is not an ostrich-like ignorance of other countries and other institutions. It is not the indulgence in ceremony — a flag salute, an oath of allegiance, a fervid verbal declaration. It is not a particular creed, a particular version of history, a particular body of economic practices, a particular philosophy.

It is a tradition, an ideal, and a principle. It is a willingness to subordinate every private advantage for the larger good. It is an appreciation of the rich and diverse contributions that can come from the most varied sources. It is allegiance to the traditions that have guided our greatest statesmen and inspired our most eloquent poets — the traditions of freedom, equality, democracy, tolerance, the tradition of the higher law, of experimentation, cooperation, and pluralism. It is a realization that America was born of revolt, flourished on dissent, became great through experimentation.

Independence was an act of revolution; republicanism was something new under the sun; the federal system was a vast experimental laboratory. Physically Americans were pioneers; in the realm of social and economic institutions, too, their tradition has been one of pioneering. From the beginning, intellectual and spiritual diversity have been as characteristic of America as racial and linguistic. The most distinctively American philosophies have been transcendentalism — which is the philosophy of the Higher Law — and pragmatism — which is the philosophy of experimentation and pluralism. These two principles are the very core of Americanism: the principle of the Higher Law, or of obedience to the dictates of conscience rather than of statutes, and the principle of pragmatism, or the rejection of a single good and of the notion of a finished universe. From the beginning Ameri- cans have known that there were new worlds to conquer, new truths to be discovered. Every effort to confine Americanism to a single pattern, to constrain it to a single formula is disloyalty to everything that is valid in Americanism.

93.

## David E. Lilienthal: This I Deeply Believe

*David E. Lilienthal, former director of the Tennessee Valley Authority (TVA), was nominated by President Truman as chairman of the Atomic Energy Commission in 1946. During the course of hearings held by the Joint Congressional Committee on Atomic Energy, Lilienthal became engaged in a celebrated confrontation with Senator Kenneth D. McKellar of Tennessee, who sought to rescind the appointment on the grounds of Lilienthal's alleged "leftist" leanings. Alfred Friendly of the* Washington Post *reported McKellar's questions and Lilienthal's response in an article published February 4, 1947.*

Source: *This I Do Believe,* New York, 1949, pp. ix-xiii.

For more than a week, Senator Kenneth D. McKellar (D., Tenn.) has used the hearings of the Joint Congressional Committee on Atomic Energy as a forum in which to attack David E. Lilienthal. The committee is considering the confirmation of the former TVA head in his new post of Atomic Energy Commission chairman.

McKellar's line of questioning has been apparently designed to portray Lilienthal as a Communist.

Yesterday, on a side excursion, McKellar demanded to know TVA's production cost of a ton of ammonium nitrate.

Lilienthal said the figures were available, that he would obtain them, but that he did not carry them in his head. McKellar professed to find this answer in itself evidence of Lilienthal's gross incompetence. He repeatedly requoted it, with heavy sarcasm.

Later, back on his original tack, McKellar snapped, "The truth is that your sympathies are very leftist."

"The truth is," Lilienthal answered, "that an answer to that assertion cannot be made in terms of 'yes or no.' "

"Well, what are your convictions on Communist doctrine?" McKellar persisted.

The witness, who until yesterday had shown no signs of emotion or anger under McKellar's barrage, suddenly wheeled in his chair to face his antagonist. He said, in a voice which was low, but electric with fervor:

"This I DO carry in my head, Senator.

"I will do my best to make it clear. My convictions are not so much concerned with what I am against as what I am for; and that excludes a lot of things automatically.

"Traditionally, democracy has been an affirmative doctrine rather than merely a negative one.

"I believe — and I conceive the Constitution of the United States to rest, as does religion, upon the fundamental proposition of the integrity of the individual; and that all government and all private institutions must be designed to promote and protect and defend the integrity and the dignity of the individual; that that is the essential meaning of the Constitution and the Bill of Rights, as it is essentially the meaning of religion.

"Any form of government, therefore, and any other institutions which make men means rather than ends, which exalt the state or any other institutions above the importance of men, which place arbitrary power over men as a fundamental tenet of government are contrary to that conception, and, therefore, I am deeply opposed to them.

"The communistic philosophy as well as the communistic form of government falls within this category, for their fundamental tenet is quite to the contrary. The fundamental tenet of communism is that the state is an end in itself, and that therefore the powers which the state exercises over the individual are without any ethical standard to limit them.

"That I deeply disbelieve.

"It is very easy simply to say that one is not a Communist. And, of course, if despite my record it is necessary for me to state this very affirmatively, then it is a great disappointment to me.

"It is very easy to talk about being against communism. It is equally important to believe those things which provide a satisfying and effective alternative. Democracy is that satisfying, affirmative alternative.

"Its hope in the world is that it is an affirmative belief, rather than being simply a belief against something else and nothing more.

"One of the tenets of democracy that grows out of this central core of a belief that the individual comes first, that all men are the children of God and that their per-

United Press International

David Lilienthal listening to testimony at a session of the Atomic Energy Commission, of which he was named chairman by President Truman in 1947

sonalities are therefore sacred, is a deep belief in civil liberties and their protection, and a repugnance to anyone who would steal from a human being that which is most precious to him — his good name — either by imputing things to him by innuendo or by insinuation. And it is especially an unhappy circumstance that occasionally that is done in the name of democracy. This, I think, can tear our country apart and destroy it if we carry it further.

"I deeply believe in the capacity of democracy to surmount any trials that may lie ahead, provided only that we practice it in our daily lives.

"And among the things we must practice is this: that while we seek fervently to ferret out the subversive and anti-democratic forces in the country, we do not at the same time, by hysteria, by resort to innuendo, and smears, and other unfortunate tactics, besmirch the very cause that we believe in, and cause a separation among our people — cause one group and one individual to hate another, based on mere attacks, mere unsubstantiated attacks upon their loyalty.

"I want also to add that part of my conviction is based on my training as an Anglo-American common lawyer. It is the very basis and the great heritage of the English people to this country, which we have maintained, that we insist on the strictest rules of credibility of witnesses and on the avoidance of hearsay, and that gossip shall be excluded, in the courts of justice. And that, too, is an essential of our democracy.

"Whether by administrative agencies acting arbitrarily against business organizations, or whether by investigating activities of legislative branches, whenever those principles fail, those principles of the protection of an individual and his good name against besmirchment by gossip, hearsay, and the statements of witnesses who are not subject to cross-examination — then, too, we have failed in carrying forward our ideals in respect to democracy.

"This I deeply believe."

The pin-drop silence which had obtained throughout Lilienthal's remarks lasted several moments more.

Then Senator McMahon (D., Conn.) said in a quiet voice, "That was the statement of a very real American."

There was still another period of complete silence. Then McKellar shuffled his papers and resumed, "Mr. Lilienthal, while you were head of the TVA, did you have any Communists in your employ?"

---

94.

# Racial Discrimination in Washington, D.C.

*In 1946 President Truman established an advisory Committee on Civil Rights to recommend "more adequate and effective means and procedures for the protection of the civil rights of the people of the United States." A year later the Committee published* To Secure These Rights, *one of the first comprehensive surveys of civil rights in America. The report, drafted by a professor of political science at Dartmouth College, resulted in little legislation, but it succeeded in dramatizing the civil rights problem. The following selection from the report deals with civil rights in Washington, D.C.*

Source: *To Secure These Rights*, New York, 1947: "Civil Rights in the Nation's Capital."

THROUGHOUT THE COUNTRY, our practice lags behind the American tradition of freedom and equality. A single community — the nation's capital — illustrates dramatically the shortcomings in our record and the need for change. The District of Columbia should symbolize to our own citizens and to the people of all countries our great tradition of civil liberty. Instead, it is a graphic illustration of a failure of democracy. As the seat of our federal government under the authority of Congress, the failure of the District is a failure of all of the people.

For Negro Americans, Washington is not just the nation's capital. It is the point at which all public transportation into the South becomes "Jim Crow." If he stops in Washington, a Negro may dine like other men in the Union Station, but as soon as he steps out into the capital, he leaves such democratic practices behind. With very few exceptions, he is refused service at downtown restaurants, he may not attend a downtown movie or play, and he has to go into the poorer section of the city to find a night's lodging. The Negro who decides to settle in the District must often find a home in an overcrowded, substandard area. He must often take a job below the level of his ability. He must send his children to the inferior public schools set aside for Negroes and entrust his family's health to medical agencies which give inferior service. In addition, he must endure the countless daily humiliations that the system of segregation imposes upon the one-third of Washington that is Negro.

The origin of the pattern of discrimination in Washington is partly explained by its location in a border area where many Southern customs prevail. Certain political and local pressure groups and the administrative decisions of municipal officials contribute to its persistence. Attempts to guarantee equal rights on a segregated basis have failed. In recent years the "separate and unequal" pattern has been extended to areas where it had not previously existed. Except where the federal government has made a few independent advances, as in federal employment and the use of federal recreational facilities, racial segregation is rigid. It extends to ludicrous extremes. Inconsistencies are evident: Constitution Hall, owned by the Daughters of the American Revolution, seats concert audiences without distinctions of color, but allows no Negroes on its stage to give regular commercial concerts. On the other hand, the commercial legitimate theater has had Negro actors on its stage, but stubbornly refuses to admit Negro patrons.

*Discrimination in education.* — The core of Washington's segregated society is its dual system of public education. It operates under congressional legislation which assumes the fact of segregation but nowhere makes it mandatory. The Board of Education and a white superintendent of schools administer two wholly separate school systems. The desire of Congress to insure equal facilities is implemented by a requirement that appropriations be allocated to white and Negro education in proportion to the numbers of children of school age. But this has not been successful. Negro schools are inferior to white schools in almost every respect. The white school buildings have a capacity which is 27 percent greater than actual enrollment. In the colored schools, enrollment exceeds building capacity by 8 percent. Classes in the Negro schools are considerably larger and the teaching load of the Negro teachers considerably heavier. Less than 1 percent of all white school children, but over 15 percent of colored children, receive only part-time instruction. Similar inequalities exist in school buildings, equipment, textbook supplies, kindergarten classes, athletic and recreational facilities.

The District superintendent of schools recently answered charges of inequality in school facilities with the statement that, "Absolute equality of educational opportunity is impossible. Reasonable equality . . . is the goal." The conditions described above eloquently document the extent to which even "reasonable equality" is impossible in a segregated school system.

Official freezing of the segregated school system is complete. The Board of Education frowns on visits by whites to Negro schools and by Negroes to white schools. Intercultural education programs are stillborn because they are considered a threat to the prevailing pattern. Interracial athletic and forensic competition is forbidden. Two cases illustrate the lengths to which the District's officialdom goes to prevent interracial contact. During the war, the Office of Price Administration asked permission to use a school building at night for in-service training of its clerks. The request was denied solely because the class would have included both white and colored employees. In the other case, a white girl was ordered to withdraw from a Negro vocational school where she had enrolled for a course not offered by any other public school in Washington.

Private universities in the District have followed the lead of the public schools. Two of the large universities and most of the smaller schools admit no colored students. American University admits them to its School of Social Science and Public Affairs, but not to the College of Arts and Sciences. Catholic University, on the other hand, presents an outstanding example of successful interracial education. In the last few years, Negroes have been admitted, and there is no color distinction in classes. Last year a Negro was elected a class officer. The presence of Howard University in Washington alleviates somewhat the problem of higher education for the District's Negroes. While Howard University is primarily a Negro institution, it also admits white students.

*Discrimination in housing.* — In the past, many of Washington's Negroes and whites have lived close together in many parts of the city, and where mixed neighborhoods still exist, incidents of racial friction are rare. Now, however, Negroes are increasingly being forced into a few overcrowded slums.

Programs for the development of highways, parks, and public buildings have often played an unfortunate role in rooting out Negro neighborhoods. There has been a commendable desire to beautify the city of Washington. But there has been little concern for the fate of persons displaced by beautification projects.

The superior economic position of whites also contributes to the shrinkage of Negro neighborhoods. In areas like Georgetown and the old fort sites, white residents and realtors have been buying up Negro properties and converting them to choice residential use. Only occasionally does this process work in reverse: in deteriorating areas, white owners can sometimes get higher prices from Negroes, who have little from which to choose, than they can from white buyers.

The chief weapon in the effort to keep Negroes from moving out of overcrowded quarters into white neighborhoods is the restrictive covenant. New building sites and many older areas are now covenanted. Some covenants exclude all nonmembers of the Caucasian race; others bar only Negroes, or Negroes and members of "Semitic races." Even where covenants do not prevail, the powerful local real estate fraternity protects white areas from "invasion." The all-white Washington Real Estate Board has a "code of ethics" which prohibits its members from selling land in predominantly white areas to Negroes, and the realtors are supported in this practice by nonmember dealers, banks, and loan companies. Two of the city's newspapers will not accept ads offering property in white areas for sale to Negroes. Because the policy of the National Capital Housing Authority is to follow the "community pattern," all public housing projects are completely segregated and housing for Negroes is built only in established Negro neighborhoods. The Authority has spent most of its funds for permanent housing to build homes for Negroes, but its appropriations have been limited.

Housing conditions are poor for Washington residents in general, but, largely because of the pressures just described, they are much worse for Negroes. According to a recent Board of Trade report on city planning, 70 percent of the inhabitants of the city's three worst slum areas are Negroes. The largest single slum in the District houses about 7 percent of the white and 30 percent of the Negro population. In 1940, one-eighth of the white dwellings in Washington and 40 percent of those occupied by Negroes were substandard; 15 percent of white-occupied and 38 percent of Negro-occupied dwellings had more than one person per room.

*Discrimination in employment.* — More than one-third of the jobs in Washington are with the federal government. Therefore, discriminatory practices of government agencies, which have already been discussed, are important to District Negroes. The District government itself has only a small proportion of Negro employees, and most of these are confined to unskilled and menial jobs. Partial exceptions to this are the Metropolitan Police, the segregated Fire Service, and the school system with its segregated staff. A ranking District official during the war told an interviewer: "Negroes in the District of Columbia have no right to ask for jobs on the basis of merit," the rationalization being that whites own most of the property and pay the bulk of municipal taxes.

Negroes are confined to the lowest paid and least skilled jobs in private employment. In 1940, three-fourths of all Negro workers in Washington were domestics, service workers, or laborers, while only one-eighth of the white workers held jobs of that type. At the other end of the scale, only one-eighth of all Negro workers were clerks, salesmen, managers, proprietors, or professionals, while two-thirds of the white workers were in jobs of this kind. There are similar striking racial differences in average income and length of workweek.

A few examples will illustrate the part discrimination has played in causing these differences. During the war, Washington's public transportation system bogged down badly for lack of qualified streetcar and bus operators. The Capital Transit Company advertised for workers hundreds of miles away and even recruited government employees on a part-time basis. In spite of this, the company would not employ qualified Negroes as operators. In building construction, one of Washington's largest industries, the various building trade unions discriminate against colored craftsmen. They are either excluded completely, allowed to work only on projects to be occupied by Negroes, admitted only as helpers to white journeymen, or not allowed to become apprentices. The numerous large white hotels employ Negroes only in such capacities as chambermaids, busboys, waiters, and coal stokers. There are no colored salespeople in the large department stores. In laundries and cleaning plants where wages are low and hours long, most of the workers are colored, but supervisors are white; where whites and Negroes perform the same work, there is a wage differential of from 20 to 30 percent. The District Bar Association and the Medical Society are for whites only.

*Discrimination in health services.* — The greatest inequalities are evident in Washington's concern for the health of its residents. Freedmen's Hospital, federally supported and affiliated with Howard University, is for Negroes only, and three-fourths of the beds in the municipal Gallinger Hospital are usually occupied by Negroes in segregated wards. Four of the twelve private hospitals in the city do not admit Negro inpatients, and the rest accept only a few in segregated wards. It is peculiarly shocking to find church hospitals practising discrimination. Far fewer hospital beds in proportion to population are available to Negroes than to whites. Sickness rates are higher among Negroes than whites, which aggravates this situation. All but the smallest clinics are segregated. Group Health Association, however, does not discriminate either in membership or services.

No Negro physician is allowed to practise in Gallinger Hospital, although it is publicly supported and the majority of its patients are colored. Nor are they allowed in St. Elizabeth's, a federal institution, or any of the private hospitals. Only Freedmen's is open to them, and then only for the care of assigned ward patients. Thus the Negro physician cannot follow his own patients into the hospital. Negro medical students are similarly discriminated against in the provision of training facilities.

Public and private agency welfare services are available to both colored and white residents, but institutional care is provided only on a segregated basis, and the institutions for Negroes are far inferior in both number and quality to those for whites. Here, again, the lower economic position of Negroes and their consequent need for care aggravates the problem.

*Discrimination in recreational services.* — In the field of public recreation, compulsory segregation has increased over the past twenty-five years. Various public authorities have closed to one race or the other numerous facilities where whites and Negroes once played together harmoniously. In 1942, the District of Columbia Board of Recreation was set up to centralize the control of public recreation facilities. Congress eliminated from the locally sponsored bill a provision that would have required the new board to continue segregation. But it took no positive stand on the issue, and the board has adopted regulations which enforce segregation in all the parks and playgrounds under its control.

Under this policy, facilities in seven out of twenty-six "natural areas" in the District have been turned over to Negroes. Because the Negro areas are disproportionately concentrated in the older, crowded parts of the city, white facilities are generally superior to those allotted to Negroes. Furthermore, whites and Negroes alike who live far from facilities open to their race have easy access to none. White residents who had shared with Negroes the use of the Rose Park Tennis Courts protested in vain against being barred from them.

On the other hand, recreation facilities under the jurisdiction of the Department of the Interior are open to all races, and serious friction is nonexistent. District officials have tried repeatedly to have these facilities turned over to the Recreation Board. The transfer has not been made because the board will not agree to refrain from imposing segregation in their use.

Most private recreational groups follow the official policy of segregation, although occasional interracial competitions have been held successfully by some. The Washington branch of the Amateur Athletic Union allows no interracial contests under its auspices. For example, no Negro may enter the local Golden Gloves Tournament, although they compete in the national tournament.

*Discrimination in places of public accommodation.* — Public transportation is provided without separation of the races, and the spectators at most professional sporting events are unsegregated. But other public accommodations are a focal point of Negro resentment, because rigorous segregation in practice means exclusion. No downtown theater except the burlesque house admits Negroes. They may see movies only in their neighborhood houses. Some department stores and many downtown shops exclude Negro patrons by ignoring them or refusing to show the stock they request or making them wait until all white customers have been served. A Negro is seldom accepted at the downtown hotels unless special arrangements are made. Although they may dine at the Union Station, the YWCA, and the cafeterias in government office buildings, the overwhelming majority of downtown restaurants are closed to them.

The shamefulness and absurdity of Washington's treatment of Negro Americans is highlighted by the presence of many dark-skinned foreign visitors. Capital custom not only humiliates colored citizens but is a source of considerable embarrassment to these visitors. White residents, because they are the dominant group, share in both the humiliation and the embarrassment. Foreign officials are often mistaken for American Negroes and refused food, lodging, and entertainment. However, once it is established that they are not Americans, they are accommodated.

*This is the situation that exists in the District of Columbia. The committee feels most deeply that it is intolerable.*

95.

# Thomas E. Dewey: Public Service

*Thomas E. Dewey was the Republican candidate for President both in 1944 and in 1948, losing on the first occasion to Franklin D. Roosevelt in the latter's bid for a fourth term, and on the second to Harry S. Truman, who beat Dewey unexpectedly in one of the closest races on record. Governor of New York from 1943 to 1955, Dewey was a successful lawyer and, even after he left the State House at Albany, a power in the Republican Party. Always deeply concerned with the importance of finding the best men for public service, Dewey delivered the address, part of which is reprinted here, during the commencement exercises at Hamilton College, Clinton, New York, on June 15, 1947.*

Source: VSD, July 15, 1947: "Government, the Nation's Biggest Industry."

OF ALL THE CHANGES that have come about since the 1920s, none is more remarkable than the growth of government. In that decade, often known as the era of wonderful nonsense, the investment market was booming and everybody was buying stocks and bonds. From 1920 to 1929, private capital in this country raised and invested the unprecedented sum of $37 billion. That figure seemed to jump right out of a page I was reading the other day, because that ten-year investment total is just about the same as the proposed budget for one year's running expenses of the federal government alone — not to mention the record cost of state and local government. Big government today spends in a year the savings of a decade invested in big business in the heyday of the boom.

No matter how little we may like it and no matter how we may long for the simplicities of a Jeffersonian state, which is considered best because it governs least, we must face the fact that government has become our biggest industry and will continue to be big.

In talking about the vast increase in government and its budgets, I am not now referring to the great burden the cost of government has placed upon the people. I am directing attention to the other side of the picture — the burden the people have placed upon government. Unless government machinery can be made more fit to carry the loads upon it, then the condition of our free society is even more sorry than it appears to be.

There is a theory widely extant today that any problem can be solved if you just turn it over to government and appropriate a lot of money. That is a dangerous illusion. Actually such action merely sets in motion a complex chain of intense effort and technical activities, which depend entirely for their success on the caliber and training of the men it is possible to recruit for the job.

To run any government today, you need lawyers of various kinds, doctors of various kinds, engineers, bacteriologists, agronomists, financiers, accountants, military men, experts in all the intricacies of labor and industrial relations, and many other specialists. Above all, you need capable, trained administrators, men who can recruit special talents, get them working together, and put a program into action without the waste effort of bogging down in governmental procedures.

Few men have ever had opportunity to develop these skills. Their scarcity is why we have seen so many manifestations of governmental incompetence or so-called bureaucracy — the loud promises with small results; the regimentation; the institutionalized patterns, forms, and routines; the excess paper work; the exasperating technicalities; the directives written in that language so elegantly described as gobbledegook. It's the age-old problem of little men in big jobs — or untrained men in highly technical jobs. Government's responsibilities have been multiplied many times over, but its supply of competent men has not multiplied.

Government cannot wait any longer to start recruiting such men, just as industry has done for many years, catching them young and giving them every chance to develop to the full extent of their powers. Almost the only field in which this has been done to any great extent is with our military and naval officers. Annapolis and West Point are only the beginning. Our officers are required to attend one school and then another, over the years, both inside the service and out, to develop their competence. To this we owe the miracles of military expansion and the triumphs of technology which recently saved our national existence. We also owe to this the anomalous fact that it has been so often necessary in recent years to go to the armed forces for the men to fill big civilian jobs.

We need the same degree of training in other fields. Fundamentally our first need is for higher education in all our colleges and universities to fit our young men and women for both private and public life. For ex-

ample, next to education itself, the biggest job of your state government is the care of the mentally ill. Our state mental-hospital system takes one-quarter of the state's operating budget. For years it has been operating under the utmost difficulties, with overcrowded, inadequate buildings for over 100,000 patients. We have a big building program to remedy that, but an even greater difficulty has been the shortage of doctors — specialists in the ailments of the human mind. We can have the best buildings in the world, but if we didn't cure people we'd be doing a bad job.

There is a great shortage of psychiatrists. The services took so many that we were 40 percent understaffed during the war. The majority came back to us, but still it wasn't enough. So last year we started a new system, appointing a class of 74 young physicians as resident psychiatrists in our mental hospitals. The state pays them $3,200 a year for their residency and they agree to stay in the state service two years, caring for all the ills which can befall a community of thousands of people. As a part of that service they receive intensive instruction at the New York State Psychiatric Institute in cooperation with Columbia University and at the Syracuse Psychopathic Hospital in cooperation with Syracuse University. The first group has recently completed its first year, and a new group of 79 has started its service, making our total 153 residents. While learning their specialty, these young medical men have greatly improved our hospital care. We will pick the best of these who will stay for our hospital staffs, and the others will go out into medical practice bringing new psychiatric skills to the communities.

That new program is already so successful that we have recently set up another project in collaboration with Syracuse and New York universities to give graduate courses, advanced training in public administration, for people in the state service generally. In addition to the professors, some of our top state officials will participate as lecturers.

In connection with this, and following up our success with the psychiatrists, we are creating a series of new positions in the state service to give graduate students an opportunity to work intimately with some of our best administrators. Borrowing a term from the medical men, we are calling these posts internships, like the work a young doctor has in a hospital before he goes out to practice. Whether or not these students remain in state service, they will reduce the scarcity of a most essential skill. And if the state gets just one topnotcher out of a year's crop, the whole experiment is worthwhile.

These two projects are beginning steps in a direction we must follow if free government is to strengthen itself from within. Vigorously rejecting the totalitarian notion that government is everything, we must be alert that our own government does not outgrow its own skills like those prehistoric dinosaurs which got too big and clumsy to survive the struggle for existence.

I need not elaborate the fact that free government is under attack throughout the world. It seems clear that the attack will continue for some time to come. In that competition we cannot rely on boasts about the efficiency of American industry. Government has become so important that it too must catch up with the competence of industry. There is no reason why it should be harder to fill out a tax blank than it is to drive a car, and the job of simplifying that and other processes is a challenge to the best ingenuity we have. Government as well as industry must give a better product for less unit cost.

This is a challenge to all young men and women who are eager to use their powers to the utmost. The public service requires the best talents that can be found. Nobody is going to get rich at it, in a money way, but it does have rich rewards in sense of accomplishment and participation in great events. I invite the class of 1947 to look for careers in government.

When I speak of careers, I am talking about the top flight, the men and women who really make things go. These fall into two categories:

First, there are the elected legislators, the chief executives and their cabinet officers. These front-window figures in public life make the policies and stand responsible before the people. They can be thrown out of office any election day. Their positions are insecure, and should be. So, I invite you to learn the hard business of politics — the job of political leadership — of statesmanship — and they are all part of the same task. But I warn you that it is the hardest work of all and the most insecure. The challenge to do great things, to make free government work is no opportunity for the lazy, the dullard, or the seeker of comforts. It is the challenge of a creative life with few thanks but great satisfaction in rendering service.

One more warning: Don't aspire to an elective public career until you have so mastered your own private profession or business that you can make more money out of office than you can in office. There is nothing more pathetic than a high public official who is scared of losing his job. And there's nothing more useless. In my own cabinet, there are men who are working for $11,000 to $17,500 a year who have earned and can any day earn again several times those salaries. They are the kind of public servants who make government a living and a useful thing.

These appointive and elective public officers provide the essential political leadership. But of the sum total of government servants, they are only a handful and those in the second category of which I speak to you have a vital and continuing role. This is the career service. It offers fine opportunity and also genuine security. Every sound speech that is made by a public officer, every policy advanced and every issue drawn requires the help and technical assistance of very able men and women. When policies have been adopted, then the tremendous job of carrying them into execution requires an ever increasing degree of high competence. Old-age assistance is useless if the checks do not go out. New hospitals are futile if they do not effect cures. Treaties are disastrous if the negotiators do not know their facts.

Every phase of government depends upon career men and women of an increasingly high degree of loyalty and competence. Whether ambition may be to cure the sick, to feed the hungry, to command an army, or to build an irrigation dam, or to do the patient day-by-day job of building in the foreign service for a peaceful world — here is a field for talents more boundless than all the frontiers we have conquered up to date.

Back in the 1920s, as I have said, none of us thought of working for the government. Not even our commencement speakers suggested it. But there were some of our generation who did do it. The young fellows who went into the Army and Navy then got no glory and little pay and there was nothing in the budget to plug the rat holes in the houses their country gave them. But they did a job, as — to our relief — we found out later on.

But our present contest in the world is not merely one of arms or of diplomacy. It is a competition between whole systems of government, of economics, of human philosophy. To win it we must excel, not only in war but in the humanities, in production, in education, and in all the other arts of peace.

If as an individual you are going to succeed, you can't rely on the mistakes, incapacities, and delinquencies of the other fellow. You have to be good yourself. The same is true for nations and for competing systems of society.

We know our system is the best in the world but we must keep on proving it. It won't do us any good to wring our hands over the atomic bomb or over the political exiles, murders, and the tragic millions in concentration camps beyond our sphere of influence. What we can do is go to work, use our best talents, and by hard work build an ever better free system. We can pool our talents, organize our efforts, use our common sense, and make out of this outsized sprawling Goliath of big government over here our tool and not our master.

This much we can do today, and tomorrow may be too late. It will call for a great outpouring of new blood, of young men and women of superb competence and deep faith in the institutions by which we live. It is the real challenge of our time. It can only be met by your generation, and that, after all, is as it should be, for to each generation falls the task of saving its own freedom. Amid a reviving strength of spiritual leadership and continuing growth of the skills of industry, we must now develop as we have never done before the skill of good government. As we do so we shall assure the onward, upward march of mankind through the preservation of the institutions of human freedom.

———◆———

*At the beginning of the World Series of 1947, I experienced a completely new emotion, when the National Anthem was played. This time, I thought, it is being played for me, as much as for anyone else. This is organized major league baseball, and I am standing here with all the others; and everything that takes place includes me.*

JACKIE ROBINSON

Bernard Hoffman, "Life," © Time Inc.

**Destruction at Hiroshima following the dropping of the atomic bomb, August 1945**

# THE COLD WAR

The end of World War II saw the losers — Germany, Italy, Japan — in ruins, and many of the victors in little better condition. Nearly all of Europe had been ravaged by the war; there was, in fact, little to distinguish the two sides in the general social and economic chaos of 1945. World power had passed to the two nations that had been outside the central battlefields of Europe and the Pacific, and who had been, nominally, allies — the United States and Soviet Russia. As the necessity of military alliance and cooperation ended, the basic divergence of aims and philosophies of the two nations became wider and painfully apparent. Military operations were super-seded by diplomatic maneuvering as each nation sought to prevent the dominance of the other; the formation of two opposing power blocs was the inevitable outcome. With a profound and constantly increasing mutual distrust permeating U.S.-Soviet relations on every level, compromise was nearly impossible; thus the United Nations, upon which much hope for lasting peace had been pinned, was crippled from the beginning. The World War was succeeded, not by an era of peace and international cooperation, but by the Cold War, conducted in secrecy and in the knowledge that another war, an atomic war, could destroy civilization.

(Above) Ruins of Warsaw's Jewish ghetto remain untouched in 1949; (left) food shortages cause Polish woman to subsist on watery potato soup

The immediate physical problem at the end of the war was the economic helplessness of most of Europe. Relief served political as well as humanitarian ends: it staved off depression at home by keeping production high, and it "fought Communism." The United Nations Relief and Rehabilitation Administration, pooling the resources of 44 nations, was scrapped in 1946, however, under charges from Congress and the State Department of inefficiency, favoritism, and subsidizing Communist factions.

(Above) Compiegne, France, lies in ruins for a second time after a war, 1945; (below) quonset huts provide temporary homes for citizens of Hamburg, Germany, after Allied occupation

(Above) Photograph admitted as evidence in the Nuremberg trials showing Nazi forces removing Jews from the Warsaw ghetto; (right) Goering and Hess, two of the German officers tried at Nuremberg

The major Allied powers agreed in August 1945 to hold an international military tribunal to try German civil and military leaders for war crimes. The trials opened in November and dragged on for more than ten months, resulting in the sentencing of 19 German officials. The revelations at the trial of the grisly details of Nazi concentration camps failed to arouse the expected public revulsion. The tribunal was the last cooperative action in the growing Cold War split; in March 1946 Churchill defined the new Western world-view in his "Iron Curtain" speech.

(Above) Big Four foreign ministers meeting in New York in 1946 to work out peace terms for Eastern Europe; (below) Winston Churchill and President Truman at Westminster College in Fulton, Mo., 1946. Churchill used the term "Iron Curtain" during speech he delivered here

(Above) Greek liberals and leftists demonstrate in Athens to protest the United Nations investigation of frontier incidents; (below) guerrillas in the mountains of northern Greece, 1947

**President Truman seeking U.S. aid for Greece and Turkey to stop Communist aggression**

In 1946 civil war broke out in Greece as Communist guerrillas repudiated the restored monarchy and the unstable government. Britain, facing a severe financial crisis at home, announced that it would be unable to maintain its forces in Greece after March 1947. Stepping into the breach and ignoring the UN, Truman requested congressional authority for a unilateral military and economic aid program to both Greece and Turkey. The Truman Doctrine, dedicated to the firm "containment" of Communism, represented a vast extension of American strategic frontiers.

**American observer giving assistance to Greek army in its campaign against the guerrillas, 1948**

(Above) Posters of Communist-supported candidates displayed during Polish elections of 1947; (bottom left) Herblock cartoon showing Russian reaction to the United States' recovery program; (bottom right) George Marshall, U.S. secretary of state, 1947-1949

**"It's The Same Thing Without Mechanical Problems"**

**Lewis Douglas, George Marshall, and V. M. Molotov relax during London conference, 1947**

By 1947 the Communist-led government of Poland was well established and had been recognized by Britain and the U.S. Despite its indigenous character, the new Polish government was regarded as a mere satellite of Russia. In the summer of 1947 discussions to organize the Marshall Plan for Western European recovery began; partly in reaction, the Cominform was organized in September by the Communist nations. Notwithstanding clear signs of independence in Poland and Yugoslavia, the myth of monolithic international Communism was born.

**Soviet Ambassador Gromyko casts a veto during the 1947 session of the UN Security Council**

(Above) May Day parade in Prague, Czechoslovakia, 1948; (below) parade honoring Tito, who succeeded in breaking Stalin's control over Yugoslavia in June 1948

Despite fears of Western pro-royalist intervention and the threat posed by the Allied occupation of Trieste, Yugoslavia resisted identifying its policies with those of Russia. In 1948 Tito closed Yugoslavia's borders to guerrillas operating in Greece and this, as much as U.S. aid, prevented a Communist takeover. Yugoslavia was expelled from the Cominform in June 1948. In April East Germany had begun the blockade of Berlin in an attempt to drive Allied forces out; after 11 months of airlift, the blockade was lifted. In April 1949 the U.S. took the final step: for the first time in history it formed an alliance with a foreign nation — twelve foreign nations, in fact — with the signing of the North Atlantic Treaty.

(Left) President Truman looks on as Secretary of State Dean Acheson signs the North Atlantic Treaty for the United States; (below) U.S. plane flies in supplies to blockaded Berlin, 1948

European Picture Service

Jacobs from Black Star

**George Marshall tries to effect mediation between Chang Chun and Chou En-lai, 1946**

The end of Japanese occupation in China allowed the shaky coalition of Nationalists and Communists to revert to civil war. The U.S. continued to aid Chiang's Nationalists while trying to arrange a compromise of some sort. Chiang refused to allow any but a Nationalist government; when the U.S. seemed to be considering the hitherto impotent Democratic League as the core of a possible coalition, Chiang suppressed the League. This intransigence, combined with the extensive corruption of the Nationalist organization and its refusal to initiate popular reform measures, doomed the negotiations arranged in 1945 and 1946 by U.S. envoy Gen. Marshall. Nationalist forces were finally driven from the mainland to the island of Formosa in late 1949.

**Nationalist Chinese infantry on the march during 1948 struggle against advancing Communists**

96.

# Paternalism in Government

*The range of the federal government's activities, as well as the cost of its operations, increased enormously during World War II. Ever since the early days of the New Deal, an important segment of the American public had objected to any increase in federal power, and their objections grew more vehement as the trend begun by Roosevelt gave promise of continuing under Truman. The following resolution, adopted by the two houses of the Indiana legislature in January 1947, reflected that attitude. In fact, the trend did continue, under the Republican Eisenhower as well as under the Democrats Truman, Kennedy, and Johnson. However, the cost of state government actually increased at a much faster rate during the twenty years after the resolution was passed than the cost of federal government.*

Source: *The Freeman*, November 1958.

INDIANA NEEDS NO GUARDIAN and intends to have none. We Hoosiers — like the people of our sister states — were fooled for quite a spell with the magician's trick that a dollar taxed out of our pockets and sent to Washington will be bigger when it comes back to us. We have taken a good look at said dollar. We find that it lost weight in its journey to Washington and back. The political brokerage of the bureaucrats has been deducted. We have decided that there is no such thing as "federal" aid. We know that there is no wealth to tax that is not already within the boundaries of the forty-eight states.

*So we propose henceforward to tax ourselves and take care of ourselves. We are fed up with subsidies, doles, and paternalism. We are no* one's stepchild. We have grown up. We serve notice that we will resist Washington, D.C., adopting us.

*Be it resolved by the House of Representatives of the General Assembly of the State of Indiana, the Senate concurring:* That we respectfully petition and urge Indiana's congressmen and senators to vote to fetch our county courthouse and city halls back from Pennsylvania Avenue. We want government to come home. *Resolved, further,* that we call upon the legislatures of our *sister states* and on *good citizens everywhere* who believe in the basic principles of Lincoln and Jefferson to join with us, and we with them to restore the American Republic and our forty-eight states to the foundations built by our fathers.

97.

# Percival and Paul Goodman: Community

*The technological and industrial advances made during World War II gave promise of a postwar society that would be increasingly urbanized and conditioned by the activities of huge corporations. To some Americans such a society meant loss of individuality, dehumanization, and a concomitant loss of the values of work and personal integrity. To combat these effects they engaged in what has been largely a losing battle to retain and even restore the conditions and values of a rural America with smaller units of production and distribution and a larger role for all individuals in the whole economic process. In 1947 Percival and Paul Goodman published* Communitas *as a plea for an integrated society blending urban and rural qualities in order to enhance and preserve both personal and communal values of life. Portions of the seventh chapter of their book are reprinted below.*

Source: *Communitas: Means of Livelihood and Ways of Life,* Chicago, 1947; "The New Commune: The Elimination of the Difference Between Production and Consumption."

## QUARANTINING THE TECHNOLOGY — QUARANTINING THE HOMES

THAT THERE IS an "instinct of workmanship," expressing itself in a desire for efficient handling of material means, surely has some truth; and it is even truer that work springs from rhythm and other spontaneous acts and retains some of the feelings of play. It is a kind of creation; it is an extension of the personality into material nature, etc. But it is also true that the capitalist relations of production, and machine industry itself as at present analyzed under whatever system, have so far destroyed the pleasures of work that economic work is what all ordinary men avoid. (At the same time, unemployment — such is our society! — is regarded as the worst of political and moral terrors.) Under capitalism — and the same holds for any society devoted to reinvestment in new machines — efficiency is measured by the surplus value rather than by the handling of the means. Mass produc-

tion, analyzing the acts of labor into small steps and distributing the product far from home, destroys the sense of creating something. Rhythm, accuracy, style, and so forth belong to the machine rather than the man. And all this is summed up in the unvarying demands of workmen for shorter hours, higher pay, and better conditions; they want less of the job and more of the profits, to enjoy at a general market unconnected with their specific work.

The division of economy into production and consumption as two opposite poles means that we are already far from the conditions in which work could be a way of life. The "instinct of workmanship" requires at least the direction of the work to an understood finished product. But a way of life requires the added principle of merging the means and the end, and the work must therefore be thought of as a continuous process of activity and satisfaction, of production and consumption. These considerations have led many moralist-economists to the desire to turn back the clock to conditions of handicraft in a limited society, whose relations of guilds and small markets give at least the master-craftsmen a hand in every phase of production, distribution, and consumption. Obviously, our problem must be rather to accomplish the same ends with modern technology, a national economy, and a democratic ideal; and to reanalyze efficiency and machine production with this aim. For machine production, too, will be part of an integrated way of life.

A characteristic of American offices and factories is the severe discipline with regard to punctuality. Now, in many cases where the workers cooperate in teams, where business is timed by the mails, where the machines use a temporary source of power, etc., being on time and on the same time as everybody else is essential to efficiency. But in many cases it would make little difference at what hour work began and ended, so long as the day's work was completed; often, indeed, the work could be done at home or on the premises indifferently, or part here and part there. Yet this laxity is never allowed, or only in the typical instances of hack-writing and commercial art — typical because just these workers have an uneasy relation to the economy in any case. The fact is that punctuality is demanded not primarily for efficiency but precisely for the discipline itself. The discipline is necessary because the work is onerous; in turn, it makes the idea of working even more onerous, but it makes the work itself much more tolerable; for it establishes it in an impersonal, secondary environment where — once one has gotten out of bed early in the morning — the self has already resigned all claims. Regulation of time, separation from the personal environment, these are the signs that the work is not a way of life; they are the methods by which, for better or worse, the work cannot be energized directly by personal concerns, or confused by personal concerns.

In many town plans we have seen what we have called "quarantining the technolo-gy" from the homes; this is part of the more general necessity of quarantining the work. Now with regard to the technology it might seem that the homes are being defended from nuisance-factories; but it is even truer to say that the factories and offices are being defended from the homes. (For instance, it is calamitous for a man's wife or children to visit him at work; this privilege is reserved for the highest bosses.) Under the usual conditions of domestic industry, we can see the intermixture of the worst features of both environments; the house is full of steam; the piecework pay is minimal; labor is atomized and unorganized. But in the old guild town (presumably) and on certain diversified farms we see the pattern of a more ideal integration.

## THE REANALYSIS OF PRODUCTION

IN PLANNING A REGION of satisfying industrial work we therefore take account of four main principles:

1. Closer relation of the personal and productive environments, making punctuality reasonable instead of disciplinary and introducing phases of domestic and small-shop production; and, vice versa, finding an appropriate technical field for personal relations which have come to be considered unproductive.

2. For all workers, a role in all stages of the production of a product; for all experienced workers, a voice in the design of the product and the design and operation of the machines; and for all a political voice, on the basis of what they know best (namely, their specific industry), in the national economy.

3. A schedule of work designed on psychological, as well as technical grounds, to give the most well-rounded employment of each person, in a diversified environment.

4. Relatively small units with a relative self-sufficiency; so that each unit enters into

a larger whole with security and independence of viewpoint.

A moment's reflection will show that these principles are mutually interdependent.

1. On the first point something has already been said. Starting from the present separation of work and home, we can achieve their closer relation from two sides: (a) returning parts of the production — which parts we must soon consider — to home-shops or to the proximity of the homes and (b) introducing domestic work and the productive part of family relations, which are now not considered part of the economy at all, into the style and relations of the larger economy.

(a) As to home-shops, we must think of the present sudden proliferation of machine tools. Previously, it could be said that the sewing machine was the only productive machine widely distributed. But now, largely because of the war, the idea of thousands of small complete machine shops, powered by electricity, has become familiar. And, in general, the change from steam power to electricity and oil has relaxed one of the greatest causes for the concentration of machines around a single driving-shaft. Which part of manufacture requires a factory (for instance, an assembly line) and which does not (for instance, turning a small part) depends on the analysis of production and the proximity of plant and homes. And, further, the new factories are themselves no longer nuisance-buildings; many are neater and certainly handsomer than the homes and monumental buildings of the same communities; therefore, the proximity of factories, home-shops, and homes is possible and desirable.

(b) Borsodi, going back to the old conception of Aristotle, has proved, often with hilarious realism, that home production, such as cooking, cleaning, mending, and entertaining has a formidable economic value. The problem is, without destroying the individuality of home production, to lighten and enrich it by the technical means and some of the expert attitudes which belong to public production. And, vice versa, to restore to the home many services that are really most humanly satisfactory there but are now unfeasible because of the drudgery, lack of tools, etc. (Below we develop an example, cooking, to show how a new combination of private and public production can be perfected.)

But the chief part of finding a satisfactory productive life in the environment of homes and families consists in the analysis of personal relations and conditions: e.g., the productive cooperation of man and wife, which exists on farms, or the productive capabilities of children and old folk, now simply excluded from the economy. But this involves sentimental and moral problems of extreme depth and delicacy which could only be solved by the experiment itself. Nevertheless, taking our lead from the well-known population figures showing that the city is replenished from the country, we try to develop a rural activity for all children.

2. A chief cause of the living meaninglessness of industrial work is that each machine worker is acquainted with only a few processes, not the whole order of production; and even worse, that the thousands of products are distributed where the worker has no acquaintance at all. Efficient production is organized from above by expert managers who assign the jobs, first analyzing the production into simple processes and then synthesizing these into combinations built into the machines themselves, arranging for the order of supplies, the location of machines, etc. And profitable distribution depends on a national market, organized by advertisers and other sales experts.

As against the efficiency organized from above, efforts have been made — especially in the Soviet Union — to give this function to the workers. But, obviously, this is feasible only if the workers have a total grasp of all the operations. Therefore, there must be a school of the industry, academic and not immediately productive, connected with the factory. Now let us distinguish apprentices and graduates; to the apprentices, along with their schooling, could be assigned more of the monotonous work; to the graduates, more of the executive and coordinating work, the fine work, and the finishing touches. The masterpiece of an apprentice, graduating him, could be just an invention, new method, or other practical contribution advancing the industry. And very important is that the masters have, as a regular part of their jobs, periods of analysis and discussion looking to changes.

Such a setup detracts greatly from the schedule of continued production in present-day factories; but it is a question whether it would not prove to be more efficient in the long run — *if the men are working for themselves and have a say in the distribution.*

"A say in the distribution" here means not merely economic democracy or even socialist ownership. These are necessary checks, but they do not give a political meaning to industrialism as such. What is required is the organization of economic democracy on the basis of the productive units, where each unit, relying on its own expertness and the bargaining power of what it has to offer, cooperates with, and delegates authority to, the whole of society. This is syndicalism. And to guarantee the independent say of each productive unit it must have a relative self-sufficiency; this is regionalism and the union of farm and factory — problems to be discussed shortly.

3. Next, machine work in its present form is stultifying and monotonous, as against the variety which makes intensive agriculture, for instance, a "way of life." The remedy for this must be to assign each man's work on psychological as well as technical and economic grounds. The object is to provide a well-rounded employment. Within any one industry, the work can be divided on such grounds (for instance, team-work and individual work or physical work and intellectual work); and the right industries can be combined in a neighborhood (for instance, cast glass, blown glass, and optical instruments — or, most important of all, industry and agriculture).

There are, of course, many kinds of psychological analysis appropriate to finding a well-rounded employment. On a social basis, there could be a combination of team, isolated, and domestic jobs. On a basis of faculties or powers, there could be physical or intellectual, routine or initiative jobs; on a Gestalt basis, every gradation of simplicity and complexity of attention and adjustment; on a cruder, environmental basis, more amenable to merely architectural planning, the variety of city and country work. It would be a hard, but not impossible, task to make such an analysis for a number of factories and would be worthwhile for some author to attempt. But the important point is to insist on the immediate relevance of such considerations if machine industry and mechanized agriculture are to be integral parts of a way of life.

The problem comes down to this: to envisage a well-rounded schedule of jobs for each man and to arrange the buildings and farms so that the schedule is feasible.

Elements of a well-rounded schedule have already appeared in what has been said; the reintroduction of domestic industry; the introduction of school work and political authority into the factory; the interdependence of city and country.

4. The integration of factory and farm brings us to the idea of regionalism and regional relative autonomy. Such a regional idea has the following main parts:

(*a*) Diversified farming as the basis of self-subsistence and, therefore, small urban centers (two hundred thousand).

(*b*) A number of mutually dependent industrial centers; so that an important process of the national economy can be under local control.

(*c*) These industries developed around regional resources of mine, field, and power.

Diversified farming alone is economically independent. Small farms have therefore always been a root of social stability though not necessarily of peasant conservatism. On the other hand, under modern conditions, as analyzed even by a Homesteader, they import power and small machines and pay with the products of domestic industry and cash crops farmed perhaps cooperatively with large machines. Such a farm then is the type of productive unit, independent in itself but linked with the larger economy of the other farms and of the town.

The problem of industry is the reverse; for every machine industry is completely dependent on the national economy. But by regional interdependence of industries and by the close integration of factory and farm workers — factory hands taking over in the fields at peak seasons; farmers doing factory work in the winter; town people, especially children, living in the country; farmers making small parts for the factories — the industrial region as a whole can secure for itself an independent bargaining-power in the national whole.

The general sign of this whole formed of wholes is the distinction of the local regional markets from the national market and the different standards of transportation for each: the local markets are served by foot, bicycle, cart and car; the national market by plane and trailer-truck.

Now it might be that all these provisions — small units, double markets, the selection of industries on political and psychological grounds, etc. — that all this is a strange and roundabout way of achieving a unified national economy, when at present this unity already exists with a tightness and efficiency that leave nothing to be desired. But first, it is always a question whether the regional and syndicalist method is not more efficient in the end, when invention, for instance, is not inhibited and the job is its own incentive. But most important of all, it must be remembered that we are here aiming at the highest and nearest ideals of external life: liberty; personal concern, responsibility, and expertness; and a say in what a man lends his hands to. Compared with these things, the present setup, that does not even make the attempt to find living meaning in its work, has nothing to offer us. . . .

## A FARM AND ITS CHILDREN

THE COUNTRY PROCREATES ITSELF, the city does not. Instead of striving to correct these trends, let us — since we are here integrating town and country anyway — proceed along with them. The plan is to rear all the children in the natural environment where they are many and furnish a society for each other — an environment whose business is plain to their eyes, not concealed in factories and accounts. The mechanism of urban production is clear to adult minds; the nature of farm production is not so much clearer, yet clear enough, to the men than it is to the children of ten or eleven.

It is necessary to remedy the present-day injustice to the country, whereby it bears the burden of rearing and educating more than its share of the population — then loses 50 percent of the investment at maturity. And then there are urban complaints that the youth have been educated according to rural standards! But if the city children are brought to the country schools, the city bears its prorata share of the cost and has the right to a say in the policy.

The parents who work in the city may live in small houses on nearby farms. When they leave for their work, their children are not alone, are with many children, but are still at home. For it is obvious (to anyone who has given the matter a second thought) that if the urban family continues to break down, there must be something better than the pathos of crèches, nursery schools, and kindergartens.

These city families are the farmers' most valuable source of money income.

Once they have reached the age of a certain awareness of themselves as persons and no longer live altogether by dependence, the best society for children is other children, older and younger by easy grades. Admittedly, it is a rough society but characterized at worst by conflict rather than by a loving absolute authority. These children, therefore, no longer sleep with their parents, but in a children's dormitory.

From quite early all are set to work feeding the chickens and to doing chores which are occasionally beyond their powers. But here the presence of urban sentiment can alleviate the condition of farm and city children both.

In general, in planning a community of integrated productive life, it would be absurd to omit, or not to give a major role to, the agricultural family that has always served as the model of such a life.

The sense in which diversified farming is a way of life has been defined and praised often enough. Nevertheless, the farm youth migrate to the city when they can. But this is inevitable when all the advertised social values, broadcast by radio, letters, and cinema, are urban values, created for and by the cities and created, often, in order to increase the volume of city business. To counteract this propaganda it is not sufficient for farmers to make their way of life more attractive, as they can by new technical means; they must likewise set up a social opinion specifically rural. The centers of this exist in farmers' cooperatives and collectives.

But best of all, of course, is for neither environment to compete with the other but for each, without losing its characteristics, to aim at some kind of integration. We must remind ourselves that even the socialist formula "the elimination of the difference between town and country" has always meant, for historical reasons, the elimination of the country as a way of life. Yet, in fact, the rural way, so tenaciously clung to by farmers of all nations when once they have gained the title to their land, has a more fundamental contribution to make.

## REGIONAL AND NATIONAL ECONOMY

THE LARGE NUMBER OF DIVERSIFIED FARMS means, on the one hand, that the region is self-providing but, on the other, that the farmers have little crop to export outside the region. (Its gross value is less, but this is not dissipated by the cost of distribution.) Their cash comes from the city market, from domestic industry, from industrial agriculture, and from housing the cityfolk. If they have a specialized crop, such as grapes or cotton, it would be processed in the town. All of this guarantees a tight local economy.

Now — even apart from politics — if there is to be a close relation between production and consumption, such a tight local economy is essential; for it means that prices and the value of labor will not be so subject to the fluctuations of a vast general market. A man's work will be meaningful to him during production, and this meaning will also carry through (more than elsewhere) into what he gets in return. That is, within limits, the nearer the system comes to a household economy, the more it can be an economy of — specific things and services rather than an economy of generalized money.

"An economy of things rather than money": this formula is the heart of regionalism. For the persons of a region cooperate with each other directly, drawing on natural resources, without the intermediary of a vast national bookkeeping with millions of clashing motives. We have already seen how the regional development of the Tennessee Valley brought together power and fertilizer for farms, navigation and the prevention of erosion, the control of floods and the processing of foods, and by this natural cooperation produced a host of ingenious inventions. All this, at least in its inception (whatever change may have resulted from financial and political pressure), was carried on in a relative autonomy, under the loose heading of "general welfare." But if the T.V.A. now has to trim its activities *in detail* to a national budget, there will be an end of intensive development and of what it stands for, although some items may show more money profits.

We see, then, that the kind of life looked for in our region depends first on the awareness of local distinctness. And this, we have already seen, is also the condition of its political independence as a group of industries and farm cooperatives rather than as a multitude of voters and consumers.

At the same time, every machine economy is a national and international economy. The fraction of necessary goods produced in a planned region is very substantial, but it is still a fraction. And this, once the region is well established, is the salvation of regionalism! For it prevents the wilful provincialism that is so nauseating in movements of regional literature and art. (These regionalist critics are truly "ignorant" in Aristotle's use of the term: they come to errors as the result of demonstration which any fool would have found intuitively in his mother wit.) To the industrialists in their meeting, it is clear that just because their industry and their region are strong and productive, they are subject to wider and wider circles of influence; and, unlike private persons, they cannot shirk the responsibility of informing themselves.

---

98.

# Jean Paul Sartre: Americans and Their Myths

*Jean Paul Sartre has been the leading exponent of the French school of philosophy known as existentialism. The most systematic presentation of his thought is* L'Être et le néant *(1943;* Being and Nothingness, *1956). By the time it appeared Sartre already had a considerable reputation in France as a novelist. From the existentialist standpoint, fiction or drama is as much a form of philosophical literature as the conventional essay, and in some ways a medium even better able to communicate the experience and meaning of existence. His play* Huis-clos *(1944;* No Exit*) was produced on Broadway in 1946. The following pessimistic observations on American society, published late in 1947, nonetheless reflected his belief in indeterminism, or "human freedom." He saw freedom as a heavy burden on mankind, since it brings with it responsibility, guilt, remorse, punishment; at the same time he regarded freedom as the source of man's nobility.*

Source: *Nation,* October 18, 1947.

Everything has been said about the United States. But a person who has once crossed the Atlantic can no longer be satisfied with even the most penetrating books; not that he does not believe what they say, but that his agreement remains abstract.

When a friend tries to explain our character and unravel our motives, when he relates all our acts to principles, prejudices, beliefs, and a conception of the world which he thinks to find in us, we listen uneasily, unable either to deny what he says or entirely accept it. Perhaps the interpretation is true, but what is the truth that is being interpreted? We miss the intimate warmth, the life, the way one is always unpredictable to oneself and also tiresomely familiar, the decision to get along with oneself, the perpetual deliberations and perpetual inventions about what one is, and the vow to be "that" and nothing else — in short, the liberty. Similarly, when a careful arrangement of those melting-pot notions — puritanism, realism, optimism, and so on — which we have been told are the keys to the American character is presented to us in Europe, we experience a certain intellectual satisfaction and think that, in effect, it must be so. But when we walk about New York, on Third Avenue, or Sixth Avenue, or Tenth Avenue, at that evening hour which, for Da Vinci, lends softness to the faces of men, we see the most pathetic visages in the world, uncertain, searching, intent, full of astonished good faith, with appealing eyes, and we know that the most beautiful generalizations are of very little service: they permit us to understand the system but not the people.

The system is a great external apparatus, an implacable machine which one might call the objective spirit of the United States and which over there they call Americanism — a huge complex of myths, values, recipes, slogans, figures, and rites. But one must not think that it has been deposited in the head of each American just as the God of Descartes deposited the first notions in the mind of man; one must not think that it is "refracted" into brains and hearts and at each instant determines affections or thoughts that exactly express it. Actually, it is something outside of the people, something presented to them; the most adroit propaganda does nothing else but present it to them continuously. It is not in them, they are in it; they struggle against it or they accept it, they stifle in it or go beyond it, they submit to it or reinvent it, they give

themselves up to it or make furious efforts to escape from it; in any case it remains outside them, transcendent, because they are men and it is a thing.

There are the great myths, the myths of happiness, of progress, of liberty, of triumphant maternity; there is realism and optimism — and then there are the Americans, who, nothing at first, grow up among these colossal statues and find their way as best they can among them. There is this myth of happiness: black-magic slogans warn you to be happy at once; films that "end well" show a life of rosy ease to the exhausted crowds; the language is charged with optimistic and unrestrained expressions — "have a good time," "life is fun," and the like. But there are also these people, who, though conventionally happy, suffer from an obscure *malaise* to which no name can be given, who are tragic through fear of being so, through that total absence of the tragic in them and around them.

There is this collectivity which prides itself on being the least "historical" in the world, on never complicating its problems with inherited customs and acquired rights, on facing as a virgin a virgin future in which everything is possible — and there are these blind gropings of bewildered people who seek to lean on a tradition, on a folklore. There are the films that write American history for the masses and, unable to offer them a Kentucky Jeanne d'Arc or a Kansas Charlemagne, exalt them with the history of the jazz singer Al Jolson, or the composer Gershwin. Along with the Monroe Doctrine, isolationism, scorn for Europe, there is the sentimental attachment of each American for his country of origin, the inferiority complex of the intellectuals before the culture of the old Continent, of the critics who say, "How can you admire our novelists, you who have Flaubert?", of the painters who say, "I shall never be able to paint as long as I stay in the United States"; and there is the obscure, slow effort of an entire nation to seize universal history and assimilate it as its patrimony.

There is the myth of equality — and there is the myth of segregation, with those big beachfront hotels that post signs reading "Jews and dogs not allowed," and those lakes in Connecticut where Jews may not bathe, and that racial *tchin*, in which the lowest degree is assigned to the Slavs, the highest to the Dutch immigrants of 1680. There is the myth of liberty — and the dictatorship of public opinion; the myth of economic liberalism — and the big companies extending over the whole country which, in the final analysis, belong to no one and in which the employees, from top to bottom, are like functionaries in a state industry. There is respect for science and industry, positivism, and insane love of "gadgets" — and there is the somber humor of the *New Yorker*, which pokes bitter fun at the mechanical civilization of America and the hundred million Americans who satisfy their craving for the marvelous by reading every day in the "comics" the incredible adventures of Superman, or Wonderman, or Mandrake the Magician.

There are the thousand taboos which proscribe love outside of marriage — and there is the litter of used contraceptives in the backyards of coeducational colleges; there are all those men and women who drink before making love in order to transgress in drunkenness and not remember. There are the neat, coquettish houses, the pure-white apartments with radio, armchair, pipe, and stand — little paradises; and there are the tenants of those apartments who, after dinner, leave their chairs, radios, wives, pipes, and children and go to the bar across the street to get drunk alone.

Perhaps nowhere else will you find such a discrepancy between people and myth, between life and the representation of life. An American said to me at Bern: "The trouble is that we are all eaten by the fear of being less American than our neighbor." I accept this explanation: it shows that Americanism is not merely a myth that clever propaganda stuffs into people's heads but something every American continually reinvents in his gropings. It is at one and the same time a great external reality rising up at the entrance to the port of New York across from the Statue of Liberty, and the daily product of anxious liberties. The anguish of the American confronted with Americanism is an ambivalent anguish, as if he were asking, "Am I American enough?" and at the same time, "How can I escape from Americanism?" In America a man's simultaneous answers to these two questions make him what he is, and each man must find his own answers.

———————◆———————

*America is everywhere. For an isolationist nation it is remarkable how she gets about.*
        EDWARD CRANKSHAW, *Russia and the Russians*, 1948

# 1948

99.

## DWIGHT D. EISENHOWER: On the Unsuitability of Military Men for Public Office

*As the presidential election of 1948 approached, the Republicans were confident that nearly any candidate they chose to nominate would win. The Democrats, on the other hand, were doubtful about President Truman's chances at the polls, especially in view of the threatened split with Southern Democrats over civil rights. One man to whom both parties turned briefly as a potential candidate was General Dwight D. Eisenhower, who until late January 1948 was chief of staff for the Army. An attempt was made to get his name on the primary ballot in New Hampshire in 1948. On January 22 Eisenhower addressed the following letter to Leonard V. Finder, publisher of the Manchester (New Hampshire) Evening Leader, disclaiming any desire to be a candidate for public office.*

Source: *Record, App.,* 80 Cong., 2 Sess., p. A745.

YOUR LETTER AND EDITORIAL have been on my desk for more than a week while I pondered the reply merited by your obvious concern for the nation's welfare, and from a personal standpoint, by the honor you had done me. Months ago I thought that unqualified denial of political ambition would eliminate me from consideration in the coming campaign for the presidency, because that office has, since the days of Washington, historically and properly fallen only to aspirants.

That some few would misinterpret or look for hidden meanings in my past expressions was expected and discounted, but my failure to convince thoughtful and earnest men such as yourself proves that I must make some amplification. This will necessarily partake of the laborious, due to the complexity of the factors that have influenced me to say no more than I have, but which dictate my decision that I am not available for and could not accept nomination to high political office.

I have heretofore refrained from making the bald statement that I would not accept nomination, although this has been my intention since the subject was first mentioned to me.

This omission seems to have been a mistake, since it has inadvertently misled sincere and disinterested Americans. But my reticence stemmed from cogent reasons. The first was that such an expression would smack of effrontery. I had and I have no desire to appear either as assuming that significant numbers of our peoples would actively interest themselves in me as a possible candidate, or to appear as lacking in respect and regard for the highest honor American citizens can confer upon one of their own body.

A second and even deeper reason was a persistent doubt that I could phrase a flat refusal without appearing to violate that concept of duty to country which calls upon every good citizen to place no limitations upon his readiness to serve in any designated capacity. On this point it is my conviction that, unless an individual feels some inner compulsion and special qualifications to enter the political arena, which I do not, a refusal to do so involves no violation of the highest standards of devotion to duty.

It was only the possible misinterpretation of my attitude that caused me concern, and as long as I could believe that mere denial of political ambition would prevent serious misunderstanding and misdirected effort, I was reluctant to say more. It would seem almost superfluous for me to add that as long as I live I shall hold myself in instant readiness to respond to any call by the government to military duty.

In full awareness, then, and not in violation of my own sense of duty, I have developed the following conclusions which are responsible for my negative decision.

It is my conviction that the necessary and wise subordination of the military to civil power will be best sustained, and our people will have greater confidence that it is so sustained, when lifelong professional soldiers in the absence of some obvious and overriding reasons abstain from seeking high

political office. This truth has a possible inverse application. I would regard it as unalloyed tragedy for our country if ever should come the day when military commanders might be selected with an eye to their future potentialities in the political field rather than exclusively upon judgment as to their military abilities.

Politics is a profession — a serious, complicated, and, in its true sense, a noble one.

In the American scene I see no dearth of men fitted by training, talent, and integrity for national leadership. On the other hand, nothing in the international or domestic situation especially qualifies for the most important office in the world a man whose adult years have been spent in the country's military forces. At least this is true in my case.

I am deeply regretful if a too simple faith in the effectiveness of a plain denial has misled any considerable number concerning my intentions and so allowed them to spend time and effort under erroneous impressions. At the risk of appearing pompous, I must say that the honor paid me cannot fail to spur me in future years to work the more diligently for America, her youth, her veterans, and all her citizens, and for the continuance of peace.

I trust that this rather lengthy explanation will convince you that my conclusions are not only sound but have been arrived at objectively and have not been unduly influenced by my own desires and convenience. In any event, my decision to remove myself completely from the political scene is definite and positive. I know you will not object to my making this letter public to inform all interested persons that I could not accept nomination even under the remote circumstances that it were tendered me.

---

*The finest prison in the world.*
Harry S. Truman, of the White House

100.

# HENRY C. SIMONS: Liberalism and a Free Society

*Henry C. Simons, a University of Chicago economist who attempted to apply the principles of classical economics to twentieth-century problems, rejected both the theorists of the "right," who he said portray "laissez faire as a merely do-nothing policy," and those of the "left," whom he regarded as "the real enemies of liberty." "A Political Credo," a portion of which is reprinted here, was written in the early part of 1945 and later revised and adopted to serve as an introduction to a collection of his essays that was published in 1948.*

Source: *Economic Policy for a Free Society*, Chicago, 1948, pp. 1-39.

### Central Versus Local Governments

INDIVIDUALISM AND COLLECTIVISM are usually discussed largely in terms of political (coercive) versus voluntary (free) association and of governmental-monopolistic versus private-competitive organizations. The range of aggregate governmental activities, however, is hardly more important, as a policy problem, than their distribution between small and large, local and central, governments. Extensive local socialization need not be incompatible with, or very dangerous to, a free society. Local bodies are themselves largely voluntary associations; people have much freedom to choose and to move among them; they are substantially competitive and, even if permitted to do so, rarely could much restrain trade. The libertarian argument against "too much government," consequently, relates mainly to national governments, not to provincial or local units — and to great powers rather than to small nations.

Democratic process is an invention of local bodies. It has been extended upward and may be extended gradually toward world organization. In any case, modern democracy rests upon free, responsible local government and will never be stronger than this foundation. Free, responsible local bodies correspond, in the political system, to free, responsible individuals or families and voluntary associations in the good society. A people wisely conserving its liberties will seek ever to enlarge the range and degree of local freedom and responsibility. In so doing, it may sacrifice possible proximate achievements. Doing specific good things by centralization will always be alluring. It may always seem easier to impose "progress" on localities than to wait for them to effect it for themselves — provided one is not solicitous about the basis or sources of progress. A community imposing good local government from above may seem to get ahead rapidly for a time. Likewise, a community may temporarily raise its economic scale of life by living up its capital. And the analogy seems closely in point. Progress to which local freedom, responsibility, and experimentation have pointed the way may be accelerated for a time and effected more uniformly by the short cut of central action.

But such short-cutting tends to impair or to use up the roots of progress in order to obtain a briefly luxuriant bloom.

The inefficiency and corruption of local government are recognized evils — which make us unduly complacent or enthusiastic about centralization. It is generally supposed that almost any function will be more efficiently and more honestly discharged by a larger unit of government. So, we readily accept increase of central responsibility, through supervision or outright transfer of functions or both. As regards corruption, the prevailing view is simply wrong — unless one sticks to a narrow, legalistic definition. Our federal government (I venture) is far more corrupt in its best years than municipal government at its worst, if one judges by the proportion of outlays (activities) which serve the common interest as against the proportion spent in vote-buying, that is, in serving special interests against the common interest. Municipal machines at worst divert a modest tribute; their graft and patronage are small fractions of the value of public services actually rendered. Our national government typically spends freely on behalf of organized, logrolling minorities, tossing in some general welfare outlays for good measure. For decades the subsidies appropriated in the form of protective tariffs probably amounted to more than the total of all other federal outlays, including silver subsidies.

The notion that large governmental units are more efficient than small ones is equally wrong but hard to attack, because efficiency is far more ambiguous or deceptive in meaning than is corruption. Large administrative units may seem more efficient than small ones, if only because they contain so many people employed to increase efficiency rather than to produce substantive services. But administrative efficiency in government, at best, is a false god and a dangerously static good. Large governments, like giant business corporations, may effec-

tively mobilize existing technology, realizing fully its current potentialities. In a short-sighted view they are instruments of progress; but they lack the creative powers of a multiplicity of competitive smaller units. They are, to repeat, at best only means for "forcing" the plant — for enriching the present at the expense of the future. . . .

The political agnostic or specialized reformer would transfer control or responsibility upward whenever proximate gains seemed thus attainable. Libertarians would counsel a bolder scheme of improving local government by enlarging local freedom and removing the props of central control — and they would join in recommending central measures for facilitating proper discharge of local responsibilities.

### Central Government Functions: War

THE MOST OBVIOUS CENTRAL FUNCTION is that of external defense. In the ultimate federalism this function disappears, and only at or near this limit can libertarian democracy be securely attained. Total war, actual or imminent, demands extreme centralization, that is, a unitary, military, collectivist state which is the antithesis of a free society. It involves moral, economic, and governmental mobilization in which all freedom may be subordinated to one overriding, concrete purpose. And such mobilization is hard to undo after the emergency is past, for it brings its own other "emergencies" and invites retention for all manner of worthy purposes. The emotional experience of war and the impressive achievements of mobilization leave us ill prepared for the prosaic processes of a free society and for renewed faith in any "invisible hand."

Fortunately, however, even the demands of external defense are ambivalent. If wars are frequent, victories will probably accrue to those who remain mobilized. Otherwise, planning for peace may also be the best planning for war. If there are vital, creative forces to be released by demobilization — by return to a free society — the nation may thereby gain enough strength to compensate handsomely for the risks involved. Victories may consistently accrue to those who bet on peace; and progress toward world order may continue secularly in spite of disastrous retrogressions.

This a libertarian must believe, for war is the great threat to his kind of society. There is simply no democratic answer to the problem of external defense, save indefinite extension of federalism, first, into a predominantly powerful supranational federation, and then gradually into inclusive world organization of all nations capable of responsible participation. Here the important next steps must be taken in the field of commercial policies; and the next conspicuous institutional innovation will be an international court with compulsory jurisdiction, albeit only among some Western democracies at the start. Libertarian democracy can survive without world order but not without secular movement toward such order.

### Other Central Functions

THE BASIC FUNCTION of central government is to sustain domestic peace. Internal order is prerequisite to external defense and, of course, is the essence of world federation. The good central government will represent a monopoly of violence; it must sustain that monopoly against both its constituent political units and all extra-governmental bodies. It must promote all kinds of peaceful intercourse, intellectual and commercial. It must articulate the prevailing moral consensus and promote enlargement of that consensus by organized, free discussion and legislative-judicial experimentation.

Two more definite central government functions are stressed by libertarians: first, the maintenance of free trade and, second, the provision of a stable currency. . . .

### The Rule of Law and Government by Discussion

IF SUCH PRESCRIPTIONS ARE FOLLOWED, government by discussion and consensus is facilitated and strengthened thereby. At higher levels, and especially at the highest level, political discussion should be focused on clear-cut, general rules of law and policy. It is such discussion that feeds the growth and diffusion of the basic moral consensus. Only from slow action out of such discussion may a nation build solidly and progressively the principles and working rules which afford political security and economic stability. Only by adherence to the rule of law and to announced rules of policy may a people have strong government without granting inordinate, arbitrary power to ruling parties, factions, or majorities of the moment. Only thus may it assure the use of governmental power in the common interest or avoid the degradation of government by logrolling, patronage-seeking, special-interest groups. Only thus may freedom be protected against large-government power and, to repeat, large-scale discussion focused on questions that can be fruitfully discussed or usefully settled by discussion.

The alternative is "plebiscitary democracy," the antithesis of libertarian government. Elections then merely choose among leaders or factions. Campaigns are mere contests for power — slogan-mongering, promising everything to all minorities save the scapegoats, absurd eulogies and vilifications. Platforms are unprincipled in themselves and binding, if at all, only during the campaign. Parties are simply organizations for promising and dispensing patronage, standing for nothing but unlimited prerogative of tactical opportunism, either as "government" or as "opposition" (if any). Such, at all events, is the meaning of government by men as the antithesis of government by law and policy rules.

These prescriptions in terms of service

functions (concentrated at the bottom) and
the rule of law (severely adhered to at the
top) are, like federalism itself, designed to
assure minimal dispersion or decentralization of power. Executive-administrative discretion in large governments is an ominous
thing — as is ad hoc legislation on behalf
of particular areas, industries, producers, or
pressure groups. Constitutional rules, enforced by courts, are one means for limiting
the exercise of power implicit in central
government. But constitutional provisions
are no stronger than the moral consensus
that they articulate. At best, they can only
check abuse of power until moral pressure
is mobilized; and their check must become
ineffective if often overtly used. . . .

### "Power Always Corrupts"

TRADITIONAL LIBERALISM, to repeat, is an optimistic faith in the potentialities of free
men and free societal process. By vulgar re-
pute, however, it is a narrow, negative, and
pessimistic doctrine perhaps by association
with "the dismal science." The charge of
pessimism is valid as regards "Malthusian"
societies, notably India. Moreover, all positive or optimistic prescriptions necessarily
have their negative corollaries. And one of
these, while implicit above, may properly be
stressed in passing.

A cardinal tenet of libertarians is that no
one may be trusted with much power —
no leader, no faction, no party, no "class,"
no majority, no government, no church, no
corporation, no trade association, no labor
union, no grange, no professional association, no university, no large organization of
any kind. They must forever repeat with
Lord Acton: "Power always corrupts" —
and not merely those who exercise it but
those subject to it and the whole society.
The only good power is that of law based
on overwhelming voluntary consensus of
free men and built and rebuilt by gradual
experimentation, organized discussion, and
tolerant compromise. They do not deny

that concentrated power may occasionally
serve human progress as a temporary or
transitional expedient. They do deny its
uses in advanced nations, save in the gravest
military emergencies and then only until the
peak of crisis has been passed — and any
libertarian who cries wolf easily or frequently is automatically disqualified.

### Liberalism and Commercial Policy

LIBERALISM IS ALSO NOTORIOUS for its uncompromising opposition to governmental restraint or manipulation of foreign trade.
This "negative" aspect of liberalism, that is,
its categorical free-trade prescription, perhaps merits a few remarks in connection
with world problems.

The main content of centralization in the
modern world has been control of foreign
trade. It was this aspect of mercantilism
that Adam Smith mainly attacked; and this
same aspect of government remains, or has
again become, the proper first concern of
libertarians. Commercial policy is not only
the hard core of bad national centralization;
it is also the necessary basis or prerequisite
of bad centralization in other manifestations.
Bad central planning begins historically in
commercial policy and, in all major aspects,
involves or requires arbitrary restrictions on
foreign trade. Free foreign trade would
largely frustrate all major enterprises in economic centralization or in direct federal
control of relative prices, wages, or production. To specify that central economic planning or regulation should proceed with a
framework of free external trade is to suggest perhaps the most useful distinction between good and bad "planning." To
achieve free trade would be to realize, directly and indirectly, most of the decentralization that libertarians propose.

Nationalism, as imposition of internal free
trade, is a means to prosperity and peace.
As imposed control of trade, external and
then internal, it is mobilization for war.

which immediately jeopardizes world order and, in the longer view, also undermines the moral basis of internal peace.

The proximate future of libertarian democracy depends crucially on the future of commercial policy, especially in the United States. This country cannot long have free internal trade without free or much freer trade across its borders; and, be that as it may, this country cannot maintain a libertarian political-economic system as an isolated island surrounded by increasingly antithetical systems. On the other hand, its power is adequate to reestablish a libertarian trend among its friends and neighbors; and, so reestablished, libertarian democracy may then resume its gradual, peaceful "conquest" of the world.

Recent decades have witnessed a steady resurgence of protectionism, culminating during the great depression in disastrous economic warfare. The subtle, substantial international organization implicit in mutual self-denying ordinances, under the rule of equal treatment or nondiscrimination, was suddenly swept away in an orgy of bilateralism, quota restrictions, clearing agreements, and exchange control. Blame for this disaster may be placed largely on the United States — on its stupid tariff legislation, on its impardonable devaluation, and primarily on its failure, as custodian of the dominant or world currency, to prevent a long and deep deflation. Whosesoever the blame for what is past, this country alone can lead the world back to decent commercial policies.

We may negotiate all manner of nobly vague resolutions and paper organizations of sovereign great powers. Much ultimate good may come from such beginnings. But the substance of supranational order will in the near future be achieved, if at all, largely in the field of commercial relations. Here organization, though subtle and obscure, is a matter of almost continuous, daily national actions; it grows or is cut away with every political decision, legislative and administrative, affecting world trade and finance. Thus commercial policies become more or less discriminatory, more or less restrictive, more or less collectivist, more or less informed by narrow national or bloc interests in relative power; and thus commercial intercourse becomes more or less subject to arbitrary controls, more or less governmental, and less or more free.

Whether such changes cause or reflect changes in the degree of international organization and stability is mainly a question of intellectual fashions among contemplators of "first causes" — a question of what abstractions or aspectual qualities are commonly hypostatized, of whether one set of "causes" is prevailingly translated into another or conversely. The prospect is that world commercial, productional, financial organization will mainly lead the way, or manifest the basic direction of change, during the next decade. Major national issues in commercial policy seem certain to obtrude themselves; momentous decisions are likely to be made; and these decisions will either fill or empty the synthetic forms of political structure.

Free trade is an essential feature of stable federation. Real international organization, removing sovereign national prerogatives of trade manipulation, must come slowly out of discussion, experiment, and compromise. The proximate means toward abolition of the prerogatives is gradual abandonment of the practices, under the venturesome leadership of the nation which is at once most influential, best able to risk the venture and likely to gain most by its success.

International organization must be pursued opportunistically on every front which offers opportunity for substantial institutional growth. Beyond the immediate problems of the enemy nations and a political *modus vivendi* lie the persistent problems of economic instability and commercial warfare. Toward progressive mitigation of economic nationalism, blocism, and commercial separatism, America might offer almost irresistible leadership. We should dismantle our tariff. We should assure the world a dollar currency highly stable in purchasing power and enlist cooperation in its stabilization. We should eschew all preferential treatment of our exports in our colonies and dependencies. We should abandon "tied" foreign lending, save possibly as loans are tied to reduction of trade barriers and discrimination in the borrowing nations. Along these lines, we might lead wisely toward an ordered world and toward a Western world economy compatible with libertarian political-economic institutions in the United States. Such bold investment of our national power offers fabulous returns to us and to the world.

### Private Property

IT SEEMS NECESSARY HERE to say something about "private property" because of its conspicuous place in ideological controversy. "The institution of property" is a kind of shorthand notation for an infinitely complicated political-economic system and, indeed, for almost any possible alternative system. Meaning both nothing and everything, it naturally is the subject of much loose talk and impassioned rhetoric, among both stupid reactionaries and romantic radicals. To say that liberal democracy rests on private property is almost pure tautology. To discuss policy problems of "property" would be to discuss almost all economic-policy problems of our society. Only a few discursive remarks on the subject are here in order.

Private property in the instruments of production is an institutional device both for dispersing power and for securing effective organization of production. The only simple property system is that of a slave society with a single slaveowner — which, significantly, is the limiting case of despotism and of monopoly. Departure from such a system is a fair measure of human progress. The libertarian good society lies at an opposite extreme, in the maximum dispersion of property compatible with effective production or, as process, in progressive reconciliation of conflicts between equality and efficiency. Such process involves increasing dispersion both of wealth among persons or families and of proximate productional control among enterprises or firms.

Basic to liberty are property rights in labor or personal capacities. The abolitions of slavery and serfdom are the great steps toward freedom — and, by the way, are striking reconciliations of apparent conflict between productional and distributional considerations. Property in one's own services, however, is a secure, substantial right only where there are many possible buyers. It thus implies private property in other resources and freedom of independent sellers of labor to choose and to move among autonomous, independent organizations or firms. It also implies a distinctively modern institutional achievement, namely, the separation or dissociation of the economic and the political — a political order that sustains formal rights and a largely separate economic order that gives them substance. Otherwise, freedom to contract for one's services is merely an anomalous, synthetic, administrative construct, resting on "platforms" or on "administrative law," that is, freedom to contract with a single buyer or to choose among the offers of a single ultimate authority.

It is advisable, for most practical purposes, to avoid or to minimize categorical distinction between "inalienable" or "personal" capital and "external" property — to regard all property rights as integral aspects of personal capacity. Both kinds of property are the result of investment; both are largely inherited and hence are bound up with the family; both are largely acquired by luck; and each is subject to deliberate transfer from parents to children and transmutable into the other for that purpose. There is no obvious tendency, at any particular income level, toward excessive relative investment in either kind of property; and it certainly is doubtful whether any social gain would result if the more fortunate families endowed their children with access to political power instead of with "material" property. It is no accident that income taxes represent the substantial modern institutional achievement among taxes; that property taxes serve a narrow special purpose unrelated to personal inequality; and that inheritance taxes should remain inelegant, inequitable, ineffective, and chock-full of ineradicable anomalies.

A society based on free, responsible individuals or families must involve extensive rights of property. The economic responsibilities of families are an essential price of their freedom and, like the inseparable moral responsibilities, are necessary to moral development. Family property, in the occidental sense of the primary family, moreover, is largely the basis of preventive checks on population and of the effort to increase personal capacity from generation to generation, that is, to raise a few children hopefully and well or to sacrifice numbers to quality in family reproduction.

Private property is practically indispensable, if only as an administrative device, in modern large-scale organization of production. This organization is national and supranational; it requires wide delegation or dispersion of managerial control, and freedom and opportunity responsibly to initiate new undertaking. Responsible control of managerial units or firms implies property against which responsibility may be enforced; and responsibility for costs implies rights to revenues, especially if there is to be venturesome enterprise and progress.

### Libertarian Socialism

MODERN SOCIALISM is avowedly concerned mainly about inequalities of wealth (and power?) and about industrial monopoly — both major concerns of libertarians. Inequality, in the sense of too much at the top, is

admittedly a matter of taxation; but taxation presents no issues which need divide socialists from libertarians — if socialist interest in the subject or its problems ever becomes substantial and informed. On monopoly problems there is at least a tactical difference: socialists talk much about enterprise monopolies; libertarians talk much about both enterprise monopolies and labor monopolies. Real difference appears only in the respective policy prescriptions for "basic industries." Socialists would "cure" monopoly problems by extending, consolidating, and "politicalizing" monopolies, that is, by abolishing competition in areas where it is relatively "impure." Libertarians would directly regulate or governmentalize only a small group of intractable "natural monopolies," leaving them largely to local bodies, and then seek, by innumerable policy devices, partly direct but mainly indirect, to render competition more and more effective everywhere else.

When socialists begin to talk about decentralization, however, even this difference promises to become empty and nominal "Decentralized socialism" has perhaps great merit as vicarious, intellectual experimentation. It may be fruitful of insights to ask what government should do if a basic industry, paralyzed by administrative disorganization, were simply dropped in its lap. The first step, of course, would be to impose organization from above, perhaps by putting the army quartermasters in charge. Vicarious experimentation, intelligently pursued, probably would lead to a financial-administrative organization in which the administrative units, if autonomous enterprises, would be numerous enough to assure effective competition. Properly decentralized in administration, a socialized industry would probably be completely ripe for alienation; indeed, alienation would be necessary to implement the administrative decentralization. Wise central control would surely come to rely more and more on competition among numerous, similar administrative units, if only to set standards. The administrative devices necessary to sustain such competition would probably transform the central authority gradually from a proprietor to a bondholder or prior claimant. At this stage the public administrative units would become private enterprises, but with the worst possible financial structures. The next obvious step would be to liquidate the government's fixed claims from the proceeds of common-stock issues — and thus to reduce the government debt.

"Decentralized socialism" may thus be regarded as a very roundabout kind of antitrust policy — and as a stimulating approach to both economic and political theory. As social experimentation, however, it is not likely to be well conducted unless it is purely vicarious. Socialist rules regarding outputs, prices, wages, and marginal cost could hardly be implemented against the inevitable pressure-group demands; no governing faction could be expected to eschew the enormous available patronage; and the desirable administrative decentralization would be blocked by central appetites for power and jobs. At best, however, the experiment would turn out to be not one of abolishing private property but one of contriving new property arrangements. If, out of such vicarious experiment, one is able better to apprehend the good property arrangements, one may attain a sound directional sense for actual experimentation and see more clearly the promising routes from here and now. The more intelligently socialists plan for decentralization, the more does socialism fall into line with an orderly, gradual, libertarian process of dispersing property and of continuous, experimental development in the institution of property itself.

### Progress and Security of Property

As IN THE CASE OF the democratic political process, the importance of continuity in property arrangements can hardly be overstressed. Property must be secure in advanced nations, if production is to sustain living standards and if real social wealth is to be conserved or accumulated. Insecurity of property means diversion of production toward precious metals and jewels, that is, high valuation of assets that permit of concealment and can be securely possessed at the price of serviceless possession. Security of property means production of highly useful things, especially improved instruments of production. In the one case, property means withdrawal of resources from socially useful production and accumulation of assets in socially useless forms; in the other, property releases resources from merely protecting possession and promotes their accumulation in forms which augment both currently useful output and the progressive accumulation of capacity.

Economic progress requires that property be secure. Otherwise, those who hold it — governments, organizations, or individuals — must or will use property (and personal capacity) largely to protect property. Such use may involve either the concealment of oriental hoarding or the gross social abuse of property in rivalrous military organization. A telling objection to collectivism is that it locates property where it is least secure and aggravates total insecurity thereby. Its extreme national centralization, if only by threatening other nations, aggravates world insecurity and, in turn, commends external threats as indispensable to domestic order. An unnatural concentration of property affords, at best, only momentary, relative external security, at the cost of greater insecurity for everyone outside; and its only real protection against either the *coup d'état* or divisive civil war is unremitting fear of external attack.

Security of property, moreover, implies a flexible institution of property and persistent, progressive resolution of problems as they obtrude themselves into the democratic discussion process. Radical movements may impair economic organization and disturb economic processes by their direct threat to security of property; on the other hand, they may mainly serve merely to keep us properly busy with the small, manageable problems which are the grist of the democratic mill. Whether radicalism is excessive or inadequate at any period is not for contemporaries to judge with confidence. Whatever the balance of benefits and costs, however, the main cost now lies in the diversion of intellectual and political talents away from urgent small problems and the dull business of particularist discussion, compromise, legislation, and experimentation. Radicals jeopardize the security of property less by attacking the institution than by neglecting it. There is nothing more insidious than the notion that big, rapid changes are easier or more fruitful than small, slow changes; it leads to talk without action, to action without talk, and perhaps to collapse of democracy under a mass of accumulated, neglected routine business. The way to multiply big problems is to neglect small ones. There is nothing seriously wrong with our institution of property or our institutional system save our proclivity to waste time in attacking or defending it and to neglect proper tasks of changing it continuously by wise collective experimentation.

### Democracy Versus Syndicalism

EFFECTIVE COMPETITION is indispensable for adequate dispersion of power within industries and functional groups. The antithesis of a competitive economy is not socialism but syndicalism. It is, to repeat, one of the deep anomalies of socialism that its political strength derives mainly from highly syndicalist labor organizations. Syndicalist organization is equally incompatible with democratic socialism and libertarian democracy and, indeed, inherently incompatible with order. It bars both concentration and dispersion of power.

All monopoly or bargaining power implies special privilege to limit production, to restrict entry into industries or occupations, and thereby to levy tribute upon the whole community. As an actual present evil, it involves a concentration of power that has little relation to the concentration of personal wealth.

In one aspect it is a matter of uncontrolled corporate imperialism and giant enterprise aggregations. The profligate dispensation of privileges under incorporation laws may have accelerated the industrialization of America. Existing corporation laws may have been somewhat appropriate to an agricultural nation bent on rapid change. They may, by their extravagances, have accelerated progress. But they are surely ill designed to sustain progress or tolerable operation of the economy they promoted. Turned loose with inordinate powers, corporations have vastly overorganized most industries. Having perhaps benefited briefly by corporate organization, America might now be better off if the corporate form had never been invented or never made available to private enterprise.

A heritage of excessive centralization may be a necessary or reasonable price to pay for rapid maturing of new industries and new technology — and the same may be true of some desirable new governmental functions or services. In any case, America should face now an urgent task of deorganizing industry and deconcentrating industrial control. Some direct dismantling of corporate empires seems indispensable. The main concern of policy, however, should be that of facilitating new enterprise and multiplication of moderate-sized firms. There are grave productional diseconomies in giant enterprises; but these are compensated by larger artificial, private "economies" which wise public policy may and should cut away. Notable are the "economies" of national advertising and vast sales organizations (a problem of consumer education, consumer-goods standards, and technical information), of differential access to technical knowledge (patent-pooling and research), and differential access to new capital funds (inordinate centralization of securities markets). All these merely private advantages of great, monopolistic size present challenges which can be met. Reasonable access to markets, to technology, and to capital funds, on the part of new and moderate-sized firms, would mean an end of serious enterprise monopoly.

Industrial monopolies are not yet a serious evil. Their organization is largely superficial; their powers, with rare exceptions, are very limited and precariously held; they tend to fall apart, though too slowly, in spite of policy. Their menace remains largely potential and complementary. In a community bent on preserving libertarian democracy, enterprise monopolies, standing alone, would be diagnosed as a simple skin disease and easily remedied.

The hard monopoly problem is labor organization. Here are monopolies, actual and imminent, with really great power, economic, political, and military. Once grown large, they cannot easily be taken apart like enterprise aggregations. Like corporations and up to about the same size or scale, unions have real social uses — which may outweigh abuses. But their size potentials and their appetites for power exceed even those of business corporations. Organized like armies rather than like businesses, and encountering no productional diseconomies of size because they produce nothing, they tend to absorb all competitors and to use power zealously and overtly while any eligible workers remain outside. Their size tendencies, moreover, are almost unamenable to the check of law or governmental policy. There would appear to be no stable or attainable happy mean. Strong labor organizations either die aborning or grow into intolerable monopolies. Moreover, labor monopolies and enterprise monopolies are ominously complementary; each tends to foster and to strengthen the other, fighting togeth-er to maximize joint exactions from the public while also fighting each other over division of the spoils.

Libertarians can offer no specific for the affliction of labor monopoly. They may propose to deal intelligently with other problems, in the hope that this one may somehow be mitigated or rendered less intractable by progress on other fronts.

An awful question here, as in the case of tariffs and other producer subsidies, is the capacity of democracy to protect the common interest or general welfare against organized minorities. Labor organization presents the hardest of the tests which democracy must meet. It can hardly meet this severest test unless it improves its record in dealing with other minorities as beneficiaries of promiscuous vote-buying and as usurpers of the coercion which all private restraint of trade involves. The old easy tests were matters of obvious corruption — government buying off groups with votes to sell. The hard test ahead involves all this plus a contest for power with organizations whose capacity for violence and coercion rivals that of the state itself. Under modern division of labor, any one of many large organizations of workers can stop or seriously disrupt the whole production process; such coercive power, resting fundamentally on violence, is an abuse (indeed, a negation) of freedom of association, which freedom must be limited by prohibition of monopoly as well as by prohibition of private armies. Here is the perennial problem of pressure groups developing into threat of civil war — the state monopoly of violence so impaired that no remedy compatible with democratic government is readily available.

### Inequality and Syndicalism

THE MODERN PROBLEM of inequality largely and progressively ceases to be a problem of ordinary property or personal wealth. Already it is overwhelmingly a problem of acquired status within organizations — parties, factions, civil service, giant corporations, labor unions, and farm organizations — and of differential access to high salaries and power. Only deorganization of extra-governmental, functional "states," along with decentralization of government, offers solution for such inequality. Otherwise, our society must offer superlative rewards of power and income to those few whose task it is to hold together organizations that should not exist — and that draw its ablest or most aggressive citizens into essentially antisocial activities. Libertarian society, with its multitude of small organizations, offers a field for millions of leaders and the prospect of moderate power differences among officials within organizations. It places a premium on personal qualities and skills which are, at worst, not grossly unbecoming to men and may properly be cultivated in the good society. It protects men from the corruption of great power by dispersing power, by avoiding large organizations outside government, and by limiting severely the exercise of power by large governmental units. In government the power of men may be limited by constitutional-conventional rules; outside, the power of men within organizations may be limited by keeping organizations loose or small. The best single device, in business organization, is to limit the power of officials by keeping their organizations under the severe discipline of competition. Moreover, wars apart, the need for exercise of central-government power varies progressively with the size and power of extra-governmental organizations. Extreme federalism becomes easiest when there are no strong extra-governmental "states."

### Prospective Changes in "Property"

LIBERTARIAN POLICY CONTEMPLATES a scheme of property law which is both stable and flexible and which, even with prompt excision of archaic elements, becomes more and more complex. There is, and always will be, obvious need for substantial changes. Our progressive personal taxes remain needlessly crude, full of loopholes, and inequitable among persons in similar real circumstances. They can easily be made more equitable, more effective in curtailing inequality of income and opportunity, and at the same time less injurious to desirable incentives. There is need for new arrangements regarding property in fugacious materials, notably oil; for reconsideration of property rights in knowledge, technology, and names; for wise experiments with laws concerning farm tenancy and urban housing; etc.

The time is more than ripe for undoing most of the complexity in property that modern corporations, and finance corporations especially, have imposed. In the good society private property would consist almost exclusively of claims against government (money and consols), unincumbered titles to tangible assets, and homogeneous equities in enterprises — together with the inevitable minimum of accounts in process of (quick) collection and of interpersonal debts. Interest-bearing government debt should be issued, if at all, only in consol form, should rise only during grave war emergencies, and should be retired rapidly thereafter. Net returns from personal wealth normally should accrue only to owners of tangible assets and to pure proprietors, partners, and common shareholders in riskful enterprises.

The problem here, to repeat, is mainly one of corporation finance, of corporate issue powers, and of financial corporations, notably banks. The recent trend in business finance has turned sharply and surely in the right direction and largely in spite of governmental policy. The policy task is thus a fairly simple one, first, of getting out of the way (e.g., by tax reform) and, second, of guiding and accelerating a trend already well established. The goal, while wisely attainable only by gradualist measures, is fairly clear: an economy where the securities of private corporations consist exclusively of common stocks, where financial corporations exist only as pure investment trusts (highly localized as to both portfolios and shareholders), and where only pure investment-trust corporations are permitted to own securities of other corporations.

Libertarian policy also calls for a currency of stable purchasing power, that is, for firm, conventional rules of fiscal policy calculated to prevent aberrations of inflation or deflation. No advanced nation has ever had a good monetary system or the financial structure and institutions necessary to stable employment and orderly economic progress. Only with firm monetary stabilization and minimal monetary uncertainty can the best potentialities of the libertarian political-economic system be released; and, incidentally, stabilization of our currency is perhaps the largest single contribution America can make to the progress of international organization.

---

101.

## Harry S. Truman: Civil Rights Message

*President Truman devoted considerable attention to the problem of civil rights for Negroes and other persecuted minorities. Following the Committee on Civil Rights report of 1947, Truman recommended congressional action to implement the committee's recommendations. On February 2, 1948, the President presented to Congress his first major civil rights program. Though Congress remained on the whole unresponsive, the program was influential in emphasizing the urgency of civil rights and in laying out the guidelines for later legislation. The President's message is reprinted here in part.*

Source: 80 Congress, 2 Session, House Document No. 516.

TODAY THE AMERICAN PEOPLE enjoy more freedom and opportunity than ever before. Never in our history has there been better reason to hope for the complete realization of the ideals of liberty and equality.

We shall not, however, finally achieve the ideals for which this nation was founded so long as any American suffers discrimination as a result of his race, or religion, or color, or the land of origin of his forefathers.

Unfortunately there still are examples — flagrant examples — of discrimination which are utterly contrary to our ideals. Not all groups of our population are free from the fear of violence. Not all groups are free to live and work where they please or to improve their conditions of life by their own efforts. Not all groups enjoy the full privileges of citizenship and participation in the government under which they live.

We cannot be satisfied until all our people have equal opportunities for jobs, for homes, for education, for health, and for political expression, and until all our people have equal protection under the law.

One year ago I appointed a committee of fifteen distinguished Americans and asked them to appraise the condition of our civil rights and to recommend appropriate action by federal, state, and local governments.

The committee's appraisal has resulted in a frank and revealing report. This report emphasizes that our basic human freedoms are better cared for and more vigilantly defended than ever before, but it also makes clear that there is a serious gap between our ideals and some of our practices. This gap must be closed.

This will take the strong efforts of each of us individually, and all of us acting together through voluntary organizations and our governments.

The protection of civil rights begins with the mutual respect for the rights of others, which all of us should practise in our daily lives. Through organizations in every community — in all parts of the country — we must continue to develop practical, workable arrangements for achieving greater tolerance and brotherhood.

The protection of civil rights is the duty of every government which derives its powers from the consent of the people. This is equally true of local, state, and national governments. There is much that the states can and should do at this time to extend their protection of civil rights. Wherever the law-enforcement measures of state and local governments are inadequate to discharge this primary function of government, these measures should be strengthened and improved.

The federal government has a clear duty to see that constitutional guarantees of individual liberties and of equal protection under the laws are not denied or abridged anywhere in our Union. That duty is shared by all three branches of the government, but it can be fulfilled only if the Congress enacts modern, comprehensive civil rights laws, adequate to the needs of the day, and demonstrating our continuing faith in the free way of life.

I recommend, therefore, that the Congress enact legislation at this session directed toward the following specific objectives:

1. Establishing a permanent Commission on Civil Rights, a Joint Congressional Committee on Civil Rights, and a Civil Rights Division in the Department of Justice.

2. Strengthening existing civil rights statutes.

3. Providing federal protection against lynching.

4. Protecting more adequately the right to vote.

5. Establishing a Fair Employment Practice Commission to prevent unfair discrimination in employment.

6. Prohibiting discrimination in interstate transportation facilities.

7. Providing home rule and suffrage in presidential elections for the residents of the District of Columbia.

8. Providing statehood for Hawaii and Alaska and a greater measure of self-government for our island possessions.

9. Equalizing the opportunities for residents of the United States to become naturalized citizens.

10. Settling the evacuation claims of Japanese-Americans. . . .

The legislation I have recommended for enactment by the Congress at the present session is a minimum program if the federal government is to fulfill its obligation of insuring the constitutional guarantees of individual liberties and of equal protection under the law.

Under the authority of existing law the executive branch is taking every possible action to improve the enforcement of the civil rights statutes and to eliminate discrimination in federal employment, in providing federal services and facilities, and in the armed forces.

I have already referred to the establishment of the Civil Rights Division of the Department of Justice. The Federal Bureau of Investigation will work closely with this new division in the investigation of federal civil rights cases. Specialized training is being given to the Bureau's agents so that they may render more effective service in this difficult field of law enforcement.

It is the settled policy of the United

States government that there shall be no discrimination in federal employment or in providing federal services and facilities. Steady progress has been made toward this objective in recent years. I shall shortly issue an executive order containing a comprehensive restatement of the federal nondiscrimination policy, together with appropriate measures to ensure compliance.

During the recent war and in the years since its close, we have made much progress toward equality of opportunity in our armed services without regard to race, color, religion, or national origin. I have instructed the secretary of defense to take steps to have the remaining instances of discrimination in the armed services eliminated as rapidly as possible. The personnel policies and practices of all the services in this regard will be made consistent.

I have instructed the secretary of the army to investigate the status of civil rights in the Panama Canal Zone with a view to eliminating such discrimination as may exist there. If legislation is necessary, I shall make appropriate recommendations to the Congress. . . .

The position of the United States in the world today makes it especially urgent that we adopt these measures to secure for all our people their essential rights.

The peoples of the world are faced with the choice of freedom or enslavement, a choice between a form of government which harnesses the state in the service of the individual and a form of government which chains the individual to the needs of the state.

We in the United States are working in company with other nations who share our desire for enduring world peace and who believe with us that, above all else, men must be free. We are striving to build a world family of nations — a world where men may live under governments of their own choosing and under laws of their own making.

As part of that endeavor, the Commission on Human Rights of the United Nations is now engaged in preparing an international bill of human rights by which the nations of the world may bind themselves by international covenant to give effect to basic human rights and fundamental freedoms. We have played a leading role in this undertaking designed to create a world order of law and justice fully protective of the rights and the dignity of the individual.

To be effective in these efforts, we must protect our civil rights so that by providing all our people with the maximum enjoyment of personal freedom and personal opportunity we shall be a stronger nation — stronger in our leadership, stronger in our moral position, stronger in the deeper satisfactions of a united citizenry.

We know that our democracy is not perfect. But we do know that it offers a fuller, freer, happier life to our people than any totalitarian nation has ever offered.

If we wish to inspire the peoples of the world whose freedom is in jeopardy, if we wish to restore hope to those who have already lost their civil liberties, if we wish to fulfill the promise that is ours, we must correct the remaining imperfections in our practice of democracy.

We know the way. We need only the will.

102.

# Harry S. Truman: Desegregation of the Armed Forces

*Even after World War II the armed forces were still racially segregated. But the notable accomplishments of Negro soldiers in the war, as well as the sense of equality they had enjoyed while off-duty in Europe, led many Negroes to protest against this discrimination. A. Philip Randolph and other Negro leaders began to make plans for a mass civil disobedience campaign against the draft unless Negro demands for integration were met. On July 26, 1948, President Truman issued the following executive order establishing a committee to report on racial conditions in the armed forces and recommend ways to promote integration. The committee's report,* Freedom to Serve, *published in May 1950, was in large measure implemented during the Korean War.*

Source: *Code of Federal Regulations,* Title 3 — The President, 1943-1948 Compilation, Washington, 1957, p. 772.

*Establishing the President's Committee on Equality of Treatment and Opportunity in the Armed Services*

*Whereas* it is essential that there be maintained in the armed services of the United States the highest standards of democracy, with equality of treatment and opportunity for all those who serve in our country's defense:

*Now, Therefore,* by virtue of the authority vested in me as President of the United States by the Constitution and the statutes of the United States, and as Commander in Chief of the armed services, it is hereby ordered as follows:

1. It is hereby declared to be the policy of the President that there shall be equality of treatment and opportunity for all persons in the armed services without regard to race, color, religion, or national origin. This policy shall be put into effect as rapidly as possible, having due regard to the time re-quired to effectuate any necessary changes without impairing efficiency or morale.

2. There shall be created in the national military establishment an advisory committee to be known as the President's Committee on Equality of Treatment and Opportunity in the Armed Services, which shall be composed of seven members to be designated by the President.

3. The committee is authorized on behalf of the President to examine into the rules, procedures, and practices of the armed services in order to determine in what respect such rules, procedures and practices may be altered or improved with a view to carrying out the policy of this order. The committee shall confer and advise with the secretary of defense, the secretary of the Army, the secretary of the Navy, and the secretary of the Air Force, and shall make such recommendations to the President and to said secretaries as in the judgment of the committee will effectuate the policy hereof.

4. All executive departments and agencies of the federal government are authorized and directed to cooperate with the committee in its work, and to furnish the committee such information or the services of such persons as the committee may require in the performance of its duties.

5. When requested by the committee to do so, persons in the armed services or in any of the executive departments and agencies of the federal government shall testify before the committee and shall make available for the use of the committee such documents and other information as the committee may require.

6. The committee shall continue to exist until such time as the President shall terminate its existence by executive order.

---

## 103.

# Universal Declaration of Human Rights

*One of the purposes of the United Nations, as stated in its Charter, was "to reaffirm faith in fundamental human rights." In January 1947 the United Nations Commission on Human Rights convened to draw up a statement implementing this aim. Mr. Mora, the delegate from Uruguay, declared: "The traditional bills of rights have a national character. It seems to me that in the twentieth century we must emphasize the international human rights . . . so that human beings might receive a certain degree of what we might almost call world citizenship." The commission drafted, after long debate, the following Universal Declaration of Human Rights, which was adopted by the United Nations General Assembly on December 10, 1948.*

Source: *Yearbook of the United Nations, 1948-49,* New York, 1950, pp. 535-537.

### PREAMBLE

*Whereas* recognition of the inherent dignity and of the equal and inalienable rights of all members of the human family is the foundation of freedom, justice, and peace in the world,

*Whereas* disregard and contempt for human rights have resulted in barbarous acts which have outraged the conscience of mankind, and the advent of a world in which human beings shall enjoy freedom of speech and belief and freedom from fear and want has been proclaimed as the highest aspiration of the common people,

*Whereas* it is essential, if man is not to be compelled to have recourse, as a last resort, to rebellion against tyranny and oppression, that human rights should be protected by the rule of law,

*Whereas* it is essential to promote the development of friendly relations between nations,

*Whereas* the peoples of the United Nations have in the Charter reaffirmed their faith in fundamental human rights, in the dignity and worth of the human person, and in the equal rights of men and women and have determined to promote social progress and better standards of life in larger freedom,

*Whereas* Member States have pledged themselves to achieve, in cooperation with the United Nations, the promotion of universal respect for and observance of human rights and fundamental freedoms,

*Whereas* a common understanding of these rights and freedoms is of the greatest importance for the full realization of this pledge,

*Now, therefore, the General Assembly proclaims* this Universal Declaration of Human Rights as a common standard of achievement for all peoples and all nations, to the end that every individual and every organ of society, keeping this Declaration constantly in mind, shall strive by teaching and education to promote respect for these rights and freedoms and by progressive measures, national and international, to secure their universal and effective recognition and observance, both among the peoples of Member States themselves and among the peoples of territories under their jurisdiction.

## ARTICLE 1

All human beings are born free and equal in dignity and rights. They are endowed with reason and conscience and should act towards one another in a spirit of brotherhood.

## ARTICLE 2

Everyone is entitled to all the rights and freedoms set forth in this Declaration, without distinction of any kind, such as race, color, sex, language, religion, political or other opinion, national or social origin, property, birth, or other status.

Furthermore, no distinction shall be made on the basis of the political, jurisdictional, or international status of the country or territory to which a person belongs, whether it be independent, trust, non-self-governing or under any other limitation of sovereignty.

## ARTICLE 3

Everyone has the right to life, liberty, and the security of person.

## ARTICLE 4

No one shall be held in slavery or servitude; slavery and the slave trade shall be prohibited in all their forms.

## ARTICLE 5

No one shall be subjected to torture or to cruel, inhuman, or degrading treatment or punishment.

## ARTICLE 6

Everyone has the right to recognition everywhere as a person before the law.

## ARTICLE 7

All are equal before the law and are entitled without any discrimination to equal protection of the law. All are entitled to equal protection against any discrimination in violation of this Declaration and against any incitement to such discrimination.

## ARTICLE 8

Everyone has the right to an effective remedy by the competent national tribunals for acts violating the fundamental rights granted him by the constitution or by law.

## ARTICLE 9

No one shall be subjected to arbitrary arrest, detention, or exile.

## ARTICLE 10

Everyone is entitled in full equality to a fair and public hearing by an independent and impartial tribunal, in the determination of his rights and obligations and of any criminal charge against him.

## ARTICLE 11

1. Everyone charged with a penal offense has the right to be presumed innocent until proved guilty according to law in a public trial at which he has had all the guarantees necessary for his defense.

2. No one shall be held guilty of any penal offense on account of any act or omis-

sion which did not constitute a penal offense, under national or international law, at the time when it was committed. Nor shall a heavier penalty be imposed than the one that was applicable at the time the penal offense was committed.

## ARTICLE 12

No one shall be subjected to arbitrary interference with his privacy, family, home or correspondence, nor to attacks upon his honor and reputation. Everyone has the right to the protection of the law against such interference or attacks.

## ARTICLE 13

1. Everyone has the right to freedom of movement and residence within the borders of each State.

2. Everyone has the right to leave any country, including his own, and to return to his country.

## ARTICLE 14

1. Everyone has the right to seek and to enjoy in other countries asylum from persecution.

2. This right may not be invoked in the case of prosecutions genuinely arising from nonpolitical crimes or from acts contrary to the purposes and principles of the United Nations.

## ARTICLE 15

1. Everyone has the right to [his own] nationality.

2. No one shall be arbitrarily deprived of his nationality nor denied the right to change his nationality.

## ARTICLE 16

1. Men and women of full age, without any limitation due to race, nationality, or religion, have the right to marry and to found a family. They are entitled to equal rights as to marriage, during marriage, and at its dissolution.

2. Marriage shall be entered into only with the free and full consent of the intending spouses.

3. The family is the natural and fundamental group unit of society and is entitled to protection by society and the State.

## ARTICLE 17

1. Everyone has the right to own property alone as well as in association with others.

2. No one shall be arbitrarily deprived of his property.

## ARTICLE 18

Everyone has the right to freedom of thought, conscience, and religion; this right includes freedom to change his religion or belief, and freedom, either alone or in community with others and in public or private, to manifest his religion or belief in teaching, practice, worship, and observance.

## ARTICLE 19

Everyone has the right to freedom of opinion and expression; this right includes freedom to hold opinions without interference and to seek, receive, and impart information and ideas through any media and regardless of frontiers.

## ARTICLE 20

1. Everyone has the right to freedom of peaceful assembly and association.

2. No one may be compelled to belong to an association.

## ARTICLE 21

1. Everyone has the right to take part in the government of his country, directly or through freely chosen representatives.

2. Everyone has the right of equal access to public service in his country.

3. The will of the people shall be the basis of the authority of government; this will shall be expressed in periodic and genuine elections which shall be by universal and equal suffrage and shall be held by secret

vote or by equivalent free voting procedures.

## ARTICLE 22

Everyone, as a member of society, has the right to social security and is entitled to realization, through national effort and international cooperation and in accordance with the organization and resources of each State, of the economic, social, and cultural rights indispensable for his dignity and the free development of his personality.

## ARTICLE 23

1. Everyone has the right to work, to free choice of employment, to just and favorable conditions of work, and to protection against unemployment.

2. Everyone, without any discrimination, has the right to equal pay for equal work.

3. Everyone who works has the right to just and favorable remuneration ensuring for himself and his family an existence worthy of human dignity, and supplemented, if necessary, by other means of social protection.

4. Everyone has the right to form and to join trade unions for the protection of his interests.

## ARTICLE 24

Everyone has the right to rest and leisure, including reasonable limitation of working hours and periodic holidays with pay.

## ARTICLE 25

1. Everyone has the right to a standard of living adequate for the health and well-being of himself and of his family, including food, clothing, housing, and medical care and necessary social services, and the right to security in the event of unemployment, sickness, disability, widowhood, old age, or other lack of livelihood in circumstances beyond his control.

2. Motherhood and childhood are entitled to special care and assistance. All children, whether born in or out of wedlock, shall enjoy the same social protection.

## ARTICLE 26

1. Everyone has the right to education. Education shall be free, at least in the elementary and fundamental stages. Elementary education shall be compulsory. Technical and professional education shall be made generally available and higher education shall be equally accessible to all on the basis of merit.

2. Education shall be directed to the full development of the human personality and to the strengthening of respect for human rights and fundamental freedoms. It shall promote understanding, tolerance, and friendship among all nations, racial or religious groups, and shall further the activities of the United Nations for the maintenance of peace.

3. Parents have a prior right to choose the kind of education that shall be given to their children.

## ARTICLE 27

1. Everyone has the right freely to participate in the cultural life of the community, to enjoy the arts and to share in scientific advancement and its benefits.

2. Everyone has the right to the protection of the moral and material interests resulting from any scientific, literary, or artistic production of which he is the author.

## ARTICLE 28

Everyone is entitled to a social and international order in which the rights and freedoms set forth in this Declaration can be fully realized.

## ARTICLE 29

1. Everyone has duties to the community in which alone the free and full development of his personality is possible.

2. In the exercise of his rights and freedoms, everyone shall be subject only to such limitations as are determined by law solely for the purpose of securing due rec-

ognition and respect for the rights and freedoms of others and of meeting the just requirements of morality, public order, and
the general welfare in a democratic society.

3. These rights and freedoms may in no
case be exercised contrary to the purposes
and principles of the United Nations.

ARTICLE 30

Nothing in this Declaration may be interpreted as implying for any State, group, or
person any right to engage in any activity
or to perform any act aimed at the destruction of any of the rights and freedoms set
forth herein.

---

104.

## ARTHUR H. VANDENBERG: Collective Security Within the United Nations

*By the spring of 1948 the ideological, or Cold War between the Communist bloc and
the Western democracies was well under way. The Russians had denounced the
Marshall Plan as an act of "American imperialism," had established the Cominform
as an agency for the spread of international Communism, and had formed defensive
alliances with their Eastern European satellites. In April the Russians launched the
first in a series of moves intended to oust the Allies from Berlin. The American
response came in the form of the Vandenberg Resolution, presented to Congress on
May 19, which urged the establishment of defensive alliances among the Western
powers. The Resolution, approved by the Senate on June 11, paved the way for the
North Atlantic Treaty Organization.*

Source: *Record,* 80 Cong., 2 Sess., pp. 6053-6054.

*Whereas* peace with justice and the defense of human rights and fundamental
freedoms require international cooperation
through more effective use of the United
Nations: Therefore be it

*Resolved,* that the Senate reaffirm the policy of the United States to achieve international peace and security through the
United Nations, so that armed force shall
not be used except in the common interest,
and that the President be advised of the
sense of the Senate that this government,
by constitutional process, should particularly
pursue the following objectives within the
United Nations Charter:

1. Voluntary agreement to remove the
veto from all questions involving pacific settlements of international disputes and situations, and from the admission of new members.

2. Progressive development of regional
and other collective arrangements for individual and collective self-defense in accordance with the purposes, principles, and
provisions of the Charter.

3. Association of the United States, by
constitutional process, with such regional
and other collective arrangements as are
based on continuous and effective self-help
and mutual aid, and as affect its national
security.

4. Contributing to the maintenance of
peace by making clear its determination to
exercise the right of individual or collective

self-defense under Article 51 should any armed attack occur affecting its national security.

5. Maximum efforts to obtain agreements to provide the United Nations with armed forces as provided by the Charter, and to obtain agreement among member nations upon universal regulation and reduction of armaments under adequate and dependable guarantee against violation.

6. If necessary, after adequate effort toward strengthening the United Nations, review of the Charter at an appropriate time by a general conference called under Article 109 or by the General Assembly.

---

105.

## Albert Einstein: An Open Letter to Russian Colleagues

*World government was advanced as a solution to the problem of the control of atomic weapons by a number of American scientists at a time — the late 1940s — when the United States still enjoyed a monopoly of such weapons. The Russians, who were doing their best to catch up in the arms race, interpreted any such suggestions as further evidence of America's alleged desire to dominate the world. Albert Einstein was the best-known advocate of world government in the American scientific community. A group of Soviet scientists attacked his idea of a "universal state" as an aggressive move on the part of "international capitalism," and Einstein replied to these charges in a letter of February 1948 that is reprinted here.*

Source: *The Atomic Age*, Morton Grodzins and Eugene Rabinowitch, eds., New York, 1963, pp. 130-134.

FOUR OF MY RUSSIAN COLLEAGUES have published a benevolent attack upon me in an open letter carried by the *New Times*. I appreciate the effort they have made, and I appreciate even more the fact that they have expressed their point of view so candidly and straightforwardly. To act intelligently in human affairs is possible only if an attempt is made to understand the thoughts, motives, and apprehensions of one's opponent so fully that one can see the world through his eyes. All well-meaning people should try to contribute as much as possible to improving such mutual understanding. It is in this spirit that I should like to ask my Russian colleagues and any other readers to accept the following answer to their letter. It is the reply of a man who anxiously tries to find a feasible solution without having the illusion that he himself knows "the truth" or "the right path" to follow. If in the following I express my views somewhat dogmatically, I do it only for the sake of clarity and simplicity.

Although your letter, in the main, is clothed in an attack upon the nonsocialistic foreign countries, particularly the United States, I believe that behind the aggressive front there lies a defensive mental attitude which is nothing else but the trend toward an almost unlimited isolationism. The escape into isolationism is not difficult to understand if one realizes what Russia has suffered at the hands of foreign countries during the last three decades — the German invasions with planned mass murder of the

Dr. Albert Einstein

civilian population, foreign interventions during the civil war, the systematic campaign of calumnies in the Western press, the support of Hitler as an alleged tool to fight Russia. However understandable this desire for isolation may be, it remains no less disastrous to Russia and to all other nations; I shall say more about it later on.

The chief object of your attack against me concerns my support of "world government." I should like to discuss this important problem only after having said a few words about the antagonism between socialism and capitalism, for your attitude on the significance of this antagonism seems to dominate completely your views on international problems. If the socioeconomic problem is considered objectively, it appears as follows: Technological development has led to increasing centralization of the economic mechanism. It is this development which is also responsible for the fact that economic power in all widely industrialized countries has become concentrated in the hands of relatively few. These people, in capitalist countries, do not need to account for their actions to the public as a whole; they must do so in socialist countries, in which they are civil servants similar to those who exercise political power.

I share your view that a socialist economy possesses advantages which definitely counterbalance its disadvantages whenever the management lives up, at least to some extent, to adequate standards. No doubt, the day will come when all nations (as far as such nations still exist) will be grateful to Russia for having demonstrated, for the first time, by vigorous action the practical possibility of planned economy in spite of exceedingly great difficulties. I also believe that capitalism, or, we should say, the system of free enterprise, will prove unable to check unemployment, which will become increasingly chronic because of technological progress, and unable to maintain a healthy balance between production and the purchasing power of the people.

On the other hand, we should not make the mistake of blaming capitalism for all existing social and political evils, and of assuming that the very establishment of socialism would be able to cure all the social and political ills of humanity. The danger of such a belief lies, first, in the fact that it encourages fanatical intolerance on the part of all the "faithfuls" by making a possible social method into a type of church which brands all those who do not belong to it as traitors or as nasty evildoers. Once this stage has been reached, the ability to understand the convictions and actions of the "unfaithfuls" vanishes completely. You know, I am sure, from history how much unnecessary suffering such rigid beliefs have inflicted upon mankind.

Any government is in itself an evil insofar as it carries within it the tendency to deteriorate into tyranny. However, except for a very small number of anarchists, every one of us is convinced that civilized society cannot exist without a government. In a healthy nation there is a kind of dynamic balance between the will of the people and the government which prevents its degeneration into tyranny. It is obvious that the danger of such deterioration is more acute in a country in which the government has authority not only over the armed forces but also over all the channels of education and information as well as over the economic existence of every single citizen. I say this merely to indicate that socialism as such cannot be considered the solution to all social problems but merely as a framework within which such a solution is possible.

What has surprised me most in your general attitude, expressed in your letter, is the following aspect: You are such passionate opponents of anarchy in the economic sphere, and yet equally passionate advocates of anarchy, *e.g.*, unlimited sovereignty, in the sphere of international politics. The proposition to curtail the sovereignty of individual states appears to you in itself reprehensible, as a kind of violation of a natural right. In addition, you try to prove that behind the idea of curtailing sovereignty the United States is hiding her intention of economic domination and exploitation of the rest of the world without going to war. You attempt to justify this indictment by analyzing in your fashion the individual actions of this government since the end of the last war. You attempt to show that the Assembly of the United Nations is a mere puppet show controlled by the United States and hence the American capitalists.

Such arguments impress me as a kind of mythology; they are not convincing. They make obvious, however, the deep estrangement among the intellectuals of our two countries which is the result of a regrettable and artificial mutual isolation. If a free personal exchange of views should be made possible and should be encouraged, the intellectuals, possibly more than anyone else, could help to create an atmosphere of mutual understanding between the two nations and their problems. Such an atmosphere is a necessary prerequisite for the fruitful development of political cooperation. However, since for the time being we depend upon the cumbersome method of "open letters" I shall want to indicate briefly my reaction to your arguments.

Nobody would want to deny that the influence of the economic oligarchy upon all branches of our public life is very powerful. This influence, however, should not be overestimated. Franklin Delano Roosevelt was elected President in spite of desperate opposition by these very powerful groups and was reelected three times; and this took place at a time when decisions of great consequence had to be made.

Concerning the policies of the American government since the end of the war, I am neither willing, nor able, nor entitled to justify or explain them. It cannot be denied, however, that the suggestions of the American government with regard to atomic weapons represented at least an attempt toward the creation of a supranational security organization. If they were not acceptable, they could at least have served as a basis of discussion for a real solution of the problems of international security. It is, indeed, the attitude of the Soviet government that was partly negative and partly dilatory which has made it so difficult for well-meaning people in this country to use their political influence as they would have wanted, and to oppose the "warmongers." With regard to the influence of the United States upon the United Nations Assembly, I wish to say that, in my opinion, it stems not only from the economic and military power of the United States but also from the efforts of the United States and the United Nations to lead toward a genuine solution of the security problem.

Concerning the controversial veto power, I believe that the efforts to eliminate it or to make it ineffective have their primary cause less in specific intentions of the United States than in the manner in which the veto privilege has been abused.

Let me come now to your suggestion that the policy of the United States seeks to obtain economic domination and exploitation of other nations. It is a precarious undertaking to say anything reliable about aims and intentions. Let us rather examine the objective factors involved. The United States is fortunate in producing all the important industrial products and foods in her own country, in sufficient quantities. The country also possesses almost all important raw materials. Because of her tenacious belief in "free enterprise" she cannot succeed in keeping the purchasing power of the people in balance with the productive capacity of the country. For these very same reasons there is a constant danger that unemployment will reach threatening dimensions.

Because of these circumstances the United States is compelled to emphasize her export trade. Without it, she could not permanently keep her total productive machinery fully utilized. These conditions would not be harmful if the exports were balanced by imports of about the same value. Exploitation of foreign nations would then consist in the fact that the labor value of imports would considerably exceed that of exports. However, every effort is being made to avoid this since almost every import would make a part of the productive machinery idle.

This is why foreign countries are not able to pay for the export commodities of the United States, payment which, in the long run, would indeed be possible only through imports by the latter. This explains why a large portion of all the gold has come to the United States. On the whole, this gold cannot be utilized except for the purchase of foreign commodities, which, because of the reasons already stated, is not practicable. There it lies, this gold, carefully protected against theft, a monument to governmental wisdom and to economic science! The reasons which I have just indicated make it difficult for me to take the alleged exploitation of the world by the United States very seriously.

However, the situation just described has a serious political facet. The United States, for the reasons indicated, is compelled to ship part of its production to foreign countries. These exports are financed through loans which the United States is granting foreign countries. It is, indeed, difficult to imagine how these loans will ever be repaid. For all practical purposes, therefore, these loans must be considered gifts which may be used as weapons in the arena of power politics. In view of the existing conditions and in view of the general characteristics of human beings, this, I frankly admit, represents a real danger. Is it not true, however, that we have stumbled into a state of international affairs which tends to make every invention of our minds and every material good into a weapon and, consequently, into a danger for mankind?

This question brings us to the most important matter, in comparison to which everything else appears insignificant indeed. We all know that power politics, sooner or later, necessarily leads to war, and that war, under present circumstances, would mean a mass destruction of human beings and material goods the dimensions of which are much, much greater than anything that has ever before happened in history.

Is it really unavoidable that, because of our passions and our inherited customs, we should be condemned to annihilate each other so thoroughly that nothing would be left over which would deserve to be conserved? Is it not true that all the controversies and differences of opinion which we have touched upon in our strange exchange of letters are insignificant pettinesses compared to the danger in which we all find ourselves? Should we not do everything in our power to eliminate the danger which threatens all nations alike?

If we hold fast to the concept and practice of unlimited sovereignty of nations it only means that each country reserves the right for itself of pursuing its objectives through warlike means. Under the circumstances, every nation must be prepared for that possibility; this means it must try with all its might to be superior to anyone else. This objective will dominate more and more our entire public life and will poison our youth long before the catastrophe is itself actually upon us. We must not tolerate this, however, as long as we still retain a tiny bit of calm reasoning and human feelings.

This alone is on my mind in supporting the idea of world government, without any regard to what other people may have in mind when working for the same objective. I advocate world government because I am convinced that there is no other possible way of eliminating the most terrible danger in which man has ever found himself. The objective of avoiding total destruction must have priority over any other objective.

I am sure you are convinced that this letter is written with all the seriousness and honesty at my command; I trust you will accept it in the same spirit.

---

106.

# House Un-American Activities Committee Report on Communism

*Since its establishment in 1938, the House Un-American Activities Committee had been engaged in investigations into the feasibility of legislation designed to outlaw, or at least hamper, the activities of the American Communist Party. On April 30, 1948, the committee reported out the Mundt-Nixon Bill, which proscribed many Communist activities but did not outlaw the party. The bill passed the House in May but failed to pass the Senate, and President Truman contended that, instead of helping in the fight against Communism, it would hamper the efforts of the FBI. Reprinted here is a portion of the committee report read by Representative Karl Mundt of South Dakota, one of the authors of the bill.*

Source: 80 Congress, 2 Session, House Report No. 1844.

THE NEED FOR LEGISLATION to control Communist activities in the United States cannot be questioned.

Ten years of investigation by the Committee on Un-American Activities and by its predecessors have established: (1) that the Communist movement in the United States is foreign-controlled; (2) that its ultimate objective with respect to the United States is to overthrow our free American institutions in favor of a Communist totalitarian dictatorship to be controlled from abroad; (3) that its activities are carried on by secret and conspiratorial methods; and (4) that its activities, both because of the alarming march of Communist forces abroad and because of the scope and nature of Communist activities here in the United States, constitute an immediate and powerful threat to the security of the United States and to the American way of life.

The conclusion that the Communist movement constitutes a threat to the security of the United States and to the American way of life is not the cry of alarmists. The Communist program of conquest

"Bringing Home the Yule Log"; cartoon by Alexander in the "Evening Bulletin," Philadelphia, 1948

through treachery, deceit, infiltration, espionage, sabotage, corruption, and terrorism has been carried out in country after country and is an ever growing threat in other countries. There is ample evidence that one of the primary objectives of the world Communist movement, directed from within the most powerful existing Communist totalitarian dictatorship, is to repeat this pattern in the United States.

There is incontrovertible evidence of the fact that the Communist Party of the United States is dominated by such totalitarian dictatorship and that it is one of the principal instrumentalities used by the world Communist movement, directed from within that totalitarian dictatorship, in its ruthless and tireless endeavor to advance the world march of communism.

The findings, which support these conclusions, and the vast quantity of evidence on which they are based, are set forth in detail in the numerous reports which this committee and its predecessors have printed and circulated. Corroboration has been supplied by independent and exhaustive research by other committees of Congress.

Concern over this threat is not limited to the legislative branch of our government. On March 17, 1948, the President asked the Congress to appropriate several billions of dollars to build up American defenses against the potential threat of the world Communist conspiracy, of which the Communist movement in the United States is a constituent element. Previously, on February 5, the attorney general, in testifying before the Legislative Subcommittee of the Committee on Un-American Activities, had stated that present laws were inadequate to deal with the subversive activities of Communist threat in the United States. To resist Communist aggression abroad and ignore it at home would be an utterly inconceivable pattern of procedure.

Concern over the Communist threat is not limited to the United States. It is mounting throughout that part of the world which still remains free. For confirmation we have only to look at the recent unprecedented steps taken by the leading nations of Western Europe toward banding together in a union, political as well as economic, which will be powerful enough to resist the Communist onslaught.

In this hemisphere the nations assembled at Bogotá, on April 22, 1948, unanimously adopted a resolution declaring that the —

> present world situation demands urgent measures to safeguard peace and defend mutual respect among states

and recommending that each participating nation —

> adopt within their respective territories and in accord with their constitutional precepts, necessary measures to prevent and uproot activities directed, assisted, or instigated by foreign governments, organizations, or individuals.

The Congress of the United States, by adopting the legislation here proposed, can set the pattern for controlling in each country the foreign-directed Communist conspiratorial activities which threaten the existence of free institutions, not only here but throughout the world. . . .

In considering the merits of the various proposals before it, the committee found that it was confronted with a most perplexing and difficult problem, one of which the framers of the Constitution could have had little conception, and one which required the most comprehensive analysis and study.

The committee approached the problem with care and restraint because it is believed essential that any legislation recommended be strictly in accordance with our constitutional traditions. How to protect freedom from those who would destroy it without infringing upon the freedom of all our people presents a question fraught with constitutional and practical difficulties. We must not mortally wound our democratic framework in attempting to protect it from those who threaten to destroy it.

There are no doubt some, whose opposition to communism is beyond question, who contend that no legislation should be adopted because of the grave constitutional questions involved. The committee believes, however, that the Constitution does not deny to the Congress the power to enact laws which will defend the nation from those who would use liberties guaranteed by the Constitution to destroy it.

In considering the problem, the committee found it necessary at the outset to distinguish those features of Communist activity against which legislation cannot and should not be directed from those in the case of which legislative restraints are clearly practicable and necessary. Communism as an economic, social, and political theory is one thing. Communism as a secret conspiracy, dedicated to subverting the interests of the United States to that of a foreign dictatorship, is another.

The committee holds no brief for the economic, social, and political theories which the Communists advocate, but we contend that, under our constitutional system, ideas must be combated with ideas and not with legislation. If communism in the United States operated in the open, without foreign direction, and without attempting to set up a dictatorship subservient to a foreign power, legislation directed against them would neither be justified nor necessary. This, however, is not the case. A careful analysis of the strategy and tactics of communism in the United States discloses activities by reason of which the committee has concluded that legislation can and should be directed toward —

1. Making unlawful all activity which has as its purpose setting up a totalitarian government in the United States under foreign control.

2. In view of its foreign-directed character, requiring the Communist movement in the United States to operate in the open rather than underground.

3. Cutting the threads which bind the international Communist conspiracy together by restricting travel of members of the American section of the world Communist movement.

4. Protecting the integrity of the government itself by denying government employment to members of the American section of the world Communist movement. . . .
The legislation herewith reported to the House contains provisions designed to accomplish the four objectives listed in the preceding paragraph.

Congress has passed several laws which were directed specifically at curbing the subversive activities of communism in the United States, but they have proved largely ineffectual in accomplishing their purpose. The Alien Registration Act in 1940 made it a crime to advocate the overthrow of the government of the United States by force and violence. While force and violence is without doubt a basic principle to which all Communist Party members subscribe, the present line of the party, in order to evade existing legislation, is to avoid wherever possible the open advocacy of force and violence. Consequently, the act has not been an effective instrument in dealing with Communist activity. The McCormack Act of 1938 required registration of individuals who are acting as agents of a foreign principal. The Voorhis Act required the registration of organizations which are agents of foreign principals.

Though these acts were directed against both Nazis and Communists, they have proved ineffective against the latter, due in part to the skill and deceit which the Communists have used in concealing their foreign ties. The attorney general pointed out some technical weaknesses in these acts in his testimony before the committee, and his recommendations have been incorporated in the registration provisions of the committee bill. The attorney general, together with a great majority of the expert witnesses who appeared before the committee during its legislative hearings, agreed that existing laws were inadequate to deal with the Communist threat and that new legislation was essential.

The committee gave serious consideration to the many well-intentioned proposals which were before it which attempted to meet the problem by outlawing the Communist Party. Proponents of this approach differed as to what they desired. Some wanted to bar the Communist Party from the ballot in elections. Others would have made membership in the Communist Party illegal per se.

The committee believes that there are several compelling arguments against the outlawing approach. There are grave constitutional questions involved in attempting to interfere with the rights of the states to declare what parties and individuals may qualify for appearance on the ballot. To make membership in a specifically designated existing organization illegal per se would run the risk of being held unconstitutional on the ground that such an action was legislative fiat.

Among the policy considerations which militate against this type of approach are the following:

1. Illegalization of the party might drive the Communist movement further underground, whereas exposure of its activities is the primary need.

2. Illegalization has not proved effective in Canada and other countries which have tried it.

3. We cannot consistently criticize the Communist governments of Europe for suppressing opposition political parties if we resort to the same totalitarian methods here.

4. If the present Communist Party severs the puppet strings by which it is manipulated from abroad, if it gives up its undercover methods, there is no reason for denying it the privilege of openly advocating its beliefs in the way in which other political parties advocate theirs. In politics as well as sports, there are certain rules of the game which must be obeyed. Daggers are out of order on the American playing field. Undercover methods and foreign direction cannot be tolerated on the political field.

This legislation does not constitute a fiat. The Communist Party of the United States is not made guilty of any offense by reason of the enactment of the provisions of this act. If, however, the Communist Party of the United States or any other party now in existence or to be formed operates in such a way that it comes within the definitions and performs activities which are proscribed under the act, then the legislation will apply to it. If such party changes its characteristics then the objectives sought by the committee will have been accomplished.

The committee wishes to emphasize that this legislation alone is not a complete answer to the Communist problem in the United States. An attack must be made upon the Communist problem on all fronts if we are to meet it successfully. It is imperative that the American people understand the true character, aims, and techniques of the Communist conspiracy. The many patriotic and fraternal organizations in the United States can be of tremendous service in developing a program of education which will inform the people of this threat. In the words of one of the outstanding witnesses before our committee:

> The people should be informed accurately and fully and continuously about the nature, activities, strategy, and tactics of communism. This educational task can be in part accomplished by qualified and concerned private citizens.

The committee has intentionally not recommended legislation which will deal with so-called theoretical communism in the United States. We are seeking rather to strike a body blow at the American cadre of the foreign-directed Communist conspiracy. We believe that if its criminal activities are prosecuted, its false fronts exposed, and its foreign assistance and direction cut away, the movement in the United States, standing alone for what it is, will be overwhelmingly defeated. We are willing to permit the theories of communism and democracy to clash in the open market place of political ideas in America, but we insist that communism not be allowed to have the unfair advantages in this conflict of the unrestricted use of illegal means, the cloak of secrecy and fraud, and the assistance and direction of a foreign Communist dictatorship.

---

107.

## Lee Hays and Walter Lowenfels: "Wasn't That A Time!"

*Strictly speaking, the McCarthy Era had not yet begun in 1948, for Joseph McCarthy did not rise to national eminence until after his speech at Wheeling, West Virginia, in February 1950. Nevertheless, the characteristics of the epoch to which the Wisconsin senator later gave his name were already evident: the suspicion of all dissent, the harrying of "liberals" as well as out-and-out Communists, the seemingly overwhelming pressures toward conformity in almost every sphere of life. Objections to this "climate of fear" were voiced by a few hardy souls, of whom Hays and Lowenfels, and their fellow folk singers in the Weavers and other groups, were notable examples. The following song, "Wasn't That A Time!" reminds its hearers that the American tradition has been revolutionary from the beginning, and expresses the belief that this tradition will win out in the end.*

### WASN'T THAT A TIME!

Our fathers bled at Valley Forge,
The snow was red with blood,
Their faith was warm at Valley Forge,
Their faith was Brotherhood.

> *Chorus:*
> Wasn't that a time!
> Wasn't that a time!
> A time to try the soul of man,
> Wasn't that a terrible time!

Brave men who fought at Gettysburg
Now lie in soldiers' graves,
But there they stemmed the rebel tide
And there the faith was saved.

The fascists came with chains and war
To prison us in hate.
And many a good man fought and died
To save the stricken faith.

And now again the madmen come
And shall our victory fail?
There is no victory in a land
Where free men go to jail.

*Second Chorus:*
Isn't this a time!
Isn't this a time!
A time to try the soul of man,
Isn't this a terrible time!

Our faith cries out they shall not pass!
We cry *no pasaran!*
We pledge our lives, our honor, all
To free this prisoned land.

*Last Chorus:*
Isn't this a time!
Isn't this a time!
A time to free the soul of man,
Isn't this a wonderful time!
Isn't this a wonderful time!

108.

# E. B. White: Sound

*In 1948 the Supreme Court agreed to review a case involving municipal restrictions on the use of sound trucks in public places. The Court ruled that the regulation in question, which had prohibited the use of sound trucks except with the permission of the chief of police, was unconstitutional because it established a constraint on freedom of speech. The following year the Court in a similar case upheld a municipal ordinance outlawing the use of all sound trucks because of the noise they made. In the interim between the two cases, humorist E. B. White published the following remarks in the* New Yorker, *dealing with the earlier case,* Saia v. New York, *and beyond that with the high level of noise in modern-day society.*

Source: *The Second Tree from the Corner,* New York, 1954.

THE SOUND TRUCK, or Free Speech on Wheels, won its first brush with the law by a close decision in the Supreme Court. We have an idea, however, that the theme of amplification is not dead and will recur in many variations. The Court found itself in a snarl; free speech became confused with free extension-of-speech, noise with ideas wrapped in noise. A sound truck, it seems to us, is not a man on a soapbox — it is Superman on a tower of suds. The distinction will eventually have to be drawn. Loud speaking is not the same thing as plain speaking; the loudspeaker piles decibel on decibel and not only is capable of disturbing the peace but through excess of volume can cause madness and death, whereas the human voice is a public nuisance only to the extent that it aggravates the normal human resentment against the whole principle of free speech. Amplified sound is already known among military men as a weapon of untried potency, and we will probably suffer from it if there is another war.

Up till now, modern man has meekly accepted the miracle of his enlarged vocal cords. He has acquiesced in jumboism. A modern baby is born amplified, for even the nursery is wired for sound and the infant's earliest cries are carried over a private distress system to the ears of its mother in the living room — along with street noises that drift in through the open nursery window. (Note to political candidates: Always park your sound truck under nursery windows and your remarks will be picked up by an interior network and carried to uneasy elders.)

One wonders, though, how much longer the human race will string along with its own electrical gifts, and how long the right to speak can remain innocent of wattage. We have a feeling that only if this issue is met will the principle of free speech survive. There are always plenty of people who are eager to stifle opinion they don't admire, and if the opinion happens to be expressed in a volume of sound that is in itself insufferable, the number of people who will want to stifle both the sound *and* the fury will greatly increase. Amplification, therefore, is something like alcohol: it can heighten our meanings, but it can also destroy our reason.

In radio it is understood that whatever else happens, there must never be a silence. This hard condition is most noticeable in the aerial forums, in which the performers are expected to offer an immediate opinion on any subject, and do. Someone must always be speaking, either the ringmaster or one of the experts. The rule seems to be: make sense if you can, but if you can't make sense say something anyway. If you listen to one of these nervous exercises in intellectual rough-and-tumble, it is plain that a large part of the effort goes simply into preventing a lull in the conversation. The Quakers take a more sensible view of silence; they accord it equal recognition with sound. We doubt that radio will ever amount to a damn as long as it is haunted by the fear of nobody speaking.

---

109.

## John Kouwenhoven: Vernacular Art

*The perennial controversy about the quality of American art was given new life by John Kouwenhoven in his study* Made in America, *published in 1948. Kouwenhoven's main thesis was stated in the Preface to the work, in which he declared that "we cannot understand either the limitations or the achievements of [American] civilization if we continue to think of it solely as the product of Western European culture, modified by the geography and the climate of the new world." Instead, Kouwenhoven maintained, we should look to the special contributions of America to the world's art — contributions that he grouped under the term "the vernacular." Portions of the first and last chapters of the book are reprinted here.*

Source: *Made in America*, New York, 1948: "Art in America" and "Stone, Steel, and Jazz."

To many Americans the arts have always seemed to have little connection with everyday life. Architecture, painting, literature, and the other arts have been regarded as rather remote things, vaguely foreign, no direct concern of ours. As a people we have been proud of American civilization and of its political and social institutions, but we have been less confident about our performance in the arts. There have been many respected American architects, painters, and poets, to be sure, but their total achievement, regarded from the conventional critical and historical points of view, has appeared to be only a somewhat crude dispersal of the western European tradition. . . .

Most historical and critical studies of the development of the arts in America have been based on some variant of John Fiske's theory of "the transit of civilization." Culture, the theory goes, is brought here from Europe by "carriers" — artists, writers, and musicians who migrate to this country from the Old World or natives who return after studying abroad. Thus American culture is regarded as an extension of western European culture, subject only to certain influences often thought of as more or less regrettable — inherent in the American environment.

The principal cramping or limiting influences to which culture has been subjected in America, according to this theory, have been the lack of leisure among a people engaged in conquering the wilderness, the gross materialism fostered by the frontier and by industrial capitalism, and the reputed anti-aesthetic bias of our Puritan intellectual inheritance. What is more, all three of these influences have been pictured as interacting with one another in a diabolic circle: Puritanism encouraging (if it did not actually breed) materialism, the frontier strengthening both, and everything conspiring to make leisure impossible.

Yet if we accept the view that American art is an integral part of a western European tradition which, in spite of national variants, is essentially a unity, we inevitably encounter a problem. On the one hand we find that although all the trends and movements and fashions of European art may be traced in work done by Americans, there is nevertheless a quality in the total sum of our painting, our architecture, our music, or our literature which is distinct from the comparative unity of tradition among the arts in the various countries of Europe. As Henry James noted, without enthusiasm, in the book which sums up the impressions he received during a visit to the United States after living abroad for almost a quarter of a century, the way things were done in America was "more different from all other native ways, taking country with country, than any of these latter are different from each other."

On the other hand, however, it is frequently said that in spite of this distinctively American element the arts have been inadequately representative of our national character. In one way or another almost everyone, native or foreign, who has commented on our artistic history has borne witness to the disparity between our achievements in the arts and in the realms of politics, economics, and social organization. . . .

Thus the theory of a transplanted culture leads us at last to the paradoxical conclusion that though art in America is American it is singularly less so than the acts and institutions which embody our history. Fruitful as the study of the interrelationship between American and European art can be, therefore, it clearly must abandon the theory that one is merely a maimed offshoot of the other. There is obviously something left out of our concept of the arts if they are unrepresentative of the civilization which produced them; for it is in the arts that a civilization most compactly and fully expresses itself. . . .

Men everywhere and at all times instinctively seek to arrange the elements of their environment in patterns of sounds, shapes, colors, and ideas which are aesthetically satisfying, and it is this instinct which underlies the creation of techniques and forms in which the creative imagination of the artist finds expression. In a given culture, such as that of western Europe, certain of these techniques and forms are more relevant than others to the life of the people, and from time to time these become institutionalized as schools of painting and sculpture, orders or styles of architecture, and types of music and literature. As long, therefore, as we are discussing a single, comparatively unified culture like that of western Europe from the Middle Ages to the Industrial Revolution, it is the tradition composed of these dominant techniques and forms which we have in mind when we talk about the arts. But in another culture, in a different kind of civilization, quite different forms and techniques might be in the ascendancy, and some of the arts which were most highly developed in western Europe might be relatively unimportant. The criteria of historical and critical judgments appropriate to the products of the western European tradition would not be adequate to the understanding or appreciation of an art produced in a different tradition. . . .

So much is pretty obvious. Yet for a hundred and fifty years the historians and critics of American culture have, in effect, been applying the established western European criteria of value to the products of a civilization which has had less and less in common with that which produced the forms and techniques from which those criteria were deduced. To the cultural achievements, and specifically to the arts, of a civilization whose dynamics originate in technology and science, they have sought to apply the standards which were appropriate to those of civilizations founded upon agriculture or handicraft commerce.

The civilization which took form in the United States during the first century after the Declaration of Independence was, more than that of any European nation, the unalloyed product of those forces which throughout the world were creating what Charles Beard calls "technological civilization": that is, a civilization founded on power-driven machinery which indefinitely multiplies the capacity for producing goods, and upheld and served by science in all its branches. At most this civilization is two hundred years old, and there has never before been any order comparable to it.

Many people, including a good many historians, like to think of the United States as having been a nation of farmers and handicrafters, relatively untouched by the so-called Industrial Revolution, during a great part of its formative period. And it is, of course, true that until about the time of the Civil War the nation's economy was predominantly based upon agriculture. But it is easy to overestimate the agrarian aspects of our early history, and it is well to be reminded that in significant respects our civilization has from the beginning been dependent upon technology.

The least mechanized of all aspects of our society — the lives of men and women on the advancing frontier — depended upon the machine-made rifles and revolvers which enabled the pioneers to kill game and outfight the Indians, upon the steamboats and railroads which opened up new country for settlement, and upon the telegraph which made rapid intercommunication possible. It was technological civilization which made it possible for our people to conquer the wilderness and which ultimately built all our continental diversities into what the Civil War made clear was an indisseverable union. And as this civilization spread westward across the New World it was free, in a way that it could not have been free in any European country, to develop with relatively little interference from the habits of mind and social conventions which had been developed in earlier civilizations, and which, like the artistic monuments they had created, persisted in Europe.

It is this fact which gives special significance to the study of American arts. As this book tries to make clear, it is not primarily because they are American that they are worth our notice. Their importance lies in the fact that because they are American, and because America is — for a number of fortuitous reasons — the only major world power to have taken form as a cultural unit in the period when technological civilization was spreading throughout the world — because of both these facts the arts in America reveal, more clearly on the whole than the arts of any other people, the nature and the meaning of modern civilization. . . .

Many Americans were aware of the need for new forms — for what they called a national literature, or art, or architecture. At first they tended to think in such nationalistic terms for the obvious reason that nationalism stood foremost in the consciousness of a people who had just fought a war for political independence. The answer to our needs seemed to many to be simply that we produce American versions of Shakespeare and paint pictures the way the European masters did — but of American subjects. Many of our early writers, on the other hand, began with a youthful determination to "forget Europe wholly," as James Russell Lowell urged in *A Fable for Critics,* and to write of native matters only, shaping their literature to the scale of the vast new continent, just as many painters like Bierstadt tried to develop an appropriate American art by simply increasing the size of their canvases. But they soon discovered that they could not forget Europe, and most of them found that they really didn't want to.

The comfortable thing to do, then, was to relax into something approximating Longfellow's ultimate assumption that since Americans were really only "English under another sky" our literature needn't be expected to differ much from theirs. Of course, he added, the English stock in America was being mixed with other nationalities, and our English thoughts and feelings would therefore be tempered by German "tenderness," Spanish "passion," and French "vivacity." But he obviously assumed that we would remain essentially English, and that all that the writer and artist need do was carry on the old traditions. After all, he concluded, "all literature, as well as all art, is the result of culture and intellectual refinement." . . .

The quest for a national tradition in this spurious sense ended inevitably in failure. But all during the early years of the Republic we, and our European critics as well, debated the question of American art as if the problem were one of cultural independence. We argued stoutly that we could achieve it; most of the Europeans who came over here to inspect the strange new Republic argued that we could not. Yet both seemed to feel that beneath the surface manifestations of our society there were the elements of an indigenous culture — something singularly and essentially non-European expressed in our everyday life. . . .

It was easy, indeed almost inevitable, in nineteenth-century America to assume that art had little relation to the affairs of everyday life. Anyone familiar with American history will recall how remote Edgar Allen Poe and Henry James found themselves from the predominant concerns of their fellow Americans. But one need not assume — as some people do — that the things which interested Poe and James were of more aesthetic importance or of greater human value than those which preoccupied their countrymen. The world from which they were remote was, after all, the world of Abraham Lincoln.

Actually the chasm between art and everyday life may well prove to have been merely one manifestation of the catastrophic split which cut right through the whole of nineteenth-century society, both here and abroad. The conflict between the new science and the traditional religion produced an apparently unbridgeable gap between what man knew and what he believed. The development of industrial capitalism tended to divorce the production and distribution of goods from the political system, thus forcing men as unregulated economic beings to commit barbarous injustices which as political beings they had to cope with in terms of an inadequate traditional system. And finally, the tradition of western European art, like that of the Church, seemed to be seriously at odds with the social forces emerging chaotically from the Industrial Revolution.

So irreconcilable have art and technology seemed that many who believe in the creative discipline of form still cut themselves off deliberately from important areas of contemporary experience. . . . For all its pseudo-scientific trappings, this is Victorian sentimentality in modern dress. So long as men persist in ordering their attitudes toward life in harmony with concepts which they merely wish were true, they will face life with emotional insecurity and dread. Only when men reckon with one another and the world in terms which take courageous account of what they *know* can they face life or death without fear.

Such wistful and perilous withdrawal from reality is evidence of a split between art and everyday life which, to many people, has seemed more complete in our generation than in any other in history. Actually that split . . . is illusory. What we really have to reckon with, at home and abroad, is a conflict between two civilizations — one maturing, the other powerless to die. If in the United States for a century and a half the arts have seemed more strikingly unrepresentative of national life than in the countries of Europe, that is because here the art forms inherited from the older culture have had to cope with the new civilization in its most uninhibited aspects. What we have overlooked is the concomitant fact that in the United States — for that same reason — the new civilization has been freest to evolve its own artistic expression. . . .

A civilization shaped by technical and industrial forces . . . working in collaboration with social and political institutions which — in spite of two world wars and a cataclysmic depression — have retained a degree of democratic equality and personal liberty unparalleled elsewhere, implies cultural values and artistic forms which are not only different from those appropriate to the agricultural and handicraft-commercial civilizations of the past, but have also originated in an altogether different way. For the process by which technological civilization has taken form has reversed that which operated in earlier cultures.

Hitherto, as Santayana pointed out in *Reason in Society* (1905), civilization has consisted in the diffusion and dilution of habits arising in privileged centers: "It has not sprung from the people; it has arisen in their midst by a variation from them, and it has afterward imposed itself on them from above." But civilization in America, insofar

as it can be identified with the vernacular influences this book has sought to define, *has* sprung from the people. What was "imposed on them from above" was the transplanted tradition of an older culture.

From the point of view of those who have been trained in the cultivated tradition, the emergence of a civilization from popular roots has been a phenomenon of dubious merit. The fear of what is often called "popular culture," in all its manifestations, is a notable feature of much historical and critical writing. To Santayana himself it seemed certain that "a state composed exclusively of such workers and peasants as make up the bulk of modern nations would be an utterly barbarous state." Indeed, those who think of culture as "the diffusion of habits arising in privileged centers" are led almost unavoidably to the conclusion reached by an anonymous writer in *Harper's* in 1928, that the future of culture in America is "clearly quite hopeless" because there is no church or aristocracy or other authority to modify or restrain what is assumed to be the human race's "natural taste for bathos." . . .

Those who might have been expected to help in the exploration of new values too often spent their time ridiculing or denouncing or lamenting what they called America's bourgeois taste. People like James Truslow Adams, whose study of the downfall of the Puritan theocracy in colonial New England should have taught him better, wrote articles urging "the upper class" to refine and elevate the middle class and not be swamped by its "obscurantist prejudices, its narrow and ignoble prepossessions, its dogmatism, self-righteousness, self-sufficiency." In an article published in a popular monthly in 1932 — after Radio City and the George Washington Bridge had both been built — one of the future editors of the *Reader's Digest* declared that anyone who looked at American architecture and manners could see that for a decade or more we had been in the throes of an "up-rising of serfs." The middle class, he an-nounced, had delusions of upper-class gran-deur to which it was giving expression in structures like the Automat restaurant up near the Bronx with its huge cathedral win-dow and elaborate vestibule, in huge, "in-sincerely magnificent" movie palaces such as New York's Roxy and Paramount, and in overelaborate business offices designed to cater to what he contemptuously called "the demand for the dignity of industrial pursuits."

That demand was real enough, and the amount of money spent in an effort to sat-isfy it is a measure of its intensity. It is cer-tainly true that there were plenty of inap-propriate guesses as to how that dignity should be expressed. But the failure to find appropriate expressions, in architecture and elsewhere, should not have been taken as evidence that the demand itself was con-temptible. The onus for buildings like the Roxy, the Gothic Automat, and the ornate business offices belonged not to those who demanded beautiful surroundings for recrea-tion and work without knowing how to achieve them, but to those who could not, or would not, share Louis Sullivan's faith that it was the architect's job to affirm that which the people really wish to affirm — namely, the best that is in them. For as Sullivan knew, "the people want true build-ings, but do not know how to get them so long as architects betray them with architec-tural phrases."

As one looks back at the twenties and thirties . . . there is something rather touching about the desperate efforts Ameri-cans made to put utilitarian architecture be-hind them and to build beautiful things. We had been effectively taught, by those who we readily agreed were our betters in aesthetic matters, that what was useful was not beautiful. The architecture of the Chica-go school — the highest manifestation of the vernacular tradition yet achieved — was

discussed by Thomas E. Tallmadge in a chapter of his 1927 history of American ar-chitecture entitled "Louis Sullivan and the Lost Cause." Such architecture was doom-ed, he said, because of its demand for origi-nality and for freedom from traditional styles. "What is the culture and genius of America?" he asked; and promptly an-swered, "It is European."

It was no wonder, then, that the ordinary citizen who wanted beauty in his dwelling frequently turned, not to the vernacular for inspiration, but to the cultivated tradition, convinced that to be beautiful a design must be both European and useless. It was in this mood that Americans built during the twenties those genial horrors that Charles Merz described in *The Great American Bandwagon*: the Italian wells that pumped no water, the Spanish balconies for houses with no rooms upstairs, and all the rest of the amiable but pointless lies of the Coral Gables era.

There were, of course, fine things being done all through this period. We were still building grain elevators and industrial plants which, as the German architect Walter Gropius had written in the *Jahrbuch des Deutschen Werkbundes* in 1913, had a natu-ral integrity deriving from their designers' independent and clear vision of these grand, impressive forms, and which were "not ob-scured by sentimental reverence for tradi-tion nor by other intellectual scruples which prostrate our contemporary European de-sign." But in the twenties this mechanical architecture, as Lewis Mumford pointed out at the time, had a vocabulary without a lit-erature. When it stepped beyond the ele-ments of its grammar — that is, when it moved from pure engineering construction ·into the field of architecture proper, it usu-ally could only "translate badly into its own tongue the noble poems and epics which the Romans and Greeks and medieval builders left behind them."

A dispassionate study of the relationships

between engineering and architecture in the twentieth century would be of great value to an understanding of our civilization. What apparently happened was that the engineers, feeling the need for something more than the purely utilitarian satisfactions which their designs provided, turned to the architects for help, while at the same time the architects, sensing the vitality of engineering construction in contrast with the sterility of traditional architecture, turned increasingly to the problems of giving architectonic expression to the forms evolved by the engineers.

Any study of these interrelationships would, to be sure, have to reckon with certain questions which are posed by such a structure as the George Washington suspension bridge across the Hudson at New York. As it stands, the bridge is concededly one of the most beautiful structures in America. Other great suspension bridges, like the Golden Gate Bridge, have more spectacular settings; but there is something about the George Washington's lofty yet sturdy towers, curving cables, and slender floor which, as the eminent bridge designer David B. Steinman said, has made this bridge, to the younger generation of Americans, a symbol of our civilization. . . . Yet, as it stands, it is unfinished; the original design worked out by the engineers and the consulting architect has never been completed.

The bridge as originally designed was the work of O. H. Amman, chief engineer; Allston Dana, engineer of design; and Cass Gilbert, architect. According to the *First Progress Report* on the bridge, issued by the Port of New York Authority January 1, 1928, the guiding motives of the design, from the engineering point of view, were "purity of type, simplicity of structural arrangement, and ease and expediency of construction" — motives which, as we have frequently observed, are characteristic of the vernacular tradition. But, the *Report* contin-

ues, in designing this bridge "it was realized that more than the usual attention must be paid to the aesthetic side," because of its monumental size and conspicuous location and because the bridge "should be handed down to posterity as a truly monumental structure, which will cast credit upon the aesthetic sense of the present generation."

Here were the reverence for tradition and the intellectual scruples which Gropius had lamented in European design, and which appeared in America wherever the cultivated tradition retained influence. The general outlines and proportions were purely vernacular in origin, dictated, as the *Report* said, "by engineering requirements." But the towers, anchorages, and approaches "called for careful architectural treatment and dignified appearance." It was here, especially in the towers, that the cultivated tradition would be called upon to create the beauty which it was assumed the vernacular alone could not achieve. The steel skeletons of the towers, designed to carry the entire dead and live load of the completed structure, were nevertheless to be imbedded in a concrete casing faced with granite, in the design of which the architect had decorated the main arch with imposts, springers, and voussoirs and had provided other ornamental details which had no reference to the structural forces at work. . . .

However, as the 635-foot steel skeletons of the towers rose from the shores of the river, something unprecedented happened. The "unexpected" functional beauty of the naked steelwork fascinated people, and there was a widespread popular protest against applying the masonry covering which, according to the original plan, was to be the chief element in the aesthetic appeal of the bridge. So far as the present writer knows, the Port of New York Authority has never taken formal action to abandon the original design, and it is still theoretically possible that the towers will be cased in concrete and stone. The protest which prevented the "aesthetic" treatment of the towers was, after all, almost entirely a popular one, and the time may come when our betters in these matters will decide to go ahead with the design which they believed would best cast credit on our generation's taste. For to many people, apparently, it still seems difficult to believe that pure mathematics and engineering expediency can by themselves produce something beautiful. Even Chief Engineer Amman himself, in his final report on the bridge in 1933, still insisted that the appearance of the towers would be "materially enhanced by an encasement with an architectural treatment" like Cass Gilbert's, though he admitted that the steel towers as they stand lent the structure "a much more satisfactory appearance" than he or anyone else connected with the project had anticipated. . . .

In all branches of architecture the influence of the vernacular has been increasingly effective during the past twenty years. First the depression and then the war created pressures which tended to overcome the retarding influence of the cultivated tradition and to encourage a bold acceptance of vernacular forms and techniques. There is increasing awareness that the best work in American architecture grows directly out of the democratic and technological necessities which force us to think in terms of economy, simplification, and fitness for human purposes. . . .

The triumph during the second quarter of this century of vernacular forms which emerged from a hundred years of firsthand experiments in patterning the elements of a new environment could be traced in many fields besides construction. In writing, for example, it would be easy to show how the tradition of reportorial journalism which first attained literary quality more than a hundred years ago in Dana's *Two Years Before the Mast* had become, since Mark Twain's time, one of the principal shaping forces in our literature and could be traced as clearly in John Dos Passos' *U.S.A.* trilogy as in John Gunther's *Inside U.S.A.* Indeed, journalism in this sense has become a distinctively American phenomenon. As Georges Bataille said in the critical journal which he publishes in France, writing like John Hersey's account of the atom bomb's aftermath in Hiroshima illustrates a characteristic American effort "to give reportage a foundation of rigorously factual detail" which is almost unknown elsewhere.

In the movies, again, one could observe the origin and development of an almost purely vernacular art form, the direct product of technology and the commercial organization of popular culture. Those who were sensitive to the changing character of our civilization had anticipated something like the movies long before the technical means had been discovered. As early as 1888 David Goodman Croly, newspaper editor and sociologist, wrote a curious book called *Glimpses of the Future* in which — fifty years before publication of *Finnegan's Wake* — he prophesied the disintegration of the novel as an art form and suggested the use of colored pictures (in his day, chromolithographs of course) to take the place of descriptions of people and places, and of phonographs to reproduce the conversations between characters. That was as near as he could come, at that stage of technical development, to foreseeing the Technicolor talking picture. But the point worth noting is that long before movie cameras or color film had been invented those who were aware of the vital forces in the new civilization recognized that the traditional art forms would be superseded by forms appropriate to a technological environment.

A study of the development of the movies, furthermore, would provide a striking example of the interaction between the cultivated and vernacular traditions. . . . In the early stages movies were produced without any conscious aesthetic aim; the men and women who made them were in the business of providing mass entertainment in a medium which had been created by machines and science. Then, sometime in the twenties, cultivated critics began discussing the films of D. W. Griffith and Charlie Chaplin as artistic achievements of the first rank. The moviemakers themselves began to wonder if they weren't artists and shouldn't behave as such, and artists who had been trained in the techniques of older art forms like the theater began to move over into movie making. With the coming of the talking picture in the late twenties the movies became more and more like photographed plays, and the confusion between what can properly be called cinema values and those of the theater still marks much of Hollywood's output in spite of the success of such movies as *The Informer* and a few of the great documentary films like Pare Lorentz' *The River*.

The role of the vernacular in creating new art forms and altering the basis of old ones could be traced, too, in other fields: in modern dance, in the evolution of the animated cartoon, of the comic strip, and of the radio serial, and in the effect of photographic techniques and movie scenarios upon fiction and poetry. But it is in music, especially in the music loosely known as jazz, that we can most clearly perceive both the extent to which vernacular forms and techniques have succeeded in modifying older traditions and the degree to which the newer forms and techniques are still limited. . . .

To begin with, then, let us agree that by jazz we mean American popular dance music, exclusive of waltzes, *as it has been performed* for the past quarter century or so. By this definition we mean to include not only the spontaneous instrumental or vocal improvising called hot jazz, epitomized by such a performer as Louis Armstrong, but also the carefully rehearsed performances,

featuring improvised solos and "breaks," which professional dance bands like Benny Goodman's or Tommy Dorsey's give to everything they play — whether it be Tin Pan Alley tunes composed in the old operetta or ballad traditions, or melodies lifted from western European concert music, or pieces composed by Tin Pan Alley in imitation of hot-jazz improvisations. In this broad sense jazz is a product of the interaction of the vernacular and cultivated traditions, but its distinctive characteristics as a form of musical expression are purely vernacular.

Jazz is fundamentally a performer's art, and in this it marks itself off decisively from the music of the western European tradition. The composer, who is the dominant figure in Western concert music, is of almost no importance to jazz, for in jazz — in its most distinctive form — invention and performance occur simultaneously as the players have their way with the melodic or rhythmic pattern. It is true, of course, that musical improvisation has flourished in other cultures, and that even Western music of the cultivated tradition had its roots in improvisatory processes. But never before have conditions favored the universal availability of a performer art. The emergence of jazz as what might be called the folk music of the American people is inextricably bound up with such technological advances as phonographic recording and radio broadcasting.

Nor is it only in making jazz available that these technological devices have been important. In the early development of jazz, for example, the player piano not only contributed to the dissemination of ragtime (a rhythmic type which popularized many of the elements of jazz) but also imposed certain characteristics of rhythmic precision and even of tonal quality which became distinctive elements of its techniques. Anyone familiar with the playing of accomplished jazz pianists knows how they can use "pianola" style, though usually only for humorous effect in these latter, more sophisticated days. Similarly, the microphone of the recording and broadcasting studios has had its effect upon the instrumental and vocal performance of jazz. The vocal techniques of singers as diverse as Louis Armstrong and Bing Crosby, Bessie Smith, and Dinah Shore, have been devised — often with remarkable inventiveness and sensitivity — to exploit the full range of possibilities in the microphone, and it is largely to the microphone's limitations and possibilities that the typical jazz band owes both its characteristic makeup and its distinctive instrumental techniques. Indeed, these techniques have become such an integral part of jazz that it is seldom performed without the use of a microphone even in small quarters like night clubs and even when the band is not on the air.

It was precisely with the beginning of recorded jazz, in 1918 and the years immediately following, that the instrumentation of jazz bands began to undergo the changes which in the early twenties produced the orchestral combination that is still standard. As long as jazz remained a localized phenomenon in the Storyville district of New Orleans, it retained the instrumentation which had first crystallized with Buddy Bolden's band in the 1890s: a combination of trumpet, valve trombone, clarinet, string bass, drums, and banjo. But as it spread to other parts of the country, and as recordings became increasingly popular after the phenomenal success which Victor made with its records by the Original Dixieland Band in 1918, new instruments were added (notably the piano and saxophone) and the balance of instruments within the ensemble underwent important changes. From about 1921 on the standard jazz orchestra has consisted of three units: the brass (trumpets and trombones), the reeds (saxophones and a clarinet), and the rhythm section (piano, guitar or banjo, string bass or tuba, and

drums). All kinds of variants have been tried on this basic arrangement; big "symphonic" bands have been organized, and there have been recurrent experiments with various "small band" combinations built around a piano, and even some highly successful trios, quartets, sextets, and so on. But the three-unit instrumentation remains the standard for both hot and sweet (or commercial) bands.

One of the most interesting aspects of jazz instrumentation is that the rhythm section tends to remain intact, whatever variations may be made in the other units. A fifteen-piece band has four men in the rhythm section, and so has an eight-piece band. What this amounts to, of course, is a recognition of the fundamentally rhythmic nature of jazz. For it is its rhythmic structure that distinguishes it from other types of music.

It is precisely this distinctive rhythmic structure which makes jazz such an extraordinarily effective musical form in our civilization, and we will be better able to understand its significance if we acquaint ourselves with the two rhythmic characteristics which give it its special quality. These characteristics are syncopation and polyrhythm.

Syncopation, in the simplest terms, is the upsetting of rhythmic expectation by accenting a normally unstressed beat and depriving a normally stressed beat of its emphasis. As such it is a device which is fairly common in western European music, and consequently people who do not understand jazz frequently assume that jazz performance has merely borrowed a stock effect from traditional music and done it to death. But in a Brahms quartet, for example, syncopation is a special effect, consciously used for its striking qualities, whereas in jazz it is — as Winthrop Sargeant says — "a basic structural ingredient which permeates the entire musical idiom."

Even so, syncopation by no means accounts for the special nature of jazz. If it did, musicians trained exclusively in the cultivated tradition would produce jazz merely by continuously employing a device with which they are already familiar — whereas all they would actually produce would be *corn*. For in addition to syncopation jazz is characterized by superimposing of conflicting rhythms which creates a peculiar form of polyrhythm. This polyrhythm, as Don Knowlton was apparently the first to recognize, consists of imposing a *one*-two-three rhythmical element upon the fundamental one-two-three-four rhythm which underlies all jazz.

This formula of three-over-four, with its interplay of two different rhythms, seldom is baldly stated in jazz melody, but it almost invariably affects jazz phraseology and gives it its unique stamp. Here, as in the case of syncopation, we are using a term which is familiar in the cultivated tradition of Western music; but, as with syncopation, the term has a distinctive meaning in relation to jazz. As Sargeant points out, the commonest form of polyrhythm in European concert music — two-over-three — *never* appears in jazz, and the almost universal three-over-four of jazz is very rare indeed in Western music. Furthermore, in European polyrhythm there is no upset of normal rhythmic expectation; strong beats remain stressed and no accent is placed upon unstressed beats. But jazz polyrhythm has the effect of displacing accents in somewhat the same way that syncopation does so.

The domination of jazz by these two characteristics means, as Sargeant makes clear, that the relation between jazz rhythms and those of music composed in the western European tradition is "so slight as to be negligible." In other respects, of course, jazz has been strongly influenced by the cultivated tradition. Both its scalar and harmonic structure are largely borrowed or adapted from western European sources, though even in these aspects jazz has developed certain peculiarities — notably the "barber-shop" or "close" harmony which it shares with other types of American music including that of the cowboys and the hillbillies. But rhythmically jazz is a distinctive phenomenon.

The source of jazz polyrhythm is almost certainly to be found in the Afro-American folk music of the Southern Negroes. But from the point of view of our discussion, the important fact is that almost all American popular music, the commercial "sweet" as well as the hot variety, has wholeheartedly adopted both polyrhythm and syncopation, *and that both of these are devices for upsetting expected patterns.* In other words this music which originated in America and spread from there to the rest of the world depends for its distinctive quality upon two rhythmic devices which contribute to a single effect: the interruption of an established pattern of alternation between stressed and unstressed beats. . . .

It is essentially this same sort of battle between unexpected, challenging melodic rhythms and the regularity of the fundamental beat which characterizes all jazz. In hot jazz, when almost all the players are improvising all the time and nobody really knows what anybody is going to do next, the exhilaration is more intense than in rehearsed performances spiced with improvised solos and breaks. But the difference is one of degree, not of kind. . . .

What we have here, then, is an art form which within its own well-recognized limits comes closer than any other we have devised to reconciling the conflict which Emerson long ago recognized as the fundamental problem in modern civilization — the conflict between the claims of the individual and of the group. Everybody in a first-class jazz band seems to be — and has all the satisfaction of feeling that he is — going his own way, uninhibited by a prescribed musical pattern, and at the same time all are performing in a dazzlingly precise creative unison. The thing that holds them together

is the very thing they are all so busy flout-
ing: the fundamental four-four beat. In this
one artistic form, if nowhere else, Americans have found a way to give expression to
the Emersonian ideal of a union which is
perfect only "when all the uniters are isolated."

By its resolution of this basic conflict jazz
relates itself intimately with the industrial
society out of which it evolved. The problems with which Armstrong and Goodman
are concerned have much less to do with
the problems of the artist, in the traditional
sense, than with those of industrial organization. . . .

In other ways, also, jazz relates itself to
the vernacular tradition out of which it
came. Like all the patterns which that tradition has created, it is basically a very simple
form. Harmonically it is little more than
the repetition of four or five extremely simple and rather monotonous chord se-
quences. Melodically, it consists of the repetition of extremely simple tunes which,
however lovely or amusing they may often
be, are not subject to elaborate development, as are the themes of western European music. They may be worried and fooled
with in hot solos till they are practically
dismantled, but they are not thematically
developed. Finally, even in its rhythm,
where jazz displays so much ingenuity, it is
restricted to four-four or two-four time.

As a musical form, then, jazz is so simple
as scarcely to be a form at all. The "piece"
being played always has, of course, at least
an elementary formal pattern — a beginning, middle, and end; but the jazz performance as such usually does not. It merely
starts and then — after an interval which
has probably been determined more by the
duration of phonograph records than anything else — it stops. But this structural
simplicity accords with the other vernacular
characteristics that jazz displays. The poly-
rhythmic and syncopated flights of hot solos
and breaks, with their abrupt, impulsive ad-

justments to ever-changing rhythmic situations, give jazz an extraordinary flexibility;
but they could exist only in a simple, firmly
established musical framework. Similarly, it
is the structural simplicity of jazz which
makes it, like other vernacular forms and
patterns, so suitable for mass participation
and enjoyment and so universally available. . . .

It is clear that these vernacular forms and
the others we have touched upon in this essay do not — by themselves — yet offer a
medium of artistic expression adequate to
all our needs. Forms inherited from an older tradition still must play an important role
if we are not to be aesthetically starved, or
at least undernourished. Opera and poetic
drama, for example, may be as moribund as
their most candid critics assert, but there
will inevitably be periodic attempts to reju-
venate them. And such attempts will be
made not only because of the cultural (and
social) prestige which attaches to these and
many other heirlooms of the cultivated tradition but also because we cannot yet afford
to let them die.

Meanwhile the techniques and forms of
the vernacular are rapidly attaining widespread influence and prestige, and their
popularity throughout the world serves to
remind us once again that it is not their
specifically American quality, in any nationalistic sense, which gives them their fateful
significance. The products of the vernacular
in America do, of course, bear the stamp of
the national character, just as the artistic
achievements of other peoples display certain national characteristics. But these are
superficial features. The important thing
about the vernacular is that it possesses inherent qualities of vitality and adaptability,
of organic as opposed to static form, of energy rather than repose, that are particularly
appropriate to the civilization which, during
the brief life span of the United States, has
transformed the world. By an accident of

historical development it was in America that this tradition had the greatest freedom to develop its distinctive characteristics. It should, however, temper any undue nationalistic pride which that fact might induce in us, to remind ourselves that people in other lands have sometimes been more ready than we to appreciate the human and aesthetic values of vernacular modes of expression. Foreign movies have, after all, frequently surpassed ours in creative realization of the cinema's potentialities, and European and South American architects sometimes seem to be more alive than our own to the expressive possibilities of vernacular construction.

As a nation we have often been hesitant and apologetic about whatever has been made in America in the vernacular tradition. Perhaps the time has come when more of us are ready to accept the challenge offered to the creative imagination by the techniques and forms which first arose among our own people in our own land.

---

110.

## SIMONE DE BEAUVOIR: Goodbye to America

*Simone de Beauvoir, the noted French novelist and critic, spent four months in the United States — most of it in Chicago — shortly after the war. One of the results of her visit was the book* America Day by Day, *which was published in France in 1948 and appeared in an English version in 1952. Mlle de Beauvoir's perceptive understanding of the country that had almost overnight become the most powerful in the world is reflected in the selection from the book reprinted here, which describes her last day in America and her arrival back in Paris.*

Source: *America Day by Day,* translated by Patrick Dudley, London, 1952, pp. 290-296.

I WENT TO DECLARE the money I had earned during my four months' tour and to pay the required taxes. In France this business would have taken many days, much coming and going. Here the matter was fixed in a personal way, as always, and settled in half an hour. The official who sat with me to check my figures asked for my word of honor, nothing more. He helped to deduct my expenses: transportation, use of shorthand typists, entertaining, hotels, washing. . . ? It was he who made the suggestions with enthusiasm that was altogether touching. He then deplored the fact that the total was not bigger and that there was still tax to pay. Two blows with a rubber stamp and lo! I was free to leave America.

I could leave, I would leave. Evening approached New York — my very last evening. America had so often irritated me, and now I was miserable to be leaving it. I had often been asked during the last few days: "Do you like America?" and I had grown accustomed to answer back: "Half and half," or else "Fifty-fifty." This simple evaluation, of course, meant little; indeed it reflected only the obvious fact that I had reservations. Never a day passed without my being stunned by America in some way, or without my feeling some kind of deception. I do not know if I could live here happily; but I felt sure I should regret it.

Columbus Circle, Broadway, Times Square. Four months had passed. There was the same crowd, taxis, cars, and shimmering lights. The drugstores and the skyscrapers lost nothing of their peculiar magic. I knew why I liked them. There is a mirage that penetrates right through its civilization of comfort and abundance: that of an existence which would not waste away in attempting to maintain itself, and which could give itself wholly to surpassing even what it has achieved. Moving about from one place to another, clothing oneself and eating, all this is done without the slightest effort or waste of time — anything can happen.

The great attraction that America holds for me, where the memory of the pioneers is strong, consists in the fact that it appears as a realm still in transcendence; its history is contracted, of course, in time, yet stretches splendidly across vast spaces; it is the history of the creation of a whole world. For this reason skyscrapers always move me; they proclaim man as a being who does not stagnate, but is filled with enthusiasm and a desire for expansion and fresh conquest. In the shameless profusion of goods that you find in the drugstores there is poetry as fantastic as in a Baroque church: man has taken matter in the raw in the toils of his desire, and declares the power of imagination over matter. New York, Chicago, both these cities reflect the existence of this demi-urge with its imperial dreams, and that is why they are indeed the most human, the most uplifting cities that I know. There is no room here for any of the dreary caution of the *petit bourgeois* in his carpet slippers, whose only object is to stay at home and wait for death, as the sonnet has it. To devote one's life to that is living death. Americans in this sense are truly

alive; inertia does not appeal to them. A man is judged by his acts: to exist you must do something. The great iron bridges, buildings, Central Station, Park Avenue, the air terminals, the roads and mines, all proclaim this faith.

It would be difficult to tear myself away from these splendid visions of hope; and yet I know their wiles. In America life also ebbs away in the effort to survive. "I am out from 10 A.M.," a taxi driver told me at 10 P.M. "You bet I want to get home!" I remember how the people rushed the ferryboat that took them across to New Jersey. All my friends told me how hard were the working days in this city of distances, especially for women who have a job to do and a home to run at the same time; they are harassed when night comes: I have often seen them too tired to accept an invitation or go out and enjoy it. I understood that if people drink so much it is not because they have a mania; they need a spur at the end of the afternoon. And death by heart failure is the most common form of all in the city of New York.

That is not all. One has an inspired feeling that anything may happen. But what is actually happening? What do they do with their time and the money they earn? No doubt I did not get to know the ruling class, those who invent, study, speculate, and struggle: but they make up only a small minority. Americans for the most part are like those that I rubbed shoulders with: they let their lives turn round and round about them. They have neither the taste nor the sense of collective life; nor have they any feeling for personal destiny. This is the source of sadness that I often felt: this world full of generous promise crushes them; and its splendor soon appears barren, for no one controls it.

Each civilization offers a means of escape in the "banality of everyday life," but that which strikes one here is the point to which this escapism is organized. Neither his education, nor the atmosphere in which he develops, are designed to shed light on the individual's inner self. He is aware of himself not only as a human body but as an organism protected and prolonged by a whole arsenal of devices: he goes from floor to floor by elevator, travels by underground, speaks into the telephone, typewrites, and sweeps the floor with a vacuum cleaner. Between his stomach and the food he eats there is a world of canned food factories, Frigidaires, electric cookers. Between his sexual desires and their fulfillment there is the paraphernalia of moral precepts and hygienic practices.

He is hemmed in by society from childhood. He seeks outside himself, and among other people, his models for conduct; hence what is called American conformity; in fact, individuals are just as different and just as separate one from another in the New World as in the Old, but they find the means to escape from their individuality and avoid the feeling of "abandonment by origin" more easily; or perhaps they do not find it, but then at least they seek it with more ardor. They know, like all the world, dissatisfaction, boredom and doubt; but they try to rationalize their own confusion by posing "problems"; instead of drawing strength from solitude, or overcoming it by plumbing its depths, they cling to given facts; the source of values and of truth they see in things and never in themselves.

Their own existence is a thing of chance to which they attach no importance. That is why they are interested in net results and not in the spirit that engenders them, like Professor T.'s students, all of whom refused to listen to his demonstration of a formula. In much the same way they think they can isolate the part from the whole, as witnessed by the call for specialization that one finds in science, technology, and education. To use Hegelian terms, one can say that the very negation of the subject leads to the triumph of understanding over the spirit,

that is to say, the triumph of abstraction. And that is why in this country, which appears to turn so decidedly toward the concrete world, the word "abstraction" so often came to my lips; the object they erect into an idol loses its human values and becomes abstract, for concrete reality is that which actually envelops object and subject at one and the same time. There is the paradox of all positivisms, all pseudo-realities which turn away from humanity to proclaim the importance of things; they are lacking in the material itself and never attain to anything more than concepts.

I often felt while listening to their jazz, or talking to them, that time itself in which they live was abstract. They respect the past, but only insofar as it is a thing embalmed; the idea of the living past, integrated with the present, is foreign to them. They only want to recognize a present cut by the course of time, and the future they visualize is that which is deduced mechanically, not that whose ripening, or whose sudden explosion, bears unforeseeable risks: they believe in the future of a bridge, for instance, or of an economic plan, but not in the future of an art or a revolution. Their time is "the physician's time," an exterior concept which doubles that of space.

Because they refuse to accept the durability of things, they also refuse to recognize their quality; it is not only for economic reasons that "craftsmanship" does not exist in the States. Even in leisured occupations qualitative success is never sought for: food is cooked, just as fruit is ripened, as fast as possible; in every walk of life one must always hurry for fear lest the result be already circumscribed at the moment it is achieved. Cut off from the past and from the future, there is no weight to the present; nothing is stranger to Americans than the idea of regarding the passing moment as a repetition of time, a mirror of eternity, and of anchoring oneself to it to grasp truths or values that are in themselves timeless. To them the content of the passing moment is as precarious as the moment itself. Because they will not admit that truths and values have their consequences, they do not know how to conserve them in the movement that leaves them behind: they just deny it.

History is a great cemetery: men, deeds, ideas are always dying as soon as they are born. Each individual existence has the taste of death; from one minute to the next the present is merely an honorary past. It must be filled unceasingly anew to dissemble the curse it carries within itself; that is why Americans like speed, alcohol, thriller films, and any sensational news: the demand for new things, and ever newer things, is feverish since nowhere will they rest. But here as elsewhere life repeats itself, day after day, so they amuse themselves with gadgets, and in default of projects cultivate hobbies; in spite of these crazes they pretend to have day-to-day habits. Sport, the movies, comic strips, all show whence they are derived. But they finish up by always being sent back to that which they tried to escape — the arid basis of American life is boredom. Boredom, and also solitude.

It has been said a thousand times and it is true: these people are lonely. Because they flee in terror from the solitude with which they were endowed, because they escape from themselves, they have not got self-possession. How then to express themselves? How to become receptive? They are open and friendly, capable of tenderness, passion, sentiment, and cordiality; but seldom do they know how to create deep love or enduring friendship. Far from having stony hearts, yet their relations with one another are superficial and even cold. Far from lacking in vitality, enthusiasm, or generosity, they do not know how to devote themselves to the business of their lives. It is for the same reason. There are very few ambitious people here; there is hero worship, capricious in itself, but no one wants to raise himself by more than a few rungs

on the social ladder; a young man who is keen to distinguish himself will wish to be distinguished as a citizen, not as a man; he will not dream of emerging far beyond the set conditions of life.

Ambitions for greatness are often the source of many deceptions and indicted by faults Americans do not know; they have virtues born of indifference to themselves. They are not embittered, persecuted, or ill-willed, envious or egotistical. But they have no inner fire. In order to lose themselves in the pursuit of an object, they find themselves without an object at all. They experience their "original independence" under another form that their civilization pretends to screen from them. It is the contrast between their secret fragility and their proud constructions that makes them so pathetic.

It is because of the abstract climate in which they live that the importance of money is so disproportionate. The people are neither mean nor avaricious — on the contrary, these are faults for which they justly accuse the French; they do not want money in order to amass it, and are prompt in spending it, for other people as much as for themselves; to give is natural. Nor are they seekers after pleasure, for they do not seek their fortunes in order to satisfy extravagant appetites. If money is the sole object for so many, it is because the other values have been reduced to this one denominator, and because in time it has become the measure of every human accomplishment; whereas in fact it is only the abstract sign of all true riches. It is because they cannot frame or declare real values that Americans are satisfied with this symbol. In fact they are not satisfied; with the exception of capitalists in the highest class, they are just as embarrassed by their wealth of dollars as by their leisure.

It is one of the reasons, no doubt, why American women resemble idols — the dollar is a doleful divinity. Man is not discontented in justifying his work and his hard-won earnings by devoting them to a being of human flesh. Yet their cult of women, like the cult of money, is only a substitute. The destiny of the American male would have no sense unless it succeeded in giving a concrete meaning to this abstract entity: his liberty. Here is a vicious circle, for to fill up this empty liberty he would have to change the social and political conditions in which he lives and which dominate his inertia. Thousands of Americans are working daily to break this circle. And naturally there are thousands to whom these remarks do not apply. But insofar as one can make generalizations, it is the vast majority who are victims of the machine — escape from solitude and boredom holds them in a vice of solitude and boredom; by longing to lose themselves somehow in the world they have lost command of themselves.

One thing which struck me was how much they hate to question themselves and existing conditions. They want to believe that Good and Evil can be defined in precise categories, that Good is already, or will be easily achieved. They refuse — even people of goodwill — to visualize the actual conflict between justice and liberty, and the necessity for inventing a compromise between these concepts; they prefer to deny injustice and the lack of freedom. The fact that the complexity of the situation creates problems beyond all virtuous solution is something they will not admit. Evil is a residuum which they will eliminate by progressive stages and by applying more rigorously certain institutions which are wholesome in themselves — that is what many idealists really think; and if this optimism appears too superficial, they will try to create a kind of anti-God: the U.S.S.R. That is Evil, and it only needs to be annihilated to reestablish the reign of Good. This explains why so many of the students, who have such respect for their fellow beings, quietly talk of subjecting Soviet Russia to attack by atom bombs.

If then, in conclusion, I advance so many criticisms, why, in spite of everything, was it so sad for me to leave? First of all, because one could formulate other criticisms (just as depressing) of our European civilization and our French civilization, to which I would return. We are unhappy in other ways than the American, and false, too, in other ways. That is all. The judgments I delivered during this journey were not accompanied by a feeling of superiority. I see their faults, I do not forget our own. Embedded in all that I like and all that I loathe in America is something which fascinates me: the tremendous opportunities it offers, the gigantic risks it actually runs today — things in which we all share. All human problems are set forth on a gigantic scale; they will be solved here for the most part — and the solutions will illumine them in retrospect with a pathetic light, or plunge them into a night of indifference. That is what moved me strongly when I took my leave: America is a pivotal point in the world where the future of man is at stake. To like America or not to like her — these words have no sense. Here is a battlefield, and one can only follow with excitement the struggle she carries on within herself, the stakes of which are beyond measure.

---

*I do not care to belong to a club that accepts people like me as members.*
GROUCHO MARX, letter of resignation

**Interviewer questioning fishermen for data to be used in a Gallup Poll**

# ADJUSTING TO PEACE

Two days after the German surrender it was announced that servicemen in Europe would be gradually released according to a complicated point system. The unexpectedly quick end of the war in the Pacific allowed the government to expand and accelerate the demobilization program. The Army, in particular, sought an orderly program of release at a rate consistent with its view of occupation obligations and national securi-ty, and in this it had the strong backing of President Truman. The public, however, de-manded a much quicker program; "Bring-Daddy-Back-Home" clubs sprang up every-where and congressmen faced a torrent of mail demanding immediate demobilization. Consequently, the Army, which at its peak had numbered 12 million and at the Japa-nese surrender 8.3 million, dropped by mid-1946 to 1.5 million.

Grover from Black Star
Henri Cartier-Bresson from Magnum

(Above) Family and friends greet veteran as he returns home from war; (left) Polish wedding in Detroit

The reabsorption of millions of servicemen into the economy was eased by the Servicemen's Readjustment Act — the GI Bill of Rights — passed in 1944 to help prevent the chaos of demobilization that had dominated 1918-1919. Under the provisions of the Act, money was appropriated for unemployment compensation, help for self-employed veterans, mortgage guarantees, veterans' hospitals, and college and vocational training. This last program proved very popular; veterans came to campus in droves and by mid-1951 the government had spent 14 billion dollars in their behalf. Economic reconversion also proved more successful than it had in 1919. Domestic controls had been more extensive and effective during World War II and inflation had been held to a minimum. Industry converted back to the consumer market quickly and easily and was even able to expand production, keeping employment and prosperity high.

(Above) "Hawkeye Village" on the Iowa River — trailer camp housing for married students, mostly GI's, attending the University of Iowa, 1947; (below) scene outside an employment agency as returning veterans swelled the numbers of unemployed in the late 1940s

(Above) View of a new housing development outside San Francisco, 1946. Postwar housing shortages led to the rapid growth of such communities where construction was aided by following one standard design for all the houses built

". . . and as you leave these tranquil, ivied walls to face the stern realities of life . . ."; cartoon by Carl Rose in "The New Yorker"

David Moore from Black Star

(Above) Television antennas line the tops of buildings as this new medium gains popularity during the late 1940s; (right) actress Mary Brien and stage manager look on as singing group, The Merry Macs, performs during a television program; (bottom) Hollywood used car lot in 1942. By the end of the war, manufacturers could not meet the demands for new cars and the consumer either paid high prices or waited many months for an automobile

Marjory Collins from Black Star

Library of Congress

Henri Cartier-Bresson from Magnum

As was the case with demobilization, a strong public demand for the end of price controls developed as the war drew to a close. War priorities had already been lifted on hundreds of materials by the end of the war and by the end of 1945 only sugar was rationed. With the consumer market eager and ready to pay for all kinds of goods, industry reconverted rapidly. As controls were removed, prices soared. Shortages were not quickly overcome, and a considerable portion of the market was taken by the government for UNRRA and the Marshall Plan; this, together with the huge reserve buying power of consumers, prevented depression. The result, however, was precisely the inflation that had been held in check during the war. Organized labor reacted swiftly; losing the fight for retention of price controls, it immediately demanded wage increase to match the rising cost of living. In this the unions were largely successful, though unorganized white-collar and salaried workers were much slower in catching up. Inflation continued generally until controls were reinstituted during the Korean War.

(Above) Ford workers read about the passing of the Taft-Hartley Act, 1947; (below) striking shipbuilders picket the Brooklyn Yard of the Bethlehem Steel Co. during walkout, 1947

UPI — Compix

"Rover, Have You Put Your Muzzle On Yet?"

Courtesy, Herblock, "The Washington Post"

(Above) Cartoon by Herblock in 1948 reflecting the status of the economy during the early postwar years. Prices fluctuated greatly but generally rose as the federal government lifted wartime controls. (Right) Scene in Pittsburgh, Pa., center of the nation's steel industry, 1948; (below) Kuekes' cartoon in the "Cleveland Plain Dealer" reflecting Truman's hope for a public rejection of the Taft-Hartley law, 1949; (bottom right) John L. Lewis appears before Presidential fact-finding board to testify on behalf of his coal miners' union, 1948

Henri Cartier-Bresson from Magnum

UPI — Compix

Courtesy, Edward Kuekes, "The Plain Dealer"

STAY 'WAY BACK, PAPA'S GOIN' T' BLOW THIS THING TO SMITHERINES!

TAFT-HARTLEY BILL

TAFT-HARTLEY BILL

Pre-Fourth Fizzle.

(Above) Chicago apartment houses rented to Negroes in 1941; (below) church service at the Pentecostal Church in Chicago; (bottom right) Negro jazz band playing in New York in 1946

World War II again raised questions of whether the United States would ever recognize at home the rights it claimed to be fighting for elsewhere. Some progress was made in the armed forces; the Navy breached its policy of restricting Negroes to menial jobs, and the Marine Corps opened to Negroes for the first time in its history. At home, city-based war industry again drew Southern Negroes to the North, with the inevitable violent incidents. Government action to eliminate discrimination in war industry hiring was only partially successful.

(Top) **Negro demonstration, Harlem, 1943;** (center) **white women protesting Negroes in their housing project, 1947;** (bottom) **whites attack Negro in Detroit race riot**

(Top) Scene along a country road outside Wake-field, N.C., about 1940; (bottom left) cells in a convict camp in Greene County, Georgia, 1941; (bottom right) waiter in a restaurant in Washington, D.C., 1941

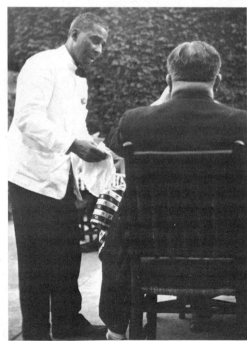

(Top) Troops rounding up Negroes following a night-long riot in Columbia, Tenn., 1946; (bottom left) cartoon by Ross Lewis for "The Milwaukee Journal," 1948; (bottom right) Sen. Theodore Bilbo campaigning for reelection in Mississippi. Bilbo, an ardent segregationist, served in the U.S. Senate and two terms as governor of his state

'The Civil Rights Bill Would Destroy Our Southern Way of Life, Suh!'

(Top) Alger Hiss (right) faces his accuser, Whittaker Chambers (left) during the 1948 hearing; (bottom left) Herblock cartoon, 1948; (bottom right) Richard Nixon examining microfilm which convicted Hiss

Griffith J. Davis from Black Star

(Top) Picket line outside New York's Wal-
dorf-Astoria during the Cultural and Scientific Peace Conference of 1949; (right)
Herblock cartoon of 1949

Courtesy, Herblock, "The Washington Post"

**"Fire!"**

The quick spread of Cold War
psychology, aided by the normal
rightward swing of public and congressional sentiment and Republican
chafing under the long years of
Democratic dominance, spawned a
new Red-hunt. Though less extensive
than that of 1919-1920, it was attended with the same disregard for
the very civil liberties it presumed to
protect. In 1947 Truman issued an
executive order for security investigations of all present and future
federal employees; the excessively
broad powers vested in investigatory
agencies held no provision for judicial review of loyalty decisions. The
sensational Alger Hiss case began in
1948; in 1949 eleven persons were
tried for membership in the Communist Party in defiance of the 1940
Smith Act.

The 1948 presidential campaign was a four-way race as the Democratic Party split into three factions. (Left) Republican candidate Thomas Dewey on the campaign trail; (center left) J. Strom Thurmond, southern Democrat (Dixiecrat) who ran on the States' Rights Ticket; (center right) Henry Wallace, former Roosevelt aide who clashed with Truman over postwar foreign policy and formed the Progressive Party. (Bottom) Winner Truman holds an edition of the "Chicago Tribune" which called the election too early

# 1949

111.

## Harry S. Truman: Inaugural Address

*President Harry S. Truman's domestic Fair Deal program contained as basic elements legislation intended to advance civil rights, provide for improved education and welfare, and establish fair employment practices; his foreign policies included the so-called Point Four program for aid to underdeveloped countries. Congress was unsympathetic to the domestic phase of these proposals, owing in part to its dislike for policies that clearly were a continuation of Roosevelt's New Deal and in part to its growing concern — and that of the public — over foreign affairs in the Cold War era. However, much of Truman's domestic program was passed under subsequent Democratic Presidents, notably during the first year after Lyndon B. Johnson's landslide victory in 1964. In his Inaugural Address of January 20, 1949, reprinted here, Truman confined himself to a general statement of the future policies of his administration, emphasizing the differences between American democracy and Soviet Communism.*

Source: *Record*, 81 Cong., 1 Sess., pp. 477-478.

Mr. Vice-President, Mr. Chief Justice, and Fellow Citizens:

I accept with humility the honor which the American people have conferred upon me. I accept it with a resolve to do all that I can for the welfare of this nation and for the peace of the world.

In performing the duties of my office, I need the help and prayers of every one of you. I ask for your encouragement and for your support. The tasks we face are difficult. We can accomplish them only if we work together.

Each period of our national history has had its special challenges. Those that confront us now are as momentous as any in the past. Today marks the beginning not only of a new administration but of a period that will be eventful, perhaps decisive, for us and for the world.

It may be our lot to experience, and in a large measure bring about, a major turning point in the long history of the human race. The first half of this century has been marked by unprecedented and brutal attacks on the rights of man and by the two most frightful wars in history. The supreme need of our time is for men to learn to live together in peace and harmony.

The peoples of the earth face the future with grave uncertainty, composed almost equally of great hopes and great fears. In this time of doubt, they look to the United States as never before for goodwill, strength, and wise leadership. It is fitting, therefore, that we take this occasion to proclaim to the world the essential principles of the faith by which we live, and to declare our aims to all peoples.

The American people stand firm in the faith which has inspired this nation from the beginning. We believe that all men have a right to equal justice under law and equal opportunity to share in the common good. We believe that all men have the right to freedom of thought and expression. We believe that all men are created equal because they are created in the image of God. From this faith we will not be moved.

The American people desire, and are determined to work for, a world in which all nations and all peoples are free to govern themselves as they see fit and to achieve a decent and satisfying life. Above all else, our people desire, and are determined to work for, peace on earth — a just and lasting peace — based on genuine agreement freely arrived at by equals.

In the pursuance of these aims, the United States and other like-minded nations find themselves directly opposed by a regime with contrary aims and a totally different concept of life. That regime adheres to a false philosophy which purports to offer freedom, security, and greater opportunity to mankind. Misled by that philosophy, many peoples have sacrificed their liberties only to learn to their sorrow that deceit and mockery, poverty and tyranny are their reward.

That false philosophy is communism.

Communism is based on the belief that man is so weak and inadequate that he is unable to govern himself and therefore requires the rule of strong masters.

Democracy is based on the conviction that man has the moral and intellectual capacity, as well as the inalienable right, to govern himself with reason and justice.

Communism subjects the individual to arrest without lawful cause, punishment without trial, and forced labor as a chattel of the state. It decrees what information he shall receive, what art he shall produce, what leaders he shall follow, and what thoughts he shall think.

Democracy maintains that government is established for the benefit of the individual, and is charged with the responsibility of protecting the rights of the individual and his freedom in the exercise of his abilities.

Communism maintains that social wrongs can be corrected only by violence.

Democracy has proved that social justice can be achieved through peaceful change.

Communism holds that the world is so widely divided into opposing classes that war is inevitable.

Democracy holds that free nations can settle differences justly and maintain a lasting peace.

The differences between communism and democracy do not concern the United States alone. People everywhere are coming to realize that what is involved is material well-being, human dignity, and the right to believe in and worship God.

I state these differences, not to draw issues of belief as such but because the actions resulting from the Communist philosophy are a threat to the efforts of free nations to bring about world recovery and lasting peace.

Since the end of hostilities, the United States has invested its substance and its energy in a great constructive effort to restore peace, stability, and freedom to the world. We have sought no territory; we have imposed our will on none. We have asked for no privileges we would not extend to others.

We have constantly and vigorously supported the United Nations and related agencies as a means of applying democratic principles to international relations. We have consistently advocated and relied upon peaceful settlement of disputes among nations.

We have made every effort to secure agreement on effective international control of our most powerful weapon, and we have worked steadily for the limitation and control of all armaments.

We have encouraged, by precept and example, the expansion of world trade on a sound and a fair basis.

Almost a year ago, in company with sixteen free nations of Europe, we launched the greatest cooperative economic program in history. The purpose of that unprecedented effort is to invigorate and strengthen democracy in Europe, so that the free people of that continent can resume their rightful place in the forefront of civilization and can contribute once more to the security and welfare of the world.

Our efforts have brought new hope to all mankind. We have beaten back despair and defeatism. We have saved a number of countries from losing their liberty. Hundreds of millions of people all over the world now agree with us that we need not have war — that we can have peace. The initiative is ours.

We are moving on with other nations to build an even stronger structure of international order and justice. We shall have as our partners countries which, no longer solely concerned with the problem of national survival, are now working to improve the standards of living of all their people. We are ready to undertake new projects to strengthen a free world.

In the coming years, our program for peace and freedom will emphasize four major courses of action.

First, we will continue to give unfaltering support to the United Nations and related agencies, and we will continue to search for ways to strengthen their authority and increase their effectiveness. We believe that the United Nations will be strengthened by the new nations which are being formed in lands now advancing toward self-government under democratic principles.

Second, we will continue our programs for world economic recovery. This means, first of all, that we must keep our full weight behind the European recovery program. We are confident of the success of this major venture in world recovery. We believe that our partners in this effort will achieve the status of self-supporting nations once again. In addition, we must carry out our plans for reducing the barriers to world trade and increasing its volume. Economic recovery and peace itself depend on increased world trade.

Third, we will strengthen freedom-loving nations against the dangers of aggression. We are working out with a number of countries a joint agreement designed to strengthen the security of the North Atlantic area. Such an agreement would take the form of a collective defense arrangement within the terms of the United Nations Charter. We have already established such a defense pact for the Western Hemisphere by the Treaty of Rio de Janeiro.

The primary purpose of these agreements is to provide unmistakable proof of the joint determination of the free countries to resist armed attack from any quarter. Every country participating in these arrangements must contribute all it can to the common defense. If we can make it sufficiently clear, in advance, that any armed attack affecting our national security will be met with overwhelming force, the armed attack may never occur.

I hope soon to send to the Senate a treaty respecting the North Atlantic security plan.

In addition, we will provide military advice and equipment to free nations which will cooperate with us in the maintenance of peace and security.

Fourth, we must embark on a bold new program for making the benefits of our scientific advances and industrial progress available for the improvement and growth of underdeveloped areas.

More than half the people of the world are living in conditions approaching misery. Their food is inadequate. They are victims of disease. Their economic life is primitive and stagnant. Their poverty is a handicap and a threat both to them and to more prosperous areas. For the first time in history, humanity possesses the knowledge and skill to relieve the suffering of these people.

The United States is preeminent among the nations in the development of industrial and scientific techniques. The material resources which we can afford to use for the assistance of other peoples are limited. But our imponderable resources in technical knowledge are constantly growing and are inexhaustible. I believe that we should make available to peace-loving peoples the benefits of our store of technical knowledge in order to help them realize their aspirations for a better life. And, in cooperation with other nations, we should foster capital investment in areas needing development. Our aim should be to help the free peoples of the world, through their own efforts, to produce more food, more clothing, more materials for housing, and more mechanical power to lighten their burdens.

We invite other countries to pool their technological resources in this undertaking. Their contributions will be warmly welcomed. This should be a cooperative enterprise in which all nations work together through the United Nations and its specialized agencies whenever practicable. It must be a worldwide effort for the achievement of peace, plenty, and freedom.

With the cooperation of business, private capital, agriculture, and labor in this country, this program can greatly increase the industrial activity in other nations and can raise substantially their standards of living.

Such new economic developments must be devised and controlled to benefit the peoples of the areas in which they are established. Guarantees to the investor must be balanced by guarantees in the interest of the people whose resources and whose labor go into these developments.

The old imperialism — exploitation for foreign profit — has no place in our plans. What we envisage is a program of development based on the concepts of democratic fair-dealing.

All countries, including our own, will greatly benefit from a constructive program for the better use of the world's human and natural resources. Experience shows that our commerce with other countries expands as they progress industrially and economically.

Greater production is the key to prosperity and peace. And the key to greater production is a wider and more vigorous application of modern scientific and technical knowledge.

Only by helping the least fortunate of its members to help themselves can the human family achieve the decent, satisfying life that is the right of all people.

Democracy alone can supply the vitalizing force to stir the peoples of the world into triumphant action, not only against their human oppressors but also against their ancient enemies — hunger, misery, and despair.

On the basis of these four major courses of action we hope to help create the conditions that will lead eventually to personal freedom and happiness for all mankind. If we are to be successful in carrying out these policies, it is clear that we must have continued prosperity in this country and we must keep ourselves strong.

Slowly but surely we are weaving a world fabric of international security and growing prosperity. We are aided by all who wish to live in freedom from fear — even by those who live today in fear under their own governments. We are aided by all who want relief from the lies of propaganda — who desire truth and sincerity. We are aided by all who desire self-government and a voice in deciding their own affairs. We are aided by all who long for economic security — for the security and abundance that men in free societies can enjoy. We are aided by all who desire freedom of speech, freedom of religion, and freedom to live their own lives for useful ends.

Our allies are the millions who hunger and thirst after righteousness.

In due time, as our stability becomes manifest, as more and more nations come to know the benefits of democracy and to participate in growing abundance, I believe that those countries which now oppose us will abandon their delusions and join with the free nations of the world in a just settlement of international differences.

Events have brought our American democracy to new influence and new responsibilities. They will test our courage, our devotion to duty, and our concept of liberty. But I say to all men, what we have achieved in liberty, we will surpass in greater liberty.

Steadfast in our faith in the Almighty, we will advance toward a world where man's freedom is secure. To that end we will devote our strength, our resources, and our firmness of resolve. With God's help, the future of mankind will be assured in a world of justice, harmony, and peace.

---

112.

# Robert A. Taft: The Republican Party

*The Republican Party suffered its fifth consecutive defeat in the 1948 presidential election, and some political analysts speculated whether the Party could survive. "The major reason why the Republicans have found it so difficult to elect a President," wrote Samuel Lubell in* The Future of American Politics, *"is because their Party has remained fundamentally unchanged, trapped by its own inner contradictions. . . . The Republican candidates have not been able to campaign as either forthright liberals or forthright conservatives." Against those who raised doubts about the party's future, Robert Taft asserted that it would survive and attributed its past defeats to its failure firmly to declare the principles for which it stood.*

Source: *Fortune,* April 1949.

SOME REPUBLICANS ARE DISCOURAGED today because for five successive elections the Republican Party has met defeat. Yet it lost by very narrow margins in 1940, 1944, and 1948. Nearly half of the voters voted for it in the recent election. And its organization is strong in many states throughout the nation. It is therefore shortsighted and cowardly to give way to despair. Political parties have a strong will to live. Indeed, the only parties that have died are those that have forgotten or abandoned the principles on which they were founded.

A party can live only if it represents a great principle or a set of great principles. The two-party system is based on the theory that a large number of men who think differently on many subjects unite in the belief that certain principles are vital to the welfare of their country and that differences on less important questions must be reconciled or forgotten in the common effort to secure those basic principles. A political party is not just an organization in which men of completely different points of view join because their parents or their friends belong to that party, or because they became members through youthful and forgotten prejudices.

No one who has been in Congress during the past ten years can doubt that the Republican Party is a party of principles. Moreover, I believe that there is basic agreement among Republicans concerning these principles, even though there are wide differences of opinion on the application of them to the complex problems of our modern world. The principles of a great party are not made by its leaders, nor by the National Committee, nor by Congress itself, but by the great bulk of the party members throughout the country.

They are interpreted by the votes cast in Congress; senators and congressmen vote the way they do because they know they are reflecting the philosophy of their constituents, and because they are imbued with the same philosophy themselves. It is Congress that is forced to apply, by actual voting, the principles of the party to particular measures, and so the record made by Congress becomes the practical expression of the philosophy of the party. If the party does not control the executive, it must run on the record made by Congress, plus the promises made at a national convention covering those measures on which Congress has not yet acted.

The defeats of the Republican Party have not been due to its principles but to its failure to present those principles effectively to the people. They are not principles that interpret themselves easily into higher prices for the farmer, higher wages for the workingman, more profits for the businessman, and government handouts from the cradle to the grave. The enemies of the party have been clever, particularly in their conversion to New Deal philosophy of columnists, editors, commentators, and other writers who have an influence on public opinion. They have obscured and confused American thinking on the very basic principles which this nation was founded to secure. They have convinced many that there are no principles involved in the position of the two parties; from which the only conclusion can be that the party making the greatest promises must receive popular approval. In the general state of public opinion, I believe it is remarkable that the Republican Party has adhered to its principles as it has. Its life depends on that adherence.

The Republican Party will continue to live and will take over the administration of the government if it dedicates itself again to the principles for which it was founded, and if it presents those principles to the people in the most forceful and effective manner, not only in elections but at all times during the next four years.

## HUMAN LIBERTY

WHAT IS THE Republican philosophy? First, and before all, it is the same philosophy of human liberty that created the United States of America. Every American today still pays lip service to the term "liberty." But he does not feel it as he did for a hundred years, when the idea of liberty inspired all Americans and they boasted of it until it became tiresome to every visiting foreigner. The examples of America and of France spread the idea throughout the world, and the philosophy of free government was accepted in nearly all sections of the globe, even where the thing itself did not really exist. But today many Americans and most people throughout the world have forgotten what it means. The limitations on liberty have grown until in many totalitarian states the substance of liberty has completely disappeared. The totalitarian theory that government must plan and direct and control dominates the thinking of today throughout the world and has made great headway here in the U.S. without a realization of the fact that it means the end of individual liberty.

What is liberty? It is freedom of speech and of the press, as the President said in his inaugural — but it is much more. It is the freedom of the individual to choose his own work and his life occupation, to spend his earnings as he desires to spend them, to choose the place where he desires to live, to take the job that fits him whether some union official is willing that he get it or not. It is the freedom of the local community to work out its own salvation when it has the power to do so. It is the freedom of cities, of counties, of school districts; the freedom to educate one's own children as one thinks best. It is the freedom of thought and experiment in academic institutions. It is the freedom of men in industry to run their business as they think best so long as they do not interfere with the rights of others to do the same. Certainly, there are limitations that must be imposed by the state to protect the liberty of others, more and more as our economy becomes complex. But a party that believes in liberty will impose such limitations only to the extent that they are absolutely necessary.

As we look back through history, we see brief periods in which liberty has prevailed, but in the major part of historical time it has been suppressed by emperors and kings, by oligarchies, by plutocracies, by so-called democracies and proletarian majorities. It is hard to gain and easy to lose — unless it is kept alive by an aggressive determination that it shall not perish from the earth. Today the battle between liberty and totalitarian government permeates every problem of life. It lies at the base of our battle with Fascism and Naziism and Communism. The American people believe in liberty, but the totalitarian creed we face abroad has insinuated itself into the philosophy of many of our labor unions and of the Democratic

Party. If it prevails it must ultimately destroy liberty here at home.

It is tragic that our people in recent elections have tended to support the theory that the government should be the source of all planning, of all control, and of bread and circuses for the multitude. It is tragic, because at this very moment we see the magnificent success of a system of liberty in the U.S. as contrasted with the comparative poverty and dissatisfaction of many foreign nations. Liberty has succeeded in the U.S. in developing original thinking, original methods, and new ideas. It has succeeded in giving a wide distribution of property and income to our people. It has succeeded in building up a tremendous production of material things and a standard of living higher than has ever been seen before in the history of the world. A man from Mars who studied the world today would of necessity come to the conclusion that only the free can solve the problems of production.

There are many other aims besides liberty to be sought by political policy and party principle, but every policy must be justified either as an affirmative policy to secure liberty or as a policy of human progress making no sacrifice to the god of the totalitarian state.

There may be many differences among Republicans as to the application of the principle of liberty to different situations. I can only explain how my belief in the vital need of liberty has led me to certain conclusions on the issues now before Congress. In my opinion the President's program, if enacted in full, would destroy great areas of freedom without even accomplishing his stated purposes. Economic freedom would be destroyed by price control, wage control, allocation control, rationing, and government operation of business as suggested in the new controlled-economy bill. So-called health insurance would socialize and nationalize medical service and the medical profession and bring the daily life of every family under the supervision of a government bureau. The tremendous burden of taxation proposed would reduce the freedom of the people, because it takes from them the right to spend the money they have earned by the sweat of their brows and spends it for something that the government thinks is good for them, whether they want it or not. Universal compulsory military training would take from a boy and his family the right to choose his own education and occupation and would impose a year of training and indoctrination determined by so-called experts in Washington.

We have many alternative programs to accomplish some of the purposes sought in this legislation, but in its present form it utterly disregards the whole principle of liberty.

## HIGHER STANDARDS OF LIVING

EVERY PARTY, of course, believes in the maintenance of full production, full employment, and a higher standard of living for all the people, and the Republican Party is no exception. In fact, in its full-dinner-pail campaign in 1900, it not only made that the issue but it convinced the workingman that prosperity could be achieved only by sound fiscal principles. In recent years the American people, or perhaps only the politicians, have almost forgotten the essential principles necessary for character and happiness in their search for more material welfare. The ideal of prosperity and material welfare is not peculiar to liberty or a free state — in fact, every dictator claims that he can provide it more effectively than a free government, and maintains his power to some extent by government stimulation of consumer welfare. Nevertheless, a reasonable prosperity is essential if the people are to enjoy the advantages of liberty. Prevention of hardship and poverty is necessary, because those who suffer them have no real freedom to determine their own lives.

Fortunately for the cause of liberty, liberty itself has constituted the most active agent in bringing about increased prosperity. It is unquestionably owing to our free economy that we have become the most productive country in the world, to which all other countries look for assistance and support. We have come where we are because the American has still the right to keep the proceeds of his efforts. There has been a constant incentive to redouble those efforts because of the reward given in material welfare. The Socialists overlook the tremendous importance of that incentive — the fact that most men do not like to work unless there is something to be gained. Lethargy has been the greatest enemy of progress in many sections of the world.

We are concerned that the government keep the economic machine running at a high rate of speed with as little friction and intermission as possible. We believe this can be brought about by sound fiscal policies, by balancing the budget, by a sound currency, and proper control of credit. We believe in incentive rewards for workingmen for good work done, such as those our system gives to the man who risks his time and money in new enterprise. To this end government should keep competition alive and prevent the destruction of freedom; it should not kill incentive. On these grounds, I am opposed to price and wage control; to the prohibition of strikes even if collective bargaining has failed; to allocation controls; and, in general, to all attempts to substitute government planning for the normal forces of competition.

To this end also I favor lower government expenses, a lower burden of taxation on the economic machine to which we look for the production of taxes themselves. Already taxation is taking more than 25 percent of our national income. Already it is discouraging the development of private industry in some fields. Already the choking effect of the tax burden on productive activity is discouraging the very energy that produces the taxes; and once a buyers' market prevents the passing on of so much of the tax burden to the consumer, the situation will be infinitely worse.

I was in Europe in December. There I observed that every European country is hamstrung by government controls, by taxation, by black markets, by the planners who forget human nature. Every country with controls is looking to the U.S. to share some part of the products of our liberty with those to whom liberty is denied.

## TO PREVENT HARDSHIP AND POVERTY

WE BELIEVE THAT government has the obligation to promote better education, better health, better housing, better security for our people, and equality of opportunity. Equality of opportunity for the children is an essential element of true liberty. These tasks are primarily the job of our states and local governments, and while federal aid is often necessary in order that they may be properly done, particularly in the poorer states, there should be no federal control or concentration of power in Washington. I believe the American people are convinced that with the tremendous productivity of our free country we can prevent extreme hardship and poverty in the U.S. today, that we can maintain a minimum floor under education, health, housing, and food. We have recognized that obligation in the past, but the job has not been systematically done. With federal aid it can be done, but there are plenty of pitfalls and dangers to liberty in the *way* in which it is done.

There are many respects in which we can promote better health and welfare for the whole population, but our efforts should not include direct or indirect subsidy to the bulk of the people or giving men something for nothing, except where we do face problems of extreme hardship. Nothing can so quickly kill the incentive and reduce the production of the people as to encourage them to look to government as their benefactor and supporter.

Aid to those in the lowest income class is necessary. But a policy of government handouts to all would impose an intolerable tax burden, would sap the energy and liberty of the people, and would destroy the American character. No people as a whole can get something for nothing. They can only be fooled into such a hope. The idea that people can get their medical care from the government without paying even a greater price than they pay today is fantastic. To the extent that we do support those at the lowest end of the income field by aid or subsidy, they can only be supported by the other four-fifths of the population; and the burden must not be so great as to discourage that four-fifths from the magnificent job they are doing today.

I favor federal aid to the states and local governments to enable them to extend medical care to all those who are unable to pay for it, but I am strenuously opposed to the system of socialized and nationalized medicine outlined in the Murray-Wagner-Dingell Bill. Organized charity or free government welfare service to the whole population can destroy the freedom and also the character of the people to whom it is extended. It can increase the power of the central government in Washington until Washington bureaus govern the daily lives of every family in the U.S. Incentive and initiative can be paralyzed. We will be ruled by people who take no personal risks and create no jobs. The people will be taxed without realizing it, through a deduction from payroll, and perhaps get some part of those taxes back in the form of government services and activity, which they may or may not want. There is real danger to liberty in the welfare state.

As in the case of federal aid to states for medical care, I believe that federal aid should be extended to enable local communities to provide decent public housing for those unable to pay the rents charged for privately owned homes of decent character. I favor the extension of federal aid to states, particularly the poorer states, so that they may provide adequate primary and secondary education for children, no matter how poor the state or community in which they live. I favor the extension of the old-age-pension plan to all those employees not now included. And there are other fields of social welfare in which the federal government can be of assistance if the proper safeguards are observed. But I cannot emphasize too strongly that these programs must be devised in such a way that they do not substitute a welfare state for a free government and a free people.

## EQUAL JUSTICE UNDER LAW

EQUAL JUSTICE UNDER LAW is a necessary corollary to liberty, for there can be no liberty if the life and property of men are subject to the arbitrary will of others.

Those who would destroy freedom in any country make the courts a tool of the government, as they are in Russia. Modern totalitarian government cannot admit the right of any court to balk its policies. Of course the Communists go further. They do not admit that such a thing as real justice can exist or that any tribunal can be truly impartial or decide cases on their merits. My objection to the Nürnberg trials was that, while clothed with the forms of justice, they were in fact an instrument of government policy, determined months before at Tehran and Yalta. Those who wrote the original draft of the United Nations Charter at Dumbarton Oaks completely forgot the ideal of justice, and even today the charter is subject to serious criticism because it gives the Security Council power to act on grounds of expediency unrestrained by justice. Fortunately, when the issue is clearly presented the American people feel deeply that we must have free and impartial courts. They reacted violently to the New Deal attempt to swamp the Supreme Court. We must oppose the powerful forces that today

are still attempting to take from the courts the power to interpret the Constitution.

The New Deal and the present administration still seek the solution of every problem by the creation of boards and commissions, with power to make regulations having the force of law, with power to file prosecutions, try the alleged culprits and condemn them, practically without recourse to the courts. Of course, in our complicated modern system there must be some control by administrative law, as in the fields of radio and air traffic, but it should be imposed in such a way as to preserve the maximum amount of freedom for those regulated; and it should subject the administrative boards to definite principles laid down by Congress on which an appeal can be taken to the courts.

Perhaps the greatest miscarriages of justice that have ever occurred in the U.S. occurred under the National Labor Relations Board in interpreting the Wagner Act. Yet today President Truman is trying to get Congress to restore the one-sided and unrestrained power of that board. The Republican Party should stand today, as it has stood in the past, for a rule of law instead of the rule of arbitrary men.

## EQUALITY AND NO SPECIAL PRIVILEGE

IN OUR DEFENSE OF LIBERTY, while today the primary threat is from totalitarian government seeking arbitrary power, we are equally determined to protect the individual from the oppression of private privilege and private power.

The Republican Party enacted the Sherman Act to prevent the economic power of monopoly. People often say that it is ineffective. My judgment is that it has an effect on all business thinking in the U.S., and has done more to maintain freedom in the economic field than any other measure ever enacted. The contrast today between conditions here and those brought about in Europe by the cartel system is striking and conclusive.

On the other hand, we have favored the increase of the minimum wage to protect the unorganized worker against the oppression of employers unrestrained by the proper power of labor unions.

Liberty may be ended by the tyranny of a majority of the people as well as by the tyranny of special groups. We are concerned that minorities shall receive fair treatment, the same rights to vote, to work, and to live their own lives as the majority. We are concerned that the economic system shall not work to the unfair disadvantage of any group, either large or small, that the small businessman shall be able to prosper if he deserves it, that the general level of farm prices and farmers' income be not out of line with the level of industrial prices, that taxation fall with substantial equality on all the people in accordance with their ability to pay. Therefore, the Republican Eightieth Congress enacted last year a bill directing the government to maintain the price of farm products in reasonable relation to other prices — the concept of parity. We enacted a fair tax-reduction bill removing seven million of the lowest-income taxpayers from the income-tax rolls. And the Republicans have sought repeatedly to enact anti-poll-tax and anti-lynching laws.

In all this kind of legislation, from the Sherman Act to the anti-lynching laws, the exact form of the statute must be such as to infringe as little as possible on the freedom of the individual and the local community. We should inject federal power only where it is absolutely necessary and we should subject any authorized action to review by impartial courts.

## PEACE

FINALLY, THE REPUBLICAN PARTY believes that peace must be the ultimate aim of our foreign policy and that no object is more important, except the liberty of this nation itself. The wars into which we have been plunged are evidence of the failure of our foreign policy, not of its success. There can be no greater tragedy than war, even for the victorious nation. No nation can really win a modern war. While war is justified only as a means of preserving liberty, it is likely to destroy the very liberty it is designed to preserve by making necessary restrictions on that liberty at home, which may be permanently fastened on the people. Horrible as have been the death and destruction caused by war in the past, they will be still worse in the future.

Of course the affairs of different nations have become so interwoven that it is not easy to keep our mind on the ultimate purposes of foreign policy, liberty, and peace. Unquestionably, we must join with other nations in any international organization that can effectively keep the peace. We have done so in the United Nations. Because the United Nations organization itself is defective, and because of the attitude of Russia, we are justified in joining other groups with a more limited membership to keep the peace within the area of their jurisdiction.

In order to protect our liberty and also to discourage others from attacking us, we have to maintain armed forces completely adequate for defense. Personally, I think, in modern times, defense is adequate only if we have an Air Force able to dominate the air over this country and for quite a long distance beyond our boundaries. But here again, the very instrument necessary to maintain liberty must not be one that can itself destroy liberty. Obviously, if we want absolutely airtight protection, our military establishment would cost from $50 billion to $100 billion a year; but this would end liberty at home and prevent the very improvement of civilian standards of living that should be the result of liberty. The size of our armed forces must be a question for decision by civilians representing the entire people and must be based on a calculated risk.

Under present-day conditions, I believe we should continue our assistance to many nations to restore their economies from the disruption arising from the war, because that disruption leads to the spread of Communism and encourages Russia to end the peace and threaten the freedom of America. We can well interest ourselves in giving economic assistance to undeveloped areas of the world to relieve extreme human misery, which may lead to war. But we must realize first that in the long run a country can maintain only that standard of living justified by its own production and cannot live on the bounty of another nation. Our aid should be confined to special fields where it can clearly be of exceptional value to the country receiving the aid. If we promise a millennium we cannot deliver, if we make other people think that they can get something for nothing, our failure will create resentment and do more harm to peace than good.

Furthermore, let us not slip quietly into using our economic power to assume political power. We have to make certain conditions on any aid that we give, and yet such conditions are soon likely to be resented and involve us in disputes that constitute a threat to peace. It is easy to slip into an attitude of imperialism and to entertain the idea that we know what is good for other people better than they know themselves. From there, it is an easy step to the point where war becomes an instrument of public policy rather than the last resort to maintain our own liberty.

## CONCLUSION

I HAVE TRIED TO outline what I conceive to be the basic principles of the Republican Party — the maintenance of liberty, equal justice under law, equality without special privilege, and the preservation of peace. There was a time when these were the principles of all American parties, while they differed on less consequential matters. Today the Democratic Party gives lip service to these principles, but its policies are certain to destroy them.

The Republican Party has done a very good job of explaining its principles or the principles of American history and government. They are the principles in which the great majority of the American people still believe today. When their liberties have been directly affected by regulation, as were those of the farmers in 1938 and the housewives in 1946, they have risen up with indignation against the party of government controls. But they have not always realized the steady reduction of liberty that is resulting from the steady advance of totalitarian methods and concepts propounded by the Democrats; nor do they yet realize the threat contained in the program that is now presented by the Democratic Party. That program, if fulfilled, would soon bring a federal tax burden of $60 billion, subject all business to detailed controls, extend the federal welfare bureaus into every home, and extend actual government operation of business into the larger industries. It would subject America to a totalitarian government. The Republican Party will survive and prevail, because it is in fact the Party of American Principles.

---

*I will make a bargain with the Republicans. If they will stop telling lies about Democrats, we will stop telling the truth about them.*

ADLAI STEVENSON, 1952

113.

## ADOLF A. BERLE: The Emerging Common Law of Free Enterprise

*By 1940 there were some forty-eight private corporations in the United States with assets of more than $1 billion. The rise of corporate power as manifested in these economic giants was of concern to many Americans, both in and out of business. It was pointed out, for example, that there was a billion-dollar corporation for every (political) state in the Union, but that many of the political states had less total wealth than a number of the "economic monsters," as they were sometimes called. Adolf A. Berle, law professor and leading authority on corporations, took issue with this gloomy view of corporate growth and size, arguing instead that it could be a promising development. In an address to the Brandeis Lawyers Society on December 13, 1949, a portion of which appears below, Berle analyzed the ways in which corporate development had altered the character of the country's total economy.*

Source: *The Emerging Common Law of Free Enterprise: Antidote to the Omnipotent State?,* Philadelphia, 1951.

EXAMINATION of the relevant economic data makes clear that private enterprise is likely to include for a good while to come a large proportion of "big" corporations. I here adopt this assumption. Engineers may, of course, take us out. Some atomic scientist may one day make it possible for anyone to make steel in a backyard blacksmith shop; some inventor may create a strange device permitting anyone to turn out automobiles in a plant the size of a small-town garage. But nothing of this is in sight now. Bigness is with us and the technicians tell us it is necessary.

Apparently, then, we are going to have to live with two phenomena: a large sector of industry concentrated in big enterprise; and a number of essential industries in which supply and distribution is dominantly concentrated in a few large concerns.

Now, great economic concentration, and great concentration within any essential industry even though privately owned, progressively ceases to be either private, or even free, enterprise. I present the thesis that corporations, under these circumstances, progressively approximate a form of nonstatist socialism.

Yet I suggest that the difference between great private concentrations, especially great concentrations within essential industries, and state- or publicly-owned industry is less than one would suppose. The two systems are similar in that both strive toward a central planning function. They differ chiefly in the groups that carry on that central planning function, and in the criteria applied to their planning.

I do not here go through the statistical evidence that concentration exists. The evidence is convincing. Further . . . we live under a tax system which tends to perpetuate it.

If you own a small business, which has grown up and got sizeable and prosperous — and you are putting your affairs in shape to meet certain death and inheritance taxes — the most advantageous thing you can do is to sell your enterprise. But you do not sell it for cash — that means paying capital gains taxes. You sell it to a large corporation, whose stock is listed on some exchange. You take in return voting stock which is readily marketable. This avoids capital gains taxes altogether. A large corporation can actually offer to the owner of a small business a lower price, payable in stock, than anyone else can offer him in cash — and the seller can benefit by accepting the offer. The large corporation thus tends to grow by acquisition.

Even without this, large corporations enjoy an advantage which small businesses do not have. They can, by appropriate handling of their affairs, generate their own capital. The industrial giants of today commonly are not seeking new investors. They conscript their capital by withholding earnings and by building up large depreciation reserves. General Electric, U.S. Steel, Standard Oil of New Jersey, General Motors, for example, have not been seriously in the market for capital for a generation.

These two circumstances alone would justify the assumption of continuing concentration. There are other factors of equal importance. But, in any case and whatever the reason, the trend is clear, and the end is not in sight.

Economic concentration in industry would be interesting as an event in itself. It happens to have occurred, however, simultaneously with another phenomenon — the phenomenon of government responsibility for the working of the economic system and for conditions of life under it. . . .

The result may be quite simply stated:

Unless the American economic system supplies at an acceptable level of prices the current needs for goods, services, and employment, the government in power is likely to be voted out of office at the next general election.

Yet the government, endeavoring to maintain a more or less stable and more or less satisfactory economic system, is forced to include the great industrial concentrations in its calculations. Production is needed; this can only be had by small-scale production, by big corporate production, or by socialist operation. Employment must be substantially full; if the government is not itself to be the employer, the private corporation must provide work. If private enterprise, balanced by competition, does not keep the economy on an even keel, the government must step in with planning and controls.

In much of the world (including most of the continent of Europe), governments have met this situation by socializing in greater or less degree the production of their respective countries. In America we have not — relying on private organization, competitive practice, and private initiative. In tangible fact, at the present state of the industrial revolution, two, and only two, great methods of productive organization have emerged: socialist collectivism, operated by government commissariats, and private collectivisms, operated by great corporations of the American type.

We seem to like it. The system has advantages as well as disadvantages. But it is fair to ask where the system is bound. The problem is whether we shall be able to avoid those developments which led England down a primrose path through concentration to cartels, and thence into state socialism — a socialism perhaps inevitable for the British, but which still seems unnecessary here.

Some commentators have propounded the theory that corporate concentration is a halfway house on the one-way road toward socialism. These believe that if concentration cannot be stopped and broken up, if small-scale production cannot be brought back, if the trend of growth continues, we have only to await the development of the corporate executive into the socialist commissar. The state may take over the corporate concentrates, or the corporate concentrates may take over the state — the result is much the same. This view, it is suggested, leaves out a possible development: the possibility that rules of law and social standards may so govern the internal as well as external functioning of the corporation that a democratic, nongovernmental economic system may emerge, capable alike of planning and stabilizing an economy and also of escaping the dangers which come from merging political and economic power. It is my belief that such rules of law and social standards are already appearing, and already are beginning to govern the corporate enterprise. I accordingly suggest . . . that there is coming into being what may be called the "intra-corporate common law" which does not regulate operations but rather sets up standards by which corporations are judged.

These standards are emerging, partly as common law and partly as applications of antitrust and similar statute laws. Enforcement of these standards, apparently, is proving to be the American alternative to the actual conduct of operations by the state. Instead of nationalizing an enterprise or industry, we set up standards of conduct for the managers of the enterprise or industry in such fashion that it will ultimately become immaterial whether it is nationalized or not. Such a result would be in the genius of the common law, as it is in line with the genius of the United States; for, fundamentally, in the United States it is the result and not the dogma that interests people.

Here we differ from our transatlantic forebears. In Europe, for years, the dogma has grown that nationalization per se was somehow good; that private ownership of production was per se an obstacle to progress. This dogma of the 19th century has been carried into, and dominates, most of European politics today. But the average American cares little about dogmatic theory. He wants certain results for his physical satisfaction; he wants certain social demands fulfilled. In method he is a pragmatist.

What results does he want?

In the first place, he wants enough of the product. He will raise all kinds of remonstrance, political and otherwise, if he does not get it, whether it consists of cigarettes or automobiles, housing or an adequate supply of steel, or any other thing that he considers necessary.

Second, he wants to pay not more than an "acceptable" price. I use the word "acceptable" because I don't want to use the word "fair." Some "acceptable" prices are anything but fair. He wants a price not so far out of range as to impose on him what he considers privation. This is realistic rather than idealistic.

Recently he has begun to make some relatively new demands. There is public insistence that at least a modicum of the Bill of Rights be applied as the standard of corporate action. Particularly he disapproves of race discrimination and wants to prevent arbitrary discrimination in choosing customers. He does not think of this as insistence on "equal protection of the laws" — but that is the origin of his demand. . . .

Still [another] social demand much in the news just now is that compensation for employment shall include provision for pensions for the old age of the employees. In economic analysis, I suppose, this is really a demand for redistribution of cost. Obviously, if a man takes a job at nineteen and works until he is sixty-three, and then is out of work, he is going to be supported from then on by somebody. Support may be in the town poorhouse; or it may be by his children or relatives; or it may be by private charity; or it may be by his own savings. The present demand is that it shall be by a pension, charged as part of the cost of his labor.

This is a new demand which some forward-looking businessmen long ago anticipated and provided for. Now it is being generally asserted by the great labor unions as a plain obligation of business. We cannot adequately analyze this demand as yet. By the time the present round of pension demands is met — they will be, in greater or lesser degree as a result of the recent steel settlements — roughly half the industry of the United States will be governed by pension agreements. An inchoate obligation is appearing, crystallizing into binding standards of practice, this time enforced through collective bargaining.

I surmise that, in addition to this, someday there will arise demand . . . that business be so handled that employment will be regular instead of seasonal, and unemployment be not as casually permitted as it is today. This is a job of industrial engineering of major proportions. . . .

Finally, I suspect that there is another demand coming up in a quite different area. Apparently there is beginning to be imposed an obligation to continue the technical development of the art of the industry. . . .

Here are . . . distinct "social demands," pushing into the field of inchoate law by various routes. Whenever stress appears, they impose themselves by one or another legal device. All, except the last, are noticeable within the everyday experience of individual people.

I submit that the phenomenon of social demands imposing themselves by process of law has gone far enough so that we are not dealing in a pure surmise when we speak of the emergence of "intracorporate" common law. . . .

How are the duties called for by social demands imposed? No clear pattern of imposition has yet emerged; a number of devices apparently can be used. One of them is worth particular attention here: the slow conversion of the antitrust laws from rules protecting small business to instruments of industrial regulation.

Antitrust law enforcement has turned away from older attempts to break up large combinations into smaller units. For a generation, indeed, no attempt of this kind was made. Now, certain actions are pending: the action to dissolve the Great Atlantic & Pacific Tea Company; to divorce the American Telephone & Telegraph Company from its wholly owned subsidiary and supplier, the Western Electric; and the pending proceeding requiring that the Du Pont Company and General Motors shall divest themselves of cross-holdings in each other's stock. The last two of these cases, even if successful, would hardly amount to prevention of concentration. The great majority of antitrust cases now follow a quite different pattern.

A great company or a concentrate is sued civilly under the antitrust laws. If found to have violated the law, the court is able to make a decree which, by way of penalty, subjects the corporation to an *ad hoc* judicial regulation. This has a certain relevance, I suppose, to the original theory of the antitrust laws; but in economic fact the regulatory decree appears to be more of a regulation of industry to get certain results than a means of restoring competition.

Thus, we have a whole body of cases in which corporations have been required not only to license their patents freely at a fixed fee, or occasionally at no fee, but also to provide personnel and know-how at cost to companies desiring to manufacture under such patents. In addition, some of the decrees give to the licensees the benefit of the further research and development which the luckless defendant is doing in his laboratories, and of any patents that may result from future research. That is to say, in a number of cases already, the result of an antitrust decree virtually makes the defendant corporation a sort of public utility to supply the know-how, patents, and even technical assistance.

The prototype is the famous International Salt case, but there are many others. Lawyers read decisions but rarely read the decrees; in this case the decree is the interesting part, for the decree, and subsequent decrees stemming from it, indicates that the social demand is not satisfied merely by depriving a company of its patent monopoly. It must so handle its affairs that it continues to disseminate its further progress in the art. I have yet to see a decree which requires a corporation to continue research and experimental work — that is, which imposes the duty to continue developing the art. Yet I suspect this development may not be far off.

Here, the antitrust law device is used as a method of conscripting a corporation or a concentrate of corporations into an era of regulation. Regulation is then worked out, situation by situation, through the Federal District courts.

It appears, then, that the pragmatic American method of dealing with its economic system prefers private ownership and operation — or, indeed, perhaps is not interested greatly in the question who is owner and who is operator, but is vividly interested in results. Put differently, the doctrine imposed by public opinion is that certain results shall be obtained; if obtained, the method of attaining them — private or public — is of only limited interest. Who cares whether the telephone is owned by the state or by the local telephone compa-

ny, provided the service is good and the price is a dime? If choice has to be made between a privately owned and a publicly owned system, the choice is in favor of the private enterprise. Yet the chief reason is that the American Telephone & Telegraph Company has lived up to, and continues to live up to, certain standards — including not only conventional public utility standards but some others as well — for instance, not tapping your wires or intruding on your conversations.

General Motors during the recent shortage endeavored to maintain its list prices. It went to trouble and expense trying to prevent its dealers from collecting black market prices so far as it could. I think this was honorably done, and was not an attempt to do good for advertising purposes; in any case, the prices collected yielded a respectable profit. I think General Motors had a very solid fear that if it let prices take their uncontrolled course in a period of shortage, the result would have been either government intervention or a row so great that General Motors would be years getting over it. . . .

Thus we are on the threshold, it seems to me, of a new superstructure of the law of the economic concentrate. It will largely be corporation law. It will sidestep, and perhaps quite properly, the problem of who ought to be the owner or who ought to head the organization. Instead, this emerging law will recognize these inchoate social demands and will translate them into accepted philosophy and workable common law. We may be finding an American answer to a problem which elsewhere has turned on sterile issues of dogma and abstract theory.

---

*Nice guys finish last.*
        Leo Durocher, when his character was criticized

114.

# BERNARD IDDINGS BELL: An Indictment of American Education

*The decade following World War II saw the publication of a number of far-reaching criticisms of American education. The critics, who often were on the fringes of the academic world and not professional educators, expressed their concern that America's schools and colleges were failing because of problems relating to financial support, teacher training, curriculum design, and administrative inefficiency. One of the more astute of these observers of the educational scene was Episcopalian Canon Bernard Iddings Bell, student chaplain at the University of Chicago during the late 1940s.* Crisis in Education, *portions of which are reprinted here, was published in 1949.*

Source: *Crisis in Education,* New York, 1949: "Is American Education Good" and "First Steps in Reformation."

## IS AMERICAN EDUCATION GOOD?

IS THE UNITED STATES today a nation composed chiefly of people who have not grown up, who think and act for the most part — and in a democracy the most part is the determining part — with the immaturity and emotional impulsiveness of adolescents? Many shrewd observers of the American scene, both abroad and here at home, are saying that this is indeed the case and that it is our educational system, defective in its understanding of man, which is largely responsible for our dangerous juvenility. I venture to add my voice to theirs.

Education is our largest American industry. Statistics furnished by the Department of Education in Washington show that there were in 1944 (the latest year in which statistics are accurate) 604,448 teachers employed in kindergarten and elementary schools, 324,190 teachers in secondary schools, and 155,000 teachers in colleges and universities. This makes 1,083,638 teachers in all. It is estimated that by 1948 this number had grown to approximately 1,200,000. The number of students engaged in *full-time* study in 1943-1944 was 28,262,248. It is estimated that there were at least 2,840,000 persons engaged in part-time study — night courses, etc. Hence the grand total of individuals studying in schools and colleges in this country would seem to be in the neighborhood of 31,000,000. Pupils and students together number certainly as many as 32,250,000. Over one-fifth of the total population are "school people." Of quantity of education we can boast, with justification for our boasting. But what of its results?

If the charge of immaturity can justly be brought against us Americans — and it is hard to deny its validity — some of us are moved to ask how we got that way and what, if anything, the nation can do, what individuals can help it to do, to insure a recovery. Peter Pan is a charming figure in fantasy; but a real community made up of little boys (and girls) who never cease to think and behave as children has nightmare possibilities. Something must be done. But what?

Obviously, nothing much can be expected in the way of growing up from most of the alleged adults who now comprise the majority of the electorate in America. Unless maturity arrives by the age of thirty or so, and those in control are well over that, it can come, if at all, only by miraculous intervention of the gods, intervention which seems too much to expect or ask. Our task is somehow to mature the rising generation; therein lies our hope. It is the basic contention of this book that this necessary job cannot be done by our character-molding institutions — the home, the Church, the school — unless these rediscover somehow that *democratic education must be not only democratic but also education.*

An increasing number of observers, some of them specialists in education and others just generally intelligent, have reluctantly become convinced that what is now being done in the schools and colleges, assisted by the churches and homes, far from being a corrective of the current immaturity, is one of the chief causes of it, and a potent source of social instability and human unhappiness. To say this is not to deny, not to disparage the magnificent work being done incidentally in and by our schools and colleges and universities and churches and homes. It is not for what they do that one must blame them but for what they leave undone. More than a few of us have begun to suspect that somehow we must rescue the American schools and colleges from those in them who are mishandling boys and girls or else be content to watch a continued deterioration of that democratically ordered society of which our fathers dreamed and for which they sacrificed and of which we boast one to another and to the rest of the world.

Because of a growing distrust of the competency of current American education, especially our higher education, there are those of us who were more than a little alarmed when we heard of the provision by our government at the close of World War II which makes it possible for any veteran to go to a college, university, or professional school almost entirely at public cost. We had reason to feel none too sure of the wisdom of this procedure. The standards of admission and of achievement at such institutions, with a few honorable exceptions, have for some time been so low, their regimens have been so stereotyped, their desire for growth in quantity rather than quality has been so great, their appetite for fees to supplement an ever-lessening income from endowment so voracious that it was, or at least it seemed to us doubters, a dreadful thing to expose a million or so veterans to their tender mercies. It might be that the GIs would think that they were going to get an education at public expense; it was a shame thus to delude them.

The effect on the universities and colleges might be equally sad. Their financial hides saved, at least for the time being, these institutions of somewhat diluted learning would probably go in more and more for uncritical expansion. They would have to engage more professors, instructors, assistants, technicians than the competently trained supply; for lack of manpower the teaching would have to be done in mass lots by the discredited lecture method; there could be little analysis of individual students or guidance of them into the particular pursuits in which they were competent to function.

We were aware, to be sure, that the proposed grants would be useful in keeping out of the labor market a group too great easily to be assimilated into industry and agriculture — that this was probably the real motive of the GI Bill of Rights. We comforted ourselves also by remembering that most of the GIs would be after only a few tools to use for the improvement of their financial status. We were fairly sure that the returning veterans were too much the product of our school system to know a decent educational discipline if they met up with it.

But what of the few who did wish an education and were competent to get one? And what of the harm that would be done to our country by throwing vast new crowds of conformist mediocrities with college degrees into a citizenry already over-blessed with such people? No good and much almost certain harm would come to America by encouraging in complacency new throngs whose attention had been directed under official sanction chiefly to concentration on superficialities.

What we dreaded seems to a large extent to be happening. Most of the collegiate GIs neither desire nor gain access to illumination or general understanding, while increasingly the cry goes up from the intelligent GI that instead of wisdom he is being sold an inferior piece of goods.

We comforted ourselves with the thought that the supply of veterans would soon be exhausted and that the evils involved in the GI Bill of Rights would come to an end. But now comes along the report of the President's Commission on Higher Education (1948) which, in spite of many valuable suggestions for improvement in education, advocates a vast extension of the privilege of getting a higher education at public expense, regardless of whether or not there is made available for this new academic population the sort of colleges which can develop their variant types of brains.

In the minds of Congress and of our people generally, back of the GI Bill of Rights and back of these new proposals is an assumption that it is a good thing for everyone to attend the American college "as is," just as it has come to be taken as beyond argument that it is highly desirable for the national welfare that every child shall go through the American high school "as is." There are those of us who insist that these assumptions are unjustified, who maintain that what is needed is a rethinking of our whole notion of democratic education — differentiation in colleges, various kinds of high schools, widely variant types of post high-school study, such education as will not stereotype on a low level every man Jack and woman Jill in the land but will rather, to use G. K. Chesterton's phrase, encourage "every potty little person to be happily and effectively his potty little self," such an educational system as will demand a clear willingness to work hard plus a demonstrated ability as prerequisites for access to the public funds. If this, our conviction, be un-American and unpatriotic, make the most of it.

Lest there be misunderstanding, it needs to be made clear that those of us who are doubters and viewers with alarm are not enamored of the little red schoolhouse or McGuffey's *Readers* or regimented classrooms or the use on pupils of the birch or the bamboo wand. We do not advocate a blind return to the educational methods of the nineteenth century — or of the thirteenth or of the fifth or of Periclean Athens. But it is no mark of wisdom either, so we think, to admire educational philosophies, programs, methods merely because their proponents insist that they are "modern" or "progressive."

Sometimes "modern" and "progressive" educators go on to say that what they advocate is "scientific" and therefore to be accepted without question. Much as one respects the good faith of those who make this claim, it is hard to see that it is justified. John Dewey and his disciples, whatever be their wisdom or lack of it, do not come to their conclusions as a result of experimentation one whit more than do, for example, the Jesuits, who are at the opposite pole in method. In both cases what is advocated and practised is derived from philosophical presupposition; it is deductive rather than inductive. We have yet to look upon a "scientific" pedagogy. Probably none is possible, at least in the sense of its being derived from measurement; human behavior is a bit too elusive for that. If by "scientific" is meant testing theoretical presuppositions by how they work, then *all* schools of thought in education are scientific. "By their fruits ye shall know them." It is an observation of the fruits which scares many of us; we see what has happened and is happening to the American mind, the American character, under the leadership of those who now set the educational pattern. A theory which works so badly *must* be wrong. . . .

## FIRST STEPS IN REFORMATION

1. *The teaching profession must be organized more widely and more definitely than it now is, to see to it that the public is aroused, first of all, to insist on adequate financial support of education and, secondly, to resist all political control, all attempts to transform the schools, colleges, and universities into agencies for the spreading of government-devised propaganda.* . . .

2. *We need to recognize that there is an inexcusable waste of student time involved in our system of schooling as now organized. Formal education takes entirely too long.*

The waste injures, first of all, those who are going on to the professions: medicine, the law, business administration, diplomacy and consular service, education, forestry, agriculture, research in science, and the rest. Consider for example the young American of today who desires to become a medical doctor. After leaving high school at eighteen years of age, he must go four years to college, then four years to a medical school (if it is a good one), then two years to an in-

ternship. By the time he is through with all this and ready to begin work, he is twenty-eight years old. Then — and probably not until then — he can get busy, settle down, marry. About the same amount of time should be required in the other professions.

The waste also hurts those who are going into business, industry, finance. These should have, and the best of them demand, four years in college, after which they must get jobs and learn how to handle themselves in terms of their jobs. This takes four or five years more. They too are well on toward thirty before they can function competently. Even young men and women who desire to learn a trade, if they are to have anything of a general education, are in their twenties before they are ready for apprenticeship.

This is obviously too long a time to spend on education apart from self-support and self-expression; and it is unduly extravagant for the country as a whole to support out of labor so many people for so many years. In consequence, the tendency has been to telescope the college and technical or professional training, with resulting restriction in the amount and adequacy of general education for citizenship and for a rich and rational enjoyment of living. When we bemoan the too utilitarian nature of our colleges and to some extent of our high schools, we might have grace to remember that this is largely forced on them by sheer pressure to get the students out and about their business at a reasonable age. If we are to have both general education and vocational training — and obviously we need them both — we must avoid all possible waste and duplication from the beginning to the end of our system.

Most observers are sure that the major waste is in the elementary schools and high schools. How to remedy this will require a great deal of study on the part of experts who are not hindered by the inertia of things as they are. It would even now seem possible and worthwhile to divide our schools somewhat differently from the way they are traditionally divided in the United States. . . .

3. *We must make it possible for highly competent students of low income or from low-income families to go on with their education through high school, college, graduate or professional school at public expense, and this without expectation that they take time off from their studies to support or partially support themselves by gainful employment.* . . .

Often our state or municipal universities do, it is true, provide free or nearly free tuition, and almost all our secondary schools are of the free-tuition type; but tuition fees are a small part of the cost of education to pupils and their families. We still handicap the poor man's sons and daughters. It is conservatively estimated that going on beyond the high school is financially possible only for one in three really bright children of parents whose family income is less than $2,500; for one in two whose family income is between $3,000 and $5,000; for one in one whose family income is over $7,000. They do not all go, of course, from the higher income group, but it can be wangled when desired. . . .

It is hard not to agree with S. E. Harris who, after study of the facts, statistical and otherwise, concludes that ". . . the loss of talent is serious. . . . We need not only free schools for all and tuition subsidies for the talented in colleges; we also need aid to finance the upkeep of those who show talent or promise at all ages." *We should, as a matter of investment for the public welfare, adequately support men and women who show evidence of superior brain power. Only thus can we really equalize and democratize educational opportunity.* . . .

4. *Forbid by law the assigning at any stage of schooling of more than twenty-five pupils to a teacher.* It is impossible really to teach more pupils than that. This is an entirely proper demand made by the better educa-

tional associations. But if we satisfy it we must have, for the same number of pupils as at present, at least 25 percent more teachers than now. Where do we get them? Whence do we pay them?

5. *We must enlist, train, and sustain both more teachers and much more able teachers than we now have, and this at every level.* The teaching profession is demanding more pay. Of the justice of this insistence, more in a moment or two. First let us ask if the teachers that we have at present, taking them by and large, are worth more than we pay them. The answer is that for the most part they are not. Many of them have not had an education, either general or professional, sufficient for effective teaching.

The average four-year college course given in American colleges and universities does not encompass an impressive amount of "higher" education, measured by, say, British standards. But only fifteen American states out of the forty-eight require a college degree for teachers; and more than half of all the teachers in the country have none. Over 6 percent of American public-school teachers have had no training beyond high school; 35 percent have had less than two years of post high-school training; and over 14 percent hold sub-standard certificates, indicating incapacity to meet even the minimum requirements of their states . . . and it is certainly no sign of progress that the average American teacher today has less college education than the average of five years ago.

Even when we recognize these low-qualification standards, however, almost any unprejudiced observer will admit that our teachers are not paid enough to live on. They were underpaid before the war; they are worse underpaid today. Between 1939 and 1948 the general cost of living rose about 55 percent; the pay of teachers, in spite of an estimated increase of $350 million in 1947-1948 over 1946-1947, has gone up only about 25 percent. Stipends will have to be raised at least a further billion dollars if we are to establish a wage for teachers of from $2,500 to $6,000 a year, a reasonable and not extravagant remuneration.

The low pay now prevailing is the largest factor in preventing the enlistment of the proper kind of women in teaching, and it prevents most men from even thinking of teaching except in university positions; it also hinders the continuance of qualified persons in the profession. But there are other deterrents beside low pay.

There is also insecurity of tenure. In most parts of the country teachers in grammar schools and high schools are "hired" year by year, their competence judged and sentence rendered annually by local school boards made up for the most part of popularly elected persons inexperienced in pedagogy and subject to political pressure and to even less reputable forms of social prejudice. Even in higher education there is insecurity for those under the rank of associate professor, which means for the greater part of every college staff.

Another hindrance to our getting enough competent teachers is the common feeling that teaching is not a profession of dignity, not a learned profession, only a sort of hack trade which receives little public honor, honor such as might help make the low pay endurable.

There is also the irksome difficulty, widely known, of a teacher's having to deal with undisciplined children. A schoolmistress whom I knew to be experienced and able, living in the Far West, a master of arts from a good university, once wrote me that at the age of thirty-five, after ten years' service in a public junior high school, she had abandoned the profession and taken a position selling blouses for a jobbing firm. I protested at the change and asked if she were doing it in the hope of more money. She replied,

Not at all. I lose my pension rights; besides, I am not sure I shall make more in the new work. The truth is that I could not stick it any longer. I could not

face the thought of being insulted for another year, day after day, by a pack of impudent and unlicked cubs of fourteen or so, the males crude enough and the females worse, whose homes did not discipline them, discipline of whom was on principle ignored by the very "progressive" and in my opinion wholly unrealistic school authorities, and whom I was forbidden by law in any way myself to punish. Life is too short and self-respect is too strong for me to go on.

I told this to a teacher in a school in the Bronx, one of the best esteemed teachers in the New York City school system. "Of course," she said. "Your acquaintance is quite right about it. The same thing is true in New York City. A woman must have the hide of a rhinoceros to teach in the public schools in our metropolis. It is a rare day that I am not insulted by some of the little beasts, cursed at, shoved and jostled, called a vile name or two. If I let myself notice, I should have to follow your friend's example. I have learned to ignore it."

In parts of the country that are more civilized than the monster cities, in smaller communities where the home has not collapsed, in places where administrators try to deal with real children instead of with the little angels imagined by a good many professors of education, teachers are not quite so trampled on by their charges; but, speaking generally, "the teacher's lot is not a happy one," and gentlemen and gentlewomen think twice before they contemplate teaching and often do not think twice about abandoning it later on for other vocations.

Coupled with this resentment against undiscipline, teachers often feel an irritation at being ordered about by theorists from schools of education who are put into posts of authority over them and who, though they have had small teaching experience themselves, continually want to change procedures to fit in with new ideas thought up in a study somewhere. Teachers think that before pedagogic changes are made, particularly changes which involve radical adjustment of philosophical approach, they who do the instructing should be consulted and persuaded and convinced of the necessity and wisdom thereof; that reforms should come not from the top down but from the bottom up.

They are weary of change and rechange. They see their pupils regarded not as growing human beings but as guinea pigs for experimentation and themselves as unwilling laboratory technicians. Inner revolt drives thousands out of teaching every year and prevents other thousands from preparing for it, and these frequently the cream of the crop. Most teachers realize the facts of the case, but it is usually considered impolitic to say anything about them in public unless one first gets out of teaching. This curious silence is good evidence of "the sickness that destroyeth in the noonday."

To sum up, if we wish teachers in proper numbers and of the right sort, we should:

a. Pay them from $2,500 to $6,000 a year and give them assurance of tenure unless incompetence can be proved, and proper pensions on retirement after service.

b. Raise the academic requirements for teachers as rapidly as possible so that teaching becomes a reputable profession. If pedagogues are paid a living wage, the public may thus be made at least a little more sure that it gets its money's worth.

c. Subsidize secondary-school and college students who show potential competence for teaching so that they may prepare themselves for it. Give them if they have need an annual allowance of at least $1,000 from the public funds, to be used toward tuition and support in reputable places of training, with a requirement that if they do not enter the profession or leave it voluntarily after less than five years' service they shall pay back all sums advanced to them at the rate of $200 a year.

d. Require that no one be given supervisory authority over teachers who has had less than five years of actual teaching experience.

e. Restore to the schools a discipline sufficiently effective to protect teachers from insult and intimidation at the hands of their pupils.

Other things are doubtless necessary for getting and holding competent instructors in sufficient numbers; but the steps just mentioned would seem almost indispensable.

6. *We need to combat the notion that the only attitude toward God which is legitimate in a tax-supported school is the attitude that ignores God as though He does not exist or, if He does exist, does not matter.*

It is of course proper that atheists should be able to send their children to atheistic schools if they so desire; but it is hard to see why atheists, few in number as they are, should be allowed to force atheistic-by-negation education on the children of the great majority of us who do pay at least theoretical attention to the Deity. As the American school system is now conducted, more and more conducted, there is no such thing as religious liberty in American education. There is liberty only to be unreligious. "In God we trust" we still put on our coins; we cannot entrust our children to Him. If the public schools must "leave religion out," then the only decent thing is to permit religious groups to run their own schools, which of course we now do, and to give them tax money to run them with, which we do not. Such a step would not in the least violate the principle, embodied in the Constitution, that there must be no established Church in the United States. No one wishes to set up an exclusive *ecclesia*. Those who think that to give public funds to a religious body for schools in which religion matters is somehow tied up with reuniting Church and State, would seem to be just plain ignorant and illogical people, and this whether they sit on cracker barrels or on the Supreme Court of the United States.

If it be contended that multiple school systems divide the body politic, which to some extent they do, then in reply it may be pointed out that the only way to retain complete unity and at the same time give freedom to those who desire that their children shall recognize God is to see to it that time is given in the public schools to a common examination by the growing children of what are the basic religious and moral ideas, all this taught objectively and with no desire to bring about conviction (which is the province of the Church and the home), and also to furnish opportunity in school hours for the various current faiths in a community to teach their own children what they themselves believe. But this is unlawful according to the Supreme Court (Scopes Case, 1948). Is the price of national unity, then, the abandonment of all religion? This is the nub of the matter.

7. *The schools should refuse to assume burdens properly parental; they have quite enough to do without that.* If the American parent is incompetent to look after the physical, social, and ethical upbringing of his or her children, which is certainly true of many parents, possibly true of most of them, then those who have the national welfare at heart, instead of piling impossible burdens on the schools, had better make homemaking and home education itself a basic part of schooling from six years of age onward and had better go in dead earnest at the education of parents who already are parents.

8. *Adult education generally is grossly neglected among us, though happily less so with each passing year.* The time never comes when a human being can justly be called an "educated person." The world is not divided into the educated and the uneducated, but rather into the educable and the uneducable. If a man were really to come to the place that he was educated, that is to say if he were to come to the end of growing apprehension and understanding, all that could rightly be done to that man would be to dig a hole and bury him. Fortunately few reach such a sad estate. The educable pro-

cess should be made available for men and women of all ages from babyhood to death.

Nor should it be regarded as enough to assist adults to improve their technical skills and so increase their incomes. There is real hunger for general knowledge, liberal knowledge, among adult persons: witness the introduction of courses in political theory for farmers in Kansas, under the joint direction of the Farm Bureau and the Institute of Citizenship at Kansas State College; witness the great success of the Peoples' High Schools in Denmark, which do *not* teach technology but devote themselves to the teaching of history, bases of Danish culture, the literature of the country, the principles of political and social organization, which admit no pupil under eighteen years of age and none who is not engaged in industry or agriculture; witness the wide spread of the "Great-books Movement"; witness the growth of lecture courses, women's clubs, town halls. There are many things which cannot be studied to much advantage or otherwise than in an atmosphere of artificiality except by people who are grown-up and at work: political science, for instance, or how to handle loneliness and frustration. A community ought to be thoroughly ashamed of itself which does not devote as much thought, time, money, to the education of adults over twenty as it provides for the nurture of children under twenty.

9. *Thought needs to be given to what may be done in respect to teaching morals and manners.*

The chief difficulty here is that our American civilization has no agreed-upon ethical standards, standards which can be assumed and taught to the oncoming generation as a matter of course. We are a people with no common world view, no generally accepted definition of the nature and purpose of man. Such being the case, it becomes a necessity for each school or college to determine the sort of moral theory to which it intends to commit itself, together with the brand of good manners which it will derive from that theory. If this is not done, the result will be the turning out of amoral graduates and unmannered boors. The ethical commitment of a college or school should be made clear to those who teach, to those who learn, to those to whom appeal is made for pupils and support.

But to whom or to what is a man responsible for his behavior? Only to himself? In spite of the dictum of Polonius, to be true to oneself does not necessarily result in being false to no other man, not unless the self to which one is true is a self devoted to more than self. Otherwise, for people to be true each to himself or herself is more apt to result in anarchy than in an ordered way of life. Is one to be responsible, for what one is and does, only to the will of majorities? This results in a conformist mediocrity. Is one to look to the total social group for standards of behavior, for sanctions? The end of this is a totalitarian setup manipulated by the ruthless and unscrupulous, a negation of just opportunity for freedom of expression and for voluntary self-investment. Is man's responsibility to mere tradition? This is deadly to creative and critical thinking, without which no society can long survive. Is it to negation of tradition? This way lies a deal of precious nonsense and preciosity. Is human responsibility to that which is beyond man? *If so, religion is involved, primarily involved, inescapably involved in education.*

We need a deeply concerned consideration of the basis of right conduct and decent manners, a consideration carried on not merely on the level of high philosophy but also on the pedagogic level of how to train for character and social cooperation. We need this immediately, demandingly; but our professors of education, our administrators, our teachers, are usually little concerned with inquiry about purpose — purpose in politics, purpose in labor, purpose in living, purpose in anything, including

purpose in education itself. This neglect is almost too absurd to be imagined; yet it is a fact. It is obviously ridiculous to try to develop growing human beings without asking what man is to aim at and why. *We might well have a moratorium on discussion of methods and organization of education until we come to some decision about the moral ends of education.*

Ideally decision about such matters should be reached by society as a whole and govern our education as a matter of course; but in a confused state of social disruption like ours in this mid-twentieth century, general agreement about morals is next to impossible. In this lies national peril; we have no agreed-upon ethical ideology; there is nothing commonly held as imperative to be promoted or defended, nothing which compels the glad devotion of lives and fortunes unless we get returns in profits and praise. It will be a long time, possibly a fatally long time, before we again have a national morality unless it be a totalitarian and secularistic morality, which God forbid. Meanwhile each school or college or university is forced to define its own concept of the good life and then strive to impart it, unless that school or college or university is content, as most are in the United States today, to deal only with secondary matters while the commonwealth drifts toward dissolution. We might at least be informing our students about what the various ethical alternatives are. *Make moral philosophy once more the central consideration in education.* Of all the steps suggested or implied for the salvation of teaching and learning, in this book or in any other book on the subject that I have read, this is both the most immediately required and the most difficult.

Would the taking of the nine steps which have just been mentioned serve to rescue American thinking and action from incompetence, insure maturity among us, enable us to avoid alternations of ignorant conceit and of a panic fear, make out of education in America what it reasonably ought to be? Obviously not; but they would help a little, more than a little. In excuse for their obvious inadequacy as a program of reform, let it be remembered again that it is the purpose of this book not to prescribe but to diagnose; perhaps to get the patient, which is all of us, to know that in respect to our pedagogics we are a sick folk, that we have been too long fooled by doctrinaire pedagogues who ignore man as he is and children as they are. In short it is our thesis that education in these United States is in crisis, that it is being judged by the relentless impact of reality, that it is being judged and found wanting. Once we realize this, we shall soon have both wisdom and bravery to set about a radical and comprehensive reform.

## 115.

# Debate on the North Atlantic Treaty

*The North Atlantic Pact, establishing a mutual defense agreement (the North Atlantic Treaty Organization, or NATO) among twelve North American and Western European nations, represented the first concerted attempt of the Western democracies to contain Communist expansion. Negotiations to establish NATO began in London in September 1948, and the treaty was made public in March 1949. Debate about the treaty and about America's participation in still another international organization besides the United Nations was carried on in Congress and in the press. The following selection includes arguments pro and con. Secretary of State Dean Acheson defended the treaty in an address of March 19, 1949, part of which is reprinted here. Senator Robert A. Taft of Ohio voiced the objections of congressional opponents of the treaty in a speech during the Senate debate of July 11, part of which is also reprinted below. The Senate ratified the treaty on July 21.*

Source: *Record*, 81 Cong., 1 Sess., pp. 9111-9113, 9205-9210.

## I.

### Dean Acheson:
### For the Treaty

The text of the proposed North Atlantic Pact was made public today. I welcome this opportunity to talk with my fellow citizens about it.

It has taken many months to work out this text with the representatives of the other nations involved. . . . Public opinion can now be formed on the basis of complete information. Only in this way can your government have what former Secretary of State [Henry] Stimson has termed "the understanding support . . . of the American people," which is essential to the success of any policy.

I think the American people will want to know the answers to three principal questions about the pact: How did it come about and why is it necessary? What are its terms? Will it accomplish its purpose?

The paramount purposes of the pact are peace and security. If peace and security can be achieved in the North Atlantic area, we shall have gone a long way to assure peace and security in other areas as well. The achievement of peace and security means more than that in the final outcome we shall have prevented war and brought about the settlement of international disputes by peaceful means.

There must be conviction of people everywhere that war will be prevented and that disputes will be settled peacefully. In the most practical terms, true international peace and security require a firm belief by the peoples of the world that they will not be subjected to unprovoked attack, to coercion and intimidation, to interference in their own affairs. . . .

The Atlantic Pact is a collective self-defense arrangement among the countries of the North Atlantic area. It is aimed at coordinating the exercise of the right of self-defense especially recognized in Article 51 of the United Nations Charter. It is designed to fit precisely into the framework of the United Nations and to assure practical measures for maintaining peace and security in harmony with the Charter.

It is the firm intention of the parties to carry out the pact in accordance with the provisions of the United Nations Charter and in a manner which will advance its purposes and principles. Already one such arrangement under the Charter has been established with United States participation. The twenty-one American republics in reorganizing their regional system have specifically brought it within the framework of the United Nations Charter. We are now joining in the formation of a second arrangement, pertaining to the North Atlantic area, likewise within the framework of the United Nations.

It is important to keep in mind that the really successful national and international institutions are those that recognize and express underlying realities. The North Atlantic community of nations is such a reality.

It is based on the affinity and natural identity of interests of the North Atlantic powers.

The North Atlantic Treaty which will formally unite them is the product of at least 350 years of history, perhaps more. There developed on our Atlantic Coast a community, which has spread across the continent, connected with western Europe by common institutions and moral and ethical beliefs. Similarities of this kind are not superficial, but fundamental. They are the strongest kind of ties, because they are based on moral conviction, on acceptance of the same values in life. . . .

Added to this profoundly important basis of understanding is another unifying influence — the effect of living on the sea. The sea does not separate people as much as it joins them, through trade, travel, mutual understanding, and common interests. For this second reason, as well as the first, North America and Western Europe have formed the two halves of what is in reality one community, and have maintained an abiding interest in each other.

It is clear that the North Atlantic Pact is not an improvisation. It is the statement of the facts and lessons of history. We have learned our history lesson from two world wars in less than half a century. That experience has taught us that the control of Europe by a single aggressive, unfriendly power would constitute an intolerable threat to the national security of the United States.

We participated in those two great wars to preserve the integrity and independence of the European half of the Atlantic community in order to preserve the integrity and independence of the American half. It is a simple fact, proved by experience, that an outside attack on one member of this community is an attack upon all members.

We have also learned that, if the free nations do not stand together, they will fall one by one. The stratagem of the aggressor is to keep his intended victims divided or, better still, set them to quarreling among themselves. Then they can be picked off one by one without arousing unified resistance. We and the free nations of Europe are determined that history shall not repeat itself in that melancholy particular.

As President Truman has said: "If we can make it sufficiently clear in advance that any armed attack affecting our national security would be met with overwhelming force, the armed attack might never occur." . . .

What are the principal provisions of the North Atlantic Pact? I should like to summarize them.

First, the pact is carefully and conscientiously designed to conform in every particular with the Charter of the United Nations. This is made clear in the 1st Article of the pact, which reiterates and reaffirms the basic principle of the Charter. The participating countries at the very outset of their association state again that they will settle all their international disputes, not only among themselves but with any nation, by peaceful means in accordance with the provisions of the Charter. This declaration sets the whole tone and purpose of this treaty.

The 2nd Article is equally fundamental. The associated countries assert that they will preserve and strengthen their free institutions and will see to it that the fundamental principles upon which free institutions are founded are better understood everywhere. They also agree to eliminate conflicts in their economic life and to promote economic cooperation among themselves. Here is the ethical essence of the treaty — the common resolve to preserve, strengthen, and make understood the very basis of tolerance, restraint, and freedom — the really vital things with which we are concerned.

This purpose is extended further in Article 3, in which the participating countries pledge themselves to self-help and mutual aid. In addition to strengthening their free institutions, they will take practical steps to maintain and develop their own capacity and that of their partners to resist aggression. They also agree to consult together when the integrity or security of any of them is threatened. The treaty sets up a council, consisting of all the members, and other machinery for consultation and for carrying out the provisions of the pact.

Successful resistance to aggression in the modern world requires modern arms and trained military forces. As a result of the recent war, the European countries joining the pact are generally deficient in both requirements. The treaty does not bind the United States to any arms program. But we all know that the United States is now the only democratic nation with the resources and the productive capacity to help the free nations of Europe to recover their military strength. Therefore, we expect to ask the Congress to supply our European partners some of the weapons and equipment they need to be able to resist aggression. We also expect to recommend military supplies for other free nations which will cooperate with us in safeguarding peace and security.

In the compact world of today, the security of the United States cannot be defined in terms of boundaries and frontiers. A serious threat to international peace and security anywhere in the world is of direct concern to this country. Therefore, it is our policy to help free peoples maintain their integrity and independence, not only in Western Europe or in the Americas but wherever the aid we are able to provide can be effective. Our actions in supporting the integrity and independence of Greece, Turkey, and Iran are expressions of that determination. Our interest in the security of these countries has been made clear, and we shall continue to pursue that policy.

In providing military assistance to other countries, both inside and outside the North Atlantic Pact, we will give clear priority to the requirements for economic recovery.

We will carefully balance the military-assistance program with the capacity and requirements of the total economy, both at home and abroad.

But to return to the treaty, Article 5 deals with the possibility, which unhappily cannot be excluded, that the nations joining together in the pact may have to face the eventuality of an armed attack. In this article, they agree that an armed attack on any of them, in Europe or North America, will be considered an attack on all of them. In the event of such an attack, each of them will take, individually and in concert with the other parties, whatever action it deems necessary to restore and maintain the security of the North Atlantic area, including the use of armed force.

This does not mean that the United States would be automatically at war if one of the nations covered by the pact is subjected to armed attack. Under our Constitution the Congress alone has the power to declare war. We would be bound to take promptly the action which we deemed necessary to restore and maintain the security of the North Atlantic area. That decision would be taken in accordance with our constitutional procedures. The factors which would have to be considered would be, on the one side, the gravity of the armed attack; on the other side the action which we believed necessary to restore and maintain the security of the North Atlantic area.

That is the end to be achieved. We are bound to do what, in our honest judgment, is necessary to reach that result. If we should be confronted again with a calculated armed attack such as we have twice seen in the 20th century, I should not suppose that we would decide any action other than the use of armed force effective either as an exercise of the right of collective self-defense or as necessary to restore the peace and security of the North Atlantic area. That decision will rest where the Constitution has placed it.

This is not a legalistic question. It is a question we have frequently faced, the question of faith and principle in carrying out treaties. Those who decide it will have the responsibility for taking all appropriate action under the treaty. Such a responsibility requires the exercise of will — a will disciplined by the undertaking solemnly contracted to do what they decide is necessary to restore and maintain the peace and security of the North Atlantic area. That is our obligation under this Article 5. It is equally our duty and obligation to the security of our own country.

All of these provisions of the pact are subject to the overriding provisions of the United Nations Charter. Any measure for self-defense taken under the treaty will be reported to the Security Council of the United Nations. These measures will continue only until the Security Council, with its primary responsibility, takes the necessary action to restore peace and maintain security.

The treaty has no time limit, but after it has been in effect twenty years, any member can withdraw on one year's notice. It also provides that, after it has been in existence ten years, it will be reviewed in the circumstances prevailing at that time. Additional countries may be admitted to the pact by agreement of all the parties already signatories.

These are the principal provisions of the treaty.

Will the pact accomplish its purpose? No one can say with certainty. We can only act on our convictions. The United States government and the governments with which we are associated in this treaty are convinced that it is an essential measure for strengthening the United Nations, deterring aggression, and establishing the sense of security necessary for the restoration of the economic and political health of the world.

It seems absurd that it should be necessary, in this era of popular education and highly developed communications, to deal with allegations which have no relation to the truth and could not stand even the crudest test of measurement against realities.

I refer here to the allegations that this treaty conceals aggressive designs on the part of its authors with respect to other countries. Anyone with the most elementary knowledge of the processes of democratic government knows that democracies do not and cannot plan aggressive wars. But for those from whom such knowledge may have been withheld I must make the following categoric and unequivocal statement, for which I stand with the full measure of my responsibility in the office I hold:

This country is not planning to make war against anyone. It is not seeking war. It abhors war. It does not hold war to be inevitable. Its policies are devised with the specific aim of bridging by peaceful means the tremendous differences which beset international society at the present time.

Allegations that aggressive designs lie behind this country's signature of the Atlantic Pact can rest only on a malicious misrepresentation or a fantastic misunderstanding of the nature and aims of American society. . . .

The United States is waging peace by promoting measures for the revival and expansion of world trade on a sound and beneficial basis. We are preparing to carry out an energetic program to apply modern skills and techniques to what President Truman has called the primitive and stagnant economies of vast areas, so that they will yield a better and richer life for their people. The United States is waging peace by throwing its full strength and energy into the struggle, and we shall continue to do so.

We sincerely hope we can avoid strife, but we cannot avoid striving for what is right. We devoutly hope we can have genuine peace, but we cannot be complacent about the present uneasy and troubled peace.

A secure and stable peace is not a goal we can reach all at once and for all time. It is a dynamic state, produced by effort and faith, with justice and courage. The struggle is continuous and hard. The price is never irrevocably ours. To have this genuine peace we must make it clear that armed attack will be met by collective defense, prompt and effective.

That is the meaning of the North Atlantic Pact.

## II.

### ROBERT A. TAFT:
### Against the Treaty

WE HAVE TO CONSIDER here the North Atlantic Treaty as it has been drafted, without the improvements senators would like to see made, but which twelve nations probably would not agree to once this treaty is ratified. We abandoned the chance of getting those when we signed the treaty in its present form. The Atlantic Treaty as drawn is certainly no improvement over the United Nations, nor can it by any stretch of the imagination be regarded as a perfection of or supplement to that Charter. From the point of view of an international organization, it is a step backward. Apart from the obligation to provide arms, the treaty is permitted by the Charter, which says:

> Nothing in the present Charter shall impair the inherent right of individual or collective self-defense if an armed attack occurs against a member of the United Nations until the Security Council has taken the measures necessary to maintain international peace and security.

The Charter merely recognizes this inherent right as necessary because the veto provision of the Charter may result in complete inaction on the part of the Security Council. But certainly in all other respects the treaty far more resembles a military alliance than it does any international association of nations. As the senator from Iowa so forcefully said, it is a step backward in the progress toward international peace and justice.

What is the nature of that treaty?

It is obviously, and I do not think it can be questioned, a defensive military alliance between certain nations, the essence of which is an obligation under Article 5 to go to war if necessary with any nation which attacks any one of the signers of the treaty. Such an attack may come from outsiders or it may come from one of the signers of the treaty itself. The obligation is completely binding for a period of twenty years. It imposes an obligation upon the United States to each member nation whether or not there is consultation or joint action by the Council, or a finding by any court that an unjustified armed attack has occurred. Our obligation is self-executing upon the occurrence of an armed attack.

Some doubt will always remain as to whether the Congress must declare war before our armed forces actually take part. I am inclined to think such action is not necessary if the President chooses to use our armed forces when an ally is attacked. But whether it is or not, the obligation to go to war seems to me binding upon the United States as a nation, so that Congress would be obligated to declare war if that were necessary to comply with the provisions of the treaty. It is pointed out that the President could fail to act and Congress could refuse to declare war, but certainly we are not making a treaty on the theory that we expect to violate it in accordance with our own sweet will.

It is correctly pointed out that the exact measures which we are obligated to take will be determined by us, and that it may not be necessary to go to the extent of a declaration of war. We do reserve a certain discretion, but as I see it, we do not reserve any discretion on the question, for instance, whether the armed attack is justified as a

reason for supporting it. If one of the members of the pact provides an attack, even by conduct which we disapprove, we would still apparently be bound to go to its defense. By executing a treaty of this kind, we put ourselves at the mercy of the foreign policies of eleven other nations, and do so for a period of twenty years. The Charter is obviously aimed at possible Russian aggression against Western Europe, but the obligation assumed is far broader than that. I emphasize again that the obligation is much more unconditional, much less dependent on legal processes, and much less dependent on joint action than the obligation of the United Nations Charter.

And yet in spite of these dangers, I have wanted to vote in favor of the Atlantic Pact for one reason and would still do so if the question of arms were not involved. . . .

It is said that the Atlantic Treaty is simply another Monroe Doctrine. I wish it were. That would be much more acceptable to me than the Atlantic Pact, arms or no arms. Let me point out the vital differences. The Monroe Doctrine was a unilateral declaration. We were free to modify it or withdraw from it at any moment. This treaty, adopted to deal with a particular emergency today, is binding upon us for twenty years to cover all kinds of circumstances which cannot possibly be foreseen. The Monroe Doctrine left us free to determine the merits of each dispute which might arise and to judge the justice and the wisdom of war in the light of the circumstances at the time. The present treaty obligates us to go to war if certain facts occur. The Monroe Doctrine imposed no obligation whatever to assist any American nation by giving it arms or even economic aid. We were free to fight the war in such a manner as we might determine, or not at all. This treaty imposes on us a continuous obligation for twenty years to give aid to all the other members of the pact, and, I believe, to give military aid to all the other members of the pact.

All kinds of circumstances may arise which will make our obligation most inconvenient. The government of one of these nations may be taken over by the Communist Party of that nation. The distinguished senator from Michigan says that we are then released from our obligation, but I see no basis whatever for such a conclusion. If that were true of a Communist government, it might also be true of a Socialist government if we did not happen to approve of socialism at the time. Presumably, it could be true of a Fascist government, one similar, perhaps, to that existing in Spain, which has been denounced recently by the secretary of state and which is not very different from the dictatorship of Portugal, which is a member of the pact and which has not a truly democratic form of government.

I cannot find anything in this treaty which releases us because we do not happen to like the officials in charge of the member nations at the particular moment. . . .

I have come reluctantly to the conclusion, therefore, that the arms program now presented to Congress must be considered an integral part of the Atlantic Treaty.

If that is the fact, we have a very different problem from the one which is urged upon us by the Committee on Foreign Relations, by its distinguished chairman, by the State Department, and by the distinguished senator from Michigan.

First, with the arms in the pact, it is even more clear that the pact is a military alliance, a treaty by which one nation undertakes to arm half the world against the other half, and in which all the pact members agree to go to war if one is attacked. It cannot be described otherwise than a military alliance. Of course, it is not like some of the alliances in the past, although many of them, such as the Franco-British alliance prior to World War I, were entirely defensive in character, or purported to be. Others were offensive and defensive alliances. I quite agree that the purpose of this alliance is not offensive and that we have no offensive purpose in mind. But it is exactly like many defensive military alliances of the past. . . .

Second, the pact standing by itself would clearly be a deterrent to war. If Russia knows that if it starts a war it will immediately find itself at war with the United States, it is much less likely to start a war. I see and believe in the full force of that argument. That is why I would favor the extension of the Monroe Doctrine to Europe. But if Russia sees itself ringed about gradually by so-called defensive arms, from Norway and Denmark to Turkey and Greece, it may form a different opinion. It may decide that the arming of Western Europe, regardless of its present purpose, looks to an attack upon Russia. Its view may be unreasonable, and I think it is. But from the Russian standpoint it may not seem unreasonable. They may well decide that if war is the certain result, that war might better occur now rather than after the arming of Europe is completed . . .

Third, the pact with the arms obligation, I believe, violates our obligations under the United Nations. The pact apparently is not made under Articles 52 to 54 inclusive, because we do not propose to consult the Security Council as there contemplated, we do plan to take enforcement action without the authorization of the Security Council, and we do not plan to keep them fully informed. . . . It violates the whole spirit of the United Nations Charter. That Charter looks to the reduction of armaments by agreement between individual nations. I do not claim that there is any direct violation of the Charter, but the Atlantic Pact moves in exactly the opposite direction from the purposes of the Charter and makes a farce of further efforts to secure international peace through law and justice. It necessarily divides the world into two armed camps. It may be said that the world is already so divided, but it cannot be said that by enforcing that division we are carrying out the spirit of the United Nations.

Fourth, the obligation to furnish arms is either a mere token obligation, or it is one of vast extent. I do not know enough about modern military equipment to make any estimate. I have heard that to provide sixty divisions, which is said to be the very minimum necessary and perhaps completely inadequate against Russian attack, would cost a total of $24 billion. We are entering on a new lend-lease. The history of these obligations has been that once begun, they cannot be easily brought to an end. . . .

We have chosen to give economic assistance. That assistance is given on the theory that the Russians do not contemplate aggressive war, but intend to fight their battle by propaganda and a production of chaotic economic conditions. I believe the undertaking of both types of assistance is beyond the economic capacity of the United States. I believe we will have to choose whether we give economic assistance or arms. The first, I believe, has contributed and will contribute to peace. The second, I think, will make war more likely.

Fifth, the justification for the arms aid rests on the necessity of defense against Russia, but remember that once these arms are provided, they are completely within the control of the nation receiving them. They are subject to the orders of those who, at the time, control the government of the country. Those governors may be Communists or Fascists, they may be peace-loving or they may be aggressors. In future years, these arms may be used against us instead of on our side. If Russia should choose to go to war within the next year or two, they might easily be captured by the Russians and turned against us. We would be playing a dangerous game if we encouraged every country in Europe to arm itself to the teeth. Modern arms are not toys. . . .

Sixth, by approving this pact with the arms program, I believe we are committing ourselves to a particular course of action in war which may be unwise at the time when a war may actually develop. It is one thing to agree to go to war with Russia if it attacks Western Europe. It is another to send American ground troops to defend Norway or Denmark or Holland or Italy or even France and England. I cannot assert positively that we are committing ourselves to a particular type of war, but I am inclined to think that we are. . . .

Seventh, finally, Mr. President, it is becoming increasingly apparent that England, at least, intends to trade extensively with Russia, and inevitably the same thing will be true of other Western European nations. They have provided airplane engines for Russia, heavy machinery and other equipment which can aid the Russians' warmaking potential. The more we take off their shoulders the burden of providing for their own defense, the more free they will be to ship steel and heavy machinery to the east. As a matter of fact, trade between Eastern and Western Europe has prevailed for thousands of years, and it is going to go on, no matter what we say about it. Of course, the recent agreement between Russia and England is very clear evidence of that fact. We are providing extensive economic assistance. To a large extent, economic assistance and aid for arms will go into the same pot. I do not think that the American people at this time desire to increase the overall aid we are giving to Western Europe with its tremendous burden on the American taxpayer.

Mr. President, since I feel that this pact is inextricably linked with the arms program, and since I believe that, so linked, the program is a threat to the welfare of the people of the United States, I shall vote against the treaty.

I am quite willing to consider the providing of assistance to particular countries, at particular times, if such aid seems at that time a real deterrent to war, and on that principle I voted for aid to Greece and Turkey. But that is a very different thing from an obligation to build up the armed forces of eleven countries, and a commitment on the American taxpayer for twenty years to give continued aid under circumstances of which we have not the slightest conception today. It is a very different thing from arming half the world against the other half.

My conclusion has been reached with the greatest discomfort. When so many disagree with that conclusion, I must admit that I may be completely wrong. I do not claim to be an expert in questions of foreign policy. I would like to be able to vote for a policy that will commit us to war if Russia attacks Western Europe. I would be glad to join in an agreement to occupy Germany indefinitely to guard against a third attack from that quarter. I would waive my other objections to the Atlantic Pact if I did not feel that it was inextricably involved with the arms program. But I cannot escape the logic of the situation as I see it, and therefore I cannot vote for a treaty which, in my opinion, will do far more to bring about a third world war than it will ever maintain the peace of the world.

---

116.

# Harry S. Truman: The Point Four Program

*The ideological battlegrounds of the Cold War were the underdeveloped nations of the earth, which were exposed to intensive propaganda activities from both sides. Russian claims that Western colonialism was the cause of economic stagnation in such areas and that its own impressive economic growth was the result of its adoption of the Communist system were alluring to the uncommitted nations and disturbing to many Americans. The American response was the so-called Point Four program, proposed by President Truman in his Inaugural Address on January 20, 1949. Whereas the Marshall Plan had been intended to promote economic recovery through capital investment in the war-torn industrial nations of Western Europe, the Point Four program was designed to foster economic development through technical assistance to the nonindustrial nations of Asia, Africa, and Latin America. On June 24 Truman sent a special message to Congress outlining the program, which was launched a year later.*

Source: 81 Congress, 1 Session, House Document No. 240.

In order to enable the United States, in cooperation with other countries, to assist the peoples of economically underdeveloped areas to raise their standards of living, I recommend the enactment of legislation to authorize an expanded program of technical assistance for such areas, and an experimental program for encouraging the outflow of private investment beneficial to their economic development. These measures are the essential first steps in an undertaking which will call upon private enterprise and voluntary organizations in the United States, as well as the government, to take part in a constantly growing effort to improve economic conditions in the less-developed regions of the world.

The grinding poverty and the lack of economic opportunity for many millions of people in the economically underdeveloped

of benefits resulting from the careful application of modern techniques to local problems. The benefits which a comprehensive program of expert assistance will make possible can only be revealed by studies and surveys undertaken as a part of the program itself.

To inaugurate the program, I recommend a first-year appropriation of not to exceed $45 million. This includes $10 million already requested in the 1950 budget for activities of this character. The sum recommended will cover both our participation in the programs of the international agencies and the assistance to be provided directly by the United States.

In every case, whether the operation is conducted through the United Nations, the other international agencies, or directly by the United States, the country receiving the benefit of the aid will be required to bear a substantial portion of the expense.

The activities necessary to carry out our program of technical aid will be diverse in character and will have to be performed by a number of different government agencies and private instrumentalities. It will be necessary to utilize not only the resources of international agencies and the United States government but also the facilities and the experience of the private business and non-profit organizations that have long been active in this work.

Since a number of federal agencies will be involved in the program, I recommend that the administration of the program be vested in the President, with authority to delegate to the secretary of state and to other government officers, as may be appropriate. With such administrative flexibility, it will be possible to modify the management of the program as it expands and to meet the practical problems that will arise in its administration in the future.

The second category of outside aid needed by the underdeveloped areas is the provision of capital for the creation of productive enterprises. The International Bank for Reconstruction and Development and the Export-Import Bank have provided some capital for underdeveloped areas, and, as the economic growth of these areas progresses, should be expected to provide a great deal more. In addition, private sources of funds must be encouraged to provide a major part of the capital required.

In view of the present troubled condition of the world — the distortion of world trade, the shortage of dollars, and other aftereffects of the war — the problem of substantially increasing the flow of American capital abroad presents serious difficulties. In all probability novel devices will have to be employed if the investment from this country is to reach proportions sufficient to carry out the objectives of our program.

All countries concerned with the program should work together to bring about conditions favorable to the flow of private capital. To this end we are negotiating agreements with other countries to protect the American investor from unwarranted or discriminatory treatment under the laws of the country in which he makes his investment.

In negotiating such treaties we do not, of course, ask privileges for American capital greater than those granted to other investors in underdeveloped countries or greater than we ourselves grant in this country. We believe that American enterprise should not waste local resources, should provide adequate wages and working conditions for local labor, and should bear an equitable share of the burden of local taxes. At the same time we believe that investors will send their capital abroad on an increasing scale only if they are given assurance against risk of loss through expropriation without compensation, unfair or discriminatory treatment, destruction through war or rebellion, or the inability to convert their earnings into dollars.

Although our investment treaties will be directed at mitigating such risks, they cannot eliminate them entirely. With the best will in the world a foreign country, particularly an underdeveloped country, may not be able to obtain the dollar exchange necessary for the prompt remittance of earnings on dollar capital. Damage or loss resulting from internal and international violence may be beyond the power of our treaty signatories to control.

Many of these conditions of instability in underdeveloped areas which deter foreign investment are themselves a consequence of the lack of economic development which only foreign investment can cure. Therefore, to wait until stable conditions are assured before encouraging the outflow of capital to underdeveloped areas would defer the attainment of our objectives indefinitely. It is necessary to take vigorous action now to break out of this vicious circle.

Since the development of underdeveloped economic areas is of major importance in our foreign policy, it is appropriate to use the resources of the government to accelerate private efforts toward that end. I recommend, therefore, that the Export-Import Bank be authorized to guarantee United States private capital, invested in productive enterprises abroad which contribute to economic development in underdeveloped areas, against the risks peculiar to those investments.

This guarantee activity will at the outset be largely experimental. Some investments may require only a guarantee against the danger of inconvertibility; others may need protection against the danger of expropriation and other dangers as well. It is impossible at this time to write a standard guarantee. The bank will, of course, be able to require the payment of premiums for such protection, but there is no way now to determine what premium rates will be most appropriate in the long run. Only experience can provide answers to these questions.

The bank has sufficient resources at the present time to begin the guarantee program and to carry on its lending activities as well without any increase in its authorized funds. If the demand for guarantees should prove large, and lending activities continue on the scale expected, it will be necessary to request the Congress at a later date to increase the authorized funds of the bank.

The enactment of these two legislative proposals, the first pertaining to technical assistance and the second to the encouragement of foreign investment, will constitute a national endorsement of a program of major importance in our efforts for world peace and economic stability. Nevertheless, these measures are only the first steps. We are here embarking on a venture that extends far into the future. We are at the beginning of a rising curve of activity, private, governmental, and international, that will continue for many years to come. It is all the more important, therefore, that we start promptly.

In the economically underdeveloped areas of the world today there are new creative energies. We look forward to the time when these countries will be stronger and more independent than they are now, and yet more closely bound to us and to other nations by ties of friendship and commerce, and by kindred ideals. On the other hand, unless we aid the newly awakened spirit in these peoples to find the course of fruitful development, they may fall under the control of those whose philosophy is hostile to human freedom, thereby prolonging the unsettled state of the world and postponing the achievement of permanent peace.

Before the peoples of these areas we hold out the promise of a better future through the democratic way of life. It is vital that we move quickly to bring the meaning of that promise home to them in their daily lives.

117.

# Alexander Meiklejohn: Professors on Probation

*The pervasive concern of the public for "security" reached into the academic community in the late Forties when several states passed laws prohibiting Communists and Communist sympathizers from teaching in public-supported schools and universities. In 1949, when the University of Washington dismissed a group of professors on the ground of their membership in the Communist Party, a heated controversy arose over the conflict between political loyalty and academic freedom. Professor Sidney Hook was a leading spokesman of the segment of the academic community that argued that Communists should be excluded from teaching because their beliefs hindered them in many cases from exercising independent and objective judgment. In the following article of March 27, 1949, Professor Alexander Meiklejohn, former president of Amherst College, analyzed the problems of academic freedom in relation to Communist theology.*

Source: *New York Times Magazine*, March 27, 1949: "Should Communists Be Allowed To Teach?"

THE PRESIDENT AND REGENTS of the University of Washington have dismissed three professors and have placed three others on probation. That statement fails to mention the most significant feature of what has been done. The entire faculty is now on probation. Every scholar, every teacher, is officially notified that if, in his search for the truth, he finds the policies of the American Communist Party to be wise, and acts on that belief, he will be dismissed from the university.

In one of the dismissal cases, the evidence is not clear enough to enable an outsider to measure the validity of the decision. But the other five cases force an issue on which everyone who cares for the integrity and freedom of American scholarship and teaching must take his stand. Cool and careful consideration of that issue should be given by all of us, whether or not we agree with the teachers in question, but especially if we do not agree with them.

The general question in dispute is that of the meaning of academic freedom. But that question has three distinct phases. The first of these has to do with the organization of a university. It asks about the rights and duties of the faculty in relation to the rights and duties of the administration. And the principle at issue corresponds closely to that which, in the Government of the United States, is laid down by the First Amendment to the Constitution. Just as that Amendment declares that "Congress shall make no law abridging the freedom of speech," so, generally, our universities and colleges have adopted a principle which forbids the administration to abridge the intellectual freedom of scholars and teachers. And, at this point, the question is whether or not the president and regents at Washington have violated an agreement, made in good faith, and of vital importance to the work of the university.

The principle of academic freedom was

clearly stated by Sidney Hook in *The New York Times Magazine* of Feb. 27, 1949. After noting that "administrators and trustees" are "harried by pressure-groups," Mr. Hook concluded his argument by saying, "In the last analysis, there is no safer repository of the integrity of teaching and scholarship than the dedicated men and women who constitute the faculties of our colleges and universities." On the basis of that conviction, the Association of University Professors has advocated, and most of our universities, including Washington, have adopted, a "tenure system." That system recognizes that legal authority to appoint, promote, and dismiss teachers belongs to the president and regents. But so far as dismissals are concerned, the purpose of the tenure agreement is to set definite limits to the exercise of that authority.

This limitation of their power, governing boards throughout the nation have gladly recognized and accepted. To the Association of University Professors it has seemed so important that violations of it have been held to justify a "blacklisting" of a transgressor institution — a recommendation by the association that scholars and teachers refuse to serve in a university or college which has thus broken down the defenses of free inquiry and belief.

It is essential at this point to note the fact that the fear expressed by the tenure system is a fear of action by the president and regents. Since these officers control the status and the salaries of teachers, it is only through them or by them that effective external pressure can be used to limit faculty freedom. To say, then, as we must, that the explicit purpose of the tenure system is to protect freedom against the president and regents, is not to say that these officials are more evil than others. It says only that they are more powerful than others. Theirs is the power by which, unless it is checked by a tenure system, evil may be done.

Under the excellent code adopted at the University of Washington, it is agreed that, after a trial period in which the university makes sure that a teacher is competent and worthy of confidence, he is given "permanence" of tenure. This means that he is secure from dismissal unless one or more of five carefully specified charges are proved against him. And the crucial feature of this defense of freedom is that the holding of any set of opinions, however unpopular or unconventional, is scrupulously excluded from the list of proper grounds for dismissal. The teacher who has tenure may, therefore, go fearlessly wherever his search for the truth may lead him. And no officer of the university has authority, openly or by indirection, to abridge that freedom.

When, under the Washington code, charges are made against a teacher, it is provided that prosecution and defense shall be heard by a tenure committee of the faculty, which shall judge whether or not the accusations have been established. In the five cases here under discussion, the only charge made was that of present or past membership in the American Communist Party. Specific evidence of acts revealing unfitness or misconduct in university or other activities was deliberately excluded from the prosecution case. And, further, since the alleged fact of party membership was frankly admitted by the defense, the only question at issue was the abstract inquiry whether or not such membership is forbidden under the five provisions of the tenure code.

Upon that issue, the faculty committee decided unanimously that, in the cases of the ex-members of the Communist Party, there were, under the code, no grounds for dismissal. And, by a vote of eight to three, the same conclusion was reached concerning the two men who were still members of the party. In the discussions of the committee, the suggestion was made that the code should be so amended that party membership would give ground for dismissal. But that action was not recommended. In its capacity as the interpreter of the code which now protects academic freedom, the committee, in all five cases, declared the charges to be not supported by the evidence presented.

In response to this judgment upon teachers by their intellectual peers, the regents, on recommendation of the president, dismissed the two party members. And, second, going beyond the recommendation of the president, they placed the three ex-members "on probation" for two years. These actions are clearly a violation of the agreement under which faculty members have accepted or continued service in the university. They deserve the condemnation of everyone who respects the integrity of a covenant, of everyone who values faculty freedom and faculty responsibility for the maintaining of freedom.

The second phase of the general question goes deeper than the forms of university organization. It challenges the wisdom of the tenure code as it now stands. It may be that though the regents are wrong in procedure, they are right in principle. Here, then, we must ask whether President Allen is justified in saying that a teacher who is "sincere in his belief in communism" cannot "at the same time be a sincere seeker after truth which is the first obligation of the teacher." In a press interview, Mr. Allen is quoted as saying, "I insist that the Communist Party exercises thought control over every one of its members. That's what I object to." Such teachers, he tells us, are "incompetent, intellectually dishonest, and derelict in their duty to find and teach the truth." Can those assertions be verified? If so, then the tenure code should be amended. If not, then the action of the university should be immediately and decisively reversed.

No one can deny that a member of the American Communist Party accepts a "discipline." He follows a party "line." As the policies of the party shift, he shifts with

them. That statement is in some measure true of all parties, whose members agree to work together by common tactics toward a common end. But the Communist discipline, it must be added, is unusually rigid and severe. Our question is, then, whether submission to that discipline unfits for university work men who, on grounds of scholarship and character, have been judged by their colleagues to be fitted for it.

For the judging of that issue we must examine the forces by means of which the discipline of the American Communist Party is exercised. It is idle to speak of "thought control" except as we measure the compulsions by which that control is made effective. What, then, are the inducements, the dominations which, by their impact upon the minds of these university teachers, rob them of the scholar's proper objectivity?

So far as inducements are concerned, good measuring of them requires that we place side by side the advantages offered to a scholar by the Communist Party and those offered by the president and regents of a university. On the one hand, as seen in the present case, the administration can break a man's career at one stroke. It has power over every external thing he cares for. It can destroy his means of livelihood, can thwart his deepest inclinations and intentions. For example, in very many of our universities it is today taken for granted that a young scholar who is known to be a Communist has not the slightest chance of a faculty appointment. He is barred from academic work. And, as against this, what has the American Communist Party to offer? Its "inducements" are the torments of suspicion, disrepute, insecurity, personal and family disaster.

Why, then, do men and women of scholarly training and taste choose party membership? Undoubtedly, some of them are, hysterically, attracted by disrepute and disaster. But, in general, the only explanation which fits the facts is that these scholars are moved by a passionate determination to follow the truth where it seems to lead, no matter what may be the cost to themselves and their families. If anyone wishes to unearth the "inducements" which threaten the integrity of American scholarship he can find far more fruitful lines of inquiry than that taken by the administration of the University of Washington.

But Communist controls, we are told, go far deeper than "inducements." The members of the party, it is said, "take orders from Moscow"; they are subject to "thought control by a foreign power." Now, here again, the fact of rigid party discipline makes these assertions, in some ambiguous sense, true. But, in the sense in which President Allen and his regents interpret them, they are radically false.

Let us assume as valid the statement that, in the American Communist Party "orders" do come from Moscow. But by what power are those orders enforced in the United States? In the Soviet Union, Mr. Stalin and his colleagues can, and do, enforce orders by police and military might. In that nation their control is violent and dictatorial. But by what form of "might" do they control an American teacher in an American university? What can they do to him? At its extreme limit, their only enforcing action is that of dismissal from the party. They can say to him, "You cannot be a member of this party unless you believe our doctrines, unless you conform to our policies." But, under that form of control, a man's acceptance of doctrines and policies is not "required." It is voluntary.

To say that beliefs are required as "conditions of membership" in a party is not to say that the beliefs are required by force, unless it is shown that membership in the party is enforced. If membership is free, then the beliefs are free.

Misled by the hatreds and fears of the cold war, President Allen and his regents are unconsciously tricked by the ambiguities of the words, "control," and "require," and "free," and "objective." The scholars whom they condemn are, so far as the evidence shows, free American citizens. For purposes of social action, they have chosen party affiliation with other men, here and abroad, whose beliefs are akin to their own. In a word, they do not accept Communist beliefs because they are members of the party. They are members of the party because they accept Communist beliefs.

Specific evidence to support the assertion just made was staring President Allen and his regents in the face at the very time when they were abstractly denying that such evidence could exist. Three of the five men whom they condemned as enslaved by party orders had already, by their own free and independent thinking, resigned from the party. How could they have done that if, as charged, they were incapable of free and independent thinking? Slaves do not resign.

At the committee hearings, these men explained, simply and directly, that, under past conditions, they had found the party the most effective available weapon for attack upon evil social forces but that, with changing conditions, the use of that weapon seemed no longer advisable. Shall we say that the decision to be in the party gave evidence of a lack of objectivity while the decision to resign gave evidence of the possession of it? Such a statement would have no meaning except as indicating our own lack of objectivity.

In these three cases, as in the more famous case of Granville Hicks who, some years ago, resigned party membership with a brilliant account of his reasons for doing so, the charge made cannot be sustained. The accusation as it stands means nothing more than that the president and regents are advocating one set of ideas and are banning another. They are attributing to their victims their own intellectual sins. And the tragedy of their action is that it has immeasurably injured the cause which they seek to serve and, correspondingly, has advanced the cause which they are seeking to hold back.

The third phase of our question has to do with the wisdom, the effectiveness, of the educational policy under which teachers have been dismissed or put on probation. And, on this issue, the evidence against the president and regents is clear and decisive. However good their intention, they have made a fatal blunder in teaching method.

As that statement is made, it is taken for granted that the primary task of education in our colleges and universities is the teaching of the theory and practice of intellectual freedom, as the first principle of the democratic way of life. Whatever else our students may do or fail to do, they must learn what freedom is. They must learn to believe in it, to love it, and most important of all, to trust it.

What, then, is this faith in freedom, so far as the conflict of opinions is concerned? With respect to the worldwide controversy now raging between the advocates of the freedom of belief and the advocates of suppression of belief, what is our American doctrine? Simply stated, that doctrine expresses our confidence that whenever, in the field of ideas, the advocates of freedom and the advocates of suppression meet in fair and unabridged discussion, freedom will win. If that were not true, if the intellectual program of democracy could not hold its own in fair debate, then that program itself would require of us its own abandonment. That chance we believers in self-government have determined to take. We have put our faith in democracy.

But the president and regents have, at this point, taken the opposite course. They have gone over to the enemy. They are not willing to give a fair and equal hearing to those who disagree with us. They are convinced that suppression is more effective as an agency of freedom than is freedom itself.

But this procedure violates the one basic principle on which all teaching rests. It is impossible to teach what one does not believe. It is idle to preach what one does not practice. These men who advocate that we do to the Russians what the Russians, if they had the power, would do to us are declaring that the Russians are right and that we are wrong. They practice suppression because they have more faith in the methods of dictatorship than in those of a free self-governing society.

For many years the writer of these words has watched the disastrous educational effects upon student opinion and attitude when suppression has been used, openly or secretly, in our universities and colleges. The outcome is always the same. Dictatorship breeds rebellion and dissatisfaction. High-spirited youth will not stand the double-dealing which prates of academic freedom and muzzles its teachers by putting them "on probation."

If we suggest to these young people that they believe in democracy, then they will insist on knowing what can be said against it as well as what can be said for it. If we ask them to get ready to lay down their lives in conflict against an enemy, they want to know not only how strong or how weak are the military forces of that enemy, but also what he has to say for himself as against what we are saying for ourselves.

Many of the students in our colleges and universities are today driven into an irresponsible radicalism. But that drive does not come from the critics of our American political institutions. It comes chiefly from the irresponsible defenders of those institutions — the men who make a mockery of freedom by using in its service the forces of suppression.

Underlying and surrounding the Washington controversy is the same controversy as it runs through our national life. The most tragic mistake of the contemporary American mind is its failure to recognize the inherent strength and stability of free institutions when they are true to themselves. Democracy is not a weak and unstable thing which forever needs propping up by the devices of dictatorship. It is the only form of social life and of government which today has assurance of maintaining itself.

As contrasted with it, all governments of suppression are temporary and insecure. The regimes of Hitler and Mussolini flared into strength, and quickly died away. The power of the Soviet Union cannot endure unless that nation can find its way into the practices of political freedom. And all the other dictatorships are falling, and will fall, day by day. Free self-government alone gives promise of permanence and peace. The only real danger which threatens our democracy is that lack of faith which leads us into the devices and follies of suppression.

---

## 118.

### ALISTAIR COOKE: A Generation on Trial

*A sensational espionage case opened in 1948 when Whittaker Chambers, a confessed Communist, charged that Alger Hiss, a former State Department official and Yalta Conference adviser, had been a member of a Communist spy ring in Washington, D.C., during the 1930s. Hiss denied the charge and was later indicted for perjury by a federal grand jury. On January 25, 1950, he was sentenced to five years in prison. Hiss protested his innocence throughout two highly public trials (the first trial ended in a hung jury in July 1949) that inaugurated a prolonged national furor concerning Communist infiltration of the federal government. The following article by Alistair Cooke, a British writer on American affairs, anticipated a book with the above title that appeared in 1950.*

Source: *New Republic,* July 4, 1949.

IT IS NEVER EASY on the conscience, and an assault on what we call our sense of reality, to come out of a trial into the daylight and the world of sunlight, business, gossip, and friendship. To come out of the paneled courtroom in New York where they are trying Hiss and limp into Foley Square is to exchange two worlds any decent citizen is meant to accept as one: a world in which every casual memory and date is screened for perjury, and a world in which dates are heedlessly made, truth is the "I said to her" of the couple on the bench, and a drunken bum failing to filch a cigarette calls you a son-of-a-bitch and staggers off, free as the dust and the smell of chicory. Then you have a soda and a sandwich and hear more headlong perjury at your elbow in a half hour than a Lloyd Paul Stryker will expose in a lifetime.

No wonder you can only give a dusty answer to friends who seize you in the evenings and the weekends and ask which is the liar, which is the guilty one? You only wish they would come into the courtroom and see terror and comedy putting on a medieval ritual. It is one of the great, and perhaps inevitable, misfortunes of this trial that it asks twelve human beings, twelve of Chesterton's "ordinary men looking on," to interpret the friendships and beliefs of the mid-1930s in the political climate of 1949. In this sense, it is not only Alger Hiss who is on trial. It is a whole generation. And whatever the verdict, there is a historical tragedy latent in the lives and careers of Hiss, Chambers, and Henry Julian Wadleigh of the same kind, and not so secular at that, as in the trial of Saint Joan.

To see just where this tragedy applies, you have first to be careful to separate the courtroom procedures and traditions that shock the layman, unused to trials, especially if he is an idealist, or a nonreligious liberal, who wants to make the courts more heroic than they can ever be; who assumes they are the guardians of a man's faith and of a way of life. Two of these procedures that hurt the sensitive are the requirements of a witness not to make assumptions or deductions but to give positive answers, and the whole tradition of cross-examination.

Charles F. Darlington, an assistant chief of the Trade-Agreements Section of the State Department, was the most conspicuous victim of the first procedure, only because he is a lawyer himself and meant to appear a very smooth article. He was asked to say what he "observed" about Wadleigh's "behavior" when he asked questions. This naturally provokes opinions. But opinions are not evidence. Has he any independent recollection of a certain document "remaining on top of the desk"? He says he thinks "it would be normal . . ." and Thomas F. Murphy, the government counsel, groans, "Will you please direct the witness, Your Honor, to answer questions?"

A layman assumes that "to tell the truth, the whole truth, and nothing but the truth" is a good and practicable oath. But as a moral command, it is clearly an impossibility. And the pathos creeps in when you see in the flesh a witness whose notion of a truthful memory is even more scrupulous than that of somebody else who possesses

the legal knack of being "a good witness."

For example, Mrs. Chambers' memories of where the Hisses lived in Washington happen to be essential to the second indictment — the charge that Hiss lied before the grand jury in saying he had never seen Chambers after January 1, 1937. She first said she and her husband had gone to a New Year's Eve party at the Hisses' when they were living at Volta Place, on December 31, 1937. It has been established that the Hisses did not move to this address until the very end of December of that year. Under ordeal by Stryker, Mrs. Chambers amended her testimony to put the date a year earlier. Then she started to wrestle with her uncertain memory of three parties — a housewarming, a wedding anniversary, and the New Year's Eve party. After long silence, she says, almost to herself, that the Volta Place party "must have been the housewarming." Stryker whisks around. "You were at the Thirtieth Street House, not Volta Place, then, on December 31, 1937. Is that your testimony now?"

Another long pause, Mrs. Chambers' eyes go to the ceiling and she drums her housewife's fingers on the rail, like a woman checking the figures on a grocery bill. She says, hopelessly, "I am trying to recall," and wanders off into the dark underground of her memory. She has been said by the press, indeed on her own confession, to be "not very good on dates." But this is only because her replies seem to spring from a premise in her own mind that the law cannot allow for. It is that, somewhere deep in her memory, if only she can concentrate her digging in the right place, the truth and the recollection will be found to run in overlapping seams. But every time she tries, she discovers to her obvious alarm that the memory is a poor miner and that the deep recesses of truth are guarded by jesting Pilate.

A little later, Stryker was trying to find

out when she had decided to include Alger Hiss on a jaunt Mrs. Hiss is supposed to have made to drop some children's things off at the Chamberses' apartment in New York. When did she have her memory refreshed? She thought it was when the FBI spoke to her.

"Was there any sort of leading question on the part of the FBI to suggest Mr. Hiss might have been there?"

She answered at once, quietly and with much dignity, "You are insulting, sir."

Murphy came snorting to his feet and the judge's head bobbed over the bench and his pink face reddened. "Mrs. Chambers," he lectured, "from the standpoint of both the government and the defendant this is a most serious case. Mrs. Chambers, I tell you again not to indulge suggestions of that kind."

You have to be a lawyer to sense the correct direction from which righteous indignation is likely to come. Anywhere outside a court, Stryker would have seemed to get what was coming to him. But sarcasm and invective are the counsel's monopoly and the witness must swallow his emotion and say yes and no. It is doubtful whether the American jurists who have cherished this inheritance from English common law ever anticipated the explosion on the legal scene of Lloyd Paul Stryker. For he prowls the shadowy fence between truth and untruth like a tomcat howling at the neighborhood to come and join in the obviously hopeless search for an honest man.

These, then, are the conventions that put any trial in a certain emotional frame and make it, I should say, even harder for the jury to eschew emotion, prejudice, bias, sympathy, and all the other admonitions that, if faithfully sworn to, would produce not twelve jurymen but a dozen saints.

What is there in this trial, more than any other, that reflects an inevitable personal tragedy which the court cannot appease or resolve? It is, I think, the fact which constantly emerges through this disheveled stockpile of memory — that the main characters were idealists at a time when the nature of loyalty — to the state, to one's beliefs, to one's family and fellowmen — was undergoing one of those historic and permanent changes. In the Western world, loyalty has simmered down to a negative assumption that a man is bound first to his family, then to his country's policies, and between these poles his yearnings toward reform swing freely within the limits of Christian charity.

The positive religious impulse of our time has been the Soviet assertion of another integrity, whose ghastly vitality the sentimental liberal has learned about only since he has come to see that Hitler produced in the Third Reich an inverted parody of the Communist state. This "integrity" is like the priest's in denying the prior loyalty of the family and the state. It is a dedication (as I think, a pathological one) to the omnipotence of the revolutionary clique, which transcends the loyalties of human love, of family, and of state. Up to now we have heard about it as a monster Displaced Person at large over Eastern Europe. We have seen our own tradition debauched by it in the figure of Rubashev, in *Darkness at Noon*. Before that, we saw it as a monstrous figure of fiction in Conrad's *Under Western Eyes*.

To be such a character, we are told, takes demoniac guile and the guts of a martyr. It is still next to impossible to watch Gromyko and Malik out at Lake Success and grant that they, in their Sears, Roebuck suits, can really be such men.

And the fascination of the Hiss trial, the weird sense of a ghoul invading a clambake, is the possibility that this sensitive editor and Maryland farmer, and the handsome young lawyer in the Brooks Brothers suit, might both some time have made that dedication.

119.

## BERNARD DE VOTO: Due Notice to the FBI

*President Truman's loyalty program resulted in a series of investigations, both by
official government agencies and by private firms, aimed at uncovering subversive
and disloyal citizens. All of the employees of the U.S. government underwent a
security check between 1947 and 1951, and many other persons found that they had
to be "cleared" in order to retain their jobs. A certain number of Americans
objected violently to this state of affairs, going so far as to assert that America was
in danger of becoming, if it had not already become, a "police state," and that in
its emphasis on security it was losing its precious liberty. The following article
by the historian Bernard De Voto, in which he stated his strong opposition to the
practices of such organizations as the FBI, was published in the fall of 1949.*
Source: *Harper's,* October 1949.

THE QUIETLY DRESSED MAN at your door shows you credentials that identify him as Mr. Charles Craig of the Bureau of Internal Revenue. He says he would like to ask you a few questions about one of your neighbors. The Harry S. Deweys are friends of yours, aren't they? Yes, you tell him. How long have you known them? Ever since they moved to Garden Acres eight or nine years ago — or was it seven? — no, thirteen. Mr. Craig says the Deweys moved into their house June 1, 1935, which makes it fourteen years. By the way, have they got a mortgage on it? Sure, you say, we all have. Harry didn't buy till about eight years ago. He is paying it off on a monthly basis; must be down to a couple of thousand by now.

Mr. Dewey's older son graduated from Yale this spring? Mr. Craig asks. Yes, you say. The daughter — she's at Vassar? Yes, she's a sophomore. And the other boy? — Exeter? Yes, first form. Mr. Dewey bought a new car last year, a Buick? Yes, he'd driv-

en that Chevrolet for nine years. Who is his tailor? Gummidge? Pretty high-priced firm. Does Mrs. Dewey spend a lot on clothes? The trash barrels were on the curb when Mr. Craig came by and he noticed several empty Black and White bottles — do the Deweys drink a lot? Didn't they have Zimmerman, the caterer, for that big party last April? — Zimmerman comes high. Have you noticed their garbage — pretty rich stuff? What labels have you seen? Bellows & Co., maybe, or Charles & Co., Inc.? Do you happen to know what Mr. Dewey's income is?

By this time you are, I hope, plenty mad. You say, for God's sake, it's none of my business. Mr. Craig explains. Investigation by the Bureau of Internal Revenue does not necessarily mean that the person being investigated is under suspicion. These checks are routine in certain kinds of cases. Orders to make them come from above; the local echelons do not initiate inquiries, they simply find out what they can. Then back in

Washington the information thus gathered is evaluated. No improper use is made of anything and of course the evaluators know that most of the stuff sent in is mixed, idle, or untrue — they simply go through the vast chaff in order to find an occasional grain of wheat. The Bureau, Mr. Craig points out, is part of the United States government. It conducts its inquiries with entire legality and under rigid safeguards. The duty of a citizen is to assist his government when he is asked to.

So you say, look, Harry is district manager of the Interstate Gas Furnace Corporation and everybody knows that IGF pays district managers fifteen thousand a year. Yes, Mr. Craig says, IGF pays him fifteen thousand but one wonders whether he hasn't got other sources of income. How can he send three children to prep school and college, buy a house and a new Buick, and patronize Gummidge and Zimmerman on fifteen thousand? And he belongs to the City Club and the Garden Acres Country Club. He took Mrs. Dewey to Bermuda last winter. He has heavy insurance premiums to pay. He had a new roof put on the house last fall and this spring Mrs. Dewey had the whole second floor repainted and repapered. How come? Does it make sense? Where's he getting it from?

Does Harry S. Dewey belong to the Wine and Food Society? The Friends of Escoffier? Has he ever attended a meeting of either group? Does he associate with members of either? Has he ever been present at a meeting of any kind, or at a party, at which a member of either was also present? Has he ever read Brillat-Savarin's *The Physiology of Taste?* Does he associate with people who have read it? Has he ever been present at a meeting or a party at which anyone who has read it was also present? Does he subscribe to or read *Daily Racing Form?* Has he ever made a bet on a horse race? A dog race? A football game? Does he play poker or shoot craps? Has he

ever been present at a meeting or a party at which anyone who makes bets or plays poker was also present? Does he play the market? Do you know whether Harry puts any cash into diamonds? Does he associate with people who own diamonds? Does he know any millionaires, or people who own cabin cruisers, or people who have accounts in more than one bank? Has he ever attended meetings of such persons? Has he ever been present at a meeting or a party at which such persons were also present? Does he read the *Wall Street Journal?* Has he ever been present at a cocktail party at which anyone who does read it was present? Is it true that Harry gave his secretary half a dozen pairs of nylon stockings for Christmas? Could she be fronting or dummying for business deals that are really his? What kind of girl is she? Does she always leave the office at five o'clock? Whom does she associate with?

Where does Harry stand on the Bureau of Internal Revenue and the income tax laws? Have you ever heard him say that the income tax laws ought to be changed or the Bureau reorganized or abolished? Have you ever heard him damn the income tax? Does he associate with people who damn it? Has he ever been present at a meeting or a party where people who want to abolish the Bureau or revise the tax laws were also present?

Let us assume that you remember nothing which indicates that Harry S. Dewey is a tax-dodger or a crook. But Mr. Craig goes a few doors down the street and interviews Frances Perkins Green, who is a prohibitionist and has suffered from nervous indigestion for many years. She has seen truffles and artichokes and caviar in the Dewey garbage. The Deweys' maid has told Mrs. Green that they have porterhouses much oftener than frankforts, that they always have cocktails and frequently have wine, that sometimes cherries and peaches come all the way from Oregon by mail. Mrs. Green has seen many suspicious-looking characters come to the Dewey house. She doesn't know who they are but it's striking that mostly they don't come till after dark, seven o'clock or later. Some of them, she says, are staggering when they leave at midnight.

So Mr. Craig tries the next house and finds Henry Cabot White at home. Cabot is doing all right now but he had tough going for a couple of years after Harry Dewey fired him. Everyone in Garden Acres is familiar with the neighborhood feud and would tend to discount Cabot's revelation to Mr. Craig that Harry's secretary used to work as a cashier at a race track. He confirms the nylons but says there were a dozen pairs. Sure Harry is sleeping with her — Cabot has seen them lunching together several times. Matter of fact Harry only took Mrs. Dewey to Bermuda because she blew up about the girl. Yes, and do you know who was on that boat? Gooks McGonigle — you remember, he runs the numbers racket and they almost got him for wiretapping. Cabot wouldn't like to say anything either way, but Harry took the same boat and Harry manages to lay his hands on money when he needs it.

I HAVE HUNG THIS FANTASY *on the Bureau of Internal Revenue precisely because it does* NOT *operate in this way.* When it suspects that someone is making false tax returns, its investigators go to the suspect's books, his bank, the regular channels of his business, and similar focal points where factual evidence can be uncovered and made good. If Harry S. Dewey reads Brillat-Savarin or serves Stilton with the cocktails, the Bureau is not interested. It does not ask his friends or enemies to report on his wife's visits to the hairdresser as a patriotic duty.

But if it did, would you be surprised? In fact, would you be surprised if any government bureau sent round its Mr. Craig to ask you if Harry Dewey reads the *New Republic* or has ever gone swimming in the nude at Bay View? I think you wouldn't be surprised. What is worse, I think that for a moment Mr. Craig and his questions would seem quite natural to you. And this feeling that the interrogation of private citizens about other citizens is natural and justified is something new to American life. As little as ten years ago we would have considered it about on a par with prohibition snooping, night-riding, and blackmail. A single decade has come close to making us a nation of common informers.

It began with the war. Candidates for commission in the services or for jobs in non-military agencies had to be investigated. If enormous asininities resulted, if enormous injustice was done, they were inevitable, part of the cost of war. They are not inevitable now. But several branches of the government are acting as if they were. Several branches of the government and far too many of us private citizens are acting as if they didn't matter.

True, we have occasional qualms. The Committee on Un-American Activities blasts several score reputations by releasing a new batch of gossip. Or a senator emits some hearsay and officially unaccused persons lose their jobs without recourse. Or another senator blackens the name of a dead man and then rejoices in his good deed, though the people he claimed to be quoting announce that they didn't say what he said they did. Or some atrocious indignity inflicted on a government employee by a loyalty board comes to light. Or we find out that the FBI has put at the disposal of this or that body a hash of gossip, rumor, slander, backbiting, malice, and drunken invention which, when it makes the headlines, shatters the reputations of innocent and harmless people and of people who our laws say are innocent until someone proves them guilty in court. We are shocked.

Sometimes we are scared. Sometimes we are sickened. We know that the thing stinks to heaven, that it is an avalanching danger to our society. But we don't do anything about it.

Do you think the questions I have put in Mr. Craig's mouth are absurd? They are exactly like the questions that are asked of every government employee about whom a casual derogatory remark has been unearthed, even if that remark was made twenty years ago, even if a fool or an aspirant to the employee's job made it. They are exactly like the questions asked of anyone who is presumed to know anything about him, whether casual acquaintance, grudgeholder, or habitual enemy. They are exactly like the questions asked about anyone outside the government of whom anyone else has reported that he has radical sympathies. Have you (has he) ever studied Karl Marx? Have you (has he) ever been present at a meeting or a party where anyone sympathetic to Communism was also present? Did you (did he) belong to the Liberal Club in college? Did you (did he) escort to a dance a girl who has read Lenin or is interested in abstract painting? Have you (has he) recommended the *Progressive* to a friend? Those questions and scores like them, or worse, have been asked of and about millions of American citizens.

The FBI — to name only one agency that asks such questions — tells us that everything is properly safeguarded. The investigators gather up what they can and send it in, but trained specialists evaluate it, and whatever is idle, untrue, false, malicious, or vicious is winnowed out. So the FBI says. But we are never told who does the evaluating and we have seen little evidence that anyone does it. Along comes the Coplon case, for instance, and we find out that a sack has simply been emptied on the table. The contents are obviously in great part idle and false, in great part gossip and ru-

mor, in great part unverifiable — and unverified. Investigator K-7 reports that Witness S-17 (for we have to cover up for our agents and our spies) said that Harry S. Dewey is a member of the Party, or wants to make the revolution, or knows some fellow-travelers, or once advised someone to read Marx, or spent a weekend at a summer resort where there were members of an organization on the Attorney-General's list. If K-7 is only two degrees better than half-witted, if S-17 is a psychopath or a pathological liar or Harry's divorced wife, no matter. And also, no one can be held accountable. If the same sack has previously emptied for the loyalty board of any government department nobody can be held responsible for that act, either, and Harry Dewey has no recourse. He will never know and neither will you and I. We will never learn who K-7 or S-17 is, in what circumstance the information was given, whether or not it is true or deliberate falsehood, how far it has been spread or by whom.

In the Coplon trial the government did its utmost to keep from the public view certain information which it was using and which had been gathered by the FBI. That was a sagacious effort. For when the judge ruled that it must be made public some of it turned out to be as irresponsible as the chatter of somewhat retarded children: it would have been farcical if it had not been vicious. For instance, some S-17 had given some K-7 a list of people whom he considered Communists or Communist-sympathizers. One of them was the president of a large university. In all candor, he is not continentally celebrated for intelligence but his economic and political ideas are a hundred miles to the right of Chester A. Arthur. He is a man of unquestionable patriotism, loyalty, integrity, and probity, incapable of any kind of behavior with which the FBI is authorized to concern itself. But it was the privilege of someone — perhaps a fool, a personal enemy, a boy who had flunked out, a maniac — to lodge in the FBI's files a declaration that he is a Red.

Well, the university president will not suffer in public esteem. But his university may be damaged in many ways, now, next week, ten years hence. And Senator Mundt or Congressman Dondero or any public official with the gleam of a headline in his eye can denounce the university, its students, and all who have acquired their guilt by contagion — on the basis of a remark which may have been made by an imbecile and for which no one can be held to account. And that remark remains permanently indexed in the FBI files. And what about humbler names on that list? How many people have been fired? How many are having their reading, their recreation, and their personal associations secretly investigated? Against how many of them are neighbors with grudges or senile dementia testifying to some Mr. Craig, hereafter and alias K-7? What redress have they got? What redress has anyone got whom anyone at all has named to the FBI or any other corps of investigators as a Communist, a Communist-sympathizer, a fellow-traveler, a bemused dupe, or just a person who happened to be in the bar at the New Willard when a subscriber to the *Nation* was buying a drink?

I SAY IT HAS GONE TOO FAR. We are dividing into the hunted and the hunters. There is loose in the United States today the same evil that once split Salem Village between the bewitched and the accused and stole men's reason quite away. We are informers to the secret police. Honest men are spying on their neighbors for patriotism's sake. We may be sure that for every honest man two dishonest ones are spying for personal advancement today and ten will be spying for pay next year.

None of us can know how much of this inquiry into the private lives of American citizens and government employees is necessary. Some of it is necessary — but we have no way of knowing which, when, or where. We have seen enough to know for sure that a great deal of it is altogether irresponsible. Well, there is a way of making it all responsible, of fixing responsibility. As one citizen of the United States, I intend to take that way, myself, from now on.

Representatives of the FBI and of other official investigating bodies have questioned me, in the past, about a number of people and I have answered their questions. That's over. From now on any representative of the government, properly identified, can count on a drink and perhaps informed talk about the Red (but non-Communist) Sox at my house. But if he wants information from me about anyone whomsoever, no soap. If it is my duty as citizen to tell what I know about someone, I will perform that duty under subpoena, in open court, before that person and his attorney. This notice is posted in the courthouse square: I will not discuss anyone in private with any government investigator.

I like a country where it's nobody's damned business what magazines anyone reads, what he thinks, whom he has cocktails with. I like a country where we do not have to stuff the chimney against listening ears and where what we say does not go into the FBI files along with a note from S-17 that I may have another wife in California. I like a country where no college-trained flatfeet collect memoranda about us and ask judicial protection for them, a country where when someone makes statements about us to officials he can be held to account. We had that kind of country only a little while ago and I'm for getting it back. It was a lot less scared than the one we've got now. It slept sound no matter how many people joined Communist reading circles and it put common scolds to the ducking stool. Let's rip off the gingerbread and restore the original paneling.

120.

ELEANOR ROOSEVELT: The United Nations

*Eleanor Roosevelt devoted most of her public efforts following the death of her husband to the advancement of the United Nations. In 1945 President Truman appointed her a delegate to the UN, and she served as chairman of the commission that drafted the Universal Declaration of Human Rights. In her lectures, both in the United States and abroad, she was an untiring supporter of the world organization against its numerous critics. In the following article, "What I Think of the United Nations," published in August 1949, Mrs. Roosevelt discussed the contributions of the UN to world peace and the challenges that it faced in the future.*

Source: *United Nations World*, August 1949.

I KNOW THAT a great many people in the United States and other nations today wonder what is the use of having a United Nations. "It is just a debating society. It doesn't do anything." Those are criticisms one can hear almost anywhere, though to my mind they are quite unjustified.

I would like to ask everyone who has made or been tempted to make some such criticism of the United Nations to remember just one fact: When the United Nations was set up in the spring of '45 we thought that as soon as the war came to an end we would make the peace. And the organization that was set up was to function in a peaceful world, maintaining the new peace and creating an atmosphere in which lasting peace could grow and develop. But peace has never been made, and because of that there is dumped in the lap of the United Nations — a large number of political questions it was never expected or designed to deal with.

In addition, in this period in which no peace has been made, a rift has developed and widened between the world's two great nations. As long as they cannot come to an agreement on certain questions, the complete organization of the UN is impossible.

For example, they cannot agree on what shall happen in the realm of atomic energy. Therefore, there can be no agreement on what kind of force there should be at the disposal of the United Nations, and until the world has force within the United Nations it is obliged to have force somewhere else. That is one reason you hear such constant complaints as, "Why do we have to pour money into Greece? — And why must we build up the armies of the Atlantic Pact nations? Why must we do this and why that? If the United Nations were really doing its job, there would be no need of our doing it."

But the United Nations cannot use force, or even the threat of force, to maintain peace until its member nations are able to complete their organization, establishing collective force. And there cannot be collective force until there is some kind of agreement as to how communism and democracy are to live in the world together.

All this means, of course, that we must look at the United Nations from a different point of view, emphasizing what it *has* been *permitted* to accomplish rather than what it *had* been *expected* to do.

The Security Council, for example, was

intended to take care of problems that were a threat to world peace. It was expected to use force if necessary. It can render decisions, and has done so, stopping or localizing warfare in a number of areas and eliminating other threats to the peace. But it has no collective force to put behind its decisions. And while moral force has value — as events in Palestine, Kashmir, Indonesia, and elsewhere have proved — moral force has not the same value as the ability to say to an aggressor, "You must stop or be stopped." When you put moral force behind something, you have to persuade — you cannot order — and persuasion takes far longer and requires far greater understanding.

Important as the Security Council is, however, I prefer to focus attention on those other parts of the organization which the Charter set up to encourage in the world an atmosphere in which peace might grow.

The people who wrote the Charter did not assume that peace was going to drop down on us like a beneficent blanket from heaven and be with us forever. They were quite realistic about it. They knew that, even though we made a peace, we would have to work year in and year out, day in and day out, to keep that peace, and to see that the atmosphere of the world was conducive to its growth. They knew that throughout the world there were tremendous difficulties, that it would take a long while, for instance, to make it possible for the people of our country to understand what was happening to someone in South Africa or in India or in Siam.

They set up, therefore, some specialized agencies, such as the Food and Agriculture Organization, to begin to do things in the world that would increase understanding and, being done on a world scale, would help bring about world understanding of special problems.

I can recall very well the days when we thought that our Great Plains were doomed to be largely desert. But we started then something which was called a "shelter belt" area. Many thought that it was the greatest nonsense in the world. At the time some of the foresters came to me and said: "The President is crazy. It just can't be." But about eight years later I saw people in the "shelter belt" region, who had not believed in it, but who suddenly found that their fields were holding soil again. And they were growing crops where they had not been able to grow them before.

That special problem of wind erosion of farmland is one a limited number of Americans now know how to meet. It is one of the multitude of agricultural problems that need to be tackled on a world scale, and for the first time it is being done. For the first time a group of nations is meeting together to find ways of holding and restoring the world's top soil. It is really exciting because it is a fundamental thing. The nations in FAO are trying to prevent, by providing more food, the wars which have resulted when hunger forced peoples to move out of devastated areas.

Another important specialized agency is the World Health Organization. To be sure all the nations aren't in it yet, but it is functioning — and very effectively. This year it is attacking a problem that a citizen of the United States may not think important because we have faced and met it pretty well. Tuberculosis isn't a terrifying disease to us. But when I was in Paris at the United Nations Assembly last autumn, I met with a good many students. One night a group came in to see me. They wanted to get in touch with young people of similar interests in this country.

In the course of conversation an older woman who was in charge said their major needs were clothes and food. I asked if they had a good deal of illness. She said, "Oh, yes, Madame. Fifty percent of our students are either tubercular or on the border."

What would you think if 50 percent of the students in an American university were either tubercular or on the border?

When I was in Holland a year ago last spring, I went with Queen Juliana to see the first and only — and small — hospital where they were caring for young tuberculous students who couldn't keep up with their university studies. Queen Juliana told me that they didn't know yet the percentage of tuberculosis among their children. She guessed that of the resistance movement youngsters who would soon attain university age there were probably between 40 and 50 percent who had the disease.

Conditions similar to those in Holland can be found in other countries, and it is vital that tuberculosis be attacked on a world scale. This would be true even if we Americans were the only ones concerned. Our children are going to have to run the world with these Dutch and French and other children and, unless physical and mental and spiritual help comes to the youngsters of all the countries in the world, our children are going to have a hard time — a harder time than we had. No matter how healthy and fortunate otherwise they may be, the world isn't going to be a normal place to live in if the peoples of other nations are warped by disease and hunger and frustration.

FAO and WHO, and eleven other specialized agencies, are connected with the United Nations through the Economic and Social Council. Under the Council also, set up almost immediately after its organization, is the Human Rights Commission. I want to cite a few of the difficulties confronting this organization, which should make you more tolerant of its operation and help you realize how trying it is to work in an international group.

Many persons feel the Human Rights Commission can be important because it has written the Universal Declaration of Human Rights which was adopted by the General Assembly in Paris and which may become one of the pillars of world peace in the future.

After I came home from Paris I had a letter from a gentleman who asked: "How could you as the United States delegate accept Article I of the Universal Declaration of Human Rights when our declaration [in the U.S. Bill of Rights] is different?"

The reason, of course, is that there were fifty-eight nations sitting around the table in Committee Three, which brought the draft to the Assembly, and there were fifty-eight nations in the General Assembly, and of these, forty-eight nations approved it. Committee Three spent four weeks on the first three articles and we made three changes. In Article I we changed the familiar, "All men are created equal," to, "All human beings are born free and equal in dignity and rights."

Why say all human beings? Because in Committee Three, which deals with humanitarian, social, and cultural matters, there are a number of women. They are the ones who changed "all men" to "all human beings." Many of them come from countries where the great mass of women have no equality and no recognition, and they are very conscious of that situation. That's the first change, and it illustrates that conditions in different parts of the world have great effect on an international document and on an international situation.

The differences in languages are another source of problems. We have five official languages — English, French, Russian, Chinese, and Spanish — into which all statements are translated. It frequently happens that there is a disagreement between the man who speaks and his interpreter. The speaker will stop the translator — we listen with earphones to whichever of the five languages we wish — and say he isn't getting the meaning, and sometimes the speaker will take over the translating for a sentence or two himself. When the Russian delegate did just this at one of our meetings, I told him his insistence on making the English translation, "no discrimination because of estate," would mean very little to us. So he changed it to, "no discrimination because of class." I said: "We think we are getting away from classes that divide human beings, so let's not say 'class'." He finally settled on "birth" as translating his idea. And then the Chinese delegate, who is much more of a stickler for proper English than most of us who speak it, said he would accept "birth" but that it must be preceded by the words, "race or —." This did not please the U.S.S.R. delegate and it took us some time, not only to get the right word but to put it in the place which was satisfactory.

Religion is another subject that creates problems for us. In our article on religion we thought we had satisfied everyone, but we found we had overlooked a final consultation with the Mohammedans. As a consequence they had very nearly decided to abstain from voting or vote against the article because of an apparently minor clause that said any person had a right to change his or her belief. But some feel the Koran does not allow a Mohammedan to change his religious belief. In the end, however, Pakistan, Lebanon, and some of the other Arab states decided that the Koran permitted a change in belief. Saudi Arabia held to the last that a change was not permissible, and it cast one of the abstaining votes.

These international differences and intricacies are all so interesting, though often discouraging, because one is constantly learning new things about other peoples — learning to understand them and cooperate with them. But the problems are so many and we need to know so much that, when an agreement is finally reached, one often wonders how it ever was achieved.

The agreements are coming, however. As the delegates learn to appreciate and sympathize with each other's points of view, one can see the growth of a new spirit of trust

— of willingness to talk frankly in an earnest search for compromise. I have not yet found this to be true with the Soviet delegates — I wish I had — perhaps because they are always conscious of being government representatives and do not permit themselves to be themselves. They are tied by the line they have to follow. But with the other delegates there is a growing urgency to find areas of understanding and agreement.

It is going to take a great deal of time to find and develop such areas with the Eastern European nations. But we have to recognize that they must be found, and that we must do much of the searching.

We know that the U.S.S.R. and the Communist parties are making promises for communism that sound very attractive to the downtrodden peoples of the world. We know that we should recognize that the fight today is in Asia, in Africa, and in the islands of the Pacific among the peoples who have felt that they are looked down on by the white race. One cannot observe the United Nations in action — one cannot look around that great table at which now sit the representatives of fifty-nine nations — without realizing that the white race is a minority race in the world and that there are more peoples believing in other religions than there are Christians.

Our first task in finding ways to get along with the Communists is to find ways to make democracy mean what we say it does. And we have to make democracy work in our own country where other peoples can see it function. They can't see inside Russia, but here they can see everything that happens and can see that freedom of information is in itself one of our first advantages.

This country can, and must, show that democracy isn't just a word, but that it means regards for the rights of human beings; that it means that every human being, regardless of race or creed or color, has equal dignity and equal rights; that it means that we care about the kind of freedom which allows people to grow, and allows them to develop their own potentialities and their own interests; that we recognize that democracy, as a basis for government, has to assume certain obligations to its citizens.

It will not be enough to establish as fact that we have military superiority. It will not be enough to prove our economic superiority. We are going to have to persuade the Russians and their friends that compromise is not only desirable but quite possible, and that it has to be reached. We must somehow convince them — and the most stub-born on our own side — that their ideology and ours can live in the world together without open conflict.

Finally, if democracy — and the blessings of it both as a way of government and a way of life — are going to win this contest for the support of the peoples of the world, we must have moral conviction and spiritual leadership. That is the challenge to America today. That is the challenge that we face in strengthening and making the United Nations work as a whole. Those are the standards that we set ourselves and, in the interest of the future, those are the standards by which we must live.

121.

# E. B. WHITE: The Capital of the World

*New York has been the leading city of America for more than a century and a half, and as such has been the subject of endless analysis, criticism, and praise. On balance, perhaps the criticism outweighs the approval, for New York is undoubtedly a difficult place to live, and the problems faced by all large cities at mid-twentieth century are particularly evident there. But there have been many paeans of praise, too, a notable example of which is E. B. White's* Here Is New York, *which was first published in the April 1949 issue of* Holiday *magazine and appeared in book form the same year. White, then an editor of the* New Yorker *and hence familiar with the city's intricacies, tried in his essay to suggest its essence, which he said was height, and to describe the precariousness of its existence. He ended by observing that the establishment of the permanent headquarters of the United Nations in New York had made the city in some sense the capital of the world — a fact that, to one who loved New York with all his heart, seemed appropriate. Portions of White's book are reprinted here.*

Source: *Here Is New York*, New York, 1949, pp. 9-10, 17-26, 50-54.

ON ANY PERSON who desires such queer prizes, New York will bestow the gift of loneliness and the gift of privacy. It is this largess that accounts for the presence within the city's walls of a considerable section of the population; for the residents of Manhattan are to a large extent strangers who have pulled up stakes somewhere and come to town, seeking sanctuary or fulfillment or some greater or lesser grail. The capacity to make such dubious gifts is a mysterious quality of New York. It can destroy an individual, or it can fulfill him, depending a good deal on luck. No one should come to New York to live unless he is willing to be lucky. . . .

There are roughly three New Yorks. There is, first, the New York of the man or woman who was born here, who takes the city for granted and accepts its size and its turbulence as natural and inevitable. Second, there is the New York of the commuter — the city that is devoured by locusts each day and spat out each night. Third, there is the New York of the person who was born somewhere else and came to New York in quest of something. Of these three trembling cities the greatest is the last — the city of final destination, the city that is a goal. It is this third city that accounts for New York's high-strung disposition, its poetical deportment, its dedication to the arts, and its incomparable achievements. Commuters give the city its tidal restlessness; natives give it solidity and continuity; but the settlers give it passion. And whether it is a farmer arriving from Italy to set up a small grocery store in a slum, or a young girl arriving from a small town in Mississippi to escape the indignity of being observed by her neighbors, or a boy arriving from the Corn Belt with a manuscript in his suitcase and a pain in his heart, it makes no difference: each embraces New York with the intense excitement of first love, each absorbs New York with the fresh eyes of an adventurer, each generates heat and light to dwarf the Consolidated Edison Company.

The commuter is the queerest bird of all. The suburb he inhabits has no essential vitality of its own and is a mere roost where he comes at day's end to go to sleep. Except in rare cases, the man who lives in Mamaroneck or Little Neck or Teaneck, and works in New York, discovers nothing much about the city except the time of arrival and departure of trains and buses, and the path to a quick lunch. He is deskbound, and has never, idly roaming in the gloaming, stumbled suddenly on Belvedere Tower in the Park, seen the ramparts rise sheer from the water of the pond, and the boys along the shore fishing for minnows, girls stretched out negligently on the shelves

of the rocks; he has never come suddenly on anything at all in New York as a loiterer, because he has had no time between trains. He has fished in Manhattan's wallet and dug out coins, but has never listened to Manhattan's breathing, never awakened to its morning, never dropped off to sleep in its night.

About 400,000 men and women come charging onto the Island each weekday morning, out of the mouths of tubes and tunnels. Not many among them have ever spent a drowsy afternoon in the great rustling oaken silence of the reading room of the Public Library, with the book elevator (like an old waterwheel) spewing out books onto the trays. They tend their furnaces in Westchester and in Jersey, but have never seen the furnaces of the Bowery, the fires that burn in oil drums on zero winter nights. They may work in the financial district downtown and never see the extravagant plantings of Rockefeller Center — the daffodils and grape hyacinths and birches and the flags trimmed to the wind on a fine morning in spring. Or they may work in a midtown office and may let a whole year swing round without sighting Governors Island from the sea wall. The commuter dies with tremendous mileage to his credit, but he is no rover. His entrances and exits are more devious than those in a prairie-dog village; and he calmly plays bridge while buried in the mud at the bottom of the East River. The Long Island Rail Road alone carried forty million commuters last year; but many of them were the same fellow retracing his steps.

The terrain of New York is such that a resident sometimes travels farther, in the end, than a commuter. Irving Berlin's journey from Cherry Street in the lower East Side to an apartment uptown was through an alley and was only three or four miles in length; but it was like going three times around the world.

A poem compresses much in a small

space and adds music, thus heightening its meaning. The city is like poetry: it compresses all life, all races and breeds, into a small island and adds music and the accompaniment of internal engines. The island of Manhattan is without any doubt the greatest human concentrate on earth, the poem whose magic is comprehensible to millions of permanent residents but whose full meaning will always remain elusive. At the feet of the tallest and plushiest offices lie the crummiest slums. The genteel mysteries housed in the Riverside Church are only a few blocks from the voodoo charms of Harlem. The merchant princes, riding to Wall Street in their limousines down the East River Drive, pass within a few hundred yards of the gypsy kings; but the princes do not know they are passing kings, and the kings are not up yet anyway — they live a more leisurely life than the princes and get drunk more consistently.

New York is nothing like Paris; it is nothing like London; and it is not Spokane multiplied by sixty, or Detroit multiplied by four. It is by all odds the loftiest of cities. It even managed to reach the highest point in the sky at the lowest moment of the depression. The Empire State Building shot twelve hundred and fifty feet into the air when it was madness to put out as much as six inches of new growth. . . .

Manhattan has been compelled to expand skyward because of the absence of any other direction in which to grow. This, more than any other thing, is responsible for its physical majesty. It is to the nation what the white church spire is to the village — the visible symbol of aspiration and faith, the white plume saying that the way is up. The summer traveler swings in over Hell Gate Bridge and from the window of his sleeping car as it glides above the pigeon lofts and back yards of Queens looks southwest to where the morning light first strikes the steel peaks of midtown, and he sees its upward thrust unmistakable: the great walls and towers rising, the smoke rising, the heat

not yet rising, the hopes and ferments of so many awakening millions rising — this vigorous spear that presses heaven hard.

It is a miracle that New York works at all. The whole thing is implausible. Every time the residents brush their teeth, millions of gallons of water must be drawn from the Catskills and the hills of Westchester. When a young man in Manhattan writes a letter to his girl in Brooklyn, the love message gets blown to her through a pneumatic tube — *pfft* — just like that. The subterranean system of telephone cables, power lines, steam pipes, gas mains, and sewer pipes is reason enough to abandon the island to the gods and the weevils. Every time an incision is made in the pavement, the noisy surgeons expose ganglia that are tangled beyond belief. By rights New York should have destroyed itself long ago, from panic or fire or rioting or failure of some vital supply line in its circulatory system or from some deep labyrinthine short circuit. Long ago the city should have experienced an insoluble traffic snarl at some impossible bottleneck. It should have perished of hunger when food lines failed for a few days. It should have been wiped out by a plague starting in its slums or carried in by ships' rats. It should have been overwhelmed by the sea that licks at it on every side. The workers in its myriad cells should have succumbed to nerves, from the fearful pall of smoke-fog that drifts over every few days from Jersey, blotting out all light at noon and leaving the high offices suspended, men groping and depressed, and the sense of world's end. It should have been touched in the head by the August heat and gone off its rocker.

Mass hysteria is a terrible force, yet New Yorkers seem always to escape it by some tiny margin: they sit in stalled subways without claustrophobia, they extricate themselves from panic situations by some lucky wisecrack, they meet confusion and congestion with patience and grit — a sort of perpetual muddling through. Every facility is inadequate — the hospitals and schools and playgrounds are overcrowded, the express highways are feverish, the unimproved highways and bridges are bottlenecks; there is not enough air and not enough light, and there is usually either too much heat or too little. But the city makes up for its hazards and its deficiencies by supplying its citizens with massive doses of a supplementary vitamin — the sense of belonging to something unique, cosmopolitan, mighty, and unparalleled. . . .

The subtlest change in New York is something people don't speak much about but that is in everyone's mind. The city, for the first time in its long history, is destructible. A single flight of planes no bigger than a wedge of geese can quickly end this island fantasy, burn the towers, crumble the bridges, turn the underground passages into lethal chambers, cremate the millions. The intimation of mortality is part of New York now: in the sound of jets overhead, in the black headlines of the latest edition.

All dwellers in cities must live with the stubborn fact of annihilation; in New York the fact is somewhat more concentrated because of the concentration of the city itself, and because, of all targets, New York has a certain clear priority. In the mind of whatever perverted dreamer might loose the lightning, New York must hold a steady, irresistible charm.

It used to be that the Statue of Liberty was the signpost that proclaimed New York and translated it for all the world. Today Liberty shares the role with Death. Along the East River, from the razed slaughterhouses of Turtle Bay, as though in a race with the spectral flight of planes, men are carving out the permanent headquarters of the United Nations — the greatest housing project of them all. In its stride, New York takes on one more interior city, to shelter, this time, all governments, and to clear the slum called war. New York is not a capital city — it is not a national capital or a state capital. But it is by way of becoming the capital of the world. The buildings, as conceived by architects, will be cigar boxes set on end. Traffic will flow in a new tunnel under First Avenue. Forty-seventh Street will be widened (and if my guess is any good, trucks will appear late at night to plant tall trees surreptitiously, their roots to mingle with the intestines of the town). Once again the city will absorb, almost without showing any sign of it, a congress of visitors. It has already shown itself capable of stashing away the United Nations — a great many of the delegates have been around town during the past couple of years, and the citizenry has hardly caught a glimpse of their coattails or their black Homburgs.

This race — this race between the destroying planes and the struggling Parliament of Man — it sticks in all our heads. The city at last perfectly illustrates both the universal dilemma and the general solution, this riddle in steel and stone is at once the perfect target and the perfect demonstration of nonviolence, of racial brotherhood, this lofty target scraping the skies and meeting the destroying planes halfway, home of all people and all nations, capital of everything, housing the deliberations by which the planes are to be stayed and their errand forestalled.

A block or two west of the new City of Man in Turtle Bay there is an old willow tree that presides over an interior garden. It is a battered tree, long suffering and much climbed, held together by strands of wire but beloved of those who know it. In a way it symbolizes the city: life under difficulties, growth against odds, sap-rise in the midst of concrete, and the steady reaching for the sun. Whenever I look at it nowadays, and feel the cold shadow of the planes, I think: "This must be saved, this particular thing, this very tree." If it were to go, all would go — this city, this mischievous and marvelous monument which not to look upon would be like death.

# Index of Authors

*The numbers in brackets
indicate selection numbers
in this volume*

ACHESON, DEAN (April 11, 1893-    ), lawyer and public official. Undersecretary of the treasury (1933) under F. D. Roosevelt; assistant secretary of state (1941-45) under Roosevelt; undersecretary of state (1945-47) and secretary of state (1949-53) under Truman; wrote *Power and Diplomacy* (1958). [115] See also Author Index, Vol. 17.

BARUCH, BERNARD M. (Aug. 19, 1870-June 20, 1965), financier and statesman. Member (1916) of the Advisory Commission of the Council for National Defense; chairman of the War Industries Board during World War I; member (1919) of the Supreme Economic Council of the Paris Peace Conference; advisor on industrial mobilization during World War II; member (1946) of the UN Atomic Energy Commission; advisor to U.S. Presidents from Wilson to Kennedy. [75]

BEAUVOIR, SIMONE DE (Jan. 9, 1908-    ), French author. Professor (1931-43) at the University of Paris; wrote *The Mandarins* (English trans. 1956), *Memoirs of a Dutiful Daughter* (1959), *The Prime of Life* (1962), *The Force of Circumstance* (1965). [110]

BELL, BERNARD IDDINGS (Oct. 13, 1886-Sept. 5, 1958), Episcopal clergyman and author. Professor of religion (1930-33) at Columbia; canon (1933-46) of St. John's Cathedral, Providence, R.I.; canon (from 1946) of St. James Cathedral Church, Chicago; general consultant on religion and education, and pastor of Episcopalians, (from 1948) at the University of Chicago; wrote *Beyond Agnosticism* (1929), *The Church in Disrepute* (1943), *God Is Not Dead* (1945), *Crisis in Education* (1949). [114]

BENEDICT, DONALD (Sept. 12, 1917-    ), clergyman. Seminary student (c. 1941) and conscientious objector to military conscription; served churches (1947-54) in New York City and (1954-60) in Cleveland; executive director (1960-  ) of Chicago City Missionary Society; instructor (1963-  ) at Chicago Theological Seminary. [19]

BENÉT, STEPHEN VINCENT (July 22, 1898-March 13, 1943), author. Wrote novels, short stories, and poetry (*Heavens and Earth*, 1920; *John Brown's Body*, 1928; *Ballads and Poems, 1915-30*, 1931; *Western Star*, 1943). [4] See also Author Index, Vol. 14.

BENTON, WILLIAM (April 1, 1900-    ), businessman, educator, and statesman. Founder (1929) with Chester Bowles of Benton and Bowles advertising agency; vice-president (1937-45) of the University of Chicago; publisher (1943-  ) of *Encyclopaedia Britannica*; assistant secretary of state (1945-47) under Truman; U.S. senator from Connecticut (1949-53); ambassador to UNESCO (1963- ). **[47]** See also Author Index, Vol. 17.

BERLE, ADOLF A. (Jan. 29, 1895- ), lawyer and diplomat. Consultant (1918-19) to the Paris Peace Commission; assistant secretary of state (1938-44) under F. D. Roosevelt; ambassador to Brazil (1945-46); professor (1927- ) at Columbia University Law School. **[113]** See also Author Index, Vols. 15, 17.

BLACK, HUGO L. (Feb. 27, 1886- ), political leader and jurist. U.S. senator from Alabama (1927-37); associate justice (1937- ) of the U.S. Supreme Court. **[37, 49, 81]** See also Author Index, Vol. 18.

BROGAN, DENIS W. (Aug. 11, 1900- ), British political scientist. Teacher at the University of London and the London School of Economics; professor of political science (1939- ) at Cambridge University; wrote *The American Political System* (1933), *The American Character* (1944), *American Themes* (1949). **[50]**

BROWN, LEW (1893-Feb. 5, 1958), lyricist. Born Russia; wrote the words to "Shine," "That Old Feeling," and "The Best Things in Life Are Free"; wrote songs for motion pictures; collaborated on musical comedies and on an estimated 7,000 songs. **[32]**

CHAFEE, ZECHARIAH (Dec. 7, 1885-Feb. 8, 1957), lawyer, scholar, and author of works on civil liberties. Professor (from 1916) at Harvard Law School; wrote *The Inquiring Mind* (1928), *Free Speech in the United States* (1941), *Government and Mass Communications* (2 vols., 1947), *Blessings of Liberty* (1956). **[18]**

CHURCHILL, WINSTON (Nov. 30, 1874-Jan. 24, 1965), British statesman. Served as soldier and journalist in Cuba (1895), India (1896-97), and Sudan (1898); undersecretary for the colonies (1906-08); president (1908-10) of the Board of Trade; home secretary (1910-11); first lord of admiralty (1911-15); secretary for war and air (1919-21) and for the colonies (1921-22); chancellor of the exchequer (1924-29); prime minister (1940-45, 1951-55); made honorary U.S. citizen by

act of Congress (1963); received Nobel Prize for Literature (1953); wrote *The Second World War* (6 vols., 1948-54), *A History of the English-Speaking Peoples* (4 vols., 1956-58). **[76]**

COMMAGER, HENRY STEELE (Oct. 25, 1902- ), historian. Professor of history (1939-56) at Columbia and (1956- ) at Amherst; wrote *The Growth of the American Republic* (with S. E. Morison, 1931-42), *Freedom, Loyalty, Dissent* (1954), *The Nature and the Study of History* (1965); edited *Documents of American History* (1934, 1940, 1949). **[92]** See also Author Index, Vol. 17.

CONANT, JAMES BRYANT (March 26, 1893- ), scientist and educator. Instructor (1917-27) and professor (1927-33) of chemistry at Harvard; president (1933-53) of Harvard; helped organize scientific research on the atom bomb during World War II; adviser to the National Science Foundation and the Atomic Energy Commission (1945- ); U.S. high commissioner for Western Germany (1953-55); ambassador to West Germany (1955-57); author of numerous works on science and education. **[7]**

COOKE, ALISTAIR (Nov. 20, 1908- ), journalist. Born England; became U.S. citizen (1941); film critic (1934-37) for BBC; London correspondent (1936-37) for NBC; American correspondent (1938-42) for the *London Times;* commentator on American affairs (1938- ) for BBC; UN correspondent (1945-48) and chief correspondent in the U.S. (1948- ) for the *Manchester Guardian;* master of ceremonies for the television program "Omnibus." **[118]**

CRAWFORD, FREDERICK C. (March 19, 1891- ), businessman. President (1933- ) of Thompson Products, Inc.; director, U.S. Chamber of Commerce; president (1943) of the National Association of Manufacturers. **[34]**

CUMMINGS, E. E. (Oct. 14, 1894-Sept. 3, 1962), poet and artist. Wrote prose works (*The Enormous Room*, 1922, and *Eimi*, 1933), plays, and poetry characterized by typographical nonconformity and stylistic originality (*XLI Poems*, 1925; *Is*

5, 1926; *&*, 1926; *Collected Poems*, 1938; *One Times One*, 1944; *95 Poems*, 1958). **[53]** See also Author Index, Vols. 14, 15.

DAVIS, STUART (Dec. 7, 1894-June 24, 1964), painter and illustrator. At the age of 19 exhibited works in the Armory Show of 1913; cartoonist for *Harper's Weekly;* paintings include murals for Radio City Music Hall, N.Y.C., and are represented in permanent collections of museums in New York, Philadelphia, and Washington, D.C. **[43]**

DESMOND, JOHN (fl. 1944), journalist. **[46]**

DE VOTO, BERNARD (Jan. 11, 1897-Nov. 13, 1955), writer, historian, and editor. Teacher of English (1929-36) at Harvard; editor (from 1935) of "The Easy Chair" in *Harper's* magazine and (1936-38) of the *Saturday Review;* wrote *Mark Twain's America* (1932), *The Course of Empire* (1952). **[119]**

DEWEY, THOMAS E. (March 24, 1902-    ), lawyer and public official. Special prosecutor in investigation of organized crime in New York (1935-37); district attorney of New York County (1937-38); governor (1943-55); twice defeated (1944, 1948) Republican Party candidate for President of the United States. **[95]**

DONOVAN, WILLIAM J. (Jan. 1, 1883-Feb. 8, 1959), army officer and public official. Infantry colonel during World War I; assistant to U.S. attorney general (1925-29); U.S. coordinator of information (1941-42); director of Office of Strategic Services during World War II; ambassador to Thailand (1953-54). **[78]**

DOUGLAS, WILLIAM O. (Oct. 16, 1898-    ), jurist. Engaged in bankruptcy studies for U.S. Department of Commerce (1929-32); professor of law (1931-39) at Yale; member (1934-36) and chairman (1936-39) of the Securities and Exchange Commission; associate justice (1939-    ) of the U.S. Supreme Court. **[37]** See also Author Index, Vols. 17, 18.

EINSTEIN, ALBERT (March 14, 1879-April 18, 1955), theoretical physicist. Born Germany; professor at the universities of Zürich, Prague, and Berlin; director of the Kaiser Wilhelm Physical Institute; to

U.S. (1933); member (1933-45) of the Institute for Advanced Study, Princeton; published accounts of his special (1905) and general (1916) theories of relativity; received Nobel Prize for Physics (1921). **[105]** See also Author Index, Vol. 15.

EISENHOWER, DWIGHT D. (Oct. 14, 1890-    ), soldier and statesman. Thirty-fourth President of the United States (1953-61); supreme Allied commander in North Africa (1942) and in the western Mediterranean (1943); commander in chief of Allied forces in Western Europe (1943-45); general of the Army (1944); member (1945) of the Allied Control Council for Germany; president (1948-53) of Columbia University; supreme commander (1951-52) of NATO forces; wrote *Crusade in Europe* (1948). **[99]** See also Author Index, Vols. 17, 18.

FARRELL, JAMES T. (Feb. 27, 1904-    ), author. Wrote *Gas House McGinty* (1933), *Studs Lonigan* (trilogy, 1932-35), *A World I Never Made* (1936), *An American Dream Girl* (1950), *Reflections at Fifty, and Other Essays* (1954), *Sound of the City, and Other Stories* (1962). **[79]**

FISCHER, JOHN (April 27, 1910-    ), editor and author. Reporter (1928-33) for newspapers in Texas, Oklahoma, and New Mexico, (1933-35) for United Press in England and Germany, and (1935-37) for Associated Press; staff member (1937-42) of U.S. Agriculture Department; associate editor (1944-47), editor in chief, and vice-president of *Harper's* magazine. **[57]**

FRANKFURTER, FELIX (Nov. 15, 1882-Feb. 22, 1965), jurist. Born Austria; professor (1914-39) at Harvard Law School; chairman (1918) of the War Labor Policies Board; legal adviser to President Wilson at Paris Peace Conference; a founder of the *New Republic* and the American Civil Liberties Union; associate justice (1939-62) of the U.S. Supreme Court; wrote *The Case of Sacco and Vanzetti* (1927) and works on law and government. **[37, 49]**

FROST, ROBERT (March 26, 1874-Jan. 29, 1963), poet. Professor of English (1916-20, 1924, 1926-38, 1949-63) at Amherst; professor of poetry (1939-43) at Harvard and (1943-49) at Dartmouth; among his books of poetry are *A Boy's Will* (1913), *North of Boston* (1914), *Mountain Interval* (1916), *New Hampshire* (1923), *West-running Brook* (1928), *A Further Range* (1936), *A Witness Tree* (1942), and *In the Clearing* (1962). **[26]** See also Author Index, Vols. 13, 14, 15.

GOODMAN, PAUL (Sept. 9, 1911-    ), author and critic. Brother of Percival Goodman; teacher at the University of Chicago, New York University, and Black Mountain College; wrote *Communitas* (with Percival Goodman, 1947), *Growing Up Absurd* (1960), *The Community of Scholars* (1962). **[97]**

GOODMAN, PERCIVAL (Jan. 13, 1904-    ), architect. Brother of Paul Goodman; visiting critic (1930-36) at the New York University School of Architecture; professor of architecture (1953-    ) at Columbia University; wrote *Communitas* (with Paul Goodman, 1947). **[97]**

GOTTLIEB, ADOLPH (March 14, 1903-    ), painter. Member of the abstractionist school; paintings in museum collections in New York, Miami, Detroit, and Tel Aviv. **[43]**

GUTHRIE, WOODY (July 14, 1912-Oct. 3, 1967), Oklahoma balladeer. Composed folk songs, including "So Long (It's Been Good to Know Yuh)," "Tom Joad," and "Union Maid." **[6]** See also Author Index, Vols. 15, 17.

HANDY, W. C. (Nov. 16, 1873-March 28, 1958), composer. Conducted his own orchestra (1903-21); established the popularity of blues music through his "Memphis Blues" (1911) and "St. Louis Blues" (1914); published anthologies of Negro spirituals and blues and studies of Negro musicians. **[21]**

HAYS, LEE (fl. 1948), songwriter and performer. **[107]**

HINES, FRANK T. (April 11, 1879-April 3, 1960), army officer and public official. Chief (1918-19) of Army Embarkation Service; director (1923-30) of U.S. Veterans' Bureau; administrator (1930-45) of Veterans' Affairs; ambassador to Panama (1945-48). **[45]**

HOOVER, J. EDGAR (Jan. 1, 1895-    ), lawyer and public official. Special assistant

(1919-24) to U.S. attorney general; director (1924-    ) of the Federal Bureau of Investigation. **[91]**

HUTCHINS, ROBERT M. (Jan. 17, 1899-    ), educator. Dean (1927-29) of Yale Law School; president (1929-45) and chancellor (1945-51) of the University of Chicago; president (1954-    ) of the Fund for the Republic and president of the Center for the Study of Democratic Institutions; wrote *The Higher Learning in America* (1936), *Some Observations on American Education* (1956), *The Learning Society* (1968). **[16]** See also Author Index, Vol. 15.

JACKSON, ROBERT H. (Feb. 13, 1892-Oct. 9, 1954), lawyer and jurist. General counsel (1934-36) for U.S. Internal Revenue Bureau; assistant U.S. attorney general (1936-38); U.S. solicitor general (1938-39); U.S. attorney general (1940-41) under F. D. Roosevelt; associate justice (from 1941) of the U.S. Supreme Court; U.S. chief prosecutor at Nuremburg war crimes trials (1945-46). **[37, 49]**

KENNAN, GEORGE F. (Feb. 16, 1904-    ), diplomat. Chargé d'affaires at Moscow (1945); ambassador (1952) to the Soviet Union and (1961-63) to Yugoslavia; member (1956-    ) of the Institute for Advanced Study, Princeton University; wrote *American Diplomacy, 1900-1950* (1951), *Russia and the West under Lenin and Stalin* (1961), *On Dealing with the Communist World* (1964), *Memoirs, 1925-1950.* **[89]** See also Author Index, Vol. 17.

KNOX, FRANK (Jan. 1, 1874-April 28, 1944), publisher and politician. General manager (1928-31) of the Hearst newspapers; publisher (from 1931) of the *Chicago Daily News;* Republican Party candidate (1936) for Vice-President of the United States; secretary of the Navy (from 1940) under F. D. Roosevelt. **[14]**

KOUWENHOVEN, JOHN (1909-    ), editor and author. Teacher of English (1936-38) at Columbia College and of literature (1938-41) at Bennington College; an editor (1941-54) for *Harper's* magazine; professor of English (1948-    ) at Barnard College. **[109]**

LAURENCE, WILLIAM L. (March 7, 1888-    ), journalist. Science reporter (1930-

56) and science editor (1956-64) for the *New York Times;* wrote first journalistic account of the significance of the discovery of uranium fission; only journalist present at first test of atomic bomb (1945); accompanied the mission that dropped the atomic bomb on Nagasaki. [68]

LESTER, RICHARD A. (March 1, 1908-    ), economist. Professor of economics at Haverford, Duke, and the University of Washington; professor (1947-   ) and chairman of the department of economics (1961-   ) at Princeton University; served on the War Manpower Commission, the National War Labor Board, and the President's Commission on the Status of Women. [85]

LILIENTHAL, DAVID E. (July 8, 1899-    ), lawyer and public official. Member (1933-41) and chairman (1941-47) of the Tennessee Valley Authority; chairman (1947-50) of the Atomic Energy Commission; wrote *Democracy on the March* (1944), *This I Do Believe* (1949). [48, 93]

LINDBERGH, CHARLES A. (Feb. 4, 1902-    ), aviator. Made first solo nonstop transatlantic flight, from Roosevelt Field, New York, to Le Bourget Air Field, Paris (May 20-21, 1927); toured U.S. for Guggenheim Foundation to promote aeronautics; worked on physiological experiments that resulted in development of the "artificial heart" (1936); consultant to U.S. Army Air Force during World War II. [17] See also Author Index, Vol. 14.

LIPPMANN, WALTER (Sept. 23, 1889-    ), editor and author. Assisted in preparation of the Fourteen Points and the League of Nations plan for the Paris Peace Conference (1918-19); a co-founder (1914) and editor of the *New Republic;* syndicated political columnist (1931-67) for the *New York Herald Tribune;* wrote *Public Opinion* (1927), *A Preface to Morals* (1929), *The Good Society* (1937), *U.S. Foreign Policy: Shield of the Republic* (1943), *Essays in the Public Philosophy* (1955). [41] See also Author Index, Vols. 13, 14, 15, 17, 18.

LOESSER, FRANK (June 29, 1910-    ), songwriter. Wrote songs for stage productions (*Guys and Dolls, The Most Happy Fella*) and motion pictures, including "Baby, It's

Cold Outside," "On a Slow Boat to China," "Praise the Lord and Pass the Ammunition," and "Spring Will be a Little Late This Year." [32]

LOW, DAVID (April 7, 1891-Sept. 19, 1963), British cartoonist and caricaturist. Staff member (1911-19) *Sydney* (Australia) *Bulletin,* (1919-26) *London Star,* (1927-50) *Evening Standard,* for which he created the character "Colonel Blimp," (1950-53) *London Daily Herald,* and (from 1953) the *Manchester Guardian;* published 30 cartoon collections; wrote *Autobiography* (1956). [29]

LOWENFELS, WALTER (fl. 1948), songwriter. [107]

MACARTHUR, DOUGLAS (Jan. 26, 1880-April 5, 1964), army officer. Commanded 42nd Division in France during World War I; superintendent (1919-22) of U.S. Military Academy; commanded Philippines Department (1928-30); chief of staff of U.S. Army (1930-35); supreme Allied commander in the Pacific (1942-45) and of occupation forces in Japan (1945-50); commander of UN forces in Korea (1950-51). [69] See also Author Index, Vol. 17.

MACLEISH, ARCHIBALD (May 7, 1892-    ), poet, teacher, and public official. Librarian of Congress (1939-44); assistant secretary of state (1944-45) under F. D. Roosevelt; professor (1949-62) at Harvard University; wrote poetry (*Tower of Ivory,* 1917; *New Found Land,* 1930; *Conquistador,* 1932; *Actfive and Other Poems,* 1948), essays, and verse plays (*The Hamlet of A. MacLeish,* 1928; *J. B.,* 1957). [1] See also Author Index, Vols. 15, 18.

MARSHALL, GEORGE C. (Dec. 31, 1880-Oct. 16, 1959), army officer and public official. Served in France during World War I and (1924-27) in China; chief of staff of U.S. Army (1939-45); ambassador to China (1945-47); secretary of state (1947-49) and of defense (1950-51) under Truman; received Nobel Peace Prize (1953). [88]

MEIKLEJOHN, ALEXANDER (Feb. 3, 1872-Dec. 16, 1964), educator. Professor of logic and metaphysics and dean (1901-12) at Brown University; president (1912-24) of Amherst College; head (1926-38) of the experimental school at the University of

Wisconsin; instructor (1938-42) in the School for Social Studies, San Francisco. [117]

MUÑOZ-MARÍN, LUIS (Feb. 18, 1898- ), Puerto Rican statesman. A founder (1938) of the Popular Democratic Party; senator (1932-49) and president of the senate (1941-48); governor (1949-65); U.S. senator (1965- ). [63]

MURPHY, FRANK (April 13, 1890-July 19, 1949), jurist and public official. Mayor of Detroit (1930-33); governor-general of Philippine Islands (1933-35); U.S. high commissioner to the Philippines (1935-36); governor of Michigan (1936-38); U.S. attorney general (1939-40) under F. D. Roosevelt; associate justice (from 1940) of the U.S. Supreme Court. [49]

MURRAY, PHILIP (May 25, 1886-Nov. 9, 1952), labor leader. Born Scotland; worked in the Pennsylvania coal mines (1902-20); vice-president (1920-42) of the United Mine Workers' Union; organizer (1936) and president (from 1940) of the United Steel Workers' Union; president (from 1940) of the Congress of Industrial Organizations. [5]

MYRDAL, GUNNAR (Dec. 6, 1898- ), Swedish economist and public official. Professor (1933-50) of economics and (1960- ) of international economics at the University of Stockholm; legislator (1936-38, 1944-45) and cabinet minister (1945-47); director (1947-57) of UN Economic Commission for Europe; wrote *An American Dilemma: The Negro Problem and Modern Democracy* (Carnegie Endowment report, 1944). [51]

NEVINS, ALLAN (May 20, 1890- ), educator, historian, and author. Editorial staff member (1913-23) *New York Evening Post,* (1913-18) the *Nation,* and (1925-31) *New York World;* professor of American history (1931-58) at Columbia; wrote books on American history and biographies (Grover Cleveland, 1932; Hamilton Fish, 1936); edited diaries of historical figures. [73]

NIEBUHR, REINHOLD (June 21, 1892- ), Protestant theologian and social critic. Brother of H. Richard Niebuhr; professor of applied Christianity (1930-60) at Union Theological Seminary; wrote

*Moral Man and Immoral Society* (1932), *The Nature and Destiny of Man* (2 vols., 1941, 1943), *The Children of Light and the Children of Darkness* (1944), *The Irony of American History* (1952), *The Self and the Dramas of History* (1955). [52]

NIELSEN, WALDEMAR A., "Michael Darrock" (fl. 1943), journalist. [36]

OCKENGA, HAROLD J. (July 6, 1905- ), Presbyterian clergyman. President (1945-54, 1959-62) of Fuller Theological Seminary, California; vice-president (1951-61) of World Evangelical Fellowship; author of books and journal articles on religion. [28]

O'MAHONEY, JOSEPH C. (Nov. 5, 1884-Dec. 1, 1962), public official. U.S. senator from Wyoming (1933-52, 1954-60); chairman (1938-41) of the Temporary National Economic Committee. [15]

POLLOCK, JACKSON (Jan. 28, 1912-Aug. 11, 1956), painter. A leader of the Abstract Expressionist movement in U.S. [43]

PYLE, ERNIE (Aug. 3, 1900-April 18, 1945), journalist. War correspondent for Scripps-Howard newspapers during World War II, covering campaigns in North Africa, Sicily, Italy, France, Iwo Jima, and Okinawa; newspaper columns compiled in *Ernie Pyle in England* (1941), *Here Is Your War* (1943), *Brave Men* (1944), *Last Chapter* (1946). [39]

RANDOLPH, A. PHILIP (April 15, 1889- ), labor leader. Organized (1925) the Brotherhood of Sleeping Car Porters; vice-president (1957- ) and member of the executive council of the AFL-CIO. [31]

RIDENOUR, LOUIS N. (Nov. 1, 1911-May 21, 1959), physicist. Professor of physics (1938-47) at the University of Pennsylvania and (1947-51) at the University of Illinois; associated (from 1956) with Lockheed Aircraft Corp. [74]

ROOSEVELT, ELEANOR (Oct. 11, 1884-Nov. 7, 1962), diplomat and humanitarian. Wife of Franklin D. Roosevelt; delegate (1945-52) to the United Nations and chairman of the commission to draft the Universal Declaration of Human Rights; wrote "My Day," a syndicated newspaper column, *This Is My Story* (1937), and

*The Moral Basis of Democracy* (1940). [120] See also Author Index, Vol. 17.

ROOSEVELT, FRANKLIN D. (Jan. 30, 1882-April 12, 1945), lawyer and statesman. Thirty-second President of the United States (1933-45) and the only President to be elected to a third (and a fourth) term; assistant secretary of the Navy (1913-20) under Wilson; governor of New York (1929-33); initiated national administrative and legislative reforms known as the "New Deal"; chief architect of the United Nations. [3, 9, 10, 11, 12, 20, 23, 25, 33, 44] See also Author Index, Vol. 15.

ROSTOW, EUGENE V. (Aug. 25, 1913-     ), lawyer and economist. Professor (1944-     ), and dean (1955-65) at Yale Law School; adviser to U.S. State Department (1942-44, 1961-   ); member (1961-   ) of the Advisory Council to the Peace Corps; undersecretary of state (1966-   ). [72] See also Author Index, Vol. 18.

ROTHKO, MARK (Sept. 25, 1903-     ), artist. Born Russia; specialist in abstract and surrealist art; paintings in museum collections in New York and San Francisco. [43]

RUML, BEARDSLEY (Nov. 5, 1894-April 18, 1960), businessman. Assistant (1921-22) to the president of the Carnegie Corp., N.Y.; director (1922-29) of the Laura Spelman Rockefeller Memorial; dean (1931-33) of the Social Sciences Division of the University of Chicago; treasurer (1934-45) and chairman of the board (1945-49) of R. H. Macy and Co. [27]

SARTRE, JEAN PAUL (June 21, 1905-     ), French philosopher, playwright, and novelist. Wrote short stories (*The Wall,* Eng. trans. 1939), novels (*Nausea,* 1949; *Paths of Freedom,* 4 vols., 1947-50), plays (*The Flies,* 1946; *No Exit,* 1946), philosophical works (*Existentialism and Humanism,* 1948; *Being and Nothingness,* 1956; *The Problem of Method,* 1964), and an autobiography, *The Words* (1964); was awarded Nobel Prize for Literature (1964) but declined. [98]

SHAPIRO, KARL (Nov. 10, 1913-     ), poet. Professor of writing (1947-50) at Johns Hopkins University; editor (1950-56) of

*Poetry* magazine; professor of English (1956-   ) at the University of Nebraska; wrote *Poems* (1935), *V-Letter, and Other Poems* (1944), *Trial of a Poet* (1947), *The Bourgeois Poet* (1964). [30] See also Author Index, Vol. 17.

SHIRER, WILLIAM L. (Feb. 23, 1904-     ), journalist and radio commentator. Foreign correspondent (1925-33) for the *Chicago Tribune* and (1935-37) for Universal News Service; European representative (1937-40) for CBS; wrote *Berlin Diary* (1941), *The Rise and Fall of the Third Reich* (1960). [40]

SIMONS, HENRY C. (1899-1946), economist. Professor at the University of Chicago; wrote a series of pamphlets and journal articles on economics and politics, collected and published as *Economic Policy for a Free Society* (1948). [100]

STEELE, BILL (fl. 1943), soldier and field correspondent for *Yank* magazine. [38]

STEPT, SAM H. (1897-Dec. 1, 1964), songwriter. Born Russia; wrote scores for motion pictures; collaborated on musical comedies; first hit song was "That's My Weakness Now" (1928), others include "Please Don't Talk About Me When I'm Gone." [32]

TAFT, ROBERT A. (Sept. 8, 1889-July 31, 1953), lawyer and political leader. Son of William Howard Taft; Ohio legislator (1921-26, 1931-32); U.S. senator (from 1939) and Republican majority leader in the Senate (1953); co-sponsor of the Taft-Hartley Labor-Management Relations Act (1947). [24, 55, 84, 112, 115] See also Author Index, Vol. 15.

TOBIAS, CHARLIE (1898-     ), lyricist. Wrote the words for "The Old Lamp-Lighter," "Sail Along, Silvery Moon," and "Don't Sit Under the Apple Tree." [32]

TRAVIS, MERLE (fl. 1947), songwriter and singer. Wrote popular and folk songs, including "Dark as a Dungeon" and "Sixteen Tons." [86]

TRUMAN, HARRY S. (May 8, 1884-     ), political leader and statesman. Thirty-third President of the United States (1945-53); presiding judge (1926-34) of Jackson County (Mo.) Court; U.S. senator from Missouri (1935-45); Vice-President of the United States (1945); succeeded to the Presidency upon the death of F. D. Roosevelt (April 12, 1945). [67, 71, 87, 90, 101, 102, 111, 116] See also Author Index, Vol. 17.

VANDENBERG, ARTHUR H. (March 22, 1884-April 18, 1951), political leader and public official. Editor (1906-28) of the *Grand Rapids* (Mich.) *Herald*; U.S. senator from Michigan (from 1928); as chairman (1947-48) of the Senate Foreign Relations Committee, helped secure passage of the Marshall Plan (1948). [66, 104]

WAGNER, RALPH B. (fl. 1945), professor of speech at St. Louis University. [59]

WALLACE, HENRY A. (Oct. 7, 1888-Nov. 18, 1965), agriculturist and public official. Vice-President of the United States (1941-45) under F. D. Roosevelt; on staff (1910-29) of *Wallace's Farmer*; editor (1929-33) of *Wallace's Farmer and Iowa Homestead*; secretary of agriculture (1933-40) under F. D. Roosevelt; head (1941) of Economic Defense Board; secretary of commerce (1945-46) under F. D. Roosevelt and Truman; editor (1946-47) of the *New Republic*. Contributed to development of hybrid corn. [56, 77] See also Author Index, Vol. 15.

WEISENBURGER, WALTER B. (Feb. 6, 1888-June 23, 1947), businessman. Executive vice-president (from 1934) of the National Association of Manufacturers. [83]

WHEELER, BURTON K. (Feb. 27, 1882-    ),

lawyer and politician. U.S. senator from Montana (1923-47); Progressive Party candidate (1924) for Vice-President of the United States. [13]

WHITE, E. B. (July 11, 1899-    ), humorist and essayist. A contributing editor to the *New Yorker* and principal author of its "Talk of the Town" column; author of "One Man's Meat" column in *Harper's* magazine; wrote *Is Sex Necessary?* (with James Thurber, 1929), *One Man's Meat* (1942, 1944), *The Wild Flag* (1946), *The Second Tree from the Corner* (1953). [54, 108, 121] See also Author Index, Vol. 15.

WILLKIE, WENDELL L. (Feb. 18, 1892-Oct. 8, 1944), lawyer, businessman, and politician. Attorney (1929-33) and president (1933-40) of Commonwealth and Southern Corp.; Republican Party candidate (1940) for President of the United States; reported on a tour of Russia, China, Egypt, and the Middle East in *One World* (1943). [8, 42]

WRIGHT, FRANK LLOYD (June 8, 1869-April 9, 1959), architect. Advocate and practitioner of "organic architecture" harmonizing buildings with their environment. Designed (1909) Robie House, Chicago; (1916-22) Imperial Hotel, Tokyo, Japan; (1936) Fallingwater House, Bear Run, Pa.; (1938) Taliesin West, Phoenix; and (1943) the Guggenheim Museum, New York (completed 1959). Wrote *An American Architecture* (1955). [60] See also Author Index, Vol. 12.